FINANCING HEALTH CARE:
ECONOMIC EFFICIENCY AND EQUITY

FINANCING HEALTH CARE

Economic Efficiency and Equity

STEVEN R. EASTAUGH
George Washington University

 Auburn House Publishing Company
Dover, Massachusetts

Library of Congress Cataloging in Publication Data

Eastaugh, Steven R., 1952–
  Financing health care.
  Includes index.
  1. Health facilities—Finance.   2. Health facilities
—Business management.   3. Medical care—Cost effective-
nes.   4. Medical economics.   I. Title.   [DNLM: 1. Cost
Control.   2. Economics, Hospital—United States.
3. Economics, Medical—United States.   4. Financial
Management.   W 74 E128f]
RA971.3.E19   1987   338.4'33621   86-22275
ISBN 0-86569-150-9

Printed in the United States of America

PREFACE

Today we are witnessing the anomaly of increased discussion of medical rationing while the number of empty hospital beds has expanded by 50 percent over the period 1982–1986. It seems incongruous that we should discuss rationing in the face of such a glut in available capacity not only of beds but perhaps also of doctors.

In preparing this book, I have intentionally cast a wide net to include managers, policy makers, health care providers, and graduate students. I anticipate that this wide audience is more interested in a synthesis of currently available study results and potential policy ramifications than new research methods. However, the footnotes and portions of seven chapters (2, 9, 13, 18, 21, 22, and 23) are intended for functional specialists and scholars with interests in technical issues. My hope is that the reader will come away with a better understanding of the medical economics and financial management literature and a renewed appreciation of the fact that the behavior of consumers and medical providers is only partially understood at this time.

The various cost-containment proposals that have been advanced in the 1980s are examined against the backdrop of the empirical research available to date. In Part One we define the elements that make up the medical cost inflation problem and survey a number of models of physician and hospital behavior.

In Part Two we discuss managerial concerns among buyers and sellers from the vantage point of a corporation (Chapter 3), a PPO or a hospital (Chapter 4), hospital accountants and purchasing agents (Chapter 5), HMOs (Chapter 7), long-term care (Chapter 8), and marketing (Chapter 9). With the demise of cost-shifting, hospitals do less production of cross-subsidized products. However, the ability of a sufficient supply of providers to serve the uninsured is called into question in our discussion of access to services and uncompensated care (Chapter 6).

With the current push for at least a 10 percent reduction in the number of hospital beds, hospital competition appears to be emerging, especially in the 12 largest urban areas, which comprise 19 percent of the U.S. population and have a mean of 81 hospitals per city. For the unprepared hospital administrators, competition and fiscal stringency are frightening developments. However, what hospital management abhors as fiscal stringency and cost containment is what American business has labeled "Normal competitive market conditions"—that is, "if you don't cut costs, don't expect to survive." Chapters 10 and 11 discuss techniques for improvement of productivity without doing harm to access or quality. In an increasingly market-driven health economy, buyers will become more aggressive about seeking value for their money and receiving information about the quality of care. Increasing consumer power to tell providers their values and preferences will be one very important by-product of health marketing activities.

Part Three on quality and productivity control discusses value shopping, quality-of-care disclosure to patients (and employers), and the need to do appropriate severity-adjusted quality measurement (Chapter 12). Part Four of the book explores health manpower issues for teaching hospitals (Chapter 13), medical schools (Chapter 14), and nursing schools and physician extender programs (Chapter 15). Part Four also provides a review of the techniques and potential applications of cost-benefit and cost-effectiveness evaluation, although the determination of indirect and intangible benefits is often an imprecise matter in medical technology assessment.

In Part Five we discuss the alleged merits and demerits of cost effectiveness, hypothetical willingness-to-pay surveys, and cost-benefit analysis. One cannot help but observe that the PPS (prospective payment system) for Medicare furnished a regulatory language, DRGs, that brought into the picture a key group of actors heretofore not directly involved in the 21-year hospital-government tug of war: the doctors. We survey physician concerns for quality and cost analysis throughout the second half of the text. As an alumnus of two graduate schools of public health, I cannot resist pointing out that health care can be conceived of as either a final output of our industry or an intermediate input in the production of "good health." Consequently, health finance could have been misinterpreted by some readers as the study of how society finances improved health in the population. However, many studies reviewed in this text have posed the tougher basic question regarding the minimal marginal impact that increased health services delivery has had on improving the health status of our citizens.

In Part Six our concerns shift to the viewpoint of the institutional manager and the impact that cost containment has had on all hospitals. Most of the emphasis is on hospital finance. Hospitals have an excessive reliance on debt relative to other sectors of the economy—for example, 80 to 85 percent of total new capitalization is debt financed. Public utilities borrow on the average about one-half of new capitalization, and manufacturing firms borrow only one-third. A number of financing alternatives are evaluated, including two types of leasing options.

Part Seven summarizes a number of future policy options and concludes that no single cost-containment strategy will be sufficient. Rather, a number of mixed strategies are suggested, including capitation.

I have depended on the ideas and assistance of others in writing this book, and credit is due them. The final stages of the manuscript were reviewed by Professors Philip Reeves, Warren Greenberg, and Kurt Darr. Parts of the manuscript were reviewed in the early stages of development by James Begun, Richard Southby, Duncan Neuhauser, and Roger Battistella. A number of research assistants over the years deserve special thanks for their help: Bonnie Horvath, David Dranove, Nancy Bohn, Kevin Smolich, Gary Selmeczi, Susan Clark, Steve Klapmeier, Carolyn Lankford, Jennifer Virnstein, Susan Cosgrove, Tom Caldwell, Jay Higham, Tina Kao, and Michael Jernigan. For errors that remain in the book I am responsible.

Finally, this book is dedicated to my wife, Dr. Janet Eastaugh, who provided moral support, a number of good ideas, and an appreciation of good scholarship.

STEVEN R. EASTAUGH

CONTENTS

Part One

ECONOMIC CONCERNS

Chapter 1

COST INFLATION: OVERTILLED AND UNDERTILLED FIELDS

In a few years utilization per 1,000 people is going to bottom out at around 500 hospital days per 1,000 people. The country started out at around 1,250 in 1982, and had declined to 950. One thing about bottoming out, however, is that the bottom seems to keep dropping. We may achieve levels like prepaid groups, in the 330–400 range.

—Paul M. Ellwood, M.D.

Every significant purchaser of medical care in the United States by 1990 should have access to price and quality information by physician and hospital name. All buyers should look at a hospital's IQ—Indicators of Quality.

—Willis Goldbeck

Change is already here, like it or not. More change is in view. Change breeds doubt. Doubt kindles choice. Choice is opportunity, opportunity to do better or worse.

—Steven Muller

Hospitals have priced themselves into the public eye. During the past 10 years annual hospital inflation has averaged 15 percent, almost triple the inflation rate that has bedeviled the rest of the economy. Prior to beginning a discussion of hospital cost inflation, it is essential first to explain how it is known that costs are in fact increasing each year. In other words, it is necessary to identify the indexes of cost inflation being used and to understand their implications. Most of the statistical evidence cited in this chapter pertains to hospital care, because the other components of medical

3

care have had a cost inflation rate more in line with the general economy.

Two indexes of the cost of hospital care are generally used. The first is used in the medical care component of the consumer price index. Published by the Bureau of Labor Statistics and called the "Index of Hospital Service Charges" (IHSC), it is a weighted average of the price indexes for several common components of hospital care. These components include room charge, use of the operating room, and eight common services such as a diagnostic x-ray and a laboratory test. The purpose of this index is to measure the change in price of a fixed basket of common services. The success of the IHSC in measuring changes in price—not quality and intensity—is limited by the extent to which improvements in the quality of care are built into the basic charges.

The second index, the Average Cost Per Patient Day (ACPPD), is published by the American Hospital Association (AHA). The intention of the ACPPD is to account for the change in the volume and mix of hospital services as well as the change in prices. This index is calculated by taking the figure for total hospital expenditures (excluding capital investment) and dividing it by the number of patient days. Total hospital expenditures include outpatient as well as inpatient care, and the AHA has therefore recently begun to publish an "adjusted" ACPPD which excludes outpatient care. However, Feldstein and Taylor (1981), who generally quote the ACPPD, view the adjustment as somewhat arbitrary and rely on the original ACPPD figure as a measure of total hospital cost inflation.

It is important to keep in mind that the IHSC and ACPPD are *not* measures of productivity, efficiency, or price increases. These two measures are only very broad indicators of the rapidly expanding amount of resources spent on medical care each year. They indicate in part the willingness of Americans to buy more and better hospital services than ever before.

Magnitude of the Cost Problem

How much has the ACPPD actually increased? Since 1950 the ACPPD has gone from $15.62 to $553.93, a 35.5-fold increase, and it has nearly doubled since 1980 (see line B, Table 1.1). Yet prices for other goods and services have increased as well. Line D of Table 1.1 gives the ACPPD in constant dollars, illustrating that, even accounting for inflation, the ACPPD is eight times what it was in 1950 but has increased only 30 percent since 1982. One indicator of the *relative* quantity of resources devoted to health care is the percentage of the GNP devoted to health expenditures. National health expenditures rose from 4.5 percent of the GNP in 1950, to 7.2 percent in 1970, to 10.7 percent in 1983, and 10.85 percent in 1986 (see Table 1.2).

Increased Intensity of Services Rendered

Aggregate expenditures on hospital care can be broken down into various components in order to facilitate discussion of hospital cost inflation. Accordingly, inflation accounts for 63 percent of the increase from 1970–1978, population growth for 7 percent, and increased "intensity" for 30 percent of the increase. "Intensity" refers to changes in the nature and quantity of services rendered (Gibson, 1979). Although the average number of days per stay in hospitals has declined, the resources utilized during each day have increased and the number of inpatient days overall has increased 8 percent since 1970. As an example of increased utilization of resources, from 1972 to 1977 the number of hospital laboratory tests nearly doubled and the number of surgical operations grew 18 percent (Gibson, 1979).

Increased expenditures on labor in the hospital setting reflect partly inflation (an increase in the *prices* of the resources employed) and partly an increase in intensity (an increase in the *amount* of resources employed). In a 10-year study of health care costs, the general inflation rate accounted for 52 percent of hospital expenses (Freeland and Schendler, 1984). Hospital price increases in excess of the general price inflation rate, as measured by the GNP deflator, explained only 13 percent of the variation in costs from 1972 to 1982.

Insurance and the Demand for Care

How, then, does the tremendous increase in expenditures on hospital care relate to the out-of-pocket costs borne by the consumer of hospital care at the time of illness? In other words, how is it that consumers are willing to bear the costs of such an increase in the intensity of hospital care without an equivalent return in the form of better health? Part of the answer lies in the fact that although there has been a great increase in the amount of national resources devoted to hospital care, there has been very little change in the cost of hospital care to the consumer at the time of illness.

In 1950 approximately 50 percent of the cost of hospital care

Table 1.1 Insurance and Net Cost of Hospital Care. Short-Term Nonfederal General Hospitals, Selected Years 1950–1985

	1950	1960	1966	1970	1972	1974	1975	1976	1977	1978	1979	1980	1981	1982	1983	1984	1985
A. Percentage of Costs Paid by:																	
1. Private Insurance	29.30	52.50	51.40	45.60	45.40	45.40	43.60	44.90	42.80	42.70	43.00	43.80	43.50	43.90	42.70	41.80	41.90
2. Government	21.10	18.80	25.50	37.80	41.10	42.80	44.50	44.00	43.60	43.00	42.90	42.80	42.50	42.20	41.80	42.50	42.30
3. Direct consumer spending	49.60	28.70	23.10	16.60	13.50	11.80	11.90	11.10	13.50	14.20	14.00	13.40	14.00	13.90	15.40	15.70	15.80
B. Average Cost per Patient Day[1]	15.62	32.23	48.15	81.01	105.21	128.05	151.53	175.08	200.29	224.53	249.20	283.13	328.42	378.20	426.99	488.90	553.93
C. 1. Net consumer cost per diem[2]	7.75	9.25	11.12	13.53	14.20	15.11	18.03	19.43	27.04	31.88	35.14	37.94	45.98	52.57	66.18	76.76	87.52
2. Net consumer cost per diem[3]	9.82	11.38	12.41	21.71	24.09	26.38	32.43	34.70	47.94	55.93	61.65	66.33	79.96	90.95	113.72	133.49	151.68
D. Average Cost per Patient Day (1967) dollars)	21.66	36.34	49.54	69.66	83.97	86.70	94.00	102.33	110.35	114.90	115.06	114.72	120.52	130.82	142.62	156.85	170.91

E. 1. Net consumer cost per diem (1967 dollars)[2]	10.75	10.43	11.44	11.63	11.34	10.23	11.18	11.36	14.90	16.32	16.16	15.37	16.87	18.18	22.10	24.63	27.00
2. Net consumer cost per diem (1967 dollars)[3]	13.62	12.83	12.77	18.67	19.22	17.86	20.11	20.35	26.41	28.62	28.35	26.88	29.34	31.46	37.98	42.83	46.80
F. CPI (1967 = 100)	0.721	0.887	0.972	1.163	1.253	1.477	1.612	1.705	1.815	1.954	2.174	2.468	2.725	2.891	2.994	3.117	3.241

SOURCES: DHHS (1986). "National Health Expenditures," *Health Care Financing Review*, Summer 1986; *Handbook of Basic Economic Statistics* (1986), Economics Statistics Bureau, Washington, D.C.

NOTE: These percentages and the corresponding figures for later years are calculated on the basis of data published by the Social Security Administration and the American Hospital Association. The Social Security Administration estimates total expenditure on hospital care and the proportions financed by government private insurance, and direct consumer spending. All of these amounts refer to care in all types of hospitals, including long-term and psychiatric institutions, and not just the short-term hospitals that are the subject of the current report. To develop estimates for short-term hospitals, we subtracted the American Hospital Association's measures of the cost of care in federal, long-term, tuberculosis, and psychiatric hospitals from the Social Security values for total and government spending. An alternative estimating procedure that started with the American Hospital Association data to estimate private expenditure directly produced almost the exact estimates as those presented here.

[2]ACPPD × (Direct Consumer Expenditures/Total Expenditures).
[3]ACPPD × (Direct Consumer Expenditures/Private Expenditures).

8 Economic Concerns

Table 1.2   National Health Expenditures (aggregate and per capita)

Year	GNP (in billions)	Health Expenditures (in millions)	Health Expenses per Capita	Health as a Percentage of GNP	Hospital Care as a Percentage of GNP*
Year Ending June 30					
1929	$ 101.3	$ 3,589	$ 29	3.5	0.7
1935	68.9	2,846	22	4.1	0.9
1940	95.4	3,883	29	4.1	0.9
1950	264.8	12,027	78	4.5	1.0
1955	381.0	17,330	104	4.5	1.1
1960	498.3	25,856	142	5.2	1.5
1965	688.0	38,892	198	5.9	1.9
1966	722.4	42,109	212	5.8	1.9
1967	773.5	47,897	238	6.2	2.2
1968	830.2	53,765	264	6.5	2.3
1969	904.2	60,617	295	6.7	2.4
1970	960.2	69,201	333	7.2	2.7
1971	1,019.8	77,162	368	7.6	2.9
1972	1,111.8	86,687	410	7.8	3.0
1973	1,238.6	95,383	447	7.7	3.0
1974	1,361.2	106,321	495	7.8	3.1
1975	1,451.5	123,716	571	8.5	3.3
Year Ending September 30					
1975	1,487.1	127,719	588	8.6	3.4
1976	1,667.4	145,102	663	8.7	3.5
1977	1,838.0	162,627	737	8.8	3.5
1978	2,107.6	192,400	863	9.1	3.6
1979	2,346.5	216,500	964	9.3	3.7
1980	2,631.7	247,500	1,049	9.4	3.7
1981	2,957.8	285,200	1,197	9.6	3.9
1982	3,069.2	321,200	1,334	10.5	4.2
1983	3,304.8	355,100	1,461	10.7	4.3
1984	3,662.8	387,400	1,580	10.6	4.1
Year Ending December 31					
1985	3,990.0	425,000	1,728	10.7	3.9
1986 est.	4,090.0	445,000	1,780	10.85	3.9
1988 est.	4,635.0	535,500	2,098	11.5	4.0
1990 est.	5,272.0	624,500	2,398	11.8	4.1

SOURCE: 1929–1985; DHHS, HCFA, Division of National Cost Estimates.
*This is an underestimate of the hospital sector's share of GNP because the figure does not include services provided by nonsalaried physicians within hospitals. Because physicians have increasingly pursued subspecialty careers that demand increased reliance on the hospital, the magnitude of the hospital sector underestimation bias has undoubtedly increased since the 1950s.

(short-term, nonfederal) was paid directly by the consumer and 50 percent was paid by third parties, including government and private insurance. By 1980 the proportion of the costs paid directly by the consumer had dropped to 13 percent (see line A.3, Table 1.1). However, after 1980 this figure increased to 16 percent by 1985 because of increases in cost-sharing provisions (covered in Chapter 3). The result of this growth in third-party coverage is that the average cost of a patient day to the consumer has only increased 69 percent from 1950 to 1982, whereas the 1982 ACPPD is more than 504 percent what it was in constant dollar terms in 1950 (see lines D and E, Table 1.1).

The nation spent $425 billion, or 10.7 percent of the gross national product (GNP), on health care in 1985. Health spending as a share of GNP was at a historic high in 1985 and is projected to increase to 11.8 percent of GNP by 1990 (Table 1.2).

There is substantial evidence to indicate that when a large proportion of medical costs are offset by insurance, doctors will recommend more services, and consumers in turn will demand more and better services. Thus as insurance increases, a higher quality of care is demanded. At this juncture, it is important to make the point that the increase in demand is for greater intensity of care per diem, rather than for more bed days.* Hospitals, as they work to fill the demand for increased services, raise prices in order to raise revenue which can be used to provide the more expensive form of care demanded. Since most consumers do not pay out-of-pocket for hospital care because they are heavily insured, they are shielded from the resulting increase in prices and do not respond in the normal way by curtailing demand. On the contrary, as consumers observe the higher prices, or cost, of medical care, their desire for insurance increases and likewise the demand for medical care increases, so the inflationary cycle continues. This six-step medical cost inflationary cycle is illustrated in Figure 1.1. The rate-limiting step, the stage in the cycle at which intervention is most effective, is between A and B, the point at which insurance stimulates demand.

It is easy to see why individuals would want to insure themselves against the risk of a very large medical bill; it is not so readily apparent why they are willing to pay the additional actuarial charges associated with insurance for small bills when these extra charges could be avoided if the small bills were paid out-of-pocket.

---

* This is not to say that there was not a dramatic expansion in the demand for days of hospitalization prior to 1975, but the demand for days abated in the 1970s (Table 1.3) and declined in the 1980s.

Table 1.3 Growth Rates in the Demand Supply of Nonfederal Short-Term Hospitals, Selected Years 1950–1985

Year	FTE Personnel per Adjusted[1] Patient Day	Patient Days (millions)	Admissions per 1,000 Citizens	Admissions per Year (in thousands)	Number of Hospitals	Number of Beds	Bed Occupancy (percent)	Outpatient Visits (millions)	Surgical Cases Outpatient (millions)	Inpatient (millions)
1950	1.62	136	111.4	16,663	5,031	505,000	73.7			
1955	1.85	149	117.3	19,100	5,237	568,000	71.5			
1960	2.06	174	129.2	22,970	5,407	639,000	74.7			
1965	2.24	205	138.8	26,463	5,736	741,000	76.0	93	na[2]	na
1966	2.37	215	138.9	26,897	5,812	768,000	76.5	96	na	na
1967	2.41	223	139.0	26,988	5,850	788,000	77.6	103	na	na
1970	2.65	242	145.6	29,252	5,859	848,000	78.0	134	na	na
1974	2.89	256	157.8	32,943	5,977	931,000	75.3	195	na	na
1978	3.23	263	161.1	34,575	5,935	980,000	73.5	204	1.9	16.6
1979	3.28	267	162.4	35,160	5,923	988,000	73.8	204	2.7	16.5
1980	3.34	279	165.8	37,562	5,905	992,000	75.4	207	3.2	16.4
1981	3.47	281	161.9	36,494	5,879	986,000	75.9	207	3.7	16.4
1982	3.52	284	156.7	36,429	5,863	982,000	75.2	214	4.3	16.2
1983	3.59	277	154.4	37,721	5,843	988,000	73.4	231	5.0	15.9
1984	3.84	252	147.1	36,260	5,810	978,000	66.6	234	5.9	15.5
1985	3.99	237	139.0	34,820	5,761	960,000	63.6	245	6.6	15.0

SOURCES: *American Hospital Association Guide*, 1986 edition (Chicago: AHA, 1986); DHHS and the Bureau of the Census.
[1]Full-Time Equivalent (FTE) personnel adjusted for outpatient visits rendered.
[2]na = not available.

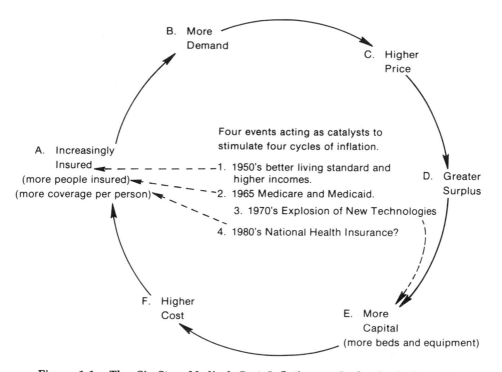

Figure 1.1 The Six-Step Medical Cost Inflationary Cycle. Both demand-pull inflation (steps ABC) and cost-push inflation (steps CDEF) have been contributing to the inflation rate in the hospital industry. Most economists agree with Martin Feldstein that the rate-limiting step is the demand-pull step AB. Hospital administrators tend to perceive only the CDEFC half of the cycle; i.e., they view the inflation as cost-push, with the various production costs forcing their prices to rise to meet the increased costs.

The reasons for the proliferation of comprehensive "first-dollar" insurance policies are twofold. First, the present tax structure encourages such policies. Second, these insurance policies can be seen as a form of precommitment on the part of policy holders.

The current tax structure encourages comprehensive health insurance in the following way. Employer-paid health insurance may be deducted from the employing company's taxable income. At the same time, employees need not include the value of health insurance policies in their taxable income, nor are the premiums subject to social security or state income tax. Thus health insurance can be considered to be a form of tax-exempt extra income. In addition, approximately one-half of the amount an individual pays for health insurance is tax deductible. The "tax break" amounted to some $7 billion for individuals and $37 billion for business in 1986. This government subsidy of health insurance premiums averages

18 percent of the premiums and, in effect, offsets all of the charges associated with private insurance as well as part of the cost of service (Enthoven, 1980; Feldstein, 1977).

Havighurst and Hackbarth (1979) have argued that when individuals select the lower cost insurance plan, they should be given the savings tax free. By eliminating the practice of requiring the employer to pay the entire premium, society can end the forced subsidy of traditional solo practice fee-for-service medicine at the expense of the more efficient modes of practice. The Federal Employees Health Benefits Program is the oldest prototype of a consumer choice health plan with a fixed dollar contribution on behalf of the employer. This program, originally promoted in 1959 by public officials in the name of fair market competition, has served both the taxpayer and federal employees well.

Health insurance can also be viewed as a form of "precommitment" on the part of individuals who do not want monetary costs to influence their choice of medical care. By precommitting themselves through insurance, individuals do not have to make the choice between expensive, highly intensive care and cheaper, less intensive care (Fuchs, 1979). In addition, insurance is a form of self-control for individuals who fear they might spend all their money now, in the short term, and not have it in the long term when they need it for medical care; it therefore acts to relieve some of the tension in the conflict between long-term and short-term goals.

The Causes of Cost Inflation

The underlying causes of the inflation in overall expenditures on hospital care can be divided into four categories: (1) increased demand (demand-pull); (2) increases in the cost of producing care; (3) increases in the prices of inputs used to produce care; and (4) changes in the markets that supply inputs, particularly the labor market (supply-push).

When a product is demanded at a rate faster than it can be produced, the product is considered scarce and its price rises. At the same time, the demand rises for factors used in its production, and so the prices of the factors rise. This form of inflation has been labeled *demand-pull* and is considered a major cause of inflation in medical costs (Salkever, 1975).

The past three decades of medical cost inflation can be divided into two basic periods: 1950–1981 and 1983–present. The demand-pull theory attracted a surplus of scholarly labor from 1950 to 1981. Health expenditures increased 2,270 percent during this period, with a marked increase in hospital usage. Analytical studies of medical cost inflation are important because such increases reflect a serious misallocation of resources toward expensive medical practice and a basic failure of the health care system to reflect individual consumer preferences (Feldstein, 1977).

The two major ingredients to understanding this inflation in health care costs are obvious: the growth in health insurance and the changing nature of the hospital. Medicare and private payers began to reverse this demand-pull incentive structure in the period 1982–83. This is not to say that the demand-pull for lifesaving technology has abated, but rather that the demand-pull is not manifest in terms of increasing admissions, patient days, and hospital bed construction. All three measures of output and capacity have declined since 1982. Competition is even more cost-decreasing—nothing new for private industry but quite a revolutionary development in the health care industry. The American public is relying less on hospital beds and more on lower-cost care settings.

Although the explosion in health insurance during the past 35 years is the single most important factor in the increased demand for medical care, other factors have had an influence as well. Growth in population and increases in the average life span have contributed to the demand for medical care. The fastest-growing age group is the 65-and-older category, whose per capita expenditures on health care are four times that of adults 19 to 64. In addition, many innovations in medical technology are extremely expensive and increase the demand for medical care in a multiplicative fashion. Although the development of antibiotics and other drugs has been cost-effective in saving lives, new developments in medical technology, such as chemotherapy and organ transplantation, require expensive equipment and skilled personnel; by prolonging life instead of curing illness, such technology can be radically cost-increasing (Eastaugh, 1983). The cost-increasing nature of medical technology will be discussed in Chapters 16–18.

Several factors, aside from nationwide inflation and excess aggregate demand, have contributed to an increase in the cost of producing medical care. Malpractice insurance, a negligible problem 15 years ago, has increased an average of 29 percent a year from 1970 to 1978 (Freeland et al., 1979). The threat of malpractice suits has caused an increase in the number of tests ordered by physicians. Some groups would like to explain the cost-control problems in terms of defensive medicine. The American Medical

Association (AMA) provided a rather high estimate of $15 billion in 1986 for such unnecessary tests. As we shall see in Chapters 16–18, that much unnecessary testing may be taking place, but all of it is not attributable to the malpractice crisis. Of the $1,820 spent on health care by the average American in 1986, $19 went toward malpractice insurance (Arnett et al., 1986). Some doctors may spend $100,000 a year in malpractice premiums, but the average doctor spends only 5.8 percent of gross income on such premiums. In fact, the average doctor pays more for an automobile than for malpractice premiums. Those who blame the "terrible for-profit insurance companies" for the malpractice crisis will be dismayed to discover that the 32 nonprofit, physician-owned companies have premiums that have been rising since 1978 at the same annual rate as the for-profit companies because of comparable claims experience. Providers should do a careful cost-benefit comparison between various claims-made coverage plans and occurrence coverage.

Many physicians have argued that the best form of malpractice prevention is through the sharing of uncertainty (with the patient) and better-informed consent (Gutheil et al., 1984). Malpractice will continue to be a problem in certain towns that cannot find enough doctors (e.g., obstetricians), but the self-serving anecdotal reports of "early retirement" forced by malpractice problems represent an ice cube floating on the surface of a lake, not the tip-of-an-iceberg "crisis." Steps to moderate the liability crisis in 1986 by federal and state governments across the entire economy may reduce the level of "crisis" rhetoric.

Rising physician expenditures also play a major role in the inflation of medical care costs. However, in some sense, hospitals have grown "richer" than physicians, especially following the passage of Medicare and Medicaid. From 1950 to 1983, the rate of physician price inflation has been less than the rate of hospital price inflation (in Table 1.4, column 2-C is always less than column 3), although both the hospital industry and the physician service industry are outperforming (inflating faster than) the general economy. Physician price inflation has been a problem of both consumer demand-pull (increased per capita usage) and pure price effects, from 1955 to 1982. However, the demand-pull impact of increased consumer demand has been lacking in the past three years, as evidenced by the negative figure in column 2-B in Table 1.4. The AMA's Socioeconomic Monitoring System reported a 16 percent decline in the number of outpatient visits per physician per week between the first half of 1982 and the first half of 1986. Physician price expansion was as much a problem in 1985–86 as it

Table 1.4   Physician Services: Annual Rates of Increase in Expenditures, Allocation of Cost Inflation to Price, per Capita Use, and Population Shifts

Time Period	(1) Annual Increase in Total Expenses for Physician Services	Sources of Physician Cost Inflation			(3) Annual Increase in Hospital Price[1]
		(2-A) Population	(2-B) Per Capita Use	(2-C) Price	
1950–1955	6.0%	1.7%	0.9%	3.5%	6.3%
1955–1960	9.1	1.7	4.1	3.3	6.5
1960–1965	9.0	1.5	4.9	2.6	6.6
1965–1968	9.8	1.1	2.5	6.2	11.3
1968–1971	10.9	0.9	2.9	7.1	14.6
1971–1974[2]	10.0	0.8	5.2	4.0	11.0
1974–1977	17.6	0.8	5.8	11.0	15.2
1977–1980	13.2	0.8	3.5	8.9	14.0
1980–1983	9.3	0.8	2.9	5.6	9.6
1983–1986	6.0	0.8	−3.4	8.6	5.8

SOURCE: Health Care Financing Administration, Department of Health and Human Services, unpublished data.
[1]Charges per inpatient day.
[2]The Economic Stabilization Program was in effect 8/15/71 to 4/30/74.

was following the Nixon price control program—the so-called five-year "catch-up" period of 1974–1979.

Cost Containment

One may approach the problem of containing rising hospital costs from two directions. First, attempts could be made to lower the cost of production of hospital care at any level of intensity by improving efficiency, by achieving greater economies of scale through building larger hospitals, or by redesigning the market to encourage competition. Second, the current trend toward more intensive care could be curtailed through programs designed to limit supply expansion (for example, the Certificate-of-Need program), through preventive medicine, or through attempts to decrease the demand for medical care by encouraging greater cost-consciousness on the part of consumers (Whitted and Torrens, 1985).

Essentially, any attempt to lower costs while not reducing the quality or intensity of care is an attempt to improve efficiency. Efficiency can be identified in three forms: technical, economic,

and allocative. *Technical efficiency* refers to the relationship between input and output, irrespective of cost. If one cannot reduce
the amount of input and still produce the same amount of output,
then maximum technical efficiency has been achieved. In a hospital context, for example, inputs might be full-time equivalent
employees, and outputs would be days of care. *Economic efficiency*
refers to the relationship between inputs and cost. When a day of
care is provided at the minimum possible cost, there is economic
efficiency. *Allocative efficiency* in health care involves determining
from among which inputs the allocation of resources would be least
costly for achieving an improved level of output (health status). A
health production function is necessary to describe the relationship between combinations of inputs and the resulting output.
Fuchs (1986) reviews the findings and limitations of a number of
studies whereby improved levels of health output are produced
using different combinations of inputs. The reader should be
careful to differentiate production functions from a closely labeled
concept—the production possibility curve—which describes the
trade-off between different outputs from a given set of resources.
We shall consider in the coming sections the impact of pricing
policies and capacity (size, equipment) decisions on efficiency.

The advent of federal and private prospective pricing has placed
hospitals at risk for their cost behavior and created a revolution in
two senses. First, and for the first time, hospitals that are the most
successful in holding down costs receive the advantages of higher
operating margins and retained earnings for future capital replacement and growth. Second, the term "price" no longer refers to the
old friendly concept of "charges" set by the hospital or in negotiation. Price has been exogeneously thrust upon the sellers—in this
case hospitals—by third-party payers interested in price competition. However, the seller could rightfully complain that the Health
Care Financing Administration (HCFA) has offered something
other than a free-market-determined price. HCFA has utilized its
monopsony power to administer a form of price controls and to act
as a "prudent buyer" on the taxpayers' behalf.

Many clinicians and hospital managers have found that the
transition from reimbursement to payment, and from cost-based to
price-based financing, has been far from smooth. The past two
decades of blank-check, pay-hospitals-what-they-spend financing
arrangements have done little to control costs. In fact, under cost
payment, voluntary efforts to cut costs became a voluntary suicide
program to shrink the assets and prestige of the hospital.

Health services delivery is emerging as a market-driven industry. The current administration at the U.S. Department of Health

and Human Services (DHHS) seems to be moving in the direction of more competition through competitive bidding and capitation contracts. Health care payers should work to devise a bidding scheme that manages cost reductions without harming quality. Before suggesting a quality-enhancing bidding system, it is necessary to survey why federal officials think that the hospital industry is currently too profitable because it earns a 14.12 percent profit margin per prospective payment system (PPS) case, according to the DHHS inspector general, Richard Kusserow (December 1985).

Sufficient Payment Rates: Our Money or Their Lives?

This section discusses some of the basic issues that limit the smooth transition to prospective hospital payment. This highly regulated industry suffers from uncertainty as to how payment rates will change. In addition, hospitals are experiencing problems in product-line planning, unbundling of services, cost accounting, and explaining these new developments to their medical staffs. Regulators and payers are enjoying the benefits of declining admission rates and duration of stay, but the equity of the payment scheme is questionable. Improvements in PPSs are suggested as a way to reap scale economies of quality and efficiency, preserve access, and encourage hospitals to develop a balanced portfolio of service lines that foster regionalization. In terms of improving efficiency and effectiveness, the hospital sector has one leg over the fence of change and the other dangling. With so much cost-containment activity, it is reasonable to ask, "Are hospital costs under control?" The answer is a complex mix of good and bad news.

The 1976–1986 trends from the AHA panel survey of 1,200 hospitals in all 50 states provide a useful sample, including all patients (not just Medicare) and more than 17 states (the sample universe for the DHHS Inspector General's audited Medicare hospital cost reports (Kusserow, 1985). One "good-news item" in Table 1.5 is that inpatient days have declined 8.9 percent (line 8) in 1984 because of a 0.3 day decline in average length of stay and 1.45 million fewer admissions. Inpatient days declined an additional 6.2 percent in 1985 as a by-product of a 0.1 day decline in length of stay and 1.46 million fewer admissions. In addition, total hospital inpatient costs increased only 3.2 percent in 1984 (line 9), the lowest rate since 1963. Hospital occupancy rates nationwide de-

Table 1.5   Trends in Hospital Capacity, Utilization, and Cost, 1976–1986

	Mean Annual Change (except lines 16, 17)			
	1976–1982	1983	1984	1985	1986 est.
Capacity					
1. Staffed beds	0.8%	0.6%	−1.1%	−1.8%	−3%
2. Total personnel FTEs	5.0%	1.4%	−2.3%	−2.3%	−2%
3. FTEs per 100 patient days	3.2%	3.8%	7.3%	4.1%	3%
Elderly Utilization					
4. Admissions (65 and over)	5.1%	5.5%	−2.9%	−5.0%	−3%
5. Length of stay (65 and over)	−1.5%	−4.3%	−7.6%	−2.0%	0
Utilization and Costs, All Patients					
6. Admissions	1.9%	−0.5%	−4.0%	−4.6%	−4%
7. Length of stay	−0.4%	−2.0%	−5.1%	−1.6%	−1%
8. Inpatient days	1.5%	−2.5%	−8.9%	−6.2%	−5%
9. Total inpatient expense	15.8%	10.2%	3.2%	4.4%	5%
10. Expense per day	14.1%	12.9%	13.3%	11.0%	10%
11. Expense per admission	13.7%	10.2%	7.5%	9.4%	9%
Marketbasket Price Trends					
12. HCFA input price index	10.0%	6.3%	5.6%	4.8%	5%
13. Consumer price index, CPI, all items	8.4%	3.8%	4.0%	3.8%	1.4%
Trends in Hospital Cost-Per-Unit-of-Output, in Real Terms Relative to CPI					
14. $ per day % Δ/ CPI	1.5×	3.4×	3.3×	2.9×	7.1×
15. $ per admission % Δ/ CPI	1.2×	2.7×	1.9×	2.5×	6.4×
Profitability (absolute values for the year, not % changes)					
16. Total operating margin (% of total revenue)	4.1%	5.1%	6.2%	5.9%	5%
17. Patient operating margin (% of patient revenue)	−0.5%	1.0%	2.0%	1.5%	1.3%
Outpatient Activity					
18. Outpatient visits and outpatient surgery	1.1%	3.3%	1.1%	4.8%	3%
19. Outpatient revenue	19.3%	16.0%	13.0%	16.0%	14%

SOURCE: "American Hospital Association Panel Survey" (1169 Hospitals), *AHA Economic Trends* 2:2 (Summer 1986); and HCFA DHHS.

clined by 8 percent in 1984 to 66.6 percent and to a record low of 63.6 percent (350,000 empty beds) in 1985. Inpatient costs increased 4.4 percent during 1985. While economists can savor these declines in hospital cost inflation and utilization, there are reasons for doubting that the improvements are either real or long lasting.

Declines in length of stay appear to have leveled off in 1986. Will the declines in admission rates continue? In 1967 the admission rate per thousand population to short-term nonfederal hospitals was 139. This figure peaked in 1980 at 165.8 admissions per 1,000 population, and it declined to 154.4 in 1983, 147.1 in 1984, and 139 in 1985. Two important points seem clear: (1) Declines in admission rates predated PPS, and (2) we appear to have returned to 1967 admission rates (with more ambulatory care, compensating for the increased demands of a more aged population). If admission rates continue to decline, there are no easy, reliable answers to the questions "Are we saving much money?" and "Is any harm being done to patient health status?" We shall consider these issues in subsequent chapters.

Ginsburg and Hackbarth (1986) conclude that PROs (professional review organizations) may also contribute to continued declines in admission rates, but they will not be as cost-effective as these alternative delivery systems facing the immediate threat of financial failure. PROs face the less immediate threat that they will lose their federal contracts. However, well-managed health maintenance organizations (HMOs), preferred provider organizations (PPOs), and the full spectrum of managed care alternatives could produce further declines in admission rates.

Inpatient costs are down, but much of the foregone costs may have simply been shifted to outpatient settings. Many of these alternative care sites are owned by diversified and restructured hospitals and may be providing a healthy contribution to total operating profit margin of the parent companies (Eastaugh, 1984). Also, the credit for much of this decline in inpatient expenses may rest with the fall in the basic national inflation rate—that is, the consumer price index (CPI). If 50 to 55 percent of all hospital cost inflation is simply a 6- to 12-month lagged by-product of the cooling of the general rate of inflation, we do not have much cause to cheer. Finally, perhaps much of the savings is simply the foregone hotel costs of 8.9 percent fewer bed days in 1984 and 6.2 percent fewer days in 1985.

Staff Reductions

If we are really serious about cutting costs in a labor-intensive industry, employment should decline markedly. Yet in 1984, employment declined by a mere 73,000 full-time equivalents (FTEs) from a high of 3.17 million hospital workers in 1983, and staff ratio per patient went up 7.3 percent (line 3, Table 1.5). In 1985, FTEs declined by 70,000, and the staff ratio per patient bed

day increased 4.1 percent. The staffing ratio should go up somewhat as length of stay declines, because the hospital is left with a
more severely acute proportion of bed days to service. But,
according to that logic, if length of stay declined 1.6 percent in
1985, one would predict that the staffing ratio (line 3) would
increase about 1 percent—not 4.1; otherwise, there is no savings in
economizing on the duration of patient stay. The goal is not census-
driven staffing; rather, the goal is workload-driven staffing.

One indication that hospital managers recognize this economic
imperative is the composition of staff layoffs. For example, full-
time hospital workers declined from 2.66 to 2.57 million during
1985, while the number of part-time employees remained stable at
0.975 million. Part-time employees are more willing to allow their
hours to be adjusted to meet the ups and downs of patient
workload than full-time workers.

Even with this reduction in work force, cost per admission (line
10, Table 1.5) increased faster in 1985 than in 1984. In fact, costs
per day are inflating 2.9 times faster than the CPI (line 14), and
costs per admission are more than double the CPI (line 15). While
some would like to throw a victory party to celebrate the decline of
hospital cost fever in line 9, a more appropriate response would be
to play the party spoiler and take away the punch bowl (lines 3, 10,
11, and 17).

Hospital costs are not fully under control, but revenues and
profits are at all-time highs. The patient operating margin doubled
in 1984 to 2.0 percent (line 17, Table 1.5) before slipping to 1.5
percent in 1985 ($2.1 billion). Although extrapolating from the
1,200 hospitals in the AHA panel survey in behalf of all hospitals is
always hazardous, dollar figures are nevertheless illuminating. For
example, total operating profit margin increased from 5.1 percent
($6.5 billion) to 6.2 percent ($8.3 billion) in 1984 and to 5.9 percent
($8.4 billion) in 1985 (line 16). Nearly $6 billion of this 1985 profit
figure was earned by tax-exempt hospitals, which are still misla-
beled by oldtimers as "nonprofit" facilities. The distinction between such tax-exempt hospitals and taxable hospitals is less a
matter of profitability and more a matter of degree, dividend
distribution, and converging management practice patterns. From
the provider viewpoint, that is good news, because hospitals need
retained earnings to modernize, keep pace with state-of-the-art
technology, and remain financially independent of hospital chains.

The optimal value for the operating margin would have to be 8 to
10 percent if tax-exempt hospitals were to keep up with the
competition and match the investor-owned, after-tax margins.
Unfortunately, the improvements in profitability gave Congress

and HCFA an excuse to freeze DRG (diagnostic related groups) payment rates for 1986–87. The logic is: We have been paying the hospitals too much; otherwise, they wouldn't have improved profits. Furthermore, unaudited cost reports were used to construct the DRGs; thus the price on average is 4.3 percent too high (Zimmerman, 1985). Policy makers should beware that arbitrarily low increases in payment rates after 1986 may erode the biomedical capacity of the nation's hospitals, even if beds close (18,000 in 1985), hospitals close (49 in 1985), and staff levels decrease. On the other hand, the hospital industry may be capable of trimming its cost behavior through productivity improvements and by closing grossly underutilized services—that is, specialize and regionalize.

The rewards imbedded in the performance incentives of PPS have been realized by the 82 percent of hospitals operating with an excess of revenues over expenses in fiscal year (FY) 1985. However, the average figures reported in Table 1.1 mask the fact that hundreds of rural hospitals and inner-city hospitals, which are often the sole source of inpatient care for their community, are in financial distress.

Unbundling of Services and the Payment Freeze

Hospitals avoid the PPS rate structure to some extent by substituting non-PPS outpatient and aftercare services for services that previously were delivered on an inpatient basis. In doing so, the hospital sector is taking the long-standing advice of health services researchers to substitute outpatient care for inpatient care (Davis and Russell, 1972). The HCFA office of medical care review in 1985 awarded PRO contracts with the explicit objective (quota) of treating 595,000 Medicare patients as outpatients rather than admitting them. However, it is not surprising that hospitals have improved profits under the PPS (also known as the "potential profit system"), because they can collect at the front end from preadmission care, collect an inpatient DRG price, and collect a third time at the back end from hospital-owned nursing homes, clinics, or home health care corporations.

PROs have the authority to review inpatient care only, and when a hospital unbundles services and performs the care in outpatient settings, the care avoids review. If it is safe and cost-effective to treat certain DRGs on a totally outpatient basis, then a great opportunity for containing costs exists. However, unbundling portions of a given patient episode to increase "net reimbursement advantages" (revenue in excess of costs) will increase total cost. This practice could lead to the worst of all possible scenarios: two-to three-year freezes in Medicare rates because HCFA and the PROs cannot control unbundling of services and transfer of costs to the preadmission and aftercare portion of the inpatient episode. Although cost transfers and unbundling will not occur equally across all DRGs, administrative simplicity and budget neutrality dictate that annual rate increases be reduced or eliminated.

Diversification and Rationing

The hospital as a core business has spun off a wide array of alternative ventures. It is a natural tendency to counter the impact of regulation with the development of less regulated sources of cash flow. If all the former hospital employees are working at alternative sites outside the mothership hospital, will the hospital produce much net savings? If some beds are closed in low-occupancy hospitals, and the hospitals continue to pay debt service on the closed decertified beds, have they realized much savings? Economic studies suggest that appreciable savings are achieved only when hospitals close out the fixed costs by closing entire facilities rather than trimming a few beds (Schwartz and Joskow, 1980). If hospitals avoid substantial productivity improvement and staff-reduction efforts, they may face the painful prescription of medical rationing as practiced in Great Britain (Aaron and Schwartz, 1985). In the American spirit of pluralism, there will probably be a mixed dose of all three: (1) increases in rationing, (2) small amounts of staff reduction, and (3) some incremental improvements in productivity. Providers may be comforted to realize that the more productivity innovation they ingest, the less rationing they will be forced to swallow.

PPS incentives clearly encourage hospitals to unbundle and diversify into a full range of health services (Eastaugh and Eastaugh, 1986). By doing so, the federal government is making capitation a more viable option. If hospitals own all comprehensive nonhospital services, why not pay a hospital to deliver total care? It would be administratively easier for HCFA to make capitation payments to 5,000 hospitals, or a small number of risk HMOs, than to pay 500,000 individuals and firms.

Akin to the airlines and banking industries, hospitals are overstaffed and overbuilt. Closures are a healthy sign because they get some of the pathology out of the system, eliminate fixed costs, and stimulate control over the total health care bill. As Egdahl (1984) has observed, in the labor-intensive hospital business bringing about significant cost savings without reducing staff and closing facilities is no easy task. Layoffs, or "managed attrition" that avoids firing people, is necessary to draw staffing in line with declining workloads. Hospitals, like airlines and banks, will continue to adapt to deregulation, trim their staffs, and close unnecessary service sites. At the same time, they will be diversifying into newly identified service product lines (Eastaugh and Eastaugh, 1986).

Uncertainty and Medicare Payment Rates

The existence of "DRG creep"—that is, the deliberate and systematic labeling of case mix so as to maximize reimbursement—was first postulated by Simborg (1981) in the context of the New Jersey all-payers system. Carter and Ginsburg (1985) studied the evidence of DRG creep and concluded that it explains 70 to 75 percent of the increase in case-mix index 1981–1984. In the initial three years of PPS, we have observed some significant shifts in popularity (prevalence) of certain DRGs. Cases of pneumonia DRG 89 increased to 274,538 in 1985, in contrast to DRG 182 cases that declined from the second to the fourth most popular DRG 1984–85 (Table 1.6). Attributing cause and effect in assessing these shifts is hard, except in a few obvious cases (DRG 39 lens procedures are increasingly done more profitably on an outpatient basis). The industry argues that most DRG creep represents honest improvement in coding practices. Furthermore, better coding of medical records is done if hospitals are paid on the basis of this coding. Needless to say, for Medicare patients the medical record determines payment (by determining the patient's DRG), not the amount collected on charge routing slips.

During the spring of 1986, the Medicare actuaries and the Prospective Payment Assessment Commission disagreed by 0.8 percent over the size of the offset for the following year's DRG rates. The issue was not trivial to the hospital industry, as a 0.8 point disagreement represents about $405 million. The more restrictive (high estimates of DRG creep) offset by the actuaries won the policy debate, and Congress confirmed a mere 1.15 percent price increase for 1987.

Why the inability to differentiate among patient types threatens to undermine the per case payment system can best be illustrated using an example. A patient with a peptic ulcer can be treated nonsurgically under DRG 176 and receive a payment of $3,600, or be treated with endoscopic therapy as a DRG 155 and receive a payment in excess of $7,000 (McMahon and Smits, 1986). The hospital earns an easy windfall profit of $3,400 for this minimally

Table 1.6   Shifts in DRG Prevalence Within the Medicare Population, Fiscal Years 1985, 1984, and CY1982

Ranking Among DRGs					Cost Weight	% of Medicare Cases		
1985	1984	1982	DRG #	Name	FY85	1985	1984	1982
Ten Increasingly Popular Medicare DRGs								
1	1	1	127	Heart failure and shock	1.03	5.1	4.7	4.5
2	6	7	89	Pneumonia and pleurisy	1.09	3.5	3.0	2.4
3	5	11	140	Angina pectoris	.75	3.4	3.0	2.0
6	10	21	296	Nutritional and miscellaneous metabolic disorders	.88	2.1	1.7	1.0
7	8	13	138	Cardiac arrhythmia and conduction disorders	.92	2.1	2.0	1.8
8	12	16	96	Bronchitis and asthma	.79	1.9	1.7	1.6
12	14	26	209	Major joint procedure	2.27	1.7	1.4	0.9
13	13	25	336	Trans. prostatectomy	.99	1.6	1.5	0.9
14	15	23	174	Gastrointestinal	.92	1.6	1.4	0.9
19	20	32	210	Hip and femur procedure	2.06	1.2	1.1	0.8
Five Decreasingly Prevalent Medicare DRGs								
4	2	2	182	Esophagitis, gastroenteritis, and digestive disorders	.61	3.3	3.7	3.8
9	7	12	243	Medical back problem	.75	1.8	2.0	2.0
10	9	5	88	Chronic obstructive	1.03	1.7	2.0	2.9
18	3	4	39	Lens procedure	.50	1.3	3.7	3.6
25	21	17	82	Respiratory	1.13	1.0	1.1	1.3

SOURCE: HCFA Division of Information Analysis.

invasive, well-established diagnostic procedure. The endoscopic approach to therapy earns a $5,500 premium at 1987 prices if bleeding esophageal varices are scoped (DRG 201) and not just treated medically. Sometimes the drift to a more profitable DRG pigeonhole (category) may be a completely paper exercise, without any real shifts in treatment patterns.

Home Care and Other Alternatives

Some researchers refer to the subacute care that hospitals had traditionally provided but which is now provided on an ambulatory basis (in response to PPS or utilization review) as *transitional care*. Transitional care can be provided in a skilled nursing facility, intermediate care facility, at home (with the assistance of home health workers), and sometimes in hospital-based, subacute care bed sections (not included under PPS). Some of the eliminated hospital days—40 million between 1983 and 1985 (Table 1.3)—may result in increased days of care in other transitional settings. The savings from shorter stays and fewer admissions among public and private patients are partially offset by the costs incurred in transitional care. Medicare enrollees, other patients, and families are finding that some of the financial burden for this transitional care has shifted onto them. By definition, some cost shift has to occur because transitional care is less well insured (more consumer out-of-pocket cost sharing) relative to hospital care.

Much of the growth in transitional care has been in the home health care arena (Table 1.7). The nature of home health service is changing. The 1986 survey of Area Agencies on Aging (AAA) reported a fivefold increase in case management services, a threefold increase in home skilled nursing care, and a twofold increase in personal care services and housekeeping following the first three years of PPS (1983–1986). In contrast, the rate of skilled nursing facility (SNF) utilization has declined over the past 15 years, despite a mild upturn in utilization these past three years. The reasons for this are probably threefold: improved mobility of the elderly population, declining preferences for institutionalization,

Table 1.7   Medicare Beneficiaries' Usage of Home Health Care and Skilled Nursing Facility (SNF)[1], by age, 1970–1985

| | *Utilization per 1,000 Medicare Enrollees* | | | |
| | *Home Health Agency* | | *Skilled Nursing Facility* | |
Patient Age	*1970*	*1985*	*1970*	*1985 (est.)*
65–69	5	34	5	5
70–74	7	51	10	6
75–79	9	79	19	12
80–84	12	98	36	20
85 and over	12	111	54	35
Total	8	66	16	12

SOURCE: Health Care Financing Administration, Bureau of Data Management and Strategy.
[1]Less than 5,000 of the national supply of SNFs are Medicare certified.

and "effective lids" on the supply of SNF beds because of the efforts of health planners and Medicaid rate setters to offer low payment levels.

Data on the development of hospital-based subacute care beds are not yet available from the American Hospital Association. HCFA officials fear that some hospitals may place financial concerns above the clinical concerns of the patients by moving some individuals prematurely so as to "game" the system and receive supplemental payments for rehabilitation or other transitional types of care. Unfortunately, it will be nearly impossible to judge how much of this is "gaming" versus a medically appropriate transfer or discharge to a lower cost service setting. These lower cost service settings not only represent an alternative source of revenue; they also help minimize losses that might have been incurred by a PPS patient sitting in an inpatient bed any longer than deemed necessary. However, when medically appropriate, transitional care is a good loss minimizer and revenue-generating strategy. If medically inappropriate, the transfer or early discharge may cause the PPS patient to relapse and be rehospitalized, much to the embarrassment (e.g., PRO oversight) and financial loss of all concerned at the hospital.

Most ethical providers argue that transitional care is more properly and less expensively delivered in less resource-intensive settings. Officials at HCFA and in the HMO industry can observe (with some smugness) that this discovery of lower cost alternative care settings was largely prompted by hospital prospective payment formulas and employer interest in prepaid care. The most critical policy question is whether this movement to transitional care will decrease total per capita costs. Three other key questions are (1) whether increasing severity-of-illness levels among transitional care patients pose a threat to patient quality of care, (2) whether access to services is a problem for certain patient groups, and (3) whether theorized continuity-of-care benefits accrue if the patients receive all their transitional care from one institution. Future research may provide answers.

Economies of Scale

In considering what happens to the level of output as the level of input increases, we are addressing the issue of economies of scale. If output grows at the same rate as inputs are increased, then there are constant returns to scale (per unit costs are the same at any given level of output). If output increases at a rate greater than inputs are increased, then there are increasing returns to scale (per unit costs decrease at high levels of output). If output grows at a rate less than the corresponding increase in inputs, then there are decreasing returns to scale (per unit costs increase as output rises).

Economies of scale are generally illustrated by the long run average cost curve (LRACC) in Figure 1.2. Hospital size is measured by either number of beds or average daily patient census. Output is typically measured by patient days, and in some cases patient discharges or admissions. The classic configuration of the LRACC is the U-shape illustrated in Figure 1.2A, Case 2. Generally, average costs are expected to decrease as output increases up

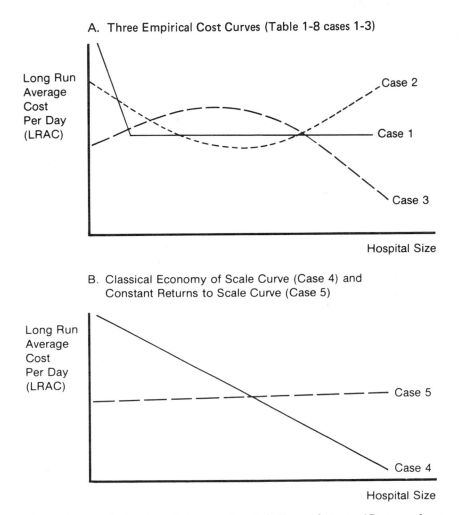

Figure 1.2 **Relationships Between Hospital Size and Cost.** (Case numbers are referred to in Table 1-8.)

to a point of minimum average costs, after which diseconomies of scale may take over. This point of minimum average costs is the optimal size for a firm or hospital (or the optimal level of output). Diseconomies beyond a certain point may be the result of inefficient management in large-scale facilities, or they may reflect the costs of increased travel time for physicians and patients (Fuchs, 1986; Eastaugh, 1986).

The central problem with applying the concept of economies of scale to hospital size is that hospitals do not produce a uniform product. Generally, the larger hospitals tend to treat more complex cases and to provide a much broader spectrum of care; thus a patient day in a small hospital is not equivalent to a patient day in a large hospital. Accordingly, any study of economies of scale must take case mix into account.

Research studies on economies of scale in the hospital sector have found five different shapes of the LRACC (see Table 1.8). Failure to account for case mix results in a U-shaped LRACC. When adjustment for case mix is made, the LRACC is found to be slightly downward sloping or flat for larger hospitals, indicating that economies of scale may exist, although the economies may not be great enough to justify much larger hospitals. An additional criticism of studies of the LRACC is that highly aggregated cost data make it impossible to separate the diseconomies due to size from those due to inefficiency, thus potentially leading to wrong conclusions regarding the optimal hospital size (Finkler, 1979).

Much more significant economies of scale have been found on a departmental basis, under conditions where the product is homogeneous, by HAS (Hospital Administrative Services) researchers. Consequently, one would presuppose that if we could perform a perfect study adjusting for heterogeneous product mix of patient cases, then economies of scale would be more significant than the 16 percent difference between the smallest and largest hospitals in Figure 1.2B, Case 4. In summary, the data on economies of scale are not persuasive enough to suggest that we close all hospitals below a certain size. The increased travel time to consumers and staff associated with closing all below-average-size hospitals would probably outweigh the benefits accrued in increasing returns to scale.

Grannemann et al. (1986) studied 800 hospital emergency departments and concluded that substantial economies of scale exist for all but the very largest urban emergency rooms. Recent results concerning the degree of inpatient economies of scale are mixed, largely because the costs that were included and the case-mix measures that were employed vary widely from study to study.

Table 1.8 Survey of Studies Concerning Economies of Scale in the Hospital Sector

Case 1. L-Shaped Average Cost Curve Found:
 Feldstein, M. S., and J. Schuttinga. "Hospital Costs in Massachusetts: A Methodological Study." *Inquiry* 14:1 (March 1977), 22–31.
 Francisco, E. W. "Analysis of Cost Variations Among Short-Term General Hospitals." In H. E. Klarman (ed.), *Empirical Studies in Health Economics*. Baltimore, Maryland: Johns Hopkins University Press, 1970, pp. 321–332.
 Lave, J. R., and L. B. Lave. "Hospital Cost Functions." *American Economic Review* 60 (June 1970), 379–395.

Case 2. U-Shaped Average Cost Curve Found:
 Schaafsma, J. "Average Hospital Size and the Total Operating Expenditures for Beds Distributed over H Hospitals." *Applied Economics* 18:1 (April 1986), 279–290.
 Carr, W. J., and P. J. Feldstein. "The Relationship of Cost to Hospital Size." *Inquiry* 4:2 (June 1967), 45–65.
 Cohen, H. A. "Variations in Cost Among Hospitals of Different Sizes." *Southern Economic Journal* 33 (January 1967), 355–366.
 Feldstein, M. S. *Economic Analysis for Health Service Efficiency*. Amsterdam: North-Holland Publishing Co., 1968.

Case 3. Inverted U-Shaped Average Cost Curve Found:
 Ingbar, M. L., and L. D. Taylor. *Hospital Costs in Massachusetts*. Cambridge, Mass.: Harvard University Press, 1968.

Case 4. Downward Sloping Average Cost Curve Throughout:
 Baron, D. P. "A Study of Hospital Cost Inflation." *Journal of Human Resources* 9 (Winter 1974), 33–49.
 Berry, R. E., Jr. "Returns to Scale in the Production of Hospital Services." *Health Service Research* 2 (Summer 1967), 123–139.
 Feldstein, P. J. *An Empirical Investigation of the Marginal Cost of Hospital Services*. Chicago, Illinois: University of Chicago, Center for Health Administration Studies, 1961.

Case 5. Constant Returns to Scale:
 Bays, C. "Specification Error in the Estimation of Hospital Cost Functions." *Review of Economics and Statistics* 42:2 (February 1980), 302–305.
 Evans, R. G. "Behavioral Cost Functions for Hospitals." *Canadian Journal of Economics* 4 (May 1971), 198–215.
 Lipscomb, J., I. E. Raskin, and J. Eichenholz. "The Use of Marginal Cost Estimates in Hospital Cost Containment Policy." In M. Zubkoff, I. E. Raskin, and R. S. Hanft (eds.), *Hospital Cost Containment: Selected Notes for Future Policy*. New York: Prodist Press, 1978, pp. 514–537.

Bays (1980), in an analysis of California hospitals, reports that if inputs of admitting physicians are excluded from the analysis, the hospital exhibits constant or mildly decreasing average costs. However, if the author includes the cost of physician inputs into the analysis, including fee-for-service billings, the average costs increase with size. Such an analysis commingles the effects of physician payment and hospitalwide economies of scale. Within individual hospital departments and product lines, substantial economies of scale are to be observed. The most common problem faced by the analysts is commingling case-mix effects with unit cost; there tends to be a correlation between more difficult case mix and size (Keating, 1984). Schaafsma (1986) studied 40 hospitals and concludes that in medium-sized hospitals (60 to 293 beds) the economies-of-scale effect (12 percent) is more than offset by a case-mix effect, and hence costs increase slightly with volume. However, in hospitals with over 300 beds the economies-of-scale effect is sufficiently powerful to swamp any case-mix effect.

In the following chapters we shall consider in some detail various aspects of social and institutional cost-containment issues. The problems of rising demand, consumer expectations, and the issue of unnecessary care are the subject of Chapter 2. Viewed in this light, no sensible analyst could conclude that medical technology per se is the cause of rising costs. However, curtailment of overcapitalization and inefficient physician-ordering habits form an increasingly important set of issues.

The concluding chapter will enable us to critically review and interrelate the disparate economic and financial management issues raised in the text. One final word of caution for those who believe that the unplanned medical economy is a "nonsystem" of scattered parts: Observe how systematically providers resist government attempts to institute change.

References

AARON, H., AND SCHWARTZ, W. (1985). "Hospital Cost Control: A Bitter Pill to Swallow." *Harvard Business Review* 63:2 (March-April), 160–167.

ARNETT, R., McKUSICK, D., SONNEFELD, S., and COWELL, C. (1986). "Projections of Health Care Spending to 1990." *Health Care Financing Review* 7:3 (Spring), 1–36.

BAYS, C. (1980). "Specification Error in the Estimation of Hospital Cost Functions." *Review of Economics and Statistics* 42:2 (February), 302–305.

CARTER, G., and GINSBURG, P. (1986). "The Medicare Case Mix Index Increase: Medical Practice Changes, Aging, and DRG Creep." Rand Corporation Report R-3292 (June). Santa Monica, Calif.: Rand Corporation.

DAVIS, K., and RUSSELL, L. (1972). "Substitution of Hospital Outpatient Care for Inpatient Care." *Review of Economics and Statistics* 54:2 (May), 109–120.

EASTAUGH, S. (1984). "Hospital Diversification and Financial Management." *Medical Care* 22:8 (August), 704–723.

EASTAUGH, S. (1983). "Placing a Value on Life and Limb." *Health Matrix* 1:1 (Winter), 5–21.

EASTAUGH, S., and EASTAUGH, J. (1986). "Prospective Payment Systems: Further Steps to Enhance Quality, Efficiency, and Regionalization." *Health Care Management Review* 11:4 (Fall), 37–52.

EGDAHL, R. (1984). "Should We Shrink the Health Care System?" *Harvard Business Review* 62:1 (January–February), 125–132.

ENTHOVEN, A. (1980). *Health Plan.* Reading, Mass.: Addison-Wesley.

FELDSTEIN, M. (1977). "The High Cost of Hospitals and What to Do About It." *The Public Interest* 12:48 (Summer), 40–54.

FELDSTEIN, M., and TAYLOR, A. (1981). "The Rapid Rise of Hospital Costs." In M. Feldstein (ed.), *Hospital Costs and Health Insurance,* Chap. 1. Cambridge, Mass.: Harvard University Press.

FINKLER, S. (1979). "On the Shape of the Long Run Average Cost Curve." *Health Services Research* 14:4 (Winter), 281–289.

FREELAND, M. S., ANDERSON, G., and SCHENDLER, C. E. (1979). "National Hospital Input Price Index." *Health Care Financing Review* (Summer), 37–52.

FREELAND, M., and SCHENDLER, C. (1984). "Health Spending in the 1980s: Integration of Clinical Practice Patterns with Management." *Health Care Financing Review* 5:3 (Spring), 1–68.

FUCHS, V. (1986). *The Health Economy.* Cambridge, Mass.: Harvard University Press.

FUCHS, V. (1979). "Economics, Health, and Post-Industrial Society." *Milbank Memorial Fund Quarterly/Health and Society* 57:2, 153–181.

GINSBURG, P., and HACKBARTH, G. (1986). "Alternative Delivery Systems and Medicare." *Health Affairs* 5:1 (Spring), 6–22.

GRANNEMANN, T., BROWN, T., and PAULY, M. (1986). "Estimating Hospital Costs: A Multiple-Output Analysis." *Journal of Health Economics* 5:2 (June), 107–127.

GUTHEIL, T., BURSZTAJN, H., and BRODSKY, A. (1984). "Malpractice Prevention Through the Sharing of Uncertainty: Informed Consent and the Therapeutic Alliance." *New England Journal of Medicine* 311:1 (July 5), 49–51.

HAVIGHURST, C., and HACKBARTH, J. (1979). "Private Cost Containment." *New England Journal of Medicine* 300:23 (June 7), 1298–1305.

KEATING, B. (1984). "Cost Shifting: An Empirical Examination of Hospital Bureaucracy." *Applied Economics* 16:3 (July), 279–289.

KUSSEROW, R. (1985). "Report of the HHS Inspector General: Performance Under the Prospective Payment System, Results from 892 Hospitals" (December 9).

MCMAHON, L., and SMITS, H. (1986). "Can Medicare Prospective Payment Survive the ICD-9-CM Disease Classification System?" *Annals of Internal Medicine* 104:4 (April), 562–566.

SALKEVER, D. (1975). "Hospital Wage Inflation: Supply-Push or Demand-Pull?" *Quarterly Review of Economics and Business* 15:33 (Autumn), 33–48.

SCHAAFSMA, J. (1986). "Average Hospital Size and the Total Operating Expenditures for Beds Distributed Over H Hospitals." *Applied Economics* 18:1 (April), 279–290.

SCHWARTZ, W., and JOSKOW, P. (1980). "Duplicated Hospital Facilities: How

Much Can We Save by Consolidating Them?" *New England Journal of Medicine* 303:25 (December 18), 1449–1457.

SIMBORG, D. (1981). "DRG Creep." *New England Journal of Medicine* 304:26 (June 25), 1602–1604.

WHITTED, G., and TORRENS, P. (1985). *Managing Corporate Health Care Expenses: A Primer for Executives*. New York: Praeger.

ZIMMERMAN, M. (1985). Testimony as Associate Director of the General Accounting Office (GAO), U.S. Congress, House Ways and Means Health Subcommittee, May 14, 1985.

Chapter 2

ECONOMIC MODELS OF PHYSICIAN AND HOSPITAL BEHAVIOR

The first step in the analysis of the medical-care market is a comparison between the actual market and the competitive model.

—KENNETH ARROW

An important general lesson in this example is that a theory can make "unrealistic" assumptions (in this case profit maximization) but still yield valid predictions. Thus a theory should not be rejected simply because its assumptions are unrealistic or even known to be wrong.

—JOSEPH NEWHOUSE

The system is always driven by the factor in short supply. We now have a short supply of patients, not doctors.

—WALTER MCCLURE

The literature on physician and hospital behavior has been characterized by two approaches: utility maximization models (Feldstein, 1970) or profit maximization models (Sloan, 1976). Supporters of the first approach view classical maxims concerning simple profit maximization as totally unrealistic. Supporters of the profit maximization approach view utility maximizers as unnecessarily fuzzy and complex. The situation is complicated because the hospital is an organizational anomaly. The principal input controlling the organization is a group of individuals—the physicians—who neither own nor work as employees of the firm. Rather than work with

the unique aspects of the doctor-hospital interaction, most conservative economists have opted for standard competitive analysis
of a two-element utility function (profit, and slack or leisure) as the
best first approximation to physician and hospital behavior (Pauly
and Redisch, 1973). Advocates of the profit maximization model
maintain that if a multifaceted model and a simple model work
almost equally well, one should prefer the simpler version. Models
with "excessive" realism are viewed as a mixed blessing, because
they complicate empirical implementation. In some cases, the
simple and complex formulations perform equally well, but their
explanatory power is too low to place any confidence in the
models.

All economic models posit some degree of profit maximization in
the physician's utility function, where profit is defined as net
earnings above practice overhead costs and above an imputed basic
wage for the profession. The specification of an imputed wage
allows for formal consideration of the clinician's trade-off of leisure
for income. The physician utility function *(U)* includes some of the
following elements:

$U = f$(profit, leisure time, professional status, internal ethics,
complexity of case mix, study time to keep up-to-date,
number of support staff under your supervision, etc.)

Sometimes the utility function is stated in negative terms; for
example, the disutility of working more or the disutility to the
physician of coercing doctor-induced patient visits. In stark contrast to more traditional markets, the percentage of patient visits
that is supplier-initiated is very high (39 percent, Wilensky and
Rossiter, 1980). We can infer little about the medical necessity of
these patient visits. Both groups of theorists, profit maximizers and
utility maximizers, agree that physician behavior is too complicated to explain merely by profit motives, but the first group is
adamant in asserting that, as in any other business, profit (net
income plus perks) is the most important element.

Another element of the physician's utility function is the desire
to treat an interesting complex of cases. Feldstein (1970) was the
first to incorporate the need for interesting cases into a model. The
inclusion of such provider taste variables in a model is often
ridiculed by conservative economists, in spite of demonstrable
physician mobility in pursuit of interesting cases. Many physicians
are able to change their subspecialty, or mode of practice, or locus
of practice (HMO, hospital-based, private office) every few years to
ensure an interesting patient case mix.

Early Evidence of Supplier-Induced Demand

The conventional wisdom among many health economists studying pre-1972 data was that excess consumer demand grants physicians an unusually high degree of discretionary power to affect both the quantity and price of their services. Contrary to traditional competitive economic analysis, higher physician density per capita has been shown to correlate with higher (Dyckman, 1978; Institute of Medicine, 1976; Newhouse and Phelps, 1974) or unchanged (Holahan et al., 1978) physician fees. One should introduce the caveat that correlation does not prove causality; for example, the direction of causality might be reversed. Physician density increases where fees are currently higher and more easily inflated in the future. However, there were three main hypotheses for explaining the mechanism by which physicians might maintain income levels in response to increased physician density and presumably somewhat more active competition among physicians.

Feldstein (1971) suggests that when physician density increases physicians simply reduce the percentage of patient need that goes untreated in this market of permanent excess demand. Recent unpublished studies by the Canadian government support this theory and suggest that you could increase physician density fivefold above the national average and still have excess demand. Feldstein and others ignore the issue of whether this excess demand is medically necessary. Health marketing practitioners are attempting to grasp the prickly nettle of how physicians affect consumer taste and induce the consumption of unneccessary medical services. In this respect, the growing discipline of marketing that we will survey in Chapter 9 goes beyond the purview of traditional microeconomics; for example, one does not assume that preferences and taste are determined independent of the economic system. A second hypothesis advanced by a number of economists (Evans, 1974; Fuchs and Kramer, 1973) is that much of this new demand is physician-generated rather than permanently existing.

Both of these aforementioned hypotheses postulate a unique ability of physicians to affect consumer demand. If physicians are unable to maintain a target level of demand, they can still maintain a target income by increasing fees in response to declining demand for their services. This third hypothesis has been reported by Newhouse (1970). These three hypotheses are not mutually exclusive. Physicians can maintain a target income by inflating prices, treating more elective conditions, or some combination of the two. As we shall see in a later section, one group of physicians (general practitioners) has been found to be less capable of maintaining a target income because the market for their particular services is relatively competitive. Therefore, they must act as price-takers.

The question of the appropriate health manpower ratios per capita has been a subject for lively debate among public policy makers since 1960. As we shall see in Chapter 14, the federal government has played a large role in providing the funds to expand medical school output. If an increased per capita supply of a given type of physician appears to cause both slightly higher prices and higher utilization, then Congress might consider more substantial controls on medical school capacity and residency training programs.

The benefits of a doctor oversupply (such as aggressive price competition) had not been flowing to the consumers because physicians would band together in tight trade union groups and payers were naive enough to pay a provider-set price. The situation has largely reversed in the mid-1980s, and payers are "calling the tune" to paraphrase Fuchs (1986). One study suggests that physicians began to disperse to relatively underserved locations in response to competitive pressures as early as 1979 (Newhouse et al., 1982).

Supplier-Induced Demand, Density, and Target Incomes

At the extreme, supplier inducement is characterized by some analysts as a sinister form of demand creation in which clinicians provide large amounts of unnecessary or marginally helpful care for their own monetary gain. On the other hand, other analysts have argued that supplier inducement is an argument for strict government regulation of medical school class size (and bed capacity) because each additional doctor represents $400,000 of additional expense in the health budget. Supplier inducement has often been simplistically explained by statements such as: "To know if you need to see a doctor you have to see a doctor, so demand does not exist but patient needs do exist." However, subsequent empirical studies have demonstrated that demand is not largely supply-determined, and both demand and supply are simultaneously driven by economic variables (Newhouse et al., 1982).

Supporters of the supplier-induced demand (SID) theory have argued that doctors can create enough physician-initiated new services to counteract a rise in the market's physician density to maintain a target income without lowering fees. One physician was so bold as to state: "The doctor glut is not a problem; it's the undersupply of patients." Neurologists and plastic surgeons seem fully persuaded that they possess enough leeway to tell patients what they should "demand" (Menken, 1983; Reinhardt, 1985). Advocates of the SID theory disregard the 6 percent annual decline in visits per physician from 1983 to 1986 because it doesn't fit with their theory; they instead argue that manipulative physicians will still make a target income by searching for frill markets and catering to consumer fantasies. This prediction may be true for noninsured services—for example, those that cater to Yuppie boutique medicine—but insurers and employers will not reimburse for these services.

The major effect of increased physician density might be a shift in referral patterns among physicians and other providers. By comparing aggregated physician utilization data in 15 Michigan market areas, Stano (1985) concludes that the availability effect is due to the larger number of providers seen by patients in physician-dense markets. Physicians are more likely to refer and patients are more likely to shop in physician-dense areas. While aggregate data conform to the SID hypothesis (e.g., a 1 percent increase in surgeon density increased per capita surgical use in the short run 0.14 percent in 1980), data from individual practices do not conform to the SID hypothesis. Data from the individual medical or surgical practices do not indicate that physicians treat their patients more intensely as physician density increases (Stano, 1985). Moreover, the aggregate short-run inducement in per capita utilization reported by Stano may be dissipated in the long run by market forces as in the dental and legal markets (Satterthwaite, 1979).

One could argue that the physician supply expansion is a major force in the development of managed care systems, HMOs, PPOs, and the entire medical community's increased susceptibility to cost-containment initiatives. If consumers are increasingly in the driver's seat in the selection of a health plan, and physicians are no longer perceived as being in short supply, the health sector will become even more market-driven. Any economic system is driven by the element in short supply: currently, patients. Increases in physician density may increase physician-initiated hospital visits or doctor visits, but as McCombs (1984) suggests, we shall begin to experience a physician-initiated attempt to restrict dollar flows to nonphysicians (e.g., anesthesiologists and CRNAs). McCombs (1984) accurately predicted a decline in hospital days per episode and a reduction in referrals to alternative providers (physician extenders, free-standing nurse practitioners) in market regions with increased physician density. Physicians are like any other professional group; they dislike competition and do not favor "professional helpers" developed in times of a doctor shortage when their volume of visits per week is on the decline.

The evidence for supplier inducement is weak in a poorly insured market segment such as primary ambulatory care. Mc-Carthy (1985) examined the primary care physician services market in over 100 cities that utilized 1975 AMA data. The sample was restricted to urban areas since competitive forces, if they are to be found, should most likely exist in large urban areas. His results using 1975 data are consistent with monopolistic competition. Given the plentiful entry of physicians into primary care since 1975, the current marketplace should be even more competitive. Demand creation seems a trivial by-product of rising physician density in both the McCarthy (1985) and Sweeney (1982) studies. What little demand creation does exist might only be on paper.

Physicians can unbundle billings into several separately reimbursable activities. Physicians are intelligent professionals who may be tempted to minimize the decline in their incomes in a period of declining patient demand. Aggressive claims review and peer review actions will reduce the prevalence of such unbundling. One of the by-products of increased overseeing of physicians' activities is the increased production of information. Whether employers, insurers, and individuals utilize this information to value shop is the subject of Chapter 12.

Fuchs (1978) has studied the surgeon manpower supply equilibrium and the problem of provider-induced demand. If surgeons do partially shift demand upward by 3 to 3.5 percent to compensate for a 10 percent expansion in surgeons per capita, and also increase price to minimize the potential reduction in income to a few percentage points, the current high number of surgical residency programs may be a major problem in cost containment. In the short term we could not reduce the supply of surgeon manhours, because the postgraduate training pipeline prevents surgical subspecialists from reaching their maximum productive level for 7 to 10 years. Surgeons have suggested from time to time that surgery should be done only by specialists, but they have not supported a policy that would discourage medical students from entering the field; rather, they minimize the effects of competition by finding new patients and new conditions on which to operate (Wennberg, 1986).

Hospital Admission Rate Variability

Wennberg (1985) has provided a classic case of the wide variability of clinical practice patterns with his small area population-based methodology. Admission rates are analyzed using epidemiologic techniques to track patients by location and not simply by hospital, such that transfers outside the service area are "charged back" to their (the patient's) home area. Wide tenfold variations in surgical rates per capita are uncovered, with little apparent reason for such variability. Some of the more recent data on variability in surgical admission rates may be explained by differential use of ambulatory surgery. A total of 11 of the 13 operations having wide inpatient operative variability in the Wennberg studies have been identified as prime candidates for ambulatory surgery (Lagoe and Milliren, 1986). However, the volume of ambulatory surgery is sufficiently low and the variation in operative rates is sufficiently wide to ask the medical community to address this issue. Physicians in Iowa and Maine have successfully adjusted their hospitalization habits in reaction to such information of atypically high rates (Wennberg, 1986). In contrast, the Massachusetts Medical Society has been rather nonresponsive following two replications of the Wennberg approach (Barnes et al., 1985).

Excessive rates of elective hospitalization are often done in the last year of life. For example, Maine urologists were stunned to discover that 47 percent of their prostatectomy patients discharged to nursing homes were dead within a year after the procedure. The Maine urologists suddenly started doing less prostatectomies the next year (10 percent fewer in 1984, 15 percent fewer thereafter). One Maine urologist summarized the educational process: "Why do the surgery if this does nothing for the quantity of life of this subgroup of surgical-eligibles, especially when the act of surgery harms the quality of life." On the more technical level, this example suggests that physicians can become more sensitive to the population-based destiny of certain patient groups. Obviously, the cost-savings potential if the operative rate for certain conditions is brought down 15 to 25 to 35 percent is substantial, and therein lies the attraction to small area analysis in comparison to DRG price controls, as a cost-reduction strategy.

The Wennberg methodology raises a number of technical questions. For example, if you pooled a number of years of data for each of the small areas, would the variability in operative rates be as significant? As Caper (1986) and Wennberg and Gittelsohn (1982) have reported, the patterns of high-usage levels for a condition are generally stable over time, even after pooling more than two years of data. Analysis of four years of data in Iowa, and five to nine years worth of data in Maine, Rhode Island, and Vermont, indicates stablewide operative variations across demographically similar populations.

The variability in practice style patterns, the "medical signatures," may be more significant outside of surgery. The admission rates for medical conditions, including chest pain, atherosclerosis, and congestive heart failure, are highly variable (CHFC, 1985; Wennberg et al., 1984). The necessity of inpatient care is less clearly defined for these conditions, and physicians differ widely from area to area as to when hospitalization is appropriate. In contrast, certain surgical procedures have low variability in operative rates—for example, appendectomy, cholecystectomy, hernia repair, lens extraction, and mastectomy.

Chassin et al. (1986) reported on geographic differences in Medicare usage of medical and surgical services for 13 regions. This Rand Corporation study team reported that use rates were not consistently high in one region, but rates for procedures utilized to diagnose and treat a specific condition did vary. Unfortunately, for those who advocate reeducation or sanctions as a policy solution, the Rand results could not be explained by the actions of a small number of physicians. One does not know whether physicians in high-usage areas perform too many procedures, or whether those in low-usage areas perform too few. One former AMA president suggests that those who believe economics alone should become the Holy Grail have a bias in favor of suggesting that the low rate is the correct rate (Boyle, 1985).

Wennberg (1986) suggests that some evidence exists in support of the low rate being closer to the "correct" rate, and that lowering the rates does no measurable harm. For example, Roos and Roos (1981) failed to show differences in reported illnesses between populations living in areas with high versus low rates of hospital use. In the context of the Rand results, perhaps we could reap significant cost savings from reducing hospitalization for conditions such as hip arthroplasty, hemorrhoids, arthrocentesis, mediastinoscopy, and coronary artery bypass surgery. Other conditions exhibit a lower variability in operative rate—e.g., prostatectomy—but perhaps should be utilized less frequently for certain population segments (such as nursing home institutionalized patients with low life expectancy). We will return to the question of provider-induced demand in a later section on physician pricing models, but first let us survey the economic literature concerning physician behavior.

Physician Supply Curves

Whether a physician works more or less as a result of an increase or decrease in physician wages is an important subject for public policy. Depending on the physicians' labor supply curve, they could decide to work harder and substitute more patient care for leisure (the substitution effect). Alternatively, physicians could decide that their income is sufficiently high to afford increased leisure time in preference to a higher workload. They would consequently work less (the income effect). An important point to remember is that even if the supply curve for a given individual physician is backward-bending (SB in Figure 2.1), the physicians' aggregate labor supply curve may instead be uniformly upward-sloping (SF in Figure 2.1), as is usually the case in most labor markets.

The research results on this issue are mixed. Feldstein (1970) finds strong support for the backward-bending supply curves. Sloan (1976) indicates no support for the position that physicians lie near the backward-bending portion of the labor supply curve and reports very low elasticities of supply. Vahovich (1977) reports empirical results intermediate between Sloan and Feldstein; he finds slightly backward-bending supply curves and low elasticities of supply. In summary, physicians will not change their workload

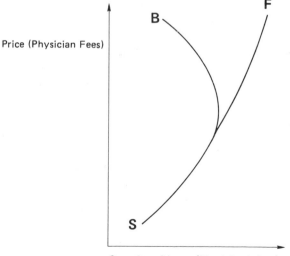

Figure 2.1 Physician Labor Supply Curve: Upward-Sloping Normality (SF) or Backward-Bending Response (SB)

significantly in response to price controls or expanded health insurance coverage.

Brown and Lapan (1979) also corroborated the backward-bending labor supply hypothesis. Although they utilized aggregate times series data, they operated under the hypothesis that physicians are price-taking utility maximizers rather than price-setters. Their findings support the view that physicians are on the backward-bending portion of the labor supply curve. A second interesting finding of this study is that nonphysician inputs (physician extenders, aides, etc.) substitute for declines in physician labor, so that the supply curve of physician-office services is always positively sloped (curve SF in Figure 2.1). These findings utilizing aggregate data corroborate the results of Reinhardt (1975) using data for individual physician practices.

Physician Supply Estimates

In 1980, the Graduate Medical Education National Advisory Committee (GMENAC, 1980) estimated that by the year 2000 the nation would have 643,000 physicians, or 29 percent more than the perceived requirement according to the panel of distinguished physicians. Whether this estimate of a glut (oversupply) of 145,000 physicians will occur in the year 2000 depends on two factors: demand and supply. The demand curve for physician services should be recalculated in response to the unexpected rapid growth in HMOs and managed care alternative delivery systems. For example, one proprietary study of a midwestern state suggests that if these prepaid systems control 80 percent of the market by 2000, 45 percent of the physicians (and 68 percent of the hospital beds) will be unnecessary. However, the market is dynamic, and conditions will change on the supply side. For example, the state medical school could admit 50 percent fewer students (following the Michigan example); physicians could work 15 to 25 percent shorter workweeks; foreign medical graduates could be substantially reduced (relative to GMENAC projections); and physicians could increasingly enter the field of administration. Therefore, hundreds of clinicians may receive training in administration, but few will resort to driving taxicabs or selling real estate because of a glut in the supply of physicians.

The original chairman of the GMENAC study amended his manpower projections recently (Tarlov, 1986). The 643,000 physician projection for the year 2000 can be downgraded by 17,000 to account for the lower number of first-year entrants to medical schools and transferees with advanced standing (from foreign schools to American schools; Crowley et al. [1985] report 255 transfers in 1984). No definitive estimates are provided as to whether the estimate of 498,000 required physicians for 2000 should be downgraded by 20 to 40 percent. The estimate is highly dependent on the growth rate of prepaid systems and to a lesser extent on the anticipated decline in the physician workweek. Steinwachs et al. (1986) utilized the GMENAC model to recalculate the requirements for certain physicians in HMOs. Extrapolating from productivity figures at three HMOs to 1990, they projected that HMOs will require only half the number of family physicians and internists and two-thirds the number of pediatricians in comparison to the GMENAC (1980) estimates.

Competition between health plans might further improve the productivity figures over time, thus further reducing the required number of physicians. Declining consumer demand for clinical physician time bears a clear reciprocal relationship to increased availability of "free time" (for some combination of leisure, education, management activities, charity services or research). Three future trends seem apparent: More physicians will be salaried, all will work less than 50 hours per week, and more will be involved in administration.

From 1966 to 1986 the estimated supply of physicians increased 99 percent, but the American population increased only 24 percent. The ratio of active physicians per 100,000 population has increased from 169 in 1975 to 195 in 1980, 214 in 1985, and a projected 233 in 1990. Regulators favor the counsel of George Bernard Shaw in his preface to the *Doctor's Dilemma:* "Make up your mind how many doctors the community needs to keep it well, and do not register more or less than this number." However, the excess supply problem is confined largely to specialists. Both the GMENAC (1980) study and Schroeder (1984) suggest that the European experience indicates that the most pressing health manpower problem is an oversupply of specialists. Whether this oversupply is a problem depends on your point of view. For HMO or PPO managers who are negotiating fee discounts, this physician oversupply provides the bargaining leverage to save money and differentially select the most cooperative specialists. Specialists left out of managed care systems in the 1990s are headed for two possible fates: serious financial trouble or membership in a union. As the formation of the AMA was a socioeconomic event to combat the cults in the 19th century, so specialty unions may form in the 1990s to combat the managed care systems and "strike for quality care" (which helps defend their declining incomes). Ginzberg (1985, p. 17) has argued for a number of years that physician incomes were bound to slide 40 percent relative to other Americans: "There is no reason for physicians to continue to earn 5.5 times as much as a skilled worker; a spread of 3.5 times is easier to justify."

Physicians' Private Pricing Decisions

Physician behavior has been presumed to vary on three very basic dimensions: (1) whether physicians act as price-setters or price-takers, (2) whether prices are sufficient to clear the market of excess demand, and (3) whether demand can be shifted or induced. Six types of physician pricing models have been developed by economists. The first three models we shall survey assume that the physician is a price-setter—that is, third-party payers' reimbursement controls are not too constraining, and lack of competition allows the professional considerable freedom to set fees. According to the longest-standing physician pricing model, Monopoly Equilibrium (markets clear so that supply is brought into equilibrium with demand and demand does not shift), physicians set prices as a discriminating monopolist (Kessel, 1958; Newhouse, 1970). Price discrimination involves charging what the individual patient can bear, not as an altruistic method of charging the poor less, but rather as a method of reaping monopoly profits by capturing all the area under the demand curve.* The growth in insurance coverage has all but eliminated the physician's ability to price discriminate, except in the case of out-of-pocket subspecialty fees paid by the rich for "star" physicians to perform transplants or heart surgery. A number of court cases made it impossible for organized medicine to maintain the discriminating pricing policies of the 1950s (Havighurst, 1980).

The second model of physician pricing, Monopolist Demand Creation, also assumes that the market clears, but demand is shifted as a result of price-setting decisions. This model assumes the physician has the most power imaginable: Like a simple monopolist the physician can set fees irrespective of what the other physicians are doing and can manipulate consumer wants and inflate demands if necessary. Evans (1974) supports this difficult-to-test theory with empirical evidence on supplier-induced demand in Canada. Evans also defends the omnipotent pricing

---

*A demand curve is the schedule of quantity sold at various prices if you offer one price to the entire marketplace. However, if a supplier could offer a spectrum of prices to the buyers so that each pays close to his or her maximum price, that would capture much more of the area under the demand curve—that is, the profits per unit of service would clearly be increased.

powers of physicians in an earlier work (Evans, 1973), which postulates that in markets with imperfect information on quality, the consumer is often led to believe that higher price means higher quality. Solid evidence of consumers searching for higher-priced providers would be a revolutionary attack against economic normality in medical markets. Recently, this pricing model has been rejected by Pauly (1980) and Fuchs (1986).

A third physician pricing model involves Simple Monopolists' Behavior in a Market of Chronic Excess Demand. This model is like model 2 in that physicians set prices irrespective of the market, but demand is not shifted and the market does not clear (excess demand is left unserved). This model is not manageable analytically; one can estimate neither a demand curve nor a supply curve. This model lacks advocates because it is largely untestable. It does have fleeting support from a number of different economists. Sloan (1976) advocates the idea of physicians acting as simple monopolists, and Feldstein (1970) in rejecting static and dynamic competitive models suggests that physician services are in a state of permanent excess demand, subject to various modes of nonprice rationing, Feldstein indicates that physicians benefit from a marketplace with permanent excess demand in which the profession can pick and choose among the most interesting case "material." In summary, none of these three models of physicians as price-setters is firmly established as empirical fact, but the first and third models do have some moderate level of support.

The last three models we shall survey are competitive models. Physicians are assumed to be such a small fraction of the marketplace that they must act as price-takers. With the exception of the market for general practitioners and family practitioners which comprises approximately 40 percent of all physicians, these competitive models are usually rejected by the econometric evidence of the authors. The fourth physician pricing model to consider is the classic Competitive Equilibrium Model. Under conditions of competitive equilibrium, the market clears and demand is not shifted. This model has been tested on 20 years of time-series data by Feldstein (1970) and on cross-sectional data* by Newhouse (1970), Fuchs and Kramer (1973), Kehrer and Knowles (1974), Newhouse and Phelps (1974), the Institute of Medicine (1976), and

---

*Time-series data can be indicative of short-run behavior because practice resources are relatively fixed in the short or middle run of 5 to 15 years. Cross-sectional analysis provides more information concerning long-run behavior, assuming the sample includes the range of various practice opportunities, in different stages of development. Analysis of a time series of cross-sections allows the researcher to construct a more complete set of structural equations for supply and demand relationships.

Dyckman (1978). All seven of these studies reject the competitive equilibrium hypothesis and report positive coefficients for physicians per capita or surgeons per capita in their price equations. The positive association between price and physician supply ratios is inconsistent with competitive models.*

Many health professionals prior to the 1980s were quick to claim that competition has been eliminated in medical markets. Some of the aforementioned studies do not include the obvious caveat that physicians are not a homogeneous group. The possibility exists that some subgroups of physicians or surgeons do exhibit competitive pricing behavior. Four studies support this proposition. Steinwald and Sloan (1974) and Sloan (1976) report mostly negative association between general practitioner (GP) density and GP fees, and a lower negative association between general surgeons' density and their fees. Holahan et al. (1978) also found the same relationships for GPs but rejected any correlation in the case of general surgeons or internists. McLean (1980) derived structural equations for both the supply of and demand for GP services utilizing the American Medical Association's eighth periodic survey of physicians. McLean rejects the hypothesis that the market for GPs is perfectly competitive, but the high net price elasticity (-1.75) indicates a considerable degree of competition in the market. This price elasticity is larger than that reported in any of the studies summarized in Table 2.1. In summary, the competitive equilibrium model appears to have had validity in the case of general practitioners and possibly general surgeons as early as the 1970s.

The fifth physician pricing model can best be summarized as the Oligopoly Target Income hypothesis. The target income theory of pricing suggests markups in prices as input costs inflate or demand declines. The model presumes that as the market clears, demand will shift, and that demand can be manipulated by the physicians. The speed of adjustment depends on a number of factors, including information collection costs. This model receives some support from Feldstein (1970) and relatively less support from Kehrer and Knowles (1974) and Vahovich (1977). The Feldstein study does not provide very strong statistical support for this theory, reporting mixed results in his demand and price adjustment equations.[†]

---

*The observed low price elasticities in Table 2.1 are also not consistent with competition or simple profit maximization theories. The price elasticity of demand for certain individual physicians will be substantially larger than the market price elasticities reported in the table.

[†]As the author (Feldstein, 1970) pointed out, reporting a low elasticity demand curve, finding a backward-bending supply curve, and inferring that price increases with excess demand seem very incompatible.

Table 2.1   Money-Price Elasticities and Time-Cost Elasticities of Eight
Econometric Studies of the Demand for Physician Services

Data Source	Dependent Variable	Price Elasticity (computed at the mean)
Newhouse and Marquis (1978)	Hospital Length of Stay	− .05
Feldstein (1977)	Hospital Days	
	(i) short run (1966–1973)	− .29
	(ii) long run (1959–1965)	− .13
Newhouse and Phelps (1976)	Hospital Days	− .23
Davis and Russell (1972)	(a) Admissions	− .5
	(b) Hospital Days	− .32 to −.46
Feldstein (1971)	(a) Admissions	− .43
	(b) Hospital Days	
	(i) short run (1963–1967)	− .26
	(ii) long run (1959–1967)	− .55
Rosenthal (1970)	(a) Length of stay (depending on diagnosis)	0.0 to −.08
	(b) Patient Days (depending on diagnosis)	− .01 to −.70
Rosett and Huang (1973), 1961 Expenditure Survey	Hospital and Physician expenditures (at 20% coinsurance)	− .35

Sloan (1976) and Steinwald and Sloan (1974) soundly reject the target income hypothesis. Green (1978) carries the argument one step further and reanalyzes the data from the Fuchs-Kramer (1973) study and fails to reject the hypothesis that physicians cannot induce demand. Unfortunately, it is almost impossible to distinguish demand shifts resulting from changes in consumer tastes from shifts caused by physician manipulation of information to the consumer, or from shifts that are simply responses to changes in time price faced by the consumer. In summary, we can infer that "physician supply creating demand" or the so-called "availability effect" is not uniform or pervasive in either model 2 or 5.

A sixth physician pricing model considered by Reinhardt (1975) and Pauly (1980) suggests the possibility of Competitive Disequilibrium under Price Controls—that is, the market does not clear and demand is not shifted under private (insurance companies) or public (Economic Stabilization Program) price controls. Supply would consistently fall short of demand if the controls were too strict. This is the traditional case of excess demand under price ceilings: Physicians acting as price-takers only produce up to the point where marginal cost equals the price ceiling (typically less than what would be demanded of the physician at that "low" price; Ginsburg, 1978). There is no empirical support for assuming that physicians presently pursue this sixth pricing model (Newhouse and Phelps, 1976). There is some limited evidence that the subset of physicians serving Medicaid patients is unresponsive to price ceilings and to a 30 percent across-the-board reduction in Medicaid fees (Schwartz et al., 1981). One might suggest that if a substantially lower level of reimbursement yields the same number of surgical and medical services 30 months later, then the initial fees were set arbitrarily high. It is heartening to learn that the only significant persistent drop in utilization occurred for the procedure most frequently labeled unnecessary, the tonsillectomy. One might question whether these results from Massachusetts would hold up over a longer time period or in other states that do not have such a high density of physicians per capita.

The early studies of the price elasticity of demand were limited by small sample size, short time horizons, and, most critically, by a control group population. Price elasticity refers to the responsiveness of the quantity of care demanded to changes in price, all other factors being held constant. For example, a -0.23 price elasticity with respect to hospital days translates into an expected 2.3 percent decline in hospital days resulting from a 10 percent increase in price. The price elasticity for minor or elective diagnoses is usually larger, but still inelastic (less than 1.0), whereas the price elasticity for life-threatening emergency care is very low— that is, price is of no consequence (Table 2.2).

In summary, there may be types of physicians for which all six of these economic models fail to work, while other significant groups of physicians behave in a manner that is reasonably consistent with a number of these models. As we shall observe in the next section, the Rand Health Insurance study provided strong support for the view that consumers are price-sensitive and physicians are increasingly price-takers (consistent with models 4 and 6 in Figure 2.2).

Rand Health Insurance Study

The $77-million Rand Health Insurance experiment attempted to put some of the major research issues concerning the desirability and effectiveness of cost sharing to rest. Unlike families in the aforementioned retrospective studies, families in the Rand experiment were randomly assigned to different insurance plans. This randomization study, with long-run follow-up of the families,

Table 2.2   Summary of Seven Econometric Studies of the Price Elasticity for
Hospital Care

Data Source	Dependent Variable(s)	Elasticity with Respect to Price or Time
Newhouse and Marquis (1978)	Physician Visits	−1.00
Newhouse and Phelps (1976)	Physician Visits	− .15 to −.20
Phelps (1975)	Physician Visits (at 25% coinsurance)	− .20
Fuchs and Kramer (1973)	Physician Expenditures	− .15 to −.35
Acton (1975)	Demand Elasticity with Respect to:	(Time Elasticity)
	(a) Travel Time to MD's Office	− .25 to −.37
	(b) Waiting Time for Services	− .12
Phelps and Newhouse (1972)	Price Elasticity for:	
	(a) Physician Home Visits	− .35
	(b) Physician Visits	− .14
	(c) Lab, X-Ray, Ancillary Services	− .07
Davis and Russell (1972)	Outpatient Visits	−1.00
Feldstein and Severson (1964)	Physician Visits	− .19

proved expensive but invaluable in overcoming the self-selection bias explicit in all previous studies of cost sharing. The experiment, which ran from November 1974 to January 1982, enrolled 7,706 people under age 62 at six study sites. Excluded from the experiment were wealthy families with incomes above the 97th percentile and persons disabled enough to qualify for Medicare. Families were assigned to one of 14 experimental insurance plans by a random sampling technique that made the distribution of family characteristics as similar as possible (Newhouse et al., 1981). Each of the 14 plans was assigned to one of four basic categories (free care, 25 percent, 50 percent, or 95 percent coinsurance). There was a maximum loss provision of 5, 10, or 15 percent of family income, or $1,000 (in some sites during some years the maximum expenditure was limited to $750).

For both ambulatory care and hospital care, as the level of cost sharing increased, the family health expenditures declined (e.g., ambulatory care annual expenses of $186 for free care, versus a $1,000 maximum out-of-pocket cap—$149 under 25 percent co-

1. Demand Shifts	2. Market Clearing Prices Achieved	3. Physicians Are Price-Setters	4. Physicians Are Price-Takers
NO	YES	**Model 1—** Monopoly Equilibrium	**Model 4—** Competitive Equilibrium
YES	YES	**Model 2—** Dynamic Demand Shifts	**Model 5—** Oligopolistic Target Income Levels
NO	NO	**Model 3—** Chronic Excess Demand Disequilibrium	**Model 6—** Exogeneous Price Ceilings

Figure 2.2   Taxonomy of Six Economic Models for Physician Behavior

insurance, $120 under 50 percent, and $114 under 95 percent coinsurance). Contrary to the prevalent assumption in the 1970s, increased cost sharing for ambulatory care did not result in more use of inpatient services or increased overall costs. The probability of hospitalization actually declined with increased cost sharing (Newhouse et al., 1981). Ambulatory care usage did not behave as a substitute or preventive service for inpatient care. The lower the cost sharing on ambulatory care, the greater the ambulatory utilization and the greater the likelihood of hospitalization. Once hospitalization began, cost sharing did not significantly affect hospital expenditures.

Insurance coverage did not affect the number of lab tests per ambulatory visit nor the duration of physician time during a visit (Danzon et al., 1984). Other Rand study team reports indicate that cost sharing or insurance does not affect the cost of an ambulatory episode (Keeler and Rolph, 1982). One should be careful about extrapolating these findings from a social experiment in which Rand patients represent less than 1 percent of provider market share to a situation in which providers might react to any activity affecting 15 to 50 percent of their patients (as in some two-company towns). In other words, Rand patients represented a very small fraction of the business in any of the six sites.

Newhouse et al. (1981) also report that expenditures by adults are more responsive to variation in cost sharing than expenditures for children. This suggests that families may not shop aggressively for price-competitive child care and, perhaps, that a high proportion of child care represents truly "necessary services." However, adults covered by higher levels of cost sharing may seek care less frequently, or if they have the information base on which to shop, may seek less costly sources of care (e.g., alternative providers). Rational consumers weigh the benefits of purchasing from their current suppliers against the costs and the benefits of searching for lower prices or better value against the cost of this search (comparison shopping). There is little evidence to suggest aggressive shopping for lower-priced providers in the Rand data. Marquis (1985) found no evidence to suggest that consumers during the period 1974–1981 shopped for lower-priced providers. As we shall see in Chapter 3, employers still promote cost sharing as a strategy to reduce the quantity, if not the direct price, of care. Perhaps the cost of search behavior will decline in the late 1980s as more referral networks are set up for comparison shopping and more consumer handbooks are disseminated. Consumer shopping for a provider, on both a price and quality basis, may become less costly and more fashionable in the near future (Eastaugh, 1986). (In Chapters 9 and 12, we will discuss the long-run impact of cost sharing and HMO care on patients in the Rand study.)

The Rand study team concluded that the poor are not more responsive to cost sharing if such payments are in proportion to family income. However, this income-related "ideal plan" may be the likely by-product of a political process that seems increasingly willing to compromise on the equity side to achieve overall cost savings in Medicaid or Medicare programs. If the probable changes in cost-sharing requirements are unrelated to family income, they will disproportionally reduce the buying power and provider contact (visits) among the sick who are poor. Data from Davis and Rowland (1984) suggest that hospital cost sharing is 27 percent of the income of hospitalized elderly poor. In the Rand study (Newhouse et al., 1981), the poor were more likely to exceed the maximum dollar expenditure of $1,000, a fact consistent with the view that the economically disadvantaged are also the medically disadvantaged, with a backlog of untreated health conditions (Brook et al., 1983). The administrative costs of a finely tuned, income-related, cost-sharing program are substantial in the public sector. Government officials have trouble informing providers of beneficiary program eligibility (for example, whether Medicaid will pay a given individual's bill). However, the private sector has a proven track record of running an income-related, cost-sharing program for more affluent employed populations. We shall discuss one such program in Chapter 3.

Generalizability of the Rand Study

One limitation in the Rand study is that subjects in the experiment faced no risk in joining the experiment. Any family assigned to a plan that offered less coverage than its current (preexperiment) insurance was reimbursed an amount equal to its maximal possible loss. This money was paid in installments every four weeks, and the family was not required to spend it on health care. Consequently, the effects of the coinsurance may be underestimated. The participants who were covered by a high rate of coinsurance could not actually lose money in the experiment. The original Rand sample may have been additionally biased by participant refusals and attrition (net 35 percent).

The Rand analysis focuses on the effects of cost sharing on consumer behavior, but what of the potential effects of cost sharing on provider behavior if a large fraction of the provider's patient population is affected? In this context, Fahs (1986) studied physician treatment patterns before and after cost sharing was implemented on United Mine Workers (UMW). She analyzed treatment patterns for three ambulatory conditions (diabetes mellitus, urinary tract infection, and tonsillitus/pharyngitus/streptococcal infections) for 1,089 patient episodes. She divided components of an episode into patient-initiated and physician-initiated categories. After 30 years of free care, the 800,000 members of the UMW agreed to the imposition of cost sharing as of July 1977. The cost-sharing package included a $250 inpatient deductible, a 40 percent coinsurance on physician and most other outpatient services, and an annual maximum liability of $500. Immediately following the imposition of cost sharing, demand for physician visits decreased substantially. Scheffler (1984) found that UMW families and retirees were 36 percent less likely to have one or more physician visits in the second half of 1977.

The uniqueness of the contribution by Fahs (1986) in reanalyzing this natural experiment is that she indicates weak support for a target income hypothesis. The UMW physicians, working in a stable group practice—the Russelton Medical Group—and serving

UMW and steelworkers, attempted to inflate the number of physician-initiated visits to compensate for declining patient revenues caused by the cost-sharing effects on 60 percent of their patients. The control group, the nonminers insurance plan, remained constant over the entire study period (1976–1979). Fahs used a fixed-effects model that controlled for each managing physician over the episode, regressing patient-initiated and physician-initiated visits, and a number of independent variables (diagnosis, disease stage, age, sex, prior visits, and insurance). While total fees per episode, both ambulatory and inpatient fees, decreased by 10 percent for the UMW, the physicians found 17 percent more business (fees) in the control group that did not increase its cost-sharing requirements. Neoclassical competitive market analysis would not predict such an increase in the total fees per episode for other patients in the group practice. However, one could argue that one decade later, the 1987 solution to this finding might be twofold: to implement more stringent utilization review within the Russelton Medical Group and to offer alternative health plans (HMOs and PPOs) so that nonminers cannot be cost-shifted onto by providers. All consumer groups, not just the providers or the employers, can then decide which health plan offers a more appealing product.

The 17 percent cost-shift of fees onto the control group in the Fahs (1986) study was barely significant at the 0.05 level. Patient-initiated visits were unchanged for the control group, but physician-initiated fees increased 11 percent in the nonminer group, and follow-up recall time improved (for the physicians) 24 percent. These results provide weak evidence for the supplier-induced demand (SID) hypothesis based on 1977 data. The SID effect manifests itself in increased physician-initiated recall visits. No published evidence involving more recent data exists to support either the target income or the SID hypotheses. Physicians are increasingly price-takers, subject to utilization review and competition in the 1980s.

Payment Alternatives for Physicians

Physician payment methods are increasingly a concern for public policy makers. Projections are that in 1987 Medicare's Part B program will cost almost $27 billion, making it the third largest domestic program. More than $22 billion of Part B benefits will be paid for physician services. The Medicare prospective payment system for hospitals has generated a major impetus to reform the fee-for-service system for paying physicians. One of the problems with DRG payments for doctors is that the system would unfairly redistribute payments from physicians with genuinely more complex and costly practices to physicians with less complex and costly practices (Culler and Ehrenfried, 1986). In contrast to hospitals that serve large numbers of patients within a DRG category, individual doctors admit few cases per DRG and thus have few opportunities to offset high-cost cases with low-cost cases. The real potential for physician DRGs might reside in assisting medical staff, HMO, PPO, and hospital managers in monitoring physician practice styles.

Mitchell (1985) argues that physician DRGs should be utilized to pay for hospital-based RAPs (radiologists, anesthesiologists, and pathologists). Folding the RAPs into the current hospital DRG prices would be a simple matter of inflating the payment rates to cover such hospital-based physician services. The hospital could then pay such physicians by their method of choice—for example, salary, base compensation with incentive pay for more productivity, or the traditional fee-for-service system. The next two professional groups to be folded into the DRGs after the RAPs (in 1988–1989 perhaps) would be surgeons and surgical assistants.

In selecting a "fair price" for physician services, four basic options are to be considered: (1) paying a variable rate for the same service depending on the professional, his or her credentials, and location, (2) paying a uniform rate per service, (3) paying a uniform rate per episode (e.g., DRGs), or (4) paying a per capita rate. The direction of public decision makers seems to be toward the last three options. Ultimately, capitation may become the most prevalent payment method because the physicians could not manipulate this system by increasing the quantity and complexity of services provided. If the private and public sectors continue to tighten physician payment rates, physicians will not be any more or less likely to treat public patients. However, the price Medicaid administrators pay in tightening physician rates excessively is that clinicians may discriminate against public patients (Holahan, 1984).

Research efforts to improve fee schedules should not be derailed by an HCFA push to promote capitation payment plans. Probably not all patients will be covered by capitation plans, and a more equitable fee schedule is required to replace the customary, prevailing, and reasonable (CPR) rates—referred to as usual, customary, and reasonable (UCR) rates in the AMA parlance and the original Medicare law. Two decades of UCR rates have exacerbated and perpetuated payment inequities among physician specialties, across geopraphic areas, on behalf of certain procedures (over medical approaches), and in a manner biased against certain health delivery settings. More importantly, the payment of a "usual" fee, if it was within the range of "customary" fees in the area (or could be considered reasonable if an independent profile of the individual's fees was lacking), is highly inflationary (Gabel and Rice, 1985).

Given that expenditures equal price times quantity, the CPR/UCR fee system is highly inflationary on both sides of the equation. As with any fee-for-service payment system, there is no restraint on volume (beyond what the professional review organizations provide). On the price side, inflationary increases from year to year compound—that is, payment rates in one year are based on physicians' actual charges in the previous year (for clinicians whose customary fees are below the Medicare prevailing fees). Consumer cost sharing has only a limited restraining effect on these fee increases because Medicare beneficiaries purchase extensive supplemental medical insurance. In 1986–1987, almost 75 percent of Medicare enrollees will purchase private Medigap insurance policies, and an additional 10 percent will be eligible for Medicaid. Therefore, Medicare increasingly has had to take a more active role in implementing fee screens and fee freezes to protect both the federal treasury and the pocketbooks of the underinsured. Medicare pays physicians based on the lowest of four calculated rates:

1. Physician's submitted charge—the billed amount.
2. Physician's customary charge—defined as the physician's median charge for that service during the previous year.
3. "Unadjusted" prevailing charge for that service in the locality—defined as the 75th percentile of the distribution of customary charges for all physicians in the locality.
4. "Adjusted" prevailing charge—defined as the prevailing charge applicable in June 1973 inflated by an index of earnings and office expenses called the Medicare Economic Index (MEI).

Medicare physician payment rates are less than submitted physician charges for 85.5 percent of patient bills under the 1985 system of customary and prevailing fee screens. The data in Table 2.3 are limited (due to reporting problems) to Medicare carriers in 39 states plus upstate New York. Some 14.5 percent of bills were paid according to rate 1 (submitted charges). Payment was reduced by rate method 2, customary screens, in 30.4 percent of physicians' services billed, and prevailing screens (payment rates 3 and 4) reduced payment in 55.1 percent of the cases. Prevailing fee screens have the most critical impact on surgical fees (line 6, Table

**Table 2.3   Percent of Physicians' Allowed Amounts and Bills Constrained by
Alternative Fee Screens, 1984–1985**

Physician Practices by Specialty and Location	Fee Screen Used to Set Payment (Percent of Allowed Amounts)			Fee Screen Used to Set Payment (Percent of Services Billed)		
	Billed Amount	*Cus-tomary Screen*	*Prevail-ing Screen*	*Billed Amount*	*Cus-tomary Screen*	*Prevail-ing Screen*
All Practices	14.5	30.4	55.1	17.4	31.4	51.2
Generalists						
General practice	23.6	27.8	48.6	22.0	26.7	51.3
Family practice	19.3	27.7	53.0	18.7	24.4	56.9
Internal medicine	15.5	29.7	54.8	15.4	27.4	57.2
Specialists						
Nonsurgical	17.3	37.3	45.4	18.1	38.0	43.9
Surgical	10.7	29.3	60.0	16.6	39.4	44.0
All Practices by Location						
Nonmetropolitan	19.5	23.3	57.2	19.8	19.3	60.9
Metropolitan	13.7	31.4	54.9	16.8	34.3	48.9

SOURCE: Congressional Budget Office (1986).

2.3). Prevailing screens in columns 3 and 6 of Table 2.3 include unadjusted prevailing, the adjusted prevailing, and lower ceilings set by seldom utilized "inherently reasonable" criteria (*Federal Register* 51:32, February 28, 1986, p. 5726). The Reagan administration's 1987 budget proposed rebasing the MEI to provide further downward pressure on specialists' fees. Current HCFA regulations specify that payment rates for certain radiology and medical services in hospitals not exceed specified percentages of those same services when rendered in physicians' offices. The clear regulatory intent is to promote treatment in the most cost-effective setting, without adding too much of a profit for services done in ambulatory care sites.

The Future Collapse of the Specialists' Dream House

It is all too apparent that this complex fee-setting structure reimburses specialists and procedures more generously relative to cognitive physician care outputs (Yett et al., 1985). The best early study of this bias in the incentive structure was provided by Hsiao and Stason (1979), who estimated that after adjusting for case complexity, the doctors were paid four to five times as much per hour for surgery as for office visits. Moreover, procedures that have become automated or routine over time are highly profitable under Medicare (or other noncapitated payment schemes) because the relative value (RV) scales were not adjusted downward as the procedure became less costly to perform. To promote efficiency, we should either recalibrate the RV scales (Stason and Hsiao, 1986; Hsiao and Kelly, 1984) or jettison the fee-for-service method of payment and move toward capitation systems (McClure, 1984; Congressional Budget Office, 1986). (The capitated systems are discussed in depth in Chapters 7 and 24.)

Obviously, the CPR payment system has been a windfall for surgical specialists, anesthesiologists, radiologists, and pathologists. Consequently, education in these areas has yielded tremendous returns (Burstein and Cromwell, 1985). Using 1983 data, the real rate of return from education in a primary care specialty averages 13 percent, which is still a better return on training than getting a nonmedical doctorate (Table 2.4). However, the real rate of return for specialists in the last four lines of the table is 20 percent (Sloan and Hay, 1986). The bias of the CPR payment method, as used by Medicare and many other payers, materially adds to the rates of returns of procedure-focused specialties. A brief example might highlight this point. A cardiac surgeon can earn $439,000 per year by performing only two cardiac bypass operations per week on Medicare patients in FY 1987. In 1987,

Table 2.4   Real Rates of Return from Medical Education

Specialty	Rate of Return to Training (in percent)
Pediatrics	9
General practice/Family practice	11
Psychiatry	13
Internal medicine	14
Obstetrics-Gynecology	16
Pathology	17
Surgery	19
Radiology	20
Anesthesiology	22
Total, All physicians	*16*

SOURCE: Sloan and Hay (1986).

this might require a time commitment of 15 to 20 hours per week. However, in baseline period 1975, the cardiac surgeon spent two- to threefold more time doing two operations per week, had little assistance from residents and fellows (because few were trained in that new field), and continuously had to think up better methods of technique and postoperative treatment. The CPR payment system pays for each procedure as if the current physician's responsibili- ties are as onerous as the original inventor of the procedure at the Cleveland Clinic. This is more of a financial dream house for specialists than one might think. Not only does the attending physician get paid at inflated rates per procedure, but the Medi- care program will also help pay for the residents and fellows who are doing the work that the senior attending physician is paid for under rates implicitly pegged to the 1975 style of medicine—when the attending physician had to do it all.

The payment system is so clearly biased in favor of procedures that reform is imminent. A gynecologist would have to perform 275 office visits on elderly women each week to achieve the income earned by one cardiac surgeon doing two operations per week. Is there any question as to why we have a maldistribution of special- ists?

One might assume that three years of Medicare fee freezes have managed to slow the growth in physician expenditures, even if a freeze could not reverse the payment bias against delivering primary care. Surprisingly, the rate of increase in physician ex- penditures per Medicare enrollee increased by 10 percent in 1985, versus only 7.4 percent in 1984 (line 2, Table 2.5). A readjustment of the physicians' relative value scales, to pay less for procedures and more for primary care, should also focus on promoting eco- nomic efficiency.

Stason and Hsiao (1986) are currently in the process of restruc- turing the Medicare payment rates to reflect current resource cost- based efforts on the part of clinicians. They are assessing the appropriate relative value units (RVUs) across a wide range of services so as not to appear unfair to any particular subspecialty. The research, being done under contract from HCFA, could presumably be used to set payment rates in 1990–1991. The results seem promising to date. If resource cost estimates devel- oped by Stason and Hsiao (1986) were used, surgeons would receive 86 percent less for cataract operations, 60 percent less for bypass operations, and 76 percent less for pacemaker implants (Table 2.6). Members of organized medicine may dislike the industrial engineered cost figures based on time required to provide the service. Stason and Hsiao are working with the

Table 2.5   Annual Rates of Growth in Reimbursements Under Medicare,
1975–1985 (in percent, 1985, 1975 Dollars)

	Annual Percentage Change				Reimbursements (millions of dollars)	
Reimbursements	*1975–1982*	*1983*	*1984*	*1985*	*1985*	*1975*
Physician Services						
Total reimbursements	19.5%	18.2%	9.8%	12.1%	$19,504	$3,760
Per enrollee	16.5	16.4	7.4	10.0	651	159
In constant dollars[1]	8.1	12.1	3.2	6.4	651	299
All Supplementary Medical Insurance[2]						
Total reimbursements	20.2	17.2	8.6	16.7	22,947	4,273
Per enrollee	17.1	15.3	6.3	14.5	766	181
In constant dollars	8.7	11.1	2.1	10.8	766	340
Hospital Insurance						
Total reimbursements	17.8	10.4	10.0	10.0	47,579	11,315
Per enrollee	14.9	8.6	8.0	8.2	1,572	470
In constant dollars	6.6	4.6	3.8	4.7	1,572	884
Total Medicare						
Total reimbursements	18.5	12.4	9.5	12.1	70,526	15,588
Per enrollee	15.5	10.6	7.5	10.1	2,337	650
In constant dollars	7.2	6.6	3.2	6.6	2,337	1,225

SOURCE: Congressional Budget Office (1986).
[1]Reimbursements per enrollee after eliminating the effects of general inflation, as measured by the GNP deflator.
[2]Physician services are a subset of Supplementary Medical Services (SMI).

American Medical Association to assess what other factors should be incorporated into the payment cost weights—for example, risks incurred by the provider, skills, or specialty training. We shall review the topic of cost-accounting methods in Chapter 5. One could argue that the payment RVs should reflect the supply of physicians in the catchment area. However, if one really wanted to reflect supply ratios in the payment system, one could pay on the basis of competitive bids. We shall discuss a quality-enhancing system of competitive bidding, based on price and quality, in Chapter 24.

Government Pricing Policies

Although Medicare patients may represent only 31 percent of the average physician's billings, with the aging of America, dependency on elderly patient revenues is a major issue in the physician

Table 2.6   Comparison of Relative Values Calculated from Medicare's Allowed
Amounts and Estimates of Resource Costs, for Selected Services,
1983

Service	Average Allowed Amount	Allowed Amounts If Based On Resource Costs	Resource Cost-Based Amounts as a Percent of Current Allowed Amounts
For Ophthalmologists			
Base service: initial			
eye examination	50	50	100
Cataract extraction	1,100	150	14
For Cardiovascular Surgeons			
Base service:			
initial office visit	80	80	100
Coronary artery bypass	3,000	1,200	40
Pacemaker implant	1,060	256	24

SOURCE: Stason and Hsiao (1986).

community. The Deficit Reduction Act of 1984 (DEFRA) froze
Medicare customary and prevailing charges for physicians' services
from July 1984 to September 1985. It was later extended through
April 1986. As of May 1, 1986, physicians who signed participation
agreements for the remainder of fiscal 1986 received an update of
nearly 4 percent in payment rates. Customary and prevailing fees
for physicians not signing such Medicare agreements will remain
frozen until 1987. Beginning in January 1987 the participation
agreements will be on a calendar year basis. The prevailing charge
levels applied to nonparticipating physicians who do not accept
Medicare as payment in full will lag one year behind those rates
applied to participating physicians. The Department of Health and
Human Services will continue to publish directories of participating physicians for appropriate local geographic areas. Such fee
freezes and marketing ploys have demoralized many American
doctors. Medical journals contain a number of impassioned cri-
tiques of Medicare and private sector managed care. The economic
forces seem to favor continued downward pressure on physician
fees. American physicians who believe they can take their case to
the public should consider the failure to garner public support in
recent Canadian physician strikes. The typical Canadian citizen
reaction is contained in the following quote: "My physician is
making a very adequate living without extra-billing, so let's cut
their fees and continue to channel them into remote geographic
areas. Cut the incomes of those who do not serve remote areas."

References

ACTON, J. (1975). "Nonmonetary Factors in the Demand for Medical Services: Some Empirical Evidence." *Journal of Political Economy* 83:3 (May), 595–614.

ARROW, K. (1963). "Uncertainty and the Welfare Economics of Medical Care." *American Economic Review* 53:4 (December), 941–973.

BARNES, B., O'BRIEN, E., COMSTOCK, C., D'ARPA, D., and DONAHUE C. (1985). "Report on Variation in Rates of Utilization of Surgical Services in the Commonwealth of Massachusetts." *Journal of the American Medical Association* 254:3 (July 19), 371–376.

BOYLE, J. (1985). "Regional Variations in the Use of Medical Services and the Accountability of the Profession." *Journal of the American Medical Association* 254:3 (July 19), 407.

BROOK, R., WARE, J., ROGERS, W., KEELER, G., DAVIES, A., DONALD, C., GOLDBERG, G., MASTHAY, P., and NEWHOUSE, J. (1983). "Does Free Care Improve Adults' Health?—Results of a Controlled Trial." *New England Journal of Medicine* 309:23 (December 8), 1426–1434.

BROWN, D., and LAPAN, H. (1979). "The Supply of Physicians' Services." *Economic Inquiry* 17:2 (April), 269–279.

BURSTEIN, P., and CROMWELL, J. (1985). "Relative Incomes and Rates of Return for U.S. Physician Services." *Journal of Health Economics* 4:1 (March), 63–78.

CAPER, P. (1986). "How Medical Practice Affects Cost Containment." *Healthcare Executive* 1:2 (January/February), 29–31.

CHASSIN, M., BROOK, R., PARK, R., KEESEY, J., FUNK, A., KOSECOFF, J., KAHN, K., MERRICK, N., and SOLOMON, O. (1986). "Variations in the Use of Medical and Surgical Services by the Medicare Population." *New England Journal of Medicine* 314:5 (January 30), 285–290.

CHFC (1985). "Variations in Hospitalization Rates in California." California Health Facilities Commission Report IV-85-9. Sacramento, California: CHFC.

Congressional Budget Office (1986). *Physician Reimbursement Under Medicare: Options for Change*, CBO Study Report (April), U.S. Congress, Washington, D.C.

CROWLEY, A., ETZEL, S., and PETERSEN, E. (1985). "Undergraduate Medical Education." *Journal of the American Medical Association* 254:15 (October 18), 1565–1572.

CULLER, S., and EHRENFRIED, D. (1986). "On the Feasibility and Usefulness of Physician DRGs." *Inquiry* 23:1 (Spring), 40–55.

DANZON, P., MANNING, W., and MARQUIS, M. (1984). "Factors Affecting Laboratory Test Use and Prices." *Health Care Financing Review* 5:4 (Summer), 23–32.

DAVIS, K., and ROWLAND, D. (1984). "Medicare Financing Reform: A New Medicare Premium." *Milbank Memorial Fund Quarterly/Health and Society* 62:2 (Spring), 300–324.

DAVIS, K., and RUSSELL, L. (1972). "The Substitution of Hospital Outpatient Care for Inpatient Care." *Review of Economics and Statistics* 54:2 (May), 109–120.

DYCKMAN, Z. (1978). *A Study of Physician Fees*, Staff Report (March), Council on Wage and Price Stability, Executive Office of the President, Washington, D.C.

EASTAUGH, S. (1986). "Hospital Quality Scorecards, Patient Severity, and the Emerging Value Shopper." *Hospital and Health Services Administration* 31:6 (November–December), 85–102.

EVANS, R. (1974). "Supplier-Induced Demand: Some Empirical Evidence and Implications." In J. Perlman (ed.), *The Economics of Health and Medical Care*. New York: John Wiley, 162–173.

EVANS, R. (1973). *Price Formation in the Market for Physician Services in Canada, 1957–1969*. Ottawa: Queen's Printer.

FAHS, M. (1986). "Physician Response to Cost Sharing." *Medical Care* 25:11, forthcoming.

FELDSTEIN, M. (1977). "Quality Change and the Demand for Hospital Care." *Econometrica* 45:7 (October), 1681–1689.

FELDSTEIN, M. (1971). "Hospital Inflation: A Study in Nonprofit Price Dynamics." *American Economic Review* 61:5 (December), 853–872.

FELDSTEIN, M. (1970). "The Rising Price of Physicians' Services." *Review of Economics and Statistics* 52:2 (May), 121–133.

FELDSTEIN, P., and SEVERSON, R. (1964). "The Demand for Medical Care." In *Report of the Commission on the Cost of Medical Care*. Chicago: American Medical Association, 56–76.

FUCHS, V. (1986). *The Health Economy*. Cambridge, Mass.: Harvard University Press.

FUCHS, V. (1978). "The Supply of Surgeons and the Demand for Surgical Operations." *Journal of Human Resources* 13 (Supplement), 35–36.

FUCHS, V., and KRAMER, J. (1973). "Determinants of Expenditures for Physicians' Services in the United States, 1948–1968." Paper Series, National Bureau of Economic Research.

GABEL, J., and RICE, T. (1985). "Reducing Public Expenditures for Physician Services: The Price of Paying Less." *Journal of Health Politics, Policy and Law* 9:4 (Winter), 595–609.

GINSBERG, P. (1978). "Impact of the Economic Stabilization Program on Hospitals: An Analysis with Aggregate Data." In M. Zubkoff et al. (eds.), *Hospital Cost Containment: Selected Notes for Future Policy*. New York: Prodist, 293–323.

GINSBURG, P., and KORETZ, D. (1983). "Bed Availability and Hospital Utilization: Estimates of the Roemer Effect." *Health Care Financing Review* 5:1 (Summer), 87–92.

GINZBERG, E. (1985). "1990s and Beyond Predictions." *The New Physician* 9:9 (September), 15–19.

GMENAC (1980). *Graduate Medical Education National Advisory Committee Report to the Secretary of DHHS*, 7 volumes. Washington, D.C.: Public Health Service (September), Health Resources Administration.

GREEN, J. (1978). "Physician-Induced Demand for Medical Care." *Journal of Human Resources* 13 (Supplement), 21–34.

HAVIGHURST, C. (1980). "Antitrust Enforcement in the Medical Services Industry: What Does It All Mean?" *Milbank Memorial Fund Quarterly* 58:1 (Winter), 89–124.

HOLAHAN, J. (1984). "Paying for Physician Services in State Medicaid Programs." *Health Care Financing Review* 5:3 (Spring), 99–110.

HOLAHAN, J., HADLEY, J., SCANLON, W., and LEE, R. (1978). *Physician Pricing in California.* Urban Institute working paper, report 998–10.

HSIAO, W., and KELLY, N. (1984). "Medicare Benefits: A Reassessment." *Milbank Memorial Fund Quarterly/Health and Society* 62:2 (Spring), 207–229.

HSIAO, W., AND STASON, W. (1979). "Toward Developing a Relative Value Scale for Medical and Surgical Services." *Health Care Financing Review* 1:2 (Fall), 23–38.

Institute of Medicine (1976). *Medicare-Medicaid Reimbursement Policies: Part III,* Volume 3. Washington, D.C.: National Academy of Sciences.

KEELER, E., and ROLPH, J. (1982). "The Demand for Episodes of Medical Treatment." Rand Report R-2829-HMS. Santa Monica, Calif.: Rand Corporation.

KEHRER, B., and KNOWLES, J. (1974). "Economics of Scale and the Pricing of Physicians' Services." In D. Yett (ed.), *An Original Comparative Economic Analysis of Group Practice and Solo Fee-for-Service Practice* (DHEW Report). Springfield, Va: National Technical Information Service.

KESSEL, R. (1958). "Price Discrimination in Medicine." *Journal of Law and Economics* 1:1 (October), 20–53.

LAGOE, R., and MILLIREN, J. (1986). "A Community-Based Analysis of Ambulatory Surgery Utilization." *American Journal of Public Health* 76:2 (February), 150–153.

MANNING, W., WELLS, K., DUAN, N., NEWHOUSE, J., and WARE, J. (1986). "How Cost Sharing Affects the Use of Ambulatory Mental Health Services." *Journal of the American Medical Association* 256:14 (October 10), 1930–1936.

MARQUIS, M. (1985). "Cost Sharing and Provider Choice." *Journal of Health Economics* 4:2 (June), 137–157.

McCARTHY, T. (1985). "The Competitive Nature of the Primary Care Physician Services Market." *Journal of Health Economics* 4:2 (June), 93–117.

McCLURE, W. (1984). "On the Research Status of Risk-Adjusted Capitation Rates." *Inquiry* 21:3 (Fall), 205–213.

McCOMBS, J. (1984). "Physician Treatment Decisions in a Multiple Equation Model." *Journal of Health Economics* 3:2 (June), 155–171.

McLEAN, R. (1960). "The Structure of the Market for Physicians' Services." *Health Services Research* 15:3 (Fall), 271–280.

MENKEN, M. (1983). "Consequences of an Oversupply of Medical Specialists: The Case of Neurology." *New England Journal of Medicine* 308:22 (May 12), 1224–1226.

MITCHELL, J. (1985). "Physician DRGs." *New England Journal of Medicine* 313:11 (September 12), 670–675.

NEWHOUSE, J. (1970). "A Model of Physician Pricing." *Southern Economic Journal* 37:2 (October), 174–183.

NEWHOUSE, J. et al. (1981). "Some Interim Results from a Controlled Trial of Cost Sharing in Health Insurance." *New England Journal of Medicine* 305:23 (December 17), 1501–1507.

NEWHOUSE, J., and MARQUIS, M. (1978). "The Norms Hypothesis and the Demand for Medical Care." *Journal of Human Resources* 13 (Supplement), 159–182.

NEWHOUSE, J., and PHELPS, C. (1976). "New Estimates of Price and Income

Elasticities of Medical Care Services." In R. Rosett (ed.), *The Role of Health Insurance in the Health Services Sector*. New York: Watson Academic, 261–312.

NEWHOUSE, J., and PHELPS, C. (1974). "Price and Income Elasticities for Medical Care Services." In M. Perlman (ed.), *The Economics of Health and Medical Care*. New York: John Wiley, 139–161.

NEWHOUSE, J., WILLIAMS, A., BENNETT, B., and SCHWARTZ, W. (1982a). "Where Have All the Doctors Gone?" *Journal of the American Medical Association* 247:17 (May 7), 2392–2396.

NEWHOUSE, J., WILLIAMS, A., BENNETT, B., and SCHWARTZ, W. (1982b). "Does the Geographical Distribution of Physicians Reflect Market Failure?" *Bell Journal of Economics* 13:2 (Autumn), 493–505.

PAULY, M. (1980). *Doctors and Their Workshops: Economic Models of Physician Behavior*. Chicago: University of Chicago Press.

PAULY, M., and REDISCH, M. (1973). "The Not-for-Profit Hospital as a Physicians' Cooperative." *American Economic Review* 63:1 (March), 87–99.

PHELPS, C. (1975). "The Effects of Insurance on the Demand for Medical Care." In R. V. Anderson et al. (eds.), *Equity in Health Services: Empirical Analysis in Social Policy*. Cambridge, Mass.: Ballinger.

PHELPS, C., and NEWHOUSE, J. (1972). "The Effect of Coinsurance: A Multivariance Analysis." *Social Security Bulletin* 35:6 (June), 20–29.

REINHARDT, U. (1985). "The Theory of Physician-Induced Demand: Reflections After a Decade." *Journal of Health Economics* 4:2 (June), 187–193.

REINHARDT, U. (1975). *Physician Productivity and the Demand for Health Manpower*. Cambridge, Mass.: Ballinger.

ROOS, N., and ROOS, L. (1981). "High and Low Surgical Rates: Risk Factors for Area Residents." *American Journal of Public Health* 71:6 (June), 591–600.

ROSENTHAL, G. (1970). "Price Elasticity of Demand for Short-Term General Hospital Services." In H. Klarman (ed.), *Empirical Studies in Health Economics*. Baltimore: Johns Hopkins University Press, 104–124.

SATTERTHWAITE, M. (1979). "Consumer Information, Equilibrium Industry Price, and the Number of Sellers." *Bell Journal of Economics* 10:2 (Autumn), 483–502.

SCHEFFLER, R. (1984). "The United Mine Workers' Health Plan: An Analysis of the Cost-Sharing Program." *Medical Care* 22:3 (March), 247–254.

SCHROEDER, S. (1984). "Western European Responses to Physician Oversupply." *Journal of the American Medical Association* 252:3 (July 20), 373–384.

SLOAN, F. (1976). "Physician Fee Inflation: Evidence from the Late 1960s." In R. Rosett (ed.), *The Role of Health Insurance in the Health Services Sector*. New York: Watson Academic, 321–354.

SLOAN, F., and HAY, J. (1986). "Medicare Pricing Mechanisms for Physicians' Services." *Medical Care Review* 43:1 (Spring), 33–45.

STANO, M. (1985). "An Analysis of the Evidence on Competition in the Physician Services Market." *Journal of Health Economics* 4:3 (September), 197–211.

STASON, W., and HSIAO, W. (1986). "A New Relative Value Scale for Physician Services." Unpublished paper, Harvard School of Public Health, Boston.

STEINWACHS, D., WEINER, J., SHAPIRO, S., BATALDEN, P., COLTIN, K., and WASSERMAN, F. (1986). "A Comparison of the Requirements for Primary Care

Physicians in HMOs with Projections Made by the GMENAC." *New England Journal of Medicine* 314:4 (January 23), 217–222.

STEINWALD, B., and SLOAN, F. (1974). "Determinants of Physicians' Fees." *Journal of Business* 47:3 (October), 493–511.

SWEENEY, G. (1982). "The Market for Physicians' Services: Theoretical Implications and an Empirical Test of the Target Income Hypothesis." *Southern Economic Journal* 48:1 (January), 594–614.

TARLOV, A. (1986). "HMO Enrollment Growth and Physicians: The Third Compartment." *Health Affairs* 5:1 (Spring), 23–35.

VAHOVICH, S. (1977). "Physicians' Supply Decisions by Specialty: TSLS Model." *Industrial Relations* 16:1 (February), 51–60.

WENNBERG, J. (1986). "Which Rate Is Right?" *New England Journal of Medicine* 314:5 (January 30), 310–311.

WENNBERG, J. (1977). "Changes in Tonsillectomy Rates Associated with Feedback and Review." *Pediatrics* 59:7 (July), 821–826.

WENNBERG, J., and GITTELSOHN, A. (1982). "Variations in Medical Care Among Small Areas." *Scientific American* 246:4 (April), 120–135.

WENNBERG, J., MCPHERSON, K., and CAPER, P. (1984). "Will Payment Based upon DRGs Control Hospital Costs?" *New England Journal of Medicine* 311:6 (August 9), 295–300.

WENNBERG, J., and SERVI-SHARE OF IOWA (1985). "A Comparative Study of Iowa Hospital Utilization, 1980–81." Des Moines: Servi-Share of Iowa.

WILENSKY, G., and ROSSITER, L. (1980). "The Magnitude and Determinants of Physician-Initiated Visits in the United States." Proceedings of the World Congress on Health Economics, September 8–11, Leiden University, the Netherlands.

YETT, D., WILLIAM, D., ERNST, R., and HAY, J. (1985). "Fee Screen Reimbursement and Physician Fee Inflation." *Journal of Human Resources* 20:2 (Spring), 278–291.

Part Two

MANAGERIAL CONCERNS FOR BUYERS AND PROVIDERS

Chapter 3

EMPLOYERS, COST SHARING, AND COST CONTAINMENT

Employers were like an absentee host who paid the bill but never showed up at the table. Now they are intimately involved in planning the menu.

—Bernard Tresnowski

Chrysler's comparable cost per employee is $5,700, or 400 percent higher health care costs than Mitsubishi. What has Chrysler gotten for its health care dollar? A health care industry that is expensive, wasteful, and inefficient. . . . The fee-for-service and cost-reimbursement systems must be eliminated and all patients must be made more cognizant of their own health care.

—Joseph A. Califano

Employment-based insurance is necessary to attract and retain skilled, highly qualified workers and to reduce sick days. However, a business that experiences excessive health costs by offering too small a dose of cost sharing in its health insurance options incurs a competitive disadvantage. Corporate health care spending exceeds after-tax total profits and should reach $106 billion in 1986. Employees are a capital asset, and health maintenance is a business cost in need of control. Corporate America should not just be concerned with those currently employed; it must also be concerned with future health care costs of retirees. Union contracts often specify financial provisions for the health care expenses of retirees and their dependents that are not otherwise provided by Medicare. The sum total of Ford's plus General Motors' future liability to retirees and their dependents exceeds $10 billion.

A business has three basic avenues for controlling health ex-

penses: usage reduction, management efficiency, and cost shifting
(Herzlinger and Schwartz, 1985). Corporations have begun to use
a number of monitoring techniques to track hospital usage and
physician expenditures (Caper et al., 1986). Researchers at the
Mayo Clinic have developed a set of comparative benchmarks
(reference points) for assessing corporate hospital utilization and
expenditures (Shaller and Gunderson, 1986). Reduction in the
usage of services can be accomplished through cost sharing, wellness programs (Schwartz and Rollins, 1985), health promotion
(Spilman, 1986; Warner, 1986), utilization review (Siu et al., 1986),
and alternative delivery systems such as HMOs (Whitted and
Torrens, 1985). The second strategy of managing costs more efficiently can be achieved through self-insurance, coordination of
benefit rules for phantom coverage, and negotiation of discounts
(Herzlinger, 1985; Eastaugh, 1986). Cost shifting, the third way of
controlling health expenses, takes two forms: (1) increasing the
employee's premium contribution or (2) "cost-transfer" off the
insurance plan and into the employee's pocketbook by increased
cost-sharing requirements.

The first method of cost shifting, cost-shifting of premiums,
fosters increased price sensitivity at the annual point of selecting
an insurance plan. Unfortunately, this mechanism provides the
consumer with no incentive to cooperate or to stimulate the more
efficient utilization of services. However, in the second method of
cost shifting, cost-sharing affects consumption at the point of
service—that is, it stimulates employees to economize and not let
excess cost transfers occur into their pocketbooks. This chapter
discusses cost sharing as a cost-control strategy and the impact of
the heightened price sensitivity on utilization.

Cost Transfer and Usage Reduction

Cost sharing not only shifts the burden onto the employee (cost
transfer), but also reduces the cost of care by deterring unnecessary services (usage reduction). As we shall see in an example of
collective bargaining, employees are highly interested in how
much cost transfer is required to buy a certain amount of usage
reduction. The trade-off can benefit all concerned, with the exception of the provider's pocketbook (but unions have a strong interest
in asking what is the balance struck between usage reduction and
cost transfer). Therefore, the firm must seek to curtail through cost
sharing what is labeled "moral hazard" in the jargon of economics
(Feldstein, 1981). The economist's term "moral hazard" does not

imply moral turpitude. In fact, employees' responses to increased insurance coverage are considered rational economic behavior in that they demand (or have demanded for them) more service when they pay less and less of the price.

Reports to date indicate that the health status of nonpoor employees and their families does not appear to suffer measurably from increased cost sharing. There is limited evidence to suggest that the poor, especially those with preexisting health problems, may have some erosion of health status under high levels of cost sharing (Shapiro et al., 1986). Consequently, this chapter should only be considered relevant for employed populations with incomes in excess of the bottom quartile of society. Cost sharing may be a prudent strategy for the "worried well," but not the poor and ill. According to the eight-year Rand study, individuals economize by being less prone to seek treatment or be hospitalized for an illness that can be treated elsewhere (Newhouse et al., 1981; Brook et al., 1984). Raising price sensitivity had no measurable impact on the health status of the employed and their dependents. Effective prices out-of-pocket should not be expected to have much effect on necessities, but 20 to 40 percent of prevailing medical practice might not be true necessities (Brook and Lohr, 1985; Williamson, 1977). In the Rand study, the average cost per hospitalization and per ambulatory episode was the same across a wide range of five high-low, cost-sharing options. However, usage was 30 to 40 percent lower with 50 percent cost sharing versus no free care (Newhouse et al., 1981).

Cost Sharing on the Increase

There have been many recent examples of significant increases in cost-sharing requirements. In 1984, Xerox instituted a 20 percent coinsurance plan for inpatient expenses, with a stop-gap provision to spend no more than $4,000, or 4 percent of salary. Hewitt Associates has surveyed a constant sample of half the Fortune 500 industrials, plus other firms, over the past seven years. The fraction of companies with substantial cost sharing, defined as requiring employees to pay more than 5 percent of their hospital bill, increased from 11 percent in 1979 to 50 percent in 1984. Until 1983, less than 18 percent of the companies required a deductible, but that percentage skyrocketed to 52 percent as of 1984. In 1982, only 5 percent of firms required deductibles of $150 or more, but this figure increased to 25 percent in 1984. To prevent a possible "catastrophic" fiscal impact of these increased employee cost-sharing requirements, companies instituted maximum out-of-pocket (MOOP) provisions. In 1979, only half the firms had instituted MOOP provisions, but by 1984 this figure had increased to 87 percent.

Given the topical importance of cost sharing, it is surprising how little econometric research has been translated into actuarial forecasts (Eastaugh, 1985). One should ask, "What is the distributional and fiscal impact under a simulated menu of cost-sharing options?" Two factors—the amount of cost transfer and the resulting total expense reduction from lower utilization—need to be studied to answer this omnibus question.

Designing an optimal cost-sharing program is particularly burdensome to small- and moderate-sized businesses, especially when they may not have the knowledge of econometric studies available to very large firms. Unfortunately, only a few benefit options were tested in the Rand study, thus making interpolation between a wide range of options necessary. Very large employers can afford to hire econometric consultants to interpolate data from dozens of other sources and come to a consensus. The intent of this chapter is to share some of this forecasting experience to help both employers and employees come to a decision about structuring their coinsurance, deductibles, and maximum out-of-pocket provisions.

Piecing Together a Forecasting Model

We shall consider the trade-offs between cost transfer onto employees and total expense reduction in health plan costs yielded by the cost transfer, in describing how forecasts can be useful in the collective bargaining process. For an anonymous company we shall consider the two original alternatives suggested by labor and management and come up with a better compromise plan. The employee fraction of total expenses, as a function of the three cost-sharing parameters, is presented in Table 3.1. Unfortunately, cost-sharing programs are often not updated on an annual basis. If these amounts remain fixed, the desired degree of price sensitivity erodes over time. One progressive way to avoid this problem is the variable deductible and variable maximum out-of-pocket, depending on the individual's salary. This makes the cost-sharing requirements equally burdensome for blue-collar and white-collar employees.

Another important consideration is how much total expense reduction occurs as cost sharing increases. Ceterus paribus, all else

Table 3.1 Fraction of Health Costs Paid by the Employee as a Function of Three Cost-sharing Provisions

Coinsurance	Maximum Out-of-Pocket per Annum	$0	$100	$250	$500	$1,000	4% of Salary
				Annual Deductible			
0%	none	0	.08	.13	.18	.25	.29
20%	$1,500	.14	.18ᵃ	.21	.24	.30	.32
	$2,000	.16	.20	.23	.26	.32	.34
	$2,500	.18	.21	.24	.27	.33	.36
	10% of salary	.20	.23	.26	.29	.35	.38
25%	$1,500	.17	.21	.24ᵇ	.27	.33	.35
	$2,000	.19	.23	.26	.29	.35	.37
	$2,500	.21	.24	.27	.31	.37	.39
	10% of salary	.22	.26	.29	.32	.38	.40
30%	$1,500	.21	.24	.27	.31	.36	.38
	$2,000	.23	.26	.29	.34ᶜ	.39	.41
	$2,500	.25	.28	.31	.36	.40	.42
	10% of salary	.26	.29	.32	.37	.41	.43
40%	$1,500	.26	.29	.32	.37	.41	.43
	$2,000	.28	.31	.35	.40	.44	.46
	$2,500	.30	.34	.38	.43	.46	.48
	10% of salary	.31	.35	.39	.44	.47	.49

SOURCE: Eastaugh (1985); all figures are in projected 1987 dollars assuming 6 percent inflation.
ᵃcurrent plan in 1986.
ᵇAlternative A: first option advanced by the union; no change in maximum out-of-pocket ($1,500), moderate increase in deductible (up from $100 to $250), small increase in coinsurance (up to 25%).
ᶜAlternative B: first option presented by the employer, substantial increases in deductible (to $500), moderate increases in coinsurance and maximum out-of-pocket expense.

equal, assuming the same population, the lowest cost-sharing option in Table 3.2 (free care) is 53 percent more expensive per employee than the highest cost-sharing option. The company we are studying currently has a moderate degree of cost sharing (20 percent, $1,500 maximum, $100 deductible), but costs per family are projected to increase next year by 10.5 percent (from $1,810 to $2,000). The question is how can we moderate this increase without achieving diminishing returns from cost transfers?

The Collective Bargaining Context

Although the collective bargaining process is never a sterile academic exercise, the projections are offered for both parties in a

Table 3.2 **Percentage Change in Total Health Insurance Plan Costs Relative to an Unchanged Benefit Plan (with a projected cost of $2,000 per employee for 1987)**

Coinsurance	Maximum Out-of-Pocket per Annum	Annual Deductible (%)					
		$0	$100	$250	$500	$1000	4% of Salary
0	none	+12	+8	+4	−2	−7	−8
20%	$1,500	+3	$2000	−3	−7	−11	−11
	$2,000	+1	−2	−5	−8	−13	−14
	$2,500	−1	−3	−6	−9	−14	−14
	10% of salary	−2	−4	−7	−9	−14	−14
25%	$1,500	−3	−5	−8[a]	−10[b]	−15	−15
	$2,000	−5	−7	−10	−12	−17	−18
	$2,500	−6	−8	−11	−13	−18	−18
	10% of salary	−7	−9	−12	−14	−19	−19
30%	$1,500	−8	−10	−13	−15	−19	−20
	$2,000	−10	−12	−14	−16[c]	−20	−20
	$2,500	−11	−13	−15	−17	−21	−21
	10% of salary	−12	−14	−16	−18	−21	−21
40%	$1,500	−14	−17	−19	−21	−24	−24
	$2,000	−15	−18	−20	−22	−25	−25
	$2,500	−16	−19	−21	−23	−26	−26
	10% of salary	−16	−19	−21	−23	−26	−26

[a]Alternative A: first option advanced by the union; no change in maximum out-of-pocket ($1,500), moderate increase in deductible (up from $100 to $250), small increase in coinsurance (up to 25%).
[b]Alternative G: the compromise plan (double underlined, Tables 3.1 and 3.2)
[c]Alternative B: first option presented by the employer, substantial increases in deductible (to $500), moderate increases in coinsurance and maximum out-of-pocket.

spirit of "more information is better than less." Baseline alternative 0 was to leave the cost-sharing requirements fixed and let costs increase at 10.5 percent. During the process of bargaining, two alternatives were developed by the employees and the employer. Alternative A, advanced by the union, had a projected cost per family in 1987 that was 8 percent less than the forecast $2,000 ($1,844). The employee pays out-of-pocket a projected 24 percent of that $1,844 ($443), instead of paying out-of-pocket 18 percent of the projected $2,000 ($360) if the old cost-sharing requirements remain unchanged. The cost-transfer burden, or extra share the employee has to pay, is $83 per family ($443 − $360) under the union alternative, but the total expense reduction is $156 ($2,000 − $1,844). In summary, $73 of the cost reduction per family results from utilization savings ($156 − $83), and $83 of the cost savings is in the form of a cost transfer from insurer to out-of-pocket expense.

Option B, advanced by the employer, would reduce total cost per employee during 1987 by 16 percent less than the forecast $2,000 ($1,677). The employee would, however, be paying out-of-pocket 34 percent of that smaller dollar figure ($1,677), instead of paying out-of-pocket a projected $360 of $2,000 of health expenses if the cost-sharing requirements remained unchanged. The cost-transfer burden, or extra share the employee has to pay, is $207 per family ($567 − $360), but the total expense reduction is $323 ($2,000 − $1,677). In summary, under the employer alternative B, $116 of the cost reduction per family is from a usage reduction ($323 − $207), and $207 of the cost savings is from a cost transfer of the burden from insurer to employee.

Reaching a Consensus

The employee representatives had three basic reasons for disliking alternative B. First, and of special importance to the union, was the increased potential financial risk of raising the maximum out-of-pocket expense to $2,000. Second, the fraction of costs paid out-of-pocket was almost double the 1986 figure (.18) and substantially higher than the union alternative (.24). Third, the employees feared that too great a cost transfer to the benefit of the employer would destroy the firm's interest in cost containment through other fledgling cost-control efforts (e.g., second opinion, home care, utilization review).

In the process of bargaining, a compromise was developed (25 percent coinsurance, unchanged $1,500 maximum, $500 deductible, plan C). Management acquiesced to the request that the maximum annual expense not be increased and that coinsurance be raised by only 5 percent; the union agreed to accept a $400 increase in the deductible. As can be seen from the double underlined figure in Table 3.2, costs were projected to be 10 percent less in 1987 than the forecast figure of $2,000 under this compromise plan C, at parity with present-year (1986) costs of $1,810 per family. The worker pays out-of-pocket 27 percent (double underlined figure, Table 3.1) of the $1,800 ($481), instead of paying out-of-pocket $360 of $2,000 in 1987 if we do not change the cost-sharing provisions. The total expense reduction, or differential cost advantage of increasing the amount of cost sharing, is $200 ($2,000 − $1,800). Therefore, $121 of the cost savings would be achieved by a cost transfer onto the employee, and $79 of the cost reduction per family would result from utilization reductions.

Lessons Learned

Collective bargaining need not be shrouded in excessive uncertainty. It is possible to achieve some good estimates of the expected cost transfer and usage reduction, in dollars, under various cost-sharing alternatives. Cost transfer, by definition, is a means for shifting health expenses off the firm's budget. But, the added benefit of cost sharing is that it stimulates cost consciousness and reduces utilization, thus reducing health expenditures. Cost consciousness, at the time the "buying" decision is made, moves unnecessary costs off the employees' and employer's budgets.

A second lesson learned involves the value of a scientific principle known as Occam's Razor: If a simple and a complex model produce the same predictions, one should prefer the simple model. Changes in the cost-sharing variables dominate moderate shifts in the demographic characteristics of the employees, as they impact health utilization and cost. A 10 percent change in cost sharing outweighs a 2 percent annual shift in the demographics by 40- to 90-fold. In a stable industry, cost-sharing provisions change more substantially than the descriptors of the work force (age, sex, race). Consequently, a more complex, expensive model with claims data buys little in terms of predictive accuracy. In the jargon of economics, the exogenous preexisting demographics of the employees are by definition worked into the baseline cost and usage figures used for projection, and they do not change much. There is endogenous control of the degree of cost sharing, however, and insurance plans should update the provisions in an attempt to control costs without reductions in care quality, access, health status, or the morale of the employees. A broad array of other cost-sharing initiatives and their estimated savings are presented in Table 3.3.

The cost-sharing strategy for reducing health care costs can work equally well for small and large firms. In contrast, management techniques for expense reduction are more dependent on business size. Self-insurance is best suited for large firms, because firms can spread the risk over many more employees. Self-insured employers, as judged by the June 1985 U.S. Supreme Court decision (53 USLW 4616), remain generally exempt from state controls and are governed instead by less constraining federal ERISA (Employee Retirement Income Security Act) requirements (Rublee, 1986). Employee leasing, when an individual is leased from a company that provides benefits at lower average cost for a large pool of workers, is well suited for small business. The Hartford Foundation is supporting a survey of Multiple Employer Trusts (METs),

**Table 3.3   Projected Marginal Cost Savings of Plan Design Changes
for Five Insurers***

Plan Design Change	Magnitude	Savings
Front-end deductible for room and board only	$450	5.2%
Coinsurance provision for surgery	70%	4.3
(as a percentage of reasonable	80%	2.8
and customary charges)	90%	1.2
Coverage for mental health or nervous	50%	2.5
disorders (as a percentage of payment with	80%	2.2
a $750 annual maximum benefit)	100%	1.8
Limit per day for mental health or nervous disorder	$90	.3
Limit per day, 15-day maximum ancillary usage only	$450	1.4
Limit per day on room and board	$300	1.0
Coinsurance provisions for lab or	70%	1.3
x-ray (as a percentage of reasonable	80%	.8
and customary charges)	90%	.4
Lifetime maximum benefit limit	$350,000	.8
	$700,000	.1%

*All figures are inflated to CY 1987 dollars, assuming 6 percent inflation. Original survey
data, 1983 Massachusetts Business Roundtable Health Care Task Force.

which aggregates small businesses to enlarge the population risk
pool and purchase group insurance. Sufficient cost-sharing provisions are essential for keeping METs financially solvent without
rejecting large numbers of high-risk applicants with poor health
status. Cost sharing need not be viewed as an assault on equity.
Cost sharing can help prevent risk selection, prevent unnecessary
utilization (and thus provider-caused iatrogenic illness), preserve a
firm's cost-competitive posture, and, ultimately, preserve jobs.

The consumer cost-sharing strategy, acting on the point of
possible consumption, makes the patient the central cost container. HMOs and managed care systems make the consumer a
major cost containment force, but acting only at an annual basis in
selecting a health plan. The health plan is ultimately the central
cost container, and to the extent that it contains costs and delivers
good service, consumers will be attracted (or disenrolled) from the
plan. For the consumer in a prepaid plan, there is no stress
concerning out-of-pocket expense each time services are required.
Some managed care systems mix the two strategies, as with PPOs,
offering annual cost-selection decisions about which plan to join. If
the consumer wishes to seek a non-PPO provider during the year,
the care is paid by the plan, but cost-sharing requirements are
substantial (20 to 35 percent of costs being paid out-of-pocket).

Table 3.4   Estimated Number of Persons with Physician's Expense Protection by Type of Insurer (in millions)

					Private Insurers		
Year	Population	All Insurers	HMOs, PPOs, Self-Insured Plans^a	Blue Cross/ Blue Shield	Individual and Family Policies	Group Policies^b	Total U.S. Population
1986	Under 65	168.2	82.2	53.6	8.9	92.4	
	65 and over	11.6	6.9	7.3	2.0	1.3	
	All ages	179.8	89.1	60.9	10.9	93.7	249.7
1981	All ages	164.1	43.3	68.1	11.2	97.3	238.3
1976	All ages	163.3	17.3	74.7	11.4	88.9	226.8
1966	All ages	114.0	8.4	52.2	8.5	56.9	205.3

SOURCES: Health Insurance Association of America, *Source Book of Health Insurance Data 1985–86* (Washington, D.C.: HIAA and DHHS); Chicago: Blue Cross/Blue Shield.

^aThese include self-administered plans, self-insured plans, and plans employing third-party administrators. HMOs assume the financial risk for unexpected payment expense, whereas PPOs shift this risk onto the purchaser. HMOs restrict reimbursed services to plan providers, while PPOs will allow patients to pay higher out-of-pocket costs and visit non-plan providers.

^bThe numbers do not sum across due to duplication among persons protected by more than one kind of insuring organization or more than one insurance company policy.

These new arrangements for consumer and provider-cost sensitivity are certainly an improvement over the old system in which insurers just paid bills and passed on the costs, patients consumed services with little regard for costs, and providers delivered services irrespective of the resource costs.

The trends indicated in Table 3.4 suggest that Blue Cross and private insurers have been losing market share to HMOs, PPOs, and self-insured plans from 1981 to 1986. In the case of Blue Cross, the slide in enrollment predates the trend for commercial insurance companies (1977–1986). The insurance concerns, nonprofit and for-profit, have not been complacent about these trends. Insurers have tried to become more price competitive, in addition to sponsoring HMO and PPO development. Hospital managers should also follow these trends closely. Assuming that beds only close at 2 percent per year, but managed care systems will grow at 10 to 15 percent per annum, 30 states could have hospital occupancy rates ranging from 20 to 35 percent by 1990. At 15 percent managed care growth rates, the average occupancy rate in Ohio and Michigan would be 27 and 29 percent, respectively. The price system may soon prove much more effective at closing beds than any system of health planning regulations.

References

BROOK, R., and LOHR, K. (1985). "Efficacy, Effectiveness, Variations and Quality." *Medical Care* 23:5 (May), 710–722.

BROOK, R., WARE J., ROGERS, W., MANNING, W., and NEWHOUSE, J. (1984). *The Effect of Coinsurance on the Health of Adults*. Santa Monica, Calif.: Rand Corporation Report to DHHS.

CALIFANO, J. (1986). *America's Health Care Revolution: Who Lives, Who Dies, Who Pays*. New York: Random House.

CAPER, P., KELLER, R., and ROHLF, P. (1986). "Tracking Physician Practice Patterns." *Business and Health* 3:9 (September), 7–9.

EASTAUGH, S. (1986). "Differential Cost Analysis: Judging a PPO's Feasibility." *Healthcare Financial Management* 40:5 (May), 44–51.

EASTAUGH, S. (1985). "Cost-Sharing Forecasts Can Assist in Health Care Collective Bargaining." *Business and Health* 3:2 (December), 52–53.

FELDSTEIN, M. (1981). *Hospital Costs and Health Insurance*. Cambridge, Mass.: Harvard University Press.

HERZLINGER, R. (1985). "How Companies Tackle Health Care Costs: Part II." *Harvard Business Review* 63:5 (September–October), 108–120.

HERZLINGER, R., and SCHWARTZ, J. (1985). "How Companies Tackle Health Care Costs: Part I." *Harvard Business Review* 63:4 (July-August), 69–81.

NEWHOUSE, J., et al. (1981). "Some Interim Results from a Controlled Trial of

Cost Sharing in Health Insurance." *New England Journal of Medicine* 305:23 (December 17), 1501–1507.

RUBLEE, D., (1986). "Self-Funded Health Benefit Plans: Trends, Legal Environment, and Policy Issues." *Journal of the American Medical Association* 255:6 (February 14), 787–789.

SCHWARTZ, R., and ROLLINS, P. (1985). "Measuring the Cost Benefit of Wellness Strategies." *Business and Health* 2:10 (October), 24–26.

SHALLER, D., and GUNDERSON, S. (1986). "Setting Benchmarks for Cost-Effective Care." *Business and Health* 3:10 (October), 28–32.

SHAPIRO, M., WARE, J., and SHERBOURNE, C. (1986). "Effects of Cost Sharing on Seeking Care for Serious and Minor Symptoms." *Annals of Internal Medicine* 104:2 (February), 246–251.

SHELTON, J. (1985). "Private Sector Conference—Costs at Ford Motor." *Journal of the American Medical Association* 254:13 (October 4), 1788.

SIU, A., SONNENBERG, F., MANNING, W., NEWHOUSE, J., and BROOK, R. (1986). "Inappropriate Use of Hospitals in a Randomized Trial of Health Insurance Plans." *New England Journal of Medicine* 315:20 (November 13), 1259–1266.

SPILMAN, M. (1986). Effects of a Corporate Health Promotion Program." *Journal of Occupational Medicine* 11:4 (April), 34.

TELL, E., FALIK, M., and FOX, P. (1984). "Private Sector Health Care Initiatives: A Comparative Perspective from Four Communities." *Milbank Memorial Fund Quarterly/Health and Society* 62:3 (Summer), 357–379.

WARNER, K. (1986). "Selling Health Promotion to Corporate America." *Health Education Quarterly* 13:4 (Winter), 22.

WHITTED, G., and TORRENS, P. (1985). *Managing Corporate Health Care*. New York: Praeger.

WILLIAMSON, J. (1977). *Improving Medical Practice and Health Care*. Cambridge, Mass.: Ballinger.

Chapter 4

PPOs AS A JOINT VENTURE

If you have seen one PPO, you have seen one PPO. They differ widely in structure and sponsors. Hospitals are starting to sponsor PPOs, and not just contract with them.

—MAX FINE

PPOs are making inroads into the utilization advantage of HMOs. Where in the past HMOs had a hospital experience 50 percent less than that experienced by their fee-for-service competitors, that margin has now shrunk. As these managed care products continue to push down the utilization curve the price attractiveness of HMOs may decline.

—DONALD COHODES

As we have observed in Chapter 1, average daily census (ADC) has declined dramatically in the past three years. One emerging strategy for financial survival under the prospective payment system (PPS) is for hospitals to increase the utilization of charge-paying patients through PPO (preferred provider organization) development. The thrust of this chapter involves suggesting how hospitals can form joint venture partnerships to initiate a successful PPO, attain a critical mass of patients, and sell the plan at some future date to an HMO network in the 1990s. PPOs are less capital-intensive than staff or group model HMOs, more akin to traditional group insurance products, and highly attractive to insurance companies and hospital chains that are initiating comprehensive networks of insurance-plus-delivery (Graham, 1986). PPOs add to the competitive pressure on HMOs (Cohodes, 1985). A comprehensive network must offer to employees the "triple option" of HMO care, PPO care, and traditional group insurance. The acronym PPO may not be long-standing (Lissovoy et al., 1986;

81

Fox and Anderson, 1986): Most PPOs will either evolve into independent practice association (IPA) model HMOs, join an HMO network, or go out of business.

Initiating a PPO

PPOs have an intuitive appeal as a mechanism for attracting fixed blocks of business (Trauner, 1986; Egdahl and Walsh, 1985). Taking on PPO patients is analogous to taking credit-card business, in that you absorb the 3 to 6 to 9 percent discounts in hopes of increasing the volume of new users to your firm. Because most PPOs are only 10 to 20 months in development, few have yet to prove themselves as a financial success from the hospital perspective; for that reason, other strategies for financial survival should not be precluded (Gabel and Ermann, 1985).

Despite the fact that PPOs are far from a proven marketing bet, their growth in numbers has been explosive: up from 123 in the spring of 1984 to an estimated 400 by July 1986. As of the fall of 1986, PPOs had enrolled an estimated 6.4 million Americans (2.5 percent of the population). Already, however, some PPOs have failed. Many single hospital-sponsored PPOs have underestimated the risk of initiating a PPO venture (Eastaugh, 1986; Kuntz, 1984). Any hospital initiating or joining a PPO should carefully weigh the strategic options, risks, and benefits or it could find itself in severe financial difficulty. Generating new sources of revenues and new users of the hospital—not merely increasing the volume of patient days labeled as PPO users—is the desideratum.

The impact of a PPO on a hospital's financial position is twofold: (1) it can generate new revenue in excess of variable costs to create a net profit from pulling in new users (PPO-generated users) of the hospital, and (2) it can forego revenue previously paid at charges by offering discounts in the context of the PPO to preexisting or "old users" of the hospital (label it discount giveaway to those who would have used your hospital with or without a PPO). The critical question for a given hospital is, Does the net profit (new user revenue above variable cost) exceed the giveaways in discounts to old users (includes any and all expected users of your facility, even if it is the first time the individual has ever been sick)? This question will be addressed in the context of three anonymous hospitals that initiated a PPO as a joint venture during 1985.

To make the venture work, all three partners must benefit from the PPO. The motivation for these three hospitals starting a PPO is twofold: (1) to be proactive in attracting more patients to offset the current declines in ADC and thus be better able to cover fixed costs (which was especially a problem at Charity Hospital, the one hospital with a high debt-service burden, and (2) to be reactive in blunting the impact of an investor-owned hospital in the same area that had the "advantage in being first" by starting a PPO in the summer of 1984.

As a note of background, the three tax-exempt hospitals (Charity, Oceanfront, and Suburban) formed an isosceles triangle 20 × 20 × 30 miles surrounding the proprietary hospital. The market geography reinforces the financial rationale for the partnership in three basic ways. First, all three hospitals can "chip away" on all sides at the investor-owned hospital's market catchment area. Second, the three potential partners in the joint venture are not in competition for patients nearly as much as they are competing with nearby hospitals. Third, employers are more attracted to a PPO that can cover a higher fraction of their employees, both geographically and seasonally (as in the summer when they migrate to beachfront property in the vicinity of Oceanfront Hospital). In summary, the more partners involved in the venture of initiating a PPO, the better their chances of success in achieving a critical mass of enrollees, and the better able they are to recoup the $900,000 initial start-up costs.

The market strategy for these three hospitals can be stated in either a positive or negative way: to maintain or slow the decline in ADC or to prevent continued erosion of their respective market shares by the competition. Our financial analysis will involve what accountants refer to as *differential cost analysis,* or what economists refer to as *marginal cost analysis*. No statement can be made concerning the financial position of the entire hospital across all payers. Our only concerns shall be how viable is the PPO strategy at improving the profitability contribution by charge payers and at reversing the downtrend in ADC.

Selecting How Much to Discount Charges

The historic trends in charges and patient census for charge payers are displayed in Table 4.1. The nine quarters of data were utilized to forecast, with seasonal adjustment, utilization in 1985–86 by exponential smoothing (McClain and Eastaugh, 1983). The single most important financial decision that management at each facility must make is the selection of an appropriate discount rate. In organizing the joint venture, it is not necessary that all partners benefit equally or discount equally but rather that each partner

Table 4.1   Charge Payers (Commercial, Self-Funded, Self-Pay), Per Quarter, Per Diem, and Average Daily Census (ADC) CY 1982–1984 (Q₁), and Estimated 1985–1986

Time Period		Oceanfront Hospital			Charity Hospital			Suburban Hospital		
		Patient Days (per quarter)	Charges/Day	ADC	Patient Days (per quarter)	Charges/Day	ADC	Patient Days (per quarter)	Charges/Day	ADC
1982	Q_1	2,975	$419	33.1	4,617	$446	51.3	2,379	$470	26.4
	Q_2	3,200	$419	35.2	4,446	$459	48.9	2,387	$478	26.2
	Q_3	3,081	$444	33.5	5,145	$472	55.9	2,561	$480	27.8
	Q_4	3,477	$453	37.8	5,053	$474	54.9	2,201	$490	23.9
1983	Q_1	3,905	$497	43.4	4,841	$524	53.8	2,172	$510	24.1
	Q_2	3,887	$503	42.7	5,320	$543	58.5	2,074	$520	22.8
	Q_3	3,521	$529	38.3	5,213	$538	56.7	2,201	$525	23.9
	Q_4	3,914	$506	37.9	4,714	$550	51.2	1,861	$530	20.2
1984	Q_1	3,185	$555	35.0	4,439	$558	48.8	2,028	$540	22.3
1985*	Estimated no PPO	2,865	$575	31.4	4,005	$580	43.9	1,907	$551	20.9
1986*	Estimated no PPO	2,573	$596	28.2	3,605	$603	39.5	1,789	$578	19.6

*Scenario 1 in our analysis assumes no PPO is started by any of the three hospitals.

benefit and trusts that the distribution of revenues and discounts is fairly distributed.

Pricing discount decisions must consider the response of PPO enrollment, and thus patient census, to a change in the rate of billed charges. The employers will consider the overall discount rate across all three facilities (DISTOTAL) in deciding whether (1) it is worth the risk to add the PPO option to their benefit plan given that a PPO may not have a long life expectancy and (2) to waive either all or only some cost-sharing requirements as a means of channeling employees to the PPO hospitals. Individual employees will react in their selection of a provider to differences in cost sharing for the PPO option, which itself is driven by DISTOTAL. But consumers will have no interest in the discount offered by each individual hospital $(D(X))$. Individuals care about their out-of-pocket risk under the plan, and not the preexisting financial arrangements that the plan has with each hospital.

As a hypothetical example, one could achieve an aggregate weighted discount across all PPO hospitals (DISTOTAL = 7 percent) in one of the following three ways:

1. Equal discount rate for all three hospitals.
2. Egalitarian—allocate higher discounts (e.g., 11 percent) to those better able to absorb them and let the partner with the worst financial health offer a lower discount (e.g., 3 percent).
3. Meritarian—based on an external standard from historical experience relative to one large payer that has required a discount (e.g., utilize Blue Cross as the yardstick).

We shall consider all three methods for distributing DISTOTAL across the three hospitals. In the first few months of the market survey, some employers indicated they would only consider a PPO if DISTOTAL was equivalent to Blue Cross, and a few indicated that they would be unresponsive to entry of another PPO in the market unless discount $D(X)$ at each hospital was at a parity with Blue Cross or better (higher discount). In this situation a brief description of Blue Cross reimbursement in this state seems necessary.

In this market, Blue Cross (BC) currently pays at cost plus 5 percent plus community service. Defacto, these cost-based BC rates are equivalent to paying 0.84 percent of Oceanfront Hospital's charges, 0.97 percent of Charity Hospital's charges, and 0.98 percent of Suburban Hospital's charges, on average during 1983–84. In 1985, Blue Cross started a prospective system, which is defacto equivalent to paying 0.84 percent of Oceanfront's charges, 0.91 percent of Charity's charges, and 0.93 percent of Suburban's charges, on average. To achieve parity with Blue Cross, the potential PPO would have to offer discounts of 16 percent, 9 percent, and 7 percent, respectively, across the three hospitals, or a total weighted DISTOTAL of 10.5 percent. Two of the hospitals suggested a "second best" pricing strategy by offering lower discounts in the initial year of the PPO—1985 (scenarios 2, 3, 4, Table 4.2)—and achieving parity with BC in the future. Immediate parity with BC is defined as scenario 5 in Table 4.2. Scenario 1, having no PPO, is projected in Table 4.1.

Marketing to Employers and Consumer Choice

Having a good estimate of the necessary "critical mass" of PPO enrollees to make the venture viable is a critical issue for all parties concerned. Just because area employers exhibit a great deal of "general interest" in the PPO "concept" does not mean they have the capacity to easily add the PPO option to their benefit packages. In our situation, the study area lacked a great number of self-funded employers with large numbers of employees. Fortunately, a number of companies are about to become self-funded, or will soon become self-funded unless their commercial insurance carriers allow special arrangements for PPO participation.

A second basic issue concerns what fraction of hospital utilization for a company offering the PPO option will actually walk into PPO facilities. The answer clearly is not 100 percent, even with the "carrot" of waived cost-sharing requirements if one uses the three PPO hospitals. If the condition is very urgent, one might rather pay the extra dollar costs of going to a non-PPO hospital than pay the time and travel costs of driving to the closest PPO facility (McGuirk and Porell, 1984). In our analysis, we assume that PPO enrollees will utilize the three hospitals either 720 days per thousand per year (low estimate), or 940 (high estimate). Obviously, one could perform a sensitivity analysis to a point where PPO usage by PPO eligibles is so low, or reductions in total days per thousand is so low due to aggressive utilization review, that even this low estimate is unreasonably high.

Given the prevailing trends in medical practice in our marketplace—namely, the lack of aggressive utilization review—the range of estimates at the bottom of Table 4.2 appears reasonable. The relative attractiveness of the PPO benefit option improves as the number of hospitals in the venture increases. If we only had a single-hospital PPO at Oceanfront, time and travel costs might so outweigh expected dollar cost savings in the consumer's mind such that the PPO could only attract a 12 percent share. The distribution of hospitals and self-funded employers and employees is a crucial point of information to gain in the market survey. The range of high-low estimates in Table 4.2 would have to be adjusted if, for example, by 1987 utilization review brought charge-patient usage per thousand enrollees down from 1,100 to 770 days, with a net share of 70 percent going to the PPO hospitals and resulting in a net yield to the three partners of only 539 days per 1,000 PPO eligibles. The current low estimate of 720 days per thousand for 1985, compared to the 1983–84 experience of 1,100, could either be achieved by (1) a 10 percent reduction in days through utilization review (UR) and achievement of a 73 percent share of that market (720/990); (2) a 20 percent reduction through UR and achievement of a 82 percent share of the market (720/880); or (3) any other linear combination that adds up to a 34.5 percent decline in bed usage at the three hospitals. One could run a PPO without discounts as long as one could convince employers ex ante that utilization review would be sufficient as a means of cost control.

Differential Cost Analysis

Discounts are a two-edged sword in the sense that if the rates are too low, the PPO will fail to attract enough employers to test whether the venture can achieve true savings by means of utilization review and price discounts in combination. Second, if the discounts are too high, the hospitals will lose money. The differential costs and revenues of the PPO venture can be analyzed in the following framework. The formula for costs and foregone charges given away to sure users (old-faithful patrons) of the hospital who now sign up for the PPO is

$$FR(X) = P(X) \cdot ADO(X) \cdot D(X) \qquad (4.1)$$

where X = the hospital
$FR(X)$ = foregone revenue from discounts for patients who would have come to X irrespective of the PPO
$P(X)$ = average charges per diem at hospital X
$D(X)$ = fraction of charges (P) discounted at X
$ADO(X)$ = average daily old user census at X (listed in Table 4.2)

Shifts in variable cost behavior will not be a factor in our analysis because we shall assume that physicians and hospitals do not treat old customers differently in intensity of service per day merely

Table 4.2 **Sensitivity Analysis of High-Low Estimates of the Impact of Discounts on PPO Daily Census by "Old Users" and PPO-Generated "New Users," 1985**

Hospital, Discount Rate (DISC)	Low Estimate		High Estimate	
	ADO (Avg. Daily Old User Census)	ADN (Avg. Daily New User Census)	ADO (Avg. Daily Old User Census)	ADN (Avg. Daily New User Census)
Oceanfront Hospital				
scenario 2, 9% discount	1.2	1.0	1.4	1.3
scenario 3, 7% discount	1.3	1.2	1.5	1.5
scenario 4, 12.5% discount	1.4	1.7	1.6	2.2
scenario 5, 16% discount[a]	1.6	2.9	1.8	3.6
Charity Hospital				
scenario 2, 4.5% discount	1.2	1.2	1.4	1.4
scenario 3, 7% discount	1.3	1.4	1.5	1.7
scenario 4, 7% discount	1.4	2.1	1.6	2.5
scenario 5, 9% discount[a]	1.5	4.0	1.7	4.8

Suburban Hospital	Assume LL	Assume HH	Assume LL	Assume HH
scenario 2, 4.5% discount	1.2	0.8	1.4	1.0
scenario 3, 7% discount[a]	1.3	0.7	1.5	0.9
scenario 4, 4.5% discount	1.3	1.0	1.6	1.2
scenario 5, 7% discount[a]	1.5	2.0	1.8	2.4

Given the Assumptions[b] on Days per 1,000:

Number of Enrollees in the PPO	Assume LL	Assume HH	Assume LL	Assume HH
scenario 2, 6.6% avg. discount	9,150	7,025	10,975	8,400
scenario 3, 7% avg. discount[c]	10,000	7,650	11,950	9,150
scenario 4, 9% avg. discount	12,350	9,475	14,850	11,375
scenario 5, 10.5% avg. discount	18,750	14,350	22,350	17,125

[a]Equivalent to Blue Cross effective rate of discount under the new payment plan, July 1984.

[b]Under assumption *LL* the number of inpatient days per 1,000 PPO enrollees at PPO-number hospitals is 720. Under assumption *HH* it is 940 (or only 5 percent below current levels). In other words, the low estimate of scenario 2 could be produced by either 9,150 enrollees being hospitalized at the rate of 720 days/1,000 per year, or 7,025 enrollees hospitalized at the rate 940 days/1,000/year.

[c]All three hospitals offer the same rate of discount, 7 percent.

because they have joined a PPO. With experience in the area of utilization review, one could modify the assumption. However, employers traditionally have more confidence in a provider's ability to discount charges rather than say with certainty that utilization review will "save Y amount of money." The net profit from PPO-generated new users to the hospital is given by the following formula:

$$NR(X) = [P(X) \cdot ADN(X) \cdot (1.0 - D(X))] - [ADN(X)VC(X)] \quad (4.2)$$

where $NR(X)$ = net profit from new users
$ADN(X)$ = average daily new user census at X (listed in Table 4.2)
$VC(X)$ = variable cost per diem at X

Three basic estimates will have to be made in our analysis. First, we assume PPO users have the same intensity of case mix and severity as previous charge-paying patients. Second, a range of variable cost estimates is provided at all three hospitals. In our sensitivity analysis, variable costs per diem as a percentage of total costs range from 50 to 60 percent (37 to 41 percent variable labor costs, 7 to 10 percent variable supply costs, and 6 to 9 percent variable overhead costs). Fixed costs account for 40 to 50 percent of average costs, as consistent with previous hospital cost function studies* (Eastaugh, 1986; Eastaugh, 1982; Atkinson and Eastaugh, 1984) (5 to 10 percent depreciation, 16 to 22 percent fixed overhead, and 18 to 20 percent fixed labor costs). Reporting one-third of your labor costs as fixed might appear high. Economists tend to report a higher fraction of costs as variable and think in multi-year time horizons, whereas managers tend to think short run and have a bias toward declaring more costs as fixed. Staff reductions are getting more prevalent in this industry. However, labor costs are variable only of they are managed in that manner (Burik and Duvall, 1985; Eastaugh, 1985). If it is the hospital's policy to accept 18 to 20 percent of average costs as fixed for a specified time period (1985), regardless of variation in patient demand, then these costs are not variable. The estimated variable costs per diem range from $287 to $345 at Oceanfront Hospital, $290 to $348 at Charity Hospital, and $275 to $331 at Suburban Hospital.

The third area of estimation involves refining the earlier work of

---

*Such analysis depends on the size and cost structure of the facility under study. One recent analysis (Bridges and Jacob, 1986) suggests that marginal cost may be as low as 0.3 to 0.39 for 14 DRGs under study.

Schmitt (1983) in assuming a fixed ratio of ADN/ADO old/new users of 54/100. Our market survey indicates that this ratio is a function of PPO growth, size, and population density. In a new, smaller PPO, the old users are naturally the first to sign up, but if the PPO should expand, the new users of the hospital will eventually outnumber the familiar old users. Moreover, the pool of potential new users is more unlimited in the dense urban environment, whereas the less populated rural areas would tend to have a higher ADO/ADN ratio, ceterus paribus. In our market the estimated old/new ratio equals 145/100 for Suburban Hospital and 100/100 for the urban Charity Hospital in the case of a fledgling PPO (8,000 enrollees). However, ADO/ADN equals 75/100 for Suburban Hospital and a projected 35/100 for Charity in the case of a mature PPO with over 20,000 enrollees. In each market situation, a finely honed conjoint measurement survey of consumer preference would be in order (Rosko et al., 1983). Moreover, as Tresnowski (1985) points out, consumers are interested in value for their money—that is, the choice is not always for the least expensive alternative.

Operational Projections

Differential costing, whether revenues from the venture would be in excess of variable costs and ignoring the $300,000 of start-up costs, is presented in Tables 4.3 to 4.5. The basic question asked by the chief financial officers of the three hospitals is, "Can our discounts be as generous as Blue Cross?" The answer seems affirmative over a wide range of assumptions. In other words, one need not hedge the bet and attempt other discount scenarios (scenarios 2, 3, 4, Table 4.2). Scenario 5 (Table 4.2), offering discounts at parity with Blue Cross, will attract between 14,000 to 22,000 PPO enrollees. The "good news" is that to move quickly and get into the PPO business in late 1984 may preempt the competiton from starting PPOs and allow the venture to gain a sufficient scale of operations. The bad news is that average daily census may increase by only 13 to 16 days, helping to halt the projected rate of decline in ADC but not enough to restore the occupancy rate to previous levels or to raise the occupancy rate much beyond 72 percent. The $300,000 per hospital investment is of little concern, since the expected payback period on the investment is under five years for the worst case scenario at the weakest case hospital.

Further analysis indicates a single-hospital PPO by any of the

Table 4.3 New Impact in Profitability per Diem in 1985 Under the Four PPO Scenarios at Oceanfront Hospital

Case Situation	Level of discounts to PPO patients (DISC[b])	Case A	Case B	Case C	Case D	PPO Daily Census Given the Demand Estimate Low[a]	PPO Daily Census Given the Demand Estimate High[a]
Variable Cost Estimate per PPO Patient Day		Low ($287.5)	Low	High ($345)	High		
Demand Estimate Assumptions[a]		High	Low	High	Low	Low	High
Scenario 2:	.09	$234.03	$173.65	$159.28	$116.15	2.2	2.7
Scenario 3:	.07	310.50	244.38	224.25	175.38	2.5	3.0
Scenario 4:	.125	359.38	265.94	232.88	168.19	3.1	3.8
Scenario 5:	.16	538.20	419.75	331.20	253.00	4.5	5.4

[a]The high estimate of demand assumes that PPO enrollees utilize 940 patient days per 1000 members at the PPO-member hospitals. The low estimate of demand assumes a more effective utilization review effort, where PPO enrollees utilize only 780 patient days per 1000 members per year.
[b]Revenue per patient day received by the hospital equals, on average, $(1 - DISC) \times \$575$.

Table 4.4 Net Impact in Profitability per Diem in 1985 Under the Four PPO Scenarios at Charity Hospital

Case Situation		Case A	Case B	Case C	Case D	PPO Daily Census Given the Demand Estimate	
						Low[a]	High[a]
Variable Cost Estimate per PPO Patient Day		Low ($290)	Low	High ($348)	High		
Demand Estimate Assumptions[a]		High	Low	High	Low		
	Level of discount to PPO patients (DISC[b])						
Scenario 2:	.045	$332.92	$285.36	$251.72	$215.76	2.4	2.8
Scenario 3:	.07	363.08	296.38	264.48	215.18	2.7	3.2
Scenario 4:	.07	558.54	466.90	413.54	345.10	3.5	4.1
Scenario 5:	.09	1052.70	872.90	774.30	640.90	5.5	6.5

[a]The high estimate of demand assumes that PPO enrollees utilize 940 patient days per 1000 members at the PPO-member hospitals. The low estimate of demand assumes a more effective utilization review effort, where PPO enrollees utilize only 780 patient days per 1000 members per year.
[b]Revenue per patient day received by the hospital equals, on average, $(1 - DISC) \times \$580$.

TABLE 4.5 New Impact in Profitability per Diem in 1985 Under the Four PPO Scenarios at Suburban Hospital

Case Situation	Case A	Case B	Case C	Case D	PPO Daily Census Given the Demand Estimate	
					Low[a]	High[a]
Variable Cost Estimate per PPO Patient Day	Low ($275.5)	Low	High ($330.6)	High		
Demand Estimate Assumptions[a]	High	Low	High	Low		
Level of discount to PPO patients (DISC[b])						
Scenario 2: .045	$215.99	$170.81	$160.89	$126.73	2.0	2.4
Scenario 3: .07	155.38	115.71	105.79	77.14	2.0	2.4
Scenario 4: .045	261.17	218.97	163.37	195.05	2.3	2.8
Scenario 5: .07	499.21	416.01	305.81	366.97	3.5	4.2

[a]The high estimate of demand assumes that PPO enrollees utilize 940 patient days per 1000 members at the PPO-member hospitals. The low estimate of demand assumes a more effective utilization review effort, where PPO enrollees utilize only 780 patient days per 1000 members per year.
[b]Revenue per patient day received by the hospital equals, on average, $(1 - DISC) \times \$551$.

partners would only attract 2,500 to 6,000 enrollees. Initiating the PPO as a joint venture seems in order, but the discount policy should be reviewed after the first year of operation. If one or two other PPOs in the market go under, the discounts may be revised downward. If competition from PPOs and HMOs heats up in the area, the discount rates may have to be raised in 1986. An iterative approach to discount selection allows the multifacility-sponsored PPO to understand its market better over time and not give away too much in ADO charges relative to gains through ADN new users. Local business groups might even help underwrite the $300,000 start-up costs. As one business coalition executive put it, "We are a marketplace looking for a product called PPOs, not a product looking for a marketplace."

The enthusiasm of senior managers may have caused many PPOs to form, but the enthusiasm of utilization reviewers and operating managers will make PPOs a winning or losing proposition (Edelston et al., 1985; Fielding, 1985). The built-in cost-management incentives, not mere discounts, are the keys to PPO success (Boland, 1985). Multiple-sponsor, vertically related PPOs can be successful but only if each partner makes a considerable effort to understand the activities of the other partners. In the example presented in this chapter, the partners are horizontally linked (three short-term general hospitals), and therefore understand the business activities of their neighbors. However, they lack business expertise in the insurance and employer relations area. In all likelihood, as Graham (1986) suggests, the hospital-based PPO will wisely sell out to a vertically related senior partner at some future date. Sales prices in this area have ranged from $250 to $400 per enrollee, and twice that price for some HMOs in their golden era (1984–85). Putting a price on a PPO is like putting a price on a rural radio station—very little is tied up in assets. What is being bought and sold is good faith and continued operating relationships. In the interest of fiduciary responsibility, we shall select the low estimate ($250) and consider whether the hospital partners should sell their successful PPO at some future date.

PPOs are relatively easy to build in the physical sense in that like radio stations or insurance companies there are few fixed assets (e.g., computer software) and only cash flow to broker or manage. The buyer is purchasing goodwill and existing relations with the provider community and the public. Many insurance companies, HMO chains, and hospital chains are highly interested in purchasing successful PPOs. Hospital chains have become health care companies, viewing the insurance companies as their ultimate competition (see Chapter 20). Chains can make money from the

Table 4.6 Leveraged Scenario: Three Hospitals Borrow $300,000 each (8.5% Interest) and Develop a PPO (1987–1992), for Sale at $250 per Enrollee in 1992–1994 (all dollar figures 000's omitted)

	1987	1988	1989	1990	1991	1992	1993	1994
Income Statement								
Enrollment	5,000	8,000	10,000	12,000	14,000	16,000	18,000	18,000
Revenues	5,960	10,108	13,267	16,716	20,477	24,572	29,025	30,447
Expenses								
Operating	6,860	9,822	12,646	15,630	18,782	22,109	25,619	26,388
Interest	76	76	76	76	76	76	76	76
Earnings Before Taxes*	-976	210	545	1,010	1,619	2,387	3,330	3,983
Net Income	-976	141	365	677	1,085	1,599	2,231	2,669
Cash Flow* Cumulative	-925	-733	-317	411	1,547	3,197	5,479	8,199
Current Liabilities								
Debt	900	900	900	900	900	900	900	900
Equity	0	0	0	0	0	0	0	0
Total	900	900	900	900	900	900	900	900

Potential Sale (@ $250/PPO enrollee)

PPO Sale Price	1,250	2,000	2,500	3,000	3,500	4,000	4,500	4,500
Net	−5,652	−4,710	−3,794	−2,566	−931	1,220	4,002	6,722
Capital Gains (22%)	0	0	0	0	0	951	3,121	5,243
Discount Rate 8%								
NPV* (net present value) without capital gains								
NPV*	−5,233	−4,038	−3,012	−1,887	−634	769	2,335	3,632
NPV with capital gains	−5,233	−4,038	−3,012	−1,887	−634	600	1,821	2,832
Discount Rate 12%								
NPV* without capital gains								
NPV*	−5,046	−3,755	−2,701	−1,631	−528	618	1,810	2,715
NPV with capital gains	−5,046	−3,755	−2,701	−1,631	−528	482	1,412	2,118

*Tax Rates 33%. Cash flow includes interest (1-Tax), $51,000 each year.

Table 4.7 Equity Financed Scenario: Three Hospitals Contribute Equally to Develop a PPO 1987–1992, for Sale at $250 per Enrollee in 1992–1994 (all dollar figures 000's omitted)

	1987	1988	1989	1990	1991	1992	1993	1994
Income Statement								
Enrollment	5,000	8,000	10,000	12,000	14,000	16,000	18,000	18,000
Revenues	5,960	10,108	13,267	16,716	20,477	24,572	29,025	30,447
Expenses								
Operating	6,860	9,822	12,646	15,630	18,782	22,109	25,619	26,388
Interest	0	0	0	0	0	0	0	0
Earnings Before Taxes*	−900	286	621	1,086	1,695	2,463	3,406	4,059
Net Income	−900	192	416	728	1,136	1,650	2,282	2,720
Cash Flow* Cumulative	−900	−708	−292	435	1,571	3,221	5,503	8,223
Current Liabilities								
Debt	0	0	0	0	0	0	0	0
Equity	900	900	900	900	900	900	900	900
Total	900	900	900	900	900	900	900	900
Potential Sale (@ $250/PPO enrollee)								

PPO Sale Price	1,250	2,000	2,500	3,000	3,500	4,000	4,500	4,500
Net	−6,510	−5,569	−4,652	−3,425	−1,789	361	3,143	5,863
Capital Gains (22%)	0	0	0	0	0	282	2,452	4,573
Discount Rate 8%								
NPV (Net Present Value) without capital gains								
NPV	−6,028	−4,774	−3,693	−2,517	−1,218	228	1,834	3,168
NPV with capital gains	−6,028	−4,774	−3,693	−2,517	−1,218	178	1,431	2,471
Discount Rate 12%								
NPV (Net Present Value) without capital gains								
NPV	−5,813	−4,439	−3,312	−2,177	−1,015	183	1,422	2,368
NPV with capital gains	−5,813	−4,439	−3,312	−2,177	−1,015	143	1,109	1,843

*Tax Rates 33%.

insurance end of the business and channel patients to their half-empty hospitals. HMOs and insurance companies are quick to respond to the challenge and have gotten into the PPO business because employers strongly favor carriers that can offer the "triple option": HMO plans, PPO plans, and traditional indemnity insurance. In considering make-versus-buy decisions, and after experiencing a number of disappointing acquisitions, all three sectors (hospital chains, HMOs, and insurance companies) are anxious to buy proven PPOs.

The first pair of questions PPO managers should answer is: (1) At what point do we begin to experience a positive cumulative cash flow? and (2) At what point is the net present value of the investment in a PPO positive? These questions are answered at two rates of discount and under two basic scenarios in Tables 4.6 and 4.7. In scenario 1 (Table 4.6), each of the three hospitals borrows $300,000 at an 8.5 percent interest rate (because no employer group is forthcoming with the funds, and physicians are unwilling to invest because of their disillusionment with the impact of federal tax reform on their tax shelters). The PPO enrollment is expected to peak at 18,000 enrollees in the seventh year of operation (1993). The enrollment in year one is expected to be 5,000, doubling in size by 1988. Expenses grow proportionately, yielding a net profit of − $925 after year one. The cumulative cash flow is not positive until 1990, and the net present value (after paying 22 percent capital gains tax) is not positive until 1992. The return on investment if the PPO is sold in 1994 (after two years of peak enrollment, 18,000) is 315 percent (discounted at 8 percent, 2,830/900). The return on investment is still a very healthy 235 percent if discounted at 12 percent (2,118/900) in Table 4.6. The return on investment declines as leverage declines. If the PPO is 100 percent equity-financed, the return on investment discounted at 8 percent is 275 percent (Table 4.7, 2,471/900); discounting at 12 percent, the return on investment is 205 percent (1,843/900). We shall utilize these same discount rates (8 and 12 percent) in analyzing buy/lease decisions in Chapter 22.

PPOs represent a mixed cost-control strategy—using provider discounts and consumer cost-sharing as a disincentive against usage of nonpreferred providers. We have uncovered a second hospital-side motivation for initiating a PPO, other than the obvious motivation of providing annual patient revenues for the mothership. If the PPO is successful in attracting patients, it can be sold to larger organizations at a profit. Two caveats are in order. The return on investment in developing the PPO is sufficient by health industry standards if one presumes that a buyer willing to pay $250 per enrollee can be found. Second, many fledgling PPOs may be acquired from within by the medical staff or other buyers and converted into IPA model HMOs in the future. Again, the PPO acronym may not even exist in the year 1995. The risks are substantial, but so are the benefits. Consequently, hospitals, insurers, and other health providers will continue to invest in PPO development in the near future.

References

ATKINSON, G., and EASTAUGH, S. (1984). "Guaranteed Inpatient Revenue: Friend or Foe to PPOs and Alternative Delivery." *Maryland HFMA Quarterly* 18:5 (May), 1–4.

BOLAND, P. (1985). "How to Negotiate a Cost-Effective PPO." *Business and Health* 2:7 (June), 18–20.

BRIDGES, J., and JACOBS, P. (1986). "Obtaining Estimates of Marginal Cost by DRG." *Healthcare Financial Management* 40:10 (October), 40–46.

BURIK, D., and DUVALL, T. (1985). "Hospital Cost Accounting: Strategic Considerations." *Healthcare Financial Management* 39:2 (February), 20–28.

COHODES, D. (1985). "HMOs. What Goes Up Must Come Down." *Inquiry* 22:4 (Winter), 333–334.

COOK, J. (1983). "Hospital Prospective Rate Setting." *Healthcare Financial Management* 37:4 (December), 67–69.

EASTAUGH, S. (1986). "Differential Cost Analysis: Judging a PPO's Feasibility." *Healthcare Financial Management* 40:5 (May), 44–51.

EASTAUGH, S. (1985). "Improving Hospital Productivity Under PPS." *Hospitals and Health Services Administration* 30:4 (July/August), 97–111.

EASTAUGH, S. (1984). "Hospital Diversification and Financial Management." *Medical Care* 22:8 (August), 704–723.

EASTAUGH, S. (1982). "The Ineffectiveness of Community-Based Health Planning." *Applied Economics* 14:3 (September), 475–490.

EDELSTON, J., VALENTINE, S., and GINOZA, D. (1985). "PPO Contracting: A California Experience," *Hospitals* 59:19 (October 1), 81–83.

EGDAHL, R., and WALSH, D. (1985). *Health Cost Management and Medical Practice Patterns*. Cambridge, Mass.: Ballinger.

FIELDING, J. (1985). "A Utilization Review Program in the Making." *Business and Health* 2:7 (June), 25–28.

FOX, P., and ANDERSON, M. (1986). "Hybrid HMOs and PPOs." *Business and Health* 3:4 (March), 20–27.

GABEL, J., and ERMANN, D. (1985). "Preferred Provider Organizations: Performance, Problems, and Promise." *Health Affairs* 4:1 (Spring), 24–40.

GINSBURG, P., and HACKBARTH, G. (1986). "Alternative Delivery Systems and Medicare." *Health Affairs* 5:1 (Spring), 6–22.

GRAHAM, J. (1986). "Insurers to Launch PPOs as a Way to Contain Costs, Protect Markets." *Modern Healthcare* 16:8 (April 11), 40.

KUNTZ, E. (1985). "Hospitals' PPOs Face Hard Times." *Modern Healthcare* 15:3 (February 1), 60.

LISSOVOY, G., RICE, T., ERMANN, D., and GABEL, J. (1986). "Preferred Provider Organizations: Today's Models and Tomorrow's Prospects." *Inquiry* 23:1 (Spring), 7–15.

MCCLAIN, J., and EASTAUGH, S. (1983). "How to Forecast to Contain Your Variable Costs: Exponential Smoothing Techniques." *Hospital Topics* 61:6 (November/December), 4–9.

MCGUIRK, M., and PORELL, F. (1984). "Spatial Patterns of Hospital Utilization: The Impact of Distance and Time." *Inquiry* 21:1 (Spring), 84–95.

MEMEL, S. (1986). "PPOs Spawn Maricopa-Phobia: Legal Issues." *Healthcare Executive* 2:2 (March-April), 51.

ROSKO, M., WALKER, L., MCKENNA, W., and DEVITA, M. (1983). "Measuring Consumer Preferences for Medical Care Arrangements." *Journal of Medical Systems* 7:6 (June), 545–554.

SCHMITT, J. (1983). "Preferred Provider Organizations: A Fiscal Perspective." *Healthcare Financial Management* 37:11 (November), 60.

TRAUNER, J. (1986). "The Second Generation of Selective Contracting: Another Look at PPOs." *Journal of Ambulatory Care Management* 9:5 (May), 13–21.

TRESNOWSKI, B. (1985). "PPOs: The Choice Isn't Always for the Least Expensive." *Inquiry* 22:4 (Winter), 331–332.

Chapter 5

ECONOMIC BUYING AND HOSPITAL ACCOUNTING

> *In some cases hospital administration tended to go off on its own, saying "worry not, cost reimbursement will pay for everything." The attitude prior to 1984 was you trustees and physicians tell us what you want to do, we will spend the money, and somebody will pay us for our costs. With DRGs the new ball game had to include good cost analysis.*
>
> —ALEX MCMAHON

> *Beware of little expenses; a small leak will sink a great ship.*
>
> —BENJAMIN FRANKLIN

Hospital accounting and financial reporting conventions have undergone two basic revolutions. The first one, from 1966 to 1968, followed the passage of Medicare and Medicaid and required that tax-exempt hospitals keep more information than a simple one-page balance sheet. The state of tax-exempt financial reporting at this time was decades behind the business world. Investor-owned hospitals also lagged behind but not as far behind as the tax-exempt hospitals. Former Speaker of the House Carl Albert once related a marvelous story of how far hospital accounting has developed in the past decade. After the passage of Medicare and Medicaid, 30 hospital "superintendents" (no one was called an executive in those days) descended on his office to "protest this socialist concern for accounting ledgers and keeping records." The prevailing wisdom was that nonprofit organizations were too "charitable in character" to waste time keeping accounting records. Hospital superintendents began to be called administrators, and hospitals slowly discovered GAAP, generally accepted accounting principles.

103

The second revolution, during 1986–87, is seeing the implementation of the Healthcare Financial Management Association's (HFMA) recommendation that hospitals record their income like any other business concern. In the spirit of true cost and revenue accounting, the hospital industry began to report revenue at expected payment level. In the past, hospitals had recorded revenue as gross revenue—that is, as if every patient paid list price (charges), with deductions for bad debt, charity care, and contractual or courtesy allowances (e.g., clergy). The pressure for this change in reporting conventions emanated from the need for the hospitals' books to make sense for trustees who had ties to the business world and for external relationships of hospitals with five other key actors: lawmakers, state regulators, discount payers (e.g., Medicaid, PPOs, etc.), bankers, and bond-rating agencies (Schlag, 1986).

Financial Reporting and Cost Accounting: Hospitals Enter the World of Business

Prior to 1987, the bond-rating agencies (e.g., Moody's and Standard and Poor's) and commercial bankers had to make numerous piecemeal extrapolations to assess a hospital's credit-worthiness or financial health. Since modern hospital executives are clearly troubled about possible insufficient access to capital, communication with these external users of hospital financial reports is a critical area of concern. One could speculate that if the hospital industry had been more proactive, reporting conventions would have changed much sooner. For example, if hospitals had been reporting charity and bad debt as expenses prior to 1987 rather than as a "hidden" deduction from gross revenue, two outcomes might have resulted: (1) state lawmakers might have included indigent care in more of their payment schemes and (2) federal lawmakers might have included expenses for indigent care in Medicare DRG rates. If legislators have no accurate estimate on the size of a problem (e.g., indigent care) because reporting conventions are deceptive, the problem often goes unresolved.

Over the past year, an increasing number of hospitals have begun to report gross patient revenue as the actual amount that the payers provide—that is, *true revenue*. The industry should have enacted this policy independent of any external reporting concerns. Such information is important if an institution is to meet the internal fiduciary responsibility of staying viable and up to date. For example, internal decision making requires one to know how much PPO payer A is paying in relation to Blue Cross Plan B. A hospital may not have any leverage negotiating better prices with Medicare, but the leverage to trade off discounts for improved patient volume does exist on a local level. Having a more accurate estimate of the benefits and costs of alternative arrangements is better than forcing the finance department to mimic the extrapolations that bond raters are put through.

Hospitals have recently come to adopt the business sector's convention of product-line and net-revenue reporting. If the hospital sector has experienced quantum leaps in financial reporting policies, the progress in managerial cost accounting has been more gradual and steady these last few years.

Some ambulatory care products are easily process-costed, like diabetes control. However, other items have a wide range of customizing, including the addition of various "options" along the treatment process. As a rejoinder to interested medical staff, one might add, that in order to avoid reductionist "cookbook" standardization of medicine, it is necessary to quantify the cost behavior ramification of the options (professional review organizations tend to ignore the subtleties of marginal costing and jump to the larger question of whether much of this care is "necessary"). For some DRGs, variability of costs within a DRG depends largely on the level of patient severity, which in turn determines the degree of customization (options selected). For example, within major reconstructive vascular surgery, including DRG 111, and to a greater degree for the more prevalent DRG 110, a wide coefficient of variation exists in cost per case, even when served by the same provider team (Rhodes et al., 1986). The range of customized options varies from proximal bypass to distal bypass for limb salvage to multiple ipsilateral surgery. The word "customized" is not intended to be perjorative; nor are the "options" frivolous.

The term "customized" denotes a situation that offers a wide range of options within the given DRG and thus a wide range of final product costs (e.g., DRGs 25, 82, 108, 169, 231, 243, 254, 296, 324, 421). Horn's (1986) computerized severity-of-illness index provides a four-level measure to improve on the definition of final products. Moreover, the Horn measure, or some other measure, could also be considered a custom option. For example, the daily room charge could be disaggregated into two basic components: (1) fixed per day hotel costs *plus* nursing costs at level-one severity and (2) variable costs for days in which the patient achieves severity-level two, three, or four. In effect, hotel cost plus level-one severity costs could be process-costed, and other severity levels (2, 3, 4) could be job-order-costed. Consider an extreme example: DRG 108 cardiothoracic procedures (except valve and bypass) might have a process-order cost of $7,000 per case, but a severity-level-two job order costs 3-fold higher, a severity-level-three job order costs 7-fold higher, and a severity-level-four job order costs 10– to 14–fold higher, depending on the senior attending physicians. Regulators, including the PROs, may wish to claim that much of this extra care is questionable, or could be provided more efficiently. In some cases, however, including DRGs 108, 110, and 111, there appear to be relatively narrow differences in the customization options selection process among equally board-qualified surgeons where case mix (DRG) is adjusted for severity level.

From the more limited perspective of cost accounting, as long as the institution can isolate the custom options in serving a patient and standardize unit cost, cost accounting is a simple matter of arithmetic. The two difficult steps in cost accounting are (1) developing standard costs for each service item option initially and (2) keeping these standards updated. We shall next consider standard costing methods. Standard costs are the direct patient-related costs in hospital operations. Today, methods for handling indirect costs are well established (Suver and Neumann, 1985). Indirect costs are simply allocated from overhead departments to patient care (revenue) departments. The four basic cost-allocation techniques for handling indirect costs, ranging from the direct method to multiple apportionment, have been well established for two decades (Berman and Weeks, 1982). Some hospitals still have problems appropriately assigning the fixed assets and labor costs of dietary or housekeeping to their respective work center of origin. However, this measurement error in the cost-assignment process of indirect overhead departments is dwarfed by the potential specification and measurement problems in calculating variable standard costs.

Standard Costing Approaches

Standard costs represent established yardsticks that should be achieved by an efficient institution and thus can be used normatively to assess economic efficiency and productivity. One cannot perform effective cost accounting without standards (Horngren, 1982). The three techniques for identification of standards vary from nonscientific/inexpensive to traditional time motion to the technically sophisticated input-output approach. The most long-standing management-sciences approach to standards involves time-motion activity analysis (microcosting) standards. The second meaningful standards-setting approach involves input-output unweighted regression analysis, or alternatively, exponential smoothing regressions that downweight the value of more historic (outdated) observations (McClain and Eastaugh, 1983). Some hospitals attempt an even more sophisticated alternative for input-output analysis, utilizing Box-Jenkins time-series analysis (Coddington and Steiker, 1986), but the results are no better than the exponential smoothing technique. A third variety of "standards" is an ad hoc negotiated opinion/standard, which for purposes of the survey instrument utilized at the end of this chapter, is defined as "cost accounting without standards." The following is a summary of the three basic categories:

1. Input-output regression measures of standard costs.
2. Time-motion-work-sampling-management-engineering approach to measuring microcosted standards.
3. Without empirical standards—ad hoc estimates of unit cost per service item based on informal work sampling (the nonscientific approach).

All three techniques in practice may involve some degree of negotiation between middle managers and senior managers, but the third technique is by definition a totally negotiated process. For purposes of our survey, we combined techniques one and two and labeled the result "cost accounting with standards," for one obvious reason. These two techniques are typically utilized simultaneously, or alternating every few years. The standard-setting technique utilized varies by cost center, by service item within each cost center, and by year. Consider two examples. One might utilize management-engineered microcosting standards, done in an annual two- to four-week work sampling, for 85 percent of the routine service items (tests) within the laboratory department. For the nonroutine 15 percent of lab tests, one might perform input-output regression analysis. Consider a second example. One might microcost half of the service items in diagnostic radiology every three to five years to keep the standards current but input-output regress the standards in other years. Actually, one-third, or 39 out of 124 service items in diagnostic radiology, capture 95 percent of the expenses in that area at one teaching hospital.

As a last resort, the standards themselves could be externally adopted from other hospitals and adjusted with regression analysis to better fit the institutional application. One might borrow standards from the state of Maryland Health Services Cost Review Commission, the New York State RMS (resource monitoring stan-

dards), or some other source. Some hospitals have discovered that
the search for analytical precision and theoretical perfection in
microcosting is too expensive to do on a regular basis. But,
differentiating levels of refinement in cost accounting is key to
determining the manner in which variable cost items are identified
and allocated. In other words, a one-time initial investment in
microcosting five to nine large departments may pay off in increased accuracy but cost a significant amount of money and slow
down implementation.

The basic question becomes: Would you like a good product
soon or a much better product for management in 12 to 24 months?
As an academic, the author prefers the second road, as was done at
Tufts New England Medical Center and at six departments at
Georgetown Hospital. To avoid embedding levels of inefficiency
into the standards (some other hospital's baseline), these two
hospitals "build up" standard costs with local firm-specific data.
This route involves management-engineered yardsticks for how
many FTEs (full-time equivalents) should really be in a department and offers targets (e.g., can we decrease direct productive
worked hours to 85 percent?). The easy method, used in the
majority of cases, is to "back in" costs based on the budget and
external standards, and thus absorb baseline inefficiency into cost
standards.

Pilot cost accounting with microcomputers to allow management
time to gain familiarity with costing methods before placing the
best (reasonable) system up on the mainframe may offer the best
option for avoiding strategic mediocrity. The concept of diminishing returns at increasing expense (administrative cost) is often
summarized in the 90/10 Pareto principle: The first 90 percent of
cost-accounting accuracy can be obtained with 90 percent of
available resources, and the last 10 percent requires an additional
90 percent effort. Are the marginal benefits in microcosting accuracy worth the increased marginal costs ($100 to $180 per patient
served), or could the system be validated and updated on a
sampling basis on a periodic basis? Do you need to microcost at the
procedural level, or could you do it every three to five years on a
20 percent sampling basis, plus do procedure-costing for each and
every newly initiated procedure? For example, at one teaching
hospital, 7 of 33 service items in hematology capture 90 percent of
expenses. Therefore, effort should be concentrated on these seven
items. A typical 200- to 400-bed Council of Teaching Hospitals
(COTH) facility ($N = 116$ nationally) may treat 1,000 separate
diseases and perform 9,000 separate procedures, with 50 new
procedures newly introduced in 1987–88 alone. Procedure-costing

would prove an onerous task. The problem is compounded in the case of 800+ bed COTH hospitals (N = 74) that offer 12,800 procedures, with 100 to 150 new procedures (service items) initiated each year.

Automation and management information systems expertise are critical determinants of standard costing capacity. For example, the 840-bed Dallas Parkland Memorial Hospital invested $150,000 in 1986 in the MEDSCAN bar-coding system that allows complete flow tracking (medical records, tests, and materials) throughout the entire facility. MEDSCAN can interface with any mainframe, meaning that bar coding can be applied to radiology, satellite clinics, and whatever else moves throughout the total hospital complex. A large hospital may require bar-code readers at 24–36 major distribution points, but a smaller hospital may need only 10.

Selective sampling and microcosting at the procedural/DRG level has allowed two innovative CFOs in our sample to develop software to reaggregate the cost information by 20–40 strategic product-line groupings (SPGs). These SPGs are utilized like strategic business units (SBUs) in the administrative sciences literature (Eastaugh and Eastaugh, 1986). Productivity and variance analysis are obviously more valid and reliable if costs can be combined at the procedural level. In this context, the purist may state that inferior costing of P&L (profit and loss) by product line can do more harm than good if one opens or expands the "wrong" service misidentified as profitable. This statistical type-one error, rejecting the null hypothesis (unprofitable) when it is unprofitable (i.e., the product line is a poor bet, but your cost-accounting system cannot recognize this), is sometimes labeled "failure to maximize specificity." Moreover, an inaccurate cost-accounting system can do harm if it closes or reduces the size of a product line misidentified as unprofitable. This is a statistical type-two error, accepting the null hypothesis (unprofitable) when it is not true. If, in fact, the product line is a good investment, this is a failure to maximize sensitivity. The only costing system that can achieve both a 90+ percent specificity and sensitivity in doing strategic financial planning is a procedural/DRG-based system. There is no such thing as a perfect system. However, misspecified costs yield poor short-run variance analysis, weak medium-run control, and inaccurate long-range financial planning.

Hospitals never have been able to charge uniformly for services in proportion to their costs. Without a measure of actual cost, it would be impossible to uniformly price markup relative to actual cost. Without standard cost accounting, charges have little association with costs. Consider the problems with such inaccurate RCC (ratio of cost to charges) costing in the context of an American auto company. The company produces two models: ADRG and BDRG. The company produces car ADRG at $12,000 and sells it at $24,000. The company produces car BDRG at $8,000 and sells it for $12,000. The company sells threefold more model BDRG cars relative to model ADRG sales.

In our example, the ratio of cost to charges across the company is 0.6, or $(3 \times 8 + 12)/(3 \times 12 + 24)$. If the company had been so unsophisticated as to allocate costs by RCC, it would have claimed that car ADRG costs $14,400 (.6 × 24), and car BDRG costs $7,200 (0.6 × 12). Such a primitive RCC methodology overstates the profitability of a BDRG case by $800 and understates the profitability of an ADRG by $2,400 (12,000 − 14,400). The principles are the same when we attempt to cost-account patient care, with two exceptions: (1) Maintenance of technically up-to-date costing standards is more of a problem for medicine and surgery, and (2) health providers typically make a better net profit on the less expensive DRGs such as DRG 86, 96, and angina pectoris (140), which exhibited a 57 percent increase in admissions in 1985. Obviously, with economies of scale any DRG can prove profitable with sufficient volume and reasonable levels of provider efficiency. However, certain high-cost DRGs are seldom reported as profitable: craniotomy (DRG 2), hepatobiliary shunt (DRG 191), kidney transplants (302), and extensive burns (457).

One should consider two final caveats in the cost-accounting process. First, charge items need to be refined into a multitude of service items. For example, one might develop a medical records service item, a discharge and/or admissions service item, and a routine (lowest level of severity or acuity) nursing service item per day. If medical records as a service item is 70 percent fixed and 30 percent variable costs, a seemingly homogeneous service item may subdivide into two separate cost accounts (fixed, variable). However, it may be more expensive to discharge a patient to a nursing home rather than to self-care, but the expense of microcosting this service item into multiple accounts may not justify the administrative expense.

The second caveat concerns reconciliation of standard costs as collected in an extended charge master file containing data on all service items. Statistical discrepancies in the aggregate across the institution should be very small, amounting to under 1 percent of expenses at most. However, one cannot be unrealistic and expect to reconcile to the last dollar. In reconciling standard costs compared against actual cost information in the general ledger accounts, the difference can either be unfavorable or favorable. This variance can be attributable to management competence, system error, or exogenous events beyond management control. In any case, the variance information can be utilized to restructure future budgets.

Variance Analysis and Flexible Budgets

As Horngren (1982) has pointed out, the essential strength of managerial cost accounting is that it links "promises" made during the budget process back to the responsibility center. For example, if a department chairperson claims that the purchase of certain equipment will result in labor savings, but no labor savings are experienced, then this shortfall in performance needs to be either (1) explained away by exogenous circumstances beyond the manager's control or (2) utilized annually to discount the judgment and/ or budget of the manager in question. Budget variance is defined as the difference between the budgeted and actual amounts and can be favorable (F = underbudget) or unfavorable (U = overbudget). The traditional business technique as presented by Horngren (1982) is to separate total variance into three component parts: (1) *price* (input expense—what it costs to pay labor or purchase supplies) *variance*, (2) mix variance, and (3) *volume variance*. In the hospital context, Finkler (1982) neatly summarizes this traditional variance analysis into an easy-to-calculate "pyramid model."

Consider a sample case where the actual radiology expenses for the month were $91,448, and the budgeted salaries were $90,576 (Figure 5.1). The chief operating officer, unfamiliar with the new flexible budgeting software, claims the radiology manager does not deserve to go to a national conference because of this $872 unfavorable variance. To defend herself, the radiology manager has to ask how this variance arose. Finkler's pyramid model, in Figure 5.1, provides a good analytical framework. The expectations when the most recent rolling budget was made were that, on average, 6 RVUs (relative value units) of radiology would be required per diem (Qi), at an expense of $20.40 per RVU (P), with a patient census of 740 (Qo). In actuality, there was an average of 7 RVUs per day, as the patients were more intensely treated in a shorter duration of stay, and more severe/sicker patients came from the recently closed public hospital's catchment area. Expense paid per RVU declined to only $18.40 per RVU thanks to the hard work of the radiology department manager to improve productivity and reduce costs. The number of patients declined to 710 (Qo) follow-

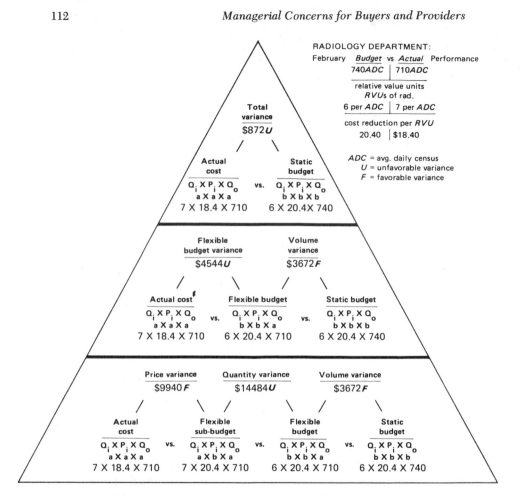

Figure 5.1   Variances in a Hospital with Flexible Budgets and Standard Cost Accounting

ing an 8 percent decline in predicted average length of stay and a 4.3 percent increase in admissions.

At the top of the pyramid in Figure 5.1, the total variance is described as the difference between the static budget (6 × 20.40 × 740) minus actual expense, for a net unfavorable $872. For simplicity, the lowercase letter *a* denotes actual, and the letter *b* denotes budgeted. For the pyramid, any time an actual cost or budget figure on the left is smaller than the number on the right, it implies a favorable variance (e.g., radiology price variance); the opposite implies an unfavorable variance (e.g., quantity per patient day variance). One might suggest from the flexible budget variance analysis that the utilization review committee consider the appropriateness of such a substantial increase in radiology services per diem. This medical staff issue is certainly beyond the control of the radiology department manager. The volume variance in the lower-right corner of the pyramid is the same as the middle level of the pyramid ($3,672 favorable). The flexible budget variance of $4,544 unfavorable has been subdivided in the bottom of the pyramid into changes in input efficiency (lower cost per RVU) and changes in radiology service mix utilized per case (more RVUs per patient, perhaps without any improvements in efficacy). The department manager is partially responsible for efficiency, in that she could purchase more cost effectively or schedule better (and so reduce overtime hours). The senior management also has an impact on efficiency. The medical staff is largely responsible for efficacy, and totally responsible for patient orders.

Both the subbudget and the flexible budget utilize the $20.40 expense per RVU and the 710 actual patient census. Thus, given the actual workload, the radiologists and other clinicians have produced an unfavorable $14,484 quantity variance. Some fraction of this might result from a more severe case mix. The remaining variance is the price variance, based on the actual cost and the subbudget. Any difference between the actual cost and the subbudget is a result of paying a different amount per RVUs produced for the total radiology RVUs needed (one could be even more refined and subdivide the pyramid on a fourth level: increased [or decreasing] RVUs caused by deteriorating [or better] quality control per procedure versus increased RVUs caused by shifts in physician ordering habits). Since quality control was unchanged in our example, the radiology manager is largely responsible for a $9,940 favorable price variance. The radiology manager cannot be assigned any responsibility for the $3,672 favorable volume variance—that is, she did not decrease the average duration of patient stay.

Because flexible budgeting is not easily understood by many managers, the best software is so "user friendly" as to present the analysis in simplified language. One of the pioneers in this area was the Tufts New England Medical Center system. The strength of flexible budgets is that they focus on what expenses would have been, had the workload output been forecast perfectly. The problem with a static budget is that it simplistically ignores variations that naturally occur as a result of circumstances outside of line management control or in the control of others (e.g., medical staff, rate regulators, and other hospitals' management).

Buying behavior and efficiency are important in the hospital sector because inventory-related costs represent one-third of the costs of providing inpatient care (Reisman, 1984). Nearly half of this cost is related to supply and movable equipment expense, and therefore to "buy smart" is to make the facility more price competitive in a prospectively paid competitive market. Buying smart includes buying at a competitive price high-value products that are convenient to receive and distribute. Prior to the enactment of PPS, the performance of hospitals in "buying smart" was less than outstanding. For example, the General Accounting Office (GAO) provided dramatic evidence of hospitals paying 200 to 300 percent more than the market price (e.g., what other hospitals and state institutions pay after seeking competitive bids) for a wide range of hospital supply items (General Accounting Office, 1983). Under cost reimbursement, if a facility paid more for an item, it would be reimbursed dollar for dollar for this excess expense. Therefore, no effective incentive existed to contain purchasing costs, especially if hospital supply companies offered extra benefits (e.g., free meals and gifts) to hospital managers and medical staff. Under prospective payment, noneconomic buying behavior is a severe liability; the hospital does not get paid more if it wastes more (Eastaugh, 1984). When hospitals in 46 states joined the PPS system at the end of 1983, there were not fewer vendors bidding for hospital business; instead, a price war started among supply firms to sell equal-quality goods at competitive prices. The hospital supply companies had to lay off employees rather than discount the quality of their goods to attract hospital buyers. Indeed, the improvement in operating profit margins from AHA member hospitals, from $5.8 billion in 1983 to $9.6 billion in 1985, was taken largely out of the bottom line of hospital supply companies.

One could postulate that the introduction of PPS had a measurable impact on management attitudes toward cost accounting and hospital purchasing (buyer) behavior. Cost accounting analyzes what it costs to bring together inputs into intermediate and final products; hospital purchasing behavior analyzes how to purchase appropriate inputs at the best value (considering price and quality). Changes in cost-accounting methods and level of detail will be analyzed first, followed by a general discussion of the concerns of chief financial officers (CFOs) in the open-ended section of the survey instrument. We consider shifts in accounting behavior initially because it is a relatively objective subject area. However, shifts in purchasing decisions represent a more subjective area since perceived shifts in self-reported attitudes may overstate actual changes in buying behavior (Lancaster, 1966). Four basic hospital buyers are surveyed at each hospital: (1) directors of nursing; (2) materials managers; (3) EDP (electronic data processing) directors, often called directors of MIS (management information systems); and (4) chief operating officers (COOs). The individual approach of these four professional groups involves, to varying degrees, three basic attributes or dimensions: cost, quality, and convenience. Buyer priorities in 1983 and 1986 are compared, followed by a multivariate analysis of manager conjoint weighted preferences. Conjoint measurement technique is a statistical approach to preference analysis borrowed from the marketing sciences business literature (Green and Rao, 1971). This type of information is of interest to external users (hospital supply firms), as well as to managers interested in optimization, and not merely satisficing.

The characteristics of the purchase alternatives from which hospital managers must select are multidimensional. Probably no alternative is superior on every dimension of interest. Therefore, managers must make decisions based on some implicit internal criterion that we shall attempt to discover. Even though conjoint measurement originally developed in the fields of psychometrics and mathematical psychology, it is the technique of choice used by market researchers to sort out the relative importance of multidimensional attributes. The technique allows decomposition of the managers' ordinal observations into separate and compatible utility scales by which the original global judgments, preference for a certain package of attributes over another option, can be reconstituted. The capacity to separate overall judgments into components provides valuable information for managers, suppliers, and policy analysts. One is provided information about the value of various levels of a single attribute or the relative importance between attributes.

Prior to PPS, hospitals were more concerned with the reimbursement aspects of costing, loading as many costs onto cost-paying patients, than actual true costs. Maximization of reimbursement translated into maximization of yield out of the Medicare cost-reporting firm. This game of maximization was not a zero-sum game, because hospitals reported to various cost payers with varying levels of detail. Cost determination prior to 1984 was essentially income determination within the framework of cost reimbursement formulas. To manipulate ("game") the system was an economically rational response to payer attempts to initiate cost controls. With the wide array of prospective payers, hospitals currently have to measure the actual specific costs of final products (patients) and intermediate products. For the unwary hospital buyer, cost accounting has posed a nightmare with two major derailment opportunities: (1) buying software systems that were "announced" but not available for 12 to 24 months or tested for 6 to 18 months, and (2) buying "flexible" systems that required the hospital to be flexible in molding its requests to fit the existing software product.

The Hospital Population Sampled

A random stratified sample of tax-exempt (nonpublic) hospitals based on 1982 AHA/AAMC/COTH survey data was selected in the summer of 1983 from the two control group states (Massachusetts and New York). Only voluntary community (or religious) hospitals with over 100 beds were included in the analysis. The nine categories, based on three classes of bed size and three levels of teaching status, are presented in Table 5.1. The 27 control group hospitals from the two waiver states were matched against 1982 data tapes for PPS-eligible hospitals (the experimental group: Connecticut, Ohio, Pennsylvania, and Washington, D.C.). The matched hospitals in the experimental group had to meet all of the following criteria:

1. Reside in the same teaching strata.
2. Reside in the same bed-size category (A–C, Table 5.1).
3. Have within plus or minus 10 percent the same average daily census in June 1983.
4. Anticipate joining the PPS program within the year.

Hospitals contacted had full knowledge of their census and could predict based on their fiscal year the month in which they would join PPS. Only 28 hospitals had to be contacted to achieve 27 matched pairs of hospitals for survey in October 1983. The attractions for hospitals joining the study were that only five one-hour interviews were required, the results of the study might yield better service from the hospital supply industry, and the hospitals were provided a "free" one-day management consult.

The market research was originally funded by a hospital supply firm interested in ascertaining how PPS might impact on its business. Since the sponsor-reported teaching hospitals with a higher "dosage" of graduate medical education purchased more items from supply firms, we oversampled COTH hospitals by 200 percent and non-COTH teaching hospitals by 100 percent. In retrospect, the "buyer" of the original pretest (1983) study was surprised to discover that PPS hospitals were now highly interested in 10 to 30 percent price discounts and less interested in associated service, such as computer-to-computer ordering and

Table 5.1 **Teaching Status and Bed Size for Hospitals under PPS (the Experimental Group) and Control Group Hospitals (non-PPS Facilities in Waiver States)**

	1983			1986		
	(A) 650+ Beds	*(B)* 400– 649	*(C)* Under 400	*(A)* 650+ Beds	*(B)* 400– 649	*(C)* Under 400
1. COTH (Council of Teaching Hospitals) Member Hospitals						
(w) waiver, non-PPS	2	2	1	2	2	2[a]
(p) PPS hospital	2	2[b]	1	2	0	5[b,c]
2. Non-COTH Teaching Hospitals						
(w) waiver, non-PPS	0	3	5[a]	0	3	4[a]
(p) PPS hospital	0	3[c,e]	5	0	1[d]	8[e,f]
3. Nonteaching Hospitals						
(w) waiver, non-PPS	0	1	13	0	1	13
(p) PPS hospitals open 1983–1986	0	1[d]	13[f]	0	0	9
(c) PPS hospitals closed 1985–1986	—	—	—	—	—	2

[a]One non-COTH teaching hospital joined COTH prior to 1985 (shift category 2-C to 1-C).
[b]Two COTH hospitals reduced bed size by an average of 19% (shift category 1-B to 1-C).
[c]Two non-COTH teaching hospitals joined COTH in 1984–1985, reduced bed size by an average of 16% (shift from category 2-B to 1-C), reflecting the 34% growth in COTH 1983–1986.
[d]One nonteaching hospital became a non-COTH teaching hospital (shift category 3-B to 2-B).
[e]One non-COTH teaching hospital reduced bed size 15% 1984–85 (shift category 2-B to 2-C).
[f]Two nonteaching hospitals became non-COTH teaching hospitals (shift category 3-C to 2-C).

inventory software programs. The posttest (1986) survey was aided by the fact that the author had maintained contacts with the original study hospitals. At the start of 1986, 52 hospitals were resurveyed, with a significant difference: Respondents were presented with flashcards to test their conjoint preferences for various product attributes. This more sophisticated marketing technique is superior to simply asking individuals to self-report their dominant attitudes and opinions (Rosko et al., 1983). The pretest-posttest study design methodology is described in Cook and Campbell (1979).

The most striking aspect of Table 5.1 is the degree of maturation and history, to use Cook and Campbell's (1979) terms, in this quasi-experimental design. If you compare how the sample is distributed between the strata, two observations are apparent: The institutions have downsized bed capacity and upgraded teaching status. For example, consider a hospital that experienced the transition going from a nonteaching to a teaching hospital (Table 5.1, note d). This could probably be explained by the PPS reimbursement system, which for each 0.1 resident and intern allowed an extra payment of 11.59 percent added on (the so-called indirect teaching factor), yet hospital expenses appeared to have increased only 8 to 9 percent (Berry et al., 1986). In other words, residents were a "sure" profit center for most hospitals under PPS until the federal government cut payment rates back to 8 percent for 1987. Not surprisingly, more hospitals initiated teaching programs or expanded teaching programs (which often made them eligible to join COTH—and 110 hospitals did join COTH during the period from 1983 to 1986).

Trends in Cost Accounting

The CFO is responsible for the detailed requirements of the definition phases for identifying the most appropriate features and functions for the institution (e.g., a small facility may not have the ability, or need, for microcosted refinements). The level of detail that is needed in identifying costs and how far the hospital should go in reporting variable standard costs is a moot point: department level, subdepartment, DRG, DRG/procedure, or product line. There is no one correct answer for all hospitals, as it depends on manager ability, taste, facility size, and the payment environment. Table 5.2 presents results for CFO attitudes concerning the most appropriate level of cost accounting. If a facility process-costed some departments but still relied on the crude RCC (ratio of cost-to-charges) for other departments, that institution would be labeled a *process-costing hospital*. If the hospital utilized both job order and process-costing methods, the facility would be labeled a *hybrid combination cost-accounting system*. Two trends are apparent in Table 5.2. First, hospitals in the two waiver states had somewhat more advanced costing methods in 1983 (six more PPS hospitals had no cost-accounting system in 1983). However, advances in cost accounting occurred much more rapidly in PPS states, so the number of facilities with no cost accounting declined to two in 1986 (down from 20 in 1983), whereas the movement to better cost accounting was much slower in the waiver states of New York and Massachusetts. The second point to gather from Table 5.2 is that no hospital eroded (downgraded) its cost-accounting capabilities over the period 1983–1986.

Table 5.2   **CFO Survey of Cost-Accounting Capability in 27 PPS Hospitals and 27 Non-PPS Hospitals, 1983–1986, Attitudinal Probability Matrix***

		Dominant Attitude January–February 1986 (number of respondents in parentheses)				
Sample 1: CFOs in 27 PPS Hospitals		No Cost Acct., but RCC (2)	Process Costing (2)	Job Order Costing (12)	Hybrid Combina- tion (9)	Closure (2)
	No Cost Acct. (20)	.10	.05	.40	.35	.10
October– November 1983 Dominant Attitude	Process Costing (3)	.0	.33	.67	.0	.0
	Job Order Costing (3)	.0	.0	.67	.33	.0
	Hybrid: Job Order & Process (1)	.0	.0	.0	1.00	.0
Sample 2: CFOs in 27 non-PPS Hospitals in New York and Massachusetts		(13)	(5)	(5)	(4)	(0)
	No Cost Acct. (14)	.93	.07	.0	.0	.0
October– November 1983 Dominant Attitude	Process Costing (7)	.0	.57	.43	.0	.0
	Job Order Costing (3)	.0	.0	.67	.33	.0
	Hybrid: Job Order & Process (3)	.0	.0	.0	1.00	.0

*Probabilities should be read across the rows (sum to 1).

Respondent hospitals in this survey, reporting only a ratio of cost-to-charges costing scheme, de facto, possess no reliable form of cost accounting. Hospital charges correlate poorly with actual costs and often reflect long-standing convention (e.g., overcharging for surgery to cross-subsidize undercharging for maternity care). These hospitals simply comply with the minimum mandate of third-party payers and allocate all direct and support costs to revenue centers. The direct, step-down, double-apportionment, or algebraic multiple-apportionment, techniques "find" department costs on a crude, aggregate basis. This traditional cost-finding methodology begs the difficult question of how costs distribute per patient, per procedure, and per product line (Williams et al., 1982). Moreover, this analysis was performed only once per year.

Consequently, even if the information were more refined, managers provided with cost information on an annual basis could not be expected to make timely monthly decisions. In the current environment, timely accurate cost accounting information is needed by the payer, and by DRG. Information on cost function variability (cost behavior) is needed in relation to changes in service volume, mix, and severity.

The basic premise behind good cost accounting is, when possible, directly allocate costs. For example, if 25 percent of your marketing expenses are directly linked to maternity cases, directly allocate such expenses to maternity patients. This is a good example of full cost accounting, sometimes labeled absorption accounting. However, if most managerial decisions involve changes at the margin, to expand, initiate, close, or reduce volume for a given program or payer group (e.g., PPO), then direct incremental costing is the method of choice. This method of marginal cost analysis is also labeled differential cost accounting (Eastaugh, 1986).

There are three basic types of cost accounting for purposes of our survey; listed in order of increasing complexity, they are process costing, job-order costing, and a combination of both methods. The most basic method, process costing, involves averaging the accumulated costs according to a specific cost center's processes and dividing cost by volume to arrive at a unit cost per item (a case, an intermediate product, e.g., radiology) for all products generated by the specific process. Process costing utilizes explicit general assumptions to allocate the bulk of costs to a department-level input per case (final product, e.g., a DRG). The process method is time- and volume-dependent, and additive—that is, as each cost center completes the specific process, the system attaches a unit cost to the patient/case.

A more complex form of cost accounting is job-order costing. Job-order costing is most appropriate for service products that vary considerably from order to order—for example, DRG 108s and Jaguars are each highly customized. Job costing treats each product or case as unique and assigns all costs to a specific individual case. An automated bar-coding system is helpful in identifying and tabulating patient-specific intermediate and final product costs.

The third cost-accounting technique is a combination of job-order and process-costing methods. Continuing the analogy to highly customized automobiles, a Jaguar radiator might be sufficiently costed with process costing, but other items are more unique and subject to job-order costing. Hybrid cost accounting at the DRG level will incorporate the average costing aspects of a process technique, such as taking the average costs of routine nursing care in treating that given DRG on average in the facility. As the Jaguar plant director can process cost 40 percent of the costs and job-order cost 60 percent of the cost—specifically, the materials and labor easily attached to production of a specific auto—so can hospital managers combine the two techniques.* If the intermediate product exhibits very little variation from week to week and across a wide number of cases, the item could be process-costed (e.g., inhalation therapy).

The descriptive summary in Table 5.3 outlines two attributes of hospital cost-accounting systems: (1) method and (2) level of detail. The most sophisticated hospitals utilize a combination of both the process and job-order methods, depending on the department. Microcosting job-order methods are not difficult if a small number of items are to be costed and there is no firmly established production function (highly stabilized) relationship in the combination of subproducts, supplies, other materials and capital. Relative value unit (RVU) process-costing methods are more applicable in labor-intensive services (e.g., nursing or physical therapy) or capital-intensive services like laboratory (i.e., have a consistent stable production function; Burik and Duvall, 1985; Martin and Boyer, 1985). The most sophisticated hospitals may utilize RVUs for many departments, but they process cost other departments at the level of 400+ DRGs or 700 to 1,000 procedures (e.g., EKG or diagnostic radiology).

The most primitive cost-accounting system simply allocates variable costs at a department level (line A, Table 5.3). This system is still superior to having no cost accounting, or operating on the outdated assumption that ratio of cost to charges measures resource costs (line 1, Table 5.3). In 1986, the seven-level scale of cost-accounting sophistication was more highly utilized in nonwaiver states relative to waiver states ($\chi^2 = 13.53$, $df = 6$). In 1983, the differences between the two payment climates were not significant ($\chi^2 = 4.7$), but hospitals in New York and Massachusetts appeared somewhat more sophisticated at cost accounting. However, these two states appear to have lagged behind hospitals in PPS climates as of 1986. This is consistent with our basic study hypothesis that nonwaiver states subjected to PPS would feel more pressure to account for costs more accurately.

Combined process/job-order cost-accounting systems, utilizing

---

*Jaguar is a classic example of the sort of productivity improvement cost reduction program we shall discuss in Chapter 10. Between 1980 and 1986 Jaguar expanded output 70 percent while trimming staff FTEs by 30 percent.

Table 5.3 **The Sophistication and Level of Detail for Hospital Cost-Accounting Methods as a Function of Time, and the Reimbursement Climate[1]**

	Waiver States, Not Under PPS		Nonwaiver States	
	1983 (n = 27)	1986 (n = 27)	1983 No PPS (n = 27)	1986 Under PPS (n = 25)[2]

Cost-Accounting Method (1, primitive; 7, most advanced)

1. Traditional RCC (Ratio of cost-to-charges)	14	13	20	2
2. Process costing without standards	4	2	2	1
3. Process costing with standards	3	3	1	2
4. Job order costing without standards	2	2	2	5
5. Job order costing with standards	1	3	1	7
6. Combined process and job order costing, without standards	2	2	0	2
7. Combined process and job order costing, with standards	1	2	1	6

Most Detailed Level of Allocation for Variable Cost (A, primitive; D, most advanced)

A. Department	2	2	2	4
B. Relative value performance measurement units by department	2	2	1	4
C. DRG	2	2	1	5
D. Procedure and DRG	7	7	1	9
E. Other (product-line, severity/stage)	0	1	2	1

[1]Random stratified sample of 27 hospitals in each group. The actual same hospitals were resurveyed. By definition lines A–E sum to equal lines 2–7 down through the columns.
[2]Two hospitals with RCC-only costing methods in 1983 closed prior to 1986.

standards, provide a refined flexible method for measuring the value of actual resources involved in patient care. Process costing might prove sufficient if the hospital were a factory, but customized job-order care is a more accurate paradigm than the assembly line. The promise of good cost accounting is that with better information one can implement operational control mechanisms that save money and improve the bottom line, thus allowing improvement in employee compensation. Contrast this capability to the primitive RCC method of multiplying patient charges by the hospital RCC, and assuming this figure equals cost per case. Such a catchall averaging approach is the ultimate in inaccurate process costing.

Priority Attributes in Purchasing

As we observe in Table 5.4, the dominant self-reported concern of COOs and EDP/MIS managers in PPS hospitals is cost. From the second row, first column, we observe that 70 percent of those listing quality as their dominant purchasing concern in 1983 switched to cost in 1986. As we observe in Table 5.5, this figure is only 21 percent in non-PPS (waiver state) hospitals. The rationale for combining COO and EDP/MIS attitudes relates to a national organizational trend. There has been a recent tendency since passage of the PPS program in April 1983 to separate management information systems (labeled EDP only in 12 hospitals) from finance. We learned on the survey instrument that in the 27 PPS hospitals, the mix of EDP or MIS managers reporting to the CFO declined from 17 in 1982–83 to 3 as of 1986. In all cases, the COO replaced the CFO in this area. Under PPS, "the medical record is your bill," charge routing slips are of lesser concern for prospectively paid patients, and utilization profiles are a central concern for a progressive COO. In the waiver states, the mix of EDP/MIS managers with direct-line responsibility up to the CFO declined less dramatically from 15 to 9, as 5 COOs and 1 CEO "volunteered" to take over.

Directors of nursing and materials managers are somewhat more likely than COOS and EDP/MIS managers to report convenience as their dominant concern, but this finding is not statistically significant in either 1983 or 1986. Table 5.4 (row five, column one) indicates that 61 percent of the nursing directors and materials managers reporting quality as their dominant buying concern in 1983 list cost as their prime concern in 1986 in PPS hospitals. The same figure in non-PPS waiver hospitals is less dramatic—36 percent, in Table 5.5.

The results in column one, row one, of Tables 5.4 and 5.5 suggest that conversion to cost consciousness as the dominant concern in buyer/agent behavior is somewhat like an absorbing

Table 5.4 Dominant Concern Among COOs and EDP Managers Compared to Directors of Nursing and Materials Managers, Attitude Probability Matrix, Transition from 1983–1986 (27 hospitals, 3 nonwaiver states)

		Dominant Attitude January–February 1986 (number of respondents in parentheses)			
Sample: COOs & EDP Managers		*Cost* (35)	*Quality* (14)	*Convenience* (1)	*Hospital Closes* (4)
October–November 1983 Dominant Attitude	Cost (6)	1.00	.0	.0	.0
	Quality (40)	.700	.300	.0	.0
	Convenience (8)	.125	.250	.125	.50
Directors of Nursing & Materials Managers		(32)	(15)	(3)	(4)
October–November 1983 Dominant Attitude	Cost (13)	1.000	.0	.0	.0
	Quality (31)	.610	.350	.030	.0
	Convenience (10)	.0	.400	.200	.40

Table 5.5 Dominant Concern Among COOs and EDP Managers Compared to Directors of Nursing and Materials Managers, Attitude Probability Matrix, Transition from 1983–1986 (27 hospitals, 2 waiver states)

		Dominant Attitude January–February 1986 (number of respondents in parentheses)			
Sample: COOs & EDP Managers		*Cost* (19)	*Quality* (32)	*Convenience* (3)	*Hospital Closes* (0)
October–November 1983 Dominant Attitude	Cost (12)	.92	.08	.0	.0
	Quality (39)	.21	.79	.0	.0
	Convenience (3)	.0	.0	1.00	.0
Directors of Nursing & Materials Managers		(26)	(23)	(5)	(0)
October–November 1983 Dominant Attitude	Cost (15)	.93	.07	.0	.0
	Quality (33)	.36	.64	.0	.0
	Convenience (6)	.0	.17	.83	.0

Markov chain. Absorbing Markov chains fall into fixed (dominant) attitudes that have the property that, once entered, it is impossible to leave them (Parzen, 1971). Indeed, of the 44 managers (6 + 13 + 11 + 14) listing cost as their dominant concern in both 1983 and 1986, 42 are still on the job, and the other two individuals were promoted from COO to CEO. If making cost your dominant buying concern had created any adverse effects on the products and services (acquired and produced), you would expect that these 44 individuals would not have such an excellent retention/promotion record. The data in Table 5.2 support this contention. Both hospitals that closed over the study period had CFOs who did not have any form of cost accounting, beyond RCC, in the fall of 1983. In addition, as we observe in Table 5.4, the two hospitals that closed employed no individuals who considered cost a dominant concern in the one to two years prior to closure.

These data suggest that those disregarding cost concerns do so at a risk to their own careers, and perhaps, at a risk to their institutions. However, one should not generalize too much from a sample of 270 managers in 54 hospitals. Under the discrete semi-Markov process, the probability of future development along a process (better accounting, more concern for economic criteria), depends on the existing situation. The probability of transition to a future state, reading across the table row, must by definition sum to 1.0 and is defined as the one-step transition probability. The transition period in our example is 2.4 years. It is highly unlikely that we have stationary transition probabilities, independent of time (year), given the one-shot initial shock of PPS on the hospital industry.

The transition probabilities in Tables 5.2, 5.4, and 5.5 summarize changes in managers' attitudes over the 2.4-year period. Table 5.2 summarizes CFO attitudes toward the three basic methods of cost accounting. The most obvious result in Table 5.2 is that the lower-left side of the probability matrix is zero in all cases, indicating that no facility "traded down" and acquired an inferior cost-accounting system during the study period. This reflects the heightened importance of cost accounting in both types of payment environment (PPS and waiver) across the period 1983–1986. The most striking finding in Table 5.2 is in row 1, columns 3 and 4, where a combined total of 75 percent (.40 + .35) of PPS facilities without a cost-accounting system acquired a high-level system, job-order or hybrid combination, prior to FY 1986. This same figure for waiver state hospitals is zero. However, if a hospital had a cost-accounting system in 1983 in a waiver state, the progression to upgrade the system is equivalent for job-order costing systems (.33), relative to nonwaiver states, and only slightly (insignificantly) slower in adopting an upgraded system for process-costing systems (two in three, row 2 versus four in seven, row 6 = 0.43). These results would seem to suggest that necessity is the "mother of innovation" for PPS hospitals, but lack of necessity appears to "impede innovation" in non-PPS hospitals. However, an innovative administrator already with cost accounting in a non-PPS facility appears to continue to upgrade the system after 1983.

Conjoint Preferences in Purchasing Decisions

The purpose of this section is to quantify manager/buyer preferences utilizing the marketing technique of conjoint analysis. Hospital managers/buyers do more than buy quality products; they also arrange for quality delivery, convenience in ordering, and convenience in inventory retrieval. Moreover, as we observed in the previous section, hospital managers are increasingly interested in discounting last year's purchasing cost and ordering costs of supplies, drugs, and equipment. *Conjoint analysis* attempts to measure the depth and direction of the attitudes of buyers toward products and cluster (bundle) the important attribute/features into homogeneous, like-thinking market segments.

The first step in our conjoint methodology involves regression analysis, as we estimate the part-worth contributions of all the attributes that underlie a hospital manager's multiattribute attitude. The six major attributes we shall analyze, listed in Table 5.6, are the only features listed by more than one-third of our 1983 sample respondents. Because of the large amount of variability in preferences among managers, conjoint analysis is performed at the individual level of analysis—not the hospital level.

The second stage in conjoint analysis involves clustering hospital managers of like attitude. Clusters of homogeneous manager attitudes, insofar as the conjoint model estimates attitudinal levels, may exist irrespective of payment environment. We have already observed in previous sections that the dominant concerns of managers differ between PPS and waiver states. However, the more salient research issue is whether underlying preferences exist that act irrespective of the payment climate. The conjoint measurement methods we employ are in some sense a practical variation of economic utility theory.

On the basis of four pretest interviews in the fall of 1985, each of the six attributes was identified at three levels (levels a, b, c in Table 5.6). The written descriptions utilized to describe the levels may appear odd to the business marketing professional, but no hospital manager in the sample could conceive of buying a below-

Table 5.6 A Comparison of Part-Worths and Attribute Importances for the Two Respondent Groups in 1986 (PPS managers—on PPS for two years; new-to-PPS in 1986—from the two former waiver states, New York and Massachusetts)

Attribute Levels # Observations*	Part-Worths Regression Clusters			Attribute Importance Clusters			Attribute-Level Weights Clusters		
	1	2	3	1	2	3	1	2	3
From PPS 3 states and Wash. D.C.	154	40	48	154	40	48	154	40	48
From former waiver states	10	57	161	10	57	161	10	57	161
1-A. Cost of the Product									
a. Discount 3–6%	0	0	0	—	—	—	.09	.12	.68
b. Discount 8–12%	2.95	1.64	.84	.51	.37	.21	.63	.56	.29
c. Discount 15–20%	.78	.84	.09	—	—	—	.28	.32	.03
1-B. Cost of Processing a Purchase Order									
a. Typical, $55–$65	0	0	0	—	—	—	.21	.25	.36
b. Good, $35–$45	1.13	.98	.57	.12	.11	.09	.42	.40	.50
c. Outstanding, <$30	1.19	1.14	.25	—	—	—	.37	.35	.14
2-A. Quality of the Product (reputation and/or prior experience)									
a. Average	0	0	0	—	—	—	.23	.33	.14
b. Very good	1.26	1.10	1.91	.17	.15	.46	.38	.36	.21
c. Outstanding	1.33	1.05	3.62	—	—	—	.39	.31	.66
2-B. Quality of Delivery									
a. Percentage of an order shipped (w/out backordering) Below average, 85%	0	0	0	—	—	—	.21	.26	.30
b. Average, 90–94%	0	−.02	.26	.07	.06	.08	.32	.27	.44
c. Outstanding, 97%+	.40	.29	.16	—	—	—	.47	.47	.26
3-A. Convenience in Ordering									
a. Below average	0	0	0	—	—	—	.20	.12	.25
b. Average (consolidate orders and shipments)	.47	1.26	.50	.08	.22	.08	.41	.37	.42
c. Outstanding (computer-to-computer order and hardcopy confirmation)	.45	.73	.41	—	—	—	.39	.52	.33
3-B. Convenience in Inventory									
a. Inventory accuracy average, 85–90%	0	0	0	—	—	—	.22	.13	.18
b. Inventory accuracy good, 92–95%	.20	.46	.35	.06	.10	.09	.37	.42	.44
c. Inventory accuracy outstanding, 98%+	.29	.61	.28	—	—	—	.41	.45	.38

*The total numbers of observations are 242 and 228 for PPS and former waiver states' profiles. The numbers of observations are based on a weighted cluster analysis; thus the number of profile observations is higher than the number of manager/respondents (135, 125).

average product. Consequently, the levels in that example are identified as average, very good, or outstanding. The six attributes and three levels were subsequently utilized in 1986 to resurvey the 52 surviving hospitals. We collected the information utilizing a full profile approach (Carroll and Gagon, 1983) rather than the more simplistic and unrealistic two-factor-at-a-time approach. A factorial design was constructed to offer descriptive profiles of the product acquisition, delivery, and storage process. Since it is not feasible to present managers with a huge number of profiles, 729 possible (3 raised to the 6th power), a fractional factorial pretest in 1985 limited the number of profiles to 27. This limited number of profiles keeps the interview to under 75 minutes and allows estimation of all parameter values. The cost of administering a purchaser evaluation study on 729 possible alternatives, not to mention the manager's fatigue and confusion, would be impractical. Therefore, we take advantage of an orthogonal array experimental design so one can test the independent contributions of all attributes and attribute levels from the selected 27 combinations (Green, 1974; Green and DeSarbo, 1978). The 27 profiles, constructed according to an orthogonal array, represented only one in 27 of the 729 possible combinations.

Managers were asked to select their single dominant concern in making purchasing decisions in 1983 and 1986. The three basic concerns were cost, quality, and convenience. The two most popular attributes listed under each of these three areas were, along with their 1983 target levels of performance for 1986, utilized to structure the 27 profiles for the conjoint measurement single survey in 1986. The most popular attributes to capture cost concerns included product cost (mentioned by 100 percent of respondents), purchase-order processing costs (62 percent), and inventory costs (30 percent) in the 1983 survey. The attributes most often cited to describe quality concerns include product reputation (88 percent), supplier delivery quality without back ordering (50 percent), and general manufacturer reputation (26 percent). The attributes most often cited to describe convenience concerns include convenience in ordering (75 percent), inventory accuracy (58 percent), contrast of actual item count versus record count, stock availability (32 percent), and location accuracy (14 percent; stored items in their assigned location as a measure of accuracy).

Computation of the utility scales of each attribute, which determines how influential each is in the manager's evaluations of what to buy for the hospital, is carried out through a search procedure. The scale values for each level of each factor are chosen so that when they are added together the total utility of each combination will respond to the original ranks as best as possible. Two constraints are readily apparent. First, only rank-order data are supplied to the algorithms. Second, the orthogonal experimental design involves only 27 of 729 possible combinations. As has been documented in the marketing science literature (Acito and Jain, 1980), despite these limitations the conjoint measurement program is capable of finding a reliable numerical representation of the utilities, thus providing an indication of each attribute's relative importance.

The 27 profiles were presented on separate index cards for the managers' evaluations. Each of the five respondents at a given hospital was shown the 27 cards, in a randomized order, and asked to evaluate each one on an 8-point scale ranging from extremely undesirable to highly desirable. The data from the 27-profile interview were fitted to a main-effects-only utility model (Green and Tull, 1984). Since the respondents' overall evaluation score is known, the part-worth utility associated with the six attributes and three levels can be solved with traditional, ordinary least-squares (OLS) regression analysis. The appropriateness of such OLS estimates, relative to five other estimation techniques, is well established in the marketing literature (Green and Srinivasan, 1978). The relative attribute weights were utilized to uncover three unique manager attitude segments through Johnson's hierarchical clustering procedure (Jain et al., 1982). The results in Table 5.6 suggest three unique manager segments:

- Cluster 1: the pure economic buyer (two-thirds of the PPS sample).
- Cluster 2: the economic/convenience buyer.
- Cluster 3: the quality/cost buyer (over two-thirds of the waiver-state sample managers).

From cursory inspection of each dendrogram in the cluster analysis, each of the four minor trees ($N = 11, 9, 7, 5$ observations) was "cut" to fit into the three large clusters. The original three clusters contained 94 percent of the sample, before these final four minor groupings were "collapsed" back into the analysis. Given the goodness-of-fit (ranging from 0.49 to 0.43 v-restricted), interpretation, and the correlations between attributes, the basic three clusters are the best representation of the sample (Johnson, 1967).

In the third and final stage of the conjoint analysis, the pooled evaluations for each of these three clusters were utilized for a segment-level analysis (similar to the individual OLS regressions) to determine part-worth utilities for each of the three clusters. The part-worths are adjusted such that the first level (*a*) within each attribute is zero. The part-worth regression coefficients for each manager cluster segment, obtained from the dummy-variable regressions, are given in the initial three columns of Table 5.6. Attribute-level weights resulting from transformation of the original unpooled regression coefficients, through a conditional logit model (Akaah and Becherer, 1983), are given in columns 7–9 of Table 5.6. One attractive feature of this transformation is that the computed attribute-level weights are invariant over an additive constant applied to each of the part-worth coefficients within any specific attribute (McFadden, 1976).

To assure comparability of the data across the sample, the standardization option of the Barr/Johnson clustering procedure was employed (Becker and Chambers, 1980). Attribute importances, indicating the relative contribution of each feature to the judged overall profile score, are presented in columns 4–6 of Table 5.6. Relative attribute importance was thus defined in terms of the range of the attribute's part-worths relative to the total ranges of all other attributes combined. In estimating the structure of hospital managers' preferences, the traditional additive composition rule was used.

With respect to attribute preference, members of cluster 1 consider purchase cost to be the single most important determinant of their behavior, with quality and processing costs ranking a distant second and third place, respectively. In the case of cluster 2 (economic/convenience buyers) cost and ordering convenience rank a close first and second in importance. For members of cluster 3 (quality/cost buyers) quality of the product is still the principal concern (weight = .46 in Table 5.6), followed distantly in order of importance by the cost of the product (weight = .21).

Discussion and Conclusions

One possible threat to the validity of this conjoint analysis is the pooling of the five major management categories. One could hypothesize that attitudes differ as a function of job responsibility and the character of the products one has to buy. For example, economic criteria might become more critical an attribute as the products become more standardized. However, the attributes did not vary significantly across manager types: from the EDP directors to the directors of nursing. This finding is surprising given the wide array of products a director of nursing has to purchase, among them surgical asepsis products, wound closure products, cardiovascular surgery products, critical care products, orthopedic products, and surgical instruments. One would not wish to generalize too extensively from this finding given the limited sample sizes. We did test the validity of the results from a holdout sample. In order to measure the comparative validity of the results, a set of nine holdout cards not used in the original card sort were evaluated by the respondents. The utility scores from the two card sorts were used to predict the rankings of the holdout cards. The majority (78 percent) of the predicted ranks were within one rank of the actual rank. It was interesting that this check on comparative validity was slightly higher (83 percent) for those with graduate professional school training (MBA, MHA, nursing) than for those without graduate training (71 percent).

Given that the future pressures for cost control are not going to ease up, even if we move to capitated limited-access systems, the "economic buyer" model may become increasingly prevalent (Malcolmson, 1986). However, there is no one correct way to purchase. Nevertheless, there are a number of totally incorrect ways to purchase, including the price-insensitive and quality-regardless schools of thought. It would be helpful if the information on quality of care was more valid and reliable. Hospital buyers should never confuse supplier claims with facts. Analogously, it is fruitless to ask only the butcher whether the "meat is fresh." The developers and promoters of a given technology or product will always claim that their quality is the "best" and that the item does what it is purported to do. Hospital managers and physicians should confirm the seller's claims elsewhere.

Future research should consider whether shifts in management attitudes lead to positive financial outcomes for their hospitals. More precise data linking changing attitudes to changed behavior and improved financial status would prove useful to policy makers. A second posttest in 1989 could be analyzed restricting the sample in one conjoint analysis to managers who did not alter their preferences until after 1986. The sample could be divided into proactive managers (reacting prior to 1986), reactive managers, and nonreactive, nonprogressive managers. One critical research question is whether one continues to sample on the basis of hospitals, with minimal job turnover of 11 percent in the 2.5-year period.* One might attempt to track people through an organization such as the American College of Healthcare Executives rather than track just hospitals. One would expect that (1) proactive

---

*There is substantial anecdotal evidence that the job turnover rates in the hospital industry are much higher since January 1986.

managers have a lower job turnover rate relative to reactive managers (1986–1989), and (2) all types of managers have a higher turnover rate in 1986–1989 compared to the relatively easy reimbursement climate of 1983–1986. The payment climate under P. L. 99-372, the Gramm-Rudman-Hollings deficit-reduction bill, may lead to higher manager stress and turnover (Rayburn, 1986). While the evidence is consistent with the general view that financial concerns have become more important these last three years, the action linkage and behavioral implications of future changes in the prospective payment environment should be more fully examined by organizational theorists (Chamberlain, 1982).

References

ACITO, F., and JAIN, A. (1980). "Evaluation of Conjoint Analysis Results: A Comparison of Methods." *Journal of Marketing Research* 17:2 (February), 106–112.

AKAAH, I., and BECHERER, R. (1983). "Integrating a Consumer Orientation into Planning of HMO Programs: An Application of Conjoint Segmentation." *Journal of Health Care Marketing* 3:2 (Spring), 9–18.

BECKER, R., and CHAMBERS, J. (1980). *Language and System for Data Analysis*. Murray Hill, N.J.: Bell Laboratories.

BERMAN, H., and WEEKS, L. (1982). *Financial Management of Hospitals*, 5th ed. Ann Arbor, Mich.: Health Administration Press.

BERRY, R., VARHOLY, S., RUSSELL, M., KELLY, N., and EASTAUGH, S. (1986). "A Study of the Financing of Graduate Medical Education." Arthur Young & Company Final Report (September), Contract DHHS:ASPE, DHHS–100–80–0155.

BURIK, D., and DUVALL, T. (1985). "Hospital Cost Accounting." *Healthcare Financial Management* 39:3 (March), 58–64.

CARMONE, F., and GREEN, P. (1981). "Model Misspecification in Multiattribute Parameter Estimation." *Journal of Marketing Research* 18:2 (February), 87–93.

CARMONE, F., GREEN, P., and JAIN, A. (1978). "The Robustness of Conjoint Analysis." *Journal of Marketing Research* 15:5 (May), 300–304.

CARROLL, N., and GAGON, J. (1983). "Identifying Consumer Segments in Health Services Markets: An Application of Conjoint and Cluster Analyses." *Journal of Health Care Marketing* 3:3 (Summer), 22–34.

CHAMBERLAIN, F. (1982). "Analysis of Panel Data." Working paper No. 913, National Bureau of Economic Research, Cambridge, Mass.

CODDINGTON, D., AND STEIKER, A. (1986). "New Tools for Healthcare Decision-Making." *Healthcare Forum* 29:5 (September–October), 25–27.

COOK, T., and CAMPBELL, D. (1979). *Quasi-Experimentation: Design and Analysis Issues*. Boston: Houghton-Mifflin.

EASTAUGH, S. (1986). "Differential Cost Accounting and PPOs: Judging the Feasibility of a Joint Venture." *Healthcare Financial Management* 40:5 (May), 44–51.

EASTAUGH, S. (1984). "Checking the Cost-Effectiveness of Unit Dose Pharmacy." *Hospital Topics* 62:2 (March/April), 24–28.

EASTAUGH, S., and EASTAUGH, J. (1986). "Prospective Payment Systems: Further Steps to Enhance Quality, Efficiency, and Regionalization." *Health Care Management Review* 11:4 (Fall).

FINKLER, S. (1982). "Increasing the Usefulness of Flexible Budgeting: The Pyramid Approach." *Hospital Financial Management* 36:2 (February), 30–39.

General Accounting Office (1983). "Hospitals in the Same Area Often Pay Widely Different Prices for Comparable Supply Items." GAO Report HRD–80–35 (January 21). Washington, D.C.: U.S. Government Printing Office.

GREEN, P. (1974). "On the Design of Experiments Involving Multiattribute Alternatives." *Journal of Consumer Research* 1:3 (September), 60–69.

GREEN, P., and DESARBO, W. (1978). "Additive Decomposition of Perceptions Data via Conjoint Analysis." *Journal of Consumer Research* 5:5 (June), 58–65.

GREEN, P., and RAO, V. (1971). "Conjoint Measurement of Quantifying Judgmental Data." *Journal of Marketing Research* 8:8 (August), 350–365.

GREEN, P., and SRINIVASAN, V. (1978). "Conjoint Analysis in Consumer Research: Issues and Outlooks." *Journal of Consumer Research* 5:9 (September), 103–123.

GREEN, P., and TULL, D. (1984). *Research for Marketing Decisions*, 4th ed. Englewood Cliffs, N.J.: Prentice-Hall.

HORN, S. (1986). "Measuring Severity: How Sick Is Sick? How Well Is Well?" *Healthcare Financial Management* 40:10 (October), 21–32.

HORNGREN, C. (1982). *Cost Accounting: A Managerial Emphasis*, 6th ed. Englewood Cliffs, N.J.: Prentice-Hall.

JAIN, A., PINSON, C., and RATCHFORD, B. (1982). *Marketing Research: Applications and Problems*. New York: John Wiley.

JOHNSON, S. (1967). "Hierarchical Clustering Schemes." *Psychometrika* 32:1 (January), 241–254.

KNIGHT, W. (1972). "Working Capital Management: Satisficing versus Optimization." *Financial Management* 11:2 (Spring), 33–40.

LANCASTER, K. (1966). "A New Approach to Consumer Theory." *Journal of Political Economy* 74:4 (April), 132–157.

MALCOMSON, L. (1986). "CFOs Put the Squeeze on the Hospital's Big Ticket Purchases." *Healthcare Financial Management* 40:8 (August), 23–26.

MARTIN, P., and BOYER, F. (1985). "Developing a Consistent Method for Costing Hospital Services." *Healthcare Financial Management* 39:2 (February), 30–37.

MCCLAIN, J., EASTAUGH, S. (1983). "How to Forecast to Contain Variable Costs: Exponential Smoothing Techniques." *Hospital Topics* 61:6 (November–December), 4–9.

MCFADDEN, D. (1976). "Quantal Choice Analysis: A Survey." *Annals of Economic and Social Measurement* 5:1 (January), 363–390.

PARZEN, E. (1971). *Stochastic Processes*. San Francisco: Holden-Day.

RAYBURN, L. (1986). "PPS Creates Job Tension for the Financial Manager." *Healthcare Financial Management* 40:2 (February), 48–53.

REISMAN, A. (1984). "Material Management Systems: A Means Toward Significant Hospital Cost Containment." *Hospital Materials Management Quarterly* 2:2 (February), 74–81.

RHODES, R., KRASNIAK, C., and JONES, P. (1986). "Factors Affecting Length of Stay for Femoropopliteal Bypass: Implications of DRGs." *New England Journal of Medicine* 314:3 (January 16), 153–157.

ROSKO, M., WALKER, L., McKENNA, M., and DeVITA, M. (1983). "Measuring Consumer Preferences for Ambulatory Medical Care Arrangements." *Journal of Medical Systems* 7:6 (June), 545–554.

SCHLAG, D. (1986). "Providing Better Understanding of the True Revenues of the Organization—Impact of Principles and Practices Board Statement No. 7." *Healthcare Financial Management* 40:4 (April), 72–81.

SUVER, J., and NEUMANN, B. (1985). *Management Accounting for Healthcare Organizations*. Oak Brook, Ill.: Healthcare Financial Management Association.

WILLIAMS, S., FINKLER, S., MURPHY, C., and EISENBER, J. (1982). "Improved Cost Allocation in Case-Mix Accounting." *Medical Care* 20:5 (May), 450–459.

Chapter 6

ACCESS AND THE UNINSURED

Americans are inherently pluralistic. We talk about the importance of every citizen being educated. To accomplish that ideal we have a mixed-up private/public education system. We utter general words about how everybody should have adequate health care, and create 47 overlapping arrangements to deal with the question of access. Our American tradition is to not do anything with a comprehensive single system. Although it may be very expensive and duplicative, this pluralistic approach is more dynamic and more adaptable to change.

—JOHN T. DUNLOP

Until we nationalize energy and transportation, we will not have national health insurance in this country.

—RASHI FEIN

Political forces for equitable provision of equitable care resemble rivers. The pressure on the dams is enormous but unseen; it is only when the public and nonprofit hospitals burst (dump patients or close) that the strain is realized. How does a malfunction in the indigent care "nonsystem" manifest itself? One recent study of patient transfers to Cook County, Illinois, revealed that 81 percent of the cases were unemployed, only 6 percent had been given informed consent for the transfer, and 24 percent were in unstable clinical condition on transfer (Schiff et al., 1986). Declines in health status may have to be horrifying and directly linked to lack of insurance coverage to engage the public interest in adequate and equitable provision of health care. Some analysts trained outside of the health arena have argued that if we have an oversupply of doctors and 360,000 empty beds, how can any segment of the public be receiving an inadequate supply of medical care?

135

Indigent care is service provided to those who are incapable of paying for all or part of their medical bill and do not qualify for medical assistance programs. Care for the medically indigent includes charity care and some fraction of the bad debts. Sloan's (1985) analysis of American Hospital Association data found that billed charges to "self-pay" patients are likely to be uncompensated care. In his Tennessee sample, the self-pay patients are most likely to be maternity or accident cases. At his local Vanderbilt teaching hospital, most uncompensated care patients had incurred small bills. However, patients with hospital bills over $25,000 accounted for 35 percent of total hospital expenses (and only 2 percent of the patients).

A number of recent analysts (Ohsfeldt, 1985; McDaniel, 1986) have pointed out that the term "uncompensated" or "indigent" care lumps both charity care and bad debt into a single category. It is hard to get any accurate national estimate as to what fraction of bad debt involves poor people financially incapable of paying their bills, in contrast to nonpoor people unwilling (because they are dissatisfied) to pay some fraction of their bill. In affluent suburban markets bad debt might involve less than 10 percent charity care, whereas in the ghetto bad debt is 95 percent charity care. In 1986, an estimated $2.5 billion of charity care will be provided by hospitals, and $5.4 billion of bad debt (1.5 and 3.25 percent of hospital gross revenues, respectively). While $6 to 7 billion of free care to the poor may seem in macroeconomic terms an insignificant amount within a nation that spends over $8 billion per week on health care, it represents an ethical and financial problem for 10 to 15 percent of the hospitals.

Uncompensated care is one of the forgotten stepchilds of our increasingly competitive medical marketplace. Hospitals compete for market share of the paying patient business, but no one competes for nonpaying patients (Bazzoli, 1986; Kinzer, 1984). The debate over indigent care will lead nowhere until we reach some consensus on whether our top priority is institutional financial support or providing access to a minimum standard of care for underinsured citizens. Institutional managers argue in terms of minimizing uncompensated care and mainstreaming the poor to all hospitals, no matter how costly and inefficient. The tenet of faith among managers, and some researchers (Hadley and Feder, 1985), that equity, efficiency, and access are a zero-sum equation, is certainly open to question. Moreover, one could question whether we can promote affordable managed-care systems for the uninsured and still maintain the dream of mainstreaming all people into "best quality" service delivery systems. We hear reports on how the poor are dumped from hospitals. Policy makers insist that indigent care is a vexing problem and insist that providers do "it" better—with hardly any consideration of the "it" we want improved. Good care for our population is the answer. But what is the question?

Wanted: Stable Financing and Better Management

A stable, sufficient source of financing indigent care is critically needed, but better management among the "suffering" providers is also a necessity. These two issues are linked, but a public policy solution for one problem will not assure the resolution of the other. The hospital sector, disturbed to varying degrees by the absence of revenue for providing service for the uninsured, is the major advocate of improved public insurance programs. The uninsured poor, often described as the medically indigent, are financially unable to pay their hospital bills. Feder et al. (1984) estimate that 17.9 million persons with incomes below 150 percent of the poverty line are uninsured. The hospital sector, in response to price competition and revenue controls, has been accused of limiting the care which it will provide to the poor (Relman, 1986; Schiff et al., 1986) or of exhibiting signs of financial distress (NAPH, 1986). However, financial distress can be reduced or eliminated by better management and cost-reduction techniques (Eastaugh, 1986). Because the poor are often more severely ill, they may be presumed to cost more per case treated. Hospitals serving a high volume of uninsured individuals, however, have the twin problems of inadequate revenues and very inefficient levels of productivity.

The best hospital managers will improve efficiency per department, while continuing the public effort to lobby for better reimbursement per patient. One cannot finance indigent care with productivity improvements alone; but without better productivity and increasing reliance on ambulatory care, the money invested in indigent care merely props up inefficient institutions. Policy analysts should be concerned with how resources raised for indigent care can be most effectively allocated. Then we can ask for increasing stewardship of public funds and a stable sufficient level of financing for indigent care.

The problem of indigent care is not simply a hospital finance and cost-shifting issue. Indigent service provision is a much broader social problem. The delivery of appropriate and effective medical care for the poor encompasses ethical issues such as the right to care, systemic issues such as access and new modes of service delivery (managed care), and financial issues such as who will pay for uncompensated care. Competition has made indigent care an important endemic "priority problem" for policy makers, rather than simply another "back burner" issue of concern for the public health community. Hospital executives have a valid point when they note that managing a facility in a system of set prices and prospective contracts for 50 to 70 percent of the patients threatens their ability to provide service to nonpaying patients. Nonpayment for charity care is already seriously limiting the ability of some hospitals to continue to provide their historic share of indigent care.

Hospital lobbyists call for a "level playing field" and argue that the current situation is like telling Bloomingdale's and Sears to compete for customers and capital with the proviso that Sears must give away its goods to the poor, while Bloomingdale's is allowed to transfer its poor customers to Sears. There is no "free lunch" in that if the poor cannot pay for their own care, and government will not, then someone else must bear the burden. Who else but the payers of the premium, businesses and the employed, and insurers with insufficient market share (and bargaining leverage) can bear this implicit burden of cost shifting? The problem is that this implicit burden priced itself into the public eye and so became a more explicit burden. As pointed out by Reinhardt (1985), the much deplored "cost shifting" for indigent care was effectively a cosmetic quick-fix to assure the poor a level of access to quality care. Now that payers are increasingly opting not to pay the cost-shift factor for indigent care—inflated charges over actual costs— the question is how shall we pay the health care bill of the poor? There is rising public interest in the issue of charity care. Carol McCarthy (1986), president of the American Hospital Association, reports that 21 percent of Americans now list medical care for the poor as a "major problem," up from only 9 percent in 1979.

The conventional wisdom among inner-city hospital managers can best be described with an imperfect syllogism: Financially distressed hospitals do a disproportionate amount of indigent care; therefore, hospital income redistribution through a "sin" tax (e.g., alcohol, tobacco) or patient surcharge will reduce the "unfair" financial distress, and redistributing income to the financially distressed institutions will address the problem of indigent care.

It would be prudent to note that our current problems are past solutions; therefore, more needs to be done than simply channel public or private funds. The major premise of the syllogism is flawed. Increasing the volume of indigent care does not cause financial distress; nor does financial distress result mainly among the institutions disproportionately serving the indigent. In fact, a number of indigent measures are poor contributors in explaining more than 1.5 to 15 percent of the variance in financial ratios (Sloan et al., 1985; Rundall and Lambert, 1985). Moreover, the minor premise in the syllogism is also flawed. While improved cash flow can ameliorate distress in the short run, it has the unfortunate side effect of keeping the pathology in the system. The pathology includes operational inefficiencies, poor-quality managers, unbusinesslike trustees, and excess hospital beds. The 1986 law that makes Texas the first state to put into effect regulations intended to minimize patient "dumping" has in the basic preamble explicit recognition that a businesslike hospital should be an ethical hospital (Relman, 1986). Patients are to be transferred only with their informed consent (when possible), and for valid medical, not economic, reasons.

Necessity may be the mother of invention, but lack of necessity impedes innovation. Many hospitals are financially distressed because they avoid workload-driven staffing, operate with excess staff, pay excessive prices for equipment and supplies, and eschew initiating employee incentives for improving productivity (Eastaugh, 1986, 1985). A major portion of the financial problems of the hospital may be the result of poor decision making and not an excess volume of nonpaying or poorly paying patients. Pouring more money into such facilities will not cure bad management. It will only delay the day of reckoning. Winston Churchill said, "Give us the tools and we will finish the job." Many indigent-care facilities lack the tools, the toolmakers, and the aggressive modern managers to act as troubleshooters and enhance quality and productivity. Moreover, politicians as a general rule disallow public enterprise accounting, destroy the incentive to operate with efficiency by decreasing budgets, disallow employee-incentive compensation, and frustrate good managers. In the case of public hospitals, the solution involves elimination of civil service "protections" for unproductive, antiproductive, or incompetent employees. The choices for many hospitals are either closing, converting, selling, contract managing, or getting their internal house in order so as to foster efficiency and quality of care. This may involve breaking a little crockery, but if the goal is to maintain autonomy, the facility that survives will reward its "best employees." If public hospitals and poorly managed teaching hospitals are not up to this challenge, they may go the way of the American buffalo. All three institutions had their golden eras, and now the latter two face extinction at the hands of entrepreneurs out to serve a public demand for less cost shifting and more cost efficiency. The public

policy may be finding enough points of access for the poor throughout the restructured hospital industry. A greater dose of unpalata-
ble demarketing medicine could, under a worst case scenario,
include "dumping" poor patients, reducing services covered, and
restricting eligibility. The medical needs of the poor would become
the big loser in such a competitive environment (Lurie et al., 1986,
1984).

Money Does Not Cure All Ills

A hospital experiencing substandard financial performance should
not confuse poor results with destiny. Just because a facility serves
a large volume of nonpaying patients does not mean that it should
also exhibit poor financial health. Indeed, in the Rundall and
Lambert study (1985) utilizing California data, three indigent-care
variables could only capture 12 to 15 percent of the variance for a
range of liquidity and leveraged financial ratios. Only one financial
ratio, total operating margin, had a significant fraction (.34) of
variance explained by the indigent-care measures. The Sloan
(1985) study was even more unsuccessful in trying to explain
institutional financial ratios. The vast majority of the variation in
financial health can perhaps best be explained by differences in
management, leading to better productivity and more aggressive
diversification. Diversification and productivity incentive systems
have been found to be much more significant predictors of financial
standing than the volume of indigent care provided (Eastaugh,
1985, 1984). Contrary to one study of New York hospitals from
1979 to 1981 (Brecher and Nesbitt, 1985), financial decay is not the
predetermined destiny of hospitals that serve a higher-than-aver-
age volume of indigent care patients. Such hospitals require both
better management and a stable "sufficient" source of financing.
We shall discuss the definition of "sufficient" in the next section. It
is clear that the old cost-shifting game has almost been played out,
and somebody or some group of bodies (federal, state, local) must
explicitly finance indigent care. Given that state governments are
in better financial shape than the federal government, most of the
action in indigent coverage reform has been at the state level these
past four years (Lewin, 1983; Colorado Task Force, 1984; NAPH,
1985).

Defining a Stable, Sufficient Mode of Funding

One should at the minimum reimburse indigent-care delivery at
marginal cost, with either a sin tax, sick tax (X percent paid by all

hospitals), or fair-share pool (different rates of X put up by all hospitals "underserving" the indigent, so that net, all contribute equally to such care). The incentives could be set asymetrically, so as to reward hospitals serving an increased volume of the indigent and penalize hospitals that demarket or discriminate against the indigent. For example, if a hospital increases the volume of indigent patients by more than 5 percent over the baseline year figure, it would be paid at 10 percent above marginal cost (.66 of average cost). However, if the facility decreased indigent care by more than 5 percent, it would be paid only half of average cost. If the volume of indigent services was relatively stable from year to year, the hospital would be paid at marginal cost (taken as 0.6 of average cost).

Two caveats are in order. First, numerous studies have been done to measure the marginal costs of hospitals (Eastaugh, 1982) and hospital educational programs (Berry, 1986). The literature on the subject can be used to justify estimates of marginal cost as a fraction of average cost ranging from 0.5 to 0.7. The 0.6 figure represents the most frequently cited mid-range figure, and it was also the figure adopted by Medicare to make outlier payments. Hospital industry representatives dislike the cost-containment rationale for paying indigent care at marginal cost rather than at actual costs or full charges. Blendon et el. (1986) suggest a more generous payment system for an expanded federalized Medicaid program. However, given that the medical care system is being leached for dollars to compensate in some way for years of free spending under blank-check retrospective cost reimbursement, a stringent formula would be the most politically feasible. In other words, the hospital sector should be happy with 0.6 a loaf in lieu of no loaf or payment at all for the nonpaying patients. Consequently, by only receiving marginal costs payments, we are as a society recognizing the burden on nonindigent patients to cover the fixed costs of operating a hospital.

Right to Care: Reaffirmation or Cremation?

During this time of health sector turbulence, many hospital managers encapsulate the policy issue under one label: "uncompensated care." This language signifies the direction, context, and vigor of the hospital lobby in generating improved cash flow for its sector. Alas, in a political world, few people will fight for the cause of cash flow. What matters is not uncompensated care in and of itself. What matters is "uncovered people" not getting the required level of care or having to settle for substandard care (Fein,

1985). Protection of equity and access in the delivery of health services will make a better election year issue than fighting to get better cash flow for hospitals. One would hope the current pre-emption of concern for access by economic priorities would erode, especially as careful studies demonstrate that short-run cost savings in ignoring the poor produce long-run life-cycle cost explosions for society 8 to 20 years in the future (Mundinger, 1985). Deterioration in health status among those with low socioeconomic status may not be significant after only a few years (Brook et el., 1983) but becomes significant over a decade (Shapiro et el., 1986). In summary, it is not cost-efficient to short shrift the poor, although it may appear so to those with a myopic, short-run vantage point.

The most prevalent change in the delivery system for the medically indigent has been the rise in managed-care networks or systems—for example, California, Massachusetts, Arizona, Oregon (Inglehart, 1983). Managed-care programs, with primary physician gatekeepers, can assure that dollars for indigent care are better channeled to ambulatory and preventive care. There has been some shortfall between program plans and performance, but in general, policy makers are pleased with the cost-containment aspects of such programs (Gelder-Kogan, 1985; Kirkman-Liff et al., 1985). For example, Arizona Governor Bruce Babbitt defended his state's managed-care program at the 1985 annual meeting of the Association of American Medical Colleges. The governor indicated that not only does the program save money, but it provides increased case coordination and better quality medical treatment. Kirkman-Liff (1985) reports that 4 percent of the poor households in Arizona self-report, during Louis Harris interviews, some degree of direct provider refusal to provide care for an individual with a serious health problem. This emergence of managed-care networks has allowed the poor to be served with more continuity of care and assured that inpatient imperatives for cash flow do not come to dominate the health agenda. Additional financial support for indigent-care programs shouldn't be a cash windfall for tax-exempt hospitals currently experiencing an operating margin of $6 billion (revenues in excess of expenses, 1986), or proprietary hospitals with a profit margin of $2.4 billion (Eastaugh and Eastaugh, 1986).

Managed care is one of a number of large-scale strategies to finance care for the uninsured. Other strategies include all-payer rate programs reallocating resources to the uninsured (New Jersey, Maryland; four additional states require an "add-on" to be paid by third-party payers—Connecticut, Maine, Massachusetts, and New

York) and, state revenue pools raised from surcharges on hospital revenues (states must circumvent section 514 of the Employee Retirement Income Security Act, ERISA, by imposing the tax on hospital net or gross revenues). If the state attempts to tax employee insurance benefits, the growing number of self-funded insurance plans can invoke ERISA 514 to avoid making any contributions. In 1986, four states had a tax on hospital revenues (Florida, South Carolina, West Virginia, and Wisconsin), and four additional states are considering such a tax in 1987 (California, Georgia, Pennsylvania, and Tennessee). The South Carolina "sick tax" on hospital revenues is equally matched by tax receipts from the state's counties. Weak financial incentives to provide a minimum level of uncompensated care at each hospital have been adopted in Arkansas and are under consideration in 1987 for Ohio and Kentucky.

Six additional piecemeal strategies are often advocated to assist the uninsured or the underinsured:

1. State risk-sharing pools to allow "uninsurable," high-risk individuals to obtain affordable health insurance coverage. For example, in 1985, Montana and Nebraska created risk pools for people denied insurance, and more state activity is expected, unless federal action is undertaken (i.e., a bill sponsored by Senator Kennedy caps premiums at no more than 1.5 times the normal rate for individual policies regardless of health status).
2. Catastrophic public insurance (Wisconsin 1987 pilot program will provide vouchers for those whose incomes are not 75 percent higher than the poverty line).
3. More comprehensive federalized Medicaid expansion to select target populations.
4. Proposed direct federal subsidies to overburdened "financially distressed" providers.
5. Mandated temporary continuation of employer insurance coverage, for the employee and family, after unemployment or a change in marital status (available after 6 to 9 months if the former employee can continue to pay the full premium cost).
6. Group insurance purchasing for small businesses through multiple employer trusts (METS) aggregating firms to enlarge the risk pool.

Of these nine alternatives, managed care is the most systematic and successful. Managed care assures more efficient use of limited resources by balancing primary care and preventive medicine on an "equal playing field" with the highly expensive inpatient care. Other keys to success are exclusive selection of clinicians and a reasonable use of cost-sharing arrangements.

Efficacy, Social Welfare, and Values

One recent study by Kelly (1985) reports that in 1977 charity patients in tax-exempt urban hospitals were less likely to have surgery and had fewer diagnostic and therapeutic procedures than privately insured patients. In addition, charity patients were discharged after only 5.8 days in comparison to a 6.7 average duration of stay for private patients. These relative comparisons might provoke some to claim that charity patients are underserved. However, the test of history seems to belie any assertion other than to say both groups were "overserved," and the efficiency and efficacy of much of this inpatient care were suspect. In 1986, the average length of stay for charity and private patients has converged to five days. The health of both groups does not appear to have suffered. This supports Feldstein's (1973) assertion that there is a multibillion dollar "social welfare loss to all society from having excess insurance" producing too much care (inpatient days, tests, procedures, and operations).

One might assume that in an "age of plenty," with so much savings from foregone unnecessary utilization and a glut of beds and doctors, policy makers would not hasten to address the problem of indigent care. After all, with so many empty beds and underutilized doctors, indigent care is something they could perform in their spare time (as part of a social contract; the public could reimburse at marginal cost for their services). We have not faced up to the shared obligation of indigent care, between both the private and public sectors, because there is little consensus as to whether health care is a desired commodity (like a college education) or a necessary commodity (like food). If health care is a desired commodity, then providers will produce service along multiple levels of amenities and technical quality. Most citizens would not begrudge the rich first-class amenities in what Reinhart (1985) refers to as "Yuppie boutique" medicine. However, public policy might consider some assurance that technical quality is not "substandard" for the medically indigent. "Boutique medicine" would involve not just better amenities, but better quality of care. Society would provide boutique medicine for those who can pay, just as we have "boutique education" at Harvard and Stanford. Those people who buy the myth that providers are roughly equivalent might be equally gullible in believing that Stanford is equivalent to the local community college. The analogy breaks down in a number of ways: The poor who merit it have some chance to get into Stanford, and the Mayo Clinic can afford to franchise itself in four locations (whereas Stanford has agreed to stay at one location). This may be an unfortunate circumstance, but it is not an unfair circumstance.

If health care is a necessary basic commodity like food, society should underwrite a minimum basic needs coverage policy for all. We have attempted to mainstream the Medicaid eligible "covered poor" into the great majority of hospitals, so equity is better served in comparison to the market for education. However, as with the food stamp program, there has been little social pressure to federalize Medicaid in an egalitarian spirit. Federal policy making has always operated on the "big wheel principle"—he who is now first will later be last, and he who is last will be first. Consequently, the winds of change may make the egalitarians powerful again in a few years. Then we may have an equitable federal indigent-care policy, even if national health insurance is judged too expensive. Americans have the highest aspirations for the right of access to the best care for everyone, but we never have the necessary amount of resources to do this on a fee-for-service basis. Managed care is one strategy whereby we institutionalize the right to care with an efficient mode of service delivery.

References

American Hospital Association (1986). *The Cost of Compassion*. Chicago: American Hospital Publishing.

BAZZOLI, G. (1986). "Health Care for the Indigent." *Health Services Research* 21:3 (August), 353–393.

BERRY, R. (1986). "Cost Functions and Production Functions in a Sample of 45 Hospitals." Final Report of the Arthur Young Graduate Medical Education Study, Vols. 2 and 3, DHHS Contract 100–80–0155 ASPE (October).

BLENDON, R., AIKEN, L., and FREEMAN, H. (1986). "Uncompensated Care by Hospitals or Public Insurance for the Poor: Does It Make a Difference?" *New England Journal of Medicine* 314:18 (May 1), 1160–1163.

BRECHER, C., and NESBITT, S. (1985). "Factors Associated with Variation in Financial Condition Among Voluntary Hospitals." *Health Services Research* 20:3 (August), 267–300.

BROOK, R., WARE, J., ROGERS, W., and NEWHOUSE, J. (1983). "Does Free Care Improve Adults' Health?" *New England Journal of Medicine* 309:22 (December 11), 1426–1430.

COHODES, D. (1986). "America: The Home of the Free, the Land of the Uninsured." *Inquiry* 23:3 (Fall), 227–235.

Colorado Task Force on the Medically Indigent (1984). "Colorado's Sick and Uninsured: We Can Do Better." Report volume 1 (January).

DUNLOP, J. (1986). "Business' Interest in Health Care Won't Wane." *Hospitals* 60:13 (July 5), 103–104.

EASTAUGH, S. (1986). "Work Smarter, Not Harder." *Healthcare Executive* 1:2 (March/April), 56–57.

EASTAUGH, S. (1985). "Improving Hospital Productivity Under PPS: Managing Cost Reductions Without Quality and Service Reductions." *Hospital and Health Services Administration* 30:4 (July/August), 97–111.

EASTAUGH, S. (1984). "Hospital Diversification and Financial Management." *Medical Care* 22:8 (August), 704–723.

EASTAUGH, S. (1982). "Effectiveness of Community-Based Health Planning: Some Recent Evidence." *Applied Economics* 14:3 (September), 475–490.

EASTAUGH, S., and EASTAUGH, J. (1986). "Prospective Payment Systems: Further Steps to Enhance Quality, Efficiency, and Regionalization." *Health Care Management Review* 11:4 (Fall), 37–52.

FEDER, J., HADLEY, J., and MULLNER, R. (1984). "Falling Through the Cracks: Poverty, Insurance Coverage, and Hospital's Care for the Poor, 1980–82." *Milbank Memorial Fund Quarterly* 62:4 (Fall), 640–660.

FEIN, R. (1985). "Equity, Efficiency Needed in Health Care for Financial as Well as Moral Reasons." *Business and Health* 3:2 (December), 60.

FELDSTEIN, M. (1973). "The Welfare Loss of Excess Health Insurance." *Journal of Political Economy* 81:2 (March/April), 251–280.

GELDER-KOGAN, C. (1985). "California's Public Hospitals and the Medically Indigent." *Quality Review Bulletin* 11:9 (September), 262–265.

HADLEY, J., and FEDER, J. (1985). "Hospital Cost Shifting and Care for the Uninsured." *Health Affairs* 4:3 (Fall), 67–80.

HYMAN, H. (1986). "Are Public Hospitals in New York City Inferior to Voluntary, Nonprofit Hospitals: A Study of JCAH Hospital Surveys." *American Journal of Public Health* 76:1 (January), 18–23.

IGLEHART, J. (1983). "Medicaid Turns to Prepaid Managed Care." *New England Journal of Medicine* 308:16 (April 21), 976–980.

KELLY, J. (1985). "Charity Care by Nonprofit Hospitals in 1977." In the *Conference Proceedings, Hospitals and the Uninsured Poor: Measuring and Paying for Uncompensated Care* (Summer). New York: United Hospital Fund of New York.

KINZER, D. (1984). "Care of the Poor Revisited." *Inquiry* 21:1 (Spring), 5–16.

KIRKMAN-LIFF, B. (1985). "Refusal of Care: Evidence from Arizona." *Health Affairs* 4:4 (Winter), 15–24.

KIRKMAN-LIFF, B., CHRISTIANSON, J., and HILLMAN, D. (1985). "An Analysis of Competitive Bidding by Providers for Arizona Indigent Medical Care Contracts." *Health Services Research* 20:5 (December), 549–578.

Lewin and Associates, Inc. (1983). *Health Care Financing for the Medically Indigent in Florida: A Proposed System*. Final Report to the Florida Task Force on Competition and Consumer Choices in Health Care (January), Washington, D.C.

LURIE, N., WARD, N., SHAPIRO, M., and BROOK, R. (1984). "Termination from Medi-Cal: Does It Affect Health?" *New England Journal of Medicine* 311:7 (August 16), 480–484.

LURIE, N., WARD, N., SHAPIRO, M., GALLEGO, C., VAGHAIWALLA, R., and BROOK, R. (1986). "Termination of Medi-Cal Benefits: A Follow-up Study One Year Later." *New England Journal of Medicine* 314:9 (May 8), 1266–1268.

MCCARTHY, C. (1986). "Coping with the Constant Challenge of Change." *Hospitals* 60:18 (September 20), 104.

MCDANIEL, J. (1986). "Charity Care: A Proposal for Reform." *Hospital and Health Services Administration* 31:2 (March-April), 124–134.

MUNDINGER, M. (1985). "Health Service Funding Cuts and the Declining Health of the Poor." *New England Journal of Medicine* 313:1 (July 4), 44–47.

National Association of Public Hospitals (1986). "Financing and Provision of Health Care to the Medically Indigent." Updated status report.

National Association of Public Hospitals (1985). "Texas Public Hospitals and Care for the Poor." Report to the Texas Association of Public Hospitals (May).

OHSFELDT, R. (1985). "Uncompensated Medical Services Provided by Physicians and Hospitals." *Medical Care* 23:12 (December), 1338–1344.

REINHARDT, U. (1985). "Economics, Ethics, and the American Health Care System." New Physician 9:10 (October), 20–28.

RELMAN, A. (1986). "Texas Eliminates Dumping: A Start Toward Equity in Hospital Care." *New England Journal of Medicine* 314:9 (February 27), 578–579.

RIESELBACH, R., and JACKSON, T. (1986). "In Support of a Linkage Between the Funding of Graduate Medical Education and Care of the Indigent." *New England Journal of Medicine* 314:1 (January 2), 32–35.

RUNDALL, T., and LAMBERT, J. (1985). "Analysis of Emerging Strategies: Hospital Behavior in Competitive Markets." Report to the Western Consortium for Health Planning Under Contract to DHHS, 232–82–0006 (March).

SCHIFF, R., ANSELL, D., SCHLOSSER, J., IDRIS, A., MOMSON, A., and WHITMAN, S. (1986). "Transfers to a Public Hospital: A Prospective Study of 467 Patients." *New England Journal of Medicine* 314:9 (February 27), 552–557.

SHAPIRO, M., WARE, J., and SHERBOURNE, C. (1986). "Effects of Cost Sharing on Seeking Care for Serious and Minor Symptoms." *Annals of Internal Medicine* 104:2 (February), 246–251.

SHERLOCK, D. (1986). "Indigent Care in Rational Markets." *Inquiry* 23:3 (Fall), 261–267.

SLOAN, F., BLUMSTEIN, J., and PERRIN, J. (1986). *Uncompensated Health Care: Defining Rights and Assigning Responsibility*. Baltimore: Johns Hopkins Press.

Chapter 7

HMOs AND COMPETITION HEALTH PLANS

The ultimate purpose of pro-competitive proposals is to motivate doctors, hospitals, and other providers to compete with each other to offer health care in less costly ways. There is merit in this theory.

—WALTER J. MCNERNEY

Consumers want value for their money, and that means shopping on the basis of quality and effective price. Much of the credit for lower rates of cost containment rests with private initiatives, not just the federal prospective payment system.

—WILLIS GOLDBECK

We do not yet know whether prepaid or prospective payment has had negative effects on quality. We have some anecdotal reports, but they could represent the tip of an iceberg or an ice cube floating on the surface of the ocean.

—MARK CHASSIN

Most countries view the United States health care system as being very market-oriented and competitive. Some of these nations look to the U.S. approach for alternatives to total government regulation. The preference in Canada and Western Europe is for some degree of private management of the national health service or national health insurance plan. In the United States, physicians and administrators who distrust regulatory approaches have advocated the injection of more competitive relationships between health care providers. However, not all physicians have a truly pro-competitive bias. Many hospital managers and doctors who

148

have had experience with competition and are now facing declining patient census and visits dream of returning to a less competitive era.

The basic rationale behind the competitive model is to keep the insurance companies, and hopefully providers, under constant pressure to find the means to provide care at lower costs (Traska and Millenson, 1986). Third-party payers and HMOs will on occasion make management mistakes, create long patient queues, or provide unacceptable patient care conditions, but the strength of competitive markets is that the good-quality, lower-cost operators will grow. Advocates of competition recognize consumer ignorance, insured consumers' indifference to costs, and strong physician influence on demands as three strong arguments for regulatory activity (Enthoven, 1980).

The public policy question is not simply one of whether to allow competition or regulation, but rather, what is the proper balance of regulation and competition and how much price and nonprice competition should be encouraged. As we have observed in Chapter 1, the strongest argument for regulatory limits on competition—significant economies of scale leading to excessive monopoly power—does not exist in the medical sector. Before we review some of the by-products of injecting competition into the health arena, let us review other markets that have faced the dilemma of choosing between further regulation or deregulation.

Oftentimes an industry will reject competition in favor of a planned solution. In the mid-1970s the airline industry had a problem of excess capacity, much like the current state of affairs in the hospital industry. The planners' solution, to fight the problem by reducing the number of flights, was a failure. In 1977, Civil Aeronautics Board Chairman Alfred Kahn suggested a radical old idea: competition. The approach that finally cured the excess-capacity problem was to deregulate and let price competition fill up empty planes. With deregulation came price competition and expanded access. Competition can make the good or service more egalitarian in its distribution. Some travelers may grumble that airports increasingly resemble bus terminals. This trend is understandable, given that the service that was once an elite enjoyment has now become as accessible as bus travel. However, it is not clear that less regulation of health care providers will lead to better access to care.

The analogy between the airline and hospital industry breaks down for one very important reason: There is more of a social cost involved in filling hospitals with unnecessary patients than filling planes with discount-paying vacationers. However, before forsaking the analogy one should point out that both sectors benefit from a degree of regulatory licensure. Society has made a decision to set a minimum standard that all airlines and hospitals must meet in order to minimize the intangible collective regret that we might feel if "something goes wrong." The deregulatory advocates have not convinced society that the public role in operating each industry should simply be dissemination of information on risks and costs, and let the buyer beware (see Chapter 18).

A number of barriers impede competition in the health field. While there is sufficient time to shop for maternity care, there is seldom enough time to shop in most hospital "purchase" situations. Conventional analysis says there is seldom a real "purchase" choice to be made, since the consumer, acting with minimal knowledge of medicine, goes to the doctor and says "save me." The doctor acts as the patient's agent. One might counterargue that an economist who purchases a jacuzzi has less knowledge of the equipment that the typical high school graduate has concerning medicine. Yet the economist, with the aid of *Consumer Reports*, can make an intelligent purchase decision. The ignorance problem does not preclude competitive markets in the case of high-technology consumer goods. However, this problem is compounded in the medical sector when "rival" providers and hospitals act in a collusive fashion—for example, when they restrict advertising or quality disclosure activities.

HMO Utilization Rates

HMOs utilize four basic approaches to controlling hospital utilization: (1) constraints on physician behavior, (2) physician incentives, (3) patient incentives, and (4) selection of physicians and a "style of practice" prototype profile for participation in the HMO. Different types of HMOs place varying degrees of emphasis on these four approaches. Homer (1986) in a survey of 93 HMOs reports these findings:

1. Seventy-three percent require prior approval of elective admissions.
2. Newer HMOs are more likely to utilize annual bonus schemes for physicians.
3. Smaller HMOs are more likely to use one type of bonus— ambulatory care incentive payments for physicians.
4. Independent Practice Associations (IPAs) are less able to select physicians who order less inpatient services and admis-

sions (conservative practice style) for the plan because participation is nonexclusive (open to any medical society member
in most cases).
5. IPAs are less able to confine treatment to ambulatory care
facilities because they do not directly operate such facilities.

Average hospitalization rates reported for HMOs—415 bed days
per 1,000 enrollees or 381 bed days for enrollees under age 65—as
with any insurer, represent the days paid for by the HMOs. Mott
(1986) lists 15 ways in which enrollees are hospitalized while their
HMOs are unaware of or not reporting these days. The quantity of
out-of-plan utilization is hard to estimate and may inflate actual
hospital usage statistics from 5 to 20 percent. Luft (1979) was the
first to point out that data concerning out-of-plan hospital usage,
while seemingly objective, are really a hodgepodge of confusing,
ill-defined figures. However, the days of hospitalization per 1,000
enrollees have declined 3 to 4 percent each year from June 1983 to
June 1986. A large part of this decline may have come about
because of heightened competition between prepaid plans, but
how much of this decline may have resulted from increased out-of-
plan hospitalizations is impossible to estimate.

HMOs have obvious incentives to curtail hospital utilizations
and specialist referrals (Ermann, 1986). The incentive-based physician as a "gatekeeper" model places the clinician under some
financial risk. For example, secondary resource pools (funds) are
set up, and if the primary physician needs to refer, the cost comes
out of his or her pocket up to a certain point ($1,500, $2,000). After
that point, reinsurance kicks in, but the gatekeeper is still liable for
enough financial risk to discourage inappropriate referrals. Some
specialists argue that this creates restricted access to some appropriate referrals. Advocates of gatekeeper HMOs argue that underutilization is not a major problem and that specialists desire a
continued supply of inappropriate referrals to guarantee their
target incomes. Short-run profit taking may not lead to long-run
inefficient referral patterns assuming ethical clinician behavior. At
the end of the year, if there is any money left in the primary pool,
the primary care physician gets a share. However, physicians
realize that failure to make appropriate referrals often results in
failure to obtain early diagnoses, resulting in more costly (and
more frequent) inpatient expenses (and withdrawals from their risk
pool fund).

In staff model HMOs, the primary care physicians are salaried.
Capitated or salaried "gatekeepers" lack the direct financial incentive to improve earnings by restraining costs. However, they may

still prove effective as gatekeepers for reasons of professional pride, preventive medicine, and long-run concern for balancing service and solvency in their HMO. However, in an understaffed staff HMO, the gatekeeper may refer too many inappropriate cases to the specialists, especially if they are very busy (or uncompensated for working any harder). Under no circumstances do HMOs offer an incentive to overhospitalize, especially given the paperwork burden of preadmission authorization and second opinions for elective surgery.

From the patient perspective, the access to specialty referrals may pose a problem. Referrals are less of a problem for the consumer in large staff or group model HMOs, where they can simply walk down the hall to the specialist's office. However, in an IPA model HMO, the consumer often has to travel to a different office building. A second potential problem involves consumer expectations. Some consumers unrealistically expect a plastic surgeon for every small cut and a specialist for every minor complaint. This segment of the market would be wise to avoid enrolling in HMOs. Moreover, any HMO that caters to such whims must either go out of business or find subspecialists willing to work for $10 per hour.

Types of HMOs

There are four basic types of HMOs: staff, medical group, independent practice associations (IPAs), and networks. Staff model HMOs hire physicians as salaried employees—for example, Group Health Cooperative (340,000 enrollees) of Puget Sound in Seattle; or ANCHOR Health Plan in Chicago (Rush-Presbyterian, 138,000 enrollees); and Group Health in Washington, D.C. (150,000 enrollees). Group model HMOs function as a medical group practice, with a number of physicians operating as a partnership or corporation that contracts with HMO management and the insurance plan to provide services, pool income, and redistribute income according to a predetermined formula. There are two basic variations of the group model HMO. In the dual group model, the group contracts with a nonrelated HMO corporation for physician services (e.g., Kaiser Health Plan with Permanente Clinic physicians, and Peak Health Plan with Colorado Springs Medical Center physician group). In the single-entity group model, the physician group constructs its own HMO, health plan, and insurance entity as separate product lines, with a budget incorporated as part of the medical group. Because they are seldom sufficiently capitalized, these second subcategory group HMOs are few in number (e.g., Western Clinic in Tacoma and the former Palo Alto Medical Clinic corporation).

The third variety of HMO, the independent practice association (IPA), is a separate legal entity from the HMO that contracts with individual physicians practicing in a traditional office setting. There are two basic subcategories of IPAs. The oldest variation of IPA contracts with a separate entity (other HMOs) to provide physician services on a fee-for-service basis with a hold-back–risk-pool provision (10 to 35 percent of charges are held in the pool to be redistributed at the end of the year if the utilization experience has been sufficiently constrained). The second variation of an IPA actually develops and controls its own separate HMO plan. This second type of IPA is increasingly popular since the federal office of HMOs recognized this model as a legitimate federally qualified HMO in 1981 (e.g., CoMed in Cedar Knolls, and Crossroads IPA in East Orange, New Jersey). Prior to 1981, the federally qualified HMO would have to operate two separate corporations, even if it had the same board and administrative staff. Both types of IPAs utilize the risk-pool–hold-back mechanism in case utilization levels break the budget.

IPAs and staff model HMOs are not frequently used with or by group practice HMOs. IPAs were often marketed to physicians as a defensive reaction by organized medicine to the spread of group or staff model HMOs in the area. IPAs are formed from state or county medical societies or hospital medical staffs to create an economic bargaining unit to negotiate with all the managed care brokers (nonprofit and proprietary HMOs).

To add further complexity to the issues, there is a fourth type of HMO called the network plan. Blue Cross/Blue Shield, five for-profit hospital chains, and two nonprofit co-ops or alliances have developed network HMO models to compete with smaller local HMOs for prepaid business. For example, the Voluntary Hospitals of America (VHA) and Aetna Life Insurance initiated a contract with the Teamsters in 1985 to provide 270,000 union members and retirees with service through a network of HMOs and PPOs. The VHA is a for-profit company owned by 79 nonprofit hospitals, each of which is affiliated with other hospitals in its region (431 affiliates). The network HMO option is franchised to local providers, IPAs, and staff HMOs, as potential partners with the regional network, to provide prepaid care. For this reason, network HMOs are best labeled "multimodel franchises" that cover a city, state, or multistate region. Networks are especially attractive to multistate employers, a factor that helps explain why this fourth hybrid model HMO has great growth potential. To improve their market share 25 pecent per year, 1986–1988, the networks increasingly will have to involve group and staff HMOs and not rely on IPAs.

HMO Growth

President Nixon's vision of 40 million American HMO enrollees by 1980 has not been realized. Only 10 million Americans were in HMOs as of 1981 (Table 7.1). In 1986, 3.2 million Americans were enrolled in staff HMOs, 6.7 million in group HMOs, 8.0 million in IPAs, and 5.4 million in network HMOs. Without adjusting for area wage differences, the staff HMOs tend to be more expensive than the other three types, averaging $214 per family premium (compared with $198 to $205 for the others). Network HMOs offer the least expensive premiums and the lowest hospital utilization rates (350 bed days per 1,000 enrollees). After adding only 400,000 members in the past year, network HMOs could utilize their price attractiveness to grow substantially in 1987–88.

The majority of Medicare HMO enrollees are concentrated in three states (California, 377,000; Florida, 180,000; and Minnesota, 82,000). The majority of the 660,000 Medicaid enrollees in HMOs

Table 7.1   National HMO Census Data from the Office of Health Maintenance Organizations—Public Health Service

Year	Prepaid Health Plans (PHP)	Enrollment (in millions)	Percentage of U.S. Population Enrolled
1970, January	26	2.9	1.4
1973, Fall*	140	5.2	2.5
1975, June	178	5.7	2.6
1977, June	165	6.3	2.9
1979, June	215	8.2	3.6
1981, June	243	10.2	4.4
1982, June	265	10.8	4.7
1983, June	280	12.5	5.3
1984, June	306	15.1	6.4
1985, June	392	18.9	7.9
1985, December	480	21.1	8.6
1986, June	560	23.3	9.4
1988, est.	700+	28–41	11–16
1990, est.	800	34–64	13–25

SOURCE: National HMO Census 1986, Interstudy. Estimates by the author. 1970 and 1973 figures by DHHS, OHMOs.
*The HMO Act, P.L. 93–222, was passed in 1973.

are located in four states (California, Illinois, Michigan, and Wisconsin). In terms of total HMO enrollment, California has nearly 7 million HMO members, and eight other states have 1 to 2 million enrollees (Florida, Illinois, Massachusetts, Michigan, Minnesota, New York, Ohio, and Wisconsin).

The most rapidly growing segment of the HMO industry is the IPA. During 1985, IPAs increased 38 percent in enrollment and 35 percent in the number of plans (Interstudy, 1986). As of December 1985, IPAs accounted for a 51 percent majority of all plans (245 of 480). As of June 1986, only half of the HMOs were federally qualified (down from 60 percent in June 1985), but these older more established plans still account for 75 percent of all enrollees (23.3 million). The fraction of enrollees in nonprofit plans is on the decline as the smaller for-profit plans grow rapidly. Nonprofit enrollees as a fraction of HMO members declined from 74 percent in June 1985, to 65 percent in December 1985, to only 58 percent in June 1986. As a fraction of the total number of plans, for-profit HMOs increased from 36 percent of all plans in June 1985 to 55 percent of plans in 1986 (Interstudy, 1986).

The federal government has promoted HMOs since 1973 by requiring "dual choice" under section 1310 of the HMO Act (P.L. 93-222) and that employers offer at least one HMO if it is federally qualified and has requested to be included in the employee benefits program. In addition to having federally assured marketing access, HMOs were eligible to receive grants, loans, loan guarantees, and technical assistance until 1982. A developing HMO received a maximum $75,000 feasibility grant, a $200,000 planning grant, and a lifetime maximum $2 million development grant. Loans and loan guarantees were available to cover initial operating deficits up to a maximum of $4.5 million. Loans were also available for the modernization, construction, or purchase of ambulatory facilities (not to exceed $2.5 million per facility acquired or renovated). Until recently, most HMOs were nonprofit, and poorly managed HMOs were swallowed up by large, well-established HMOs. For example, in September 1980 the Georgetown Community Health Plan became the Kaiser-Georgetown HMO (55,000 enrollees).

Rural communities are less likely to be served by HMOs, presumably because of the lack of a critical mass (volume) of potential enrollees. This generality is not valid in all rural communities; for example, some rural areas have active business coalitions that have fueled the development of HMOs with sufficient initial start-up resources and promotional campaigns. An HMO offers certain rural areas the opportunity to retain resources and patients within the community. The percentage of rural communities served by HMOs has been on the increase: An estimated 15 percent of counties with less than 10,000 residents had HMOs in 1986 (up from only 4 percent in 1980); 25 percent of rural counties with 10,000–49,999 residents had HMOs in 1986 (up from 11 percent in 1980). Virtually 100 percent of urban communities had one or more HMOs available by 1985.

HMOs Go Increasingly For-Profit

Prior to 1981 the HMO industry was wedded to nonprofit ownership status and the sanctity of federal qualification. With the end of federal grants for HMOs in 1982 and the need for access to capital markets, the number of for-profit HMOs increased from 39 to 106 over the period 1981–1984. U.S. Health Care, with 270,000 enrollees in New Jersey and Pennsylvania, was the first HMO to be brought public (into the stock market) early in 1983. Shareholders were not sold on the basis of profits, since the firm had virtually none, but on the basis of continued growth. The stock price tripled from $20 to $60 in three months and was a "wild high flier" in the jargon of Wall Street, with a price-to-earnings ratio of over 100. Faced with substantial increases in employee and retiree health care costs, businesses jumped on the bandwagon as both HMO supporters and investors (Reisler, 1985).

Stock prices for HMOs have cooled over the 1985–86 period, which might best be labeled the fourth generation of HMO development. The progressive overlapping steps can be summarized as follows:

1. Prefederal government involvement. Prior to federal involvement a number of large prepaid groups were established (Group Health of Puget Sound; Kaiser Permanente, Health Insurance Plan of Greater New York; Harvard Community Health Plan). Initially, rural cooperatives in Oklahoma and other states began prepaid plans in 1928–29. Kaiser grew out of wartime projects in California and opened to the general public in 1946. The term HMO may have been invented on an airplane in 1970 by Paul Ellwood, but the concept was not an invention of the federal government.

2. Congressional support and sponsorship by large insurance companies. President Nixon launched the HMO initiative in 1971, and Congress passed the HMO Act of 1973 for grants and loans to facilitate development ($390 million in eight years). Large insur-

ance companies saw the need to become players in this new marketplace. Blue Cross, CIGNA, and Prudential, along with other companies, became major sponsors of HMOs in the late 1970s.

3. For-profit ownership. Rapid growth in for-profit ownership of HMOs marked the start of an era of managerial entrepreneurs in the HMO business in 1983. The release of contracts for Medicare HMO business in February 1985 marked the end of an era when many HMO stocks were trading at price-to-earnings ratios of 50–100. The promise of the HMO market segment was built on the observation that an elderly enrollee has almost fourfold the premium payment of an employed enrollee, so the revenue potential among 30 million elderly citizens was enormous. In such a heady period of growth, little was said about the risk of having 30 to 60 percent of an HMO's revenues at the mercy of federal regulators.

4. The managerial mentality. The year 1986 marked the end of the "honeymoon" period for HMOs and HMO stocks (which began trading at more reasonable price-to-earnings ratios of 20–35). The investor community began to react to frequent earnings disappointments resulting from insufficient capitation rates, poor forecasting, and inadequate control and communication. The for-profit managerial mentality has come to dominate an HMO market originally founded by idealistic advocates of preventive medicine. However, now the managerial mentality must produce results in terms of trimming cost behavior, cementing loyalties with employers and investors, and maintaining good relations with the physicians.

Major Players in the HMO Market

Kaiser is still the dominant firm in the HMO industry, but its 4.9 million members in 1986 represent only 42 percent of enrollees in national HMO firms (compared to an 82 percent share in 1981). The big four proprietary HMOs, and their projected enrollments by the end of 1986 include: HealthAmerica, 800,000 enrollees; United Health Care, 790,000; Maxicare, 690,000; and U.S. Health Care, 670,000. In examining these firms in Table 7.2, a number of trends become apparent. HealthAmerica tends to be low on hospital admissions but high on inpatient expenses. Maxicare tends to be the least costly on physician expenses and other medical expenses. U.S. Health Care spends the least share of its premium dollar on inpatient care and reports the best profit margin. This is consistent with the long-standing observation that

Table 7.2   Comparison of Operating Expenses as a Percentage of Premium Revenues in Four Large National HMOs, 1986

	Health America	Maxicare	U.S. Health Care	United Health Care
1. Inpatient hospital	39%	34%	26%	29%
2. Physician services	38%	36%	38%	37%
3. Ambulatory care	7%	9%	5%	6%
4. Other medical	6%	3%	8%	6%
5. SGA overhead	6%	12%	10%	8%
6. Total operating expenses	95.9%	94.0%	87.1%	86.3%
7. Pretax profits	4.1%	6.0%	12.9%	13.7%
8. Number of plans	31	12	4	15
9. Number of states	19	9	5	10*
10. Year the company became a national firm	1981	1976	1983	1979
1' Inpatient days per 1,000 enrollees	422	403	356	378
2' Physician visits per 1,000 enrollees	3.9	3.6	3.8	3.7

*Has IPA management contracts for physician groups in 15 other states.

controlling inpatient costs is "what makes HMOs tick." These aggregate comparisons are intended to be descriptive only, and a more detailed analysis would be required to standardize the data by age, payer class (e.g. HealthAmerica has 20,000 Medicaid enrollees; the other three plans have none), and geographic input price differences.

These four large HMO firms have projected after-tax 1986 profits that range from 2.2 to 6.5 percent. The HMO market will experience major competitive strains and shakeouts over the next four years. As a rough estimate, the net profit margins may settle at between 2.5 to 3.5 percent of gross revenues, or an estimated $400 to $560 million nationally in 1991. Approximately 30 to 45 percent of profits will be distributed from the corporate HMO to numerous joint venture partners (insurance companies, hospitals, hospital chains, and physician groups). With so much joint venturing going on in this industry, the fund-flow analysis will be exceedingly complex over time.

Analysis of HMO corporations is hampered by the "moving target" syndrome—that is, they change structure and partners so rapidly that it is hard to get a firm grasp on the industry. Indeed, much of the analysis in this section may be outdated by 1988–89, as these HMO chains ride a fast life cycle and mature quickly into broker/insurance companies. Given that HMO chains and hospital chains are viewing their bulk buyers as employer personnel offices, it should come as little surprise that they purchase life and casualty insurance products. U.S. Health Care, one HMO firm with 670,000 enrollees, has moved in this direction.

A number of insurance companies have significant HMO market share. In 1986, CIGNA had 900,000 enrollees, PruCare had 400,000, and Hancock Dykewood had 155,000. There are also a number of corporate HMOs such as Sanus (35,000 enrollees in 1986) and Jurgovin & Blair (50,000 enrollees expected by January 1987). This latter company was purchased by the hospital chain NME (National Medical Enterprises) in July 1986. Combined with NME's preexisting HMO capacity (112,000 enrollees as of the fall of 1986), the chain should have 200,000 enrollees by mid-1987.

Moran and Savela (1986) analyzed the financial structure of 217 HMOs. Over the past 36 months, 40 percent of these HMOs had negative profit margins, in contrast to the 32 HMOs that had profit margins over 7.5 percent. Because HMOs are relatively inexpensive to start up compared with other businesses, the long-term debt levels are very low. Furthermore, most HMOs have significant amounts of working capital and cash held in reserves.

The enrollment and profit trends of the "big four" HMO firms are presented in Table 7.3. The profit margins of the four firms are estimated using proforma income statements and balance sheets. HealthAmerica started in early 1981 as an HMO management company. Through management contracts, joint ventures, and acquisitions it has expanded into the most locations (19 states) of the big four firms. Unfortunately, HealthAmerica has had the most difficulty controlling costs and has the worst profit margins of the four firms. Maxicare is the oldest of the four firms. Started originally as a nonprofit HMO in California, the firm became for-profit five years later so it could secure additional capital through stock offerings. Maxicare acquired CNA Health Plans (a four-state network of group practices) and Armour Life Insurance. Although Maxicare claims to have the best information systems and cost-monitoring program, its profit margins rank a distant third behind United Health Care and U.S. Health Care.

U.S. Health Care was originally founded in 1974 as HMO Pennsylvania, a nonprofit IPA. The firm became a for-profit HMO corporation in 1983. U.S. Health Care's major risk factor is its heavy reliance on Medicare enrollment. The firm anticipates having 160,000 Medicare enrollees by the end of 1987. Not surprisingly, U.S. Health Care is the most diversified of the big

Table 7.3   Profile of Four Large HMO Chains, 1981–1988 est.

	1981	1982	1983	1984	1985	1986	1987	1988
1. *HealthAmerica*								
Enrollment (000's omitted)	98	269	403	487	790	970		
enrollment, high estimate							1,140	1,420
enrollment, low estimate							1,020	1,270
price/earnings P/E estimate						21	20	20
Operating Margin		3.3%	8.1%	12.5%	4.9%			
Profit Margin		—	4.7%	7.0%	2.5%			
pretax profit estimate						4.1%	3%	2.5%
2. *Maxicare*								
Enrollment	117	227	288	460	687	840		
enrollment, high estimate							960	1,130
enrollment, low estimate							880	1,030
price/earnings P/E estimate						27	25	23
Operating Margin		3.6%	5.3%	6.2%	5.4%			
Profit Margin		2.1%	2.8%	3.4%	3.8%			
pretax profit estimate						6.0%	5%	3.5%

3. U.S. Health Care

Enrollment	87	126	222	368	542	640	
enrollment high estimate							780	930
enrollment low estimate							740	870
price/earnings P/E estimate						29	26	24
Operating Margin	.1%	1.3%	4.3%	8.1%	13.1%		
Profit Margin	.6%	2.1%	3.4%	5.4%	8.0%		
pretax profit estimate						12.9%	8%	4.5%

4. United Health Care

Enrollment	101	125	133	317	469	822	
enrollment, high estimate							1,160	1,420
enrollment, low estimate							1,110	1,350
price/earnings P/E estimate						19	19	19
Operating Margin	9.8%	10.8%	22%	18.9%		
Profit Margin	4.1%	3.3%	2.6%	8.8%		
pretax profit estimate						13.7%	8%	3.5%

*In the fall of 1986 Maxicare doubled in size after purchase of Health America for $372 million and the purchase of Health Care USA for $66 million. Maxicare will bring central budgeting and control to both companies. Health America and Health Care USA were loose grouping of many separate HMOs, with little central direction and no uniform policies on contracting, pricing, or personnel.

four into long-term care. However, its long-run profitability is heavily dependent on the generosity of federal Medicare contract payment rates. The fourth firm in Table 7.3, United Health Care, started in 1977 as the parent company of Charter Medical. United Health Care has specialized since 1980 in managing IPAs for physician groups.

Each of the four firms' stock values were analyzed in 1986 using the traditional analyst's best estimate method. These firms are too new to apply Monte Carlo simulation or trend analysis. (The methodological approach will be different for for-profit hospital chains in Chapter 20, where there is no paucity of historical data.) Five points become clear in the determination of the appropriate value for the stock:

1. The "big four" HMO firms operate with enormous amounts of liquid assets, and U.S. Health Care and Maxicare have especially healthy current liquidity ratios.*
2. HealthAmerica and United Health Care have most of their cash tied up in working capital and are not as available for acquisitions as U.S. Health Care and Maxicare (U.S. Health Care has by far the best returns on equity—18 percent, versus 9 to 12 percent for the other three firms).
3. The return on assets for U.S. Health Care (12 percent) is also double the other three firms (5 to 6 percent).
4. The returns on these stocks to shareholders are negligible. For our projections over the nine quarters until the end of 1988 it is assumed that the price/earnings (P/E) ratio declines to the midpoint between the August 1986 value and the general market value.
5. Even assuming the P/E ratios in the 1986 column of Table 7.3, plus an assumed (generous) expected return of 15 percent, these HMO stocks are hopelessly overpriced. Maxicare and United Health Care are selling at over twice what would be expected given a normal P/E; U.S. Health Care is 60 percent overpriced, and HealthAmerica is 30 percent overpriced as of August 1986.

Creative Partnerships

After going through a honeymoon period of rapid growth and remarkably receptive investors, the HMO companies are mimick-

---

*These financial notes are not displayed in Table 7.3. In September 1986 Maxicare acquired HealthAmerica of Nashville for $400 million. Maxicare will be the largest for-profit HMO, with 2 million enrollees in 32 states (Stein, 1986).

ing the insurance companies in pursuit of the "triple-option" strategy. A provider of triple-option insurance sells a full range of HMO, PPO, and traditional insurance. The key issues are what firms will be in control and who will be the senior and junior partners. Two national HMO firms have purchased insurance concerns to broaden their product offerings to all three of the options. Small, weaker HMOs, PPOs, and insurance companies will be bought out by stronger players in the other sectors over the coming years. However, it may not always be easy for a firm to control an unrelated venture, such as running a small insurance company. Many firms might prefer joint venturing with a number of firms rather than owning an equity share in these companies.

In addition to the business risk of involving other companies, the triple-option strategy may not always be viewed as attractive by the employer community. Currently, the employers prefer the simplicity in marketing for one firm that offers all three alternatives. But in the future the quality of some of these plans may erode their popularity in the eyes of the employees and the employers. From an economic perspective, the HMOs should come to realize that these products are substitutes. Meshing the three activities not only poses an obvious business risk but also a revenue risk. For example, offering a cheaper product like PPO care may cannibalize more profitable HMO enrollment bases (Eastaugh, 1986). The market may quickly winnow out the losers, and many losers in playing the triple-option strategy may be acquired or recommit back to the base business in the 1990s. Regional HMOs (eg., Sierra Health Services and Pacificare) may be wise to leave the risk of triple-option play to the national HMO companies. In the short run, the risk-averse strategy will be to joint venture, not acquire, the complementary firms needed to broaden the range of products. The buyers cannot help but enjoy this situation: less cost inflation and more freedom of choice.

Controlling Provider Utilization

In the instances in which IPAs have instituted strong utilization review programs and restructured the reimbursement incentives to place the physicians at risk if the plan overutilizes services, the premium costs and hospital admission rates have been comparable to closed-panel HMOs (Moore, 1979; Egdahl et al., 1977). The two principal positive attributes of IPAs are that they avoid the large start-up costs of group or staff model HMOs and offer a mode of reimbursement, per unit-of-service, that is more attractive to private practitioners. Physicians prefer IPAs because they offer the benefits of utilization controls without the discomfort of closed panels and the economies of scale of a large group without forego- ing the convenience of private offices. Physicians do not like being placed under a financial risk. However, the IPAs that survive and grow reimburse physicians at only 70 to 80 percent of customary fees during the fiscal year as a hedge against potential operating deficits. If the control of utilization was stringent enough to allow a year-end budgetary surplus, then a fraction of the 30 to 20 percent discount fees is returned to the physicians. However, seldom is an IPA profitable enough to allow the physicians to receive their full customary fees.

Why do physicians join IPAs? Most of the 100 existing IPAs were started by the local medical society in response to declining patient volumes induced by the introduction of successful HMOs in the area. Some of the larger corporations have provided seed money for IPA development programs, often with the conditions that the clinicians are paid on a capitation rather than a fee-for-service basis. Employers and employees are also interested in utilization and quality audits of HMO care. A number of interesting studies have been done in this area.

The ordering habits of physicians appear to differ in HMO and fee-for-service settings. Epstein et al. (1986) studied ambulatory ordering behavior on comparable samples of patients among inter- nists in large fee-for-service groups versus internists in a large HMO. After adjusting for age, sex, blood pressure, severity, and duration of illness, the authors reported that 40 percent more chest radiographs and 50 percent more electrocardiograms were obtained among fee-for-service patients. The size of the group is not a confounding variable in explaining these wide differentials. The comparison is not one of "raisons versus watermelons," in that the groups are large in both the prepaid and fee-for-service sector. Epstein et al. (1983) have shown that the use of ambulatory tests may be twice as high in large group practices versus smaller groups. Their 1986 study suggests that the use of high-cost, high- profit ambulatory tests are 40 to 50 percent higher in large fee-for- service groups than in large HMOs. Given that much of this extra service is medically unnecessary, revising the fee schedules to downweight the profitability of such tests seems appropriate for charge-paying patients.

The style of medicine may differ in the newer, less financially solvent HMOs compared to the older, large, established HMOs. In large HMOs, where the risks are widely shared and capital investment has been largely amortized, there may be no more denial of beneficial care than under a fee-for-service payment system (Yelin et al., 1985). There is an obvious incentive for all HMOs to curtail nonbeneficial care, but there is a presumption that weak HMOs may succumb to financial incentives and shave the costs of some beneficial care. We do not have any hard evidence in this area because HMOs are not about to release such data and the professional review organizations will not begin to review HMO care until 1987–88.

One major study has been done to assess the income elasticity of HMO enrollees. Welch and Frank (1986), using the national data set, report a − .64 income elasticity of HMO enrollment and suggest that families of modest means are a natural clientele of HMOs. They found that families with lower reported health status are less likely to enroll in HMOs. One may never ascertain from retrospective analysis whether this is the result of favorable selection (by the HMO of the healthy), weak marketing of the HMO in areas with a sicker clientele, or simply a variant of natural selection (sicker people desire to remain with their current provider and not join an HMO plan). The limits of retrospective research designs are the major reason why the recent Rand health insurance study (Ware et al., 1986) of HMOs is so interesting to policy makers. On the positive side, the Rand study is a randomized controlled trial (see Chapter 2 for more detail); however, the HMO portion of the study involved less than 1,000 individuals in one HMO in one city (Seattle).

For-profit HMO firms may increasingly have to worry about more aggressive competition from tax-exempt HMOs with stringent utilization review programs. Schlesinger et al. (1986) suggest that for-profit HMOs have average costs that are 10 percent higher than their tax-exempt counterparts, primarily due to higher expenses for ambulatory care. In addition to better utilization review, one strategy to control ambulatory costs is to initiate co-payments. More recently, Welch (1986) reports that the demand for HMO enrollment is a negative function of the co-payment charged by the HMO for an office visit. Therefore, the co-payments must be balanced and modest in amount to make enrollment in the HMO desirable for the individual or the family.

The style of medicine practiced in HMOs may reduce expenditures by 15 to 25 percent, principally through a 25 to 40 percent reduction in hospital admissions (Luft, 1979), but is this style of medicine quality-neutral? In other words, for certain patient groups does the quality of care seem to be worse (or better) in HMO settings relative to fee-for-service care? One recent study by Ware et al. (1986) suggests that for one HMO the economical style of care may erode patient health status for the sick poor over a period of years. The Puget Sound HMO, a well-established plan, was studied as part of the Rand Insurance Experiment, 1975–1982. The initially sick (at enrollment), low-income (bottom 20 percent of the population) participants appeared to fare better for the group randomized into fee-for-service settings relative to HMO care. However, the sick and nonsick, high-income participants (top 40 percent of the income distribution) experienced a higher health-rating index for the group randomized into HMO care relative to traditional care. So, for the high-income enrollees, there are two reasons for joining an HMO: cost savings and gains in health status. The observed increases over time in bed days and serious symptoms were confined to the low-income, initially sick HMO enrollees. The sick poor appeared worse off at the end of the study period than both the free care and cost-sharing-care patients who were treated by traditional fee-for-service providers.

One lesson that could be drawn from the Rand study is that HMO care places more responsibility on the patient for compliance than the more aggressive and paternalistic fee-for-service system. Fee-for-service providers may cost more, but they have strong financial interests to coerce the additional follow-up care by telephone and mail. A follow-up study by Davis et al. (1986) suggests that poor people in the Puget Sound HMO are less likely to maintain continuity with the same physician relative to Medicaid patients in the fee-for-service sector. In addition to problems in communication or continuity of care, the poor may also have greater difficulty in arranging transport to the HMOs' centralized locations. What is disturbing about these two studies is that the Puget Sound HMO has two decades of experience in treating the poor and providing outreach programs. In HMOs without such an established track record and social orientation, the initially sick poor may not fare as well as the Puget Sound enrollees.

There are a number of study limitations in the Rand data base. The authors (Ware et al., 1986) point out that one should not conclude that Medicaid patients are better off in fee-for-service settings than in HMO care. The Rand experiment had a supply-side effect on Seattle physicians in that they paid fee-for-service providers charges that were 20 to 60 percent more generous than the Washington state Medicaid program. Consequently, physicians would be potentially more aggressive in following up a more profitable Rand/Medicaid patient than an ordinary Medicaid patient. That initially sick poor enrollees in the Rand study would have fared better under the standard Medicaid program seems unlikely.

In reflecting on the Rand study of Puget Sound enrollees, there is no clear relationship between quantity of care and health status. Contrast this careful research approach to the arguments put forth by critics of HMOs (1) that underprovision of care must be endemic in HMOs, (2) that HMO primary care "gatekeeper" physicians unduly restrict access to specialists, and (3) that quantity of care is critical to health status. Members of the media often cite these undocumented fears, promulgated by fee-for-service physicians, as if they were documented facts. The second point may be true, but this simply reflects the fact that better patient triage can be done in a managed-care setting than in the fragmented fee-for-service system. Underlying many media reports lurks the presumption that the quality of patient outcomes is directly related to the quantity of care provided. No such link that "more is better" has ever been established.

Prepaid Medicare

Slightly under 3 percent of the Medicare population, or 710,000 enrollees as of August 1986, were signed up with 150 risk contracts (HMOs, CMPs), and 66 more contracts are pending. The competitive medical plans (CMPs) are nonfederally qualified HMOs that serve Medicare patients. Over two-thirds of these so-called risk HMOs offer the following services as part of their basic or high option plans: eye care, preventive care, medications, and extended hospital days. Approximately 40 percent of the CMPs are offering ear care and extended mental health benefits as part of their basic option. According to the theory of consumer choice, under the assumption of perfect information, the elderly would pick the CMP or HMO that best meets their needs. Unfortunately, the elderly are a high-cost cohort of individuals operating with less than perfect information (on their providers, and concerning their future health needs). However, the HMO option may be a great deal for patients with serious chronic illnesses. Medicare supplemental insurance plans are poorly coordinated, overpriced, and poorly designed (Berenson, 1986). Therefore, it would be difficult for the sick elderly not to find a better deal in joining prepaid plans. However, the elderly with many preexisting conditions seem most concerned with staying with their existing sources of care and not shopping for an HMO unless their current physician is a member of a plan. Participating in CMPs or HMOs offers an ethical dilemma for the clinicians, because to do what is best for the elderly may minimize their long-run income.

If low disenrollment rates are any indication of the enrollees' acceptance of HMOs and CMPs, it is apparent that the elderly are satisfied with the services they receive. Advocates of prepaid Medicare are fond of pointing out this fact, in addition to pointing out an actuarial phenomenon known as "regression to the mean" (Shafer and Gocke, 1983). If the plan experiences adverse selection (expensive cases), its cost experience tends to regress down to the mean (get lower over time). Lubitz et al. (1985) report that high-risk elderly experienced Medicare costs 4.7 times higher than the mean, but by the next year their experience had fallen to 1.8 times the mean of all beneficiaries. On the other hand, favorable selection of the low-risk elderly also results in a regression up to the mean (in year one the low-risk group may spend 1.8 percent of the national average Medicare expenses but within a year this figure has risen to 55 percent). Moreover, if the HMO/CMP can only selectively market to a small fraction of its enrollees and their behavior tends to regress to the mean, the selection bias question may be labeled "much ado about nothing" by the health plans (Wilensky and Rossiter, 1986). However, if the prepaid business evolves into a highly competitive market, a few percentage points difference in cost behavior could mean the difference between plan growth, stagnation, or closure. Four rural plans have already announced they will stop their Medicare contracts because the rural AAPCC (adjusted average per capita cost) rate was $110 lower than the local urban rate, and their enrollees were heavy users of the expensive urban hospitals.

The General Accounting Office (GAO) is obviously concerned with offering too much of a profit in the market with a generous AAPCC formula. However, the GAO will have a difficult task determining whether the plans underpromote to the elderly sick, overpromote to the low-risk elderly, or work with their physicians to improve utilization review activities. Is any reduction in utilization the result of patient selection or provider education?

Future HMO Growth Rates

If HMO growth from 1986 to 1990 were to equal 30 percent per annum, 78.4 million Americans would be enrolled in HMOs by the end of 1990. Few analysts agree with the Bernstein report of July 1985 that predicted this blistering growth rate for HMOs (Abramowitz, 1985). HMO growth depends on the popularity of that form of prepaid care, competition from PPOs, and possible additions from PPOs (as many consider converting to IPA model HMOs or joining HMO networks). Table 7.4 depicts three possible growth

Table 7.4   Three Possible Growth Scenarios for the HMO Industry and PPOs, 1986–1990

	Enrollment Levels (in millions)				
	1986	*1987*	*1988*	*1989*	*1990*
Scenario 1: Highest Growth					
HMO growth: high; and a					
number of PPOs are converted to IPAs					
HMO census	23.3	30.4	41.4	54.8	64.0
HMO % of population	9.4%	12.1%	16.3%	21.4%	24.7%
PPO census	6.4	7.6	3.8*	1.3*	1.4
PPO % of population	2.5%	3.0%	1.5%	.5%	.5%
Scenario 2: High Growth					
HMO growth: high; PPOs stable/					
growth declining CY 1990					
HMO census	23.3	29.9	36.3	45.8	52.2
HMO % of population	9.4%	11.9%	14.3%	17.9%	20.2%
PPO census	6.4	8.1	10.2*	12.7*	13.2
PPO % of population	2.5%	3.2%	4.0%	5.0%	5.1%
Scenario 3: Low Growth					
HMO growth: low					
HMO census	23.3	25.5	28.2	31.0	34.1
HMO % of population	9.4%	10.2%	11.1%	12.1%	13.2%

*80% of the decline in PPO enrollees between scenarios 2 and 1 are assumed to stay with HMOs.

scenarios for HMOs. In scenario 1, HMOs grow at 29 percent per year by acquiring PPOs until the market washes out and growth is reduced to 17 percent per annum in 1990. In scenario 2, PPOs act as competitiors to HMOs, and average growth rate over the four-year period is 22.5 percent. In scenario 3, HMOs grow at a sluggish 10 percent per annum. Advocates of scenario 3 argue that PPOs and managed-care, fee-for-service hybrids will experience the most substantial growth, not HMOs. The fraction of the American public enrolled in HMOs varies from 25, 20, and 13 percent, respectively, under the three scenarios in Table 7.4.

HMO firms will not grow at equal rates—that is, there will be winners and losers in the shakedown and shake-up of the HMO industry. Partnerships between HMO networks and large employers are more capable of absorbing the search costs associated with shopping for the insurance option that offers the best long-term value. Institutions provide information to networks that is not typically allowed in advertising campaigns. The less informed small firms or consumer groups could benefit by observing the negotiations and behavior of the informed large employers and networks. Private individuals lack the resources and time required for an adequate search of the options.

Wide variation in consumer tastes is one major argument for advancing competition health plans—that is, if planners knew what individuals wanted, we could mandate the result and be done with it. Utilizing data from 6,200 University of Pennsylvania employees, Benjamini and Benjamini (1986) suggest that HMOs are a more efficient way of providing medical insurance for a relatively homogeneous group. The economics profession is in general agreement that consumers should be encouraged to make a choice among as many plans as feasible to enable more people to take advantage of their preferred plan. A single national uniform HMO plan of insurance cannot be optimal, as it is impossible for one plan to approximate the choice of most people when the group is as large and as diversified as a nation (e.g., Britain, 40 million). Many suggest that the optimal system consists of various local prepaid plans (HMOs, PPOs), coexisting with fee-for-service traditional insurance coverage. However, some analysts fear that this competitive ideal may consolidate and merge into an oligopoly/monopoly nightmare, with a few national "Supermed HMOs" totally dominating the market. Seven national Supermeds serving 280 million Americans may prove as insensitive to consumer tastes as the British National Health Service. On the other hand, local HMOs and local mini-chains of a few hospitals may stave off the current trend toward large national chains. We will discuss this issue further in Chapters 20 and 24. We will also consider alternative methods to improve the AAPCC formula in Chapter 24.

HBOs—The Newest Acronym

The continuing emphasis on cost containment has nourished a variety of new delivery systems: PPOs, CMPs, and the generic concept of managed care. The newest acronym to add to the list of so-called alternative delivery systems is the HBO, which stands for health benefit organizations. HBOs have been proposed for 1987–88 by Senator Durenberger (R., Minn.) and DHHS Secretary Otis Bowen to offer more profit incentive to the providers and the Medicare enrollee (in the form of cash rebates). Benefit packages contained in HBO plans would be highly flexible but actuarially equivalent to Medicare's under 1986 Senate bill S 1985. HBOs would offer more incentive for prepaid plan coverage of the elderly by giving the plan's managers more control over the distribution of their profit margin. Currently, Medicare law in 1986 requires the HMO or CMP to commit the profit margin to expanded service benefits, lower beneficiary cost sharing, or returning the money to Medicare. HBOs would have more flexibility to retain profits and return cash rebates (up to a maximum of $500) directly to the beneficiaries in their plan. In theory, HBOs would have more incentive to conduct effective utilization review and restructure cost-sharing provisions to yield more rational consumer incentives (within the constraint that the average cost sharing by beneficiaries would be no higher than under traditional Medicare).

HBOs have a number of potential problems, including how Medicare would appropriately price the HBO plan per Medicare beneficiary, given that the plan has an obvious incentive to enroll the healthy elderly. The tendency to attract healthy individuals is termed "favorable selection" or, if it is done deliberately, "skimming." Apparently, the federal government has overpriced the 1984 HMO contracts for the elderly by at least 5.5 percent. A July 1986 GAO study of 27 HMOs in which Medicare beneficiaries enrolled in 1984 suggests the plans attract the healthier and nonpoor elderly (GAO, 1986). This study indicated that mortality rates for Medicare enrollees in the 27 HMOs were 74 percent of the projected level adjusted for age, sex, and other demographic factors. Moreover, HMO users among the elderly had a significantly lower percentage of low-income individuals relative to the general Medicare population. Consequently, the Medicare program could be losing money under the rate formula set by the 1982 law. Premiums were set by law at 95 percent of the AAPCC the government would expect to pay for regular Medicare benefits in the traditional Medicare plan.

The AAPCC is computed according to 120 different HCFA payment rates (e.g., institutionalized male, aged 75–79; noninstitutionalized female, aged 70–74, etc.). The 120 rates are based on historical cost experience in the area and are published by HCFA in the *AAPCC Rate Book* each September. In addition to the calculated AAPCC rate, the CMPs/HMOs must calculate their own adjusted community rate (ACR), including a profit (and a reasonable contribution to a contingency reserve fund if they contribute nonelderly premiums to such a fund), which is the fair market rate the plan would have charged Medicare beneficiaries if the provider extrapolated from the rates charged to nonelderly enrollees. If the ACR of the CMPs/HMOs is less than 95 percent of the computed AAPCC rate, the plan must either provide its

Medicare enrollees with additional benefits (including lower out-of-pocket charges) or accept lower federal monthly payments. Risk is rather asymmetrically shared, in that all losses must be fully absorbed by the HMO, but any savings below the 95 percent of AAPCC must be shared with the Medicare program. Provisions of the 1985 HMO regulations allow the CMP/HMO to place some funds in a no-interest-earned "HCFA benefit stabilization fund," up to a maximum of 15 percent of the difference between the ACR and 95 percent of the AAPCC.

By setting the premium payment to HMOs at 95 percent of the AAPCC, the federal government expected to save 5 percent (100 minus 95). This assumption is valid if the HMOs enroll a representative cross section of the elderly population, but they do not. The 1986 GAO study reports that Medicare enrollees signing up for the 27 HMOs would have cost the government an average of 89.5 percent of the AAPCC if they had stayed in the regular Medicare fee-for-service program. Consequently, the HMOs had reaped an implicit 5.5 percent profit margin (95 minus 89.5) that the plan need not redistribute back to enrollees in terms of reduced cost sharing, increased services covered, or return of funds directly to the Medicare trust fund. Policy analysts are left with a number of unanswered questions, such as: (1) Doesn't it make sense to cut the AAPCC formula back to the 90 percent level (or 85 percent level if Medicare wants the plans to reduce utilization further)? (2) Don't health plans have enough profit incentive if we keep the AAPCC payments as generous as 92 percent to avoid resorting to HBO consumer rebates to the elderly? and (3) Would rebates to the elderly of up to $500 encourage the prepaid plans to attract more healthy elderly (leaving the HBO population even more unrepresentative relative to the general Medicare population, and redistributing Medicare funds to the HBO plans and the pocketbooks of healthier and richer elderly citizens)?

Conclusions

None of the competition health plans promises substantial immediate relief from the medical cost inflation problem. However, with medical costs inflating at approximately 2 to 3 points above the consumer price index, advocates of competition argue that society should not rush to a judgment on behalf of a more traditional regulatory approach. Many analysts see better potential long-run effectiveness in pro-competition incentive schemes than in quick-fix, short-term regulatory intervention. Many liberals still argue that long-term regulation in the form of global (health sector) regional budgets is the better alternative.

One of the reasons why "competition" rhetoric is currently popular is because the idea connotes so many different things to different people. However, if competition begins to make things rough for some providers, or if it fails to contain costs, a large fraction of the pro-competition camp will become embittered. The competition mind-set has one political advantage: If you go bankrupt, you cannot blame it on external regulations. Bankrupt service institutions in a purely competitive environment have only two scapegoats: poor management or poor provision of service.

The competitive capitation systems are only as good as the underlying price system, whether there are administered prices or market prices. Not surprisingly, Medicare's administered prices have posed problems for some providers. There has been some attrition from the Medicare risk contracting program. ChoiceCare and five other plans during 1986 declined to continue their prepaid Medicare contracts. ChoiceCare reported losses of $7 million and claimed that the adverse risk selection problem would retard HMOs' growth in the elderly markets unless some of the aforementioned health status measures are used to compute AAPCC rates. In theory the ideal AAPCC rate would eliminate all cost variations caused by patient risk but not those caused by plan inefficiency. A number of practical questions include: (1) How much would it cost to collect health status information regularly? (2) Would it infringe on the legal rights of the impaired elderly? and (3) Could the information be utilized to "game" the enrollment process and select favorable risks?

References

ABRAMOWITZ, H. (1985). *Bernstein Report on Health Care Growth Sectors of the Future*. New York: Sanford C. Bernstein & Company, New York Stock Exchange Member.

BALOFF, N., and GRIFFITH, M. (1982). "Managing Start-up Utilization in Ambulatory Care." *Journal of Ambulatory Care Management* 5:2 (February), 1–12.

BEEBE, J., LUBITZ, J., and EGGERS, P. (1985). "Using Prior Utilization Information to Determine Payments for Medicare Enrollees in HMOs." *Health Care Financing Review* 6:3 (Spring).

BENJAMINI, Y., and BENJAMINI, Y. (1986). "The Choice Among Medical Insurance Plans." *American Economic Review* 76:1 (March), 221–227.

BERENSON, R. (1986). "Capitation and Conflict of Interest." *Health Affairs* 5:1 (Spring), 141–146.

CUNNINGHAM, F., and WILLIAMSON, J. (1980). "How Does the Quality of Health Care in HMOs Compare to Other Settings?" *Group Health Journal* 1:1 (Winter), 2–23.

DAVIS, A., WARE, J., BROOK, R., PETERSON, J., and NEWHOUSE, J. (1986). "Consumer Attitudes Toward Prepaid and Fee-for-Service Medical Care: Results from a Controlled Trial." *Health Services Research* 21:2 (July), 429–452.

Department of Health and Human Services (1985). "Medicare Program: Payment to HMOs and CMPs—HCFA Final Rules and Comment Period." *Federal Register* 50:7 (January 10), 1314–1418.

EASTAUGH, S. (1986). "Differential Cost Analysis: Judging a PPO's Feasibility." *Healthcare Financial Management* 40:5 (May), 44–51.

EGDAHL, R., TAFT, C., FRIEDLAND, J., and LIND, K. (1979). "The Potential of Organization of Fee-for-Service Physicians for Achieving Significant Decreases in Hospitalization." *Annals of Surgery* 186:9 (September), 288–396.

ENTHOVEN, A. C. (1980). *Health Plan*. Reading, Mass.: Addison–Wesley.

EPSTEIN, A., BEGG, C., and McNEIL, B. (1986). "Use of Ambulatory Testing in Prepaid and Fee-for-Service Group Practices: Relation to Perceived Profitability." *New England Journal of Medicine* 314:17 (April 24), 1089–1094.

EPSTEIN, A., BEGG, C., and McNEIL, B. (1983). "The Effects of Group Size on Test Ordering for Hypertensive Patients." *New England Journal of Medicine* 309:7 (August 16), 464–468.

ERMANN, D. (1986). "HMOs: The Future of the For-Profit Plan." *Journal of Ambulatory Care Management* 9:2 (May), 72–84.

FELDMAN, R., DOWD, B., McCANN, D., and JOHNSON, A. (1986). "The Competitive Impact of HMOs on Hospital Finances: An Exploratory Study." *Journal of Health Politics, Policy and Law* 10:4 (April), 675–697.

General Accounting Office (1986). "Medicare Issues Raised by Florida HMO Demonstration and 26 Other HMO Demonstrations." General Accounting Office Report (July 16), HRD–86–97, Washington, D.C.

GOLDBERG, L., and GREENBERG, W. (1979). "The Competitive Response of Blue Cross and Blue Shield to the HMOs in Northern California and Hawaii." *Medical Care* 17:10 (October), 1019–1028.

GOLDFIELD, N., and GOLDSMITH, S. (1985). *Financial Management of Ambulatory Care*. Rockville, Md.: Aspen.

HOMER, C. (1986). "Methods of Hospital Use Control in Health Maintenance Organizations." *Health Care Management Review* 11:2 (Spring), 15–24.

HORNBROOK, M., and BERKI, S. (1985). "Practice Mode and Payment Method." *Medical Care* 23:5 (May), 484–511.

Interstudy (1986). *National HMO Firms, 1986*. Excelsior (January). Minnesota: Interstudy.

KAZAHAYA, G. (1986). "Risky Business: The Risk-Based, Risk-Sharing Capitated HMO." *Healthcare Financial Management* 40:8 (August), 70–73.

LUBITZ, J., BEEBE, J., and RILEY, G. (1981). "Improving the Medicare HMO Payment Formula to Deal with Biased Selection." In R. Scheffler and L. Rossiter (eds.), *Advances of Health Economics and Health Services Research*. Greenwich: JAI Press.

LUFT, H. (1979). *Health Maintenance Organizations: Dimensions of Performance*. New York: John Wiley.

McCLURE, W. (1978). "On Broadening the Definition of and Removing Regulatory Barriers to a Competitive Health Care System." *Journal of Health Politics, Policy and Law* 3:3 (July), 303–327.

McGUIRE, T. (1981). "Price and Membership in a Prepaid Group Medical Practice." *Medical Care* 19:2 (February), 172–183.

McNERNEY, W. J. (1980). "Control of Health Care Costs in the 1980's." *New England Journal of Medicine* 303:19 (November 6), 1088–1095.

MOORE, S. (1979). "Cost Containment Through Risk-Sharing by Primary-Care Physicians." *New England Journal of Medicine* 300:24 (June 14), 1359–1362.

MORAN, D., and SAVELA, T. (1986). "HMOs, Finance and the Hereafter." *Health Affairs* 5:1 (Spring), 51–65.

MOTT, P. (1986). "Hospital Utilization by HMOs: Separating Apples from Oranges." *Medical Care* 24:5 (May), 398–406.

REISLER, M. (1985). "Business in Richmond Attacks Health Care Costs." *Harvard Business Review* 63:1 (January–February), 145–155.

SCHLESINGER, M., BLUMENTHAL, D., and SCHLESINGER, E. (1986). "Profits Under Pressure: The Economic Performance of Investor-Owned and Nonprofit HMOs." *Medical Care* 24:7 (July), 615–627.

SHAFER, E., and GOCKE, M. (1983). *Going Prepaid.* Denver: Center for Research in Ambulatory Care.

SHOULDICE, R. (1986). "HMOs: Four Models Profiled." *Medical Group Management* 33:3 (May–June), 8–33.

SORENSEN, A., SAWARD, E., and WERSINGER, R. (1980). "The Demise of an IPA: A Case Study of Health Watch." *Inquiry* 17:3 (Fall), 244–253.

STEIN, J. (1986). "How HMOs Adapt: A Perspective from the Inside." *Business and Health* 3:10 (October), 44–46.

Survey of Current Business (1986). Monthly Report of the U.S. Department of Commerce 66:8 (August), Bureau of Economic Analysis, Washington, D.C.

TRASKA, M. (1986). "HMOs: A Shake-up and Shake-out on the Horizon?" *Hospitals* 60:3 (February 5), 42.

TRASKA, M., and MILENSON, M. (1986). "Managed Care: Will It Push Providers Against the Wall?" *Hospitals* 60:19 (October 5), 66–71.

VIGNOLA, M. (1986). "Health Maintenance Organizations: Performance in a Crowded Market." Report T–05 (February 28) of L. F. Rothschild, Unterberg, Towbin, New York.

WARE, J., et al., (1986). "Comparison of Health Outcomes at a HMO with Those of Fee-for-Service Care." *Lancet* 8488 (May 3), 1017–1022.

WELCH, W. (1986). "The Elasticity of Demand for HMOs." *Journal of Human Resources* 21:2 (Spring), 252–266.

WELCH, W., and FRANK, R. (1986). "The Predictors of HMO Enrollee Populations: Results from a National Sample." *Inquiry* 23:1 (Spring), 16–22.

YELIN, E., HENCKE, C., KRAMER, J., NEVITT, M., SHEARN, M., and EPSTEIN, W. (1985). "A Comparison of the Treatment of Rheumatoid Arthritis in HMOs and Fee-for-Service Practices." *New England Journal of Medicine* 312:15 (April 11), 962–967.

Chapter 8

LONG-TERM CARE: ISSUES AND OPTIONS

Those who care for the old partake of divinity, since to preserve and renew is almost as noble as to create.

—Voltaire

Palliative chronic care is as noble and necessary an undertaking as curative "make-a-save" heroic medicine for television. The "Cinderella services," as the British define them, may not get the budget or respect of high technology medicine at my Massachusetts General Hospital, but they are just as important for society.

—John Knowles

The nursing home industry, the largest long-term care market sector, spent almost $39 billion in 1986 (Arnett et al., 1986). Spending for nursing home care increased by 10.6 percent in 1985. This chapter outlines some of the financial possibilities for the long-term care sector. We shall emphasize the nursing home sector and six other, higher growth segments of this industry: life care facilities (LCFs), continuing health care communities (CHCC), congregate housing, home health care, hospice facilities, and social HMOs (SHMOs).

The elderly represent a growing segment of the population. If "elderly" is defined as age 65 and over, there were 20 million elderly in 1966, 31 million by the end of 1986, and a projected 60 million by the start of 2010. According to DHHS Secretary Otis Bowen, if FY 1987 federal entitlement programs remain unchanged, with no new federal commitments, 67 percent of the entire federal budget will be devoted to the elderly. The Medicare trust fund will be solvent through the year 2000, and $990 billion in the red by 2010. Consequently, while the supply of elderly citizens is definitely expanding, who will finance their care is a moot point. One obvious answer is that private funds will finance care for the elderly, as $2,200 billion in pension funds are paid over the coming four decades. However, federal and state governments still represent the principal financing source for many of the elderly. We will in this chapter survey the prospectus for long-term care insurance, which represents one sensible financial hedge that nonelderly workers could purchase against the possibility that sufficient public commitments to expand benefit programs are not forthcoming.

The American Association of Homes for the Aging (AAHA) predicts a need for 1.05 million additional nursing home beds (compared with the existing supply of 1.35 million in 1986) by the year 2000. The AAHA also projects a needed expansion of 800,000 units in retirement centers, representing a doubling in the supply per capita ratio. The AAHA projection is more conservative in the case of life care communities, suggesting that 116,000 more need to be built. Currently, 1060 life care communities serve 350,000 residents. Laventhol and Horwath (1985) suggest that 2,000 more LCFs need to be constructed. There will probably be a disequilibrium between need, professionally defined by self-interested parties, and supply (due to insufficient financing and payment sources).

Life Care Facilities (LCFs)

What LCFs Offer

LCFs are private-sector initiatives for the elderly to purchase housing and insurance for health and support services. The LCF population is basically healthy, typically between 69 and 76 years old, with a life expectancy of 12 to 17 years. LCFs are structured to meet the elderly's demand for independent living and to offer the guarantee of affordable life-long health and support care. LCFs offer the health insurance lacking in public programs and a brand of social insurance foreign to most Americans. The packages of housing and health services can be bought in three ways: (1) with a one-time entrance fee, (2) on a full rental basis, and (3) with an advance fee with periodic rental fees.

Under the first method, residents pay a prospective one-time entrance fee that covers housing, health care, and all services for the duration of their stay. The elderly should clearly understand that the entrance fee does not represent an ownership interest in the LCF—only a license to occupy. No additional fees beyond this lump sum are charged if the residents live longer or require more care than anticipated by the LCF actuaries. Most LCFs under this payment method have had to close or initiate a periodic rental fee, sometimes including a la carte health insurance premiums (method 3, entrance fee plus other periodic payments). Nonrefundable advance fees represent payments for future service and should always be considered deferred revenue. They should be amortized to income on a systematic rational basis, using a method that matches revenues with expenses. Because the LCFs' expenses will increase as the residents age, an increasing change method—amortizing a lower amount of revenue in the residents' initial years of occupancy—is the most appropriate method.

An LCF under the second method, on a full rental basis without any endowment fee, charges a single monthly or quarterly fee for housing and the use of all covered services. There is no obligation to render services beyond the contract period. A rental LCF carries no actuarial risk beyond the short-term package, so the owners need not be concerned with inferior rates of attrition or adverse selection problems. One selling point of the full rental approach is that the prospective residents need not sell their own homes to raise the entrance fee, in contrast to payment methods 1 and 3.

LCFs utilizing method 3, a one-time endowment fee with periodic payments, offer the most flexibility for all parties concerned. The rent can be fixed or adjustable (with inflation), and the endowment advance fee may be fully or partially refundable. Any portion of fees subject to refund should be credited to a liability account and are paid from noncurrent assets (the liability is long term for accounting purposes). In contrast to the one-shot endowment in method 1, the long-term liabilities should not be amortized. Some LCFs refund unused fees upon termination (dropout or death), while other LCFs issue refunds only during a specific 6- to 30-month trial period. When any contingency period passes, a transfer from a liability account to deferred revenue should be made. The refunds should also be contingent on whether the LCF apartment is reoccupied within a few months.

Any viable LCF should be sufficiently capitalized to assure maintenance of adequate reserves to tide the facility over the actuarial peaks and low points of occupancy. A few basic "derailment opportunities" threaten the viability of any LCF. For example, an LCF should never utilize the endowment fees to subsidize periodic variable costs or to finance the costs of capital expansion.

If growth-oriented dreamers would so cannibalize the advance fee pool, current service deteriorates and the attrition/withdrawal rate skyrockets; the LCF must then close.

A number of highly publicized bankruptcies occurred in the LCF industry in the early 1980s (Topolnicki, 1985). In their wake, nonrefundable advance fees are being displaced by more appropriately priced higher rental fees (Curran and Brecht, 1985). The confidence of the elderly and the investment community has begun to return for three basic reasons: LCFs are beginning to employ better financial managers, interest rates have declined, and health care costs are rising at lower rates of annual increase. The LCF market generally breaks into six tiers, depending on when the facility was built and whether the owners are for-profit or tax-exempt. Approximately half of the 1,060 LCFs are tax-exempt, but they do not represent the growth segment of the market. For-profit LCFs are growing at the rate of 50 per year. Hotel chains are also getting into the LCF business. In 1987 the Marriott Corporation will build a 324-unit facility in San Ramon, California. The LCF will be built next to a 112-bed new nursing facility (skilled nursing beds, personal care beds, and intermediate care beds). Entrance fees to the LCF start at $125,000, a portion of which may be refundable to residents (or their estates), and $90,000 of which is nontaxable.

LCF facilities built prior to 1978 are generally lower priced, having been built when interest rates were low and tax-exempt sources of financing were plentiful. Not only are the older LCFs better priced, but prospective residents perceive less risk in signing up with a facility that has a proven performance record of one generation.

Hospital chains are also diversifying into the LCF field. LCFs provide the multihospital system's parent hospitals with built-in access to a population who are generally affluent and can pay for services rendered. Potential residents concerned with access to quality health care may consider affiliation with a good hospital as an attractive selling point for the LCF. Many individual hospitals are also well capitalized, have a strong interest in after-care postdischarge services, continuity of care, and assurance of a high rate of return business from their elderly patients. Purchasing a minority share or an eventual controlling interest in an LCF is a prudent strategy for many large hospitals. However, old-line LCF advocates fear that hospitals may "medicalize" their system by bringing expensive procedures and unnecessary hardware into what should remain a "low-technology" service sector. The marriage of the doctor/medical model with the palliative/chronic care model represents another interesting side effect of Medicare payment policies. A traditional LCF may have two to three employees serving every ten residents, but the ratio may be twofold higher in a medical model LCF. The medical model is most popular in Medicaid states that offer generous nursing care payment policies. An LCF can be rather profitable if it can collect $55 to $80 per day for intermediate care, and $80 to $110 per day for skilled care, provided at a nursing facility adjoined to the LCF.

Future of LCFs

Growth of LCFs, as with other health facilities, is highly dependent on continued public support in the form of mortgage insurance, bond issues, and tax incentives. If a sufficient level of indirect public subsidy is not maintained, many LCFs may have to manage cost reductions and retrench the scope of services offered. Because of the uncertainty presented by tax reform, developers are being increasingly restrictive in their market segmentation and location decisions. From a financial perspective, it is better to target the elderly population over age 70 in the upper 20 percent income bracket. An estimated one-third of this population may be interested in LCFs. Some LCFs may attempt to target as a secondary market the 65- to 69-year-old population.

If only 4 percent of the elderly population finally subscribe to organized LCFs, it would take an elderly market of 100,000 to fill a 270-bed facility. Certain areas have experienced a more substantial degree of market penetration (e.g., 15 percent in Philadelphia; Coopers and Lybrand, 1985). As the LCF sector becomes a more mature industry over the next five years, failure to target the middle-class elderly with $50,000 to $90,000 in assets may result in facilities taking years to fill vacancies. According to a recent study by Laventhol and Horwath (1985), LCFs require more than a year of preconstruction marketing, at a median marketing cost of $2,800 per unit. With insufficient marketing, the proposed LCF will never achieve the 50 percent occupancy level of reservations necessary to begin construction.

Even though federal tax reform may inhibit the growth of for-profit LCFs in the future, a number of strong underpinnings remain to project growth for LCFs. The "graying," or "tinting," of America spells opportunity for developers who view LCFs as a chance to capitalize on the "last-time home buyer." Many LCFs will be built and operated as joint ventures, with the various parties placing a different emphasis in their marketing of the facility. Hospital developers of LCFs will emphasize continuity of care and the medical "campus" atmosphere, while real estate developers will market a "country club" spa and recreation atmosphere. Advocates of the medical model may be disappointed to find out that the spa life-style model sells much better in the marketplace. The image of the elderly is increasingly healthy and affluent—just ask Medicare enrollee actor Paul Neuman. Illness is not the unvarying accompaniment of aging. Moreover, aging only eliminates the capacity to live in the community for 5 percent of those over 65.

Financing Life Care

This section surveys the four basic financing options for LCFs: mortgages, taxable bonds, tax-exempt bonds, and federal financing. Conventional mortgages have two basic advantages. First, the deal can be done quickly; hence, the developer may be able to open units before the competition reaps a strong initial market position. Second, because of a lack of government regulations, mortgages can finance both the nursing home portion of the LCF and the residential units. Unfortunately, mortgages typically finance only two-thirds of total project cost, require a substantial equity or cash contribution, and involve relatively high interest rates.

The availability of taxable bond issues is a function of the bond market conditions and the credit rating of the facility. Neither Moody's nor Standard & Poor's rates LCFs because they find the concept "speculative and risky." Fitch Investor Services, in addition to doing most of the nursing home ratings, is the primary rating agency for LCFs. California and five other states issue insurance for taxable bond issues to reduce the speculative nature and interest rates of these bonds. Interest rates for taxable debt are still two to three points higher than tax-exempt debt, to compensate the investor for the tax liability.

Tax-exempt revenue bonds have been the primary source of LCF capital financing. Tax-exempt bonds can finance up to 100 percent of the project costs, even including the initial construction costs, in stark contrast to taxable debt and bank mortgages. However, tax-exempt bonds require considerable up-front financing for underwriting, legal fees, and debt service requirements. Tax-exempt financing is generally slow and involves sales to multiple bond buyers unless the offering is done as a private placement with only a few buyers.

Not surprisingly, the slowest method of long-term financing and the one involving the most paperwork is federal financing. Housing and Urban Development (HUD) recently reentered the LCF capital market after a 19-year absence (1966–1985). HUD issued a new regulation permitting FHA (Federal Housing Administration) mortgage insurance for LCFs and other continuing care or congregate housing centers, under the section 221 (d) (4) program. The FHA-insured loans are written to exclude financing projects that require residents to pay entrance or endowment fees. The financing of any LCF built under these covenants must be structured as a pure rental agreement, with health services insured separately. The facility built under section 221 (d) (4) regulations would be limited to elderly tenants who can afford market-rate housing, provided that 20 percent of the units are set aside for a reduced rental rate. Such federal programs are available to finance housing units but not nursing or medical facilities. Sponsors can offer a support services package of health services and meals at an additional rental fee. The distinction between life-care and adult congregate living facilities begins to blur under such restrictive covenants. The Agriculture Department's FmHA (Farmers Home Administration) also does a limited volume of LCF and congregate housing underwriting in a few rural communities.

In summary, the traditional LCF approach—charging a high entrance fee—has been replaced by increasing reliance on rental arrangements and a la carte purchase of health and support services. The survival of the life-care concept of comprehensive health care tied to housing is assured. Private investors are still attracted to LCFs, not for reasons of tax shelter but as a method of access to the tremendous purchasing power of many elderly citizens.

Continuing Health Care Communities and Congregate Housing

LCFs are the Cadillacs of the long-term care industry. Many individuals and families cannot afford such expensive housing and service delivery settings. Two affordable alternatives to LCFs are continuing health care communities (CHCC) and congregate housing (CH). CHCCs are similar to LCFs but thrust more of the financial risk for finding and purchasing health insurance and support services onto the residents. The elderly in CHCCs act as a co-op, meeting most of their own needs by living together and helping each other. Among the 460 CHCCs the prices vary widely, from a $45,000 entry fee with a $1,000 monthly fee, to a $160,000 entry fee with a $200 monthly fee. Publicly financed congregate housing is a more affordable alternative than CHCCs or LCFs. HUD offers rental subsidies through the Section 8 program to qualifying low-income citizens. Under this program the family pays a rent of 15 to 25 percent of its gross income, after deductions for health and child-care expenses. Assets are not taken into account in the calculation of gross income.

Nursing Homes

Patient volume in the nursing home industry has doubled in the last 12 years, even as the number of operating nursing homes has declined 16 percent since 1974. A number of nursing homes closed (2,900) in the late 1970s following the scandals concerning the maltreatment of helpless elderly patients (Vladeck, 1980). Currently, in 1986, the nation has 15,900 nursing homes; 77 percent are for-profit and serve 1.6 million residents at an annual projected expense of $39 billion. This volume dwarfs the $2 billion annual expenditures for life-care, $9 billion for other alternative care/housing settings, and home health care. However, nursing homes have had trouble attracting good managers. The low esteem with which nursing homes are held by many health workers is largely a function of the frequent stories of inappropriate utilization and abuse (Johnson and Grant, 1985).

One provider response to this criticism has been the increasing number of academic teaching nursing homes (Wieland et al., 1986). While this development is encouraging, the potential number of teaching settings is limited in a market where only 30 percent of the homes are Medicare-certified. The Health Care Financing Administration (HCFA) has made modest inroads (1985–1986) in improving its facility surveys by training state and regional surveyors to conduct their new survey instrument PaCS (Patient Care Services). In the private sector, the American Health Care Association has developed a comprehensive "Quest for Quality" program for nursing home managers and staff.

An estimated 68 percent of the 1.6 million nursing home beds are for-profit; and two-thirds of these are members of for-profit chains. The six largest nursing home chains in 1986 include Beverly Enterprises (911 facilities, 113,000 beds, and $1.3 billion in revenues); Hillhaven (a division of National Medical Enterprises, 331 facilities); ARA Health Facilities (a division of the Philadelphia-based ARA food service conglomerate, 294 facilities); Manor Care (157 facilities); Health Care Retirement (HCR, 149 facilities); and CareCorp (133 facilities). There is limited evidence available on the efficiency of for-profit nursing home chains. The recent National Academy of Sciences (1986) study group on for-profit medicine was able to cite only one unpublished study of 1,100 nursing homes drawn from the 1977 National Nursing Home Survey (Hiller and Sugarman, 1984). Chain for-profit homes had the lowest average cost, operating cost, and nursing cost per resident per day. The results summarized in Table 8.1 indicate that chain for-profit nursing homes have the highest before-tax net profit per resident per day after inclusion of nonpatient care revenues. (We shall review the for-profit hospital systems in Chapter 20.)

The popular notion that nursing homes are used exclusively by terminal patients ignores the fact that 28.3 percent of cases are discharged to community settings (Weissert and Scanlon, 1985). Good quality nursing care can result in higher rates of discharge back to the community. The Institute of Medicine (1986) study report, "Improving the Quality of Care in Nursing Homes," concludes that government and the industry have failed to maintain adequate quality standards. Quality assurance activities in skilled nursing facilities (SNFs) and intermediate care facilities (ICFs) are almost nonexistent in most cases. The report does note that the scandals of the mid-1970s are not common now, but significant room for improvement still exists. The principal recommendation of the two-year study calls for eliminating the regulatory distinction between SNFs and ICFs and using a single high standard to certify all homes. Under current law, SNFs are required to have a nurse on duty at all times, and ICFs are required to have a nurse on duty only during the day. Obviously, this distinction never

Table 8.1   Selected Nursing Home Cost and Profit Measures by Ownership and Affiliation, National Nursing Home Survey, 1977

	For-Profit		Not-for-Profit	
Measure	*Chain*	*Independent*	*Chain*	*Independent*
Net profit (before tax) per resident day	$ 1.00	$ 0.19	$ 0.32	$ − 0.66
Average cost per resident day[1]	22.38	31.43	40.50	37.38
Operating cost per resident day[2]	4.67	7.52	9.87	8.18
Nursing cost per resident day	7.25	10.14	13.71	12.06

SOURCE: National Academy of Sciences, *For-Profit Enterprises in Health Care* (Washington, D.C.: NAS Press, 1986), p. 90.
[1]Includes all costs (including operating, labor, and fixed).
[2]Operating cost includes the cost of food, drugs, and services such as laundry or nursing services purchased from outside sources. Excluded are labor costs (payroll) and fixed costs of capital expenses and rent.

represented an adequate mechanism to assess the functional, mental, and social demands of the residents. A state like Oklahoma, with 98 percent ICF homes, would be most dramatically affected by this proposed change in policy. Other states are already 100 percent SNFs (e.g., Arizona) or have implemented state Medicaid minimum nursing hour requirements for ICFs that closely correspond to SNF standards (e.g., Pennsylvania). The two-year Institute of Medicine study also suggested adding conditions of participation concerning the quality of life and measuring the quality of care (process, outcomes) for all homes.

The nursing home industry is being pressured to serve more acutely ill, post-hospital discharge patients because of recent changes in Medicare hospital payment policies. A number of analysts have argued that DRG payments under PPS systematically undercompensate hospitals for treating the frail elderly (Berenson and Pawlson, 1984). Hospitals have been discharging the elderly at higher levels of need for care (severity) since 1984. Nursing homes were not prepared for the onslaught of early-discharge patients, but PPS has also produced some benefits. On the positive side, a Rip Van Winkle, ready to doze for five years in 1982, could not wish for a better incentive system than DRGs to stimulate capital investment by hospitals in long-term care. Hospitals were not about to invest significantly in long-term care and purchase nursing homes and other facilities (e.g., home health centers) until it was in their best interest financially. According to the AHA annual survey, hospital-sponsored nursing facilities and home care programs have tripled in number, and health promotion and hospice programs have doubled since 1983.

Many nursing home residents start as private pay patients before they "spend down" and become eligible for public support. Approximately 38 percent of all Medicaid expenditures are for nursing homes, and 87 percent of all nursing home patients are Medicaid cases. Medicare, in contrast, covers less than 2 percent of all nursing home patients. The nursing home industry is de facto a Medicaid industry, a quasi-public utility that depends on state rules and federal payment guidelines. State rate regulators and health planners strictly control the supply of nursing home beds. In 1986, 13 states had declared moratoriums on the building of new beds. One recent study targeted four states as having an acute undersupply of nursing home beds: Arizona (21 beds per 1,000 aged), Florida (23), West Virginia (26), and Nevada (29), relative to the national average of 57 beds per 1,000 aged. The study's authors, Swan and Harrington (1986), identified 15 other states as having an undersupply of beds in terms of negative residuals when bed supply was regressed against seven population characteristics, hospital supply, and physician supply. These 15 states had a collective mean nursing home supply of 43 beds per 1,000 aged, and a range of 31–53. It would be interesting to see this study replicated with data more recent than 1981 and substitute provider supply variables included in the regression analysis (e.g., home health care, psychiatric care). Medicaid programs have a high degree of discretion with beneficiary coverage of inpatient psychiatric care, so nursing home beds and psychiatric services are substitutes for each other to varying degrees across states (Sheffler, 1985; Intergovernmental Health Policy Project, 1986).

The basic issues underlying any nursing home rate program involve setting sufficient levels of payment that assure adequate quality of care, an adequate return on investment to owners, and, consequently, an adequate supply of beds for the aged population. Within a homogeneous cluster of patients, any variation in profitability to the home under a fair payment system should be the result of efficient management, and not the result of differences in patient characteristics among nursing homes. Setting fair rates for ICFs, free-standing SNFs, and hospital-based SNFs is no easy task. Facility characteristics differ widely, but these differences do not explain the majority of cost differences per diem between homes. Sulvetta and Holahan (1986) report that very substantial cost differences remain even after controlling for both case mix and staffing patterns. Industry claims that cost differences are primarily attributable to a more intensive case mix could not be confirmed, even with a direct analysis of patient characteristic data (e.g., bedfast, requirements for assistance in eating, in-dwelling catheters, intravenous lines, incontinence, disorientation).

A number of states have recognized the importance of case mix in designing a more appropriate higher level of payment for the severely ill patient groups. The preferred approach for the 1990s might be to adjust rates directly in proportion to the quality of care, and resulting quality of life, for the residents. However, until such a very refined data system can be designed at reasonable cost, a DRG clustering system for nursing care patients represents a short-run solution to the problem. Fries and Cooney (1985) used the original DRG cluster program to partition 1,469 Connecticut nursing home patients into nine resource utilization groups (RUGs). The nine RUG clusters explained 38 percent of the overall variance in cost per diem. A more refined version of RUGs, with 16 clusters, explaining 55 percent of the variation in cost, is being utilized to pay New York State Medicaid patients starting in 1986.

One intrinsic problem with the Fries and Cooney (1985) RUGs

system is that it relies on subjective staff estimates of patients' requirements for nursing care. Asking the worker to rate the workload utilizing a 5-point scale can become a self-serving activity—that is, one works less hard on the unit if the patients are rated more acutely in need of nursing care. A better case-mix classification system has been advanced by Cameron (1985). He analyzed data from 1,151 patients in 23 California SNFs to develop a patient classification system made up of 13 homogeneous groups. The 13 groups, formed on the basis of nine independent patient characteristics, explained 68.5 percent of the overall variance in resource use.

Most recently, Arling and Nordquist (1986) developed a simple and reliable case-mix measure on a random sample of 12 nursing homes in Virginia. Two independent observers were present at all times during the data-gathering process, and a work sampling study was conducted for control purposes. Actual care delivered to 558 Medicaid patients was recorded over a 52-hour period spread over eight days. Cluster analysis revealed six uniquely defined patient groupings. The strengths of this Virginia six-group classification scheme reside in the reliability and validity of the dependent variable and the parsimony of the model. These Virginia case groups capture, without resorting to discarding outliers, the same amount of explained variance as complex models with double the number of resource groups. This is a classic example of "Occam's razor"—that is, choose the simple model if it performs approximately equivalent to a more complex model. This model explains over 55 percent of the variance, even with outliers in the model. The six groups should be tested on other patient populations in other states.

To enhance nursing home quality through reform in the payment system, Nyman (1984) suggests that nursing homes be paid a fixed percentage of the price they charge private patients, and that this percentage should be allowed to increase with the percentage of private patients in the home. Empirical results by Nyman (1985) suggest that quality is higher, and both average costs and the private price are lower in homes with a larger percentage of private patients. The fewer private patients, the more cost shifting must occur onto them to compensate for low Medicaid payment rates. If the nursing home can attract a substantial proportion of private pay patients, it need not overcharge each patient so much. One strategy that a few dozen homes have used to attract private patients—and to sensitize the medical profession to the special needs of the elderly—is the teaching nursing home. However, the private nursing home buyer is a price-sensitive buyer, as we observed in Chapter 2. Therefore the teaching nursing home may attract the elderly and their families on a quality basis but remain financially unattractive if the price is too high. Teaching nursing homes must strive to keep their cost behavior in line with a price structure that a sufficient number of private patients can afford.

Payment Rates to SNFs: How Much for Capital?

In 44 states, nursing home Medicaid payments are set on a prospective basis, or some hybrid combination of prospective and retrospective systems. Considerable variation exists across states as to how to treat capital costs, varying from a single payment to a three-way payment for interest, plus depreciation, plus a return on equity for the investors. Industry representatives argue that nursing homes should have the opportunity to earn a return on Medicaid patients equal to the return earned on private pay patients. Rate regulators counterargue that the charges paid by private pay patients are "excessive." A few Medicaid programs have progressively offered incentive "carrots" for efficiency. For example, in Maryland the difference between the Medicaid payment ceilings and the actual cost per diem is shared by the state and the facility 60/40; the home retains 40 percent of the differential. The Medicare hospital payment system under PPS is much more generous, allowing the hospital to keep 100 percent of the cost savings below the price line. Maryland officials should not be surprised that nursing home cost behavior clusters come near the maximum ceilings for payment, given that a 40 percent "carrot" is not a sufficient enough stimulus to promote productivity and cost reductions among most home operators.

The effect of insufficient return-on-equity payment rates on nursing homes has long been controversial. Rate regulators argue that nursing homes are sufficiently profitable. Economists argue that nursing homes have the worst profitability and cash flow among 167 business sectors (Buchanan, 1982). Regulators make a mistake commingling issues of operating profitability with return on equity invested in the nursing home business. A few states have faced up to the obvious problems with historic accounting cost treatment for capital payments. The so-called "fair rental" capital payment systems in West Virginia and Maryland explicitly recognize (1) that nursing home assets are increasing in value over time, (2) that accounting values do not rise with inflation and thus have been eroding (undervaluing) assets over time, and (3) that no incentives should exist for property manipulation and resale merely to extract, in a "backdoor" fashion, a return on equity out of the payers. Under fair rental systems, a simulated rent is paid based on the current value of assets, irrespective of the sales history or financing methods.

A cost-based or flat-rate-of-return payment system encourages frequent sales of nursing homes to revalue assets following sales at inflated prices and to restart the depreciation "game." Depreciation payments improve as a result of each sale, and many homes change owners every few years. The industry refers to this game as "trafficking," with many nursing home chains buying each other's homes in addition to investing in free-standing independent homes. However, adopting fair rental payment systems encourages ownership for longer periods of time, and more importantly, stronger incentives to invest in the quality of the physical plant and the services within the institution. Without fair rental capital payments, there is no incentive to invest in quality and upgrade the facility's reputation if the owners have to sell the facility every two to three years. According to Cohen and Holahan (1986), neither the West Virginia gross rental approach nor the Maryland net rental approach needs to increase aggregate payment levels to the industry over the life cycle of the assets, and both systems can provide acceptable (market) rates of return on equity. Fair rental capital payments create incentives for owners to seek the most efficient financing arrangements, because they reap the cost savings (and need not manipulate property ownership for maximization of reimbursement). Payers must not "rob" the homes by setting the rental rates too low, thus paying a return on equity that is below comparable investments elsewhere in the economy. If the payment rates are too low, capital will flee the nursing home industry.

Tight Rates and Structured Incentives

In many states Medicare payment was traditionally more generous than Medicaid payment rates. However, the May 1986 Medicare payment limits, instituted eight months earlier than had originally been proposed (January 1987), set tight limits for both hospital-based and free-standing SNFs. Free-standing SNF cost limits equal 112 percent of the mean per diem labor and nonlabor costs. The hospital-based SNF cost limits equal the free-standing limit plus 50 percent of the difference between that limit and 112 percent of the mean per diem routine service costs for hospital-based facilities.

Rates that are too low will encourage the SNFs and ICFs to avoid public patients. The larger nursing home chains are espe-

cially adept at minimizing their Medicaid market segment to 65 to
75 percent of cases, relative to the national average of 87 percent.
The federal government has funded a number of projects to reduce
the level of discrimination against serving Medicaid patients. Case-
mix-based SNF reimbursement has recently been promoted as a
strategy to encourage facilities not to discriminate against the
sicker Medicaid patients. A recent National Center for Health
Services Research study offered 36 San Diego SNFs special pay
incentives to treat the sicker (more dependent) Medicaid cases
(Meiners, 1986). The provision of incentives, through higher payments, created an increase in admissions and market share (from
.11 to .17 share) for patients with special nursing care as well as
help with daily living activities. Contrary to expectations, admissions did not increase for the much larger category of heavy-care
Medicaid patients who require help with all activities of daily
living. Perhaps the incentive "carrot" was of insufficient magnitude. On the other hand, perhaps society would be wiser to spend
its limited resources on alternative care organizations, such as
home health care.

Home Health Care

One major stimulus to the current rapid growth in Medicare home
health payments, in addition to the PPS hospital payment scheme,
was the P. L. 96-499 bill to liberalize home health benefits in 1980.
This bill for the first time provided coverage for an unlimited
number of home health visits and eliminated the three-day prior
hospitalization requirement as a condition for the receipt of home
health services. Since 1977, Medicare home health expenditures
have risen from under $100 million to almost $2 billion in 1986. In
this period the number of Medicare certified facilities doubled
(Table 8.2). Medicaid expenditures for the same decade have risen
from less than $30 million to over $550 million. From all payment
sources, home health care is a $5 billion industry in 1986, 51
percent financed by Medicare and Medicaid. Frost and Sullivan,
an international market research firm, estimate that by 1990
Americans will spend $18 billion on home health care.

The policy debate concerning home care versus institutionalization has raged since precolonial Elizabethan poor laws. In the
American context, pioneering hospitals developed home care "hospitals without walls" in the 1950s to compensate for the decline in
the rate of physician housecalls. Physicians in markets of oversupply have provided a modest rebirth of the home health care

Table 8.2   Medicare-Certified Home Care Agencies by Type, 1977–1985

Type	1977	1985	% Change
Proprietary	146	1793	1128
Private nonprofit	394	793	101
Hospital-based	319	1098	244
Skilled nursing facility (SNF) based	8	158	1875
Visiting Nurse Association (VNA)	494	527	7
Official health agency	1278	1224	(4)
Rehabilitation-based	7	23	229
Combination	48	57	19
Other	48	9	(81)
Total	2742	5682	

SOURCE: *Alternate Site Providers—An Encyclopedia*, Health Industry Manufacturers Association, 1986.

market, but home care is unlikely to become physician-dominated. If anything, experts argue that physician involvement has been too minimal (Burton, 1985; Koren, 1986). Housecalls as a percentage of the 1.1 billion physician visits with noninstitutionalized Americans have increased from 0.6 percent to 2 percent, from 1982 to 1986. Payment rates will limit the expansion in housecalls. Rates set for a home visit by a physician will never be commensurate with those for other hospital or office visits.

HCFA is playing its part in curtailing the growth of a booming home health market (DHHS, 1986). The rate increases fall substantially short of any inflation adjustment levels, and the regulatory requirements are increasing. In 1985, HCFA reduced the number of intermediaries from 47 to 10 designated to serve free-standing home health agencies. Reporting requirements are increasing, and inconsistent interpretations are prevalent. Still, many hospitals plan continued expansion into home health care, which leads analysts at Kurt Salmon Associates (1985) to predict a glut of home health care agencies in the future. Lower payment rates are the traditional payer response to any glut in supply.

Policy trends in home health care currently point in all different directions, like a pile of jackstraws. The marketplace is littered with the wreckage of well-intentioned home health agencies and "meals on wheels" programs. On the other hand, high-tech home care has been rapidly promoted by manufacturers. Insurers, HMOs, and PPOs are eager to pay for these high-tech services if they substitute for higher-cost hospital care. Antibiotics, chemotherapy, central intravenous lines, peripheral lines, cardiac pressor agents, and parenteral nutrition have become major product lines in home health care since 1983. For example, some 200,000 Americans have digestive problems each year and require total parenteral nutrition (TPN). If TPN can be done for $5,000 at home, it is substantially more cost-effective relative to paying $9,000 to $12,000 per month for inpatient TPN. Home health care has a number of major market segments: parenteral/enteral nutrition ($450 million in 1986), respiratory therapy ($500 million), dialysis ($360 million), cardiac monitoring ($70 million), blood pressure control ($60 million), and bone growth stimulation ($30 million). However, the majority of home health care services are still low-tech: incontinence ($1.2 billion in 1986), rehabilitation ($550 million), pressure sores ($400 million), urologic ($300 million), and durable medical equipment ($300 million). Projected growth rates, according to the Health Industry Manufacturers Association, are provided in Table 8.3.

The structure of the home health care market, as characterized by ownership, has also changed dramatically. From 1978 to 1980 there was an average annual growth rate of 7 percent in the number of home health agencies reporting to *Home Health Line*,

Table 8.3   Change in Compound Annual Growth Rate for Home and Self-Care Products and Services by Product Type, 1982–1985 and 1985–1987 (estimated; constant 1982 retail dollars)

Type of Home Care	1982–1985*	1985–1987
Durable medical equipment (DME)	13	10
Rehabilitation	13	10
Respiratory therapy	13	10
Ostomy	5	4
Incontinence	33	20
Urologicals	6	5
Pressure sores	15	10
Enteral and parenteral nutrition	40	30
Dialysis	16	14
Bone growth stimulation	18	8
Nerve stimulation	15	11
Apnea	9	5
Blood pressure	18	8
Cardiac monitoring	25	12
Diabetes	20	16
Total $/average %	18%	15%

SOURCE: Health Industry Manufacturers Association.
*$4.4 billion retail in 1985.

in contrast to a 14 percent growth rate from 1981 to 1983 and a 19 percent growth rate from 1984 to 1986. The most significant growth rates in the market have been hospital-based home health agencies (349 in January 1980, compared with 2,100 Medicare-certified agencies at the end of 1986); proprietary agencies (185 in 1980, 2,200 in 1986); and private, nonprofit agencies (443 free-standing in 1980, 1,000 in 1986). The most stagnant sectors in the home health market are the Visiting Nurse Association agencies (511 in 1980, 530 in 1986), and the government home health agencies (1,274 in 1980, 1,100 in 1986).

Some 5.5 million elderly require help in the tasks of daily living. Approximately 80 percent of this help comes in the form of unpaid assistance from friends and relatives. Home health care assists all concerned in maintaining the activities of daily living, such that the elderly are not forced into an institution (Haug, 1985). According to one recent survey, home health care patients are younger and less functionally disabled than nursing home patients (Kramer et al., 1985). For years, advocates of home health care had hoped that "low-tech" provision of services would prove cost-effective relative to inpatient care.

Hedrick and Inui (1986) recently surveyed 12 economic evaluations of home health services. Home health care has no impact on patient functioning, mortality, nursing home placements, and acute hospitalization (in three studies hospitalization actually increased with home care provision). The total cost of care was either not affected, or it actually increased by 15 percent. Poor organization and fragmentation of services could explain why home health care has yet to live up to its promise for cost benefit. For example, Hughes (1985) points out that Medicare-reimbursed home health care not only lacks homemaker/chore services, but also requires stringent case management and referral services to prevent fragmentation. A new delivery style called *managed care* allows the broker or case-managing agency to assess needs for care, develop a comprehensive care plan, refer the patient, and monitor the individual's situation so that the care plan can be readjusted if necessary.

Case management in home health care has typically been very poor. Medicare requires that a beneficiary be homebound and in need of skilled nursing, physical therapy, or speech therapy in accordance with a physician's treatment plan, but physician involvement is so minimal as to involve only a few minutes of time (Koren, 1986). This is not to suggest that the case manager must be a physician, but more importantly, cost benefit is only achievable if the case manager takes the time to monitor the case closely. If the case manager does not get the appropriate services delivered on an intermittent basis, the patient faces very costly events (hospitalization or nursing home placement). The challenge for home health has become particularly strong since 1984. Because of the DRG payment system, home health patients are sicker, and coordination of care is even more critical than before (Kornblatt et al., 1985). Nurses or social workers, who may work for the organization to which they refer patients, have not been effective as case managers seeking to maximize either quality or cost-efficiency.

Our understanding of home health care agencies' shortcomings is equally matched by federal analysts' misunderstanding of the patient population. Very few patients who use home-based services will become long stayers in nursing homes (Weissert, 1985). Long stayers tend to be older, more dependent, and poorer in social resources than those who use home care. Few patients who actually use home care have their institutional stay averted or shortened. Patients who use "high-touch, low-tech" home care are most often using it as an add-on (complement) to existing services, rather than as a substitute for institutional care. The sickest and most dependent cases may be less expensive to serve in a nursing home or a clinic than in the home, except in the case of a few high-tech home health conditions.

Public support for home health care might best focus on functionally dependent people rather than on the aged per se. Home health agencies might be able to market their services on a cost-benefit basis with better case management. However, "low-tech" home health care might still have to resort to intangible quality-of-life benefits resulting from home care. Economics is not life, and the home care setting might offer benefits such as reduced feelings of isolation, better psychiatric support, and improved cognitive functioning. We all grow old, and it would be nice to do so in the best possible way. The current $5 million home health care study at Johns Hopkins, under the direction of Karen Davis, might shed some light on these issues in 1988.

Hospice Services

Hospice services for the terminally ill, emphasizing care in the home, were largely supported by charitable contributions until the 1982 passage of P.L. 97-248. Prior to this change in the law, hospice reimbursement for home care was insufficient because the visits required two- to fourfold longer duration of time to complete relative to the average home visit. The hospice benefit is available to terminally ill Medicare patients who have been physician certified as having less than six months to live. This estimate of when a case is terminal is no easy task for physicians (Brody and Lynn, 1984). The hospice will be reimbursed for two 90-day periods and one 30-day period during the patient's lifetime. The hospice faces a substantial financial risk if it admits terminal patients who need care longer. The patient may revoke the hospice benefit at any time and return to the previously waived standard Medicare benefits. In 1985 a cap of $6,500 per hospice patient was established, with the amount adjusted annually for inflation. The hospice faces a 80/20 minimum blend of home-to-inpatient care guideline and cannot discontinue care.

Religious sponsors and other advocates of hospice care have long argued that hospice care yields "obvious" cost savings by substituting for expensive hospital services (Paradis, 1985). In the view of many, those who are to die benefit little from intensive inpatient interventions to save their life when they suffer greatly in the process (Angell, 1982). Unfortunately, physicians are afflicted with a tendency to "oversave" and overtreat the terminal case.

A number of third parties have followed Medicare's lead and now offer the hospice benefit. Many insurance plans also cover family bereavement counseling. Medicare regulations require the hospice to offer bereavement counseling for the family but do not allow its reimbursement by Medicare. Such services can be paid for by the family or by other sources. Medicare cannot pay for such services, because the Medicare trust fund is targeted to provide services for Medicare beneficiaries.

Almost two-thirds of all hospice programs in 1986 were hospital-based or strongly hospital-affiliated (e.g., the hospital invests in the hospice and sometimes acts as a junior partner). Seven percent of the estimated 1,330 hospices are proprietary. The number of purely hospital-based hospice programs increased from 487 in the fall of 1982 to over 800 in 1986. Not surprisingly, larger hospitals tend to have hospice programs (21 percent of the hospitals with over 400 beds) in contrast to only 6 percent of the hospitals with less than 200 beds. Hospice programs are dependent on volunteers to help contain their labor costs, both in the facility and at home. Hospices rely heavily on a primary care person (PCP) to assist in all aspects of care for the patient. The PCP is typically a family member who must devote much time to the care of the terminal patient. The opportunity cost of PCPs should be estimated (shadow priced) in any comprehensive cost-benefit analysis of hospice care.

Mor and Kidder (1985) report results from a national hospice study of 5,853 terminal cancer patients in 25 hospices and 14 conventional oncology departments (the control group) over a 2.5-year period. As expected, the authors report that hospice patients consistently cost less than conventional care during the last month of life, but the cost advantage declined over the months for longer-surviving patients. If the data are analyzed from a prospective of cost and utilization over the last 12 months of life, the findings differ for home versus hospital-based hospice programs. Cost savings relative to conventional care accumulated in the first month for home care hospice patients persist and are even increasing slightly over the last year of life, for a net savings of 20.6 percent ($2,221) in the last year of life. The initial savings observed in the hospital-based hospices are considerably reduced over the months, to the point at which the cost advantage relative to conventional care ($12,700) is only 4.6 percent ($585).

These observed differences in cost for the two groups cannot unequivocally be attributed to the hospice, as hospice admission may reflect earlier patient choices made about the style of care desired. The patients in the hospice group, if they had been forced to receive conventional oncologists' care, might have been capable of forcing the providers to practice a less costly style of medicine than $12,700 (1982 dollars) in the last year of life (4.6 percent less costly than conventional care). However, the patient and family would not have received the same high-quality product, more bereavement counseling, and pain-killers that a hospice provides. As with home health care, quality of life becomes a principal argument for the less conventional care setting. Mor and Kidder (1985) also question whether the home care hospice would not have been less than 20.6 percent cost-effective if such programs were not able to attract individuals prone to low inpatient utilization. Good case management and "inverse adverse selection" (selection of short-living cases) are potential keys to financial survival in the financially unstable hospice industry.

Social HMOs for the Elderly

Protection from catastrophically high health care costs is becoming an increasingly recognized public problem. One alternative delivery system, the Social HMO (SHMO), attempts to efficiently coordinate care for older people who are most likely to have multiple health problems requiring the attention of multiple providers. SHMOs are prepaid managed care systems for long-term care and medical care geared toward elderly enrollees. The sponsoring organization takes responsibility for integrating a wide range of services for a membership. Under the 1982–1987 SHMO Demonstration Project with HCFA, a representative sample of the elderly, both disabled and able-bodied, were paid on a prepaid capitation basis at four SHMOs (Kaiser Portland, Elderplan Brooklyn, Ebenezer Minneapolis, and Senior Care Action Plan Long Beach). The SHMO is at risk for service costs, taking responsibility for operating within a budget, and generating a profit (or loss) depending on how effectively costs are managed.

If the SHMOs are successful, it is hoped that they will interest employers, insurance carriers, and government to encourage greater prefunding of long-term care (Greenberg et al., 1984). We shall discuss long-term care insurance in the next section, but HMOs face a number of the same generic problems (e.g., adverse selection). An SHMO can protect itself from attracting a disproportionate share of the sicker elderly enrollees in three ways. First, the SHMO can provide less than full chronic care benefits and a lower premium (to attract the healthier elderly). Second, the SHMO can cheat the system by screening potential enrollees on the basis of health factors outside the HCFA adjusted average per capita cost (AAPCC) formula, although the HCFA demonstration project prohibited such skimming behavior. Third, queuing, with a significant waiting period to join the SHMO, is a formal mechanism to minimize adverse selection, be fair to the payer, and collect a representative share of high-risk elderly.

Some of the SHMOs in the demonstration project may not achieve the projected financial break-even level of 4,000 enrollees by the end of four years. The SHMOs are enrolling Medicare-only beneficiaries and Medicare beneficiaries who receive Medicaid assistance. SHMOs are also designed to be budget-neutral for both payer groups. Considering a recent study demonstrating how one long-standing HMO appears to have discounted quality for poor enrollees (Ware et al., 1986), the Brandeis University researchers will be especially watchful of the SHMO experience of the Medicaid elderly.

The innovative impulse behind SHMOs resides in the integration of services and funding sources, so that the elderly are not shuffled from one provider to another. The business community should be attracted to the idea of "living within a budget," and consumer groups like the idea of reduced fragmentation of services. The HMO incentive structure encourages the substitution of earlier, less expensive, "low-tech" services prior to the need for expensive inpatient services. Reducing hospital use is essential to the ability of the SHMOs to support expanded long-term care benefits. In addition to promoting increased use of community-based alternatives, SHMOs should (1) decrease inappropriate nursing home admissions and (2) slow the Medicaid "spend-down" rate at which elderly beneficiaries expend personal resources. To advise Congress on what levels of cost sharing are most appropriate for the elderly, the SHMO demonstration sites offer different cost-sharing packages (Leutz et al., 1985).

Gerontologists and psychologists will be interested in the degree to which the SHMO case management system strengthens, or erodes, the informal, principal care person and family support system for the enrollee. In theory, as the difficulty of caring for frail elders increases due to the stress of precipitating events, the informal support network should be less likely to break down. Such a prediction assumes the extensive SHMO case management placement system works well. However, the system could break down if the case manager is perceived as an enemy who is forcing a too severely ill patient to be treated at home by overworked family and friends. SHMOs have a clear financial incentive to shift more burdens on the family, even while their efficient placement service should be faster and more effective at final institutional placement. There comes a point when very sick home care patients are better served in an institution; yet SHMOs have a financial incentive to underadmit such cases.

If the SHMOs are not providing good service or if they are overextending the patience of unpaid family and friends, one would predict that disenrollment levels would be high. If the demonstration proves a success, perhaps in the 1990s Congress will enact a SHMO entitlement for Medicare enrollees that will do for long-term care what P.L. 97–248 did for hospice care. Such thoughts are uplifting, but it may be hard to generalize from four SHMO demonstration sites. These four sites have extensive prior experience with long-term care; three have experience in case management, and two own their nursing homes and agencies. Consequently, the four sites have an above-average degree of experience and concern for their long-run reputation. If we enact a national SHMO program, shoddy "fast buck" operators may have less interest in ethics, equity, and service. One would hope that shoddy operators in the emerging SHMO industry are as rare as they are in the mature HMO industry, and consumers would shop to avoid plans with high disenrollment rates.

Financing Long-Term Care

Slow Growth for Long-Term Care Insurance

The aging of the population clearly represents a major public policy challenge, and new public programs may have difficulty getting funded in an era of budget austerity. Therefore, increasing attention has turned to the development of private insurance funds for long-term care (Getzen and Elsenhans, 1986). The pioneer in the private long-term care insurance business was Acsia Insurance Services. Acsia of California issued policies through Fireman's Fund Insurance Company starting in 1976. Consistent with the casualty insurance tradition of market segmentation, Fireman's targeted wealthy and middle-class residents in California who were capable of paying the premiums. The policies currently cover 120,000 families in the ten western states where it is approved for sale. Fireman's Fund is reluctant to market the plan in more states or to sell the policy to people over age 79. Fireman's will issue the policy to a person over age 79 if the spouse is under age 80 and insured for an equivalent or greater amount of indemnity (Phillips, 1984). Applicants of all ages are carefully screened to make sure they are not an immediate risk for institutionalization. At prevailing prices, a 65-year-old could pay $60 per month for a policy that would cover up to $400 per week in nursing home costs for up to four years. Individuals aged 50 to 79 can buy insurance for $35 to $170 per month that would pay $70 per day for nursing home care, covering an estimated two-thirds of the cost per diem for such care in the 1990s.

Insurance to cover the costs of long-term care has failed to develop in the private sector for a number of reasons. While a total of 44 companies sell some form of long-term care insurance for 200,000 individuals, the market penetration in any given state was disappointingly small in 1986. The group for which the premiums are the most reasonable, the middle aged, have little incentive to purchase such insurance in our prevailing youth culture. They have numerous other pulls on their income, from the mortgage to their children's education. The insurance industry would have to structure premiums to reflect actual risk at a certain age, rather than the lifetime risk, in order to encourage greater participation by the 45 to 69 population. Moreover, some public subsidy would be required to encourage significant market growth. The Heritage Institute has advocated an individual retirement medical account (IRMA) to encourage prefunding of long-term care. The investment return would be taxable, and although earmarked for health care would be owned by consumers to do with as they choose. DHHS Secretary Otis Bowen has suggested a voluntary individual medical account (IMA) to operate like an IRA (individual retirement account) for insuring individuals against catastrophic chronic care expenses (Bowen and Burke, 1985). However, Congress does not appear predisposed to support the IRMA or IMA concept given the tax reform debate concerning IRAs in 1986.

Bet the House on Long-Term Care

Home equity conversions are another possibility to finance long-term care. The elderly could tap the equity accumulated in their residence to free up resources for long-term care. If home equity and other property were taken into account, 40 percent of the elderly have potential annual incomes of $20,000 or more. Moreover, reverse mortgages and sales-leasebacks could increase available funds. The "catch 22" paradox is that people of modest means may jeopardize Medicaid benefits, food stamps, and other income by converting their home equity into monthly income. The average elderly household had a net worth of $67,000 in 1985, but one-third of the elderly do not own a home (8.3 million). Nearly 24 percent of the elderly have a net worth in excess of $100,000, but 5.6 million elderly do not own their home outright. Elderly homeowners rode the inflation curve to higher property values. The average adult aged 25 to 35 paid more for that first new car than his or her parents paid for their first house. Even if 90 to 95 percent of the elderly are no longer "ill-clad, ill-housed and ill-nourished," to quote both Presidents Roosevelt and Kennedy, one still needs to worry about the poorest elderly.* For example, we have a "feminization" of elderly poverty with almost one million women over age 70, living alone, in poverty. Isolation and depression were major problems among the 8.3 million elderly living alone in 1986 (80 percent female).

The American pluralistic tradition has been to offer partial solutions. Meiners (1983) advocates merging gap-filling Medicare supplementary insurance with catastrophic long-term care benefits so as to raise, in 1987 dollars, the premiums from $30 to $60 monthly to $65 to $95 for the typical 65- to 75-year-old individual. One should be concerned with issues such as, Do enough elderly have the purchasing power to afford such insurance? Is there a willingness to pay for such coverage? Certain elderly individuals have the risk-aversion to pay for such insurance. If one attends any public hearing on the topic, one is struck by the number of elderly who purchase four to fourteen duplicative medigap policies "just to be sure." Although these are atypical individuals, in general the elderly are highly sensitized to long-term care issues. Certainly, they have a good financial reason to be sensitized: The income of

---

*One can utilize statistics to argue in many directions. The poverty rate for the elderly (12.5 percent) is lower than the poverty rate for those under 65 (14.5 percent). Alternatively, if one considers the "near poor" within 125 percent of the poverty line, the elderly have 2 percent more poverty (19 percent of the nonelderly, versus 21 percent of the elderly).

the elderly increased only 7.1 percent between 1978 and 1985, while their out-of-pocket expenses for health services grew 12.1 percent per annum (AARP, 1986). In 1986, estimates were that the elderly population's out-of-pocket health care costs represented 15 percent of mean income and 22 percent of median income. The elderly were paying a much smaller share in 1979: 12.5 and 18.5 percent, respectively. This situation may worsen in the short run. The Medicare deductible for hospitalization went up from $400 in 1985 to $492 in 1986, and $520 in 1987. Medicare beneficiaries must pay the average first-day hospitalization costs as a deductible. Because PPS has restrained costs per admission, the government has substantially increased the cost per first day (from 16 to 23 percent).

Long-term care insurance is more of a product in search of a market than an emerging growth industry. If the nonelderly do not have the motivation to purchase long-term care insurance, the elderly have a number of basic misconceptions concerning their current insurance. In a survey conducted by the American Association of Retired Persons, 80 percent of senior citizens incorrectly believed that Medicare fully covers nursing home care (Fackelmann, 1985). In fact, Medicare covers less than 44 percent of the health care costs for the elderly. Medicare only provides 2 percent of nursing home revenues. The majority of the elderly erroneously believe that private Medigap coverage includes nursing home care (Lane, 1985).

Summary

We have surveyed a number of alternative delivery modes and financing mechanisms for providing long-term care. If we continue our bankrupt policy toward the nonrich elderly, there is little doubt that continued reliance on fragmented programs and expensive institutional care will return to haunt us in the future. We shall be richer as a society if we commit resources to improve the quality of life in our "golden years" and postpone morbidity and disability. We must still decide the parameters of our private and public investment in better health services for our elderly. Some analysts fear a demand-pull inflation and a flood of demand. Kane and Kane (1985) provide some evidence for this expectation in a study of the initiation of universal long-term care benefits in Canada. Three Canadian provinces added long-term care to their package of benefits at different times, and the expenditures for such care increased substantially. Nursing home expenditures increased at double the rate of hospital expenditures (e.g., 14 percent for nursing homes versus 8 percent for hospitals in British Columbia, 1982). Home health care visits per capita increased threefold over the first three years, leveling off from 1982 to 1984. Even with extensive usage of case workers to constrain cost increases, costs did increase substantially. However, the Canadian people proudly observe that they initiated universal coverage for long-term care because the role of a good society is to provide for those most in need.

The financing of long-term care is one area in which little progress has been made in the United States since 1966. American analysts often question the wisdom of enacting a national program to shift responsibility to a federal agency and away from what sociologists label "mediating structures" for private charity and joint undertakings involving the spouse, family, friends, the church, and other voluntary organizations. On the other hand, maybe the voluntary support system cannot keep pace with the aging of the population and needs public funds or tax incentives to assure quality care for the elderly. Our geriatric demographic imperative seems capable of outstripping our capacity for voluntarism.

References

ABEL, E. (1986). "The Hospice Movement: Institutionalizing Innovation." *International Journal of Health Services* 16:1 (January), 77–88.

American Association of Retired Persons (1986). *Aging America: Trends and Projections*. Washington, D.C.: AARP.

American Hospital Association (1985). "Life Care Industry Grows Despite Costs." *Hospitals* 59:23 (December 1), 41.

ANGELL, M. (1982). "The Quality of Mercy." *New England Journal of Medicine* 306:2 (January 10), 98–99.

ARLING, G., and NORDQUIST, R. (1986). "Nursing Home Case-Mix: A Model for Defining Intensity of Nursing Resource Use." Paper given at the Annual Meeting of the Association of University Programs in Health Administration, April 5, Washington, D.C.

ARNETT, R., McKUSICK, J., SONNEFELD, S., and COWELL, C. (1986). "Projections of Health Care Spending to 1990." *Health Care Financing Review* 7:3 (Spring), 1–36.

BALINSKY, W. (1985). "A Comparative Analysis of Agencies Providing Home Health Services." *Home Health Quarterly* 6:1 (Spring), 45–61.

BENJAMIN, A. (1986). "Determinants of State Variations in Home Health Utilization and Expenditures Under Medicare." *Medical Care* 24:6 (June), 535–547.

BERENSON, R., and PAWLSON, L. (1984). "The Medicare Prospective Payment

System and the Care of the Frail Elderly." *Journal of the American Geriatrics Society* 32:11 (November), 843–848.

BERESFORD, J. (1986). "The Future of Hospice Care: What Will Be the Costs?" *Healthcare Financial Management* 40:8 (August), 74–78.

BOWEN, O., and BURKE, T. (1985). "Cost Neutral Catastrophic Care Proposed for Medicare Recipients." *Federation of American Hospitals Review* 18:6 (November/December), 42–45.

BRODY, H., and LYNN, J. (1984). "The Physicians' Responsibility Under the New Medicare Reimbursement for Hospice Care." *New England Journal of Medicine* 310:14 (April 5), 920–922.

BUCHANAN, R. (1984). "Medicaid: Family Responsibility and Long-Term Care." *Journal of Long-Term Care Administration* 11:3 (Fall), 17–25.

BUCHANAN, R. (1982). "The Financial Status of the New Medical-Industrial Complex." *Inquiry* 19:4 (Winter), 308–316.

BURTON, J. (1985). "The House-Call: An Important Service for the Frail Elderly." *Journal of the American Geriatrics Society* 33:3 (March), 291–293.

CAHAN, V. (1985). "The Big Boys of Insurance Move into Nursing Home Care." *Business Week* (August 12), 79.

CAMERON, J. (1985). "Case-Mix and Resource Use in Long-Term Care." *Medical Care* 23:4 (April), 296–309.

COHEN, J., and HOLAHAN, J. (1986). "An Evaluation of Current Approaches to Nursing Home Capital Reimbursement." *Inquiry* 23:1 (Spring), 23–39.

Coopers and Lybrand (1985). "Continuing Care Retirement Communities: A Guide to Health Care Facilities." New York: Coopers and Lybrand.

CUNNINGHAM, R. (1985). "The Evolution of Hospice." *Hospitals* 59:10 (April 16), 124–126.

CURRAN, S., and BRECHT, S. (1985). "A Perspective on Risks for Lifecare Projects." *Real Estate Financial Journal* 25:2 (Summer), 65–71.

DEANE, R. (1985). "Principles of Nursing Home Reimbursement." *Healthcare Strategic Management* 3:9 (August), 25–33.

Department of Health and Human Services (1986). "Limits on Home Health Agency Costs—Final Notice." *Federal Register* 51:104 (May 30), 19734–19741.

DRANOVE, D. (1985). "An Empirical Study of a Hospital-Based Home Care Program." *Inquiry* 22:1 (Spring), 59–66.

EISDORFER, C. (1985). "Health Care and the Elderly." *Health Matrix* 3:4 (Fall), 25–28.

FACKELMANN, K. (1985). "Insurers Should Be Urged to Market Long-Term Care Policies." *Modern Healthcare* 15:1 (January 4), 62.

FRIES, G., and COONEY, L. (1985). "Resource Utilization Groups: A Patient Classification System for Long-Term Care." *Medical Care* 23:2 (February), 110–122.

FRIES, B., SCHNEIDER, D., FOLEY, W., and DOWLING, M. (1986). "A Classification System for Medicare Patients in SNF Facilities." Paper presented (October 1) at the annual meeting of the American Public Health Association, Las Vegas.

GAUMER, G., BIRNBAUM, H., PRATTER, F., BURKE, R., FRANKLIN, S., and ELLINGTON, K. (1986). "Impact of the Long-Term Health Care Program." *Medical Care* 24:7 (July), 641–653.

General Accounting Office (1985). "Simulation of a Medicare Prospective Payment System for Home Health Care." Washington, D.C.: U.S. Government Printing Office, Publication No. HRD–85–110.

GETZEN, T., and ELSENHANS, V. (1986). "Insuring Against Poverty from Long-Term Care." *Business and Health* 3:10 (October), 20–21.

GREENBERG, J., LEUTZ, W., and WALLACK, S. (1984). "The SHMO: A Vertically Integrated Prepaid Care System for the Elderly." *Healthcare Financial Management* 14:10 (October), 76–86.

HARRINGTON, C., and SWANG, J. (1984). "Medicaid Nursing Home Reimbursement Policies, Rates, and Expenditures." *Health Care Financing Review* 6:2 (Fall), 40–49.

HAUG, M. (1985). "Home Care for the Ill Elderly—Who Benefits?" *American Journal of Public Health* 75:2 (February), 127–128.

HEDRICK, S., and INUI, T. (1986). "The Effectiveness and Cost of Home Care: An Information Synthesis." *Health Services Research* 20:6 (part II, February), 851–880.

HILLER, M., and SUGARMAN, D. (1984). "Private Nursing Homes in the U.S.: Effects of Ownership and Affiliation." Unpublished monograph, University of New Hampshire, Durham.

HUGHES, S. (1985). "Apples and Oranges? A Review of Evaluations of Community-Based Long-Term Care." *Health Services Research* 20:4 (October), 461–488.

Institute of Medicine (1986). *Improving the Quality of Care in Nursing Homes.* Washington, D.C.: National Academy of Sciences.

Intergovernmental Health Policy Project of the National Governors' Association (1986). "Recent and Proposed Changes in State Medicaid Programs: A 50-State Survey." Washington, D.C.: George Washington University (Fall).

JOHNSON, C., and GRANT, L. (1985). *The Nursing Home in American Society.* Baltimore: Johns Hopkins University Press.

KANE, R., and KANE, R. (1985). "The Feasibility of Universal Long-Term Care Benefits." *New England Journal of Medicine* 312:21 (May 23), 1357–1364.

KERSCHNER, P. (1986). "Are DRGs Affecting Just the Elderly?" *Business and Health* 3:5 (April), 31–35.

KNICKMAN, J., and McCALL, N. (1986). "A Prepaid Managed Approach to Long-Term Care." *Health Affairs* 5:1 (Spring), 90–103.

KNOWLES, J. (1973). "The Hospital." *Scientific American* 229:3 (March), 128–137.

KOBLE, R., and DWYER, F. (1986). "Diagnosing the Physician as Gatekeeper in Hospice Marketing." *Journal of Health Care Marketing* 6:1 (March), 23–24.

KOREN, M. (1986). "Home Care—Who Cares?" *New England Journal of Medicine* 314:14 (April 3), 917–920.

KORNBLATT, E., FISHER, M., and MACMILLAN, D. (1985). "Impact of DRGs on Home Health Nursing." *Quality Review Bulletin* 11:10 (October), 290–294.

KRAMER, A., SHAUGHNESSY, P., and PETTIGREW, M. (1985). "Cost-Effectiveness Implications Based on a Comparison of Nursing Home and Home Health Case Mix." *Health Services Research* 20:4 (October), 387–405.

Kurt Salmon and Associates Survey of Home Health Care (1985). "Could America Have a Home Care Glut?" *Home Health Journal* 6:3 (March), 5.

LANE, L. (1985). "The Potential of Long-Term Care Insurance." *Pride Institute Journal of Long-Term Home Health Care* 14:3 (Summer), 18.

Laventhol and Horwath (1986). "Sixth Annual Report on the Life Care Industry." National Health Practice Group, Philadelphia.

LEGG, D., and Lamb, C. (1986). "The Role of Referral Agents in the Marketing of Home Health Services." *Journal of Health Care Marketing* 6:1 (March), 51–56.

LEIKEN, A., SEXTON, T., and SILKMAN, R. (1986). "A Model to Assess the Quality-Cost Tradeoff in Nursing Homes." *Health Services Research* 21:2 (June), 145–160.

LEUTZ, W., GREENBERG, J., and ABRAHAM, R. (1985). *Changing Health Care for an Aging Society: Planning for the SHMO*. Lexington, Mass.: D. C. Heath.

MANHEIM, L., and HUGHES, S. (1986). "Use of Nursing Homes by a High-Risk Long-Term Population." *Health Services Research* 21:2 (June), 161–176.

MEINERS, M. (1986). *Nursing Home Admissions: The Results of an Incentive Reimbursement Experiment*. National Center for Health Services Research, Long-Term Care Studies Program Research (March) Report Number 1 (PHS), 86–3397.

MEINERS, M. (1983). "The Case for Long-Term Care Insurance." *Health Affairs* 2:2 (Summer), 55–79.

MOR, V., and KIDDER, D. (1985). "Cost Savings in Hospice: Final Results of the National Hospice Study." *Health Services Research* 20:4 (October), 407–422.

MORAN, D., and KENNELL, D. (1986). "The Developing Market for Long-Term Care Insurance." ICF Inc., Washington, D.C.

MOSS, F., HALAMANDARIS, V. (1977). *Too Old, Too Sick, Too Bad: Nursing Homes in America*. Germantown, Md.: Aspen.

National Academy of Sciences (1986). *For-Profit Enterprises in Health Care*. Washington, D.C.: NAS Press.

New York State Department of Health and Rensselaer Polytechnic Institute (1986). "New York State Long-Term Case-Mix Reimbursement Project." Quarterly report to HCFA (Fall), DHHS.

NYMAN, J. (1984). "The Effects of Medicaid Reimbursement Policy and Information Costs on the Quality of Nursing Home Care." Unpublished doctoral dissertation, University of Wisconsin, Madison.

PARADIS, L. (1985). "Hospice: The First DRG." *Health Matrix* 2:4 (January), 32–34.

PEREGRINE, M. (1986). "Is Long-Term Care Protected from Imputed Interest Rules?" *Healthcare Financial Management* 16:7 (July), 50–55.

PHILLIPS, R. (1984). "The Fireman's Fund Experience." In P. Feinstein, M. Gornick, and J. Greenberg (eds.), *Long-Term Care Financing and Delivery Systems: Exploring Some Alternatives*. Washington, D.C.: HCFA, 37–44.

RODERICK, S. (1984). "A Vision of Long-Term Care in the Future: A Look at the Year 2020." *Journal of Long-Term Care Administration* 11:4 (Winter), 17–26.

ROSE, A. (1984). "Entrepreneurs Reshaping Lifecare." *Modern Healthcare* 14:7 (July), 150.

SCANLON, W., and FEDER, J. (1984). "The Long-Term Care Marketplace: An Overview." *Healthcare Financial Management* 14:1 (January), 18–36.

SHAUGHNESSY, P., SCHLENKER, R., and POLESOVSKY, M. (1986). "Medicaid and Non-Medicaid Case Mix Differences in Colorado Nursing Homes." *Medical Care* 24:6 (June), 482–495.

SHEFFLER, R. (1985). "Mental Health Services: New Policies and Estimates." *Generations* 9:2 (Summer), 33–35.

SIMS, W. (1984). "Financing Strategies for Long-Term Care Facilities." *Healthcare Financial Management* 14:3 (March), 42–54.

SKELLIE, F., MOBLEY, G., and COAN, R. (1982). "Cost-Effectiveness of Community-Based Long-Term Care." *American Journal of Public Health* 72:4 (April), 353–358.

STEPHENS, S., and CHRISTIANSON, J. (1986). *Informal Care of the Elderly.* Lexington, Mass.: Lexington Books.

SULVETTA, M., and HOLAHAN, J. (1986). "Cost and Case-Mix Differences Between Hospital-Based and Free-Standing Nursing Homes." *Health Care Financing Review* 7:3 (Spring), 75–84.

SWAN, J., and HARRINGTON, C. (1986). "Estimating Undersupply of Nursing Home Beds in States." *Health Services Research* 21:1 (April), 57–83.

TOPOLNICKI, D. (1985). "The Broken Promise of Life-Care Communities." *Money* (April), 150–157.

VLADECK, B. (1980). *Unloving Care.* New York: Basic Books.

WARE, J. et al. (1986). "Comparison of Health Outcomes at a HMO with Those of Fee-for-Service Care." *Lancet* 8488 (May 3), 1017–1022.

WEISSERT, W. (1985). "Seven Reasons Why It Is So Difficult to Make Community-Based Long-Term Care Cost-Effective." *Health Services Research* 20:4 (October), 423–433.

WEISSERT, W., and SCANLON, W. (1985). "Determinants of Nursing Home Discharge Status." *Medical Care* 23:4 (April), 333–343.

WIELAND, D., RUBENSTEIN, L., OUSLANDER, J., and MARTIN, S. (1986). "Organizing an Academic Nursing Home: Impacts on Institutionalized Elderly." *Journal of the American Medical Association* 255:19 (May 16), 2622–2627.

WINKLEVOSS, H., and POWELL, A. (1983). *Continuing Care Retirement Communities: An Empirical, Financial, and Legal Analysis.* Chicago: Richard D. Irwin.

Chapter 9

MARKETING, PRICING, AND SPECIALIZATION

> *People do not care how much you know until they know how much you care. Quality work does not always mean quality service.*
>
> —DAVID H. MAISTER

> *Marketing involves the identification and satisfaction of consumer needs. Marketing activity should not be regarded as an expensive, speculative drain on the resources, but rather as a planning process that can guide the allocation of these resources toward a more effective result. At the same time, marketing practitioners must clearly understand the value system of the health care professionals with whom they are collaborating; the existence of different criteria for the measurement of success; and the unique problems of consumer behavior.*
>
> —PHILIP D. COOPER

> *Producers and consumers do not need more expensive inpatient products. Give the public more ambulatory and alternative care products they can afford. Hospitals must once again become in step with the marketplace. Hospitals that develop services just to fill beds are going to be losers. We need a better specialty focus.*
>
> —JEFF GOLDSMITH

Pressure on health service providers to control costs and close facilities has stimulated interest in health marketing activities. Marketing consultants take the public stance that their activity can help the firm provide better service and be more responsive to

consumers' demands. Marketing is defined operationally as the set
of activities designed to satisfy consumer needs and wants, including delivery, advertising, selling, and pricing. In the past, providers seldom considered measuring and satisfying consumer preferences. During the mid-1970s, consumer groups in a few states
initiated programs for bland informational advertising in "Medical
Yellow Pages," giving schedules, fees, and location. In the late
1970s a few large urban hospitals, facing increased competition
from suburban hospitals, bad debts, and the added responsibility
of having their emergency rooms serve as the sole source of
primary care for the poor, initiated competitive advertising
schemes. The approach was usually linked to quality: "Buy our
product (for example, open-heart surgery) or our service (for
example, maternity and pediatrics) and you'll have a better chance
of survival, thanks to our experienced staff and teaching hospital
physicians." In one case, the publication of differential survival rate
statistics at two institutions caused the closing of the higher
mortality suburban service and slight expansion of the previously
underutilized urban hospital's service, much to the delight of the
medical school officials who needed additional patients for the
education of their students and residents. The slow/reactive administrators will continue to adopt a plodder strategy to pursue
"quiet" competition—for example, to accept slight changes in
customer mix as a fait accompli that should not result in open
predatory reaction among hospitals, because no single competitor
is strong enough to disturb the silence.

Many health professionals balk at the term *marketing* because it
runs counter to their feelings that health care is "special"—not to
be treated like a marketable commodity or service. The nonprofit
hospital industry has been criticized by Carlson (1975) and by
other advocates of holistic medicine for having a static, limited-
scope, product orientation that does not provide the consumer
with the necessary information concerning the product (health
services).

Marketing is seldom understood by large segments of the health
care profession. Marketing need not involve superfluous treatments and promotional gimmicks, or a legion of medical hula
hoops, pet rocks, and Cabbage Patch dolls. Real health marketing
involves consumer preference evaluation and better service delivery, with advertising playing a minor role. Viewed in this light, the
medical staff can become the hospital's service-line development
group, and HMOs or PPOs should be viewed as wholesale buyers.
A professional can still remain a professional and adopt some of the
techniques of the common merchant. No egregious harm will be

done to the professional practice of medicine if we trade a philosophy of paternalism for consumer sensitivity. The 1985 president of the Wisconsin Medical Society summarized this obvious point during his inaugural address: "Marketing is an admonition to do right by your patient; virtue is a companion of competition" (Scott, 1985).

Conflicts Between Marketing and the Nonprofit Ethos

Some nonprofit managers have the misconception that marketing is simply selling a fixed given product. Selling is only one aspect of the marketing process. Marketing is a process of assessing consumer wants by changing the product and/or the distribution channels. Marketing is not always a process designed to increase demand.

Marketing involves managing demand and improving consumer satisfaction. For example, a public utility may decide to decrease (demarket) demand for its product in the name of energy conservation. In the case of health care, a given institution or business coalition may wish to demarket nursing home care while promoting home care, or demarket inpatient surgical or psychiatric care in order to promote the substitute product—ambulatory care. One could postulate that the invisible hand and competitive pressures might induce a given firm (for example, a nursing home) to demarket its product to some extent and to promote substitute products (home health care). However, due to institutional inertia, the invisible hand often turns out to be all thumbs; nursing homes might prefer to maintain the status quo rather than to face charges of predatory marketing behavior that pulls demand away from their neighbors.

Marketing activities that are designed to communicate with and motivate the public to consume health care services have some unique problems in health services delivery. First, the consumption of health services is frequently remembered in negative terms; pain is often a deterrent to seeking medical care. Second, even if the physicians make the major consumption decisions, health managers should increasingly treat patients as customers and potential sources of return business or word-of-mouth advertising. If the emphasis of the marketing program is to redirect the locus of care to less costly sites and to improve patient education and compliance, society will benefit.

Hospital marketing has risen steadily in popularity during the

1980s. In one published survey, 56 percent of hospitals had actual marketing departments (Steiber et al., 1985). The annual hospital budget for marketing had tripled in one year (1984–85). Some hospitals have reanalyzed their exclusive focus on bed days filled or inpatient market share. Hospitals are now in the health business, not just the inpatient, high-tech business. It may be only a minor victory for a hospital to attain a higher inpatient market share while the competition achieves a dominant position in ambulatory, chronic, and long-term care services. No market segment is too small to overlook in this current financial recession for many hospitals. For example, one Miami hospital closed 16 beds and opened a "Sniffles and Sneezes" center—day care for sick children. Working parents can leave their children for 12 hours at a cost of $20 and receive a staff pediatrician's exam for an additional $10. To minimize nursing staff reductions, nurses in the 224-bed hospital have been making "missionary marketing calls" on day-care centers and schools. Marketing is giving the public a better service, at more flexible hours, at a lower cost.

Hospital marketing is not simply the maximization of hospital admission rates or patient census. Marketing tailored to this industry, often called "social marketing," implies a service orientation (better health)—not a product orientation (more patient bed days). The smart administrator need not decrease firm size or net revenues by diversification away from inpatient care to other services. The three major rationales for diversification are (1) to acquire profit-making services (such as laboratory, radiology, alcohol rehabilitation care, and inhalation therapy); (2) to increase production volume, and consequently decrease unit costs, by contracting with other firms to supply services (such as laboratory, laundry, and food services); and (3) to develop a feeder system into the hospital. Although ambulatory care clinics are loss leaders, most institutions operate clinics as a feeder system into the hospital. Further, the product portfolio of the hospital can be diversified to include health promotion and health education activities designed to improve patient compliance. The problem of patient compliance and health education is a major growth area in our health care system. Problems with patient compliance to medical regimen was a contributing factor in 21 percent of the hospitalizations in one study (Mason et al., 1980). One unquestioned benefit of health marketing activities is the resulting increased sensitivity to consumer needs for amenities, information, and emotional support. Some fear that marketing health care as a commodity will ultimately demean it. In transplanting marketing techniques from the business sector, one must be careful to avoid hucksterism while pursuing competitive consumerism.

Marketing activities aimed at potential health care consumers are necessary for a number of reasons. First, people concerned with day-to-day living often underestimate the value of early diagnosis and preventive medicine and have to be reminded of the potential benefits of screening activities. Second, the daily news accounts of malpractice suits and second-opinion surgery studies have shaken the public faith in the medical establishment. While some skepticism is in order, unbridled skepticism can keep some people away from the health care system for too long a period. Some of the health care providers can regain public trust through customer preference analysis and integrated market planning. For example, Humana Corporation performed a market survey of patient preferences and concluded that (1) people want to see a triage nurse or physician within minutes of their arrival at the emergency room and (2) people resent being hassled for financial and insurance coverage information upon arrival. Consequently, the 90 Humana hospitals guarantee that a triage nurse will see the patient within 60 seconds after arrival at the emergency room and that the financial information will be collected in due time (10, 20, or 60 minutes later).

Health care institutions might borrow their marketing principles from the following three basic points in the "Penney Idea," adopted by J. C. Penney in 1913:

1. To serve the public, as nearly as we can, to its complete satisfaction.
2. To expect for the service we render a fair remuneration.
3. To do all in our power to pack the customer's dollar full of value, quality, and satisfaction.

Market Analysis

Marketing is a multistage process with many potential audiences. A hospital's marketing audience might include patients as consumers, physicians as direct customers of the institution, and physicians as middlemen. The first step in any marketing program is the assessment of market structure. One needs to assess the distinctive role the facility plays in meeting consumer demand in various market segments (market positioning). The existing and potential catchment area and service mix should be identified. The attractiveness and specificity of the service or product line must also be defined (market definition). The analyst should also partition the market into fairly homogeneous segments, any one of which can be expanded as a primary target market with a marketing strategy tailored to the situation. This concept of market segmentation may imply multiple marketing efforts or marketing to only one segment area.

The second step in the typical marketing effort involves an analysis of consumer tastes and attributes. The provider of service should assess the intensity of demand for various products, perceptions of specific services and the entire facility, and the casual link between consumer behavior and image. Consumer satisfaction and multi-attribute consumer preferences should be determined through conjoint measurement techniques (Reidesel, 1985; Wind and Spitz, 1976). The next three steps in building a marketing approach involve assessment of the product line, presentation of differential advantages relative to the competition, and development of the initial marketing program design (integrated market plan).

Management must consider the following seven stages in evaluation and periodic reexamination before making decisions about promotion, pricing, product, and place (location):

1. Market catchment area definition—demographic and geographic areas that are served or could be served.
2. Physician customer preference analysis—what physicians require and desire for a health care facility.
3. Patient customer preference analysis—what potential patients seek in a health facility.
4. Product definition objectives—assessment of the present and future product line of the health facility.
5. Differential advantages marketing—definition of what services and reputation are marketable to advance facility prestige in the eyes of customers (doctors and potential patients), including providing different messages to different customers or regulatory agencies to best project the facility image.
6. Integrated market planning and promotion—coordination of actions resulting from assessment in Steps 1–5. For example, we might conclude that integration between uncoordinated hospital departments is necessary to achieve a reliable and more efficient organization. The forthcoming management ideas are often quite simple—for example, placing nuclear medicine next to the x-ray department so that the patient transporters in each department can assist the other during peak demand periods. Efficient transportation and scheduling can significantly contain costs and increase consumer perception of the quality of the institution. The marketing

program promotes the message to the two basic customer groups: consumers and physicians.

7. Market activity evaluation—assessment of the costs and benefits of marketing activities and making timely corrective action. Management and trustees must ultimately decide whether the long-run intangible benefits and discounted cash flows justify reorganizing priorities.

The first stage, market catchment area definition, is a familiar process for most health care facilities. Hospitals have been performing this element of the marketing process under the title of needs assessment for over twenty years. However, certain elements of the marketing function, such as informing the public of the availability of new services and departments, is a task that most administrators fail to perform effectively.

In performing a physician customer market survey (stage 2), the hospital must make basic decisions as to which preferences they should weight highest. If the objective function of the hospital is to maximize the patient census, then it should give highest priority to the preferences of physicians who admit the largest number of patients—general surgeons and family practitioners. If the objective function is to operate the hospital as a feeder system for the hospital-based specialists, then general surgeons who require less assistance from these specialists would have a lower priority relative to internists and other specialists.

Historically, market research of consumer preferences (stage 3) has been done by the health planners. While the old style health planners of the 1950s and 1960s did not use marketing jargon, their mission was to assess consumer needs, promulgate new product lines, and open new service points. Planners utilized the jargon of needs assessment and increased accessibility, but the approach was vintage health marketing (Eastaugh, 1982). Consumers value access, but they also value amenities such as well-decorated rooms, better food, and friendly personnel. Ease of exit can also help provide the patient with an overall positive impression of the institution. A courtesy discharge policy that avoids stops at the accounts receivable department on the final day of hospitalization is one potential approach.

Some analysts tailor the marketing approach to the physician as the ultimate client, while others emphasize studying the preferences of consumers. A dual approach of studying both groups is probably warranted. The Humana Corporation applied a two-pronged approach in Louisville, Kentucky. Initially it performed a market survey of consumer preferences by telephone and interview. After discovering that over one-third of the families did not have a physician, Humana published an ad in the paper stating: "If you need help finding a doctor fill out this coupon." The consumers' referral coupons were provided only to the doctors affiliated with Humana. As a result of the coupon referral program, the patient census increased 8 percent. In the second prong of their market survey, Humana assessed physician preferences by asking existing Humana-affiliated physicians and potential new physicians how Humana may satisfy the physicians' needs.

A facility should look at the product-market competencies of neighboring facilities in the process of assessing internal product definition objectives (stage 4). Some product lines may need to be expanded, contracted, or phased out of existence. The decisions are seldom simple—for example, the maternity or emergency room services are seldom cost-beneficial unless one includes off-setting revenue from estimated return business and ancillary services. If diversification of the product line seems in order, the decision should be made in consultation with the four internal publics (trustees, physicians, volunteers, employees) and the numerous external publics (bankers, unaffiliated physicians, philanthropists, suppliers, consumers, regulators, competitors). Depending on the service area demographics, new product lines for consideration might include rheumatology, multiphasic annual physicals, alcoholism treatment, prenatal clinics, nuclear medicine, nephrology, and mental health services. (We shall cover diversification activities in Chapter 19.)

Targeting more resources to certain segments of the market where you have a differential advantage (stage 5) and contracting resources from other segments can reap a larger market share for facilities that previously provided a whole range of services. In the recent era of more stringent forms of reimbursement, to ignore market segmentation increases the risk of falling behind in the purchase of state-of-the-art equipment. In other words, the rate regulators may allow a facility the slack to purchase expensive updated replacement equipment in three to five departments but not in all areas. Rate regulation programs provide incentives for increased specialization in the hospital industry.

Stage 5, differential advantages marketing, should involve an honest self-assessment of the institution. One must carefully differentiate poor quality "centers of nonexcellence" from the ego requirements of some physicians and managers to "offer all things for all DRGs"—even if done poorly. For a hospital to underspecialize is to renege on any commitment to quality and economy. To discard certain services does not renege on the principle of patient access when other hospitals already offer those services. The resistance of hospitals to participate in regionalization plans has retarded both the quality and efficiency of care. The increasingly market-driven hospital sector will soon make the price system the "planner," and regionalization dreams of public health officials 30 to 40 years ago will rapidly become a reality. Petty ego-turf considerations among medical staff, managers, and trustees will slow the rate at which service-line specialization occurs. Some faculty members may suggest that medical education cannot be as efficiently accomplished in a world with fewer teaching beds and more specialization across hospitals. As we shall observe in Chapter 14, finance will soon drive function and organization in many academic centers. The style of the $5 billion medical education system must adapt to a hospital economy fast approaching $200 billion, and not vice versa. Excess capacity and substantial fixed-cost investments in underutilized product lines make hospital underspecialization an irresponsible market strategy.

Stage 6, integrated market planning, includes more than tactical within-institution decisions. After the hospital has decided on a course of action, it must inform both the public and the physician community via a promotional campaign. The health care institution must extoll the virtues of its new market position plan in terms of optimum cost, service, and quality patient care. The promotional campaign should not tell consumers things that they already know—for example, "Our emergency room is open 24 hours a day." Promotion should establish in the consumer's mind a point of difference between your institution and the competition. The desired target audience plus the message will determine the media of choice (magazines, television, newspaper, billboards, radio, directories). Teaching hospitals would do well to inform potential patients that they do not have to be referred in order to receive services. The marketing plan should also be consumer-directed. For example, patients at the Cleveland Clinic are informed that if their physician is more than 15 minutes late, the bill gets cut in half. The message to the public is clear: We run an efficient system that respects consumers' time and money. The quality of amenities in a good hospital should not be different from the quality of amenities at a good hotel—you don't have to serve poorly prepared food to be called a hospital.

Prior to the 1980s, marketing was viewed as "image" advertising or glorified public relations. The hospital's public relations director would put forth a general image of institutional caring and compassion. This timid approach was characterized by the generalization that physicians drive the consumers to "need" services and that all demands are professionally defined. The current strategy is more aggressive and tailored to appeal to the informed consumer—that is, find out what consumers want and offer it, at the right place, right price, and with the right style. If the institution continues to promote only general messages about "quality caring care," its consumer image will become indistinguishable from the competition. Hospitals that promote certain special areas of excellence often improve utilization across a number of service lines. These hospitals, by distinguishing their institutional comparative advantages in the minds of the consumers, benefit from a "halo effect" across a wider range of departments.

Consumers increasingly choose to select a new hospital or physician rather than return to the same provider. Patients also exercise more power in selecting which services will be "purchased" (Miaoulis, 1985; Inguanzo and Harju, 1985). The market promotion campaign should communicate to all employees as well as consumers. Many hospitals educate employees in better guest relations. Promises are made to all concerned—for example, that the nurses will respond to the call bell within 30 seconds, that the food will be served hot, and that people will knock before entering a patient's room. All these concerns are merely an application of the golden rule: Treat the patient as you would wish to be treated. Comparison shoppers may represent a minor fraction of the institution's potential patient mix, but one needs every possible patient. The most irrational management decision would be to invest millions to develop a new program and then to cut the promotional campaign designed to tell the community what has been done for them. Some administrators may wince at investing $60,000 per 100 beds per year on marketing activities, but the greater danger comes from underinvestment. If one was promoting a leisure good rather than a necessary service, the marketing budget could well run 20 to 50 times higher.

Promotional activities can also be organized by product line (Ruffner, 1986). Most hospitals with over 200 beds could benefit from a product-line manager who wears two hats: one in operations and one as a marketer. If the potential job applicant thinks that marketing is "selling and advertising," you know that you have a "dud" job candidate. Product-line management is a critical function that requires some degree of marketing background. The good product-line manager will continue to evaluate the effectiveness of promotional campaigns, suggest new and creative ways to communicate with the various market segments (including physicians), and cross organizational lines informally to assess all activities that affect the product/service (Wixon, 1985).

Linking Declining Admission Rates to Product-Line Planning

Much of the decline in admission rates has to be explained by factors other than a simple substitution of ambulatory care for inpatient care. Many analysts predicted that admission rates would increase with PPS, but the opposite effect has been observed for all age groups. Is the decline in admission rates a perverse result of PPS? Indeed, if there existed only one DRG, and payment was on a per case basis, one would expect the admissions for that condition to increase. However, when there are hundreds of DRGs, with varying degrees of hospital-specific profitability depending on product-line volume, price, and cost behavior, some profitable DRGs will have higher admission rates and some unprofitable DRGs will have declining rates. The net effect on admissions is hard to predict in the short run. Decisions in 1983–84 to trim or close product lines based on ex ante cost analysis may have produced the net decline in admission rates under PPS. This product-line profitability issue has been around for years among academics (Neuhauser, 1972), but until PPS, the incentive to actually change behavior and trim departments was buried under the comfortable blanket of cost reimbursement.

Two hypotheses may explain hospital decisions to shrink, divest (close), initiate (open), or expand a service line. One hypothesis is that hospital managers exhibit an asymmetry in confidence in their cost-accounting information in that they trust the information much more when it suggests the facility is losing money on the service. For example, managers have only a 60 percent confidence in the information if the experimental cost-accounting system reports money is being made on the product line, and thus they are slow to act. But if the cost analysis reports product-line losses, managers have 95 percent confidence in the information out of fear for financial survival, and they will definitely act on the information by trimming or closing the service. This asymmetrical concern in favor of the downside is best captured in one physician/manager's observation: "Dump those big money-losing services. That way you don't need to dump individual patients; you can just say you do not offer services in those areas." Such a policy would be good for the patients and good for the institution. To balance service and solvency, hospitals must eliminate their low-volume, low-quality services.

Consider the following example. A hypothetical hospital has three types of cases in 1983: 10,000 profitable cases, 10,000 money losers (unprofitable cases), and 20,000 break-even cases. In 1984, if the hospital expanded profitable service volume by 4 percent and cut back unprofitable service volume by 20 percent, the net impact on admissions could be a 4 percent decline. The portfolio of profitable/neutral/unprofitable admissions would have changed from 10,000/20,000/10,000 by 1984 to 10,400/20,000/8,000 for a net decline of 1,600 admissions. Profitability is influenced by volume, operating costs, utilization review, and payment rates. Profitability is dynamic, so that which is labeled a "loser" based on historic data could turn out to be highly profitable if neighboring hospitals drop that service or only pick up enough volume to achieve scale economies. For example, single DRG product lines like DRG 88, 132, and 294 could be highly unprofitable at 60 percent of all hospitals, but could prove to be profitable due to the achievement of sufficient volume, resulting in scale economies, at 15 percent of the hospitals. Conversely, single DRG product lines like DRG 148, 174, 209, and 336 could be profitable at 65 percent of hospitals, but unprofitable due to insufficient volume and consequent higher unit costs at 10 percent of hospitals.

The second hypothesis is that pressure to decrease admissions for nonelderly patients has affected physician behavior concerning Medicare cases. Declining under-65 utilization rates are largely the result of increased consumer cost sharing and growth in prepaid plan (HMO, IPA, PPO, EPO) market share. But, if these two factors fully explained the downslide in utilization, one would not expect hospital operating margins to have improved over $1.8 billion in CY 1984. Rosko and Broyles (1984), reflecting the 1984 conventional wisdom, predicted that profit margins would decline. However, margins greatly improved, suggesting some respect for basing product-line expansion or contraction decisions on profitability. In fact, a number of recent studies have demonstrated that product-line management has proved effective in cutting costs, capacity, and duplication of service (Nackel and Kues, 1986; Fackelman, 1985; Goodrich and Hastings, 1985; MacStravic, 1986).

Quality and Unit Cost by Service Product Line

Two findings, which economists and physicians accept as valid, lead to a third supposition of interest to both groups. First, economies of scale exist and unit cost falls as volume increases. Second, quality increases with scale—that is, it improves as volume of a product line increases. This second finding has been confirmed in numerous studies tracking post hospital and hospital mortality and morbidity (Flood et al., 1984a, 1984b; Wolfe et al.,

1983; Farber et al., 1981; Shortell and LoGerfo, 1982; Luft, 1980; Luft et al., 1979; Maerki et al., 1986). To paraphrase Peterson et al. (1956), "in-practice," high-volume providers do the best-quality work, and low-volume, "out-of-practice" providers do poorly. The causal effect might be a two-way street: Low-volume providers perform poorly, and poor-quality providers receive fewer referrals and therefore cannot increase volume. Both laws of scale—efficiency and quality enhancement—are outlined in Figure 9.1. Figure 9.1–a is the well-known law of economies of scale; unit cost (V) declines with a larger scale of output. In Figure 9.1–b, open heart surgery provides a classic example of curve A, and cholecystectomy provides an example of curve B. Transurethral prostate resections provide an example of curve C. These operations flatten

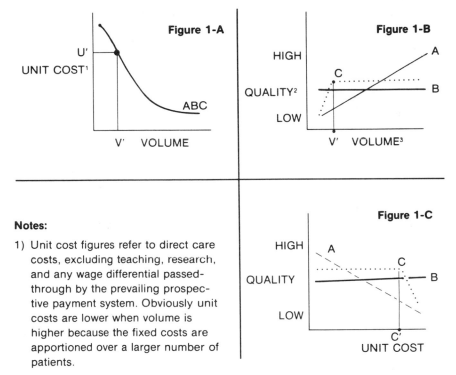

Notes:

1) Unit cost figures refer to direct care costs, excluding teaching, research, and any wage differential passed-through by the prevailing prospective payment system. Obviously unit costs are lower when volume is higher because the fixed costs are apportioned over a larger number of patients.

2) Quality index would include outcome measures such as mortality rates correcting for case severity, morbidity rates, and serious adverse patient occurrence rates.

3) Point V′ is the point along hypothetical curve C at which volume increases no longer improve the quality of service.

Figure 9.1   Three Potential Relationships Between Hospital Service Quality, Volume, and Unit Cost

out at a scale of 100 to 200 (V') annual cases, whereas hip replacements flatten out at a relatively low scale of 30 to 50 cases (Luft et al., 1979). These scale effects will shift with time and technology, but it is important to note that Peterson's original work was in primary care (Peterson et al., 1956). Hence, the scale effect is not exclusive to surgery.

The supposition in Figure 9.1–c is that good medicine is also good economics, with higher volume yielding better quality and lower unit costs. It may seem counterintuitive that facilities with lower unit costs (exclusive of their other special missions such as teaching or indigent care) also have higher-quality outcomes. But "economies running in hand with quality" are prevalent in the market for most ordinary consumer goods. You don't need to own a Porsche 928 or American TV to know that higher initial expense often buys higher rates of malfunction. For example, Whirlpool washing machines are substantially cheaper and of higher quality than General Electric. *Consumer Reports* labels the higher-cost GE product as the lower-quality product.

The impact of increases in volume on mortality is difficult to assess. For example, in the context of surgical studies limiting the sample framework to in-hospital mortality may be a problem. Following patients for 60 days after surgery removes any possible confounding effects of length of stay, patient transfers, and other factors. Riley and Lubitz (1985) examined the relationship between volume and mortality 60 days after surgery and found a mortality decline with increased volume for coronary bypass, transurethral resection of the prostate, hip arthroplasty, and resection of the intestine. Their analysis was repeated using only inpatient deaths as the dependent variable, and the results indicated a considerably stronger association between volume and mortality.

Doubts About Cost and Quality Scale Effects

Economies of scope have been postulated as a countervailing force to consider before trimming product lines in the name of specialization. Economies of scope, the efficiencies of joint production of a wide variety of product lines, have been found in other industries. However, if such benefits do exist among physician areas of specialization, the evidence is not statistically significant (Bays, 1986; Conrad and Strauss, 1983; Cowing and Holtman, 1983). Some analysts have suggested that the causal direction between high volume and better quality has been reversed and volume does not breed quality. Alternatively, quality attracts volume, and facilities do more surgery because they have lower mortality rates (Dranove, 1984). This speculation might become more accurate in the 1990s, as consumers receive more information on quality (Eastaugh and Eastaugh, 1986). (Quality will be considered in Chapters 12 and 18.) However, there is currently no evidence that patients or their physicians select hospitals based on their low mortality rates for specific conditions (Greenberg, 1986; Flood et al., 1984a; Eraker and Sox, 1981). The results of Flood's analysis concerning the volume effects on quality were strengthened, not weakened, by inclusion of teaching status and size into the analysis (Flood et al., 1984a). This suggests that consumers and their physicians do not shop effectively on the basis of quality for the better hospitals. Perhaps with more physician competition, comparison shopping, and information disclosure, consumers will be able to shop more effectively for quality and value.

One should note that scale is measured by volume of the product-line output, not by capacity of the total institution. Thus a large hospital with many product lines may not have enough volume to achieve sufficient scale economies, while each line in a smaller, more specialized hospital may achieve a good scale volume. For instance, an 800-bed hospital offering 460 DRGs and 90 basic product lines with a net volume of 900 admissions per week would have an average scale of ten admissions per product line. A 400-bed hospital offering 250 DRGs and 25 basic product lines might have a net volume of 500 admissions per week, or an average scale of 20 admissions per product line. The smaller hospital has double the scale per product line compared to the 800-bed facility. Scale by product line, not scale of the hospital, is the key to good medicine and good economics.

Clustering DRGS into Strategic Product-Line Groupings (SPGs)

Hospitals are in need of two forms of increased management control. First, line managers strive for better efficiency management in the production of intermediate services, such as nursing care or lab tests. The second crucial stage of management control is effectiveness management, including utilization review and quality assurance. The goal is to enhance quality and avoid the overtreatment of patients with costly intermediate services. From an ethical and economic viewpoint, what ultimately counts is the final product: a patient treated and returned to good health. It does little good to focus only on the intermediate components of the hospital service production function (Figure 9.2). What matters from an analytical viewpoint is effectiveness and efficiency within clusters of "peer" (like) final products or strategic product-line groupings (SPGs). It is important to know what it costs to start an SPG, contract an SPG, close an SPG, or expand an SPG in a hospital.

An SPG is defined as a clustering of similar DRGs performed by an identified subset of the medical staff. Trustees and managers have a responsibility to ask what it costs to trim, expand, open, or close a given SPG. Consequently, profitability and growth opportunity must be determined periodically. Unlike the business world, a hospital's service product line cannot sponsor its own

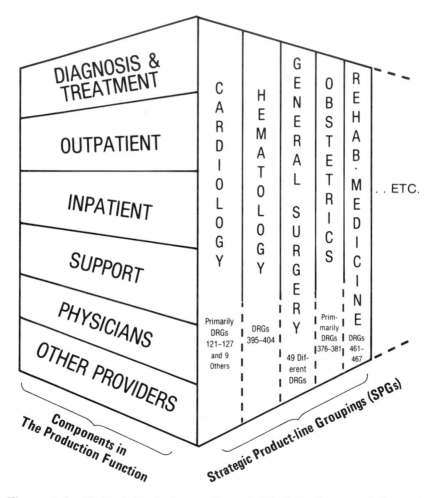

Figure 9.2 Vertical Cost Accounting of Final Products and Strategic Product-Line Groupings (SPGs) of DRGs

autonomous marketing division. Service lines in the hospital sector are clearly more jointly interconnected (interdependent) in the provision of inpatient care. Insufficient realization of this interdependency is what caused zero-based budgeting to fail.

The definition of SPGs should be institutionally specific and should involve strong input from medical staff. Allowing each hospital's medical staff to "reinvent the wheel" offers the following three advantages: (1) identifying SPGs would be a first step toward effecting change in the organization; (2) physician partners in strategic financial planning must contribute in defining the unit of analysis if they are to gain some sense of "ownership" and defend the plan; and (3) medical practice habits vary considerably across regions. For a given SPG, the relevant type of physician to include in the process may vary. For example, in one northeastern city the service line of endoscopy is 85 percent controlled (performed) by gastroenterologists. However, in one southern city, endoscopy is evenly divided 35/35/30 percent market share between general surgery, internal medicine, and gastroenterology, respectively. In the case of one western hospital, endoscopy is 75 percent controlled by internal medicine. Suggested changes in the medical staff composition or marketing of an SPG will have to take into account local habits and physician supply characteristics.

SPGs are based on physician peer grouping criteria for two reasons. First, they have interconnected referral patterns that require a "critical mass" of certain cases to make the line economically viable for all parties concerned. Second, doctors are the most important input in the delivery of patient care. SPGs are operationally useful in making physician recruitment and retention decisions. If the hospital is aggressively growing in a given area, either because the market potential is good or because profitability is high, it could experience a high return on investment in attracting or keeping clinicians in that SPG. Medical staff revenue projections by area are critical in staff development planning (Shortell, 1985). If DRGs are the new language of rate setting, SPGs will soon follow as the new language of marketing, budgeting, and mission statements. Judging by the reports that trustees are the single most important factor in hospital price setting (Bauershmidt and Jacobs, 1985), trustees may often be averse to closing an SPG.

In evaluating profitability versus market opportunity potential, as shown in Figures 9.3 and 9.4, decision making often becomes more of an art than a management science. The language can often get quite crass, especially in the area of marketing. For example, a CEO with a short-run focus might be reluctant to jettison two

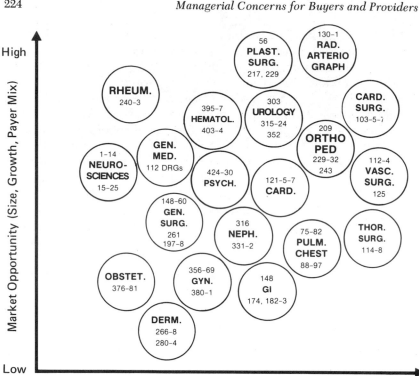

Figure 9.3   Hospitals Organize by Strategic Product-Line Groupings (SPGs) According to Clusters of DRGs. (Twenty are shown in this Hypothetical Hospital for FY 1985.)

mediocre clinicians if they currently have fair to average profitability, even if they are "maxed out" (lack volume growth potential). To use the language of the other AMA, the American Marketing Association, these two doctors offering the SPG would be given the label "cash cow," because of their short-term profitability. The better hospital CEO would take the long-run perspective, consider life-cycle costing, and concentrate on safeguarding the reputation of the institution. If one factors in the malpractice expense of mediocre performers, a big loss in the courts could more than wipe out ten years of "cash cow" profits. Profitability should include

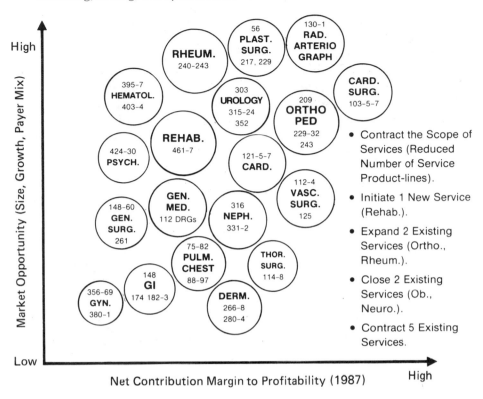

Figure 9.4 **PPS Stimulates Specialization and Regionalization over the Life-Cycle of the Institution, 1985-1987**

Notes:

1) Medicare declines to only 35% of patient days.

2) Top 50 DRGs account for 98% of days.

some life-cycle costing adjustment for malpractice risk and facility reputation risk (impacting census across all SPGs).

Closing an SPG will not be an easy task politically. There are the problems of pride and ego. Clinicians invest three to nine years of their lives in graduate medical training to specialize in an SPG. Even if the market for the service is saturated, they still feel justified in prompting the hospital to continue offering the uneconomical SPG. However, why should the hospital be run down because the supply of specialists has run up? Currently, many underutilized SPGs are incapable of achieving economies of scale or volumes sufficient to support quality care. Hiring more health care planners is not a solution for hospitals. Duplication, the oversupply of hospitals offering an SPG, is a problem not cured by external, community-based health care planning (Eastaugh, 1982; see also Chapter 23).

Internal facility planning, under the pressure of tighter payment schedules, will reduce duplication and prompt regionalization. Both efficiency and effectiveness impact net profitability, as does the payer mix. Physicians must realize their part in the process. If they wish to save an SPG, they must do a better job of effectiveness management. It is impossible to run a hospital if too many SPGs lose money. Hospitals will have to pick and choose among SPGs, rather than choose between high- and low-cost patients.

Specialization and Regionalization

Hospital trustees and managers are socially responsible individuals. One would predict, therefore, that they would choose to drop services (SPGs) rather than lower the quality of service. The most unprofitable patients will not be left out in the cold. Instead, they will be better served at regional facilities that specialize in their SPG. Patients will have longer average travel time, but unit costs will be lower and quality will be higher. Insurance plans might consider covering travel costs for patients referred to a regional center, as is done in Canada (Luft, 1985). This utopian summary of the possible effects of PPS-induced regionalization is all fine in theory, but the impact on access must be closely watched. One should not expect too much from the price system.

One important public policy question involves the degree to which patients would have to be concentrated in select hospitals to achieve significant reductions in preventable deaths. If society selects a realistic target, such as a 50 percent mortality reduction, the disruption in the hospital marketplace might be small (and consumer travel cost minimal). A study by Maerki et al. (1986) shows that averting half the preventable deaths would require varying degrees of patient dislocation for different conditions. Patient shifts from low-volume to high-volume hospitals would involve 15 percent of the cirrhosis patients, 27 percent of the fracture-of-the-femur cases, 35 percent of the respiratory distress syndrome patients, 35 percent of the cardiac bypass cases, 23 percent of the gastric surgery cases, 22 percent of the appendectomies, and 15 percent of the transurethral prostatectomies. For other conditions a more realistic goal might involve only a 25 percent reduction in preventable deaths through shifting of patients (42 percent of peptic ulcer cases, 38 percent of hernia repair cases, 37 percent of total hip replacements, 33 percent of hysterectomies, 27 percent of catheterizations and angiography cases, and

18 percent of cholecystectomies) in Maerki's national sample. Maximal regionalization that would minimize mortality yet neglect time and travel costs for the patient and visiting relatives would suggest that patients be treated only at 10 percent of hospitals.

The burden is on the HCFA to set the price so that the last institution to offer an SPG in a local market does not drop that product line because the price is too low. Prices should be set so that access does not suffer, travel and time costs do not prove too onerous, and quality is not negatively affected. PPS prices will be most effective in stimulating specialization in nonemergency SPGs. However, the prices should not constrain emergency care, such as abdominal aortic aneurysms. For much of medicine, the price system can be used to close out low-volume, low-quality, high-cost SPGs. Will access be harmed under payment-system-induced regionalization? It will not, if the regionalization is for nonemergency conditions, judging from the Canadian experience. Roos and Lyttle (1985) report that in the case of hip replacements, there may be some minor differential access based on distance to the closest regional facility. However, in the cases they studied, the access differential disappeared rapidly, and the only patients who were temporarily denied service had controversial indications for surgery.

Comparisons can be made to other sectors in which competition has bred higher quality, efficiency, and access. Hospital specialization may breed regionalization similar to the airline industry's hub-and-spoke concept. A dominant medical center may have pruned a small percentage of its SPGs to act as keystones for inpatient care in the area, with affiliations to smaller, highly specialized, few-frills, low-cost hospitals. On occasion, the hospitals that are "spokes" may pick up the SPGs that the hub hospital cannot provide as effortlessly or as effectively. Two hub hospitals might implicitly trade SPG areas of specialization, while avoiding anti-trust litigation. This concept has been carried out in the airline sector where maintenance and cost per mile are substantially cheaper if companies "swap" SPGs and service fewer product lines. For example, last year Pan Am traded 15 DC-10s to American Airlines for eight 747s.

Specialization brings lower costs and fewer mistakes. As small hospitals back out of the SPGs they never should have initiated, medical centers will inherit most ICU (intensive care unit) cases, to the benefit of quality care. Indeed, medical centers could become large ICUs. The ego-turf concerns of the professionals, whether they be physicians or pilots, will be emphasized under regionalization. For example, the "poor" 747 pilot now has to settle for flying a DC-10. What of the ego concerns of managers and providers who have to work in hospitals on a financial diet of staff reductions and trimming the number of SPGs? To address this problem, incentive compensation—both financial and nonmonetary—has been proposed.

Deregulation and price competition do indeed have a habit of raising service quality and driving costly excess capacity out of the market—witness the airline, trucking, banking, and railroad industries. Judging by the 350,000 empty hospital beds, acute short-term hospitals are plagued by excess capacity. Hospitals are further plagued by reregulation in the form of DRG-administered prices, but we cannot achieve "pure" competition by taking every citizen's insurance coverage away. The term "market competition" may sound to some as if philistine commercialism is being introduced to our medical system. All that is really advocated in the name of competition is to stop running hospitals like "gentlemen's clubs," immune to management science and lacking concern for productivity, efficiency, and effectiveness.

No longer will many hospitals be able to function as full service institutions offering almost every DRG. Within the context of business history, an analogy can be drawn between hospitals and urban department stores 15 years ago. Those stores that offered a full scope of services ranging from high fashion to toasters, soda drinks to yarn, and hardware to silk went bankrupt. Stores that identified and specialized in their most productive product lines prospered. Stores that maintained 500 product lines and poor satellite locations fell to the vicissitudes of the market.

Farming provides another useful analogy to the hospital sector. Farmers who shunned excessive diversification in favor of productivity enhancement have prospered. They realize that maximum portfolio scope does little if all product lines are inefficient or experience declining utilization. Farms saddled with debt and diversified product lines have gone under. Hospitals saddled with 50 SPGs, serving over more than 400 DRGs, will soon discover that broadness and facility size do not ensure survival. In the jargon of economics, moving up the learning curve because of higher volumes in areas of specialization not only will increase productivity and cut costs, but also will improve service quality (Eastaugh and Eastaugh, 1986).

Pitfalls of Underspecialization and Overspecialization

Hospitals on the vanguard of product-line planning have gone through one of two basic stages of misadventure: under- or overspecialization. Both groups fall prey to what Alfred North Whitehead (1932) termed the "fallacy of misplaced concreteness." The first group, occupancy maximization caretakers, place excessive faith in the slogan, "Anything beats cold sheets." They will develop any SPG and underspecialize, believing that higher occupancy rates are more important than profitability. The second group, short-run profit-maximizing risk takers, will place excessive faith in specialization, marketing, and the ability to attract new demand to compensate for closing other SPGs. They will overtrim SPGs based on short-run profitability without careful analysis of what this does for long-run profitability. It is possible, however, to balance the two approaches.

The practitioners of underspecialization and occupancy maximization in group 1 have a false sense of security in reasoning "a posteriori" that hospitals are like airlines in that if the hospital is filled to capacity everything will be fine. Hospital beds are somewhat like airline seats in that they cannot be stocked as inventory, so if they are not sold today, the revenue is foregone. However, should the strategy be to offer an indiscriminately high number of SPGs in hopes of filling beds? That idea is too clever by half. Actually, a hospital can offer so many SPGs that the majority are utilized well below capacity and the net profitability contribution is negative. Hence, increased volume does not prevent bankruptcy and may actually hasten closure. In finance, the ratio of volume to capacity by SPG is a critical concern. One should avoid the mania of declaring that all is well if census rises.

Group 2, profit-maximizers through overspecialization, finds false security in believing that dropping all the unprofitable SPGs improves the long-run bottom line. These short-run managers are unimpressed with the argument that profitability of the facility next year can be damaged by excessive concern for retrospective product-line profit reports. They are misled by a shallow reading of the business literature. Hospitals are more interdependent than most organizations, whereas business divisions can jettison a line without much concern for the core corporation's fixed-cost burden. Unfortunately, those foregone patients in SPGs that are closed no longer make a contribution to cover fixed costs. The remaining product lines must pick up more of a burden of the fixed costs and thus may become less profitable or unprofitable. For example, a "star" product line with fixed costs of $2,400 and profits of $275 per case can suddenly have fixed costs of $2,700 and a $25 net loss per case. The crucial task is getting compensated through increased volume in remaining SPGs after closing last year's unprofitable SPGs. In other words, enough patients must be pulled from the competition to fully compensate for the empty beds caused by discontinued SPGs.

Good marketing can go only so far in improving volume. As a general proposition, group 2 managers would do well to trim SPGs in a slow, phased manner and come to understand their market better over time. Hospitals face a morass of problems, of which self-induced rapid declines in occupancy rates are both an outcome and a contributing cause. Long-run profitability should be the focus of financial managers. A hospital may close some unprofitable SPGs but not so many that the patient census erodes to the point of harming the financial health of the institution. Moreover, certain slow-developing SPGs may be misidentified as poor long-run performers. Such slow-starter SPGs can be like weak-kneed quarterbacks: Eventually, they may save the franchise (Eastaugh and Eastaugh, 1986).

Excessive pruning of SPGs in pursuit of overspecialization can cause as many financial problems as underspecialization. Overspecialization can decrease patient census and impact negatively on long-run profitability. Classic cases of occupancy reductions being a self-induced problem are found among three investor-owned chains that finished 1985 with 38 to 43 percent occupancy rates. Hospitals that succumb to the "big picture" paralysis of underspecialization invite either closure or a takeover.

Strategic Price Setting

Although price elasticity of demand for hospital care is low, price decisions are still important to consumers. Consumers might be attracted by a more liberal credit policy, health education programs, or single-priced "packages" for underinsured services (for example, maternity care). One major threat to the success of hospitalization package pricing is the possibility of excessive variation in resource costs across patients. For example, the facility could unwittingly attract a biased sample of admissions that represent the more complex and costly cases because they perceive the price as a bargain.

Marketing strategy involves a number of basic questions: what services to offer (product); where to serve (place); whom to serve and how to communicate to buyers and providers (promotion); and what to charge (price). These "four P's" of marketing strategy were often softened by health marketers: service selection (product-mix decision), access (place), public information (promotion), and "service consideration" (price). In this next section we discuss objective functions in selecting prices in the medical context and avoid renaming well-known constructs with euphomisms such as "ser-

vice consideration." Hospital market planning was formerly inpatient-oriented: getting the right patient in the right bed at the right
time following the right promotion, and sometimes following
communication of a right price. Marketing activities are increasingly concerned with pricing decisions—not merely for inpatient
care but for ambulatory and alternative care. Currently, there is
less reliance on bed filling and more reliance on getting the patient
to the most appropriate cost-effective channel of service distribution (including home care) so that society and the individual both
get the most value for the investments. This trend is often labeled
"social demarketing" (less institutional care), which should be
contrasted with its antilog, "negative demarketing" (a sleazy attempt to discourage the poor or underinsured patients from coming to the facility).

A review of Porter's (1980) seminal book on competitive strategy
unveils six basic categories of competitive forces. In the context of
pricing hospital products, those forces include:

1. Rivalry among existing competitors.
2. Potential new entrants to the market (e.g., ambulatory surgery).
3. Bargaining power of buyers (e.g., bulk buyers eliciting PPO
   price discounts.
4. Bargaining power of physician/suppliers.
5. Bargaining power of other suppliers.
6. Rivalry from substitute products or services (may include
   self-care).

In pricing hospital products, the first three factors are most critical.
For each service product line, the institution should consider
developing a tactical implementation plan. The hospital may un-
dertake nine different pricing strategies for nine product lines,
depending on existing competitive conditions, the possibility of
new entrants, and forecasted buyer response to price changes
(price elasticity, Chapter 2). The nine strategic pricing options are:

1. Predatory penetration pricing—short-run, to gain market
   share, with no change in the product.
2. Slash pricing—long-run lower prices; change the product to
   make the price slashes supportable in the long run.
3. Follower pricing—not much of a strategy; simply price relative to the market leader (i.e., do not initiate a price war).
4. Phase-out pricing—price high, which may only be at true
   cost, to eliminate a seldom-utilized, often poor quality, service product line from the institution.

5. Preemptive pricing—lower the price to make the service less attractive to potential new entrants.
6. Skim pricing—price high for a unique service (unique because quality is outstanding); or the probability of short-run declines in market share is low.
7. Segment pricing—charge higher prices when so-called "snob effects" exist, that is, charging a vastly different rate for a slightly different service like VIP suites.
8. Slide-down pricing—traditional price discrimination of moving down the pricing policy to tap successive layers of consumer demand when the service is highly price-sensitive and/or significant economies of scale exist.
9. Loss-leader pricing—price low relative to your average profit margin, but hopefully not below cost, to attract customer flow to the service or in complementary service.

Some mixture of these nine strategic pricing strategies is superior to the old-fashioned policy of hospital wide pricing rules. For example, old style cross-subsidization through public enterprise pricing was never statistically defensible (policies of markdowns for maternity care or markups for radiology or elective surgery were passed down through the generations of hospital superintendents on stone tablets). Likewise, public utility pricing at marginal cost always made such charitable institutions appear capital-consuming, wasteful, and inefficient to the taxpayers who had to underwrite their operations by picking up all the other costs associated with the facility. Lastly, fair-share average cost pricing with an equal percentage markup across all products suffers from two defects. First, it disallows the marketplace the opportunity to dictate a buyer-driven, cross-subsidization policy—for example, accepting a higher profit markup in cosmetic surgery to support preventive medicine (e.g., mammography screening of high-risk groups). Second, it takes away all the requisite flexibility needed by management to initiate, expand, or close a service line through prudent use of different pricing strategies over time.

How these pricing strategies might be used in a sequential fashion over the life cycle can be offered with reference to a specific example. If the hospital has no market share (Table 9.1) in starting a new product, it may wish to attempt the most aggressive pricing strategy, especially if this is a high-growth service. Strategy 1, predatory pricing, is a short-run, price-slashing strategy to gain initial market entry and hopefully gain significant market share. The new firm on the block should not expect the dominant firms always to react. For example, IBM seldom reacts to a price-cut

Table 9.1 Seven Basic Strategic-Pricing Methods; Listed within Each Box According to Strategic Preference (the numbers refer only to order of listing in the text)*

Market Growth Potential	Market Share (Zero, Low, Moderate, High)			
	Zero	Low	Moderate	High
A. High	1. Predatory penetration pricing (no change in product) 2. Slash pricing and change the product	2. Slash pricing 1. Predatory penetration pricing	5. Preemptive pricing 3. Follower pricing	5. Preemptive pricing 7. Segment pricing
B. Moderate	2. Slash pricing 1. Predatory penetration pricing 3. Follower pricing	3. Follower pricing 1. Predatory penetration pricing	6. Skim pricing 3. Follower pricing	6. Skim pricing 5. Preemptive pricing
C. Low	3. Follower pricing 2. Slash pricing	4. Phase-out pricing 3. Follower pricing	6. Skim pricing 7. Segment pricing	6. Skim pricing 7. Segment pricing

*Two other pricing methods are discussed in the text: slide-down pricing and loss-leader pricing.

campaign from smaller firms because it would rather take a "wait and see attitude" to observe if the new entrant (1) can survive, (2) pick up a significant market share, and (3) equilibrate back to a higher price level that still might beat IBM's prices but doesn't threaten to take much more market share away. Any hospital should raise its prices after short-run experimentation with predatory pricing in order to solidify its market position. If weaker rivals in the marketplace decide to stop offering a given service, one can charge substantially higher prices (maybe even reaping monopolists' profits). If existing firms maintain this service line (but don't counterpunch or appear as potential losers in a price war) after the new firm's successful entry into the market, one may wish to attempt strategy 2: slash pricing in the longer run.

Slash pricing invites a price war. In almost every case slash pricing should involve a change in the product in order that the price structure proves sustainable over time. For example, People's Express airline changed the product called air travel by making the public pay for certain a la carte services (food, a checked bag) and pay through nonmonetary mechanisms (e.g., the time costs of flying through Newark). However, the quality of the basic product, air travel, was in no sense discounted. Indeed, the slash-pricing strategy can result in a social good by opening up the product to new users, including first-time users.

People's Express underestimated the ability of other existing competitors to employ strategy 5: preemptive pricing. For example, United Airlines could sharply reduce the prices on 11 new routes that People's moved into, or were about to move into. Preemptive pricing is a strategy to preserve market share by preventing competitive entry or expansion. Preemptive pricing is typically used by firms with above-average market share, for services with above-average market growth potential. For example, if the People's Express of the local health market catchment area is attempting to open a nearby urgent care center or expand into coronary angioplasty, one can preempt the firm's plans with pricing strategy 5. To maintain preemptive price levels that make market expansion into the specific service line seem unattractive, the firm would have to trim its cost behavior in line with the reduced prices and/or make money to cross-subsidize the discounted prices elsewhere in the organization. With sufficient economies of scale, the firm may still make a profit at a price that would be unprofitable for new entrants.

To not have a strategy is itself a strategy. Consequently, pricing strategy 3, follower pricing, is the easiest alternative. If the service offers little potential for product differentiation, and what it proposes to offer is a "me-too" or "copy-cat" entry (e.g., endoscopy), a facility can simply price relative to the industry leader. Needless to say, this is a timid strategy that invites, or almost guarantees, low growth. For example, one cannot name a single company that exists by offering copies of IBM products at IBM prices (under those circumstances consumers would rather buy from IBM). To paraphrase a college coach, follower pricing is a "chill out" strategy, to mend and heal before deciding on a new strategy.

If all else fails and the service line has proven a financial failure, the best strategy to close out a product is strategy 4: phase-out pricing. This strategy should never be employed if any harm would come to the health of the community, perhaps because only one hospital is offering the service. However, phase-out pricing can quickly allow the price-sensitive patients to close an existing service when flat-open withdrawal of the service would result in a negative reaction from certain trustees, physicians, or local citizens. For example, if the hospital offers poor-quality cardiac surgery once every three weeks at an actual cost that is 200 percent higher than the local teaching hospital, one can phase-out price the service at actual cost. So few customers will come to visit the hospital for poor-quality cardiac surgery at a premium high cost that the hospital would have to close the service. The results of phase-out pricing are both good medicine and good economics. (A more detailed discussion of quality of care is found in Chapter 12.)

For certain providers unaccustomed to the business strategy literature, the talk of closing services or engaging in price wars seems unprofessional. However, the public will avidly support the price wars among health care providers circa 1985–1995 the way they supported aggressive competition among airlines and banks. The public benefits from such activity. Managers and providers must recognize the dynamic quality of health care markets. All the constant change, competitive action, and reaction will make any pricing strategy out of date very rapidly. Failure to grasp this point and readjust the pricing (and promotion) plan every 4 to 6 to 8 months will contribute to the closing of a number of hospitals.

Strategy 6, skim pricing, offers the institution an opportunity to reap profits by attracting "cream buyers" to a unique quality product. The product has to have consumer perception of high value for the money, and marketing researchers have uncovered this image in everything from lithotripsy (kidney stone treatment) to Maytag washing machines. Skim pricing is most effective for the hospital if the price elasticity of demand is low (e.g., consumers care little about price in avoiding chest pain or kidney stone pain). The market barriers to entry are usually high because of the substantial fixed costs associated with acquiring the service. However, skim-pricing policies will be hard to maintain if competitors enter and achieve a comparable high-quality "unique reputation" in the eyes of the consumer. However, if your brand name reputation is so firm that you can continue to skim price indefinitely, the institution should continue to price high (e.g., the Cleveland Clinic in cardiac surgery). Analogously, Maytag washing machines will continue to sell at a very high price because their breakdown (quality) rate is substantially better than the competition.

Pricing strategy 8, slide-down pricing, is a mechanism by which the facility can tap successive layers of demand at different price levels. For example, one may wish to sell mobile mammography screening to high-risk women at $111 in the three wealthy neighborhoods in Washington, but in the poor neighborhoods the van can change the list price to $39. This strategy makes sense when there is a substantial price and income elasticity of demand. Moreover, the investment has a better net present value if the van is utilized to scale. In addition, this pricing policy does substantial social good if it brings a necessary service to new customers. Insurance plans often prevent the practice of price discrimination, but the strategy can be pursued if the service is not insured or if the provider wishes to forego aggressive collections of cost-sharing payments from poor or elderly patients. As with any form of price discrimination, the rich can beat the system by driving to the lower-cost point of service (e.g., for $39), but few if any do so.

Finally, strategy 9, loss-leader pricing, has two basic variations. Some hospitals sell loss leaders at below actual costs, which is a less than prudent strategy in an increasingly competitive marketplace. Other hospitals "loss-leader" price in the sense that they charge 50 to 75 to 100 percent less than their average hospitalwide profit margin, but they never price at less than average cost for the service. The loss-leader approach is often rationalized as a marketing tool to pick up complementary demand. For example, one can sell baby care as a loss leader to attract the parents to have adult care at the facility. Alternatively, a dentist or optometrist could sell the initial visit charge as a loss leader in hopes of making a substantial profit on the follow-up care.

In a service industry such as health care, consumption and production typically occur in the same location. Consequently, vertical pricing decisions within distribution channels are seldom relevant except in the case of independent practice associations or other contract service situations. Horizontal pricing decisions are made at the retail level by commercial insurance plans or Blue Cross plans paying negotiated charges. Governmental payers and half of the Blue Cross plans simply pay cost or the health industry equivalent of wholesale prices.

Advertising and Demand Creation

In principle, to inform the public is the essence of advertising. The most frequently misunderstood concept concerning the marketing process is that consumers are so ignorant and gullible in the health care business that they can be duped into asking for services they do not in fact need. No study has demonstrated that advertising merely stimulates medically unnecessary utilization. A number of 1986 surveys suggest that Americans are well informed about health and hygiene matters but believe that modern medicine has the miracle techniques and spare parts to fix them no matter how they live their lives. Future reseach should consider the question of whether the excessive faith the public has in technology makes them susceptible to misleading advertising campaigns or whether public faith is on the wane. Malpractice stories in the media might be eroding the public faith in medical technology.

One should not suggest that advertising will induce consumers to suddenly shop for health plans and providers as methodically as they shop for automobiles. It is clear that many individuals will opt for the protection and security of the status quo and not shop among competition health plans. Most consumers will not immediately abandon their current providers, even after being convinced that a new health delivery option will save the family a few dollars per week. However, over time if the family has a "bad" experience with their doctor or hospital, they will be more likely to upgrade the importance of cost considerations in their future annual enrollment decisions and move to the plan that provides the best buy with all factors considered. Consumer tastes concerning what is "valuable" in health care service delivery will vary widely in American society. Not all individuals will agree with the "average" group consensus concerning medical care, because it is in many ways an "experience good"—that is, a good that must be experienced in order to value its intangible and tangible attributes.

Expanded services or new inclusive pricing packages should be promoted in a well-managed institution. The perceived style of advertising is important in the health area. Noncompetitive "natural" advertising, sometimes labeled "social marketing," is generally more acceptable to health providers than competitive advertising ("buy our product"). Hospitals should go beyond the product orientation of selling inpatient or hospital-based services and realize that their one chance for expansion may reside in taking a broader market orientation. The hospital could then better serve the latent demands of the community with independent ambulatory surgicenters, home health care services, and health education and promotion (Eastaugh, 1984).

Five basic rationales for advertising include (1) public education about health care, (2) information on service availability, (3) accounting to the community, (4) seeking support, and (5) employee recruitment. The industry also lists guidelines for acceptable advertising content: truth and accuracy, "fairness" in avoiding any quality comparisons with the competition, and avoiding "claims of prominence." The hospital industry has been rather slow in recognizing the need for differential advantages marketing. In the minds of the authors of the advertising code, the public has no right to know if a competitor has less modern facilities, a less well-trained staff, or inferior quality of care. Most hospital marketing campaigns should be more consumer-oriented and less physician-oriented.

Physician-induced investment, leading to overcapitalization, is a frequently mentioned problem of the hospital industry. Granfield (1975) was the first to suggest that the hospital industry is subject to the Averch-Johnson (1962) hypothesis: Hospitals are regulated, protected from competition, and consequently overcapitalized. In Chapter 23 we shall test an econometric model for positive or negative effects of regulation on hospital capital investment.* The entire network of health planning and Certificate-of-Need regulations has been designed in theory to give nonphysicians the wherewithal to reject physician requests for excessive capital investment. From the standpoint of physician utility preferences, overcapitalization in the hospital sector is helpful if it increases slack capacity (and thus the certainty that physicians can get their patients admitted) and increases technology availability. Having an excess capacity of diagnostic and therapeutic equipment is "efficient" for physician utility maximization because it increases income from interpretation of test results and decreases waiting time for information to be acquired.

Hospital overcapitalization may be optimal for the physician staff, but the investment pattern is seldom socially optimal. One ramification of the Averch-Johnson hypothesis is that we would expect that firms would be regulated or constrained from maximizing profit. One corollary of the Averch-Johnson hypothesis is that the cost of capital to the hospital is less than the cost of capital in less regulated private markets. That hypothesis will be confirmed in Chapter 21, and the policy implications of tax-free hospital bonds and "free" fully reimbursed interest charges will be discussed.

We can make one quick test as to whether the Averch-Johnson (A-J) effect might be operating in the hospital sector. If the A-J effect is operating in the hospital industry, those physicians who are most frequent users of the hospital as their workshop should find their incomes improved the most. This hypothesis is supported by national average increases in physician income, where the most hospital-based specialties had the highest growth in income (Table 9.2). This result is certainly consistent with the Averch-Johnson effect, but it does not prove the A-J hypothesis. In summary, the probable allocative distortions produced by the combined effect of increased health insurance coverage and the A-J effect have yielded hospital overcapitalization and physician over-

---

*To place the issue in a broader context, Bower (1966) reviewed the Averch-Johnson hypothesis for the electric utility industry and found a professional agent of the public interest, the engineer, whose power over the investment structure is at least as impressive as the physician community's influence over hospital trustee boards.

specialization. There are too many specialists and two few generalists. We will discuss health manpower issues in a broader context in Chapters 13–15, but it seems plausible to suggest that a reduction in hospital overcapitalization might yield a reduction in returns for hospital-based specialists, and thus reduce the incentive to enter subspecialty training programs.

Physicians have an incentive to keep their retailer—the local hospital—afloat and well equipped. Many physicians view their relationship with the hospital as analogous to the relationship of a free-lance mechanic to a garage, except that the clinical setting must be substantially cleaner. The medical staff, like the mechanic, is not required to pay rent for user privileges. In this context, we shall review three basic models for describing the patient service production process.

If one assumes that the physicians control the medical-hospital producer-retailer channel, the clinician can achieve maximum profits by forcing the retailer (hospital) to purchase inputs and produce services that just cover the hospital's costs. The physician as the producer (manufacturer) controls the supply in the distribution channel and can largely dictate the price for nonphysician providers in the channel. It is in the physicians' interest to have the retailers (hospitals) provide a very expensive, technologically intensive style of service. The professional fees of the physicians are proportionally higher when interpreting and performing the more technologically intensive tests and procedures. Prevailing fee-for-service medical care involves a one-level distribution channel (where the number of intermediaries determines the length of the channel) consisting of the physician (manufacturer) and the hospital (retailer) providing care to the consumer. Medical care provided in the inner city is typically a two-level channel of physician (manufacturer), teaching hospital (wholesaler intermediary), and satellite clinic (retailer) providing the product to the consumer. The physician must set prices in reference to the demand function for professional plus hospital services combined, since physician and hospital services are complements. Consequently, making maximum use of hospital resources, collecting maximum possible fees for test interpretation, and supporting profit minimization in the hospital supports profit maximization for individual physicians.

Alternatively, if one assumes that the retailer controls the production channel, as in the case of a Health Maintenance Organization (HMO), the plan can achieve maximum profits by hiring physician services at below market prices. A third alternative is to assume that the physicians and hospitals or HMO plans

Table 9.2   Trends in Net Income by Specialty, Indexed to Pediatrician Income, 1968–1986

Specialty	1968	1971	1974a	1978	1982	1986 est.	Percentage of Patient Visits at a Hospitalb
Anesthesiology							
(a) Average Net Income (ANI)c	$35,954	47,293	54,365	67,000	131,400	155,000	84
(b) ANI as a % of Pediatricians' ANI	114.0	122.8	129.1	132.9	186.9	199	
(c) Growth in ANI Since 1968 (%)	—	31.5	51.2	86.3	265.5	331	
Surgery							
(a) Average Net Income	$43,907	54,045	60,510	75,800	130,500	153,000	66
(b) ANI as a % of Pediatricians' ANI	139.3	140.4	143.7	150.4	185.6	196	
(c) Growth in ANI Since 1968 (%)	—	23.1	37.8	72.6	197.2	248	
Internal Medicine							
(a) Average Net Income	$35,552	42,869	51,390	64,300	86,800	91,000	49
(b) ANI as a % of Pediatricians' ANI	112.8	111.3	122.0	127.6	123.5	117	
(c) Growth in ANI Since 1968 (%)	—	20.6	44.5	80.9	144.2	171	
Obstetrics and Gynecology							
(a) Average Net Income	$40,572	51,062	61,693	70,600	115,800	127,000	26
(b) ANI as a % of Pediatricians' ANI	128.7	132.6	146.5	140.1	164.7	163	
(c) Growth in ANI Since 1968 (%)	—	25.9	52.1	74.0	185.4	213	

General Practice							
(a) Average Net Income	$33,671	39,823	44,727	52,400	71,900	77,000	24
(b) ANI as a % of Pediatricians' ANI	106.8	103.4	106.2	104.0	102.3	99	
(c) Growth in ANI Since 1968 (%)	—	18.3	32.8	55.6	113.6	129	
Pediatrics							
(a) Average Net Income	$31,527	38,503	42,112	50,400	70,300	78,000	18
(c) Growth in ANI Since 1968 (%)	—	22.1	33.6	59.9	123.0	147	
Average American Worker[d]							
(c) Growth in Family Income Since 1968 (%)	—	23.2	66.3	126.7	202.2	244	
(d) Growth in the Consumer Price Index, All Items, Since 1968 (%)	—	16.4	41.7	87.5	177.5	213	

[a]The Economic Stabilization Program was in effect from 8/15/71 to 4/30/74.

[b]Health Care Financing Administration, DHHS.

[c]*Profile of Medical Practice* (1986), annual source book, Center for Health Services Research and Development. Chicago, Illinois: American Medical Association.

[d]U.S. Department of Commerce, Bureau of the Census (1986). *Statistical Abstract of the United States 1986*. Washington, D.C.: U.S. Government Printing Office.

pursue profit maximization while allowing a "necessary" profit margin to the other party. Such a compromise may result in an inefficient equilibrium at a price between P' and P'' producing a quantity of service ranging between Q' and Q'', as shown in Figure 9.5. To maximize profits physicians set marginal physician revenue equal to their marginal costs, implying a transaction with the hospital involving Q' units of care at price P'. To maximize hospital revenues in excess of costs, hospitals would prefer a transaction with the physicians involving fewer units of service (Q'') at a higher level of reimbursement (P'').

Prepaid group health plans are one of the few markets where health facility managers and physicians are on a relatively equivalent bargaining basis. The management of new HMOs must frequently report to the private risk bearers who supplied the venture capital.

The HMO sponsors are always putting on the pressure and searching the market for better managers. The market for HMOs is

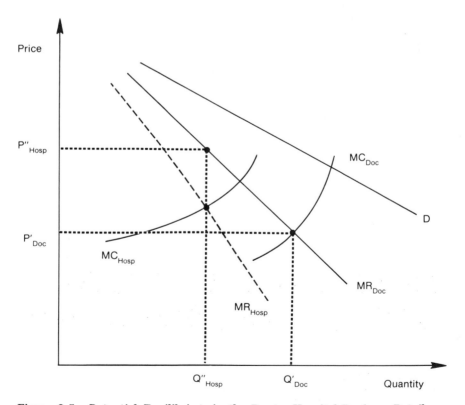

Figure 9.5   Potential Equilibrium in the Doctor-Hospital Producer-Retailer Production Channel for Hospital Services

less stable than the hospital industry, in that there is a higher chance of exit (going out of business). However, the opportunity for growth is very large. Consequently, the owner-sponsors of the HMO search for the best quality managers to deal with the potential growth opportunities in the market for prepaid group health care.

Market Surveys

For the hospital initiating a program, one natural place to begin a marketing research effort is in the patient representative department. The institution will benefit more from a survey of the needs and values of its consumers than listening to planners or consultants speculate on what they think market preferences should be.

HMOs that have taken heed and listened to potential new enrollee preferences have grown substantially. Historically, innovation in the area of health marketing for HMOs has been retarded for fear of retaliation by organized medicine. For example, in the mid-1970s the HMOs in Boston and New York would promote only the physician perception of what consumers value: good, comprehensive care. Beginning in 1982, these same HMOs ran ads mentioning the major advantage of their product from a consumer viewpoint: cost savings, reduced out-of-pocket premiums, and less paperwork than fee-for-service billings procedures. The advertising had a positive effect on consumer response; that is, the HMO had an increased enrollment.

For customer preference surveys to be usable to management, some aggregation of individual responses has to be made. The customers can be algorithmically clustered according to similarity in benefits preferred. Alternatively, they can be a priori clustered according to observable demographic or utilization characteristics—for example, urban-rural or high-user versus low-user, or physician-referral versus self-referred.

Physician preferences also need to be aggregated into clusters. Physicians could be partitioned into four basic groups: clinicians who are hospital-based, clinicians who frequently utilize their privileges at hospital X, clinicians who seldom utilize their privileges at hospital X, and area physicians who have never sought treatment privileges at hospital X. The hospital can organize a marketing program after identification of the sources of physician dissatisfaction. Some physician complaints may not be easily resolved: unacceptable nursing care, demands for additional equipment, or unpredictable availability of same-day surgery. Frequently, the hospital attracts new physicians with a capital project: satellite clinics, inclusion of a family practice department, provision of part-time office space, and ambulatory surgicenters. The marketing ideas need not involve capital acquisitions; marketing the hospital with coupons in the newspapers for families can act as a practice-building source for the physicians.

Marketing in a traditionally nonprofit industry will be fraught with a number of technical and political pitfalls. Some critics may argue that the academic advocates of marketing and competition have substituted benevolent descriptions of success stories for critical analysis. Future health marketing evaluation studies may conclude that the assumptions that were basic to the competition health plan argument fail to hold in all smaller communities and many larger communities. The process of doing market surveys may help on a national scale to convince providers that we should aggressively market caring services and demarket or decrease the marginal curing services that seldom "cure"—for example, heart transplants or heroic medical procedures that prolong for months suffering in a hospital bed. (We shall cover this topic in Chapter 18.)

Physicians as Customers, Middlemen, and Employees

The hospital can meet the needs of its office-based physician-customers in a number of ways. The oldest physician-marketing technique is to provide low-rent office space next to or within the hospital grounds. A more recent technique is to set up a loan fund from philanthropic funds to attract physicians. The monies from the loan fund are "loaned" to fill the gap between the actual annual income of the physician and the individual's targeted yearly income. In highly competitive areas, hospitals and hospital chains are even going so far as to purchase physicians' practices—that is, have the doctor work for the hospital. Young physicians are the best targets for loans or equipment gifts, because they work the longest hours and can provide a steady, high flow of patients to the hospital over the coming years. These "perks" or inducements for physicians are seldom formalized in a written agreement, since such behavior would be considered unethical and sometimes illegal in most states. This situation leaves physicians in the enviable position of being able to request new equipment and take advantage of underutilized facilities, while retaining the flexibility to break the unwritten agreement with the hospital if they get a better deal elsewhere. With the increasing cost of new equipment and medical education, physicians can be expected to make decisions among competing offers on a financial basis. Most physicians cannot be expected to stay with a poorly equipped and poorly staffed neighborhood clinic for altruistic reasons, and some of those who do stay end up doubting the marginal value of their services.

Clinics should be considered in market terms as middlemen or facilitating intermediaries. Satellite clinics seldom have a written agreement with the individual hospital that financed much of their development. However, in providing money and management expertise, the hospital would be foolhardy not to demand a return on its investment. Typically, the clinic is managed by an individual who represents the hospital by informing physicians whenever the occupancy level is low and by providing information regarding which type of beds are most underutilized. In some cases the clinics are not placed where the patient need is higher, such as a poorly insured neighborhood of the working poor (too wealthy to qualify for Medicaid and too poor to afford commercial insurance). Instead, the clinics are placed where the population has the best insurance coverage for hospital reimbursement, or in a location near a competitor's clinic to prevent potential hospitalization cases from straying to another facility. There is legitimate skepticism in the nonprofit sector as to whether location decisions should be made in a fashion that dumps unprofitable poorly insured patients on the facilities with an open-door policy.

Physicians as Employees in a Competitive Marketplace

Some representatives of organized medicine claim that younger physicians are too flexible and cooperative with the "hospital bureaucracy." Increasing numbers of physicians are becoming "employees," and by 1986, 30,000 will be members of unions. According to the AMA, the percentage of practicing physicians working as employees has increased from 23 percent in 1983 to 26 percent in 1986. However, a sense of individuality and independence, combined with a measure of arrogance, still exists in the physician community under age 50. Contacts with medical staff would be less interesting if this were not the case. Entrepreneurialism is still alive within the younger cohort of clinicians, but the avenue for expression has changed. Physician entrepreneurs sell utilization review and quality-assurance activities, initiate PPOs and HMOs, and enter joint-venture investment opportunities. The tendency of some older solo practitioners to balk at terms like "customer," "provider," and "marketing" indicates an inability to adjust with the times. Society made a number of commitments to providing access to mainstream medicine for all. Medical care has become readily accessible to 90 percent of the population, and physicians are now working according to schedules convenient for the patients. Consumers are increasingly receiving more information on which to shop. Even the "hotel side" of hospital services production has improved in the 1980s.

Respect for patient/consumer/customer was a marketing revolution. The revolution was bloodless; Doctors Marcus Welby and Ben Casey lost. During two decades of cost reimbursement, with little pressure to market, the cost "crisis" was a by-product of the system and the incentive structure and not cost per se. One could ignore consumers, run up a big bill, and get paid dollar for dollar. What a great deal? However, competition, with emphasis in purchasing on an economic basis, had to rear its head. We all like competition in what we buy, not what we sell, and health care providers were no different. With the rise of competition came a rising interest in customer satisfaction, marketing, discovering what the patients wanted, cutting excess costs, and offering the service at a favorable price. Innovation occurred on five major fronts:

1. Competitive pricing and contracting (HMOs, PPOs, managed care).
2. Staffing in proportion to workload (dumping unproductive staff).
3. Financial disincentives against overhospitalizing and testing.
4. Incentives to finally invest in aftercare and long-term care.
5. Sufficient supply of both doctors and empty hospital beds.

This new competitive world is not without risks—for example, for dumping patients, eroding the professional ethic, and a myriad of other problems (Colombotos and Kirchner, 1986). However, one can work as a salaried physician, and even join a union, without losing one's professional ethic and interest in safety. The prototype for physician groups in the next century may well be the airline pilot unions. Health care costs may decline since doctors will earn less individually and as a group. Airline pilots have experienced a drop in earnings, but their workweek is shorter, less hectic, and allows more time for family life. And the pilot unions have done an admirable job in the area of quality assurance and customer safety, despite the rise in terrorist activities.

Whereas a physician like Ben Casey disliked the interference of managers and work schedules far too much to work as anybody's employee after finishing his residency, today's young doctors currently see a number of benefits in working within a well-managed system. For one thing, physicians can schedule their work lives with regularity, in contrast to the frequent "on call" round-the-clock status of private practitioners. They are also spared the pain of paying any overhead, doing the billings, and paying malpractice premiums. Increasing numbers of physicians may encounter such "headaches" on a part-time basis as managers themselves.

As more physicians exhibt a preference for salaried positions over private practice, one might ask whether professional autonomy will suffer. Judging by the experience of group practice physicians, the important elements of autonomy need not suffer. Physicians will still have an atypical degree of control over their workload, deciding what patients to admit and how long to spend with each patient. The Group Health doctor strike in Washington, D.C., during the spring of 1986 provided a classic example of the folly of nonphysicians attempting to set quotas for clinical workload. Assembly-line medicine will never exist outside of the Soviet Union as long as we continue to grant MD degrees. The general practitioner who ruled his fiefdom with near total autonomy is an anachronism. Marketing and competition have revived the Marcus Welby housecall, but solo practice is rapidly becoming as unviable and unpopular as blank-check cost reimbursement.

Statistical Techniques in Marketing

Statistical techniques are increasingly directed at causal modeling of consumer behavior. For example, how long is a consumer willing to wait at a clinic without seeing a contact person of any sort before deciding not to return or to repeat elective service? Path analysis is one technique that might be applied to such consumer behavior problems. The technique of path analysis allows the analyst to decompose the correlation between any two relevant factors into a sum of compound and simple paths (Wright, 1960). The decomposition of the correlation has three basic components: direct effects, indirect effects, and spurious effects from compound paths that are not interpretable but are mathematically part of the decomposition. For example, the finding that more liberal maternity benefit packages attracts more enrollees to an HMO (Hudes et al., 1980) may or may not be a spurious relationship. However, if one had built a path model, the efficacy of liberalizing maternity benefits might be found to be spurious if the correlation between benefits and number of enrollees vanished when the effects of income and other socioeconomic variables were controlled.

Customers' preferences and objectives are multifaceted, and consequently require very sophisticated methods of analysis. Customers providing preference judgments about a set of hypothetical questions may produce errors in the responses provided. In considering the percentage of error variance in the criterion variable, one would expect an inverse relationship between errors and individual involvement in the process of providing preference judgments. One would expect lower degrees of error if the choice is among alternatives of substantial importance to the individual, for example, among potential customers for open-heart surgery or among radiologists concerning preferences toward purchasing CAT scanners. High rates of error probably result from situations where the decisions have minimal impact, such as patients' decisions concerning vaccinations or pediatricians' preferences concerning whether the hospital should have a CAT scanner.

No single technique is appropriate for all marketing problems. One technique, conjoint measurement, is probably the most underutilized and promising technique in the health services marketing arena. Conjoint analysis is a major technique used to assess what combination of service or product attributes the users, consumers, or providers most prefer. It summarizes the preference ranking information as an index that is easily understood by nonquantitative decision makers. Wind and Spitz (1976) were the first to utilize conjoint measurement techniques in a health service market to analyze the effect of a number of independent variables on a single (response) dependent variable: "consumers' hospital selection decision." The authors cite the previous work of Green and Rao (1971) concerning conjoint techniques for quantifying judgmental data. In a conjoint measurement study, the respondent (hypothetical consumer) is presented with a set of multiattribute alternatives and is asked to rank or rate combinations of attributes on the basis of some desired dependent variable (intention to buy, preference to utilize). Contrary to traditional attitude measurement approaches in psychology, the respondent is asked to provide an overall evaluation of a product basket or combination of various attributes, rather than simply providing only the relative rating on each individual attribute. The resulting internal trade-offs that each respondent makes among the various attributes can be decomposed into internal, scale-derived, utility judgments of given attributes and reconstructed to impute the consumer's predicted preference for new combinations of attributes.

The early applications of conjoint measurement techniques in the health sector (Wind and Spitz, 1976) provided insight into what consumers value. The consumers' three most important factors in evaluating a hospital were, in order of importance: proximity to home, prestige of the physician(s), and physical appearance of the hospital. It may be surprising to some that the least important factor was whether the hospital was a teaching hospital or had some affiliation with a major university. This corroborates the anecdotal testimony of many multihospital system managers, that consumers place a slightly positive miniscule value on whether or not a hospital is a teaching facility.

Conjoint analysis has more recently been applied to a number of HMO market research projects (Akaah and Becherer, 1983; Carroll and Gagon, 1983). Irrespective of what institutional market segment is under study, ignoring health marketing is an increasingly hazardous style of management that frequently leads to retrenchment of services or fiscal insolvency. However, refinements will be required to sell the industry on marketing techniques. As increasing numbers of health services administration students are being introduced to marketing, these activities will increase and the public and the managers will be better able to assess needs and improve efficiency. As with any management science technique, poorly applied marketing can be a disaster for the institution (Reidesel, 1985). The reasons why health marketing is underdeveloped range from a lack of adequately trained manpower to the hesitancy of trustees to support marketing efforts due to pejorative "business world" connotations. The health institutions that grow in the 1990s will be forward-looking and market-wise; these institutions will not be simply reacting to the immediate demands of regulators and local physicians. A good marketing program can increase consumer satisfaction, improve efficiency, and deliver better quality health services.

References

AKAAH, I., and BECHERER, R. (1983). "Integrating a Consumer Orientation into Planning of HMO Programs: An Application of Conjoint Segmentation." *Journal of Health Care Marketing* 3:2 (Spring), 9–18.

AVERCH, H., and JOHNSON, L. (1962). "The Firm Under Regulatory Constraint." *American Economic Review* 52:4 (December), 1052–1069.

BAUERSHMIDT, A., and JACOBS, P. (1985). "Pricing Objectives in Nonprofit Hospitals." *Health Services Research* 20:2 (June), 153–162.

BAYS, C. (1986). "The Determinants of Hospital Size: A Survivor Analysis." *Applied Economics* 18:4 (April), 359–377.

BOWER, R. (1966). "Rising Capital Cost Versus Regulatory Restraint." *Public Utilities Fortnightly* 65:5 (March 4), 31–33.

BURIK, D. (1983). "The Changing Role of Hospital Prices: A Framework for Pricing in a Competitive Environment." *Health Care Management Review* 8:2 (Spring), 65–71.

CARLSON, R. J. (1975). *The End of Medicine*. New York: John Wiley.

CARROLL, N., and GAGON, J. (1983). "Identifying Consumer Segments in Health Services Markets: An Application of Conjoint and Cluster Analysis." *Journal of Healthcare Marketing* 3:3 (Summer), 22–34.

CLARKE, R., and SHYAVITZ, L. (1983). "Strategies for a Crowded Marketplace." *Health Care Management Review* 8:3 (Summer), 45–52.

COLOMBOTOS, J., and KIRCHNER, C. (1986). *Physicians and Social Change*. New York: Oxford University Press.

CONRAD, R., and STRAUSS, R. (1983). "Multiple-Output Multiple-Input Model of the Hospital Industry in North Carolina." *Applied Economics* 15:3 (June), 341–352.

COOPER, P. D. (ed.) (1978). *Health Care Marketing*. Germantown, Md.: Aspen Systems.

COWING, T., and HOLTMANN, A. (1983). "Multiproduct Short-Run Hospital Cost Functions: Empirical Evidence and Policy Implications from Cross-Sectional Data." *Southern Economic Journal* 49:3 (January), 637–653.

DRANOVE, D. (1984). "A Comment On: Does Practice Make Perfect?" *Medical Care* 22:10 (October), 967.

EASTAUGH, S. (1984). "Hospital Diversification and Financial Management." *Medical Care* 22:8 (August), 704–723.

EASTAUGH, S. (1982). "Effectiveness of Community-Based Hospital Planning: Some Recent Evidence. *Applied Economics* 14:3 (September), 475–490.

EASTAUGH, S., and EASTAUGH, J. (1986). "Prospective Payment Systems: Further Steps to Enhance Quality, Efficiency, and Regionalization." *Health Care Management Review* 11:4 (Fall), 37–52.

ENTHOVEN, A. (1980). *Health Plan*. Reading, Mass.: Addison-Wesley.

ERAKER, S., and SOX, H. (1981). "Assessment of Patients' Preferences for Therapeutic Outcomes." *Medical Decision Making* 1:1 (January), 29–39.

FACKELMAN, K. (1985). "Cleveland Hospital on the Road to Product-Line Management." *Modern Healthcare* 15:24 (November 22), 70–71.

FARBER, B., KAISER, D., and WENZEL, R. (1981). "Relation Between Surgical Volume and Incidence of Postoperative Wound Infection." *New England Journal of Medicine* 305:4 (July 23), 200–204.

FELDMAN, R., and BEGUN, J. (1980). "Does Advertising of Prices Reduce the Mean and Variance of Prices?" *Economic Inquiry* 18:3 (July), 484–492.

FLOOD, A., SCOTT, W., and EWY, W. (1984a). "Does Practice Make Perfect? Part I: The Relation Between Hospital Volume and Outcome for Selected Diagnostic Categories." *Medical Care* 22:2 (February), 98–125.

FLOOD, A., SCOTT, W., and EWY, W. (1984b). "Reply to the Dranove Comment." *Medical Care* 22:10 (October), 967–969.

GOLDSMITH, J. C. (1980). "The Health Care Market: Can Hospitals Survive?" *Harvard Business Review* 8:5 (September–October), 100–112.

GOODRICH, R., and HASTINGS, G. (1985). "St. Luke's Hospital Reaps Benefits by Using Product-Line Management." *Modern Healthcare* 15:4 (February 15), 157–158.

GRANFIELD, M. (1975). "Resource Allocation Within Hospitals: An Unambiguous

Analytical Test of the A-J Hypothesis." *Applied Economics* 7:4 (December), 241–249.

GREEN, R. E., and RAO, V. R. (1971). "Conjoint Measurement for Quantifying Judgment Data." *Journal of Marketing Research* 8:3 (July), 355–363.

GREENBERG, W. (1987). "The Importance of Location in Choice of Hospital." *American Journal of Law and Medicine* 12:1 (May), forthcoming.

GREGORY, D., and KLEGON, D. (1983). "The Value of Strategic Marketing to the Hospital." *Healthcare Financial Management* 13:12 (December), 16–25.

GUTERMAN, S., and DOBSON, A. (1986). "Impact of the Medicare Prospective Payment System for Hospitals." *Health Care Financing Review* 7:3 (Spring), 97–114.

HAYS, R., and WARE, J. (1986). "My Medical Care Is Better Than Yours: Social Desirability and Patient Satisfaction." *Medical Care* 24:6 (June), 519–525.

HILLESTAD, S., and BERKOWITZ, E. (1984). *Healthcare Marketing Plans: From Strategy to Action*. Homewood, Ill.: Dow-Jones-Irwin.

HUDES, J., YOUNG, C., SOHRAB, L., and TRINH, C. (1980). "Are HMO Enrollers Being Attracted by a Liberal Maternity Benefit?" *Medical Care* 18:6 (June), 635–648.

INGUANZO, J., and HARJU, M. (1985). "Affluent Customers Most Discriminating." *Hospitals* 59:19 (October 1), 84–86.

KAUFMAN, N. (1984). "Product Integrity: The Missing Unit in a Hospital's Marketing Process." *Health Marketing Quarterly* 2:1(Spring), 29–32.

KEITH, J. (1984). "Personalized Care Helps Facilities Compete." *Health Progress* 65:10 (October), 36–61.

KELLY, J., and HELLINGER, F. (1986). "Physician and Hospital Factors Associated with Mortality." *Medical Care* 24:9 (September), 785–800.

KOCH, C., and CUNNINGHAM, L. (1986). "Physicians in Product-Line Marketing." *Healthcare Executive* 1:2 (January–February), 41–43.

KOTLER, P. (1984). *Marketing Management: Analysis, Planning, and Control*, 5th ed. Englewood Cliffs, N.J.: Prentice-Hall.

LUFT, H. (1985). "Regionalization of Medical Care." *American Journal of Public Health* 75:2 (February), 125–126.

LUFT, H. (1980). "The Relation Between Surgical Volume and Mortality: An Exploration of Causal Factor and Alternative Models." *Medical Care* 18:9 (September), 940–959.

LUFT, H., BUNKER, J., and ENTRHOVEN, A. (1979). "Should Operations Be Regionalized? The Empirical Relation Between Surgical Volume and Mortality." *New England Journal of Medicine* 301:25 (December 20), 1362–1369.

MACSTRAVIC, R. (1986). "Product-Line Administration in Hospitals." *Health Care Management Review* 11:2 (Spring), 35–44.

MAERKI, S., LUFT, H., and HUNT, S. (1986). "Selecting Categories of Patients for Regionalization." *Medical Care* 24:2 (February), 148–158.

MAISTER, D. (1982). "Balancing the Professional Service Firm." *Sloan Management Review* 23:3 (Fall), 15–21.

MASON, W. B., BEDWELL, C. L., ZWAAG, R. V., and RUNYAN, J. W. (1980). "Why People Are Hospitalized." *Medical Care* 18:2 (February), 147–163.

MIAOULIS, G. (1985). "A Model for Hospital Marketing Decision Processes and Relationships." *Journal of Healthcare Marketing* 5:2 (Spring), 37–45.

NACKEL, J., and KUES, I. (1986). "Product-Line Management: Systems and

Strategies." *Hospital and Health Services Administration* 31:2 (March–April), 109–123.

NEUHAUSER, D. (1972). "The Hospital as a Matrix Organization." *Hospital Administration* 17:4 (Fall), 8–25.

PETERSON, O., ANDREWS, L., SPAIN, R., and GREENBERG, B. (1956). "An Analytic Study of North Carolina General Practice." *Journal of Medical Education* 31:12 (Part 2) (December), 12–20.

PORTER, M. (1980). *Competitive Strategy: Techniques for Analyzing Industries and Competitors*. New York: Free Press.

REIDESEL, P. (1985). "Conjoint Analysis Is Worthwhile Tool, But Be Sure the Data Are Valid." *Marketing News* 19:37 (September 19), 41–42.

RILEY, G., and LUBITZ, J. (1985). "Outcomes of Surgery in the Medicare Aged Population: Surgical Volume and Mortality." *Health Care Financing Review* 7:1 (Fall), 37–60.

ROBINSON, L., and COOPER, P. (1981). "Roadblocks to Hospital Marketing." *Journal of Health Care Marketing* 1:1 (Winter), 18–24.

ROOS, P., and LYTTLE, D. (1985). "The Centralization of Operations and Access to Treatment: Total Hip Replacement in Manitoba." *American Journal of Public Health* 75:2 (February), 130–133.

ROSKO, M., and BROYLES, R. (1984). "Unintended Consequences of Prospective Payment: Erosion of Hospital Financial Position." *Health Care Management Review* 9:3 (Summer), 35–43.

RUFFNER, J. (1986). "Product-Line Management." *Healthcare Forum* 29:5 (September–October), 11–14.

SCOTT, J. (1985). "Virtue a Companion of Competition." *American Medical News* (August 16), 4.

SHORTELL, S. (1985). "The Medical Staff of the Future: Replanting the Garden." *Frontiers of Health Services Management* 1:3 (February), 3–48.

SHORTELL, S., and LOGERFO, J. (1981). "Hospital Medical Staff Organization and the Quality of Care: Results for Myocardial Infarction and Appendectomy." *Medical Care* 19:10 (October), 1041–1055.

STEIBER, S., BOSCARINO, J., and JACKSON, E. (1985). "Hospital Marketing More Sophisticated." *Hospitals* 59:21 (November 1), 73–77.

STRUM, A. (1984). "Who's Your Target? The Answer Will Help Trigger Effective Ads." *Modern Healthcare* 15:4 (April), 98–102.

STURN, A. (1984). "Selling the Medical Staff and Hospital as a Package." *Hospitals* 58:10 (May 16), 98.

WHITEHEAD, A. (1932). *Science and the Modern World*. London: Collier-Macmillan.

WILSON, A., and WEST C. (1980). "The Marketing of Unmentionables." *Harvard Business Review* 59:1 (January–February), 91–102.

WIND, Y., and SPITZ, L. K. (1976). "Analytical Approach to Marketing Decisions in Health Care Organization." *Operations Research* 24:5 (September–October), 973–990.

WIXON, D. (1985). "Product-Line Management Requires a Full-Time Worrier." *Hospitals* 59:21 (November 1), 46–47.

WOLFE, R., ROI, L., FLORA, J., FELLER, I., and CORNELL, R. (1983). "Mortality Differences and Speed of Wound Closure." *Journal of the American Medical Association* 250:6 (August 12), 763–766.

WRIGHT, S. (1960). "Path Coefficients and Path Regressions: Alternative or Complementary Concepts?" *Biometrics* 16:5 (June), 189–202.

ZEITHAML, V., PARASURAMAN, A., AND BERRY, L. (1985). "Problems and Strategies in Services Marketing," *Journal of Marketing* 49:1 (Spring), 33–46.

ZUCKERMAN, A. (1977). "Patient Origin Study Profiles Service Area, Evolving Patterns." *Hospitals* 51:14 (July 16), 83–86.

Part Three

QUALITY ASSURANCE AND PRODUCTIVITY CONTROL

Chapter 10

HOSPITAL PRODUCTIVITY: MANAGING COST REDUCTIONS WITHOUT HARM TO QUALITY OR ACCESS

> *Do not confuse bad management with destiny. You can improve your position with the right management and incentives.*
>
> —ALFRED SLOAN

> *Thinking that the facility cannot improve productivity substantially is the principal affliction of the health care industry. Productivity is the first test of management's competence. One should get the greatest output for the least input effort, better balancing all factors of service delivery to achieve the most with the smallest resource effort.*
>
> —PETER F. DRUCKER

In this chapter we explore a number of "tenets of faith" concerning hospital productivity improvement—for example, "cutting staff harms service quality," "more staff buys more quality," "reducing staff translates into reduced employee morale," and "performance gains accrue only to those who work harder." Alternative mechanisms by which the organization may work "smarter" rather than work harder are also advanced. The implementation of efficient scheduling systems and work unit reorganization, especially when reinforced by an incentive pay plan, has led to significant scale cost reductions. We shall discuss the topic of incentive pay in the next chapter.

The hospital sector's incentive structure has been revolutionized by Medicare's switch from payment based on recovery of costs to payment based on a fixed price per DRG. In the future, productivity will not be just a minor part of the management job or simply an area for added emphasis; it is, to quote Karl Bays (1984), "the whole job for hospital managers."

Hospitals have been thrown into a new game with new rules. Prior to the enactment of PPS, the hospital manager emphasized revenue enhancement, maximization of reimbursement, and, often, real declines in productivity. If the department-level decision was either to improve the productivity of 22 employees or hire 4 more, the response was typically to hire, because the added cost was a pass-through under cost reimbursement. In the future, however, the only "game in town" will be cost reduction through productivity improvement—not old-style growth and revenue maximization.

Productivity, in its simplest form, equals output divided by resource inputs. Productivity can be improved either by expanding output or contracting inputs, or by having the rate of change in output volume outperform the rate of change in input resources. For example, the ratio of output per input improves (that is, we do more with fewer resources) if volume increases 8 percent and staff hours increase less than 8 percent. Alternatively, if staff hours decline 10 percent and volume decreases less than 10 percent, productivity increases. Thus, productivity can be improved either by reducing costs or by increasing output, or by doing both.

Hospital services are a special kind of output. Producing more services than are medically necessary, even if they are produced at a lower unit cost, has little to do with a real increase in productivity. A hospital's production of unnecessary services is inefficient, and the institution will not be compensated for them under PPS. The federal government and other third-party payers will be cooperating with professional review organizations (PROs) to curtail the production of unnecessary services. Cost reduction, not output expansion, is the key to future productivity improvement in most hospital markets.

One measure of hospital output, patient days, is currently declining at a rather alarming rate. The "recession" in patient days may represent a permanent shift in provider behavior rather than a cyclical recurring problem. With less patients in bed, one obviously needs less staff, although some of these "extra" employees can be trained to work in ambulatory care or other settings. In the past, hospital managers have tried to soften the impact of sudden cuts and rehires (Wood, 1984). However, the future may not allow much in the way of rehiring. Even after we net out the shift in employees to other settings, many of the staff reductions of the mid-1980s will be permanent. For all but the most efficient hospitals, some unpleasant staff reductions are, lamentably, inescapable if we are to avoid closure.

The Inadequacy of Present Productivity Measures

A hospital manager was recently heard to exclaim: "So what if patient census dropped 10 percent last year? All departments are reporting more units of activity, so productivity is up and staff should be increased, not decreased!" On the contrary, the efficiency of activity production is essentially irrelevant. Another service industry, police protection, affords an interesting comparison: The important variable for the public is crimes prevented and solved, not staff hours of internal office activity generated, tabulated, or filed. It is easy to get lost in a mass of numbers, producing measures of insignificant activity that turn out to have no meaning. The reporting and analyzing process saps endless hours of management time throughout various departments, and such productivity information systems do not by themselves bring about real cost reductions (Sumeren, 1986).

In the new world of PPS, the basic unit of productivity is the DRG case treated—not the activity units accumulated. There has long been a need for a final product perspective in health care. Counting relative value units (RVUs) misses the target completely. It is largely irrelevant to measure "the product" with nurse relative intensity measure (RIM) points (Grimaldi, 1982), GRASP points (Meyers, 1981), or laboratory standardized unit value College of American Pathologists (CAP) points accumulated (Eastaugh, 1985a). Although RVUs are an improvement over simple procedure counts and tallies, the appearance of high levels of activity can result from inefficient allocation of responsibilities rather than from the group being understaffed or "overproductive." When talking in terms of RVUs, the productivity experts lapse into a jargon that is an industrial engineer's version of the secret lodge handshake. Even the most technically savvy senior managers are likely to doze off when bombarded with indecipherable RVU trends dear only to the heart of the management engineer. Who cares if RVU workload is improving because overreporting is on the increase? What matters to the CEO is that patient census has declined 10 percent, cash flow is down 11 percent, and the hospital will be running a big deficit. We in academia lecture on pristine systems development, but the analysis of RVUs and other activity measures are largely unproductive contributions to the management process in times of stress.

The compilation of activity measures is of little use in setting staffing levels and even less useful for cost accounting. Perhaps more dangerous, management has been lulled into believing that "productivity must be sufficient if we reside in the happy middle range of Monitrend normative standards." Under PPS incentives to "meet or beat" the DRG prices, many hospitals will find the "happy middle" staffing levels fostered by cost reimbursement severely inflated for an institution that wants to survive after 1988–1989.

To summarize, overemphasis of small activity measures is the principal weakness of traditional productivity analysis, and the normative staffing study is not very useful in getting cost-saving results. But if these traditional means of dealing with the issue of productivity are not going to work in hospitals' new environment, what can we do to ensure that services are provided at the lowest cost?

Improving Productivity

The basic requirement of a successful productivity program is that the senior managers and trustees must really want cost reduction. They cannot follow the path of least resistance. As the noted physician and administrator Dr. Richard Egdahl (1984) remarked in the *Harvard Business Review*, a cost-reduction program will likely result in reducing the number of employees and may involve reducing facility capital stock (beds and equipment). If it is true, as Peter Drucker has said a number of times, that productivity is the first test of management's competence, we should reward managers who do more with less—those who reduce staff rather than those who increase staff each year. Productivity improvements should include the following measures:

1. *Move rapidly.* The best productivity programs are rapid, large in scale, cost-beneficial, and provide benchmarks for assessing future performance. Productivity improvement studies do not need to be multiyear and very costly. The first stage of operational assessment can be rapid (three to five months) and quite cost-beneficial. Substantial cost reductions can be obtained in the short run, while second and third stages of more refined improvements (scheduling systems, for example) and incentives are put in place for permanent, long-run cost containment. Timing depends on the size and scope of the facility and areas under study, but rapid plan

development and implementation are essential both for financial and nonfinancial reasons. Allowing the assessment to go beyond a few months would create undue uncertainties among anxious employees.

2. *Start big.* The departments under study should be large if the gains are to be large. A 5 percent improvement in nurse productivity would dwarf a 30 percent improvement in labor productivity of central supply, pharmacy, housekeeping, laundry, plant, and maintenance, for example. The frequent management complaint, "We have the best laundry costs and the worst hospital cost increases," only illustrates a major point. Significant cuts in the big cost areas in a hospital cannot be avoided in the vain hope that cost containment can either be easy or confined to cosmetic reductions in staff. Merely conducting an overhead variance analysis and cutting the number of housekeepers, administrative residents, and summer interns will not get to the heart of a hospital's problems in bringing about productivity improvements.

3. *Ask the right questions.* Trustees and senior management should ask critical questions like these: What staffing ratio do we really need? How did other hospitals get expanded output with much lower growth in staff? What new equipment and organizational changes can be used to reduce staff and make the work force more effective? Examples from other institutions convince management that new methods of organizing and scheduling can be made to work. Normative comparison of "best actors" among peer hospitals (those exhibiting the best levels of productivity) can also be useful in making ballpark "guesstimates" of the potential for staff reductions.

4. *Use a conceptual approach.* The program that produces lasting, significant change, however, must be based on a conceptual rather than a consensus approach. First, the simplistic percentile "peer" comparison approach of productivity by department has little impact on management unless the facility is a severely overstaffed or understaffed outlier (everyone reports being close enough to the "happy middle"). Second, the hospital's unique employee skill mix and patient case mix is seldom captured by the phrase "peers of the same size." Third, the consensus method assumes that other hospitals have approximately the right staff organization and staffing levels for emulation. Fourth, the "quick and dirty" consensus approach typically prescribes motivating individual employees to work harder or faster to produce more units of activity (Eastaugh, 1986).

Programs that focus on the activities of individual workers ignore the two greatest keys to productivity improvement: organization and work-team scheduling. Much can be achieved by examining what is being done and how employees are being organized into work teams (stage 1), and how middle-level managers can schedule more efficiently (stage 2).

Stage 1: Operational Assessment

The conceptual approach argues that it is possible to determine, rather precisely, the number and types of employees a given hospital needs to supply quality patient care and meet its other objectives (teaching and research, for example). Exceeding this number does not increase quality; it simply creates unnecessary costs. Stage 1, the initial operational assessment, involves finding answers to two basic questions: (1) How many people should really be working here? and (2) What is the best mix of staff and other resources?

Four basic actions make up the formal operational assessment:

1. Review historical, current, and budgeted staffing levels.
2. Evaluate facility layout, equipment, intraunit functional relationships, and interdepartmental coordination.
3. Identify operational deficiencies and recommend improvements.
4. Analyze all current forms and management reports for appropriateness and timeliness of the information.

It is the hospital management's ability to focus on those actions and ideas that highlights unnecessary costs that determines the real usefulness of the assessment, however.

Focus on Basic Problems. The study should be based on the following principles:

1. Do not organize for what is done only 5 percent of the time.
2. Streamline overlapping functions and excessive layers of supervision.
3. Reduce those departments that exhibit excess capacity.

The efficiency of standing orders and standard operating procedures (SOPs), such as letting nurses restart IVs, need to be assessed. Nurse activities that need increased delegation to other staff, such as patient transport, running errands, or making beds, should be evaluated. Situations worsened by rigid specialization (for example, a small water spill that takes less time for a nurse to clean up than to make three calls to housekeeping) also should be identified (Eastaugh, 1985*b*).

Reorganize and Retrain for Improved Productivity. Nursing and ancillary departments should reorganize and retrain for improved productivity. Flexibility in staffing is the key to adjusting to the flux in demands during peak periods while keeping staffing levels down. Japanese hospitals, for example, use the "utility infielder" approach; they cross-train all staff in two areas, so that other departments can be cross-covered within the same day or within the same month. Staffing can be reduced 20 percent by using the approach; at the same time, workers with two roles to play experience improved job satisfaction and morale.

Define the Necessary Staff Qualifications. A good operational assessment of any work unit should study each task and determine the actual level of staff qualifications required. Aggregate numbers of recommended FTEs (full-time equivalents) are not the principal output of stage 1 analysis. Let us return to nursing as an example. Equally important to the staffing ratio of nurses per patient is an optimal mix of nurses employed for the given tasks assigned. An excess number of RNs, in the name of quality enhancement, is the biggest problem in nursing cost containment. Nurse administrators who think "quality" depends on how many of their nurses have B.S.N degrees are as mistaken as college presidents who judge "quality" by the number of faculty with Ph.D.s. It is the organization of the work to be done and the skill mix of the employees doing it that are the crucial issues in staffing (Shukla, 1985). Although the emergency room needs critical care nurses, delegation of more tasks to aides and clerks helps to control payroll expenses.

Use an Adequate Reporting System. Functional procedural flowchart analysis and task evaluation are two key tools in operational assessment. Development of standards and the training of personnel to help establish realistic standards are critical (Suver and Neumann, 1986). Nursing productivity studies, in particular, are often hampered by poor information systems and support systems. Although some facilities allocate float nurses' work effort back to the home department rather than to the understaffed units or subspecialty areas (like the operating room), other facilities draw all float pool personnel from an outside registry and define float time as a cost center, with no information concerning where the work effort should actually have been allocated. Useful operational assessment depends on accurate, comparable information. The essential elements in stage 1 of a productivity improvement program are summarized in the top portion of Figure 10.1.

Stage 2: Who Can Be Scheduled Better?

Stage 1, operational assessment, yields better work assignments, identifies "lost resources" and unnecessary activities, and suggests

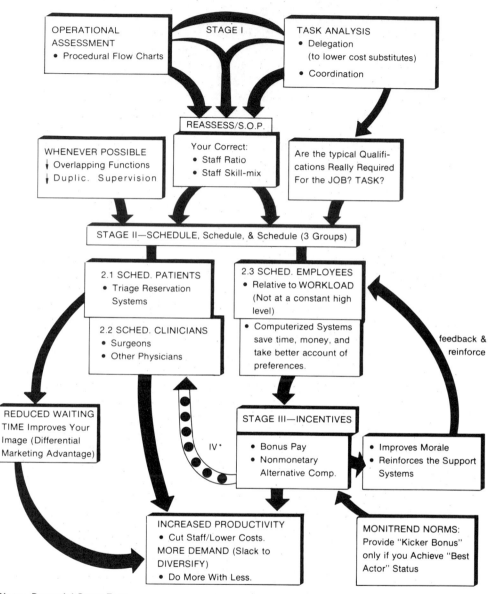

Note: Potential Stage Four,
   *IV—Either form of incentive compensation can be paid to physicians with appro-
   priate attention to IRS restrictions (link it to a productivity index, and *not*
   "profits", "gross" or "net income" if your institution is tax-exempt).

Figure 10.1   Three-Stage Approach to Productivity Improvement

ways to foster efficient interdepartmental coordination. Major productivity improvement, however, depends on one basic element: scheduling. Three critical actors—the patient, the employee, and the physician—must be scheduled for improved productivity. Better scheduling of all three groups, or stage 2, can reduce unnecessary activity flow, reduce unit costs, improve patient satisfaction, and reduce waiting time for both providers and patients (Sahney, 1982; Deguchi et al., 1984; Martin et al., 1985).

Forecast Actual Workloads. Staffing-level assessment in stage 1 refers to the numbers of personnel; scheduling refers to when the personnel are working and when patients are expected to arrive. Obviously, the staffing ratios should be set in proportion to forecasted workloads. In scheduling nurses, for example, if there is a threefold higher workload on day shifts than on night shifts, it would be illogical to provide the same number of nurses over all three shifts. Similarly, even when workload is unscheduled, as in the emergency room, there are predictable patterns of utilization. A sample survey over a few months will demonstrate the days and shifts which have the highest workload, and staffing should be proportionate to this predicted demand. Additional adjustments for seasonal changes and case-mix severity can be made, of course (McClain and Eastaugh, 1983). The result will be that the emergency room will not be staffed so that the day shift experiences 12 visits per nurse per shift and the night shift experiences only 4 visits per nurse.

Preserve Employee Morale. A basic requirement of a scheduling system is that it preserve morale and meet the personal needs of employees for days off, vacations, birthdays, and holidays. In addition, employees must believe that the scheduling process is fair and that it is carried out competently.

Use an Automated Scheduling System. Unfortunately, many hospitals use manual scheduling systems that are unresponsive to subtle shifts in workload and that are perceived as being unfair. It is amazing that personnel are still manually scheduled in an industry that spends over $3 billion each week and that has such complex scheduling problems. For example, if 12 nurses are being scheduled over a month so that each nurse works 22 days, disregarding all other constraints, there would be 1.5 million possible schedules. It is hard to imagine any human being who, even under "no other constraints," could find the best schedule. A computerized scheduling system, however, can select the best schedule without hours of paperwork, hassles, and appeals. The computer can provide convincing documentation of fairness, demonstrating that weekend assignments and shift changes (A.M. to P.M. to nights) have been equalized. Frequently, one finds capable employees being promoted to "scheduler" without ever having been taught the importance of or techniques for efficient scheduling. Computer-generated schedules are guided by efficiency and equality—not by the individual "pet" friend of the scheduler.

One needs to allocate nurses by a methodology which accounts for acuity or the level of care a patient needs. The goal is acuity-driven workload staffing—not merely census-driven staffing (Eastaugh, 1985*b*). However, even the most refined industrial engineering methodology can be undercut if management eschews flexibility in favor of a fixed decision rule—for example, each nurse is allowed every other weekend off. Such a rule results in overstaffing on the weekend and on one or two of the weekdays. One can reduce nursing costs and improve morale by fostering nontraditional staffing arrangements. Flexible use of part-time staff and a combination of two 12-hour shifts and two 8-hour shifts for some full-time nurses can assure a better match between workload and FTEs. The worst of all possible worlds exists when you force nurses to overstaff your facility on weekends and some weekdays and run short of staff on the busy weekdays. The four most prevalent nurse scheduling systems of the 54 hospitals surveyed in Chapter 5 were MEDICUS, CSF Ltd., CASH, and Saskatchewan University.

On a more macrolevel of analysis, we observed in Chapter 1 that the volume of inpatient days in the AHA panel survey (1984) declined 9.1 percent, and admissions declined 4 percent, but personnel declined by only 2.3 percent. Consequently, the phrase "census-driven" flexible staffing became popular in 1984. However, staff per patient day increased by 7.3 percent. There is some truth in the argument that staff per patient day should increase somewhat as length of stay declines (5.1 percent), because the hospital is left with a larger proportion of acute (severe) bed days to serve. As more staff is considered a variable cost, to be cut in line with declines in workload, the staffing ratio should have leveled off in 1985. In fact, in 1985 we observed 2.3 percent decline in total staff, a 6.1 percent decline in inpatient days, and a 4.1 percent increase in FTEs per diem (see Table 10.1). The critical point is that our objective should not become census-driven staffing. A staffing and scheduling system based on monitoring case-mix complexity, such as at Riverside Hospital, is a better alternative (Shukla, 1985; Eastaugh, 1985*b*). To be output-driven (workload-based) in setting staff levels is superior to simply linking staffing to the census.

Table 10.1   Aggregate Annual Changes in Utilization, 1 ÷ Productivity,
Staffing and Capacity, 1983–1985 (AHA Panel Survey)

		1984	1985
A.	Utilization		
	Inpatient days	−9.1%	−6.1%
	Admissions	−4.0	−4.6
	Length of stay	−5.1	−1.6
B.	$\dfrac{\text{Labor Input}}{\text{Output}} = \dfrac{1}{\text{Labor Productivity}}$		
	FTEs/patient days	7.3	4.1
	FTEs/admissions	1.8	2.4
C.	Staffing and Capacity		
	Personnel (FTEs)	−2.3	−2.3
	Staffed beds	−1.1	−1.8
	Payroll expense per FTE	5.3	7.2
	Total payroll expense	2.9	4.8
	Part-time workers	−.8	−.1
	Full-time workers	−2.6%	−2.7%

SOURCE: AHA Panel Survey.

Shukla has demonstrated at the Medical College of Virginia that a computerized nurse scheduling system achieves a far superior match between workload and staffing levels, thus improving the quality of patient care. Nursing costs are reduced, peak periods of overstaffing are "smoothed-out," and staffing levels can be reduced. Further, morale improves because the shift changes can be reduced by 75 percent or more, and minimal staffing levels are achieved 10 to 50 percent more often. With regards to possible changes in quality of service, a tight ship is usually a quality ship— that is, we should not be surprised at the report that quality improves in more productive units or departments.

Schedule Physicians Better. Scheduling systems for physicians can also reduce costs through a reduction in the downtime (wasted time). When an operating room mishandles scheduling of cases, cost overruns result from either underutilization and/or overtime wages. Sahney has instituted highly successful scheduling systems in the operating room and in a number of other settings. For example, he describes how one can easily implement a triage reservation system for ambulatory clinics: scheduling 25 percent more patients per hour (five per hour instead of one every 15 minutes); at staggered times (easy cases at 10 and 10:05, two cases at 10:20/10:25, respectively, with the hardest case served from

10:40–11:00); and with varying duration of forecasted necessary visiting time with the physician (Sahney, 1982). The organization works "smarter," but no individual experiences a perceptible shift toward working harder. Slack periods or downtime simply declines in frequency and duration (Eastaugh, 1986).

Stage 3: When Can Incentives Be Provided?

It is a relatively easy task to cut costs by cutting services or service quality. We have outlined a two-stage strategy that undertakes the hard tasks of managing cost reductions without service reduction or quality reduction. Little attention, however, has been paid to the use of motivational tools. Incentives can improve employee attitudes concerning the innovations implemented under the first two stages. Monetary incentives involve the provision of alternative compensation to individual employees or to departments (the bonus pool is divided up among specific individuals). Stage 3, the provision of incentives, will reinforce the new scheduling systems and new modes of work units. Adherence to reorganization into efficient work units (stage 1) and compliance with scheduling systems (stage 2) have been very successfully reinforced through the payment of incentive compensation.

Put Incentives in Context. In the hospital industry there are many jobs in which individuals have considerable discretion over how they manage their work. Employees and medical staff have control over their personal commitment and their productivity. They can withhold their effort or they can give it in exchange for something they value (cash, vacation time, nonmonetary rewards). Management needs to present with care a philosophical and financial context for the announcement of incentive programs. Employee perception is critical. A system of perceived "bribes" will not change behavior, but "incentive pay" as a substitute for even more belt-tightening does improve productivity and morale.

Communicate the Benefits of Cost Reduction. Many hospital administrators believe that "reducing staff results in working harder and translates into lower employee morale." Indeed, it is true that if the staff cuts appear abrupt and arbitrary and offer no incentive "carrot" to maintain performance, morale may decline and the most outstanding workers may look elsewhere for job security. Staff cuts can improve morale, however, if employees share in the benefits of cost reduction and understand the new incentives and why things must change. For example, the institution and the employees can both be in a better financial position following a 15 percent reduction in employees and an average 9 percent increase in compensation per employee.

Help Employees "Work Smarter." Management should explain to the employees why fiscal realities make net cost and employee reductions an imperative rather than an elective course of action. If the remaining employees receive significant incentive bonuses, they are less likely to unionize and/or strike. Incentive pay offers substantial benefits beyond the reductions in rates of absenteeism. One recent study at Henry Ford Hospital outlines how incentive compensation formulas can be provided to the three critical actors: employees, medical staff, and managers (Eastaugh, 1985). The keys are to provide bonus incentive pay by work subunits, thus reinforcing friendly acceptance of the efficient work and scheduling system, and to "work smarter" not harder, thanks to these systems.

In the case of Henry Ford Hospital's (HFH) incentive program, over 80 percent of the gross improvement in efficiency was returned to employees (including physicians), and only about 18 to 19 percent was retained by the hospital. In industry the facility or firm would generally retain 50 to 75 percent of the savings (Eastaugh et al., 1983). One could speculate that the spirit of a greater sharing of the benefits is more customary in nonprofit hospitals, and that professional and support staff in nonprofit institutions need large incentive rewards to alter existing patterns of behavior. Perhaps hospitals need to be more generous than industry to change the psychology engendered by cost reimbursement.

The HFH alternative compensation plan has four important features. First, it is department-based (not individual-specific until the department divides the bonus pool). Reliance on a department or work subunit level of incentive reward encourages teamwork, relaxes central control, and encourages initiative and autonomy. Second, the program involves no "downside" risk of reduced salary, although business analysts fantasize that poor productivity performance should be rewarded with reduced wages. However, in the hospital context, the no-wage-reductions "riskless" approach was utilized to maximize acceptance of these new incentive payment concepts.

Third, the bonus pay plan was originally operated for clinicians and employees before being expanded to include managers. Not surprisingly, incentive pay is an equally powerful motivator of performance for managers as well as employees. Although often overlooked, manager morale is just as important as employee morale. One encounters many managers who seek new opportunities because their employees received consecutive 9 or 11 percent wage increases, and management wages had been frozen or constrained to under 5 percent per annum increases. One should not simply align employee and firm interest under incentive pay schemes and avoid aligning the financial status of the manager with the productivity performance of the organization. Managers who do more with less should be paid more. Inferior managers should have to face the economic consequences of their extravagance or inefficiency.

The fourth feature of the HFH bonus pay plan is that, if the department or division achieves a target level of very high efficiency relative to carefully controlled HAS Monitrend peer comparisons, a special bonus should be provided each year or each quarter, whether or not they continue to improve. The rationale for such a special "kicker bonus" is that it will maintain the incentive to economize. The alternative—paying no additional bonus after a group has reached a certain maximum or optimal level of performance—implies that the benefits of the incentive plan would fade when the incentive pay is no longer provided. If improvement has been made, why should a department or division maintain such high performance standards? Why not just let performance slide for two or three years, establish a new baseline, and earn a bonus relative to improvements on this new yardstick? This problem was addressed at HFH by providing a "kicker bonus" for achieving target level of efficiency—that is, giving a bonus for maintaining great performance. The approach avoids long-run motivation problems of constantly "chasing your own tail" in trying to forever reduce staff to earn a bonus. We shall discuss other incentive systems in the next chapter.

Use Incentives to Improve Quality of Care. Incentives are quite effective at stimulating the best employees to push the existing standard operating procedures (SOPs) to the limits of efficiency without harming service quality. Who are the best employees? They are those innovative employees who exhibit episodic rule-breaking under the SOP, not merely to add variety to their work life, but to demonstrate that SOP or JCAH (Joint Commission on Accreditation of Hospitals) standards do little to foster efficiency or quality. Incentives implementation, following a conceptual study on task requirements, common skills, job training, flexible staffing, and scheduling, causes the total organization to focus on making a given line of work most productive. With the help of incentives, a hospital can establish and maintain a dedication to high levels of productivity, craft excellence, and quality service.

Physicians and Productivity Improvement

Physicians must be a part of the new drive for productivity under PPS. When physicians order unnecessary RVUs of activity that provide no marginal information gain in diagnosis or treatment decisions, real productivity declines. If the hospital's product is now a DRG case treated, and the total payment and clinical outcome are the same whether 1,000 or 7,000 RVUs of activity are ordered, the extra marginal resources drive up costs without any benefit to the patient or the hospital. Having employees work harder in ancillary departments will not be useful unless the extra information resulting from that work is valuable.

Some unnecessary RVUs will always be produced because of the uncertainties implicit in medical practice. The drive to contain hospital costs, however, will increasingly influence the judgment concerning what is acceptable slack versus what is waste. As the president of the AMA, Frank Jirka (1984, p. 1867), said:

> *We can find ways to eliminate the frill, the waste, the excessive treatments and tests, the unnecessary surgery, and the expensive extras of medical care. We have an obligation to do it, because we cannot put ourselves above or beyond the needs for more economy and efficiency.*

Innovative physicians and other care providers are coming to realize that both efficiency and quality can coexist. Unfortunately, most labor-intensive institutions, including hospitals, often believe that "you cannot cut staff without harming quality." The corollary is the belief that "more staff will buy more quality service." But quality does not improve merely by increasing the number of staff available. Poor response time to a patient's call bell, slow transport time, and slow lab turnaround time are almost never resolved by adding more staff. Continual management oversight is needed to balance all the factors of service delivery if the greatest output for the smallest resource effort is to be achieved. Previously, the unequivocal message from society to hospitals was to expand access and technology. The equally unequivocal mandate in the 1980s is to cut costs by improved productivity management. One is hard pressed to cite a single example of where the decline in staff caused a real increase in adverse patient occurrence (APO) rates or mortality rates (InterQual, 1986). Moreover, the one basic lesson that Japanese management should have taught American managers is that you can rapidly improve productivity and enhance quality simultaneously (Eastaugh, 1985a).

The Search for Productive Product Lines

One handicap for hospital productivity analysis is that we do not know the resources per product line that go into our operations.

Hospital administrators are very familiar with cost reimbursement and per diem averaging, but the PPS market dictates increased concern for true cost accounting and productivity resource consumption controls. Consider two analogous service industries. One could not manage a rent-a-car operation by charging $110 per diem regardless of whether the vehicle being rented was a compact car or a 30-foot truck. One could not manage a restaurant by charging $14 per meal irrespective of whether the consumer ordered toast or steak or lobster. However, in hospital finance we have been uniformly allocating more than 30 percent of inpatient costs as per diem nursing, room and board, and routine daily services. With the advent of DRGs, such a per diem catch-all costing method assumes that all patients utilize equal amounts of nursing time, whether the case is simple or complex. Each patient utilizes a near-uniform amount of laundry and linen, but a crude costing system that has more than one-fourth of costs in per diems is nearing invalidity. Managers and clinicians need to know how much we are wasting resources in the production of intermediate products (e.g., radiology, lab) and how this waste might be reduced. Since hospital care is becoming more competitive and businesslike, nonprofit managers will be reassured to know that every dollar invested in good control systems can be paid back many times annually in reduced waste. In other words, it is cost-beneficial to take the time and perform true cost accounting, whether one deals in compacts or trucks, toast or lobster, or in our case, LPNs and aides or RNs, or lab equipment versus manhours, in the selection of production-mix input decisions (Wood, 1984).

Expanding Output or Cutting Inputs?

PPS has provided strong incentives to expand alternative delivery system (ADS) activities, including surgicenters, PPOs, and free-standing emergency centers. Productivity improves if equal numbers of employees can provide increased output by shifting staff out of the inpatient care business and into ADS activities. However, nonhospital-based providers of ADS services, including physicians, may rapidly saturate this course of output expansion.

The new Medicare PPS system offers ample incentive to expand volume. The PPS system implicitly assigns a 100 percent variable cost factor—that is, hospitals receive 100 percent of the payment for each additional case and, conversely, lose 100 percent of the payment for each case lost. This provides a clear incentive for individual hospitals to increase admissions, since the additional revenue they will receive for the extra cases will greatly exceed the additional costs incurred to treat the extra cases. To make this point clear, consider two hypothetical low-cost firms, hospital ABC and hospital XYZ.

If hospital ABC experiences a 1 percent increase in annual volume, its costs may only increase very slightly, probably by the costs of the supplies used per extra patient. Additional revenue may exceed additional cost by a ratio of 10:1, and an economist studying the firm might conclude that the short-run variable costs are 10 percent of average costs in this one year at ABC. Next consider hospital XYZ. It is experiencing a 20 percent increase in volume over three years. The hospital may have to increase staff (depending on the situation, staff may increase, for example, by 5 to 15 percent), probably increase its administrative capacity (say, 2 to 10 percent), and increase supplies plus square feet of space available pro rata. Additional revenues at XYZ may exceed additional costs by a ratio of anywhere between 2:1 and 5:4. An economist studying the firm might conclude that the medium-run (three-year) variable costs are 50 to 80 percent of average costs, respectively (McClain and Eastaugh, 1983). The essential three points are that variable costs depend on the size of the volume change, management's resolve to improve productivity, and the time frame. That second point, doing more with less, cannot be had with a CEO acting as a "superintendent" by saying: "If volume increases 7.5 percent, I expand my staff by over 9.5 percent, but when volume declines 10 percent in a year, I do not reduce my staff."

The Effect of Labor Relations

One of the basic tenets of good management is that deferring action, albeit painful action, often makes the situation worse over the long run. For example, one director of nursing involved in the Minneapolis nursing strike of 1984 stated that "the wimpy CEO could not lay off 80 nurses in January, so he waited five months and was forced to announce layoffs for 140. This proves that hospital managers do not manage effectively." Needless to say, a good labor representative might call for the "CEO's head" if the layoffs were for 80, or 140, or even 20. However, in implementing the productivity improvement program, senior management will have to fully communicate their concerns to department managers if they desire lasting cost reductions. Each specific action must be placed in a framework of what should be done, by whom, and when. To some extent, department managers should assist in developing the action plan. Too frequently, the department managers are perceived as not really part of hospital management for three reasons. First, they have problems identifying with the management group and instead identify and socialize with the people with whom they work. Second, they therefore resist staff reductions or job/task reorganization in the name of protecting their people. Third, they believe the larger the department FTEs, the higher their prestige within the organization. It is not uncommon for a department manager to proclaim, with pride, that the number of employees in his or her area has doubled in five years. This phenomenon is typical of nonprofit organizations. Again, we should reward managers who do more with less rather than inflate the number of employees each year (Eastaugh, 1986, 1983).

Doing More with Less

The productivity improvement issue has been around for two decades, but until now the will to act has been buried under the comfortable blanket of cost reimbursement. The economic shock to hospitals of prospective price payment may produce a flurry of petty, short-sighted cost reductions. Hiring freezes may prevent facilities from acquiring talented people who have the requisite management science skills to save the institution. Morale will decline if continuing education programs are sharply reduced, anticipated raises are chopped, and marketing and reorganization plans are canceled. Fruitful cost reduction should not be so short run, superficial, and spasmodic as to "cut a little fat," or so ruthless and indiscriminate as to impair the hospital's ability to survive in the long run (Suver et al., 1984; Sumeren, 1986). Any significant cost-reduction effort must involve a significant reduction in the number of employees. Touting the snake oil of "cost containment without pain and staff cuts" is a very poor guide to survival under PPS.

Because hospitals are a labor-intensive service industry, we have emphasized labor productivity. However, productivity has a capital and materials management component. For example, one should care about the hundreds of years of "reduced available equipment life" in poorly managed hospitals with inferior maintenance programs. Under PPS, the hospital industry cannot afford to perform as poorly as the Department of Defense in the area of capital maintenance.

There is little question that it is more difficult to be a hospital manager today than ever before. That difficulty is going to be compounded many times over under the PPS pressure to downsize and "downstaff" hospital operations. We now have a system for closing out excess beds, and it is called "Prospective Poverty System" (PPS) DRG prices. Cost reimbursement and health planning prevented bed closures, which kept the pathology in the system and inflated hospital costs. In the future, hospitals can trim costs through productivity programs and/or contract their scope of product lines by closing the less productive elements in their DRG portfolio. If a hospital does not do a good job in either of these areas, it may have to close. Closure would be tragic to all concerned, for as we know, a closed hospital does nobody any good. Without a doubt, employee incentive systems are our best tool to trim costs and maintain morale.

References

BAYS, K. (1984). "A Common Sense Approach to Productivity." *Trustee* 37:5 (May), 29–32.

DEGUCHI, J., INUI, T., and MARTIN, D. (1984). "Measuring Provider Productivity in Ambulatory Care." *Journal of Ambulatory Management* 7:2 (May), 29–38.

DRUCKER, P. (1976). *The Unseen Revolution*. New York: Harper & Row.

DRUCKER, P. (1970). *Technology, Management and Society*. New York: Harper & Row.

EASTAUGH, S. (1986). "Work Smarter, Not Harder." *Healthcare Executive* 1:3 (March–April), 56.

EASTAUGH, S. (1985a). "Improving Hospital Productivity Under PPS: Managing Cost Reductions Without Harming Service Quality or Access." *Hospitals and Health Services Administration* 30:4 (July/August), 97–111.

EASTAUGH, S. (1985b). "Organization, Scheduling Are Main Keys to Improving Productivity in Hospitals." *FAH Review* 18:6 (November/December), 61–63.

EASTAUGH, S., SAHNEY, V., and STEINHAUER, B. (1983). "Alternative Compensation Incentives for Stimulating Improved Productivity." *Journal of Health Administration Education* 1:2 (Spring), 117–137.

EGDAHL, R. (1984). "Should We Shrink the Health Care System?" *Harvard Business Review* 62:1 (January-February), 125–132.

FERA, M., and FINNEGAN, G. (1986). "Building a Productivity Improvement Team Through MIS Leadership." *Hospital and Health Services Administration* 31:4 (July/August).

GRIMALDI, P., and MICHELETTE, J. (1982). "RIMs and the Cost of Nursing Care." *Nursing Management* 13:12 (December), 19–20.

InterQual (1986). *Hospital Risk Management and Malpractice Liability*. Westborough, Mass.: MediQual & InterQual, Inc.

JIRKA, F. (1984). "Three Major Challenges: Quality, Cost, and Balance," *Journal of the American Medical Association* 251:14 (April 13), 1867–1868.

MARTIN, J., DAHLSTROM, G., and JOHNSTON, C. (1985). "Impact of Administrative Technology on Acute Care Bed Need." *Health Services Research* 20:1 (April), 63–81.

McCLAIN, J., and EASTAUGH, S. (1983). "How to Forecast to Contain Your Variable Costs." *Hospital Topics* 61:6 (November/December), 4–9.

MEYERS, D. (1981). *Grasp Two*. Morgantown, N.C.: MCS.

PALASCO, P. AND EASTAUGH, N. (1986). "Effective Utilization of Operating Room Services," *Health Matrix* 4:3 (Fall), 29–32.

SAHNEY, V. (1982). "Managing Variability in Demand: A Strategy for Productivity Improvement." *Health Care Management Review* 7:2 (Spring), 37–42.

SHUKLA, R. (1985). "Admissions Monitoring and Scheduling to Improve Work Flow in Hospitals." *Inquiry* 22:1 (Spring), 92–101.

SHUKLA, R., and O'HALLARON, R. (1986). "AM Admissions/PM Discharges Can Reduce Length of Stay." *Hospital and Health Services Administration* 31:4 (July/August).

SORKIN, A. (1986). *Health Care and the Changing Economic Environments*. Lexington, Mass.: Lexington Books.

SUMEREN, M. (1986). "Organizational Downsizing: Streamlining the Healthcare Organization." *Healthcare Financial Management* 40:1 (January), 35–39.

SUVER, J., and NEUMANN, B. (1986). "Resource Measurement by Health Care Providers." *Hospital and Health Services Administration* 31:5 (September/October), 44–52.

SUVER, J., OPPERMANN, E., and HELMER, F. (1984). "Using Standards to Predict Nurse Staffing Patterns." *Healthcare Financial Management* 38:9 (September), 48–50.

WOOD, C. (1984). "Productivity in Health Care." In C. Wood (ed.), *Health Care: An International Perspective*, Chapter 12. New York/Geneva: International Economics and Management Institute.

Chapter 11

INCENTIVES FOR PRODUCTIVITY IMPROVEMENT

> *Incentive programs can hold together a productivity program and make it work better. If the employee compensation incentives are sufficient, the employee will work smarter. . . . One has to assume that the individual human being at work knows better than anyone else what makes him or her more productive. Even in routine work the only true expert is the person who does the job.*
>
> —Peter F. Drucker

> *PPS is the flag of the army of cost containers. Whether we will welcome these changes will depend on the ability of the institutional managers and physicians to safeguard the humane values of this most human of human service organizations.*
>
> —Sye Berki

Implementing a successful employee incentive system requires that the health institution already have a strong value system. Senior managers should express in their work the values of trust, excellence, open communication, participation, consistency, recognition, personal fulfillment, innovation, and financial responsibility. Some hospitals are overmanaged, but very few have an excess of leaders skilled at enhancing both morale and efficiency. As an industry, hospitals need less of the style and more of the substance of being "businesslike." On the positive side, many businesses have much to learn from excellent health care institutions in implementing employee incentive programs. Innovation in incentive compensation has been rapid. Wyatt Company (1986), benefit consultants, report that 26 percent of the 447 health care institutions reporting in 1986 had incentive bonus pay plans, as compared to only 7 percent in 1985.

One basic question is at what level should the incentive pay be offered: to individuals, to physician groups, to a single medical staff group, or to physician-nonphysician teams? Another critical question is whether morale is adversely affected if the incentive pay potential is most generous for the individual doctors with the most preexisting room for improvement? Or conversely, is it fair to have little incentive available to those already doing a good job, working efficiently and effectively? These criticisms are partly eliminated by offering the incentive contract between the institution and the departments, with bonus payments offered to the group, and not individuals. Internal group pressure to earn a quarterly or annual bonus reward will compensate for the fact that each individual does not derive 100 percent of the benefits for his or her individual actions. Moreover, the above average performers will have the incentive to assist those not doing as well, because the net monetary benefit is shared by all. The sum total of doctor-specific practice habit shifts in behavior and department productivity improvements will determine the amount of incentive compensation earned.

One final concern is whether the "group" at the department or subdepartment level should include only the "top dogs"—that is, senior managers and physicians. What is at stake if the hospital does not include a wide spectrum of employees in the incentive scheme? Five basic things are at risk: middle manager morale, other employees' morale, institutional market image, scheduling efficiency, and the resulting downtime from inefficient scheduling. While incentives can be the glue that holds an efficiency and effectiveness program together ("working smarter" on productivity improvement and utilization review), to exclude those who are paid less than $50,000 per annum would undermine the best of plans. The so-called "little people" can sabotage the process and throw a "monkey wrench" into a program from which they derive no benefits. The incompetent receptionist or scheduler can go along with the good ideas of the entrepreneur thinkers, or continue to mismanage provider and patient time. For example, the quality of the first contact link in the employee-patient-physician interaction will partially determine whether the institution receives repeat business. In an era of low occupancy rates, repeat business is an important issue for all concerned. Moreover, all of the problem areas are interrelated: poor morale can yield decreased scheduling efficiency, longer patient waiting time, increased consumer dissatisfaction, decreased efficiency, consequently higher costs, and reduced business from cost-conscious payers. In summary, an incentive plan open to the majority of employees seems the best compromise to support harmony and efficiency, while trading off the administrative costs of offering the plan to everyone.

The Do's and Don'ts of Structuring an Incentive Plan

One of the great unanticipated benefits of a well-designed incentive compensation program is the potential for enhanced physician and employee loyalty. Hospital employees are an important implicit component of the marketing program, as "word-of-mouth" advertising is important in any service industry. If employees are jealous of an incentive plan that excludes them, they may act in a more abrupt or uncaring manner. Likewise, if employees believe that pay has no relation to performance, they will "bad-mouth" the institution. But if employees are offered incentives, morale typically improves and all concerned get about "doing the things that really need doing." This action includes minimizing unnecessary activity, working "smarter," and, in the process, cooperating to reduce levels of staffing to more closely approximate case-mix-adjusted workload. Physicians are traditionally an important element of marketing, and if offering an incentive plan enhances physician loyalty, that translates into more patients for the hospital. As a general rule, for every one physician who believes that incentive plans are a mistake and threatens to admit patients elsewhere, there are many other physicians who will actually take the initiative and refer more patients to the hospital with the better incentive plan.

As mentioned earlier, the incentive plan should be groupwide, and not individual-specific. An individual-specific plan, especially if it is so short run as to also be patient-specific, can rapidly erode medical staff support for the incentive plan. A classic example of "what not to do" is the 1985–86 Paracelsus Healthcare Corporation physician incentive plan. The program had two basic faults: (1) compensation was physician-specific and (2) bonus pay was short run (monthly). Paracelsus, a 14-hospital proprietary chain of California and Nevada hospitals, was highly criticized by the December 1985 American Medical Association House of Delegates for creating "monetary temptation" to generate unnecessary admissions. Ron Messenger, president of the West-German-owned

Paracelsus chain, argued that the payment to the physician for each individual patient was so small that clinicians would not want to jeopardize their reputations from a malpractice or peer review standpoint. While the California Board of Medical Quality Assurance concluded that the incentive plan did not violate tough state restrictions prohibiting rebates or kickbacks for patient referrals, the public relations damage was immense. The Paracelsus plan beat the letter of the law by not explicitly connecting payment to the referral of individual patients.

The plan paid individual physicians a defined amount each month if all of the physician's admissions during that month exceeded 75 percent of the hospital's charges. For AMA physicians, including James Sammons (executive vice president), the plan co-opted the existing DRG system by creating incentives for physicians to channel (cream-skim) DRG "winners" to Paracelsus hospitals. Moreover, a physician acting as a perfect economic actor would not admit DRG "losers" to Paracelsus facilities so as not to pull the monthly average profit profile down. Paracelsus' financial managers had calculated that, prior to the 1986 Gramm-Rudman budget cuts, on average Medicare prospective payments run at about 75 percent of charges (list price). For example, for a case in which the Medicare payment equaled 85 percent of the patient's charges, the hospital would pay an incentive bonus of 0.1 of the amount over the trigger point $[0.1 \times (85 - 75) = 1$ percent]. In the 85 to 95 percent patient charge range, the hospital would pay 0.15, and over 95 percent, the hospital would pay the physician 0.2 of the hospital's financial benefit.

Consider a hypothetical patient with a DRG payment of $6,000 from Medicare, actual retail charges of $6,000 in a Paracelsus facility, contrary to historical expectation of charges being generated for that condition equaling $8,000. If PPS paid the hospital $6,000, then $1,500 of that figure would go into computing the incentive payment. The individual admitting physician receives 10 percent of the first $600 ($4,500 to $5,100), plus 15 percent of the next $600 ($5,101 to $5,700), and 20 percent of the next $300 ($5,701 to $6,000). Consequently, the physician pockets $210 and the hospital pockets ($1,290).

The traditional AMA perspective is that "ethical physicians" do not need financial inducements to manage the treatment of their patients efficiently. However, physicians are not immune from incentives. A good incentive compensation plan is good for the institution, the individuals involved, and society as a whole. The Paracelsus plan suffers in this third regard, especially if money-losing DRGs are simply dumped to nonchain member hospitals and net efficiency across all patients is not affected positively. Reducing detrimental or nonbeneficial excess utilization is the major goal of the physician component of a total incentive compensation plan. However, curtailed utilization is a necessary, but not sufficient, condition to improve the institution's financial position. If the hospital does not cut its cost function (paid hours, FTEs, supplies) as the utilization rates decline, no economic benefit is generated from which to pay out an incentive bonus to the critical actors. Bringing key actors on stage is never easy, but the challenge is even greater when the actors represent physicians, financial officers, management engineers, and personnel. The three themes of the play are productivity improvement, cost reduction, and enhancement of service quality. Therefore, each group must reduce costs and improve efficiency to underwrite bonus compensation.

Insufficient understanding of the incentive structure and uncertainty concerning the benefits are the two principal impediments to successful compensation plan innovation. There is an intrinsic dichotomy of economic incentives between a hospital and the medical staff. Three basic situations exist, depending on the patient payment methodology. If the physicians are reimbursed fee-for-service (FFS), and the hospital is not (e.g., Medicare DRGs), doctors have an incentive to inflate the amount of chargeable services, even if it harms the financial status of the hospital. Second, in the case of prepaid per capita care, both the physician and the institution have an incentive to curtail the amount of service offered. Third, if both the hospital and the doctors are paid FFS, all parties have an incentive to inflate services within the constraint that the charts may be "red flagged" for retrospective denial of payment by a utilization review audit.

From a financial standpoint, should the hospital design an incentive compensation program that sends two conflicting messages to the medical staff: to generate more chargeable services when it helps the hospital but curtail chargeable services per case when the hospital is paid a fixed price per episode? Ignoring such concerns as public relations impact, the message serves to confuse the medical staff. The majority of clinicians from 1984 to 1987 appear to have operated in one direction: to curtail duration of patient stay and also admission rates, across a wide range of payer groups, even if some would actually make the hospital money if clinicians would inflate admission rates on non-Medicare patient days. The physician community is responding to pressure from Medicare PPS and PRO programs (Fielding, 1984) and pressure from private utilization review efforts.

Some hospitals have offered a way of obfuscating the idea of a differential style of medicine by payer class. In this type of incentive compensation plan, the hospital calculates three target lists of high-volume DRGs, ignores low-volume DRGs, and claims to pay bonus compensation independent of payer source. In the case of the first list, the hospital generates a Medicare-intensive (e.g., more than 45 percent of the patient days serve Medicare patients) list of DRGs, offers a "carrot" (positive) incentive to bring in more DRGs on this specific list, and at the same time offers a disincentive to generate more cost per case. The hospital also generates a second list of prepaid-intensive DRGs (disproportionate share of capitated patient cases), and offers an incentive to minimize costs per case (and perhaps admissions) for the DRGs on this list (within the constraint of not producing such consumer dissatisfaction as to reduce per capita payer source income). For the third list, the hospital generates a list of DRGs with a high proportion of fee-for-service patients and offers positive incentives to generate more chargeable services, more admissions, and more services per admission.

Rather than sending conflicting signals to the medical staff through three-tiered differential incentives by type of DRG, or payer type, a more simple and honest incentive plan pegs bonus pay to economic efficiency for labor. Such a plan has been developed in a number of contexts (Eastaugh, 1985a). The plan is based on an improvement (decline) in a unit's compensation ratio, equal to the unit's total staff compensation divided by adjusted gross revenue (a fraction typically between 0.35–0.85). The work unit in question can equal a clinic, department, or strategic product-line grouping (SPG) of jointly produced DRGs. An SPG cluster is identified as a clearly defined list of DRGs performed by a defined subset of the providers and staff. In order to avoid risking loss of the tax-exempt status of an institution, one has to avoid paying a bonus based on "profits" or "cost savings relative to income" (Eastaugh et al., 1983, Eastaugh, 1985b) and instead pay a bonus for improvements in the CR (compensation ratio, labor expense/ net revenue) relative to an external target.

Allocation of Incentive Pay to a Work Unit

The external target is the desirable compensation ratio (DCR), or lowest ratio (best economic efficiency), for peer work units across peer institutions (e.g., compare the Cleveland Clinic to the Mayo Clinic, Lovelace Clinic, and Henry Ford Hospital clinics). This

DCR ratio is equal to total labor compensation in the "best actor" (lowest CR) unit nationally or locally, divided by adjusted gross revenue (Eastaugh et al., 1983). Adjusted gross revenue equals actual collected revenue—that is, gross revenue less contractual allowances, bad debt, or retrospective denial of payment from the utilization reviewers. The DCR is set on a prospective annual basis by the policy and planning and finance committees, based on the recommendation of a compensation committee that utilizes historic department/unit/clinic performance data and comparative data on other "efficient" peer institutions to set up targets.

These three committees work on the basis of monthly or quarterly mutual feedback. An incentive pay share (fraction) is paid for any percentage improvement in lowering the DCR ratio (CR equals actual monthly or quarterly total labor compensation divided by adjusted gross revenue), plus a "kicker bonus" for merely achieving the DCR ratio. If the compensation committee has set a DCR ratio that is too easily achieved, the finance committee may consider reducing the slope of the incentive payment if necessary (so as not to "give away the store" and pay more compensation relative to economic gain). If the compensation committee has set the DCRs in certain areas very high, the finance committee may calculate a more generous incentive pay slope for any percentage improvement (decline) in CR performance, even when performance falls short (excess cost above) the given DCR target. For example, if actual CR is 0.77 and the DCR at two efficient "peer" hospitals is 0.48, the benefits of any lowering in CR between the hospital and those involved in that area (including physicians) could be shared. The share of the benefits going to individuals might have to be higher (70 to 80 percent) to get inefficient departments that exceed the DCR by more than 20 percent to improve their behavior. However, if this department or clinic lowers its CR to within 0.48 ± 0.096, the benefits should be shared 50/50 (equally) between the hospital and those employees and clinicians involved.

In setting the targets across hospitals, one can find a tight range of DCR variability, such as 0.45 to 0.50 for strategic product-line groupings (SPGs): colon and rectal surgery, vascular surgery, or obstetrics-gynecology (Eastaugh et al., 1983). However, in comparing hospitals, the range of DCR variability for an SPG can vary from 0.45 to 0.70 for pediatrics or pediatric surgery to 0.55 to 0.80 for internal medicine. This approach has been tried in a wide range of facilities (Eastaugh, 1986, 1985a). If the SPG group achieves its DCR target, there should be a small (3 to 5 percent) additional "kicker" bonus (expressed as a percentage of adjusted gross revenue). If an SPG group improves its DCR to below the target, it will generate an additional bonus payment (slope set by the finance committee, with approval by the board of trustees). One might ask: Why pay a "kicker bonus"? One long-term problem for departments that serve as the industry standard for efficiency (DCR in department X) is that the best performers will have a diminished motive for improving efficiency in the future. Without any incentive, the best departments or clinics will not have any motivation to take risks or innovate when the opportunity arises. Efficient SPGs should generate some incentive pay, whether or not they continue to improve. Moreover, without a "kicker bonus" there is a clear incentive to "game" the system—that is, let the department or clinic have a bad year, and then "clean up" the next year by reachieving the DCR target.

Allocation Within the Work Unit of Incentive Pay

Whereas the decision as to how much incentive pay to allocate to a work unit should be based on performance outcome criteria, the division of incentive pay within the group typically involves process criteria. Employee criteria are usually developed, with a weighting scheme, in four basic areas: (1) attendance (e.g., score two performance criteria points for the year if unplanned absences are 0–3, one point if 4–7), (2) quantity of work per hour, (3) quality of work, and (4) team effort (e.g., score two criteria points if the employee willingly accepts new processes and team methods; subtract one criteria point if the employee passively resists new directions or changing work methods). All criteria points should be scaled relative to the work unit minimum level of performance— that is, zero points are earned if the employee just does the minimum. The performance appraisal should be numerically scaled so as to avoid words that carry perjorative meaning that might anger employees (e.g., poor, fair, good, so outstanding as to be "administrative material"). The rater will always encounter negative reactions in telling the employee "you have achieved minimum standards; congratulations, you are 'a slightly below average.' " Consequently, the scoring form should list numbers only, not words.

Too wide an array of possible ratings should also be avoided, as this only invites excessive subjectivity into the performance appraisal process. The form should also be kept short, so that performance appraisal is viewed as a management tool and not a management burden. In addition, the form should be somewhat task-specific, so that individual employees know where to improve their performance. Finally, as the hospital allows departments to earn a "kicker bonus," so should department managers allow good performance by employees on the top end of the pay and performance scale to receive a "kicker" bonus. As a hypothetical example, your department might receive $176,000 of bonus pay, and the pay is allocated at the rate of 2 percent of base salary paid to an individual per criteria point earned; and, in addition, two exceptional employees receive a $1,200 "kicker" bonus. The performance criteria point system will always need to incorporate a significant degree of subjectivity. For example, research articles produced might be a subcomponent of team effort, which added to the output of the department but had nothing to do with the improved economic performance (the $176,000 earned).

Managers should be evaluated with four analogous criteria: (1) department planning, direction and marketing; (2) budget management and control per quarter; (3) personal professional development; and (4) human resources development. Managers do react to incentives, which is why incentive compensation has become so popular in the health sector since the enactment of PPS. The weights for various measures should be provided ex ante (up front). For example, a senior manager's performance could be composed 30 percent based on improvements in the operating margin, 20 percent for improved market share, 10 percent for improved inventory turnover, etc. Does incentive pay yield improved market share or financial performance? The CEO of Beverly Hospital outside of Boston attributes his 14 percent increase in admissions and 5 percent decline in FTEs over 30 months (1984–1986) to just such an incentive pay scheme. Incentive pay can act as a counterveiling force to competitive pressures (e.g., when seven HMOs and PPOs entered the Beverly Hospital market). Managers, other employees, and physicians are much more likely to evolve, proact, improve standard operating procedure, and joint venture if they receive direct compensation. Hospitals without incentive plans experience an erosion in morale and market share.

Spirit of Teamwork

Incentive plans are often a response to competition between organizations that in turn create more productive cooperation within the organization. Superior output (quantity and quality of care) does not require dog-eat-dog competition, but incentive plans can reward cooperative and productive behavior. Antiproductive employees may view all incentive plans as "Yuppie victory behavior," but the institution is better off without such individuals on staff. Team-specific incentive plans establish the ethic that (1) others are depending on you and (2) your lazy behavior will adversely affect other members of the team. Incentive compensation should reinforce the love of doing both better quantity and quality of work. Competition between departments or hospitals may increase, but incentive plans typically enhance cooperation between team members. It is pop-sociology nonsense to suggest that incentive plans produce anti-cooperative or anti-productive "vying behavior" between workers. However, incentive plans can reward what Peters and Austin (1985) refer to as "skunks," or "disruptive champions of innovation" (the entrepreneurs referred to in Chapter 10 are in effect salaried "skunks" attempting to do things more productively, and promote better forms of efficient cooperation).

One could consider nonmonetary incentive programs, but they typically have little impact on behavior. The one exception to that generality is religious hospitals. In the case of religious hospitals, the incentive might be educational (e.g., extended management development programs). If the nonmonetary incentive is too trivial, it will do more harm than good. The classic example is offering "pins" on nurse appreciation day, while the competition offers incentive pay at the local hospital. On one such occasion, a nurse stood up and said "They don't have a doctor's appreciation day— those people get money—and my spouse in the factory gets a semiannual bonus check, so why not us?" Financial incentives are quite new in the tax-exempt hospital industry, as are the forces that make them increasingly necessary. These forces include unilateral price payments (e.g., Medicare PPS) and aggressive price discounters (e.g., PPOs). We often sugarcoat the title of our incentive programs with phrases like "gain sharing" and "global hospitalwide incentive sharing," as if certain segments of the hospital could not improve efficiency with autonomy. In contrast, most business executives are quite aggressive about the use of incentives. Many business executives receive half of their total compensation from incentive provisions. Having the firm, the hospital, keep 20 to 50 percent of the economic gain may seem overly generous by industrial standards. Judson (1982) reports on business incentive programs that retain at least 66 percent of the gross economic benefits for the company. One could argue that professionals and support staff in tax-exempt hospitals need a larger incentive reward to alter inefficient patterns of behavior. Alternatively, the spirit of a greater sharing of benefits is more customary among health care institutions, in which case the institution should accrue a minority share of any labor productivity gains.

Incentive Plans of the Future

In the 1990s, tax-exempt managers may increasingly have to mimic investor-owned motivational plans and issue not only bonus compensation, but also stock options. Conveying a "sense of ownership" may evolve increasingly into giving an equity share in the organization. Managers, employees, and doctors may come to own stock in their core business (the hospital itself), or some co-op subchapter T corporation of the hospital, or a for-profit subsidiary of the hospital. Defenders of the status quo in nonprofit hospital administration will resist this trend in 1990, just as they resisted pay increases for hospital employees in the 1960s and resisted calling administrators "managers" in the 1970s and "executives" in the 1980s. These archaic individuals are often wrong, thus demonstrating a remarkable degree of consistency. Times change and economic efficiency must improve, but this need not result in any erosion of the hospital mission.

The challenge for senior management and trustees is to find a means whereby all parties are motivated to work toward a common goal. Counterproductive workers might be weeded out, so that creative entrepreneurs can do a lot more. Reductions in salary expenses by firing nonproductive employees would provide the resources for offering incentive compensation and, more important, the resources for institutional survival and better quality care in an era of total revenue controls. Four crucial features are outlined in the incentive plan:

1. Departments requesting more financial support will have to face some of the economic consequences of their extravagance (inefficiency is no longer a reimbursable expense).
2. The plan should involve no downside risk of reduced salary.
3. The plan should offer a "kicker bonus" for those who receive the target (DCR) level of performance in order to maintain the incentive to economize.
4. The plan should be group-specific until the department divides the compensation pool among individuals.

The department-level director in charge of the compensation pool can also reward excellent noneconomic performance, such as incentive pay for research and teaching. This builds a spirit of harmony in the teaching hospital context (Eastaugh et al., 1983) and helps to underwrite improvements in graduate medical education and encourage biomedical research. The incentive compensation system should be viewed as a means of relaxing central control and encouraging local department initiative and autonomy. Management must be vigilant, however, to prevent departmental "turfing" behavior—that is, shifting work to others to appear more efficient on paper.

Fairness and Efficiency

If some clinical areas are viewed as intrinsically lucrative, one could consider pooling 10 to 20 percent of the net institutional bonus compensation pool and distributing it equally to all employees. This would add to an institutional feeling of cohesion and teamwork and make the program de facto 10 to 20 percent "gain sharing," and 90 to 80 percent department sharing. Innovation in cost control may be quantum, in leaps and spurts (Eastaugh, 1981). For example, if an individual department does not perform well in 1988 but earned a great bonus payment in 1987, at least it shares in some small bonus in 1988 under a limited gain-sharing program.

Many old-line administrators might fear that clinicians and/or managers might be tempted to understaff their departments in order to minimize the compensation ratio (CR), thus maximizing their incentive plan income. There are a number of arguments against these fears, apart from the fact that this behavior has not been observed (Eastaugh, 1985a, 1985b; Shyavitz et al., 1985). One can explain this finding within the context of economic utility theory or Herzberg's (1974) construct of two motivating factors: satisfiers and dissatisfiers. If one really does understaff—the classic dissatisfier—an erosion in the quality of the workplace will come into play. For an educated professional, the hassles associated with running an understaffed department or clinic far outweigh the potential gain in income. Satisfiers include income, local and national peer status, recognition, and reputation.

Cutbacks on the compensation ratio to the detriment of the quality of service would have a terrible impact on prestige and reputation. Insensitive practitioners of the "cowboy school of management," irrespective of quality concerns, fortunately do not last long in the health field. Concern solely for short-run income would have a negative impact on long-run income and reputation. It appears from recent trends in staffing FTEs and workload that in the jargon of economics there is enough X-efficiency (slack) to improve productivity closer to the level of an efficient "peer" facility without harming quality (e.g., Shukla and O'Hallaron, 1986). Departments and institutions in any industry attempt to optimize slack in order not to work too hard, but our industry has grown a high degree of slack under the safe blanket of cost reimbursement. For most, reputation is more important than a few extra dollars, but the few extra dollars in bonus compensation reinforce the decision to trim excess costs and initiate productivity innovations, all without harm to one's reputation. Therefore, until most slack X-efficiency is exhausted, we have in the health sector a number of effective, related incentives that act as checks against domination from purely monetary concerns. Tax-exempt hospitals that ignore incentive reward systems will find productivity and the financing of quality-enhancing programs as elusive as the golden fleece. Moreover, health facilities that do not reward their managers and effective employees sufficiently will find their best employees going to other facilities. When you consider the joint costs of the search process (for a replacement) and training, incentive pay is typically more cost-beneficial than having a high turnover rate. Proprietary health care facilities have realized for decades that they "get what they pay for" in terms of the correlation between pay and performance.

Other Incentive Compensation Plans

The DCR incentive plan outlined offers a blend of four traditional gain-sharing incentive plans: Scanlon, Improshare, Rucker, and profit sharing. These gainsharing plans engender bottom-to-top employee involvement and are considered a component part of a total compensation plan (Table 11.1, lines 1–5). However, an alternative innovative reward system can be run independently of the compensation program (lines 6 and 7, Table 11.1). Performance management systems (PMS) offer equal payout to work unit members for achievement of various financial or physical corporate objectives. PMS programs typically result in a modest 4 to 6 percent across-the-board improvement in manager incomes. Second, team suggestion programs (line 7, Table 11.1) pay out a fixed percentage (20–25) of work units' successfully implemented cost savings or business-expansion ideas. In contrast to monthly PPS programs, team suggestion programs are paid out as earned. (For the interested reader, Laliberty and Christopher (1984) provide a good introductory survey to employee work study methods and incentive plans.) The team suggestion payout is typically made with merchandise, and not cash, as the employee earns "recognition credits" redeemable for items in the Green Stamp award book. While human resources personnel point to the "cute reaction" of employees who bring their gifts to the workplace to "show them off," such merchandise incentive plans have a number of drawbacks. Operating the gift plan has significant administrative costs, and employees come to resent the limited lists of available items. One New Jersey hospital reported good long-run financial

Table 11.1 Seven Alternative Incentive Compensation or Reward Systems

Reward Plan	Formula Basis	Goal(s) (type of situation)	Level (timing)	Sharing Split of Benefits	Reserves
1-5 Gain-Sharing Incentive Compensation Plans					
1. Scanlon	$\dfrac{\text{Labor costs}}{\text{Sales}}$	A. Reduce labor expenses B. Suggestion committee C. Common-fate atmosphere (crisis situation)	Firmwide (quarterly)	75% to labor	10% set aside
2. Desirable compensation ratio (Henry Ford Hospital)	$\dfrac{\text{Total labor costs}}{\text{Net revenue}}$ (kicker bonus—if this DCR ratio equals the best, lowest, among peers)	A. Reduce labor input expense or expand rev. B. Merit-based pay for performance (ongoing situation)	Work group (annual)	60–80% to labor & MDs	10% distributed hospitalwide the following year
3. Improshare (J.F.K. Hospital, Edison, N.J.)	Nonfinancial base productive hours factor (BSF)	A. Improve productivity B. Reduce nonproductive hours (ongoing situation)	Work group (weekly)	50% to labor	10–25% rolling average

	Labor costs Sales-allowances- materials-supplies		Firmwide (monthly)	100% to labor	25%
4. Rucker		A. Reduce costs fast B. Suggestion committee C. "Open books" spirit of trust (short-run/crisis)			
5. Profit sharing (Humana)	Bottom-line profits	A. Control cost behavior B. Expand operating profits (ongoing situation)	Work group (quarterly)	10–40% to labor	50/50 deferred income available

6–7 Innovative Reward Systems (Independent of the Compensation System)

6. Team suggestion (Raritan Bay Med. Center, N.J.)	5–20% split of the savings among team members	A. Suggestion system B. Earn points to purchase merchandise (ongoing situation)	Work group (payout as earned)	15–20% to labor	Possible
7. Performance management system (NME)	% share of the value of improvements (sales, cost)	A. Highly customized for a big firm/chain B. Driven by senior management objectives	Strategic business units	10–30% to labor	Possible

and employee performance from a suggestion program. The 550-bed Raritan Bay Medical Center improved productivity 10 percent (1983–1986), generated a net savings of $4 million, and paid out $1.1 million in merchandise to employees.

Cash is a much less paternalistic form of incentive. However, one of the disadvantages of cash as a motivator is that the bonus checks are perceived to be too modest in size if delivered weekly (Improshare) or monthly. The DCR plan and traditional profit-sharing plans avoid this problem by offering annual payouts and quarterly accounting reports of bonus earnings. A number of other plans overemphasize timing—that is, the need to have the payout within weeks of the performance improvement (Scanlon, Rucker, Improshare). The concerned individual can keep a tally of how much bonus pay he or she has earned, and directly realize the connection between actions and benefits, without having the cash in-pocket under the DCR plan.

One of the central strengths of the Improshare gain-sharing plan, like the DCR plan, is that the incentive payout is work-unit specific (those who earn it receive it). The Scanlon and Rucker plans suffer from being hospitalwide in focus. Improshare incentive programs do have their downside. Improshare managers report that their employees are doing departmental functions that they "never had time to do." However, in the documentation of more relative value units (RVUs) of activity, these employees can generate more useless activity that does not "impro-" actual productivity. The DCR incentive plan offers incentive pay to streamline and eliminate useless departmental functions and free up more productive hours of nonadministrative activity. The DCR plan offers a less generous payout sharing with employees than the Rucker plan (100 percent to the employees, but usually for only 6 to 12 months). The team suggestion and PMS plans offer only 10 to 20 percent of the benefits to those who earn them, which suggests the incentive "carrot" might not be sufficient as a long-run motivator. The DCR plan offers a more generous payout to the employees, while retaining a 10 percent hospitalwide reserve fund to be shared by all employees.

As a thought experiment one could hypothesize that the simplest method of offering direct incentives for better performance would be if those involved divided up the proceeds every time $25,000 in cost reduction was achieved, or five to ten extra patients were brought in (cost variance and volume variance, respectively) compared to the forecasts. Unfortunately, the Internal Revenue Service would question the inurement provisions that no private individual (employee, physician) benefits from the tax-exempt status of the institution under 501(c)(3) of the tax code. In preparing a report on the incentive plan, the institution should be able to demonstrate that the plan contains maximums for salary improvement each year (e.g., 33 to 40 percent), and that the institution will always benefit under the compensation plan. The actual payment of the bonus may be offered in a number of ways, ranging from a check to payment into each employee's tax-sheltered annuity account.

Summary

Incentives are an important third stage in any comprehensive productivity improvement plan. A successful plan must attract the enthusiastic support of the employees and the physicians. Behavior will not change if the plan is viewed as merely a short-run management gimmick. According to a number of IRS rulings, tax-exempt institutions may not have an incentive plan involving the distribution of "profits," "net income," "gross receipts," or "cost savings" (Groner, 1977; Eastaugh et al., 1983). However, the plan can pay for performance relative to technical efficiency (productivity) or a desirable compensation ratio (proxy variable for labor productivity). One merely needs to demonstrate to the IRS that the plan does no financial harm to the institution by paying out too much incentive compensation ("giving away the store").

One critical requirement of any good productivity program is that the facility have comprehensive and timely management information systems (Fera and Finnegan, 1986). Moreover, the program should build on a preexisting strong human resources program and involve strong support from senior management.

A 1985 AHA survey revealed that 40 percent of nonsmall hospitals are utilizing, or plan to utilize, incentive compensation plans. One should infer from this chapter that a well-designed plan should have five E-Q-U-I-P attributes:

1. Establish a merit-based performance climate with pay for performance rewards for superior workers and idea makers (entrepreneurs).
2. Quality emphasis—to overcome the antiproductive orientation that if "you try, come to work, you should all get the same pay"—by making the incentive bonus pay significant in size (and linked to a quality-enhancing customer orientation).
3. Unproductive workers should face sanctions and no pay increases, so they hopefully will leave the facility (and go to the competition).

4. Incentives should be offered in the spirit of a "cut of the action"—or if you prefer less entrepreneurial rhetoric—a common-fate atmosphere that requires change and continuous improvement if the institution is to survive.

5. Promote a spirit of job security and trust, built upon the preexisting compensation system and performance appraisal framework.

Further research is needed to analyze how these incentive reward programs affect the total institution. Organizational theorists have developed a number of competing hypotheses to explain explicit and implicit contractual relationships between senior managers, middle managers, employees, and independent contractors (Murphy, 1986; Coughlan and Schmidt, 1985). Response to incentives can be analyzed under two alternative hypotheses: (1) where productivity depends on difficult to observe efforts and (2) where ability is unknown and is revealed (learned) over time. If the preexisting productivity measurement system is crude or continues to remain highly imperfect (e.g., due to the nature of the job), past performance may remain irrelevant in predicting current or future performance. Under the second hypothesis, incentive compensation could merely unlock the door of innate managerial ability, which is initially unknown but revealed over time. The two hypotheses are not mutually exclusive, and individual incentive payment profiles should reflect some mix of both incentives and learning.

A number of noted members of the economic profession have written extensively on the relationship between progress and the "law of comparative advantage": If each good or service is supplied by the most productive producer, all in society will be richer. To be against productivity is to be against medical progress. Productivity gains will help underwrite our future improvements in service delivery and technology. These programs will provide the linchpin to ensure that we continue to deliver a quality service at an affordable cost for all concerned.

References

BERKI, S. (1985). "DRGs, Incentives, Hospitals, and Physicians." *Health Affairs* 4:4 (Winter), 70–76.

COUGHLAN, A., and SCHMIDT, R. (1985). "Executive Compensation, Management Turnover, and Firm Performance." *Journal of Accounting and Economics* 7:1 (January), 43–66.

DRUCKER, P. (1979). *Adventures of a Bystander*. New York: Harper & Row.

DRUCKER, P. (1964). *Managing for Results*. New York: Harper & Row.

EASTAUGH, S. (1986). "Work Smarter, Not Harder." *Healthcare Executive* 1:3 (March-April), 56.

EASTAUGH, S. (1985*a*). "Improving Hospital Productivity Under PPS: Managing Cost Reductions Without Harming Service Quality or Access." *Hospitals and Health Services Administration* 30:4 (July/August), 97–111.

EASTAUGH, S. (1985*b*). "Organization, Scheduling Are Main Keys to Improving Productivity in Hospitals." *FAH Review* 18:6 (November/December), 61–63.

EASTAUGH, S., SAHNEY, V., and STEINHAUER, B. (1983). "Alternative Compensation Incentives for Stimulating Improved Productivity." *Journal of Health Administration Education* 1:2 (Spring), 117–137.

FERA, M., and FINNEGAN, G. (1986). "Building a Productivity Improvement Team Through MIS Leadership." *Hospital and Health Services Administration* 31:4 (July/August), 7–17.

FIELDING, J. (1984). *Corporate Health Management*. Reading, Mass.: Addison-Wesley.

GRONER, P. (1977). *Cost Containment Through Employee Incentive Programs*. Germantown, Md.: Aspen Systems.

HERZBERG, F. (1974). "The Wise Old Turk." *Harvard Business Review* 52:2 (March-April), 70–80.

HERZBERG, F., MAUSNER, B., and SYNDERMAN, B. (1959). *The Motivation to Work*. New York: John Wiley.

HRANCHAK, W. (1985). "Incentive Compensation and Benefits of Profit Sharing Plans." *Topics in Health Care Financing* 13:1 (Fall), 33–40.

JUDSON, A. (1982). "The Awkward Truth About Productivity." *Harvard Business Review* 60:1 (January/February), 93–97.

LALIBERTY, R., and CHRISTOPHER, W. (1984). *Enhancing Productivity in Health Care Facilities*. Owing Mills, Md.: National Health Publishing.

MILKOVICH, G., and NEWMAN, J. (1984). *Compensation*. Plano, Texas: Business Publications.

MURPHY, K. (1986). "Incentives, Learning, and Compensation: A Theoretical and Empirical Investigation of Managerial Labor Contracts." *Rand Journal of Economics* 17:1 (Spring), 59–76.

PETERS, T., and AUSTIN, N. (1985). *A Passion for Excellence: The Leadership Difference*. New York: Random House.

ROGERSON, W. (1985). "The First-Order Approach to Principal-Agent Problems." *Econometrica* 53:11 (November), 1357–1367.

SHUKLA, R., and O'HALLARON, R. (1986). "AM Admission/PM Discharges Can Reduce Length of Stay." *Hospital and Health Services Administration* 31:4 (July/August), 74–81.

SHYAVITZ, L., ROSENBLOOM, D., and CONOVER, L. (1985). "Financial Incentives for Middle Managers." *Health Care Management Review* 10:3 (Summer), 37–44.

SMITH, H., OTTENSMEYER, D., and PATERNAK, D. (1984). "Physician Incentive Compensation." *Health Care Management Review* 9:1 (Winter), 41–50.

VERGARA, G., and BOURKE, J. (1985). "Reward Employees, Achieve Goals, with Incentive Compensation." *Healthcare Financial Management* 15:8 (August), 50–53.

WHITTED, G., and EWELL, C. (1984). "Survey of Hospital Management Incentive Programs: What Will Motivate the Motivators?" *Hospitals* 58:5 (March 1), 90–94.

WILLIAMS, J., and KING, M. (1985). "Executive Compensation Trends." *Hospitals* 59:19 (October 1), M14–M16.

Wyatt Company (1986). "Survey of Benefit Trends in 447 Health Care Facilities." Monograph report (July) of the 1985 and 1986 survey results. Boston: Wyatt Company.

Chapter 12

QUALITY DISCLOSURE, VALUE SHOPPING, AND HOSPITAL QUALITY SCORE CARDS

About 10 to 15 percent of the physicians in New York state have their medical judgment impaired at some point in their career. Medicine has its quality problems with inefficient and unnecessary care. In the medical "gray areas," with a high degree of uncertainty and disagreement, medical anarchy may err on the side of ordering too much costly care.

—David Axelrod, M.D.

Physicians doing unnecessary care for reasons of added income is not the problem. We are startled to find how poor the level of medical knowledge is oftentimes. There are a lot of doctors out there who really need help.

—John Davis, M.D.

The state medical society is essentially a trade union. They have a very narrow outlook, viewing utilization profiles or quality reports as information that should be kept from the public.

—Benjamin Barnes, M.D.

Should the health sector place more emphasis on physician reeducation, credentials, PRO review, or public disclosure of quality score cards? Irrespective of your viewpoint, the hospital "price wars" of the 1980s may well give way to the provider "quality wars" of the 1990s. Quality is a difficult-to-measure attribute that has only recently pushed itself into the public eye. In 1981, the Public Citizen Health Research Group issued a policy statement calling on the federal government to assist Medicare beneficiaries in avoiding high-priced physicians. Consumerism should extend beyond simple price disclosure activities to include expanded information on quality and availability of care. The libertarian-conservatives in the Reagan administration should be supportive of any efforts designed to promote informational equality between providers and patients. Improved informational equality is a necessary condition for stimulating competitive markets. However, the traditional-conservatives in organized medicine may resist any efforts to supply patients with more information concerning cost, quality, and access (Relman, 1978).

On April 17, 1985, the Health Care Financing Administration (HCFA), in control of almost $100 billion in medical expenditures, announced that the 54 local peer review organizations (PROs) would be required to release data on hospital quality, by DRG and department, to the public (HCFA, 1985). Confidentiality would be maintained as to the identity of specific doctors and patients. PROs and hospitals could provide their own interpretations concerning the quality of care. From a political perspective this is a unique issue, in which strange bedfellows like Ralph Nader and Milton Friedman (1965) are in agreement that consumers must be provided with information as a basis for shopping for health care. For both liberals and conservatives, data that are collected with public funds must be made available to consumers, employers, and insurance companies. Consumer information is the fuel that fosters cost-decreasing competition, quality enhancement, and innovation in the marketplace. Improving quality and productivity through improved information to the multiple buyers, especially in a local service market (e.g., health care), puts into practice the economic theory concerning the benefits of a better buyer's knowledge of the supplier (Stigler, 1961). For consumerists, the battle cry is "select your providers on facts, not just hopes."

Provider concern for quality is not new. However, the type of systematic inquiry that characterizes the contemporary quality assurance field has evolved within the health services research community over the past two decades. Donabedian (1968) and Roemer et al. (1968) laid the groundwork for quality measurement and quality-control activities. Donabedian outlined three basic approaches to quality assessment: *structure* (credentials, accreditation, licensure, and certification); *process* (what is done for patients, checklists or criteria-mapping protocol, including the coordination and sequence of the activities); and *outcomes* (fatality, infection, other adverse events or positive results, assessed from medical records or interviews). As a number of Rand Corporation researchers in the quality arena attest, measures of care by outcome are the best yardstick, as this reflects net changes that occur in patient health status (Brook and Lohr, 1985). Roemer, as a strong advocate of both outcome measures and consumerism, proposed in 1968 a hospital quality index based on fatality rates crudely adjusted for case severity. A more refined version of that index may soon be published on a regular basis, by hospital product lines, in local community newspapers (Eastaugh, 1986).

Injecting Quality into the Cost-Containment Equation

Are consumers smart enough to interpret quality statistics? The most basic answer to that question is yes, if we make the summary statistics comprehensible to the nontechnical reader. Just as buyers weigh a multitude of attributes in complex purchases from televisions to cars, so payers and patients can shop for providers with better information at their fingertips. Many hospital visits cost as much as luxury cars, and some outpatient visits cost as much as televisions. Sensitivity to quality is even more acute in the case of health care. Consequently, buyer awareness is high, and the resources invested are not trivial.

A comprehensive review of the entire range of quality measurement techniques is beyond the scope of this chapter. We shall briefly review methodological issues first, followed by an examination of the federal role in information data collection and dissemination. The danger of employers utilizing Medicare PRO quality measures is that they may represent inappropriate tracers for overall facility quality. Employer groups may privately contract with the PROs to gather information on younger patient populations. The Commission on Professional and Hospital Activities (CPHA) offers normative quality data on 17 million nonelderly patients from a national sample of 1,230 hospitals (1984–1986). The CPHA data base also includes discharge abstracts for elderly patients.

The prevalence of empty beds across the board has destroyed a low cost (easy to get) signal of quality—the degree of empty beds in a facility. Many hospitals, of good and bad quality, currently have low occupancy rates much of the year. Consumers may close inferior quality hospitals and reward quality facilities. A high level of unnecessary and inappropriate care has contributed to the litigious atmosphere in our medical care system. Redoubling our efforts in the area of quality control is not only consumerist but assists in reducing the headaches and prestige-deterioration implicit in a high malpractice volume. During their September 1986 meeting, the Joint Commission on Accreditation of Hospitals (JCAH) voted to evaluate clinical outcomes as part of its ongoing accreditation process, starting in 1988. In five years the commission plans to survey all hospitals on the quality of clinical activities as frequently as quarterly. The JCAH will have to choose from a number of competing measures of severity of illness which are most appropriate for its quality assessment. Future research should attempt to measure whether there is any significant correlation between malpractice volume and outcome measures of the quality of care. The relative merits of more direct regulation of care quality (e.g., minimum standards) versus the market philosophy of providing information only (i.e., let the "buyer beware") will be surveyed in this chapter.

Quality Statistics: Large Statistical Problems

Inaccurate quality measures, either because the case is one of a hundred conditions that requires a severity adjustment in the analysis or because the sample is too small, can yield an unjustified slur against or recommendation for a given hospital. For example, the March 1986 DHHS Health Standards and Quality Bureau report on 269 "atypical" hospitals nationwide identified providers with abnormal fatality rates (Krakauer, 1986). The *New York Times* coverage of this story focused on two cases: (1) inferior hospital A, having a mortality rate of 6.0 percent when the predicted DRG-adjusted national average rate should have been 2.7 percent, and (2) good hospital B with a 4.4 percent mortality rate, relative to the national standard rate of 6.2 percent (if the average hospital treated the same mix of DRGs) (Sullivan, 1986). However, these statistical estimates were based a 5 percent sample of Medicare patients. The 95 percent confidence interval for hospital A is as low as 1.9 percent fatality rate, and is as high as 7.3 percent fatality rate for hospital B. In other words, hospital A may not be worse than the national average, hospital B may not be better than average, and there is a small chance that hospital A might be better than hospital B. For instance, two very severely ill heart attack or gastrointestinal hemorrhage cases could be making hospital A look bad. In summary, one should not be quick to generalize from 5 to 20 percent samples; analysts and consumer groups need the full data tape. Moreover, the performances of small hospitals may have to be analyzed with two to three years of compiled data to make statistically significant statements about the 10 to 20 most popular DRGs treated.

A brief example will highlight the shortcomings of a quality report card rating system that does not adjust for both case mix and severity. Consider a simplified 2 × 2 contingency situation (Table 12.1), where the first dimension consists of case-mix severity dichotomously labeled easy or hard, hospitalwide. Dimension 2 consists of the "true" quality of care as measured by the perfect study (RAND, circa 2020 A.D.), labeled good or bad, hospitalwide. God has provided the true quality ratings of the four hospitals letter graded as A −, B +, C −, D + (God, being forgiving, seldom gives away grades below D +). The local PRO, having ignored recent research, offers only severity-insensitive, but DRG-adjusted, quality grades for the four hospitals of B −, A, B, and F, respectively. Hospital 1 (Table 12.1) resides in the severe (difficult) case-mix category, with very good (A −) true underlying quality. However, due to the insensitivity of the DRG system at capturing severity, hospital 1 appears to have mediocre quality (B −), when in fact it is doing a great job considering the severity of its patient mix (*error 1:* understating the teaching/referral hospital's quality).

Hospital 2 resides in the low-severity category, with high underlying (true) quality (B + rating by God). However, the imperfect PRO gives this hospital a quality score of A, largely because it has such an easy patient mix and incorrectly appears to be superior to hospital 1 (*error 2:* overstating the good community hospital's quality of care). Hospital 3 is an example of a low-severity patient mix, with truly low underlying quality (C −). This hospital only

Table 12.1 Hypothetical Difference Between Quality Scoring Report Cards, DRG-Adjusted (but with and without appropriate adjustments for severity)

	Quality Score Without Severity Adjustment			Quality Score with Severity Adjustment		
Hospital	*Fatality Rate per 10,000 Cases*	*Morbidity Rate per 100 Cases*	*Total Score* FR&MR*	*Fatality Rate per 10,000 Cases*	*Morbidity Rate per 100 Cases*	*Total Score FR&MR*
1	13	20	33 (B −)	6	12	18 (A −)
2	7	8	15 (A)	9	12	21 (B +)
3	10	18	28 (B)	12	40	52 (C −)
4	21	54	75 (F)	15	48	63 (D +)

*As in golf, the lower the score the better (combined FR fatality rate and MR morbidity rate score). As with golfers, providers also have handicaps.

receives a respectable quality grade from the PRO of B because its patient mix is so easy to treat without complications and high fatality rates (*error 3:* labeling a poor quality hospital as fair/good). Last, hospital 4 has a difficult severity level given its DRG case mix, and low true underlying quality (D+), so it receives an abominable quality grade of F from the PRO. A poor grade is reported at an even lower level of performance because the difficult cases compound its already poor performance (*error 4:* labeling a poor hospital as lower quality than it deserves).

Error 4 is not a major problem for public policy, but the other three errors are cause for concern. Error 1 risks doing real harm to the patient census and financial viability of some of the 447 members of the Council of Teaching Hospitals. Error 2 falsely directs patients to vote with their feet to be cared for at suburban hospitals with a less severe case mix. Error 3 may cause some potential "shoppers" in the market for quality care to not shop, because their local familiar grade B hospital is good enough for most DRGs, when in fact this is a grade C− facility. Table 12.1 makes these points clear with a hypothetical aggregate scoring system. The March 1986 federal report highlights three other possible scenarios: hospitals without any fatality because their case mix is easy and/or their sample size is so small, and specialized hospice/hospitals with enormous fatality rates.

The quality yardstick should focus on comparisons between acute short-term medical and surgical hospitals, not terminal case treatment. There is an eighth possible case: the teaching hospital with a great quality score and complex case mix. For example, in the March 1986 report, the predicted death rate for Georgetown Hospital Medicare patients was, if equal to national average performance, 5.4 percent (Krakauer, 1986). The actual death rate was 1.9 percent, making this facility one of the fifty hospitals rated best. However, these ratings only considered case fatality rates, DRGs, and patient demographics. In reality, hospitals would have differing scores and severity ratings across departments, and from year to year. The challenge for researchers is to make the rankings meaningful both statistically and for consumers trying to choose a hospital.

There are a number of severity-of-illness measures, including the Horn et al. (1985) severity-of-illness (SOI) index, Brewster et al. (1985) key clinical findings, Gonnella et al. (1984) disease staging, and Young (1984) patient management categories. A fifth severity measure, done by Knaus et al. (1986), the APACHE (acute physiology and chronic health evaluation) index, has been validated on intensive care patients. This APACHE index is the only severity-of-illness measure that has been validated using clinical outcomes such as mortality and morbidity. The streamlined version II of APACHE requires only 12 routine physiologic measurements, patient age, and chronic health status. The Knaus study contained 10 teaching and 3 nonteaching hospitals. The best hospital had 41 percent fewer deaths among ICU patients than predicted, utilizing the physiologic severity index. This particular teaching hospital had 69 predicted fatalities, but only 41 observed deaths, statistically significant at the 0.0001 level. In contrast, the worst-rated teaching hospital in the sample had 27 percent more deaths than expected (predicted 44, observed 56). The worst nonteaching hospital in the sample had 58 percent more deaths than expected (predicted 33, observed 52).

Severity Must Be Balanced with Appropriateness Review

Quality score cards without severity measures may lead to needless apprehension among patients for the one-third of DRGs that are severity-sensitive. However, a severity-adjusted quality score card is incomplete if one cannot document that the extra increments of severity are not caused by bad quality medicine, or poor medical judgment (e.g., doing an elective operation on a terminal cancer case). For example, one teaching hospital defended its high fatality rates on the HCFA outlier list (Krakauer, 1986) as being the result of seven unfortunate (fatal) operations on six terminal cancer cases and one total hip replacement operation on a wheelchair-bound patient with above-the-knee amputations. The fact that these cases were more severe explains why the fatality rates were high, but why were the operations done at all? Was the hernia operation going to cure the cancer? Was the hip operation going to allow the patient to walk? All concerned agreed that the answer to these questions was "no." However, provider motivation to perform inappropriate care had two aspects: senior attendings desired the additional income, and residents desired the extra patient volume since the teaching hospital occupancy rate had declined rapidly.

Such ethical problems, producing needless pain and suffering, can be addressed with more aggressive appropriateness review. The more basic question is, Do we run our medical care system for doctors or patients? The question is raised not so much to nettle as to alert teaching hospitals that attempt to misuse "severity" as a defense for their high fatality rates. Such hospitals will discover that the "defense" that their patients are more severely ill may get the hospital into more "hot water" if the public discovers the elderly were overtreated.

Each year, according to the Center for Disease Control, 20,000 Americans die because of nosocomial infections. One-third of these hospital-acquired infections could easily be prevented with better quality-control techniques, saving society an estimated $2 billion in direct hospital care costs (not counting the billions of dollars of others costs, foregone earnings, pain, and suffering). The very nature of Medicare PPS payments fuels renewed interest in investing in quality control. Fewer hospital-caused complications translate into a shorter patient stay, at lower cost, more in line with the prospective payment price for the case. Consider one simple example, the common "catheter fever" nosocomial infection. One should take a catheterized patient's urine specimen out of the plastic bag with a syringe, rather than unhooking the bag and draining the urine into a specimen cup. This example also highlights the fact that quality is a function of both medical staff and hospital employee behavior (Eastaugh, 1986).

The Federal Role

Federally financed PROs are surveying a wide array of quality measures, including the following:

1. Department fatality rates for cases with length of stay in excess of one day (given that some hospitals receive a disproportionate share of critically ill patients who cannot be immediately stabilized).
2. Abnormally high rates of inpatient admission following outpatient surgery.
3. Abnormally high readmission rates 30 to 60 days following discharge.
4. Abnormally high rates of transfer for medical complications after the hospital treated the patient for more than two days.
5. Excessively high rates of adverse patient occurrences (APO) morbidity events (i.e., infection not present on admission, unexpected cardiac or respiratory arrest, unexpected deterioration leading to transfer into a critical care unit, unplanned return to the operating room, or pathology tissue diagnosis not matching the patient diagnosis).

If all these alternative measures of quality agree, then they provide independent confirmation of the validity of labeling a hospital good or bad.

Consumers also have their foibles. Just as individual doctors have a practice style pattern or "clinician signature," so do certain consumers have a consumption pattern or "demander signature" (e.g., to get the inappropriate drug or procedure done). Increased consumer education is warranted. If the federal government cannot afford it, employers may have to finance the effort (Eastaugh, 1986; McClure, 1985). If consumers are to reap the benefits of information disclosure on quality, they could assist the effort through personal word-of-mouth advertising and alert value shopping for the best providers to meet their needs.

Shifting Concerns in Consumer Behavior

Health care consumers are beginning to learn that "what you don't know *can* hurt you." Current questioning of the traditional model of the physician acting as the patient's agent, called *agency theory,* offers a number of challenges to the medical profession. If doctors do not send their patients to the best hospitals, but in fact make decisions for reasons of income maximization or travel minimization, as suggested by a number of recent studies (Greenberg, 1986; Flood et al., 1984; Haug and Larin, 1983), consumers should bury the idea that "doctor knows best." Hospital quality does vary widely, and the public would benefit from reading a valid summary score card on quality, disaggregated by logical groupings of similar elective conditions (high, moderate, low risk; probable surgical versus nonsurgical). Information on nonelective conditions would be less valuable for shopping considerations, especially for trauma cases. Consumers are increasingly coming to realize that it would be desirable to have the facts before choosing a hospital, and in turn, a doctor. This is a reversal of past tendencies to select the doctor first, and let the doctor make the subsequent decisions. Surveys by the American Hospital Association suggest that physicians made only 39 percent of all nonemergency hospital selections in 1983 (PRC, 1984). Consumers over the last four years have become even more involved in selecting the hospital at which they are to be treated. Consequently, this AHA figure now may be well below 25 percent. Consumers often make the de facto selection of a hospital by selecting certain HMOs or managed care options.

Consumers select providers with imperfect information, and the extent of their rational (and semirational) search behavior suggests an ongoing process in which they seek their own balance between technical quality (e.g., outcome statistics), personal care-giving quality, and out-of-pocket price. If perceptions of these three attributes become, on balance, sufficiently unattractive, consumers will search for new providers. Shock waves would resonate through the provider community if merely 10 to 20 percent of patients comparison shopped.

The health care delivery system has always been controlled by the element in short supply: previously, the doctors; currently, the patients. A lack of response from the majority of consumers could be predicted if two basic conditions occur: (1) information overload from too many conflicting and divergent sources and (2) information "underload" because the informational content of the data is low. Information disclosure will be most effective when the data are packaged in nontechnical simplified ratings and reported for a list of possible local providers. The data presentation could be popularized in a convincing manner with a five-star rating system for a number of inpatient service lines. Five stars imply excellent quality, one star implies poor quality, and zero stars implies dangerously insufficient quality. Currently, the JCAH provides a crude dichotomous estimate of the zero stars (nonaccredited) versus some stars (accredited) hospitals.

The statistical power of the estimates may not be capable of differentiating between a three-star and a two- or four-star hospital. Consequently, the ratings could be summarized by excellent (five stars), moderate, low quality (one star), and poor (zero stars). For hospitals with more than 100 beds, a different rating might be presented for six broad-scope popular service lines:

1. High mortality surgical (valve, coronary bypass, bowel, DRGs 104–7, 148).
2. Low mortality surgical (DRGs 161–2, 195–6, 336).
3. High mortality nonsurgical (cancer cases, stroke, pneumonia, heart failure, and shock; DRGs 82 and 296, 14, 89, 127).
4. Moderate (2 to 5 percent national average) mortality nonsurgical (chronic pulmonary obstruction, gastrointestinal hemorrhage, renal failure, arrhythmia, diabetes; DRGs 88, 174, 320, 138, 294).
5. Low mortality nonsurgical (bronchitis, transient ischemic attacks, angina; DRGs 96, 15, 140, 182).
6. Negligible mortality conditions (DRGs 39, 121, 243) where morbidity, infection, and complication rates would be the only available quality yardsticks.

Provider Reaction

This six-category, five-star rating system can be improved over time. However, the greatest intangible benefit of any rating system may be the degree to which it stimulates patients to ask questions.

The more questions, the fewer mistakes and the higher the pressure on the hospital sector to invest in quality-enhancing systems and procedures. Patients who ask assertive questions avoid unnecessary procedures and reduce needlessly long waits (Haug and Larin, 1983). The hospital is not a healthy place to wait, as the iatrogenic risks are substantial. The pressure might become so powerful among the medical staff and trustees that they acquire the courage to throw the "rascals" (inferior quality doctors) off the medical staff. For example, when the *Washington Post* published fatality rates among area hospitals doing heart surgery in 1981, two major teaching hospitals with poor ratings refused to renew admitting privileges for six low-quality surgeons.

Quality disclosure appears to have two basic supply-side effects: (1) improving the medical staff composition and (2) providing quality-control muscle to a "quality assurance program" that previously existed in name only. Quality assurance, in contrast to quality assessment, involves systematic identification of shortcomings in quality service delivery and designing activities to overcome the problems. One must implement follow-up evaluation to guarantee that no new problems have been introduced and that corrective activities have improved patient care outcomes. Quality research is often slow to lead to quality-enhancing action plans unless the reaction to quality disclosure by the public makes inaction a costly strategy for the hospital.

Health care organizations justifiably fear that quality report cards might further undermine public confidence in providers. Recent sensationalized press accounts of malpractice or misconduct cases have heightened the public appetite to read quality report cards, question their current choice of providers, and question alternative methods of treatment. In highly competitive markets, hospitals may publish quality statistics as part of their marketing ad copy. In two-hospital towns where both facilities are half full, one could expect the better-quality facility to advertise such statistics on a monthly basis. If nearly 1,000 hospitals will not survive the coming decade, why not make it the low-quality hospitals that fail? Public policy should be concerned with sufficient points of access to service, including the indigent. However, a large number of hospitals can close in a market with 350,000 empty acute care hospital beds.

Alternative Yardsticks and Standardized Rates

Hospital mortality is a relatively uncommon event and, as such, a rather limited measure of quality. Rehospitalization and patients' return to function may be more sensitive indicators, although they are costly to measure with accuracy. Anderson et al. (1986) have suggested a quality of well-being (QWB) scale. Unfortunately, the costly interviewer-administered instrument, using question algorithms, is necessary if health status quality-of-life data are to have sufficient reliability and validity.

One can utilize a standardized mortality score for hospitals or hospital departments based on an "expected" (standardized) par value figure. This standardized fatality rate figure would be stated relative to the facility's case mix if it had been serviced by the national average death rates applied to each patient category (DRG, age, sex, and severity class or category). This overall score might be appropriate for bulk purchasers of hospital care (i.e., employers). However, individual patients do not consume "general hospital care"; they consume specific types of care. In going from the general to the specific, the number of patients at each hospital becomes small. Luft and Hunt (1986) analyzed the experience of patients undergoing cardiac catheterization at 151 hospitals for 12 categories of patients. The authors stress some of the sample size problems with more detailed and, consequently, more accurate analysis. For example, if the base rate (par value standard) is 0.10 (10 percent fatality for this patient category, age 70+), and there are 100 patients, then an observed death rate 1.5 times above the average (.15) is statistically significant at the 10 percent level. However, in a larger hospital, the death rate on 500 patients need only be 1.2 times higher (.12) to be statistically significant at the same 10 percent level.

The frequency of the event also plays a part in the definition of "excessive" death rates. For example, if the patient category has a standard mortality of only 0.01, and there are 100 patients, then an observed death rate threefold above the average (.03) is necessary to be statistically significant. This threefold markup above the average contrasts with a mere 1.5-fold markup above the average being necessary to demonstrate statistically poor performance if the event is tenfold more common (.10 fatality versus .01). Moreover, in a larger hospital the death rate on 500 patients need only be 1.8-fold higher (.018 or 9 dead in 500) to be significantly inferior to the par value expected rate of .01 fatality.

The problem of low sample sizes can be partially overcome by pooling years of data, but at the possible cost of rendering the result less relevant to current evaluation. For example, some of the smaller hospitals requiring many years of pooled data to achieve statistically significant statements about low/high quality may claim certain poorly performing members of the medical staff have retired, therefore "invalidating" (in their minds) any historical quality scores. Low-scoring hospitals might also point to recent acquisitions of technology that have improved diagnostic accuracy and treatment effectiveness.

Profile Analysis: Comparing Related DRGs

Within any given service product line, quality may differ across components; a hospital may provide good care for one DRG but perform poorly for a closely related DRG. While a given service line may include 2 to 22 DRGs, only a few DRGs will have sufficient sample size to make statistically significant statements (Eastaugh, 1986). For example, if one considers the most popular cardiac bypass DRG 106 in the Medicare data base, hospitals with over 200 beds only have sufficient sample sizes for two related DRGs (127, heart failure; 121, acute myocardial infarction). The intent of a profile approach is to check the validity of conclusions about a given DRG (106) based on the (hopefully) parallel performance of medical staff in treating related DRGs. If the profile, or pattern, across related DRGs does not agree, one might be less confident in the results.

Profile analysis does not substitute for the possible need to measure patient severity. For example, one could perform equally poorly (or above average) across a number of DRGs merely because the patients are more (or less) severe across all the DRGs. However, fatality rates two to four times above the national average will seldom be explained away by patient severity, especially if the hospital is not a university medical center. Situation 1, market A, in Table 12.2 yields highly ambiguous results, with poorly performing hospital 4 in DRG 106 performing in the top quartile for two related DRGs. One is less confident in criticism of hospital 4 for having 1.9-fold the national average mortality rate for DRG 106. It may be conceptually possible to operate an institution with incompetent cardiac surgeons and good cardiologists. However, 18 deaths in 155, relative to an expected fatality rate of 5.9, is barely significant at the 0.11 level. In other words, hospital 4 may simply have had a bad year, by chance, for DRG 106 admissions.

Situation 2, market B, is only somewhat ambiguous. The worst hospital in this area, hospital 6, is inferior to hospital 5 for DRGs 106 and 127 but performs well on DRG 121. One is left with the question: How did hospital 6 perform so well on DRG 121 care? Perhaps the patient mix for that DRG has a relatively easy severity or acuity level, and/or the cardiologists at this facility are atypically

Table 12.2   Quality Rates for a Single DRG (106) and Two Related DRGs (121, 127) in the Same Service Product Line, 4 Markets (4 different regions of the U.S.), 1984 HCFA Medicare Data

Market/Hospital (hosp. avg. daily census)	Medicare DRG 106 Bypass Cases 1984				Survival Ranking	
	Cases	Deaths	Mortality Rate	Excess Deaths*	DRG 127, Heart Failure & Shock	DRG 121, Acute Myocardial Infarction
A. Market Area A—Eastern City						
1. Hospital 1 (595 census)	163	5	.0306	—	top 25%	top 25%
2. Hospital 2 (586)	133	7	.0526	ns	top 25%	top 25%
3. Hospital 3 (575)	169	9	.0532	ns	top 25%	top 25%
4. Hospital 4 (240)	155	18	.1161	13.3	top 25%	top 25%
B. Market Area B—Lacrosse City						
5. Hospital 5 (890)	128	6	.0469	—	top 25%	top 25%
6. Hospital 6 (550)	82	10	.1219	6.2	60th percentile	25th percentile
C. Market Area C—Ski City						
7. Hospital 7 (320)	44	2	.0454	—	top 25%	top 25%
8. Hospital 8 (154) beds	51	9	.1765	6.7	70th percentile	median
D. Market Area D—Dust City						
9. Hospital 9 (259)	99	5	.0505	—	top 25%	top 25%
10. Hospital 10 (274)	34	5	.1471	3.3	worst 10%	70th percentile

ns = not significant.
*Excess deaths relative to the first listed (best) hospital in the area.

good relative to the remainder of the medical staff. Ten deaths in 82 at hospital 6, relative to an expected rate of 5.9 percent for DRG 106, is significant at the 0.10 level (two-tailed test). The third situation, present in markets C and D (Table 12.2), is one of consistency. The worst quality hospital in treating one DRG is also the worst in the market for related DRGs, strongly suggesting that the quality of care is deficient at hospitals 8 and 10.

Organized Medicine and Regulatory Philosophy

In practice, hospitals will trim low-quality, low-volume departments before they consider closing the entire hospital. For these low-volume, poor-quality, high-cost departments, the best solution may well be competition through information disclosure. Patients can break the habit of going to such a facility, whereas professional groups often try to hide the problem. For lack of competition and information, low-quality operators have been able to avoid bankruptcy; cost reimbursement underwrote their unit costs, no matter how high. If one in six hospitals goes out of business, how will this affect the careers of physicians?

Organized medicine has offered a festoon of arguments for not releasing report cards on provider quality. Analysts are correct in pointing out that without a severity adjustment per patient, one may not be able to discriminate between a 38th percentile two-star hospital and a 62nd percentile four-star hospital. In such cases where the measurable differences in quality may be small, and fluctuate up and down from year to year, the differences in cost may be more relevant to the purchaser of care. Consequently, one could advise employees and employers to utilize economic criteria, access, and other criteria to differentiate two- to four-star hospitals. Users of the ratings should be confident that a one-star hospital is in fact a below-average hospital. Likewise, a five-star hospital is in fact an above-average hospital. What will happen if we do not taut the good news about five-star hospitals? Patient flow to such hospitals may decline in a price-competitive marketplace. One business executive of a large Fortune 500 company had a chilling rejoinder: "I don't care if 900 to 1,000 hospitals close over the coming five years, just as long as 100 of those Council of Teaching Hospitals members close. They are too expensive in the states we do business." Valid quality report cards, and not economics, may well be the trump card for survival among the expensive five-star hospitals.

Wanted: Quality Enhancement

Five-star hospitals might gain more patients than they can, or wish, to accommodate. However, higher volume will allow the hospital departments to, in the jargon of economics, slide down their average cost curves and take advantage of economies of scale (Eastaugh and Eastaugh, 1986). Because consumers are constrained by travel costs, time costs, and out-of-pocket care costs, the problem of too many patients going to good hospitals seems a minor problem in the current low-occupancy marketplace. On the other end of the scale, perhaps the low-quality hospitals will be "disciplined" by the marketplace to go out of business. Those patients who shop deserve, and receive, better value for their money. Conservatives would suggest that those who remain with their inferior quality providers deserve whatever they receive. Regulators would argue that the government should close some low-quality hospitals. If the medical profession gets more serious about its own independent investigations and fulfills Friedson's (1963) paradigm of the self-policing professional, licensing groups will give out more sanctions, expulsions, punishments, and mandatory exams and education.

If the medical profession does not police itself and protect the public from low-quality performers, physicians should not expect any additional legislation to provide relief from rising malpractice premiums. Market philosophy views technical quality as being simply another attribute, taken together with price, place (access), bedside manner, and hospital religious orientation, as being another factor on which customers may, or may not, choose. Government's role is limited to breaking the information asymmetry between providers and consumers by providing PRO statistics and data for private reanalysis on care quality.

One of the difficult problems for researchers is that it will be hard to discriminate between a hospital that has two to three unethical senior attendings, versus a facility where the majority of physicians and nurses could benefit from a substantial upgrade in performance quality. A retrospective data base may never be capable of pinpointing whether quality is a problem with 3 or 40 people in the organization. In which case, researchers may have to expose the quality shortfalls and leave it up to the hospital to develop an effective remedial quality-control program. The hospital can then decide whether it desires to be ranked poor or excellent in the eyes of its public, in which case many hospitals may finally get tough with providers of inappropriate care who in the past produced appropriate revenue for the hospital and infrequent reprimands.

One could ask, especially if we have a doctor surplus, how many doctors should be disciplined by the marketplace? And, should the discipline end careers? Some substantial fraction of physicians suffer from problems that significantly impair their functioning at some point in their careers. The number so impaired at any one time may remain small, perhaps under 5 percent. Who do we have to monitor competence? As one "60 Minutes" television segment documented in November 1985, the state of Massachusetts has two medical licensure investigators in contrast to eight hairdresser investigators. When compared to the hairdressing profession, health service consumer awareness is higher, and the dollar amounts are more significant. Physicians tend to be dedicated, hard-working individuals, subject to human foibles and fearful that quality disclosure will further erode the patient-physician relationship.

One could ask if there is a way to obtain consumer attention without resorting to overstatement? Politicians often sensationalize issues such as "premature discharges" and hospital deception concerning "what day your Medicare benefits run out under DRGs." Senator John Heinz (R., Pa.), chairman of the Senate Special Committee on Aging, claimed frequently during 1985–86 that "seriously ill Medicare patients are catapulted out of hospital doors prematurely." However, in the vast majority of these "documented abuse cases," physicians kept their patients in the "facility" until it seemed safe to discharge them.

The definition of what is included in the "facility" has substantially changed as hospitals diversify, initiate less expensive and more appropriate settings for patient care, and "unbundle" the patient episode. For example, hospitals increasingly transfer patients to "swing beds" (lower-cost nursing beds), thus maintaining the elderly patient within a more appropriate setting, yet preserving continuity of care across the hospital/campus. When appropriate, providers often discharge the patient with follow-up home health care services (often owned and marketed by the hospital). In the marketing literature this situation is often summarized by the rather unattractive word "demarketing"—that is, directing the patient to more appropriate channels of cost-effective service distribution. If the measures of quality for the individual patient do not erode under this demarketing/diversification strategy, then no harm is done. Customers would be left to decide whether a differential advantage, or shortfall, in comparing providers is substantial enough to change their behavior. For some Americans a small differential on fatality or infection rates may be substantial, but to other customers this difference is insignificant, even if it is statistically significant at the 5 percent level.

Direct Regulation, or Buyer Beware

The chief failing of the pro-regulatory school is in defining a "significant" national, or local, cutoff point beyond which the quality of care is judged so substandard as to justify closing the provider. The issues are more complex in medical care because the quality measures are more complex and subject to future refinements than truck safety or meat safety. In the 1986 case of naval heart surgeon Donal Billig, a fatality rate 1.24-fold above the national average was judged "terrible." If 18 fatal cases among 240 is terrible because the national average performance is 5.9 percent (or 14 cases in 240), should the regulatory protectors of the quality of care be charged to find those four bad results? In the Billig case, they tried him on five and convicted him on three cases. In some sense a 7.3 percent fatality rate was surprising, considering Donal Billig was legally blind with vision of 20-400—certainly a handicap for a member of the surgical profession.

Reactionary providers lobbying against consumer disclosure argue that patients should be interested in two attributes: access and continuity of service. They refuse even to call patients "consumers." In other words, consumers should know as much about the quality of health providers as they know about the quality of electricity. One might recall the ad copy "all you need to know about electricity is that it is there when you need it." Considering the highly personal and potentially final (critical, life-threatening) nature of health care, most of the population would desire more comprehensive information concerning provider quality. Everyone likes competitive information about what we buy, not what we sell (provide).

Ultimately, it is a question of regulatory philosophy as to whether you make normative or absolute judgments about quality of care. The liberal pro-regulatory school of thought suggests that the national PRO should make absolute judgments as to what is a minimum standard of care and close those 5 to 20 percent of hospitals that do not meet this standard. However, any imposed national standard is by definition arbitrary—for example, should we set it such that it closes 8 or 16 percent of hospitals? On the other side, the conservative, market-oriented school would suggest that we simply publish the information, promote consumer awareness, and let the customers vote with their feet to close poor-quality hospitals.

Advocates of more regulation ask whether market mechanisms and the courts will close providers fast enough. Regulators, while having problems defining minimum standards or "fast enough," do have a point. Low-quality providers will be harmed by consumer disclosure in two ways—business volume and further quality erosion—but will not close if enough patients continue to visit. With a more informed public, low-quality providers will lose even the patient volume necessary to maintain their substandard level of performance and decline further in quality rating (if they can stay in business). At this point Peterson's "out of practice" (negative impact on quality) effects come into play (Peterson et al., 1956), and it may be in the best interest of society to close the provider. However, most economists would counterargue that the press and the provider's financial state could close things quicker than the courts.

Consumerism and Rationing

Are hospitals to be more like restaurants, in which the public servant assures us against food poisoning, and the PRO critic provides a zero to five-star rating of the quality before the discriminating consumer decides to trust the kitchen? Or do we leave the decision totally up to government regulators to, as with taxi cabs, save us from making personal calculations on car safety and cost before consuming the service? Considering this mixed metaphor, physicians and hospital managers should consider which hassle they least dislike: (1) answering the critics and improving the kitchen or (2) being rationed like taxi cabs and burdened with substantially more paperwork. The facts seem to suggest that medical care providers are more like restaurants than taxi cabs: The variability in quality is substantial, and taste is highly personalized. Sorting single-handedly through a barrage of restaurant or hospital ad copy is an onerous task. But, having a five-star hospital guide available seems prudent. The guide would have a brief summary section for 6 to 12 basic hospital case types, followed by what will be a seldom-used, lengthy appendix listing actual numerical quality scores on a number of measures by hospital department for popular DRGs.

People spend more time shopping for restaurants in comparison to selecting health care providers. Good information concerning quality has heretofore not attracted much attention. Customs will change over time. As the population listens to friends who summarize or share consumer reports on health care provider quality, behavior will change. "Excess deaths," to utilize a very frank term, will decline. If providers attempt to falsely discredit consumer reports on quality, they will experience the lament of deregulated bankers and airline executives: Information talks, people walk (to those with the better numbers). Doctors can either steer patients to the best quality hospitals for which they have admitting privileges or try to gain privileges at better hospitals.

The cash flow now channeled to low-quality hospitals and doctors is destined to decline because of better consumer information. If society lets the low-quality providers fail, closing out their fixed costs, the average quality of care level improves. This method would cost less than any regulatory method of rationing through price controls done by Medicare DRGs or alternative delivery systems. If we trust consumers with an array of quality ratings, the public will have the ability to insist on better quality care. The surviving providers would function in a better-equipped and less tightly reimbursed environment. Resources dedicated to health care would certainly be better spent, which is good economics and good medicine.

Payers Shopping for Quality Providers

Some employers should be uneasy with the idea of utilizing Medicare patient quality statistics (even if they represent one-third of all hospital cases) as tracer "proxy" indicators of hospital quality. If the patient sample were expanded to include nonelderly patients, the resulting quality report cards could change significantly. From the hospital perspective, the "good news" is that large employers are paying state PROs to expand their review functions to nonelderly cases under private contract. Under federal contract, the PROs only review inpatient Medicare cases, but the sponsoring firms sell their utilization review services to employers, insurers, HMOs, and PPOs. However, for hospitals with bad-quality ratings, the "bad news" is that employers will shop aggressively, ask for larger discounts, or exclude the bad performers from their selective contract listing. Employees will also be strongly encouraged to shop on cost and quality (Bodendorf and Mackey, 1986). Large employers are already setting up advisory offices where employees can obtain advice on the "best" providers to utilize (McClure, 1985). As bulk purchasers attempt to teach individual purchasers to "buy right," they should also invest in PRO research and development of better-quality assessment tools. Experts in quality assessment lament that their measures are imperfect and that investment in this area is insufficient. However, in this era of reduced public spending, private sector investment must finance the bulk of new basic research.

If researchers overcriticize the potential uses for quality-of-care measurement systems, private purchasers of health services will become totally preoccupied with cost concerns. Some large employers have argued that the provider selection process can focus either on price or quality attributes, and attempting to achieve a balance of both concerns would lead to strategic mediocrity. The rejoinder reads: Tell us you cannot measure quality, and we shall ignore it. Discounting quality measurement efforts may lead to government takeover of the accreditation and licensure business for health professionals, and mandate of a federal minimum standard of care.

Over time, wide changes in quality ratings relative to the standard could reflect small sample sizes among the assessed DRGs (and natural chance variation), or substantial improvements (or erosions) in provider quality. Sloan, Perrin, and Valvona (1986) report procedure-specific in-hospital mortality was only weakly predictive of mortality associated with the same procedure and institution in subsequent years. One can only hope that professional review organizations and consumer shopping may have reduced these wide swings since 1981–82. Future increases in consumer shopping and disclosure of quality score cards, no matter how painful to low-quality providers, seem preferable to further government intrusion into medicine.

Aggressive use of information on quality and cost has always been the principal advantage of any competitive industry (Dunlop, 1980; Stigler, 1961). Valid quality measures that provide easily understandable rankings for public consumption will prove eye-opening for patients, payers, and physicians. Hospitals and physicians will have to exist in a world of more aggressive comparison shoppers, including individuals, employers, and insurance companies. The major weakness that researchers perceive in the current vision of score cards and directories is a failure to adjust for patient severity of illness within DRGs. Consumer power, from the provider viewpoint (more irritating, but better informed) will force institutions to invest more in quality-enhancing efforts.

In a quality-competitive marketplace, it becomes even more important for clinicians to ally themselves with good quality hospitals. The health establishment should well fear a coming era of price wars and quality disclosure. Medical societies and the JCAH, created to defend and promote the status of the profession, have always been hesitant to discipline members. Hospitals could appeal their quality ratings to CPHA, HCFA, and their local newspapers. Validity of quality rating schemes could be analyzed by the JCAH, CPHA, HCFA, and the local PROs. Until recently a simple doctrine existed that said competition would not work in health care, patients would not shop, and all "credentialed" doctors and hospitals offer approximately the same quality of care. The simple doctrine has died. Consider the popular joke among medical school students concerning what they should call the lowest-quality graduate in their class? Answer: doctor. A quality physician is as unhappy as anybody else about incompetent clinicians who give physicians a bad name. Future research should consider how accurately performance in residency programs and medical school predict postgraduate quality of care in practice.

Summary

Results of an anticipated second attempt by the federal government at Medicare fatality ratings in 1987 may prove equally disappointing if the analysts do not focus more attention on sample size and patient severity issues. Unless the information selected discloses only targets that are statistically defensible, in terms of low- or high-quality care, results will fall short of the uplifting rhetorical promises on behalf of comparison shopping and consumer choice. Employers and consumer groups are also making modest attempts to disseminate information before there is any well-defined, accurate methodology. Aggressive consumer groups are interested in "price wars" and "quality wars" and with the battle cry, "Select your hospital and doctor on facts, not just hopes." If such competition does occur, it would be beneficial to have it based on accurate analysis. Future critics may well argue that information score cards done incorrectly do more harm than providing no information at all. More basic research needs to be done if we are to avoid such mistakes.

References

ANDERSON, J., BUSH, J., and BERRY, C. (1986). "Classifying Function for Health Outcome and Quality of Life Evaluation." *Medical Care* 24:5 (May), 454–470.

BODENDORF, F., and MACKEY, F. (1986). "Evaluating a Hospital's IQ: Indicators of Quality." *Medical Benefits* 3:9 (May 15), 1–3.

BREWSTER, A. et al. (1985). "MEDISGRPS: A Clinically Based Approach to Classifying Hospital Patients at Admission." *Inquiry* 22:4 (Winter), 377–387.

BREWSTER, J. (1986). "Prevalence of Alcohol and Other Drug Problems Among Physicians." *Journal of the American Medical Association* 225:14 (April 11), 1913–1920.

BROOK, R., and LOHR, K. (1985). "Efficacy, Effectiveness Variations and Quality: Boundary-Crossing Research." *Medical Care* 23:5 (May), 710–722.

Center for Disease Control (1985). "Study on the Efficacy of Nosocomial Infection Control." SENIC 85-2 (February). Washington, D. C.: DHHS.

DANS, P., WEINER, J., and OTTER, S. (1985). "Peer Review Organizations: Promises and Potential Pitfalls." *New England Journal of Medicine* 313:18 (October 31), 1131–1137.

DONABEDIAN, A. (1968). "Promoting Quality Through Evaluating Patient Care." *Medical Care* 6:1 (January), 181–202.

DUNLOP, J. (1980). *Business and Public Policy.* Cambridge, Mass.: Harvard University Press.

EASTAUGH, S. (1986). "Hospital Quality Scorecards, Patient Severity, and Consumerism." *Hospital and Health Services Administration* 31:6 (November/December), 85–102.

EASTAUGH, S. (1983). "Placing a Value on Life and Limb: The Role of the Informed Consumer." *Health Matrix* 1:1 (Winter), 5–21.

EASTAUGH, S., and EASTAUGH, J. (1986). "Prospective Payment Systems: Further Steps to Enhance Quality, Efficiency, and Regionalization." *Health Care Management Review* 11:4 (Fall), 37–52.

FLOOD, A., SCOTT, W., and EWY, W. (1984). "Does Practice Make Perfect?" *Medical Care* 22:2 (February) 98–125.

FRIEDMAN, M. (1965). *Capitalism and Freedom.* Chicago: University of Chicago Press.

FRIEDSON, E. (1963). *The Hospital in Modern Society.* Glencoe, Ill.: Free Press.

GONELLA, J., HORNBROOK, M., and LOUIS, D. (1984). "Staging of Disease: A Case-Mix Measurement." *Journal of the American Medical Association* 251:5 (February 3), 637–644.

GREENBERG, W. (1986). "The Importance of Location in Choice of Hospital." *American Journal of Law and Medicine* 11:2 (December), forthcoming.

HAUG, M., and LAVIN, B. (1983). *Consumerism in Medicine: Challenging Physician Authority.* Beverly Hills, Calif.: Sage Publications.

Health Care Financing Administration (1985). *Federal Register* 50:12 (April 17), 312–322.

HORN, S., et al. (1985). "Interhospital Differences in Severity of Illness: Problems for Prospective Payment Based on DRGs." *New England Journal of Medicine* 313:1 (July 4) 20–24.

KNAUS, W., DRAPER, E., WAGNER, D., and ZIMMERMAN, J. (1986). "An Evaluation of Outcome from Intensive Care in Major Medical Centers." *Annals of Internal Medicine* 104:3 (March), 410–418.

KRAKAUER, H. (1986). "The Prediction of Statistical Outliers Based on Medicare Fatality Rates, Report (March) Office of Medical Care Review." Health Standards and Quality Bureau, Health Care Financing Administration, DHHS.

LUFT, H., and HUNT, S. (1986). "Evaluating Individual Hospital Quality Through Outcome Statistics." *Journal of the American Medical Association* 255:20 (May 30), 2780–2784.

McCLURE, W. (1985). "Buying Right: The Consequences of Glut." *Business and Health* 2:9 (September), 43–46.

MYERS, L. and SCHROEDER, S. (1981). "Physician Use of Services for the

Hospitalized Patient: A Review with Implications for Cost Containment." *Milbank Memorial Fund Quarterly/Health and Society* 59:3 (Summer), 481–507.

O'LEARY, D. (1986). "JCAH New Series of Quality Indicators Based on Outcome, Clinical Standards." *Federation of American Health Systems* 19:3 (May/June), 26–27.

PETERSON, O. et al. (1956). "An Analytic Study of North Carolina Medical Practice, 1953–54." *Journal of Medical Education* 31:12 (December), 1–165.

Professional Research Consultants, Inc. (1984). "Marketing Surge Tied to Consumers." *Hospitals* 58:12 (June 16), 33–35.

RELMAN, A. (1978). "Professional Directories—But Not Commercial Advertising—As a Public Service." *New England Journal of Medicine* 299:9 (August 31), 476–478.

ROEMER, M., MOUSTAFA, A., and HOPKINS, C. (1968). "A Proposed Hospital Quality Index: Hospital Death Rates Adjusted for Case Severity." *Health Services Research* 3:2 (Summer), 96–118.

SHARP, K., and FLOOD, A. (1986). "Causal Model of the Volume-Outcome Relationship for Patients Receiving a Cholecystectomy." Paper presented at the American Public Health Association Annual Meeting (October 1), Las Vegas.

SLOAN, F., PERRIN, J., and VALVONA, J. (1986). "In-Hospital Mortality of Surgical Patients: Is There an Empirical Basis for Standard-Setting?" *Surgery* 99:4 (April), 446–454.

SLOAN, F., VALVONA, J., PERRIN, J., and ADAMACHE, K. (1986). "Diffusion of Surgical Technology: An Exploratory Study." *Journal of Health Economics* 5:1 (March), 31–62.

STIGLER, G. (1961). "The Economics of Information." *Journal of Political Economy* 69:3, 213–225.

SULLIVAN, R. (1986). "Leading Hospital Accused of Poor Care." *New York Times*, March 4, B-3.

WEBBER, A. (1986). "Status of the PRO Program." *Federation of American Health Systems Review* 19:3 (May/June), 28–29.

WILLIAMSON, J. (1978). *Assessing and Improving Outcomes in Health Care: The Theory and Practice of Health Accounting.* Cambridge, Mass.: Ballinger.

WOLFE, S. (1986). "Consumer Information on Hospital Quality." *Public Citizen Health Letter* 2:4 (September/October), 1.

YOUNG, W. (1984). "Incorporating Severity and Comorbidity in Case-Mix Measurement." *Health Care Financing Review* 5:4 (Supp.), 23–32.

Part Four

HEALTH MANPOWER EDUCATION

Chapter 13

GRADUATE MEDICAL EDUCATION AND THE TEACHING HOSPITAL

> *Producers and consumers do not need more expensive inpatient products. Give the public more ambulatory and alternative care products they can afford. Hospitals must once again become in step with the marketplace. Hospitals that develop services just to fill beds are going to be losers. We need a better specialty focus.*
>
> —JEFF GOLDSMITH

> *Future research that explicitly recognizes variations in medical staff characteristics and organizations may be fruitful in discovering reasons underlying variations in hospital performance in response to regulation. Put another way, is "control" of medical staff a necessary condition for containment of hospital costs?*
>
> —FRANK A. SLOAN

Stressed by the continued emphasis on cost containment, teaching hospitals appear to be facing serious problems in financing traditional levels of patient care, education, and biomedical research (Schwartz et al., 1985). The problems have different etiology in all three areas—for example, declines in Medicare payments for graduate medical education (residents and interns)—but they are all described in the language of revenue shortfalls (Petersdorf, 1985; Chin et al., 1985; Foley and Mulhausen, 1986). In order to preserve their mission, teaching hospitals increasingly need to streamline their activities, so as to price their services competitively through promotion of cost-consciousness to their residents, attending physicians, and employees. Some teaching hospitals appear to be adjusting to the new competitive era better than others. A number of well-known teaching hospitals with annual gifts and grants in excess of $100 million have had to reduce staffing by 700 to 1,300 full-time equivalent employees.

In the first half of this chapter we attempt to disaggregate the full cost of graduate medical education (GME) and discuss the impact of patient severity on cost per case. In the second half of the chapter we survey the health services research literature to discern how much of the extra patient care in certain hospitals is excessive, inappropriate, or unnecessary. A reduction in optional or redundant hospital workups and elimination of nonsystematic usage of unproven procedures (those not tested in a legitimate clinical trial) not only will save money but also will increase patient satisfaction. Teaching hospitals will always offer somewhat different treatment protocols than nonteaching facilities because of differences in patient severity, research trials, innovative techniques, and sometimes, better quality of care. Teaching will always require some legitimate extra costs, such as (1) the surgical resident expending an extra 20 to 90 minutes in the operating room learning to do a technique from the more experienced mentor attending surgeon or (2) the apprentice resident ordering a liberal large number of tests to avoid making a mistake or missing a rare interesting condition (that is, before learning how to better balance risk aversion and wasted effort and not follow every "wild goose chase"; Eeckhoudt, 1985; Eastaugh, 1979). These so-called learning effects are legitimate costs of training the next generation of competent, high-quality clinicians. The indirect cost of education requires more than simply an additional increment of variable patient care costs. Teaching hospitals require additional fixed costs, beyond simply the additional space required to house biomedical research projects. For example, because the teaching function requires additional space in the patient's room for groups of residents and medical students, builders typically allocate 30 to 50 percent more square feet of space per bed to accommodate the traffic.

The GME Quandary: Who Should Pay?
And How Much?

The educational component of medical care costs is frequently given adequate earmarked support via Department of Education funds in Canada and Europe (Relman, 1984; Eastaugh, 1980). The

American tradition is to subsidize indirectly such costs through the "back door" of patient hospital bills. For example, the 1986 survey of the Association of American Medical Colleges (1986) reports that 82 percent of residents' stipends and fringe benefits were derived from hospital patient revenues. The Commonwealth report (1985), a two-year project by a 16-member national task force of teaching hospital professors and managers, suggests that a tax on all hospital admissions should be collected to reimburse hospitals for doing graduate medical education. This is a rather attractive payment "solution" for teaching hospitals because it involves minimum disruption of "business as usual" (e.g., don't look at what we do, just pay us). Such a proposed tax on hospital admissions, a sort of "sick tax" for education, has the administrative advantage of distributing the costs of teaching hospitals across all inpatients, without disaggregating how much of this cash flow underwrites (1) appropriate treatment of a more severely ill case mix (Newhouse, 1983), (2) charity care for the poor (Epstein, 1986; Rieselbach and Jackson, 1986), or (3) inappropriate high-cost care.

In fairness to the Commonwealth report (1985), Congress has not had much success in weighting the relative importance of the various reasons for the higher costs observed in teaching hospitals. The U.S. Senate Finance Committee report (1983) on Medicare reform explicitly included a lump-sum payment for graduate medical education in recognition of teaching hospitals' higher burden of charity care cases and the inability of the DRG classification system to account fully for patient severity of illness. The largest group of teaching hospitals, the Council of Teaching Hospitals (COTH), accounted for 6 percent of the hospitals, 18 percent of the admissions, and 52 percent of the charity care in 1983 (Iglehart, 1985). Anecdotal reports suggested that teaching hospitals had more severity of illness within each DRG category, and this assertion was confirmed by a number of recent studies (Horn et al., 1985; Horn et al., 1986; McGinnis et al., 1986).

The initial DHHS adjustment formula for the indirect cost of graduate medical education was based on a multiple regression analysis by two researchers at HCFA. Pettengill and Ventrees (1982) analyzed 1980 Medicare cost reports from 5,071 hospitals and concluded that costs rise 5.795 percent for each increase of 0.1 in the ratio of residents to beds after adjusting for DRG mix and local wage levels. Pressure from the Council of Teaching Hospitals led Congress to double this adjustment rate to 11.59 percent. The stated reason was that this extra payment factor would help underwrite uncompensated care and increased severity of illness not captured by the DRG categories (U.S. Senate, 1983). Non-teaching hospitals in the shadow of major teaching hospitals with

0.8 residents per bed would receive half the Medicare payment for the same DRG case treated. Because this payment formula was excessively generous to the 136 hospitals that provide 55 percent of the residency slots in the nation, payment rates for the indirect cost of graduate medical education were reduced in 1986. As part of the Consolidated Omnibus Budget Reconciliation Act (COBRA) effective April 7, 1986, the indirect teaching adjustment was reduced to 8.1 percent for FY 1986 and FY 1987. This reduction was made in part because the DRG rates would recognize, for the first time, hospitals serving a disproportionate share of charity cases. COBRA included a provision to increase the federal DRG rates for hospitals serving a disproportionate share of low-income patients.

When this disproportionate share provision expires at the end of FY 1987, the teaching adjustment factor for graduate medical education will rise to an 8.7 percent increase in residents per bed ratio (R) applied on the following curvilinear basis: $2 \times [(1 + R)^{.405} - 1]$.

Anderson and Lave (1986) present a good case for why resource costs increase at a slower rate as teaching programs get larger. This curvilinear formula takes into account the basic fact that teaching costs less than double as R doubles (e.g., R increases from 0.3 to 0.6). For example, under the old linear formula, two teaching hospitals in the same location were receiving quite different payment rates if they had different levels of R—even though they were both experiencing approximately the same factor markets, comparable severity of illness, elderly case loads, and equivalent amounts of charity care. As the authors point out, the larger teaching hospitals still have a good deal until the curvilinear formula is phased in (1988). For administrative ease HCFA oversimplified its regression results as a 10 percent increase in the R ratio translating into an 8.1 percent increase in cost per admission. Because the independent variable in the log linear equation was $(1 + R)$, this interpretation is incorrect and leads to continued overpayments to hospitals with large teaching programs.*

Payment Issues and Better Cost Analysis

The indirect costs of graduate medical education under the Medicare program amounted to an estimated \$1.2 billion in 1986. In

---

*Few teaching hospitals have taken advantage of one obvious revenue enhancement strategy: Close beds so as to increase the R ratio. The implementation of a curvilinear formula in 1988 will diminish the marginal benefits of this strategy.

addition to paying this portion of indirect costs, whether they have anything to do with education or not, the Medicare program also pays direct costs (resident and intern salaries and fringe benefits). In 1986, an estimated 54,000 residents and interns received $2.0 billion in salary and $360 million in fringe benefits (AAMC, 1986). Medicare paid an estimated $0.95 billion of this sum in 1986, with payment in subsequent years capped under COBRA in line with the consumer price index. (Congress did not collectively think that residents were overpaid but rather wished to cap the federal financial liability in paying for expansion of residency programs.) Congress also placed limitations on foreign medical graduates (FMGs) in COBRA. As of July 1987, FMGs will not be counted as residents for payment purposes if they fail to pass the FMG Exam in Medical Sciences (FMGEMS).

In summary, managers of residency programs will be under pressure to provide residents a superior educational experience based on a reasonable workload supervised by senior attendings. Continued requests for more federal aid could lead to massive intervention in medical education. The federal government would want more control over the quantity, quality, and type of residency slots (e.g., more primary care and less surgical residency positions). This trend has already been noted by Petersdorf (1985), Iglehart (1985), and a number of politicians. Faculty and hospital managers may have to face the trade-off of some loss of autonomy for stabilization of revenue sources. Nonfederal payers of inpatient care seem less willing to generously underwrite residency training; therefore, teaching hospitals' revenue may decline without an expansion in competitive bidding schemes. Manpower training program decisions may increasingly be made by federal (or state) government rather than by institutional decision makers. Smaller and leaner teaching programs may soon be mandated by legislation.

The need for better cost analysis in an era of fluctuating payment policies should be obvious to all managers and providers in teaching settings. One of the basic problems with the aforementioned cost studies is that true cost accounting systems at the institutional level are lacking. In the next section we will survey the results of a more recent study which offers the analytical advantages of a good cost accounting framework, uniform accounting across 36 teaching hospitals and 9 control (nonteaching) hospitals, plus uniform measurement of severity of illness, disease stage, and quality of care (Arthur Young study, 1986). The next four sections will survey joint production activities, standard costing, results of the AY study, and the role of severity-of-illness measures.

Joint Products and Total Cost per Case

Pfordresher (1985) reports that it is very difficult to partition joint activities such as teaching, research, and patient care. *Joint activity* is a phrase used to describe the simultaneous production of multiple outputs during a given activity. Joint activity is most obvious when multiple individuals are involved in multiple tasks at the patient bedside. However, joint activity also occurs in instances in which a single individual is involved in multiple tasks or activities. Here, a joint product may be indicated by comparative amounts of time taken to perform a task. If an attending physician acting alone, for example, performs a patient care task in an average of 12 minutes and a second-year resident takes an average of 18 minutes, then the resident's time may be attributed in part to patient care and in part to education. The attending physician's average time in this example is presumed to have no educational content. Thus, if the task is performed in that given period of time, whether by attendings or second-year residents, it is taken entirely as an input to patient care. But if the time taken is greater, then a portion becomes an input to education, on the normative premise that the individuals performing the task are not yet, on average, as skilled as the attending physicians and therefore must still be learning.

The most basic question to consider is, Why do joint production institutions exist? Joint production most often derives from economies of simultaneous production. Joint production may also arise, especially in a profession like medicine, from joint factor supply. For example, if a factor required to produce instructional outputs, like faculty members, was to be made available only if allowed to produce research, a phenomenon labeled joint factor supply exists. One should see the folly in postulating the existence of a Godlike dean who is capable of determining the minimum amount of research time to buy if the only objective is hiring a teaching faculty.

Fortunately, deans in the real world are concerned with the quality and quantity of patient care, research, and education. Deans must consider issues such as how much additional faculty practice plan effort on patient care must be requested to (1) restrain tuition rate increases, (2) secure adequate faculty resources, and (3) optimize the prestige of the research program, and still produce the level of educational output that the residency program is committed to produce.

Two caveats are in order. First, the sum of pure time spent on each of the three activities has to be less than total time effort, and the sum of pure and joint time has to be more than total hours worked. Second, one could obviously optimize the production of one activity and erode the quality of the other two activities. It is obviously not desirable to reduce research and patient care to the minimum levels actually required for educational purposes. Consequently, we shall include measures of the quality of patient care in the following cost functions.

Measuring Total Cost per Case

Unbiased cost analysis of teaching hospitals must focus on total costs: physician costs plus inpatient costs per illness episode. It has often been stated that residents and interns save money on their patients' physician fees even as they raise hospital costs (Cameron, 1985). In teaching hospitals these salaried residents and interns are paid by the hospital and provide many services that could otherwise be performed and billed separately by an attending senior physician. On the other hand, services are sometimes largely performed by the resident and also billed by the attending physician, so the payer is stuck with the problem of "paying twice" (Garg et al., 1982). If net total cost per patient episode is higher among teaching hospitals, this higher price might in turn purchase an added benefit. Perhaps patients receive better quality care through continuous 24-hour availability of residents and the immediacy of their responses to patient care problems. Irrespective of whether any quality-enhancing activities turn out to be cost-savings or cost-increasing, regulatory forces and business will continue their vigilant attempts to minimize double billing.

Some evidence points to greater utilization of ancillary services at teaching hospitals without any obvious improvement in quality of care (Frick et al., 1985; Garg et al., 1982; Eastaugh, 1979). It has also been argued that graduate medical education programs introduce operational inefficiencies into the activities of senior attending physicians. The teaching hospital as a complex organization may exhibit cost-decreasing or cost-increasing behavior. On the positive side, teaching facilities may be the first to question "tenet of faith" habits (Chapter 10)—for example, the evening-before-surgery shave has proven to be harmful and costly (Brown et al., 1984). On the downside, Beck (1986) has suggested that teaching hospitals have a cost-increasing bias to employ overly expensive nonclinicians, wasting millions by using highly trained expensive labor to perform tasks that require only moderate or minimal skill.

Determining the cost (and benefits) of graduate medical education is complicated by all these confounding factors. Moreover, our sample of 36 hospitals selected from a national sample of four strata of teaching facilities and 50 nonteaching hospitals (rather than only nine) would have substantially more statistical power. However, the Arthur Young analysis has the advantage over Cameron (1985) of measuring hospital costs as accurately as possible in the 1982–1984 period. In contrast, previous studies from Salkever (1970) to Cameron (1985) have had to create "costs" from patient charge claim data for each case. Charges are not an accurate approximation of costs (see Chapter 5). In addition, our sample is not restricted to Medicare and Medicaid patients only. Our analysis also collects severity-of-illness and cost information for a population sample of patients (Eastaugh and Cosgrove, 1986, in Arthur Young, 1986).

Standard Costing Methods in the Arthur Young Study

There is no uniform system for hospital cost allocation and standard cost accounting. Cost reimbursement systems of the major third-party payers, most notably Medicare and Medicaid, have a substantial influence on how hospitals define, accumulate, and allocate costs (Eastaugh, 1980). Commercially available software programs were designed to maximize reimbursement by defining the statistical basis for the allocation of overhead costs through sensitivity analyses. Therefore, we found different allocation bases among hospitals for the same overhead department costs with great variability in the final costs allocated to each department. These differences presented a standardization problem in comparing patient costs among different facilities, at both the hospital and departmental levels.

Four basic types of data are needed to produce a uniform and accurate comparison of hospital costs: (1) hospital expense data, (2) hospital revenue and statistical data, (3) nonhospital financial data from other institutions within a medical complex, and (4) estimated and imputed physician cost data. In order to accurately compare these four types of financial data across all hospitals in the study sample, two uniform matrices were developed. The first is a standard matrix of 26 ancillary service and 21 general service cost centers. A cost center is defined as the basic unit of cost aggregation on the hospitals records. The cost data were then allocated to programs and departments using a standardized statistical basis across all study hospitals. The second matrix necessary for the study is a uniform hospital chargemaster. Because the hospital case costs are developed using a bottom-up approach from actual patient service profiles, a standard chargemaster was necessary to

ensure comparability between hospitals at the case and departmental level.

The second type of financial data collected is hospital revenue
and statistical data. Hospital revenue is identified as patient revenue, nonpatient operating revenue, and other revenue. Patient
revenues are standardized by the 26 ancillary service cost centers
and by payer.

The third type of financial data collected consists of those costs
or services provided and those revenues received from nonhospital
components of a medical complex. An example of this type of fund
flow analysis would be derived from an associated medical school
and/or university affiliation relationship. For example, the hospital
could receive free computer support in exchange for picking up
administrative staff labor expenses. Faculty members may be paid
by the medical school. Administrative services may be provided by
a university. In more complex teaching hospitals any one of a
number of other related party cost flows may occur.

The fourth type of financial data collected was "imputed" physician cost data. Various services performed for the hospital may not
be paid for by the hospital. A significant portion of the teaching
effort in smaller teaching institutions is performed by volunteer
physicians.* It is necessary to collect sufficient data to be able to
impute a reasonable cost to the time spent by those volunteers.
These data were collected both from primary sources within the
hospital and from various secondary sources, such as the DHHS
Regional Charge Screens on a regional and local level. At each of
the 36 teaching hospitals, the department chairmen provided
source data on the number of faculty hours replaced by volunteer
faculty and estimated salary levels of equivalent faculty at various
ranks. In addition to this site-specific data, AAMC data on faculty
salaries by position by region, AMA data on physician earnings by
specialty by region, and local intermediary physician price data
were collected. For each individual voluntary physician the salary
equivalent was calculated—that is, hours times salary estimate.
The department chairman's salary estimate is the preferred data,
although this is tested against other payment data.

Faculty salaries are a major expense to both graduate and
undergraduate medical education programs. Although faculty salaries are usually paid by medical schools, some clinical faculty
members receive a portion of their salaries directly or indirectly

---

*Cameron (1985) and other previous studies did not have the resources to
incorporate the necessary funds flow and voluntary physician time adjustments,
thus biasing the results for major teaching hospitals. The Arthur Young study
included data from 45 hospitals 1982–1984, and cost over $6 million under federal
contract.

from a teaching hospital in return for administration, teaching, and supervisory services. Since Medicare and Medicaid patient service payments are the largest source of funding for graduate medical education programs, federal reimbursement for these services has become a major source of medical school faculty salaries (discussed in further detail in Chapter 14).

As medical school funding levels become difficult to maintain and teaching hospitals face more difficult financial times, the search for alternative means of funding faculty salaries has intensified. Professional fees associated with patient care activities have become an increasingly important source of alternative funding. Physicians do not, in general, share compensation data. Even within organized group practices, the department chairman and group practice administrator frequently will be the only individuals who have access to individual physician compensation levels. To physicians, their compensation levels are a measure of "success." Physicians and physician groups were assured that information provided would not be used in a punitive way and that confidentiality would be maintained.

Hospital cost allocation is a politically less sensitive task relative to physician cost allocation. Indeed, from the institutional perspective, the cost-finding and accounting expertise of Arthur Young and Company offered a major incentive for participation in this study. One crucial intermediate step necessary in determining both cost per case and cost per unit of service is to assign to various procedures weighted values representative of their consumption of resources. In order to do this, we standardized the output measurement, by cost center, in all hospitals in the study sample. The relative value weights (RVUs) by procedure are based, for the most part, on standard unit-of-service criteria used by the state of Maryland. For example, laboratory units are weighted by RVUs for test complexity. After assigning weighted units by quantity of procedures performed, procedures with high relative value unit per procedure are matched. The assignment processes will, as a minimum, assign 80 percent of the relative value or other weighted unit-of-service measurement to any given cost center. All other procedures were assigned an average weight. These units were then keyed into a tape which includes units of service weighted by procedures, by 26 GME cost centers.

Arthur Young GME Results

Our focus is on average unit cost per episode: hospital plus physician costs. We are not concerned with the typical HCFA specification for how inpatient costs of production vary among hospitals. The dependent variable in our regressions is total cost per case. Average cost is measured as a function of nine independent variables (Berry and Russell, 1986, in Arthur Young, 1986): R (resident and intern full-time equivalents per bed); DRG cost weight (1.0 national average); Horn et al.'s (1985) severity-of-illness index; other case variables (length of stay, and whether the individual was covered by Medicaid or self-pay); a department-level quality index (using percentage of adverse patient outcomes divided by at-risk potential adverse patient occurrence opportunities) (the APO rate done by the same raters across the sample hospitals); and three input price wage indices for physicians, nurses, and technicians. To avoid problems of multicollinearity in our cost-estimation procedure, we did not include resident wage rates (because this is already captured through the 0.91 correlation with nurse wage rates), and we excluded capital prices (because it had a 0.8 correlation with technician wage rates).

The last three variables are included in the analysis to separate the cost of education effect from input price effects driving up the costs of care. Better quality of care could be cost-increasing or cost-decreasing. For example, Haley et al. (1981) report that the surgical department saves the hospital seven days of variable cost for every wound infection APO avoided. Length of stay is included in the analysis because patients within a DRG category have a wide variation in length of stay (McGinnis et al., 1986; U.S. Senate, 1983) not captured by the DRGs, case severity, or acuity. DRG conditions that have higher cost weights are by definition more complex and expensive to treat than those with lower weights (e.g., bypass surgery has a 13-fold higher weight than lens procedure DRG 39). The Medicaid/self-pay variable is included in the analysis because poor people often have inadequate prior medical care, deficient nutritional status, more complications, and secondary health problems (i.e., net a level of additional acuity not captured by severity of illness or length of stay).

To capture at least part of the effect that the teaching function has on case costs, independent variable 1, (R) interns and residents per bed, is included.* To improve the econometric fit of this variable in the regression model, we multiplied the observed value in each facility by 1,000. Table 13.1, column 1, presents the regression results for a random sample of 300 to 375 patients at

---

*The second half of this chapter will introduce two additional components of teaching status—medical students and faculty senior attendings—into a more limited analysis of 19 hospitals.

Table 13.1 Cost Per Case Regressions for a Random and Tracer Sample at 45 Hospitals (Arthur Young Study, 1986)

Variable (units of measurement)	Random Sample	1. Acute Myocardial Infarction	2. Upper G.I. Hemorrhage	3. Asthma	4. Gastro-enteritis Acute Colitis	5. Complicated Delivery	6. Gall-bladder	7. Hyster-ectomy[a]	8. Benign Prostatic Hypertrophy[a]
# Patients	n = 13,436	n = 857	n = 827	n = 821	n = 704	n = 793	n = 951	n = 833	n = 848
Average Cost	$4,150	$8,407	$5,633	$2,040	$1,693	$4,001	$7,890	$6,329	$6,818
• Variable (units of measurement)									
Residents per bed (1 per 10 beds)	7.2	10.5	5.7	2.5	0ns	0ns	5.4	4.2	4.1
Severity (.1 change in 4 point SOI)	3.2	4.0	3.6	2.5	2.4	2.7	5.2	3.3	3.2
DRG Cost Weight (.1 change)	7.7	11.7	6.2	1.5b	4.9	8.4	1.7	-3.4b	3.7
Length of stay (1 Day)	5.0	21.1	22.2	8.9	24.2	4.5	14.1	20.0	17.3
Medicaid or self-pay patients	.1ns	.41	-.2ns	.43	.89	1.7	-.02ns	.21ns	-.16ns
Quality of care (APO actual/at risk)	-.01ns	—	—	—	—	—	—	—	—
RN wage (1% change)	1.1ns	18.2	5.6	4.2	2.3ns	-8.3b	-4.4b	5.6b	1.5ns
Physician wage (1% change)	5.1	7.6	3.7	1.9b	-1.1ns	10.0	7.4	.6ns	2.4
Technician wage (1% change)	12.0	31.3	-.5ns	5.7ns	14.6	52.1	35.3	10.1	11.2
R-squared (fraction of variance explained)	.541	.523	.585	.438	.735	.628	.606	.508	.680

NOTES: Coefficients are mean elasticity estimates. APO = Adverse Patient Occurrence 15-item inventory. All variables significant at the .01 level, except those marked b and c.

[a]Surgical cases; b = .05 level of significance; c = not significant at 0.1 level.

each of the 45 hospitals. Columns 2–9 in Table 13.1 present the results from patients in the eight tracer diagnoses under study. The maximum tracer sample size within each group was 25 cases per hospital (e.g., if only 14 cases of tracer 2 could be found at a given hospital in the year 1984, then only 14 cases would be included for analysis). The impact on average cost of increasing residents per bed by 0.1 ranged from 4.1 percent for benign prostatic hypertrophy to 10.4 percent for nonsurgical treatment of acute myocardial infarction. The value for the random sample was a 7.3 percent increase in cost.

The impact of quality of care had a negative, but statistically insignificant, impact on patient costs. One would not want to read too much into this finding, but perhaps the net cost to society of investing in quality-enhancing activities is self-financing. Superior quality care may cost a little bit more, but it avoids the costly consequences of fixing poor quality care through prolonged duration of stay. The cost of treating Medicaid and self-pay patients was only 1 to 2 percent higher, given that the equation already included a measure of severity of illness. This could best be described as a proxy measure of "social acuity."

The Horn et al. (1985) severity-of-illness index had the expected positive and significant impact on average cost. A 0.1 unit increase in the index was associated with a 2 to 5 percent higher cost per case. If severity of illness has a case mix and cost effect within DRGs, rather than across DRGs, it suggests that Horn's measure may be a fine-tuning mechanism to add on or supplement the DRGs. In the context of an inventory control problem, DRGs may capture broad-based product lines, but severity measures a second dimension (degree or amount). We will survey some competing measures of patient severity in the next section. We will not be able to answer the critical question of how much does the reduction in variance of unexplained cost have to be to justify the data collection. However, Horn is already marketing a less expensive alternative measure, the computerized severity index (CSI), to 80 hospitals. If the marginal cost of collecting the information begins to decline enough to equal the marginal benefits of running a more equitable payment system in the minds of federal officials, perhaps PPS will collect such information (Gustafson et al., 1986). However, as we observed in Chapter 10, a severity measurement is highly useful for individual hospitals in managing a workload-driven, fair employee scheduling system. Severity measurement is also useful for quality assurance activities, documenting quality-of-care audits for JCAH site visits, as well as reanalysis of patient outcome data.

Severity-of-Illness Measures

The key attribute of the manual severity-of-illness (SOI) system is that it attempts to capture how ill a patient is within a specific disease condition—not just that the patient has the specific condition. As a result, it predicts resource use somewhat better than DRGs alone (Horn et al., 1986).

The severity-of-illness (SOI) measure was developed by a panel of physicians and nurses who were asked to define patient severity and develop the requisite list of parameters that would be necessary to implement the definition. The panel suggested 32 variables, which were ultimately reviewed and collapsed into seven dimensions, each having four levels of increasing severity. The decision to include certain parameters was based on the relationship of the parameter to patient severity. Parameters not directly related to the patient, such as those related to the skill or experience of the physician, were excluded. Four levels of severity were chosen for each variable, and for the overall severity index (rather than five or some other odd number), to avoid the problem of having most responses fall naturally at the middle level. An even number of levels forces the rater to chose decisively between two middle points and hence provides more distinction among patients. Raters require careful initial training (and periodic follow-up) to become proficient in coding SOI. Horn et al. report (1986) that almost all raters score 90 percent or greater agreement with blind re-ratings of the same records with an average agreement of 93.5 percent across 90 raters in 18 hospitals.

A suitable severity adjustment to the DRGs would provide all hospitals with an equitable incentive to become more efficient. Currently, hospitals that admit an atypically high proportion of high-severity patients and are paid the DRG average have an "excessive" incentive to become more efficient. However, they might never be able to lower costs to the DRG average payment levels without harming the quality of care. Consequently, teaching hospitals with a higher severity of illness might be faced with the choice of eroding either their financial health or the quality of care provided. Conversely, hospitals that presently admit an atypically high proportion of low-severity patients and are paid the DRG average have little incentive to become more efficient.

There are a number of systems in use, based on discharge abstract data, that provide hospitals with measures of case mix and severity, including DRGs and the PAS-A list from the Commission on Professional and Hospital Activities (CPHA). In the PAS-A list system, severity is quantified by the existence of a secondary diagnosis and/or the existence of an operating room procedure and/ or age. Although there are almost 8,000 groups in the PAS-A list, they are about as predictive of resource use as the 467 DRGs, because the existence of secondary diagnoses, procedures, or the age level tells very little about the actual severity of illness of a patient (Ament et al., 1982). Diagnosis related groups go beyond the PAS-A list approach by selecting a special list of secondary diagnoses (the complications/co-morbidity conditions) that are thought to cluster isoresource cases. Moreover, DRGs differenti- ate types of operating room procedures in different DRGs, rather than just noting the existence or nonexistence of an operating room procedure.

Two newer systems have been analyzed in the current study: disease staging and the manual severity-of-illness (SOI) index (Horn et al., 1985). The SOI index is a more complex measure and captures more patient information than disease staging. Advocates of the disease-staging approach would disagree (Gonnella et al., 1984). The only inputs to disease staging are ICD-9-CM diagnosis and procedure codes, whereas the SOI system uses information based on laboratory values, radiologic findings, vital signs, etc., found in the medical record but not captured in the current five- digit discharge abstract data base. In addition, disease staging has no mechanism to combine all of a patient's diseases together to form a single overall stage for a patient. Disease staging as a case- mix measure has been found to be substantially less predictive of resource utilization per case than DRGs. Even when combined with DRGs, disease staging has added little predictive power (Coffey and Goldfarb, 1986).

Several new severity measurement systems have appeared in very recent years, including the computerized severity index six- digit coding system (CSI, Horn, 1986), Western Pennsylvania Blue Cross PMCs (Patient Management 800 Categories; Young, 1986) and MEDISGRPS (Brewster et al., 1985). Brewster et al.'s MEDISGRPS system goes beyond traditional five-digit discharge abstract data. This parallels the two Horn systems (SOI, CSI) and PMCs. It uses about 500 "key clinical findings" to designate the severity of a patient on a scale of 0 to 4. These key clinical findings are recorded by trained hospital personnel on the third day of hospitalization (the MEDISGRPS authors refer to this as "on admission"), and the information is processed by a computer program that determines the severity of the patient on admission to the hospital. The MEDISGRPS system designates one rating for the severity of the patient on admission and another with data collected at ten days, if the patient is still in the hospital. The developers of MEDISGRPS claim the system searches for the maximum key clinical finding to determine the severity level, but the precise rules that specify which key clinical findings fall into which severity levels are proprietary (unavailable for independent study). In this present study we will examine the relative ability of disease staging and SOI to enhance the resource consumption predictive power of DRGs, but no assessment can be made of the MEDISGRPS, PMC, or CSI systems.

The Horn SOI Measure

The severity-of-illness measure was developed by a panel of physicians and nurses who were asked to define patient severity and develop the criteria to implement the definition. The panel suggested 32 variables, which were collapsed into seven dimensions, each with four levels of increasing severity. An even number of levels forces the rater to chose between two middle points and creates a finer-tuned measure. Raters require careful training to become proficient in coding SOI, but once they learn, they are very accurate. The seven SOI dimensions are:

1. The stage of the principal diagnosis at admission, including the greatest extent of organ involvement.
2. Complications that developed during the hospital stay due to the principal disease or as a direct result of the therapy or hospitalization.
3. Preexisting problems other than the principal diagnosis and its complications (e.g., diabetes in a patient admitted with acute myocardial infarction).
4. The degree to which the patient requires more than the minimal level of direct care expected for the principal diagnosis. A dependency score above level 1 indicates that the stage of illness, complications, or preexisting diseases require extra monitoring or care.
5. Diagnostic and therapeutic procedures performed outside of the operating room. The highest level of procedure, such as those required for life support, rather than the total number of procedures performed, determines the score for this dimension. The need for such a procedure also should be reflected in one or more of the first three dimensions (stage, complications, and/or preexisting problems).
6. Patient's response to hospital treatment for the principal diagnosis, complications, and interactions. This relates to treatments for acute illness or acute manifestations of chronic

illness that one expects to manage during a hospital stay. It does not relate to improvement in underlying chronic conditions for which there is no expectation of either cure or significant progress during the hospitalization.

7. The extent to which a patient shows residual evidence of the acute injury or illness at the time of discharge.

Disease Staging

The severity-of-illness (SOI) measure uses a generic instrument that can be applied to all cases and generates a four-level measure of severity. In contrast, disease staging covers most cases in our sample but not all conditions. SysteMetrics (Louis et al., 1983), under contract to the National Center for Health Services Research, developed stages for 480 specific disease conditions. The recent efforts by SysteMetrics include the development of the staging process using not only data drawn from the medical records, but also ICDA codes from computerized discharge data sets. Staging is a system of categorizing patients into one of four levels of severity based on pathophysiological parameters primarily obtained from the medical record abstract (computer software has been developed to enable staging to be done using discharge abstract data). Disease staging has three basic limitations in the context of the Arthur Young study:

1. Stage I conditions are by definition patients with a single uncomplicated diagnosis, and often the hospitalization is questionable. Since teaching hospitals might only rarely deal with such patients, the remaining levels of staging may be inadequate for measuring severity for a particular condition.
2. Garg et al. (1978) suggest that the construct validity of staging is supported because an increased stage correlates with increased cost. However, there is little evidence to determine whether the various stages have statistically significant differential charges and whether these differences would remain when charges are adjusted to costs.
3. While the method is sensitive to complications of the principal diagnosis, it is insensitive to patients in whom multiple diseases (not related to the principal diagnosis) interact in an additive, multiplicative, or other way.

One central conceptual strength of disease staging is that the severity measure is independent of provider behavior (e.g., treating a condition medically or surgically). By utilizing only diagnostic information to define stages of specific diseases and neglecting procedure classification, disease staging does not confound treatment preference with case-mix severity. In only three situations are procedures used to form stage classifications, and only because this identified the diagnoses more precisely (e.g., Caesarean deliveries). This conceptual strength of the disease staging process, however, leads to a practical problem. Because the technique does not distinguish surgical from nonsurgical patients, costs within the same diagnosis and stage vary widely.

We shall limit our literature review of the familiar DRGs. The new 467 DRGs, like the old DRGs, utilize length of stay as the primary dependent variable to reflect resource use. DRGs as a case-mix measure differentiate surgical from nonsurgical cases and consequently exhibit significant differences in case complexity between teaching and nonteaching hospitals. The Goldfarb and Coffey (1986) retrospective regression study of 144 teaching hospitals and 226 nonteaching hospitals reported that teaching institutions admitted a 1.4-fold higher proportion of surgical candidates relative to nonteaching hospitals after differences in disease staging between hospitals were controlled. A more extensive commitment to teaching (e.g., membership in COTH or a medical-school-based hospital) does not significantly increase surgical intensity (.46 versus .33 of cases). The intent of the calculation was to get away from the surgery/nonsurgery distinction embedded in the DRGs and standardize for disease stage of the patient population. The authors also reported no differences between hospital types in case-mix standardized fatality rates, despite the greater use of resources in teaching hospitals. This result concerning patient outcomes is surprising given the conventional wisdom that the continuous all-day availability of residents and the immediacy of their responses to problems should result in increased quality of service. One could speculate that a more sensitive measure, such as an inventory of adverse patient occurrences (APO*), would better detect differences in the quality of care than a crude measure (fatality). In this study, we collected APO data on the random case sample to provide a measure of quality of care at the case level. The APO measure will be used in the following analysis due to the unavailability of the disease-specific (tracer sample), quality-of-care measures presently being assessed by the Rand Corporation (report due in 1987).

---

*APO items include iatrogenic adverse reactions, complications, incomplete clinical management, unexpected cardiac or respiratory arrest, unplanned return to the operating room, nosocomial infection, iatrogenic neurological deficit, death, and other dysquality events, infections, etc. (Panniers and Newlander, 1986).

One recent study of case mix and cost differences between 11 teaching and 20 nonteaching hospitals concludes that cost per case is 60 percent higher in teaching facilities, with only 23 percent of the cost differential accounted for by differences in the DRG mix (Frick et al., 1985). All the sample hospitals were in New York State, and the study examined only the 30 highest volume DRGs (representing 20 percent of the patient admissions). Two other recent studies of the impact of graduate medical education on inpatient costs conclude that teaching hospitals are cost-increasing (Jones, 1985; Garber et al., 1984). All three of the aforementioned studies conclude that for similar patients, costs in the GME programs are higher mainly through increased numbers of diagnostic tests or procedures. Although the increased usage of tests and procedures is highly correlated with residents per bed, this increased utilization of hospital inputs is not directly proportionate to increased total cost because of the low marginal cost per test and moderate marginal cost per procedure (Eastaugh, 1981). Horn et al. (1985) report generally the same findings but interpret the findings somewhat differently: A more costly treatment pattern may indicate a more severe case mix (burden of illness). However, in the Horn study, the average charge differential between non-teaching and teaching hospitals did not disappear when severity of illness (SOI) was controlled. Horn and her associates also found that the distribution of patients in four of six examined diseases was not more severe for a university teaching hospital in comparison to a nonteaching community hospital.

Methodological Concerns

One of the basic conceptual problems with the SOI index is the inclusion of treatment decisions in the measure—that is, if more is done, the case must be more severe. Some components of the severity score reflect higher ancillary utilization by providers, and the researcher cannot tell how much of this is independent of the medical status of the patient. The SOI is less effective than disease staging in providing a case-mix measure attributable purely to patient differences and independent of provider practices due to the treatment standards of the hospital's medical staff. Medical staff selects the workload, draws on hospital inputs to provide care consistent with peer standards, and generates positive outputs (live discharges, education, research, etc.). One difficulty in analyzing the effects of the SOI is that it commingles the case mix and provider practice behavior into one measure (labeling it "severity"), confounding the separation of patient-driven treatment actions from medical staff-driven decisions about the treatment process that might be affected by demand for graduate medical education.

It would be difficult to collapse the seven-dimension SOI measure into a scale that is independent of treatment preferences of attendings, residents, and interns. For example, dimension 4, the dependency score, is a measure of illness requiring extra monitoring or care. We have no independent verification of whether that extra care is medically appropriate if assessed by some unbiased peer reviewer. One study suggests that teaching hospitals do not have a more severe case mix if the severity measure is itself independent of resource consumption (Goldfarb and Coffey, 1986). Using 1977 data, the authors report that severity is no higher in teaching hospitals with a national sample of 9 medical-school-based hospitals, 44 other COTH member hospitals, 91 community teaching hospitals, and 226 nonteaching hospitals. While the sample size is impressive, the data are more limited than this study (based on 8-year-old discharge record abstracts), and the measure of severity is crude. The health services researcher is firmly placed on the horns of a dilemma: The measure of severity must by definition be increasingly crude as it is made unbiased for provider practices (independent of physician resource decisions driven by GME needs, or driven by the idiosyncratic preferences of the medical staff unrelated to GME). In a multiple analysis of variance context, the SOI measure has a clear identification of the patient's idiosyncratic factor (individual response to therapy), but how much of the residual behavior is the provider's idiosyncratic behavior and not truly patient severity?

There is ample evidence that provider taste can dominate treatment behavior patterns (Fielding, 1985; Brook et al., 1984; Wennberg and Girrelson, 1983; Pauly, 1978). For example, if a patient resides in a community teaching hospital ICU, does that prove the patient is more severely ill? If Medicare PPS has created a tendency to treat more cases in less costly channels of service distribution (out of the ICU, even out of the hospital), does that mean these patients are suddenly less severely ill because they command fewer resources (relative to habits under pre-1984 treatment practices)? One should note that a nonteaching hospital might have wide latitude to eschew a more conservative style of medicine, and so be able to report a more severe case mix. In the Horn et al. (1985) study, contrary to expectations, the one nonteaching hospital had severity scores that exceeded the two community teaching hospitals. It is difficult to state how much of the extra severity is attributable to (1) poor medical practices; (2)

physician preferences to avoid the new and untried without harm to quality-of-care outcomes; or (3) differences in actual patient severity.

Regression analysis was used to examine the relative power of the three case-mix measures available to the study (DRG, SOI, and disease staging) in explaining variation in total (combined hospital and physician) cost. The results of the regression analysis showed that DRG as a case-mix measure was more effective in explaining variation in cost than either of the other measures alone. In the random case sample of all hospitals in the study, DRGs explained approximately 15 percent of total cost per case, versus 4.7 percent for SOI and 2.0 percent fo disease staging. One might suggest that DRGs and disease staging are measuring much the same construct (product-line categories), whereas the SOI measure offers a more substantial improvement in explained variation in costs (i.e., it measures a second construct—acuity amount of illness within a product line).

Further analysis of DRGs shows a marked difference in explanatory power by hospital department. Table 13.2 presents a summary of the reduction in unexplained variance in cost for DRGs, as a case-mix measure, and for the two severity measures in combination with DRGs. The result, comparing surgical to nonsurgical cases, is pronounced. For surgical cases (all cases in the random sample assigned to the department of surgery), the DRG accounts for greater than 25 percent of the total variation in cost, while explaining only 2.1 percent for the nonsurgical cases. (The differences in explanatory power of the DRGs between any of the four nonsurgical departments was minimal. For this reason, the results are presented as surgical versus nonsurgical cases, rather than by department.) While this result is not surprising, given the inputs to the algorithm used to construct DRGs, it does support the findings of previous studies which suggest that DRGs might not be an effective measure for differentiating resource utilization and by extension, cost for cases that do not involve extensive surgical intervention.

Curtailing the Inappropriate

One of the conceptual problems that economists have had in the area of utilization in hospitals is understanding the wide range of heterogeneous products that physicians identify in the teaching hospital setting. In teaching hospitals, physicians simultaneously produce the joint products of education, research, and patient

Table 13.2 Percent Distribution of Cases and Costs, Random Sample (300–375 cases per hospital) (Arthur Young [1986])

Hospital Type		Severity-of-Illness Index				Disease Stage*				Residents Per Bed (average)
		1	2	3	4	1	2	3	4	
COTH medical centers (T4) (n=12)	Patients	26.5	65.8	7.1	0.6	53.5	30.0	12.6	3.9	0.65
	Costs	20.6	64.2	14.0	1.2	49.0	34.7	12.2	4.1	
Major teaching hospitals (T3) (n=16)	Patients	31.9	60.9	3.4	0.8	61.7	26.9	9.1	2.3	0.29
	Costs	26.2	63.6	8.3	1.8	55.5	29.5	12.3	2.7	
Moderate teaching (T2) (n=4)	Patients	30.8	64.0	4.5	0.7	60.7	26.4	11.1	1.8	0.18
	Costs	25.0	65.0	8.4	1.7	55.0	29.1	13.6	2.3	
Minor teaching (T1) (n=3)	Patients	31.0	65.2	3.1	0.7	64.7	21.7	10.1	3.4	0.09
	Costs	24.8	67.2	6.4	1.7	56.2	21.7	19.3	2.8	
Nonteaching hospitals T0 (n=9)	Patients	29.9	66.5	2.9	0.7	69.0	22.1	7.3	1.6	0.0
	Costs	28.1	64.0	6.3	1.6	66.9	20.2	9.6	3.3	
All types	Patients	30.2	64.9	4.2	0.7	61.5	26.2	9.8	2.5	—
	Costs	23.2	65.7	9.4	1.6	55.9	28.7	12.1	3.3	

*Rounded down to nearest integer.

care. Even within the category of patient care, the care "produced" is quite diverse, due to the great variance in the complexity of cases handled. Thus physicians have largely ignored medical economics studies because they do not capture the diversity of patient care within hospitals or across different hospital types. For example, the product of a hospital cannot be captured with just four figures: inpatient days, operative cases, out-patient visits, and number of residents on staff.

Any efficiency comparison between hospitals must involve a perfect matching of patient characteristics and a more complete treatment of physician characteristics. The objective here is to explore ways in which economists might cooperatively work with physicians in microanalytical studies with the individual patient as the unit of analysis. Variation in cost and utilization of days of stay and tests per admissions will be explained by three sets of factors: product-type (patient) characteristics, input-type hospital characteristics, and input-type physician characteristics. The study results presented in this chapter have the advantage of capturing the multiproduct nature of the firm with more direct measures of physician input. This is in stark contrast to previous econometric work, which provided very crude measures. For example, the Cowing and Holtmann (1983) measure of physician input—the number of doctors with admitting privileges at each hospital— acted as an imperfect proxy for the actual attending physician input and performed poorly in regression studies.

Excessive numbers of tests and long lengths of stay are two central issues in the public debate about rising hospital costs. Excessive use of tests and procedures is a source of concern not only because it is costly but because it is unnecessary. Evidence that American medicine has a high degree of unnecessary utilization has frequently appeared in the literature. One study by Jonsson and Neuhauser (1975) found that the American physician orders three times as many tests to decide upon a simple elective surgical diagnosis as does a comparable Swedish physician. One possible explanation is that American surgeons do more testing because they are more discriminating in deciding to operate. Unfortunately, this is not consistent with the fact that the operation rate per 10,000 population is 18 percent lower in Sweden relative to the United States for inguinal hernia, and 25 percent lower for cholecystectomies and prostatectomies. The Swedish patients have the same age and diagnosis-specific mortality rates as their American counterparts, so that the additional utilization of ancillary services observed in American hospitals may not be medically necessary.

Excessively long lengths of stay are a source of public concern not only because they are costly, but also because such care is often unnecessary. It has even been suggested that reduction of unnecessary or excessive amounts of care could raise the general health status of the population by decreasing the likelihood of iatrogenic complications. Reducing the length of stay minimizes the chance of exposure to antibiotic-resistant bacteria peculiar to hospitals; thus the number of difficult-to-treat infections may be lessened. Shortened lengths of stay are a morale builder for adult patients; and in the case of children, the trauma of separation from their parents is minimized, even when there are liberal visiting privileges (Innes et al., 1968). One study suggests the marginal benefit of excessive days of hospitalization is negative, with 20 percent of the patients being exposed to some hazardous episode (Schimmel, 1974). Clearly, the problem of cost and iatrogenic disease played a major part in the congressional commitment to the PSRO program enacted in 1972 and the PRO program of the 1980s. A number of cost-reduction patient-care strategies will be surveyed in Chapters 16 and 17. For example, Brown et al. (1984) demonstrated that significant cost savings can be obtained by reducing the time involved in preoperative skin preparation. Beck (1986) suggests an annual variable cost savings of $700,000 per 10,000 surgeries per year. He goes on to critique a number of aseptic "fetishes that continue to be used despite repeated proof of their lack of value."

Utilization patterns are not merely a function of patient characteristics and the requirement of "good medicine." Medical care requirements can be met with different amounts of resources and lengths of hospitalization. How these requirements of good medicine are met depends in some part on the physician characteristics and the hospital environment. Surgical utilization is probably affected by hospital characteristics such as the laboratory turnaround time, the availability of hospital beds, the availability of a surgical suite, and the type of hospital ownership (federal, voluntary, municipal).

Physician background characteristics are also determinants of physician behavior. The duration of stay and number of tests per patient are likely to be affected by the educational background of the surgeon and the strength of the affiliation with the local medical school (Eastaugh, 1979). The process outlined in Figure 13.1 implies a causal sequence. Differing combinations of physician and hospital characteristics lead to different styles of medicine, which in turn lead to different utilization patterns. For example, one might presuppose that medical school faculty members involved in patient care have a professional interest in curtail-

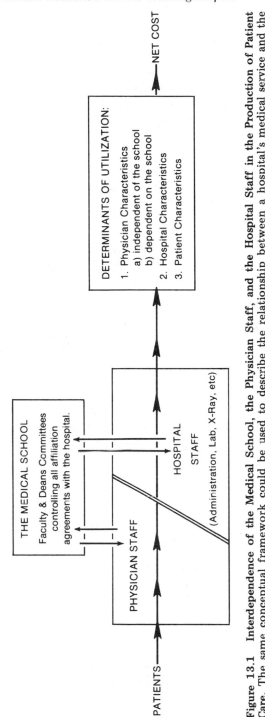

Figure 13.1 Interdependence of the Medical School, the Physician Staff, and the Hospital Staff in the Production of Patient Care. The same conceptual framework could be used to describe the relationship between a hospital's medical service and the medical school, or the affiliation of a psychiatric service with the medical school, or a hospital's department of radiology or pathology affiliation with the medical school. Each department or service within a hospital could have a different degree of affiliation with the medical school.

ing inappropriate prescriptions, but it might not always be in the faculty members' interests to curtail all types of excessive utilization. Faculty members and attending physicians might have an interest in maximizing their revenues.

A large volume of more consistent descriptive studies that correlate patient variables to the length of hospitalization is available. Patients without any hospital insurance coverage are reported to have longer lengths of stay. In a recent study by Goldfarb et al. (1980), diagnostic-specific length-of-stay equations were developed from a sample of 64 hospitals in 41 areas. The three significant factors positively affecting length of stay were fraction insured, general hospital beds per capita, and an index for the scope of services available at the hospital.

Most of the previous multivariate hospital cost regression studies emphasize the effect of insurance coverage on various hospital output and cost measures (cost per diem, laboratory charges per episode, length of stay). These studies vary with respect to objectives and methodology. The customary approach involves an aggregate cross section of individual state or hospital observations, for each of a number of years. Davis (1971) found a positive relationship between insurance and the length of hospitalization and cost per episode. Feldstein (1971) and Hu and Werner (1976) provide corroborative evidence that more highly insured areas have higher costs per episode and longer stays, on the average. Feldstein estimated an average length-of-stay equation from a cross section of the 50 states, for each of 10 years. Hu and Werner studied hospital and demographic characteristics in 70 hospital regions in Pennsylvania. Price per diem and mean patient income had no effect in the Hu-Werner length-of-stay equation, but insurance has a length-of-stay elasticity of 0.41 measured at the sample mean.

In addition to the foregoing econometric studies, a number of the early industrial engineering studies have suggested several practical ways to contain costs and length of stay. Much of the literature of the 1960s suggested that better discharge and admission planning could reduce length of stay. One such suggestion was to eliminate elective admissions on weekends or Fridays. This was supported by McCorkle (1970) and Gustafson (1968), who studied the effect of day of the week admission on preoperative and total length of stay.

Other recent studies have analyzed the impact of occupancy rate on the average length of stay and admission rates of various hospitals. Rafferty (1971) examined data from Indiana hospitals to estimate the length-of-stay elasticity and probability for admission elasticity, by diagnosis, with respect to hospital occupancy rate. The author found that the less serious medical conditions and the elective surgical cases have negative elasticities—that is to say, when the occupancy is higher, the length of hospitalization or chance of admission is lowered. A few studies focused on the actual labeling of unnecessary ("misutilized") days of stay. Querido (1963) studied a sample of patients admitted to ten teaching hospitals and concluded that one-quarter of the misutilized hospital days (as judged by implicit physician review of medical records) were associated with bottlenecks (delays) in the laboratory and x-ray departments.

In summary, the studies reviewed above provide a fair amount of empirical evidence about the influence of a number of physician and hospital characteristics on tests, costs, and length of stay. The approach taken in the remaining sections of this chapter is to perform a more disaggregate analysis of differential cost and utilization patterns across matched patient pairs from different hospitals. By analyzing matched patient data for a limited number of diagnoses, the study reported in this chapter avoids the need for any crude case-mix index. The problem in interpretation with our matched pairs approach is that a number of factors—some related to patient characteristics, some to hospital inputs, some to the physicians—all tend to influence total cost, tests, and length of stay. Multiple regression analysis will provide the tool to splice out the degree of impact that each factor exhibits on cost and utilization of hospital services.

Matched Pairs Study Design

The data for the analysis were drawn from 780 records obtained at 19 hospitals for elective herniorrhaphy, prostatectomy, and cholecystectomy patients. The 12 VA hospitals in the study represented a 9 percent random stratified sample of VA hospitals performing surgery (National Research Council, 1977). The patient pairs were drawn from among two samples: 360 VA patients from 12 VA hospitals, and 420 nonfederal patients from 7 nonfederal hospitals. The 360 VA patients were drawn as a random sample, but the 420 nonfederal patients were selected in order to have patient characteristics that were as nearly similar to the federal patients as possible (Rubin, 1973). The research rationale was to minimize the variance in patient case-mix characteristics in order to measure the effects of staff and hospital characteristics on utilization and cost.

The first step in the matching process was to select the covariables on which the two samples were to be matched. The six patient characteristics under consideration were age, sex, primary diagnosis, secondary diagnosis, socioeconomic status, and distance from the hospital. The first stage in the matching process was to have nurse abstractors of patient records enter the nonfederal facility with information on the already selected federal patient pool and select a nonfederal sample that had the same sex, primary diagnosis, and welfare status. Stage 2 in the matching process was to apply Caliper matching methods based on predefined ranges of what constitutes an acceptable match—for example, any nonfederal partner had to be within four years, plus or minus, of the federal patient's age (Rubin, 1970).

Stage 3 in the sampling design involved using nearest available matching methods after the data collection stages were completed, for final pairing of the nonfederal and VA patient groups on the basis of age, secondary diagnosis, and five-digit zip code number. Two of the 11 patient characteristics were different in the nearest available matched sample (258 pairs) relative to the original onsite data (720 patients). Matched patients tended to be less complex cases with fewer secondary diagnoses; they also tended to reside in zip code regions closer to the hospital (Table 13.3). Patients with a preadmissions visit to the hospital (9 percent) had their medical record abstracts coded with a -1, so that in the matching process, only patients with equivalent preadmission workups were matched with one another. One of the explanations for the tendency of private insurance patients to have fewer tests and days of preoperative stay is that their admission was preceded by a preadmission visit, but 91 percent of the patients in our sample entered the hospital without any preadmission tests. In the final analysis, 102 VA patients remained unmatched, compared to 162 unmatched nonfederal patients, and 258 VA nonfederal patient pairs were formed (Eastaugh, 1980).

The multiple regression approach was designed to determine how much of the variation in tests, length of stay, and cost per case are patient related, hospital related, or staff related. Sixteen dependent variables were studied:

1. Ratio between pairs in prostatectomy preoperative length of stay.
2. Ratio between pairs in herniorrhaphy preoperative length of stay.
3. Ratio between pairs in cholecystectomy preoperative length of stay.
4. Ratio between pairs in preoperative length of stay for all surgical patient pairs cited above.

Table 13.3 Mean Values for 11 Characteristics of the Matched Sample and the Original Data

	Matched Pairs After Three Stages of Matching Mean	Original Onsite Data[1] Mean
Sample Size	516 (258 pairs)	720
Fraction of Surgeons Who Are FMGs	0.27	0.28
Fraction of Surgeons on Faculty	0.08	0.08
Fraction of School's Students Doing Required Clerkship at Hospital	0.11	0.10
Lab Turnaround Time (hours)	18	19
Occupancy Rate	76%	77%
Number of Beds	412	420
Patient Census	313	323
Adult Admissions per Year	5,335	5,186
Distance Home-Hospital (miles)[2]	12	18
Number of Secondary Diagnoses[2]	1.1	1.7
Patient Age	54	51

SOURCE: Reprinted with permission of the Blue Cross Association from Eastaugh, S.R. (1980). "Organizational Determinants of Surgical Lengths of Stay," *Inquiry* 17:1 (Spring), 85–96. Copyright © 1980 by the Blue Cross Association. All rights reserved.

[1] After the second stage of matching, onsite Caliper matching.
[2] The differences between matched and unmatched samples are significant at the 0.05 level.

5. Ratio between pairs in prostatectomy length of stay.
6. Ratio between pairs in herniorrhaphy length of stay.
7. Ratio between pairs in cholecystectomy length of stay.
8. Ratio between pairs in total length of stay for all surgical patient pairs.
9. Ratio between pairs in number of elective tests ordered preoperatively (PT) for prostatectomy patients.
10. Ratio between pairs in PT for herniorrhaphy patients.
11. Ratio between pairs in PT for cholecystectomy patients.
12. Ratio between pairs in PT for all surgical patient pairs.
13. Ratio between pairs in costs (charges reimbursed or costs imputed in the case of hospitals lacking a patient-based accounting system) for prostatectomy patients.
14. Ratio between pairs in costs for herniorrhaphy patients.
15. Ratio between pairs in costs for cholecystectomy patients.
16. Ratio between pairs in costs for all surgical patient pairs.

Implicit in this analysis is that to do more tests or to require higher costs for producing the same product was inappropriate or wasteful behavior; the behavior was unnecessary in that the marginal benefits of more tests or days of hospitalization are minimal.

The definition of an unnecessary test in this context is one that did not make the partner better off relative to his match, undergoing the same operation, with the same outcome. Operationally, an unnecessary test is one that was provided to only one member of the pair and that Payne (1976) defines as unnecessary for a partner with given case-mix characteristics—that is, age, sex, and diagnoses.

Operationalization of the Variables

Product definition is a most complex problem in the field of medical economics. An operational definition of a required intermediate product would be a test that was required in nearly 100 percent of the patients in the diagnostic category under study. For example, cholelithiasis is almost always confirmed in our sample of cholecystectomy patients by radiologic evidence of single or multiple gallstones, or by evidence of a nonfunctioning gallbladder by observing the movement of concentrated amounts of gallbladder dye. Some tests are elective, such as a serum amylase assay, because the majority of clinicians do not believe that this test is necessary to rule out the possibility of pancreatitis (Payne, 1976).

The information on costs came in two forms, depending on whether or not the hospital had a patient-based system of charges. For example, four hospitals in the sample had patient-based accounting systems for billing purposes; thus one only needed to ask for the costs and charges. Costs were assigned to the surgical department by means of the multiple apportionment algebraic method of cost allocation (Berman and Weeks, 1982). However, 12 VA hospitals and 3 municipal hospitals in the sample had no need for itemized billing, and thus had no need for a price list or a charge-to-cost ratio. Consequently, a relative value scale* for assessing imputed charges was developed (Table 13.4).

All patients sampled were middle-aged males eligible for Medicaid and free VA hospital care. Three patient characteristics are included in the regression analysis as independent variables:

---

*The hospital and ancillary costs were reduced to a relative value scale by averaging prevailing hospital charges in the region. Then the surgeon's fee for the area was taken from the Social Security Administration Survey of Prevailing Charges (Institute of Medicine, 1976). Finally, in the case of the 12 federal hospitals and 3 municipal hospitals, the resources utilized in the elective surgical episode were multiplied by the relative value scale and multiplied by the conversion factor measured in dollars per relative scale unit to obtain dollars per episode (Eastaugh, 1979).

Table 13.4   **Relative Value Scale for Costing Out Elective Surgical Services at the 12 VA Hospitals and 3 Municipal Hospitals without a Schedule of Charges**

	Relative Value Scale
I. Fixed Charges	
Surgeon's Fee:	
Incisional Prostatectomy	5.6
Cholecystectomy	4.2
Unilateral Inguinal Hernia	2.5
Anesthesiologist	1.75
Operating Room	1.2
Recovery Room (2–4 hours)	0.5
Anesthesia	0.26
II. Variable Charges[1]	
Basic Room Rate (per day)	0.75
Pulmonary Function Test	0.60
Cholecystogram	0.47
Cystourethrogram	0.40
Intravenous Pyelogram	0.35
Upper Gastrointestinal Series	0.32
Barium Enema	0.29
Sigmoidoscopy (Proctoscopy)	0.22
Chest X-Ray	0.16
Serum Amylase Assay	0.14
Creatine Clearance	0.11

SOURCE: Eastaugh, S.R. (1979). "Cost of Elective Surgery and Utilization of Ancillary Services in Teaching Hospitals," *Health Services Research* 14:4 (Winter), 290–308.

[1] Excluding tests necessary for admission at all 15 hospitals and the 4 voluntary hospitals.

P_1 Distance from hospital to home in miles.
P_2 Dummy variable for lack of unmatched secondary diagnoses, between pairs.
P_3 Patient age.

The independent variables selected for inclusion in this study were chosen for reasons of either past performance in other studies or future relevance for public policy. For example, a dummy variable for affiliation with a medical school and the percentage of physicians with more than 10 years of clinical experience were omitted from this study because they were considered poor proxy measures for our medical school student and faculty variables.

The list of independent variables, which will also be expressed as a ratio of the nonfederal patient's value for the data item divided by the patient's matched federal partner's value, includes the following three physician-staff characteristics:

S_1 Fraction of surgeons (excluding anesthesiologists) at the facility who are foreign medical graduates (FMGs).

S_2 Fraction of the attending physicians on the surgical service with actual teaching faculty appointments at the local medical school who receive salary from the school (intended as an index of the hospital's dependence on the medical school for physicians).

S_3 Fraction of the affiliated medical school's students who did their required core clinical clerkship on the hospital surgical service (intended as an index for the school's dependence on the hospital as a training ground).

Frick et al. (1985), Eastaugh (1980), and others have suggested a strong positive association between the teaching function and more frequent utilization of tests and hospital days in U.S. hospitals. In contrast, Detsky et al. (1986) in their study of 10 Canadian hospitals during a residents' strike conclude that there was no significant teaching effect on test usage per case. In the foregoing regression analysis a number of new variables are analyzed.

The fraction of the medical school's students depending on the individual hospital as a source of clinical education is intended as a proxy measure of the school's dependency on the hospital. One might suggest that if the school is highly dependent on a hospital for teaching cases, the students, interns, residents, and attending physicians, acting as agents of the school's interest, would have added reason to increase length of stay or tests ordered in order to maximize the number of teaching days available and to maximize tests and cost per case in order to serve a technological interest in maximizing revenues for new equipment.

Three hospital characteristics included in the list of independent variables are

H_1 Laboratory turn-around time on the average for seven basic tests.

H_2 Hospital occupancy rate.

H_3 Federal ownership of the hospital (in this specification, the equation intercept).

Overutilization of tests and unnecessary days of stay presumably may be due to the inadequacies of the hospital in providing ancillary laboratory support or surgical suites. Inappropriate utilization can be attributed to both a "systems" failure of the institution and/or a staff behavior problem. The research question then becomes one of asking how much staff improvement can be expected for a given change in the independent variables holding the following factors constant: patient age, sex, primary and secondary diagnoses, welfare status, distance from the hospital (six patient characteristics), bed availability (occupancy), and lab turnaround time. Unless one considers all these factors simultaneously, one really is not measuring the variance truly attributable to staff characteristics.

The model is estimated by the ordinary least squares method. The 16 equations were developed for the 16 dependent variables mentioned earlier, where *VA* denotes Veterans Administration patient member of the pair and *NF* denotes nonfederal hospital patient member of the pair, under the following log-linear multiplicative specifications:

$$
\begin{aligned}
\ln(LOSVA/LOSNF) = {} & \ln(P_1VA/P_1NF) \\
& + \ln(P_2VA/P_2NF) \\
& + \ln P_3 \\
& + \ln(S_4VA/S_4NF) \\
& + \ln(S_5VA/S_5NF) \\
& + \ln(S_6VA/S_6NF) \\
& + \ln(H_7VA/H_7NF) \\
& + \ln(H_8VA/H_8NF) \\
& + \ln(H_9VA/H_9NF) \\
& + \ln(E)
\end{aligned}
$$

This log-linear form, sometimes called the double log form, implies that the effect of the error term (E) is multiplicative, as are the effects of the independent variables. The intercept term is X_3.

Results of the Cost and Test Regressions

The results of the regression analysis for cost per case, displayed in Table 13.5, indicate that federal ownership had the largest elasticity. The dummy variable coefficient implies that federal hospital cost per matched surgical case was 52.3 percent higher than nonfederal hospital care, ceteris paribus [the estimated coefficient is 0.4231 which equals $\ln(1 + 0.523)$]. The average total cost per case was $3,174 in federal hospitals, $1,980 in municipal hospitals, and $2,217 in voluntary hospitals (Table 13.6). The average per diem cost was $198 in federal hospitals, $187 in municipal hospitals, and $216 in voluntary hospitals. The finding that the voluntary hospital per diem is 9 percent higher than the federal per diem is consistent with a National Academy of Sciences study finding, using almost the same group of hospitals, and 1975 prices.

Table 13.5   Cost Equation Regression Result (*t* values in parentheses)

Type of Surgery	Transurethral Prostatectomies	Unilateral Inguinal Hernias	Cholecystectomies	Elective Surgery (columns 1–3)
Type of Surgeon	Specialist	Generalist	Generalist	Specialist or Generalist
Sample Size (patient pairs)	109	99	50	258
R-Squared	0.8145	0.5199	0.7300	0.6441
Elasticity Coefficients for the Following 9 Independent Variables:				
Staff Characteristics				
1. Fraction of Surgeons Who Are FMGs	-0.117[1] (4.09)	-0.081[1] (2.02)	-0.088[1] (2.04)	-0.097[1] (4.25)
2. Fraction of Surgeons with Faculty Appointments at a Medical School	0.198[1] (5.72)	0.076[1] (1.99)	0.167[1] (2.69)	0.063[1] (4.74)
3. Fraction of the Medical School's Students Doing Their Core Clinical Clerkship in Surgery at the Hospital	0.311[1] (11.31)	0.108[1] (2.89)	0.285[1] (5.48)	0.213[1] (9.70)
Hospital Characteristics				
1. Laboratory Turnaround Time (hours)	0.073[1] (7.74)	0.105[1] (7.70)	0.083[1] (3.16)	0.092[1] (11.69)
2. Occupancy Rate	-0.207[1] (4.85)	-0.064[2] (1.70)	-0.100[1] (1.10)	-0.063[1] (2.05)
3. Federal Ownership of the Hospital[3]	0.134[1] (3.43)	0.696[1] (7.01)	0.721[1] (1.98)	0.523[1] (8.17)

Table 13.5 (continued)

Type of Surgery	Transurethral Prostatectomies	Unilateral Inguinal Hernias	Cholecystectomies	Elective Surgery (columns 1–3)
Type of Surgeon	Specialist	Generalist	Generalist	Specialist or Generalist
Sample Size (patient pairs)	109	99	50	258
R-Squared	0.8145	0.5199	0.7300	0.6441
Elasticity Coefficients for the Following 9 Independent Variables:				
Patient Characteristics				
1. Distance from Hospital to Home (miles)	0.073[1]	0.044[1]	0.055[1]	0.060[1]
	(6.55)	(3.13)	(2.48)	(6.87)
2. Lack of Unmatched Secondary Diagnoses, Present or Absent, Between Pairs	−0.085[1]	−0.079[2]	−0.044	−0.049[2]
	(2.04)	(1.79)	(0.54)	(1.65)
3. Patient Age	0.009	0.339	0.044	0.155[2]
	(0.07)	(0.99)	(0.14)	(1.69)

SOURCE: Eastaugh, S. R. (1979). "Cost of Elective Surgery and Utilization of Ancillary Services in Teaching Hospitals," *Health Services Research* 14:4 (Winter), 290–308.

[1] $p < 0.05$, two-tailed test.
[2] $p < 0.10$, two-tailed test.
[3] The coefficients imply a VA/non-federal percentage differential of 14.3%, 69.6%, 72.1%, and 52.3%, respectively.

Table 13.6   Average Number of Elective Tests Done, Cost per Case, and Average and Preoperative Lengths of Stay, by Hospital Ownership (sample size in parentheses)

Type of Surgery Type of Surgeon	Transurethral Prostatectomies *Specialist*	Unilateral Inguinal Hernias *Generalist*	Cholecystectomies *Generalist*	Elective Surgery (columns 1–3) *Specialist or Generalist*
I. Average Number of Elective Pre-operative Tests				
a. VA Patients	5.1 (109)	1.8 (99)	6.0 (50)	4.4 (258)
b. Municipal Hospital Patients	4.2 (47)	0.6 (41)	2.2 (23)	2.5 (111)
c. Voluntary Hospital Patients	4.4 (62)	0.7 (58)	2.4 (27)	2.9 (147)
II. Average Cost (in dollars)				
a. VA Patients	$3,299	$2,628	$3,469	$3,074
b. Municipal Hospital Patients	2,823	1,456	1,758	1,930
c. Voluntary Hospital Patients	2,932	1,660	2,021	2,117
III. Average Length of Stay (in days)				
a. VA Patients	17.0	13.2	18.1	16.0
b. Municipal Hospital Patients	14.5	8.0	11.3	10.6
c. Voluntary Hospital Patients	14.2	7.6	10.8	10.3
IV. Average Pre-operative Length of Stay				
a. VA Patients	7.1	5.6	7.2	6.6
b. Municipal Hospital Patients	4.6	2.2	3.8	3.1
c. Voluntary Hospital Patients	4.4	1.9	3.6	2.8

The NAS study group found that on the average the nursing costs per diem for voluntary hospital surgical patients exceeded federal surgical per diems in nursing by 19.8 percent (National Research Council, 1977). Expressed in terms of nursing costs per surgical case, the federal hospitals were $262 more costly than voluntary hospitals. Nursing costs represented only 30 percent of total per-episode costs.

The following five findings summarize the results obtained in comparing utilization efficiency between different hospitals producing the same product.

1. The federal ownership hospital characteristic was consistently the most significant variable in explaining the variance between matched patient pairs in tests utilization (Table 13.7) and cost per case (Table 13.5). On the average, VA patients had 104 percent more preoperative elective tests performed per case, all else being equal in the equation. VA patients also had 52 percent higher costs per elective surgical case for the same operation, ceteris paribus. One policy implication of these results is that shifting surgical patients from federal to nonfederal facilities may be cost effective and may also prove quality-beneficial according to the National Research Council (1977) study of VA hospitals.

2. The size of the coefficient for the federal ownership variable was much smaller when the surgery is done by a specialist, compared to the sample of surgical cases treated by nonspecialists. However, the federal ownership variable was still the most statistically significant variable in all the regressions. The finding that the federal ownership coefficient was five to nine times larger in cases on nonspecialty surgery, compared to specialty surgery, suggests that the specialist was more independent of the effects of working in a federal facility than his nonspecialist colleague. In other words, the specialist was more likely to exhibit the same utilization patterns, independent of whether he operated in a federal, municipal, or voluntary institution. The issue of professional autonomy is a vast and complicated problem, but some descriptive observational studies suggest that the nonspecialist is much more likely to adjust his style of medicine to reflect the more predictable, slower-paced, federal schedule for getting things done (Lindsay, 1975). Our findings suggest that the specialist is also affected, but to a lesser extent, by working within the framework of a federal institutional base.

3. The fraction of the medical school's students doing their required clinical clerkship in surgery at the hospital proved to be the second most significant factor in the regressions and had the

Table 13.7 Number of Tests Regression Results (*t* values in parentheses)

Type of Surgery	Transurethral Prostatectomies	Unilateral Inguinal Hernias	Cholecystectomies	Elective Surgery (columns 1–3)
Type of Surgeon	Specialist	Generalist	Generalist	Specialist or Generalist
Sample Size (patient pairs)	109	99	50	258
R-Squared	0.7655	0.6256	0.7239	0.6374
Elasticity Coefficients for the Following 9 Independent Variables:				
Staff Characteristics				
1. Fraction of Surgeons Who Are FMGs	0.322[1]	0.211[1]	0.232[1]	0.255[1]
	(6.48)	(3.16)	(2.88)	(6.26)
2. Fraction of Surgeons with Faculty Appointments at a Medical School	−0.157[1]	−0.200[1]	−0.213[1]	−0.218[1]
	(2.61)	(2.30)	(2.15)	(4.43)
3. Fraction of the Medical School's Students Doing Their Core Clinical Clerkship in Surgery at the Hospital	0.359[1]	0.070[2]	0.512[1]	0.244[1]
	(7.54)	(1.83)	(6.14)	(6.23)
Hospital Characteristics				
1. Laboratory Turnaround Time (hours)	0.073[1]	0.236[1]	0.104[1]	0.156[1]
	(4.51)	(10.42)	(2.48)	(11.02)
2. Occupancy Rate	0.197[1]	0.271[1]	0.342[1]	0.029[1]
	(2.66)	(3.04)	(2.36)	(0.48)
3. Federal Ownership of the Hospital[3]	0.165[1]	0.609[1]	0.769[1]	0.712[1]
	(2.52)	(11.10)	(2.40)	(6.83)

Table 13.7 (continued)

Type of Surgery	Transurethral Prostatectomies	Unilateral Inguinal Hernias	Cholecystectomies	Elective Surgery (columns 1–3)
Type of Surgeon	Specialist	Generalist	Generalist	Specialist or Generalist
Sample Size (patient pairs)	109	99	50	258
R-Squared	0.7655	0.6256	0.7239	0.6374
Elasticity Coefficients for the Following 9 Independent Variables:				
Patient Characteristics				
1. Distance from Hospital to Home (miles)	0.032[2]	0.030[2]	0.013	0.017
	(1.67)	(1.78)	(0.36)	(1.09)
2. Lack of Unmatched Secondary Diagnoses, Present or Absent, Between Pairs	−0.295[1]	−0.361[1]	−0.375[1]	−0.295[1]
	(3.88)	(3.22)	(2.91)	(4.57)
3. Patient Age	0.963[1]	1.008[2]	0.752[2]	0.382[1]
	(4.24)	(1.89)	(1.77)	(2.07)

SOURCE: Eastaugh, S. R. (1979). "Cost of Elective Surgery and Utilization of Ancillary Services in Teaching Hospitals," *Health Services Research* 14:4 (Winter), 290–308.

[1] $p < 0.05$, two-tailed test.
[2] $p < 0.10$, two-tailed test.
[3] The coefficients imply a VA/non-federal percentage differential of 18.2%, 184%, 116%, and 104%, respectively.

expected positive impact on excessive utilization. One possible explanation for this finding is that as dependency of the school on the hospital for teaching beds increases, the school's need to help the hospital maximize patient days, admissions, and revenues (or budgets in the case of VA hospitals) also increases. The coefficients suggest that a 25 percent decline in students would be associated with a 6.2 percent decline in elective tests per case, and a 5.3 percent decline in cost per case.

4. The third and fourth most significant variables in the regressions were, respectively, the percentage of FMGs and faculty members on the surgical service. If the values of these coefficients were confirmed on a broader scale, and over a more complete collection of diagnoses, the predicted impact of a 10 percent increase in faculty participation on the surgical service would be a 2.2 percent decline in tests performed, but a 1.3 percent increase in cost per case. It is indeed heartening to learn that the most educated manpower category, the board-certified full-time teaching faculty member, had some propensity to emphasize parsimony in the utilization of ancillary tests. Faculty may have required fewer tests to treat the same matched case, but they had a significantly higher demand for longer periods of patient hospitalization in the post-operative phase of care. The percentage of FMGs was also an important variable in explaining the variance in tests and cost per case. There might have been some within-hospital selection bias—for example, specialist FMGs got easier cases than nonspecialist USMGs. Problems of intrastaff-class correlation remain a subject for future research. The issue of FMG utilization of hospital resources has received somewhat less attention than the more emotional debate about the quality of FMG care. The estimated impact of a 25 percent decline in FMGs on the typical surgical service would be a 6.5 percent decline in the average number of tests, but a 2.4 percent increase in costs per case. In contrast to the highly educated faculty members, the FMG manpower pool of attending surgeons utilized more tests,* but fewer days of hospitalization for the same case mix, with the net effect being a slightly lower average cost per case. The FMG and faculty staff characteristics explained nearly 40 percent of the variance in tests and costs per case.

---

*FMGs might also be expected to require more tests per case because their training is not as extensive or as diagnosis-oriented as that provided by the typical American medical school. Presumably, an inferior education is associated with greater uncertainty in affirming a differential diagnosis and the need for more time between sequential decisions and perhaps the need for more information (more tests).

5. Age was the most significant patient characteristic in the analysis. Age had its predicted positive impact on utilization. On the average, the 60-year-old man also had 19 percent more preoperative tests than his 40-year-old counterpart with the same condition. It has been suggested that older men need more testing per admission. Some of the elective tests are recommended by the Payne (1976) process criteria standards on a nonelective basis if the patient is over the age of 50. For example, Payne considers ECG to be necessary for a cholecystectomy patient over the age of 50.

Results of the Length-of-Stay Regressions

The results of the regression analysis for preoperative length of stay displayed in Table 13.8 indicate that federal ownership is the most significant variable. The dummy variable coefficient implies that federal hospitals have 158 percent longer preoperative lengths of stay, ceteris paribus [the estimated coefficient is 0.9496, which equals In(1 + 1.58)]. This is consistent with an average preoperative duration of stay that is 6.6 days in federal hospitals, 3.1 days in municipal hospitals, and 2.8 days in voluntary hospitals (Table 13.6). Again, we find empirical support in Tables 13.8 and 13.9 to suggest that specialists appear to be increasingly autonomous of the institutional variable of federal ownership. If this finding is confirmed in different settings and for different sets of diagnoses, it would suggest that the specialist is more independent of the effects of working in a federal facility than his or her nonspecialist colleague. Nevertheless, both nonspecialists and specialists are affected by working within the framework of a federal institutional base, with consequent poor utilization of staff time, patient time, and federal money.

The fraction of the medical school's students doing their required clinical clerkship in surgery at the hospital proved to be a significant positive factor in the regressions. The size of the coefficients for this student affiliation factor was not especially dramatic. The coefficients suggest that a 25 percent decline in students would produce only a 2.2 percent decline in total length of stay, and a 6.5 percent decline in preoperative stay. Another independent variable for strength of affiliation, whether or not the hospital was a member of the Council of Teaching Hospitals, was omitted from the analysis because this variable was insignificant and interacted with the student and faculty variable to make each less significant (0.10 level).

FMGs have a slight, negative (downward) impact on preopera-

Table 13.8   Preoperative Length of Stay Regression Results (*t* values are in parentheses)

Type of Surgery	Transurethral Prostatectomies	Unilateral Inguinal Hernias	Cholecystectomies	Elective Surgery (columns 1–3)
Type of Surgeon	Specialist	Generalist	Generalist	Specialist or Generalist
Sample Size (patient pairs)	109	99	50	258
R-Squared	0.8403	0.6680	0.6346	0.676
Elasticity Coefficients for the Following 9 Independent Variables:				
Staff Characteristics				
1. Fraction of Surgeons Who Are FMGs	−0.138[1]	−0.017	−0.048	−0.056[2]
	(3.61)	(0.26)	(0.60)	(1.82)
2. Fraction of Surgeons with Faculty Appointments at a Medical School	0.186[1]	0.028	0.143[2]	0.063[2]
	(4.01)	(0.33)	(1.79)	(1.69)
3. Fraction of Medical School's Students Doing Their Core Clinical Clerkship in Surgery at the Hospital	0.405[1]	0.153[1]	0.319[1]	0.259[1]
	(11.03)	(2.45)	(3.88)	(7.31)
Hospital Characteristics				
1. Laboratory Turnaround Time (hours)	0.114[1]	0.227[1]	0.113[1]	0.182[1]
	(9.10)	(12.21)	(2.72)	(14.30)
2. Occupancy Rate	−0.454[1]	−0.162[1]	−0.300[1]	−0.147[1]
	(7.98)	(2.01)	(2.09)	(2.70)
3. Federal Ownership of the Hospital[3]	0.785[1]	2.381[1]	1.623[1]	1.577[1]
	(4.86)	(12.51)	(2.38)	(5.74)

Table 13.8 (continued)

Type of Surgery	Transurethral Prostatectomies	Unilateral Inguinal Hernias	Cholecystectomies	Elective Surgery (columns 1–3)
Type of Surgeon	Specialist	Generalist	Generalist	Specialist or Generalist
Sample Size (patient pairs)	109	99	50	258
R-Squared	0.8403	0.6680	0.6346	0.676
Elasticity Coefficients for the Following 9 Independent Variables:				
Patient Characteristics				
1. Distance from Hospital to Home (miles)	0.045[1] (3.00)	0.034[2] (1.74)	0.012 (0.36)	0.043[1] (3.05)
2. Lack of Unmatched Secondary Diagnoses, Present or Absent, Between Pairs	−0.341[1] (5.84)	−0.312 (0.25)	−0.021 (0.17)	−0.228[1] (3.91)
3. Patient Age	0.504[1] (2.87)	0.248 (0.43)	0.064 (0.13)	0.480[1] (2.33)

SOURCE: Reprinted with permission of the Blue Cross Association from Eastaugh, S. R. (1980). "Organizational Determinants of Surgical Lengths of Stay," *Inquiry* 17:1 (Spring), 85–96. Copyright © 1980 by the Blue Cross Association. All rights reserved.

[1] $p < 0.05$, two-tailed test.
[2] $p < 0.10$, two-tailed test.
[3] The actual coefficients for this intercept term are 0.580, 1.219, 0.964, and 0.950, respectively.

Table 13.9 Total Length of Stay Regression Results (*t* values are in parentheses)

Type of Surgery	Transurethral Prostatectomies	Unilateral Inguinal Hernias	Cholecystectomies	Elective Surgery (columns 1–3)
Type of Surgeon	Specialist	Generalist	Generalist	Specialist or Generalist
Sample Size (patient pairs)	109	99	50	258
R-Squared	0.4911	0.4202	0.5457	0.4592
Elasticity Coefficients for the Following 9 Independent Variables:				
Staff Characteristics				
1. Fraction of Surgeons Who are FMGs	−0.053[2]	−0.033	−0.041	−0.042[1]
	(1.76)	(0.78)	(0.87)	(1.98)
2. Fraction of Surgeons with Faculty Appointments at a Medical School	0.059[2]	0.071[2]	0.039	0.066[1]
	(1.73)	(1.81)	(0.66)	(2.17)
3. Fraction of the Medical School's Students Doing Their Core Clinical Clerkship in Surgery at the Hospital	0.112[1]	0.081[1]	0.057[2]	0.088[1]
	(2.98)	(2.07)	(1.75)	(3.71)
Hospital Characteristics				
1. Laboratory Turnaround Time (hours)	0.057[1]	0.094[1]	0.107[1]	0.074[1]
	(4.45)	(6.62)	(4.28)	(8.70)
2. Occupancy Rate	−0.196[1]	−0.010	−0.018	−0.082[1]
	(3.36)	(0.18)	(0.22)	(2.26)
3. Federal Ownership of the Hospital[3]	0.270[1]	0.879[1]	0.842[1]	0.690[1]
	(2.97)	(7.36)	(3.97)	(7.50)

Table 13.9 (continued)

Type of Surgery	Transurethral Prostatectomies	Unilateral Inguinal Hernias	Cholecystectomies	Elective Surgery (columns 1–3)
Type of Surgeon	Specialist	Generalist	Generalist	Specialist or Generalist
Sample Size (patient pairs)	109	99	50	258
R-Squared	0.4911	0.4202	0.5457	0.4592
Elasticity Coefficients for the Following 9 Independent Variables:				
Patient Characteristics				
1. Distance from Hospital to Home (miles)	0.003	0.008	0.004	0.007
	(0.22)	(0.55)	(0.18)	(0.24)
2. Lack of Unmatched Secondary Diagnoses, Present or Absent, Between Pairs	-0.080[2]	-0.234[1]	-0.054	-0.115[1]
	(1.73)	(3.34)	(0.71)	(2.95)
3. Patient Age	0.314	0.038	0.040	0.185[2]
	(1.99)	(0.10)	(0.13)	(1.71)

SOURCE: Reprinted with permission of the Blue Cross Association from Eastaugh, S. R. (1980). "Organizational Determinants of Surgical Lengths of Stay," *Inquiry* 17:1 (Spring), 85–96. Copyright © 1980 by the Blue Cross Association. All rights reserved.

[1] $p < 0.05$, two-tailed test.
[2] $p < 0.10$, two-tailed test.
[3] The actual coefficients for this intercept term are 0.239, 0.630, 0.609, and 0.524, respectively.

tive and total length of stay. The effect of laboratory turnaround time on the duration of patient stay also is statistically significant. The expected impacts of a 25 percent improvement in turnaround time would be a 4.6 percent decline in average preoperative length of stay and a 1.8 percent decline in total length of stay.

Age is the most significant patient characteristic in the analysis. All other factors being equal, for the three surgical conditions studied, a 60-year-old man will have a preoperative length of stay that is 24 percent longer than that of a 40-year-old man, both having the same conditions and surgery within the same facility.

One final caveat must be introduced in the discussion. The study design would need to be adjusted if it ever were applied to private patients in the voluntary hospital sector, since the majority of private patients would have been admitted with a preadmissions diagnosis already established. Balintfy (1982), for example, found a median preoperative length of stay in his sample of only one day. The comparison of utilization patterns in private/voluntary hospitals versus federal/municipal hospitals typically ignores the differences in operational style between the two systems. In the governmental sector, the patient tends to enter the hospital without prior examination and testing. The private hospital patient tends to have fewer tests and days of preoperative stay, because the admission was preceded by preadmission visit(s) and tests (Dumbaugh and Neuhauser, 1976). Consequently, in this study, all the public patients (Medicaid or VA) with a preadmission visit to the hospital (9 percent) had their medical record abstracts coded with a -1; thus, in the aforementioned matching process, only patients with equivalent preadmission workups were matched with one another.

Policy Implications

Multiple regression analysis provided considerable insight into the roles of specific independent variables in explaining differences between hospitals along the four utilization measures (preoperative length of stay, total length of stay, tests, and costs). The increasing concern for curtailing hospital costs and renewed interest in reducing the number of hospital beds make it increasingly important for health services researchers to learn more about how to affect physician behavior in a direction that enhances hospital efficiency. PRO (professional review organization) review efforts might be targeted to those surgical services in federal hospitals, or in nonfederal teaching hospitals that provide over 10 percent of the local medical school's students with a required clinical clerkship in surgery. A continuing education program that emphasizes reduced ancillary utilization might best be targeted to surgical services with a high percentage of FMGs or high percentage of students. Although PROs do not specifically fund continuing education programs, the facilities with an abundance of excessive utilization relative to the norms would seem most in need of continuing education programs.

The basic premise of the economic model emerging from this study is that physicians are influenced in patient management decisions by the economic advantage of actions to them or their hospital, or perhaps to their medical school. We should guard against overutilization that results from physician pursuit of less explicit forms of economic advantage than income maximization tendencies under a fee-for-service system of reimbursement. The subtle incentives to overutilize are much more insidious and affect salaried and private entrepreneur physicians equally.

There are six basic methods by which hospital-based specialists are reimbursed for professional services: (1) fee-for-service billings to the patient, (2) fee-for-service compensation from the hospital, (3) salary from the hospital, (4) salary negotiated with the department chief or specialty group practice unit, (5) a fixed percentage of net department revenues, or (6) a fixed percentage of gross department billings (Roe, 1985). These six methods of reimbursement often exist in hybrid form; salary plus percentage provides the comfort of a minimum guarantee for the clinician. There are differences in the popularity of these methods of reimbursement. Pathologists prefer straight salary or fee-for-service billings done by the hospital. Radiologists are increasingly entering into leasing arrangements with the hospital whereby they compensate the hospital radiology department for the rental of staff and equipment, and all billings are generated from the specialty group. Historically, radiologists preferred a fixed percentage of billings or revenues, but over the last five years fee-for-service reimbursement has become more popular. Cardiologists are more likely to be reimbursed on a percentage of gross billings basis, after deductions for bad debts, discounts, and charity.

For managers of federal hospitals, the future appears to hold good news and bad news. The good news is that physician recruitment should be less of a problem in the future because of downward pressure on physician incomes in the private sector (as reviewed in Chapters 1 and 2). The bad news is competition from nonfederal hospitals. For example, the CEO of the Washington Hospital Center, in his survey of reforms to improve charity care, suggests "a reduction in the number of public hospitals, including the elimination of most hospitals in the VA system" (McDaniel, 1986). A more disinterested analyst, focusing on patient access, might question the wisdom of such a policy proposal in many regions of the country. However, cut-throat, head-to-head competition is inevitable in a market with 360,000 empty acute short-term hospital beds. There is some evidence that hospital beds could be utilized more efficiently. For example, the August 1986 General Accounting Office study of VA hospitals reported 43 percent of the hospital days at VA hospitals are medically avoidable.

Controlling DRG-specific lengths of stay is also a problem for Department of Defense (DOD) hospitals. Army and Air Force hospitals reduced their lengths of stay only 4.4 percent in the 1983–1986 period. However, nonfederal hospitals reduced their length of stay 12.1 percent over the same time period, such that duration of stay is 30 to 50 percent shorter than DOD hospitals. Nonfederal hospitals are doing many procedures on an outpatient basis. As of 1986, major ligament repairs and hysterectomies are often done on an outpatient basis in nonfederal hospitals. Consequently, DOD is considering paying for Civilian Health and Medical Program for the Uniformed Services (CHAMPUS) care by means of competitive contracts to three "Supermed" private sector chains. Three regional contracts covering the nation would virtually privatize all military health care ($2 billion budget) for dependents (family) and military retirees by 1988–89. The pressures are great on a number of federal facilities to reduce costs per case. But the federal health care managers are constrained by civil service rules to implement the sort of incentive plans for appropriate cost-reduction behavior outlined in Chapter 11.

Hospital-based specialists are interested in maintaining distribution channels that ensure "interesting" product assortment, efficiency (whenever possible), and progressiveness (including the ability to foster technological change). Elimination of a service or department should be analyzed in light of risks and benefits, response from the competition, and alienation of internal hospital-based vested interests. The hospital-based physicians frequently lobby for revitalization rather than elimination.

If we presume that the surgeon wishes to maximize prestige or popularity within the profession, rather than overutilize for the sake of overutilization, then the problem for policy makers becomes one of framing a set of incentives that makes prestige maximization incompatible with overutilization. Underutilization that has a detrimental effect on quality would injure the physician's prestige and image among his or her peers.

Three sets of dynamic, interacting interest groups seem to affect utilization patterns: the physician staff, the medical school faculty, and the hospital staff. The hospital is not an institutional island unto itself. Hospitals are influenced by a second multiproduct institution: the local medical school. Conventional wisdom has it that the affiliation is mutually beneficial (Culler and Bazzoli, 1985). The school, for example, depends on the hospital for teaching sites, while the hospital depends on the school as a source of manpower. It also is the style of some hospital administrators to drop subtle hints to physicians, such as: (1) The hospital occupancy rate is too low; consequently, start increasing lengths of stay; or (2) Laboratory utilization is too low to cover costs; consequently, increase the average number of lab tests. Both of these statements are indications of how a physician might shift his or her decision at the margin, without being provided with a dictum as to how to treat a given patient.

One might like to think that physician faculty members are too professional to be affected by pressures from within the hospital. Any relationship of mutual dependence implies vulnerability: The greater the degree of dependence between hospital and school, the greater the vulnerability. Resources and teaching beds obtained from the hospital therefore may not represent a large portion of the school's budget, but may in the short run be perceived by the school as necessities that are critical. Patient care revenues also play a part in the medical school's objective function, because such funds can be used to purchase future tertiary care equipment. New and better equipment always is considered by the medical school dean's committee to be a critical requirement for teaching the increasingly technological style of American medicine.

Future Research

The high statistical significance of both affiliation measures suggests that it is conceptually false to view the school, hospital, and physician staff as independent entities providing services in functionally segmented medical markets. The fact that the coefficients for the faculty variable are inelastic and negative for tests per surgical case suggests that dispersal of faculty members to less affiliated hospitals would decrease the average amount of excessive testing. However, the surgical student variable has a positive inelastic coefficient, suggesting that it is better to concentrate students on surgical rotation in as few hospitals as possible in order to minimize the regionwide impact that this factor has on tests per case and costs per case. For example, if a medical school shifts 1 percent of the surgical clerkships from a hospital serving 20 percent of its students to a hospital serving 5 percent of its students, the marginal increase in utilization (tests, dollars, days) at the hospital going from 5 percent to 6 percent students is greater than the marginal decrease in utilization at the hospital going from 20 percent to 19 percent.

Future research might consider whether physicians operate under the norms hypothesis (Pauly, 1978), making length-of-stay decisions based on the average or modal staff characteristics within their hospital, and their region, rather than handling these decisions on an individual basis. In particular, a fair test of the norms hypothesis would be to take a sample from teaching and nonteaching hospitals and compare staff characteristics for one surgeon to characteristics of everyone who made decisions about a given patient. From there, the study would proceed to characteristics of surgeons in the surgical service of a given hospital, to characteristics of all surgeons in the health service area, for a sample of both teaching and nonteaching hospitals.

One of the basic strengths in this matched pair study design was the assignment of staff characteristics to the entire surgical service. Previous studies have treated the individual patient and one individual physician as the unit of analysis; consequently, little variation has been explained. All of the phases of care from admission to discharge are not in the hands of one physician. The decisions are in the hands of a group of physicians in a teaching hospital.

The objective of the surgical study has been to discover some of the factors contributing most to excessive utilization of hospital beds. The foregoing analysis was intended to advance our understanding of the problem of unnecessary utilization and clarify the need for and nature of particular policy alternatives. Two areas for further investigation have been suggested by the regression results. The two fundamental public policy issues raised in the study involve changing the hospital reimbursement incentives, and changing the content of graduate and undergraduate medical school education.

References

AMENT, R., BREACHSLIN, J., KOBRINSKI, E., and WOOD, W. (1982). "The Case Type Classifications: Suitability for Use in Reimbursing Hospitals." *Medical Care* 20:5 (May), 460–467.

ANDERSON, G., LAVE, J. (1986). "Financing Graduate Medical Education Using Multiple Regression to Set Payment Rates." *Inquiry* 23:2 (Summer), 191–199.

Arthur Young and Policy Analysis, Inc. (1986). *A Study of the Financing of Graduate Medical Education: Final Report*, 3-volume study of 45 hospitals, DHHS 100–80–0155 (October). Washington, D.C.: U.S. Government Printing Office.

Association of American Medical Colleges (1986). *Financing Graduate Medical Education*, Final Report of the AAMC Committee on Financing GME (April). Washington, D.C.: AAMC.

BALINTFY, J. L. (1962). "Mathematical Models and Analysis of Certain Stochastic Processes in General Hospitals." Unpublished dissertation, Engineering Department, Johns Hopkins University.

BECK, W. (1986). "Asepsis and DRGs." *Infections in Surgery* 8 (August), 425, 448.

BELL, R. M., and SLIGHTON, R. L. (1975). "The Total Cost of Medical Care in Teaching and Nonteaching Settings." Santa Monica, Calif.: RAND Corporation.

BERMAN, H., and WEEKS, L. (1982). *The Financial Management of Hospitals*, 5th ed. Ann Arbor, Mich.: Health Administration Press.

BERRY, R. (1974). "Cost and Efficiency in the Production of Hospital Services." *Milbank Memorial Fund Quarterly* 52:3 (Summer), 291–313.

BREWSTER, A., KARLIN, B., JACOBS, C., HYDE, L., BRADBURY, R., and CHAE, Y. (1985). "MEDISGROUPS: A Clinically Based Approach to Classifying Hospital Patients at Admission." *Inquiry* 22:4 (Winter), 377–387.

BROOK, R., LOHR, K., CHASSIN, M., KOSECOFF, J., FINK, A., and SOLOMON, D. (1984). "Geographic Variations in the Use of Services: Do They Have Any Clinical Significance?" *Health Affairs* 3:2 (Summer), 63–73.

BROWN, T., EHRLICH, C., and STEHMAN, F. (1984). "A Clinical Evaluation of Chlorhexidine Spray as Compared with Iodophor Scrub for Preoperative Skin Preparation." *Surgery, Gynecology, and Obstetrics* 158:4 (April), 363–366.

CAMERON, J. (1985). "The Indirect Costs of Graduate Medical Education." *New England Journal of Medicine* 312:19 (May 9), 1233–1238.

CHIN, D., HOPKINS, D., MELMON, K., and HOLMAN, H. (1985). "The Relation of Faculty Academic Activity to Financing Sources in a Department of Medicine." *New England Journal of Medicine* 312:16 (April 18), 1029–1034.

COFFEY, R., and GOLDFARB, M. (1986). "DRGs and Disease Staging for Reimbursing Medicare Patients." *Medical Care* 24:9 (September), 814–829.

Commonwealth Task Force on Academic Health Centers (1985). *Future Financing of Teaching Hospitals: A Framework for Public Policy* (October). New York: Commonwealth Fund.

COWING, T., and HOLTMANN, A. (1983). "Multiproduct Short-Run Hospital Cost Functions: Empirical Evidence and Policy Implications from Cross Section Data." *Southern Economic Journal* 49:5 (Fall), 637–653.

CULLER, S., and BAZZOLI, G. (1985). "The Moonlighting Decisions of Resident Physicians." *Journal of Health Economics* 4:3 (September), 283–292.

DAVIS, K. (1971). "Relationship of Hospital Prices to Costs." *Applied Economics* 3:2 (June), 115–121.

DETSKY, A., MCLAUGHLIN, J., ABRAMS, H., ABBE, K., and MARKEL, F. (1986). "Do Interns and Residents Order More Tests Than Attending Staff?" *Medical Care* 24:6 (June), 526–534.

DUMBAUGH, K., and NEUHAUSER, D. (1976). "The Effect of Pre-admission Testing on Length of Stay." In S. Shortell and M. Brown (eds.), *Organizational Research in Hospitals*. Chicago: *Inquiry*—Blue Cross Association.

EASTAUGH, S. (1981). *Medical Economics and Health Finance*. Dover, Mass.: Auburn House.

EASTAUGH, S. (1980). "Organizational Determination of Surgical Lengths of Stay." *Inquiry* 17:2 (Spring), 85–96.

EASTAUGH, S. (1979). "Cost of Elective Surgery and Utilization of Ancillary Services in Teaching Hospitals." *Health Services Research* 14:4 (Winter), 290–308.

EASTAUGH, S. (1977). "An Econometric Model for Predicting the Future VA Patient Census." Unpublished appendix to the study *Health Care for the American Veteran* performed by the National Academy of Sciences, presented to the U.S. Congress, pursuant to Section 201 (c) of Public Law 93-82, to the Committee on Veterans' Affairs, U.S. Senate, June 7, 1977.

EECKHOUDT, L., LEBRUN, T., and SAILLY, J. (1985). "Risk-Aversion and Physicians' Medical Decision-Making." *Journal of Health Economics* 4:3 (September), 273–281.

EPSTEIN, A. (1986). "Socioeconomic Characteristics and Utilization for Hospitalized Patients: Do Poor People Cost More?" *Clinical Research* 84:1 (January), 360–373.

FELDSTEIN, J. (1971). "Hospital Cost Inflation: A Study of Nonprofit Price Dynamics." *American Economic Review* 61:5 (December), 853–865.

FIELDING, J. (1985). "A Utilization Review Program in the Making." *Business and Health* 2:7 (June), 25–28.

FOLEY, J. and MULHAUSEN, R. (1986). "The Cost of Complexity: The Teaching Hospital." *Hospital and Health Services Administration* 31:5 (September/October), 96–109.

FRICK, A., MARTIN, S., and SHWARTZ, M. (1985). "Case-Mix and Cost Differences Between Teaching and Nonteaching Hospitals." *Medical Care* 23:4 (April), 283–295.

GARBER, A., FUCHS, V., and SILVERMAN, J. (1984). "Casemix, Costs, and Outcomes: Differences Between Faculty and Community Services in a University Hospital." *New England Journal of Medicine* 310:19 (May 10), 1231–1237.

GARG, M., ELKHATIB, M., KLEINBERG, W., and MULLIGAN, W. (1982). "Reimbursing for Residency Training: How Many Times?" *Medical Care* 20:7 (July), 719–726.

GARG, M., LOUIS, D., GLEIBE, W., SPIRKA, C., SKIPPER, J., and PAREKH, R. (1978). "Evaluating Inpatient Costs." *Medical Care* 16:3 (March), 191–201.

GAUS, C. R. (1976). "Hospital Costs, Stays Vary Widely Across U.S." *American Medical News* 19:12 (March), 10–12.

GAUS, C. R. (1970). "Hospital Use Prediction Based on Population and Medical Resource Factors." Unpublished Sc.D. thesis, Johns Hopkins School of Hygiene and Public Health.

GOLDFARB, M., and COFFEY, R. (1986). "Casemix Differences Between Teaching and Nonteaching Hospitals." *Inquiry* 23:4 (Winter).

GOLDFARB, M., HORNBROOK, M., and RAFFERTY, J. (1980). "Behavior of the Multi-Product Firm: A Model of the Nonprofit Hospital System." *Medical Care* 18:2 (February), 185–201.

GOLDSMITH, J. (1984). "Death of a Paradigm: The Challenge of Competition." *Health Affairs* 3:3 (Fall), 8–17.

GONNELLA, J., HORNBROOK, M., and LOUIS, D. (1984). "Staging of Disease: A Case-Mix Measurement." *Journal of the American Medical Association* 251:5 (February 3), 637–641.

GORNICK, M. (1975). "Medicare Patients: Regional Differences in Length of Hospital Stays 1969–1971." *Social Security Bulletin* 38:7 (July), 16–33.

GUSTAFSON, D. H. (1968). "Length of Stay: Prediction and Explanation." *Health Services Research* 3:1 (Spring), 12–34.

GUSTAFSON, D., FRYBACK, D., ROSE, J., YICK, V., PROKOP, C., DETMER, D., and MOORE, J. (1986). "A Decision Theoretic Methodology for Severity Index Development." *Medical Decision Making* 6:1 (January-March), 27–35.

HALEY, R., SCHABERG, D., and CROSSLEY, K. (1981). "Extra Charges and Prolongation of Stay Attributable to Nosocomial Infection." *American Journal of Medicine* 70:1 (January), 51–58.

HENDRICKSON, L., and MYERS, J. (1973). "Some Sources and Potential Consequences of Errors in Medical Data Recording." *Methods of Information in Medicine* 12:1 (January), 30–39.

HORN, S. (1986). "Measuring Severity: How Sick Is Sick? How Well Is Well?" *Healthcare Financial Management* 40:10 (October), 21–32.

HORN, S., BUCKLEY, G., SHARKEY, P., CHAMBERS, A., HORN, R., and SCHRAMM, C. (1985). "Inter-Hospital Differences in Patient Severity: Problems for Prospective Payment Based on DRGs." *New England Journal of Medicine* 313:1 (July 4), 20–24.

HORN, S., HORN, R., and MOSES, H. (1986). "Profiles of Physician Practice and Patient Severity of Illness." *American Journal of Public Health* 76:5 (May), 532–535.

HOUGH, D., and BAZZOLI, G. (1985). "The Economic Environment of Resident Physicians." *Journal of the American Medical Association* 253:12 (March 22), 1758–1762.

HU, T., and WERNER, J. (1976). "The Effects of Insurance on Hospital Utilization and Costs: A Simultaneous Equation Model." Paper presented at the Econometric Society Meetings, Atlantic City, New Jersey, September 17.

IGLEHART, J. (1985). "Difficult Times Ahead for Graduate Medical Education." *New England Journal of Medicine* 312:21 (May 23), 1400–1404.

INNES, A., GRANT, A. J., and BEINFIELD, M. S. (1968). "Experience with Shortened Hospital Stay for Postsurgical Patients." *Journal of the American Medical Association* 204:8 (May 20), 647–652.

Institute of Medicine (1976). *Medicare-Medicaid Reimbursement Policies*, February Policy Report. Washington, D.C.: National Academy of Sciences.

JONES, K. (1985). "Predicting Hospital Charge and Stay Variation." *Medical Care* 23:3 (March), 220–235.

JONSSON, E., and NEUHAUSER, D. (1975). "Hospital Staffing Ratios in the United States and Sweden." *Inquiry* 12 (Supplement), 128–135.

KELLEY, D. C., WENG, J., and WATSON, A. (1979). "Effect of Consultation on Hospital Length of Stay." *Inquiry* 16:2 (Summer), 158–161.

KIRZ, H., and LARSEN, C. (1986). "Costs and Benefits of Medical Student Training to an HMO." *Journal of the American Medical Association* 256:6 (August 8), 734–739.

LEVIN, P. J. (1964). "Physician Characteristics and Use of Hospital Services." Unpublished doctoral thesis, Johns Hopkins School of Hygiene and Public Health.

LINDSAY, C. M. (1975). *Veterans Administration Hospitals*. Washington, D.C.: American Enterprise Institute.

LOUIS, D., BARNES, C., JORDAN, N., MOYNIHAN, C., PEPITONE, T., SPIRKA, C., SREDL, K., and WESTNEDGE, J. (1983). "Disease Staging: A Clinically Based Approach to Measurement of Disease Severity," Final Report to DHHS (NCHSR 233–78–3001), Rockville, Maryland (August). Washington, D.C.: U.S. Government Printing Office, NTIS–PB83–254649.

MCCORKLE, L. P. (1970). "Duration of Hospitalization Prior to Surgery." *Health Services Research* 5:2 (Summer), 114–131.

MCDANIEL, J. (1986). "Charity Care: A Proposal for Reform." *Hospital and Health Services Administration* 31:2 (March/April), 124–134.

MCGINNIS, G., OSBERG, J., DEJONG, G., SEWARD, M., and BRANCH, L. (1986). "Predicting Charges for Inpatient Medical Rehabilitation: Toward PPS." Paper presented at the annual meeting of the American Public Health Association (September 30), Las Vegas.

National Research Council (1977). *Health Care for American Veterans*. Washington, D.C.: National Academy of Sciences.

NEWHOUSE, J. (1983). "Two Prospective Difficulties with PPS of Hospitals, or, ' 'It's Better to Be a Resident Than a Patient with a Complex Problem.' " *Journal of Health Economics* 2:3 (September), 269–274.

PANNIERS, T., and NEWLANDER, J. (1986). "Adverse Patient Occurrences (APO) Inventory: Validity, Reliability, and Implications." *Quality Review Bulletin* 12:9 (September), 311–315.

PAULY, M. (1978). "Medical Staff Characteristics and Hospital Costs." *Journal of Human Resources* 13 (Supplement), 77–111.

PAYNE, B. (1976). *The Quality of Medical Care: Evaluation and Improvement*. Chicago: Health Research and Education Trust.

PETERSDORF, R. (1985). "A Proposal for Financing Graduate Medical Education." *New England Journal of Medicine* 312:20 (May 16), 1322–1324.

PETTENGILL, J., AND VENTREES, J. (1982). "Reliability and Validity in Hospital Case-Mix Measurement." *Health Care Financing Review* 4:2 (December), 101–128.

PFORDRESHER, K. (1985). "Clinical Research and Prospective Payment," Report of the Council of Teaching Hospitals, monograph (January). Washington, D.C.: American Association of Medical Colleges.

QUERIDO, A. (1963). *The Efficiency of Medical Care: A Critical Discussion of Measuring Procedures*. Amsterdam: Leiden Stenfert Knoose.

RAFFERTY, J. A. (1971). "Patterns of Hospital Use: An Analysis of Shortrun Variations." *Journal of Political Economy* 79:1 (January–February), 154–165.

RELMAN, A. (1984). "Who Will Pay for Medical Education in Our Teaching Hospitals?" *Science* 226:1 (October 5), 20–23.

RIESELBACH, R., and JACKSON, T. (1986). "In Support of a Linkage Between the Funding of Graduate Medical Education and Care of the Indigent." *New England Journal of Medicine* 314:1 (January 2), 32–35.

ROE, B. (1985). "Rational Remuneration." *New England Journal of Medicine* 313:20 (November 14), 1286–1289.

RUBIN, D. (1970). "The Use of Matched Sampling and Regression Adjustment in Observational Studies." Unpublished dissertation, Statistics Department, Harvard University.

SALKEVER, D. S. (1970). "Studies in the Economics of Hospital Costs." Unpublished dissertation, Economics Department, Harvard University.

SCHIMMEL, E. (1974). "Hazards of Hospitalization." *Annals of Internal Medicine* 60:1 (January), 100–110.

SCHWARTZ, W., NEWHOUSE, J., and WILLIAMS, A. (1985). "Is the Teaching Hospital an Endangered Species?" *New England Journal of Medicine* 313:3 (July 18), 157–162.

SLOAN, F. (1976). "A Microanalysis of Physicians' Hours of Work Decisions." In M. Perlman (ed.), *Economics of Health and Medical Care*. New York: John Wiley, 302–325.

STUART, B., and STOCKTON, R. (1973). "Control Over the Utilization of Medical Services." *Milbank Memorial Fund Quarterly* 51:3 (Summer), 341–394.

TWADDLE, A. C., and SWEET, R. H. (1970). "Characteristics and Experiences of Patients with Preventable Hospital Admissions." *Social Science and Medicine* 4:1 (July), 141–145.

United States Senate Finance Committee (1983). *Social Security Amendments of 1983*, Report 98–23 (March 11), 52.

VANSELOW, N., and KRALEWSKI, J. (1986). "The Impact of Competitive Health Care Systems on Professional Education." *Journal of Medical Education* 61:9 (September), 707–713.

WENNBERG, J., and GITTELSOHN, A. (1982). "Variations in Medical Care Among Small Areas." *Scientific American* 246:4 (April), 120–135.

YOUNG, W. (1986). "Measuring the Cost of Care Using Patient Management Categories," HCFA Publication Number 86–03228 (June). Washington, D.C.: U.S. Government Printing Office.

Chapter 14

FINANCIAL CONCERNS IN MEDICAL SCHOOL MANAGEMENT

A little publicized but interesting and important trend over the past ten years has been an increasing dependence of many schools on fees for service from Medicare and Medicaid as well as private patients. Many medical schools are making an organized effort to increase this source of income to compensate for the loss of research and training grants and in some it has already become the principal source of funds.

—RONALD V. CHRISTIE

He who pays the piper can call the tune.

—OLD ENGLISH PROVERB

Changes in the availability of federal funds have already led to some dramatic changes in the way medical schools support themselves. To survive and to prosper in the decade to come, medical academe must adjust to a period of no growth and change imaginatively to allow progress to continue.

—DAVID E. ROGERS

The peak year for new enrollment in medical schools was 1981 (16,757 first-year students). In the fall of 1986, for the fifth consecutive year, medical schools in the United States admitted fewer students than the previous year. Financial pressures on the nation's medical schools have been outlined most recently by MacLeod and Schwarz (1986) and Iglehart (1986). Surprisingly, in

378

the face of declining student demand, the medical schools have increased the number of full-time faculty from 53,748 in 1982 to 61,372 in 1986. The intent of this chapter is to provide a brief survey into the financial standing of medical schools, by school type. Suggestions are also advanced as to how school management should respond to calls for reductions in class size, reductions in commercialism at the university, and reductions in research support.

The Policy Context

As the supply of physicians per capita more than doubled between 1962 and 1979, there is no longer justification for the federal medical school capitation program. This form of subsidy, paid to the school per head (per student enrolled), created an obvious incentive to expand class size. The public believed more doctors were needed, and more of any trained professional group in society must be good for society (Fein, 1967). In this chapter we question the value of a uniform program of financial assistance to medical education and research. Medical schools have an uneven ability to compensate for declining federal capitation and research grants. We also utilize financial ratio analysis and cluster analysis, 1974–1984, and suggest four adaptive responses to future financial pressures. The four potential avenues of response involve reducing faculty size, expanding faculty involvement in medical practice plans, raising tuition, and in some cases increasing state-government support. Medical schools will also have to strive for better financial management if the 66 schools revealed to be in poor financial health are to survive.

The 1980s have become a time of great stress for American medical education. Schools have had to grant substantial salary increases to enable their employees to maintain purchasing power. Moreover, the certain decline of federal capitation support grants and the potential decline of future federal research grants threaten the financial health of the nation's medical schools. Private medical schools are especially vulnerable. The private medical schools and their parent universities have watched the market value of their invested assets decline. The lack of data concerning the financial state of the medical schools seriously inhibits our ability to assess the impact of policy alternatives.

Medical schools are multiproduct institutions that produce patient care (21 percent of expenditures), research (23 percent of expenditures), and instruction (56 percent of expenditures) (Jolly,

1986). Most experts agree that a decline in medical school student capitation support cannot be compensated for by a growth in funding for research activities. The Reagan administration's proposed 1987 budget decreases biomedical and behavioral research 20 to 40 percent below the 1983 levels. There will not be any increases in National Institutes of Health research grants and appropriations for research projects, research centers, and biomedical research support.

The federal government predicts that the enrollment expansion already achieved is sufficient to meet the national demand for physicians. It is withdrawing its previous level of support for medical education and cutting general institutional operating subsidies. Reduced funding will require some reaction on the part of the medical schools and university medical centers. Grants that induced changes in academic health centers presumably increased reliance of those institutions on the federal government. It has been said that, with grants, a cut in revenues means an equal cut in expenditures, but this does not follow. Grants pay for many of the indirect costs of running an institution. When grants are reduced or eliminated, funds must come from some other source to cover these indirect costs (Eastaugh, 1980). Action can come in the form of changes in programs or shifts to greater reliance on alternative sources. One source is the student on whom the federal government explicitly wishes to place more of the burden of financing medical education.

The Historic Policy Context

Behn and Sperduto (1979) reviewed the growth of a medical school "entitlement ethic" since passage of the first health manpower bill in 1963. In response to the national perception of a doctor shortage, the 1965 amendments to the 1963 Health Professions Education Assistance Act required only that the school expand enrollments by 2.5 percent per annum. In the following years, Fein (1967) questioned the validity of the assumption that a doctor shortage existed regionally or nationally. However, Congress was predisposed to respond to the 1970 Carnegie Commission assertion that the nation had a shortage of 50,000 doctors. The 1971 Health Manpower Act replaced the basic improvement grants of the 1960s with a program of capitation grants to stimulate rapid growth in class size. The capitation grant program stipulated that small schools with less then 100 students per class expand the class by 10 students, and larger schools expand class size by 5 percent.

These financial incentives to expand class size were a smashing success story. By 1968, the nation had already exceeded the American Medical Association's declared appropriate supply ratio of 154 physicians per 100,000 population (Carnegie Commission, 1970). By 1975 the national supply of physicians exceeded the Carnegie Commission's (1973) most optimistic projection of 171.3 physicians per 100,000 population for 1982. In renewing the capitation program in 1976, Congress expressed concern over the doctor surplus in the preamble and concluded that the nation had a maldistribution, but not a shortage, of physicians. Stevens (1971) and Reinhardt (1975) had argued that productivity, and not supply ratios, was the more salient public policy issue. Stevens went so far as to suggest that the physician supply could be reduced 12.5 percent if all U.S. physicians had the same level of productivity as physicians in the Kaiser Health Plan, or reduced 42.5 percent if U.S. physicians had Kaiser productivity and patient utilization rates.

Medical education policy was formulated in various statements to the effect that medical schools were a precious national resource in need of federal aid. From 1971 to 1980, Congress ignored the arguments of economists and accountants to terminate capitation grants. Congress followed the advice of social activists to address the specialty maldistribution problem, and the advice of medical lobbyists to perpetuate the entitlement ethic and foster increased government funding. Paradoxically, federal support had not kept pace with the inflation in medical school expenditures. From 1966 to 1976, federal research support declined from 34.1 percent of revenues to 19.6 percent, and federal grants for teaching and recovery of indirect costs declined from 18.5 percent of revenues to 17.5 percent. Social activists' concerns for the overproduction of specialists were placated by the 1976 Capitation Bill provision that specified annual national targets for percentage of filled residencies in primary care. If the targets of at least 35 percent primary care residencies by 1977, 40 percent by 1978, and 50 percent for 1979 were not met in any given year, then each school had to meet the target in succeeding years as a mandatory condition for capitation supports.

One important policy question concerns how medical schools can cope with the anticipated substantial reduction of the research funds in the late 1980s. Protecting the public interest requires that the resulting short-run financial problems of the schools be managed in ways that have the fewest adverse long-run effects on medical education. To accomplish this the schools must devote more systematic attention to financial ratio assessment. It is equally important for school administrators and federal officials to realize that different clusters or categories of medical schools must be treated differently. The uneven ability of medical schools to compensate for declining federal support cannot be overemphasized.

Most private medical schools began to exceed five-digit tuition charges per year by 1983. The impact of rapidly escalating tuition figures on the finances and attitudes of students is unclear. Loans are always available to students, but the thought of being $80,000 in debt upon graduation may frighten some of them away from private medical schools. Private schools may find that they have a student body composed of a few scholarship students from lower-class backgrounds, many students from upper-middle-class backgrounds, and no one in between (Iglehart, 1986). Perhaps the greater danger lies in the probability that some new physicians who may otherwise have chosen family practice, or a practice in an underserved area, may opt for a specialty practice that promises a better cash return on their investment.

From 1962 to 1985, the number of medical schools increased by 42 (a 49 percent increase), medical students increased by 128 percent, housestaff increased by 238 percent, and full-time faculty increased by 447 percent (Jolly, 1986). This unprecedented golden era of growth will undoubtedly enter an era of retrenchment, as many schools reduce class size, reduce faculty, and perhaps reduce research faculty (as research funds decline in real dollar terms). Many individual schools would rather have their peers or their neighboring schools reduce class size. If too many schools refuse to undergo a voluntary cost-reduction program, called by some a "voluntary suicide program," the future disruptions to schools may be draconian. Some medical schools lacking any clearly defensible market niche may have to close.

Medical schools are not structured to be managed. Future organizational theorists doing a postmortem on financially troubled schools (e.g., South Dakota) may well conclude that a medical faculty represented the "bumblebee of organizations" (e.g., no rule can be written without a dozen exceptions) and no engineer can ever figure out how they fly. Less flattering analogies might characterize medical schools as the dinosaur of educational organizations. In any case, medical schools will have to downstaff and downsize, or rapidly diversify their portfolio of ventures (e.g., faculty practice plans, bioengineering) to survive in the 1990s. Medical school faculty may have to become either more commercial or organize like pilot unions (i.e., demanding cuts in workweek hours with disproportionately lower percentage cuts in salary).

There will be no easy government solution to the coming medical school financial crunch. Given the retrenchment of state governments in health professional education, in part because they have little perceived financial slack, and given the federal deficit morass, medical schools will have to rely on their own ventures for survival. MacLeod and Schwarz (1986) pose this question: Will the welfare of the medical school and its programs take precedence over the financial well-being of individual faculty members?

The objective of this chapter is to suggest potential management strategies which different types of medical schools might consider implementing in the late 1980s.

Financial Ratio Analysis

Financial ratio analysis is suggested as a tool that would enable medical school deans to assess their financial position in absolute and normative terms. The appropriate ratios, calculated from data reported in balance sheets and income statements, may be used to determine an organization's profitability, liquidity (ability to meet short-term obligations), and leverage (ability to meet debt obligations). Any institution can monitor its performance by comparing financial ratios over time or by comparing its ratios against industry norms. Ratios that change significantly or are markedly different from the industry norms serve as warning signs, indicating that an evaluation of the institution's financial position is warranted (Cleverley, 1986). For example, a school that is already capital-intensive, reporting a high fixed assets/total assets ratio indicates that the school might achieve greater efficiency with better use of short-term funds (working capital).

Until now, no attempt has been made to establish national norms to facilitate ratio analysis of medical schools. At a time when many medical schools are facing fiscal crises, it is important that deans and financial officers have the data base to enable them to assess their school's financial position. A comparison of ratios over time, or between schools, might prove helpful in understanding why some medical schools are being forced to erode their endowment in order to survive.

Financial Data

Financial data utilized in the ratio analysis were obtained from an Association of American Medical Colleges (AAMC) annual questionnaire. Included in the questionnaire are data items from the financial statements. These cash-flow items indicate the schools' sources and uses of funds. No balance sheet information, however, is provided about fund balances, assets, and liabilities. The AAMC provided the author with data for the following ten ratios in the years 1974, 1979, and 1984, expressed in percentages:

1. *Profitability:* total revenues minus expenses as a percentage of total revenues.
2. *Tuition and fees:* total student tuition and fees, including undergraduate medical programs as well as other degree programs, as a percentage of total revenues.
3. *Restricted revenues:* current revenues that are designated to be spent for specific projects, as a percentage of total revenues. Since very little federal money is unrestricted, this classification covers virtually all federal sources of revenue.
4. *Government appropriations:* unrestricted revenues made available to the school by legislative act or local taxing authorities and restricted revenues from the same sources used for general operations.
5. *Federal appropriations:* federal revenue as a percentage of total revenues.
6. *Private gifts, grants, and contracts:* includes all unrestricted and restricted gifts from nongovernmental sources as well as contracts for the furnishing of goods and services of an instructional, research, or public service nature, as a percentage of total revenues.
7. *Medical practice plan:* patient care reimbursement for faculty service to the medical practice plan (MPP), as a percentage of total revenues (also called faculty practice plans).
8. *Instruction and departmental research:* expenditures for all activities that are part of the school's instructional program, and departmental research expenditures that are not separately budgeted, as a percentage of total expenses.
9. *Sponsored research:* includes all expenditures for research activities that are externally commissioned or separately budgeted, as a percentage of total expenses.
10. *Administration and general expenditures:* includes academic and institutional support and funds for student support services, as a percentage of total expenses.

Table 14.1 presents the average values of these ten basic ratios for the years 1974, 1979, and 1984 for public and private medical schools.

The best indicator of the medical schools' financial problems is the sharp decline over the five-year period in profitability margin, the excess of revenues over expenditures expressed in percentage terms. Public schools had a substantial income or profit margin of 3.7 percent in fiscal 1974. Private schools earned far less on each dollar of revenue—just 1.2 percent. By 1979 the income margins of public and private schools had fallen precipitously, to 1.2 percent and 0.7 percent, respectively. The percentage of schools with a net margin of 2 percent or higher declined from 44 percent to 8 percent. Fewer and fewer schools, therefore, have any margin for inefficiency before they operate in the red. The conclusion from these data is that all medical schools are facing increasing fiscal pressures, but private medical schools are in far greater fiscal danger than public medical schools.

Moreover, there has been an observable decline in sponsored research support over the past five years. This may be due to a change in priorities among both big business and government. The benefits of medical research are often not realized for dozens of years. In a period of fiscal belt-tightening, medical research has been assigned a low priority.

Private schools have always relied heavily on sponsored research projects for the bulk of their revenues. These revenues pay faculty salaries and support new technologies for tertiary care medicine and basic research. The rapidly escalating costs of biomedical research leave little room for an excess of revenues over expenditures (profit). As these sponsored programs are cut back, as they were from 1974 to 1984, and the machinery and personnel remain, the financial squeeze begins. A gap is created between funds available and funds necessary for operation of the school. This hits most private schools harder than public schools, but it is felt everywhere.

Appropriations from state and local governments, and grants and appropriations from the federal government, have also fallen off sharply over the last five years. These items accounted for 80 percent of public schools' revenues and 49 percent of private schools' revenues in 1974, but fell to just 72 percent and 36 percent, respectively, by 1979 and 57 percent (public schools) versus 33 percent (private schools) in 1984.

Filling the financial gap between funds available and funds required is a major problem for medical school deans and budget officers. The tactics used have been partially successful but often create additional problems. One tactic that has gained virtually universal acceptance is the expansion of medical practice plans (MPPs). In private schools, especially, often 25 to 35 percent of the

Table 14.1 Medical School Ratios (percent)

	1973–74		1978–79		1983–1984	
	Public	*Private*	*Public*	*Private*	*Public*	*Private**
Profitability	3.7	1.2	1.2	0.7	1.1	1.9
Tuition and fees	2.6	12.6	2.7	10.1	3.3	9.5
Restricted revenues	42.3	54.1	33.8	47.1	31.5	42.4
Government appropriations	47.8	10.1	43.2	7.8	32.4	4.4
Federal appropriations, grants, and contracts	32.6	38.5	22.9	28.2	19.9	28.2
Private gifts, grants, and contracts	7.6	11.5	5.6	9.3	4.1	6.9
Medical practice plan	6.8	6.9	10.3	15.5	17.6	23.2
Instruction and departmental research	38.3	24.3	37.9	23.7	34.9	21.5
Research	19.0	28.3	17.8	24.5	17.5	21.9
Administrative and general expenses	11.4	11.5	13.0	12.3	14.4	13.1

*In 1984 the sample included 75 public schools and 50 private schools.

schools' revenues come from patient services rendered by the faculty. At first these MPPs were justified to the physicians as a way of keeping up to date with new techniques. Now most faculty involved realize that these MPPs are a critical source of funds to the medical school and some schools could not survive without them.

Another issue, as yet unresolved, is whether medical researchers become better researchers and/or teachers when exposed to a few hours of clinical medicine daily. It is clear that medical school faculty now must wear three hats—the traditional ones of teacher and researcher and now the additional one of practitioner. Salaries are not necessarily commensurate with the job responsibilities. The time available for research is reduced, and individuals interested purely in biomedical research have much to consider before agreeing to a medical school staff appointment. Thus, it is conceivable that the explosion of MPPs may adversely affect the quality of biomedical research at medical schools.

The financial figure with which the public is most familiar—tuition—has skyrocketed as well. As expenses have gone up, all medical schools have raised tuition to meet them. Much of the state appropriations to public schools are tuition subsidies. Nationwide, tuition in 1984 accounted for only 6.0 percent of school revenues and an estimated 9.9 percent of the actual cost of instruction.

The Eight Types of School Clusters

Cluster analysis is a technique that groups firms or subjects together according to shared characteristics. The Department of Health, Education and Welfare (McShane, 1977) performed a cluster analysis of medical schools and devised eight clusters for 1978, grouped according to six factors. These clusters were redeveloped from AAMC data and characterize different kinds of medical schools (Eastaugh, 1980). The groupings were not developed on the basis of any of the financial ratios. The specific objective of this chapter is to study the shifts in financial ratios across clusters and time periods.

Schools were divided into eight clusters based on the following six shared characteristics:

1. *Emphasis on graduate medical education program.* Schools that are strong in this area have high ratios of interns and residents to undergraduates, a high proportion of faculty with

M.D. degrees, and a low ratio of undergraduates to faculty. A disproportionately small number of graduates of these schools go into general practice.

2. *Size and age of school*. This factor includes the rate of growth of the school, with low growth being considered a sign of age.
3. *"Control."* Public schools rate low and private schools high on this factor. Included is the proportion of in-state students in the school.
4. *Research funding success*. This is proxied by the approval rates for grants from the National Institutes of Health.
5. *Developmental stage of school*. This is a better measure of maturity than size and age.
6. *Research emphasis*. This is the level of sponsored research activity.

The eight clusters contain schools that are roughly similar in the six aforementioned factors. Several schools were excluded from this analysis because of lack of data. Descriptions of the eight clusters are listed below:

1. Cluster 1 contains 19 public medical schools. These are all established schools with few other distinguishing characteristics. They have below-average emphasis on graduate medical programs and research, and are below average in research funding success.
2. The 8 schools in Cluster 2 are the oldest and largest medical schools. Six are public with average total enrollments of around 800 undergraduate medical students. These schools do not place much emphasis on research or graduate medical education.
3. The 17 public schools in Cluster 3 have a high degree of emphasis on research and have good research funding success. There is less emphasis on graduate medical education. They are of moderate size with little growth, except in research funding.
4. Cluster 4 has 15 large well-established medical schools with strong education programs at all levels.
5. Cluster 5 contains the 11 newest schools. It should be interesting to examine how their finances differ from the rest of the medical schools.
6. Relatively new public schools experiencing rapid growth are in Cluster 6. Research support is not a substantial fraction of revenues but is growing rapidly for these 15 schools.
7. Cluster 7 contains mainly older private schools with low emphasis on research and graduate education. These 21

schools have the highest tuition but the lowest annual revenues.

8. The 19 schools, mostly private, in Cluster 8 have strong
   research and graduate medical education programs. They are
   smaller than average and have the highest house-staff to
   student ratio of any cluster. They rely on federal support
   more than any other cluster.

Table 14.2 presents the values of various ratios for each cluster in
the years 1974, 1979, and 1984. The data presented are only for the
81 medical schools in 1984 that subscribed to the uniform financial
reporting practices of the AAMC. It can be readily observed that
the decline in profit margin present in all medical schools as a
whole is present in most of the clusters. Only one group of schools,
Cluster 2, experienced an increase in profit margin. Apparently,
the inertia present in these older, larger schools gives them a
unique fiscal stability. With this exception, the decline in net profit
margin is a broad-based phenomenon.

The percentage of expenditures for restricted purposes, such as
sponsored research programs, declined significantly in all clusters
except for Cluster 6 (the newer public schools). Sponsored revenues declined in all clusters in the period. This cutback in research
funding is perhaps the biggest cause of medical schools' fiscal
problems and it has not struck medical schools selectively.

The prestige schools (Clusters 4 and 8) do not attract much state
or local money, but they still attract their share of state and federal
research funds. Most of these schools continue to run in the black.
The schools with the deepest trouble are the less prestigious
private schools. The schools in Cluster 7 actually showed a net
income loss for fiscal year 1979. Reduced government appropriations coupled with major cutbacks in sponsored programs are the
chief culprits. The ability of these schools to survive in the future is
uncertain.

The growth in medical practice plans (MPPs) has been dramatic
in all eight clusters. MPPs have been expanded to fill the gap
between educational expenses and tuition dollars; for example,
observe the across-the-board reduction in percentage of revenues
coming from tuition. Medical practice plans were a major source of
funds only in Cluster 3 in 1974; despite the fact that this cluster
contains strong public schools with good research programs, the
physicians were called on to perform a large amount of clinical
work. The increasing percentage of medical school revenues derived from MPPs obviously indicates that the faculty is expected to
spend more time on patient care. Alternatively, it could be that

Table 14.2 Cluster Analysis of Medical School Finances, 1973–1974, 1978–1979, and 1983–1984, for Nine Financial Ratios, Expressed in Percentages

Item		Mean 1973 Cluster Values[a]							
	I	II	III	IV	V	VI	VII	VIII
Sample Response	9/17	2/8	6/14	5/14	3/4	11/12	7/17	12/17
Revenue Ratios[b]								
Profitability Ratio (percent)	1.7	0.95	1.3	1.0	8.3	10.7	0.25	2.0
Tuition Ratio	12	11	12	10	23	6	16	9
Restricted Revenue Ratio	41	43	49	61	45	26	52	58
State Government Ratio	41	38	28	17	40	60	15	5
Federal Government Ratio	30	28	38	33	39	27	39	42
Medical Practice Plan Ratio	6	4	13	6	1	4	8	7
Expense Ratios[c]								
Instruction and Departmental Research	39	34	34	19	48	47	27	23
Sponsored Research	17	20	24	28	7	15	27	34
Administration and General Expense				Data Not Available in 1973				

Item		Mean 1978–1979 Cluster Values							
	I	II	III	IV	V	VI	VII	VIII
Sample Response	8/17	4/8	10/16	8/14	2/5	8/13	9/19	11/17
Revenue Ratios[b]								
Profitability Ratio (percent)	0.5	1.4	0.79	1.0	0.75	2.1	− 0.17	1.0
Tuition Ratio	4	6	2	5	19	2	15	6
Restricted Revenue Ratio	34	39	36	49	17	26	44	51
State Government Ratio	41	38	33	18	54	51	9	3

Item	I	II	III	IV	V	VI	VII	VIII
Federal Government Ratio	21	20	27	26	28	19	29	31
Medical Practice Plan Ratio	11	6	18	10	9	12	16	16
Expense Ratios[c]								
Instruction and Departmental Research	40	36	35	22	69	42	25	21
Sponsored Research	15	17	23	27	13	17	22	32
Administration and General Expense	10	12	9	10	20	17	14	9

				Mean 1983–1984 Cluster Values				
Item	I	II	III	IV	V	VI	VII	VIII
Sample Response	12/19	5/8	12/17	9/15	7/11	11/15	12/21	13/19
Revenue Ratios[b]								
Profitability Ratio (percent)	0.4	1.6	0.6	2.6	2.2	1.8	0.5	2.4
Tuition Ratio	6	6	3	4	16	3	16	5
Restricted Revenue Ratio	27	34	32	41	15	22	37	42
State Government Ratio	35	28	28	6	36	40	4	1
Federal Government Ratio	16	16	20	18	21	14	27	30
Medical Practice Plan Ratio	16	13	22	16	14	16	25	24
Expense Ratios[c]								
Instruction and Departmental Research	38	34	34	21	54	38	24	21
Sponsored Research	13	14	23	23	11	14	20	29
Administration and General Expense	12	13	11	11	17	17	14	10

[a] Definitions of the 8 clusters appear in the text.
[b] Expressed as a percent of total revenues.
[c] Expressed as a percent of total expenditures.

more schools within clusters are establishing schoolwide MPPs, redistributing faculty designation from geographic full-time to strict full-time. The growth in MPPs has not been consistent across clusters; for example, in Cluster 8 the plans have become much more important than they have in Cluster 4. The schools in both clusters are private, prestigious schools. The main difference between them is size—the schools in Cluster 8 are small and the educational programs are de-emphasized. As MPPs grow, it will be interesting to see from where the faculty's work time in these plans is taken. In less prestigious schools which no longer can attract as much research funding, the faculty may discover that hours previously spent on research need to be dedicated to clinical work if the school is to survive.

Potential Adaptive Responses by the Schools

After the elimination of federal capitation grants (1983–84) and the reduction in research grant support, it appears probable that most schools will face difficulties in meeting increasing direct costs. Expanded graduate medical education and continuing education programs have not contributed significantly to the medical school financial picture. Rogers and Blenden (1978) have pointed out that the academic medical center is becoming a stressed institution that cannot find relief from any of the financial pressures it is facing. Given that hospital-rate regulators will not allow teaching hospitals to bail out medical schools, the schools have three potential avenues of response: raise tuition, induce faculty to devote more time to reimbursable patient services in MPPs, or reduce faculty size.

The first possible response in the minds of many school administrators is to raise medical school tuition. In 1984 tuition and other student fees represented a mere 6.0 percent of school revenues—an increase from 4.6 percent in 1979. Net present value computations of the returns on investment in a medical education are in excess of the dollar returns on an education in other professions (Mennemeyer, 1978). In view of the fact that medicine is the most lucrative profession and is the only profession in which students' tuition fees are less than 9 percent of expected average future earnings, the general feeling is that medical students can absorb potential tuition increases. However, the tuition increases may exacerbate the financial burdens of poor and minority students, and the medical schools may have to resort to a policy of price discrimination in their tuition decisions (Eastaugh, 1980). For example, the schools could pursue a policy of three-tiered tuition pricing for poor ($2,000), middle class ($8,000), and rich students ($30,000 per annum). The growing numbers of rich students willing to pay exorbitant tuitions and the existence of large pools of qualified rejected medical school applicants and students willing to undertake the expensive task of attending a foreign medical school suggest that schools can raise tuition substantially.

One potential problem of increasing the tuition burden is that newly graduated physicians may charge excessively higher fees to compensate for unmanageable debt burdens. Raising the debt burden of students exacerbates two existing problems for the medical schools. University-sponsored loans typically subsidize medical education by not requiring interest payments or repayment of principal until completion of a postgraduate residency or entrance into practice. Second, many university officials have observed that even following payment of the debt principal, the debtor is less likely to donate to the medical school than the average alumnus.

Two other potential responses to declining federal financial support involve changing the composition or size of the faculty. Medical school faculties are divided into three major categories: (1) full-time teaching and research, (2) part-time, and (3) geographic full-time (faculty members allowed to have private practices). One response would involve inducing faculty members to devote more time to medical practice plan activities and spend less time in research activities or independent private practice. Rather than raise revenues, a fourth response would be to decrease costs by reducing faculty size. The number of full-time clinical faculty in the United States increased over 475 percent from 1960 to 1986, according to unpublished AAMC statistics. The prime candidates for elimination are full-time faculty members who do not contribute substantially to the medical practice plan, and part-time faculty members who receive a school salary out of line with their limited teaching activities. Faculty members in "soft-money" areas that lack a solid base of political support in negotiating with the dean are most likely to be eliminated. Unless the federal government is willing to provide increased targeted financial support, a number of new programs and faculty may be eliminated in the areas of ghetto medicine, rural medicine, and family practice, and in cost-effective clinical decision-making instruction (Hudson and Barslow, 1979). Fein and Weber (1971) indicate that innovative curriculum areas are infrequently supported by extracting a percentage of the cash flow from established departments and activities. Medical schools may no longer be able to subsidize the educational activities of nursing, pharmacy, and allied health schools.

The clusters separate into three groups according to dependence on capitation grants. Clusters 2 and 6 are financially sound, highly dependent on state grants, and not in serious need of capitation grants. The second group, Clusters 1, 3, and 5, were highly dependent on federal capitation grants but had the option to appeal for more state support. All 47 schools in this second group could have compensated for total elimination of the federal capitation program by increasing tuition 20 to 80 percent or revenues from the medical practice plans 10 to 120 percent or state grants 4 to 29 percent. The members of Cluster 3 might be most resistant to an expansion of medical practice plans since their faculties are perceived to be above-average-quality researchers. Schools in Cluster 5 are the newest and most publicly supported institutions and consequently might find negotiations with state government for increased support to be their easiest course of action.

A third group of medical schools, Clusters 4, 7, and 8, are facing the tightest fiscal squeeze because these schools were the most dependent on federal capitation grants and are largely unable to increase state support if they maintain private-school status. All 55 schools in this group could have compensated for total elimination of the capitation program by raising tuition 40 to 140 percent or by increasing revenues from medical practice plans by 30 to 180 percent. These schools will be in a particularly vulnerable position if the faculty is resistant to MPP expansion or if the students fight large tuition increases. The 55 schools in these three clusters would be the most likely to cut faculty size in response to the student argument that tuition is a small percentage of revenues, and the faculty is too large and overpaid. A study by Hall and Lindsay (1980) of 16 medical schools over a 14-year period suggests that excessive increases in tuition could decrease the number and quality of medical students. The authors suggest that for each 10 percent rise in tuition, there will be a 4 percent decline in the number of qualified applicants, all other factors held constant.

Problems for the Future

The federal government has effectively resisted pressure to bail out medical schools despite the fact that they are a precious national resource. The basic dilemma faced by the medical schools is whether they can acquire renewed federal support and maintain their current degree of autonomy from government bureaucrats.

Congress' problem is how to allocate resources effectively among many competing high-priority national needs in the face of limited discretionary funds. The presence of financial exigencies felt by government and the schools means that careful attention must be paid to find a solution that is cost-effective. A segmented approach for different categories of schools may be better than the traditional uniform approach to federal financing of medical school operations.

Many adaptive response tactics have not been explored in this study. For example, increasing the number of non-M.D. graduate degrees and offering more continuing education programs could increase school revenues. Most analysts assume that medical schools' primary response will be to increase revenues by raising tuition charges. But the schools should not ignore the importance of reducing costs. The earlier Carnegie Commission (1970) on Higher Education has made a number of recommendations for program changes that would lead to reduced costs, including making fuller use of facilities by having year-round programs and entering two classes each year. A number of medical schools did institute the three-year curriculum but found it unsatisfactory and have reverted to the four-year program (Beran, 1979).

The second Carnegie Commission report (1973) recommended that medical schools be organized into university health science centers responsible for coordinating the education of all health care personnel in their respective geographic areas. The commission also recommended that these health science centers be treated as a national resource, protected and supported by the federal government. Since it appears that the federal government is not prepared to support medical schools and ensure their existence, medical schools will have to become better managers of their resources.

Most medical schools will find it difficult to preserve their financial position through the 1990s. In the 1980s the schools tended to erode their limited endowments, withdrawing funds for operations and capital projects. Many poor capital expansion and stock investment decisions were made, and there were large investments in new facilities. As the endowments began to shrink, they became increasingly harder to rebuild, and the resultant income from investments declined. Drucker (1973) was one of the first to point out that diagnosing schools as "inefficient" because they operate on the basis of a service ethic rather than a business management ethic is overly simplistic. Nevertheless, there is an obvious need for more medical school managers with business training. However, such individuals would have to be sensitive to the health service ethic so as not to put considerations for revenue maximization and cost minimization ahead of quality education. Talented management personnel might compel schools to respond to the public cry for more primary care services. However, their real challenge would be to trim the fat from tertiary care medicine without harming the basic research and development functions of medical schools.

As medical schools become increasingly reliant on patient care revenues, corporate strategic planning must be utilized. Academic medical centers have already had a tough time adjusting to increasingly competitive markets (Kassebaum, 1986). Competition has segmented the medical marketplace into a number of managed care systems that explicitly target nonemergency patient demand to specific hospitals and physician groups. HMOs and PPOs will increasingly restrict referrals. Medical centers that wish to remain state of the art and cost competitive will have to redouble their efforts in the areas of strategic planning, departmental coordination, and ambulatory care diversification (Vanselow and Kralewski, 1986). Given that patients seem to like the cost savings of care systems that preselect their referral options, few teaching hospitals can survive by attracting the shrinking number of unenfranchised patients.

The message is clear: If you want enough patient volume to fill your teaching beds, the medical center better enroll enough people in its own managed care health plan. This will require more teaching and patient care in the area of ambulatory care. Therefore, if the financial future of the medical center and medical school is increasingly dependent on their emergency and family practice programs, the whole power structure of medical school faculties may undergo a revolution in the coming decade. Those "low status" ambulatory care types may save the franchise and feed sufficient cash flow to underwrite capital-intensive inpatient care programs. Ambulatory teaching faculty and staff should also demand high pay and fringe benefits. This is the natural economic response in any profession. For example, in football when passing (ambulatory care) became more important than running (inpatient care), we began to pay quarterbacks (ambulatory care faculty) more than running backs (hospital inpatient care specialists).

References

Association of American Medical Colleges (1986a). "Medical Education in the United States, 1984–85, Part III." *Journal of the American Medical Association* 240:12 (September 27).

Association of American Medical Colleges (1986b). *Association of American Medical College Final Report: Financing Graduate Medical Education* (April). Washington, D.C.: AAMC.

BEHN, R. D., and SPERDUTO, K. (1979). "Medical Schools and the 'Entitlement Ethic.' " *Public Interest* 14:57 (Fall), 48–68.

BERAN, R. L. (1979). "The Rise and Fall of Three-Year Medical School Programs." *Journal of Medical Education* 54:3 (March), 248–249.

Carnegie Commission on Higher Education (1973). *Priorities for Action: Final Report of the Carnegie Commission on Higher Education*. Los Angeles: Maple Press.

Carnegie Commission on Higher Education (1970). *Higher Education and the Nation's Health Policies for Medical and Dental Education*. New York: McGraw-Hill.

CLEVERLEY, W. (1986). "Hospital Financial Condition Under State Rate Regulatory Programs." *Hospital and Health Services Administration* 31:2 (March-April), 135–147.

CLEVERLEY, W. (1978). *Essentials of Hospital Finance*. Germantown, Md.: Aspen Systems, 53–80.

DRUCKER, P. F. (1973). "Managing the Public Service Institution." *Public Interest* 9:33 (Fall), 43–60.

EASTAUGH, S. (1980). "Financial Ratio Analysis and Medical School Management." *Journal of Medical Education* 55:12 (December), 983–992.

EGDAHL, R., and TAFT, C. (1986). "Financial Incentives for Physicians." *New England Journal of Medicine* 315:1 (July 3), 59–61.

FEIN, R. (1967). *The Doctor Shortage*. Washington, D.C.: Brookings Institution.

FEIN, R., and WEBER, G. I. (1971). *Financial Medical Education: An Analysis of Alternative Policies and Mechanisms*. New York: McGraw-Hill.

General Accounting Office (1978). "Federal Capitation Support and Its Role in the Operation of Medical Schools." Washington, D.C.: U.S. Government Printing Office.

HALL, T. D., and LINDSAY, C. M. (1980). "Medical Schools: Producers of What? Sellers to Whom?" *Journal of Law and Economics* 22:22 (April), 55–80.

HUDSON, J. I., and BARSLOW, J. B. (1979). "Cost Containment Education Efforts in United States Medical Schools." *Journal of Medical Education* 54:11 (November), 835–840.

IGLEHART, J. (1986). "Federal Support of Health Manpower Education." *New England Journal of Medicine* 314:5 (January 30), 324–328.

Institute of Medicine, National Academy of Sciences (1974). *Cost of Education in the Health Professions*. Washington, D.C.: U.S. Government Printing Office.

JOLLY, P. (1986). "U.S. Medical School Finances." *Journal of the American Medical Association* 256:12 (September 27).

KASSEBAUM, D. (1986). "Adjustments and Opportunities for Academic Medical Centers Under Health Care Competition and Cost Containment." *Journal of Medical Education* 61:5 (May), 421–423.

KELLY, J. F. (1978). "Options for Financing Graduate Medical Education." *Journal of Medical Education* 53:1 (January), 26–32.

MacLEOD, G., AND SCHWARZ, M. (1986). "Faculty Practice Plans: Profile and Critique." *Journal of the American Medical Association* 256:1 (July 4), 58–62.

McSHANE, M. G. (1977). "An Empirical Classification of United States Medical Schools by Institutional Dimensions." Final Report of the Association of American Medical Colleges to the Department of Health, Education and Welfare, Publication HRA 77-55. Washington, D.C.: Health Resources Administration, Bureau of Health Manpower.

MENNEMEYER, S. (1978). "Really Great Returns to Medical Education?" *Journal of Medical Education* 13, 73–90.

PERRY, D. R., and CHALLONER, D. R. (1979). "A Rationale for Continued Federal Support of Medical Education." *New England Journal of Medicine* 300:22 (January), 66–71.

RABKIN, M. (1986). "Reducing the Cost of Medical Education." *Health Affairs* 5:3 (Fall), 97–104.

REINHARDT, V. (1975). *Physician Productivity and the Demand for Health Manpower*. Cambridge: Ballinger.

ROGERS, D. E. (1980). "On Preparing Academic Health Centers for the Very Different 1980's." *Journal of Medical Education* 55:1 (January), 1–12.

ROGERS, D. E., and BLENDON, R. J. (1978). "The Academic Medical Center: A Stressed American Institution." *New England Journal of Medicine* 298:17 (April), 940–950.

STEVENS, C. (1971). "Physicians Supply and the National Health Care Goals." *Industrial Relations* 10:5 (May), 119–144.

United States Congress, Office of Technology Assessment (1980). *Forecasts of Physician Supply and Requirements*. Washington, D.C.: U.S. Government Printing Office.

VANSELOW, N., and KRALEWSKI, J. (1986). "The Impact of Competitive Health Care Systems on Professional Education." *Journal of Medical Education* 61:9 (September), 707–713.

Chapter 15

HEALTH MANPOWER POLICIES, PHYSICIAN EXTENDERS, AND NURSING EDUCATION

*The study of costs for nursing education, in a decade
which forecasts curtailing enrollments in general and
further economic retrenchment, cannot be overemphasized.*

—ELSA L. BROWN

*Hospitals have shifted an increasingly costly nurse
training program onto the public sector. . . . With a
decline in subsidy many programs will have to close.
To the extent that the earnings of an RN plus the
nonmonetary benefits of nursing provide a "surplus"
above the most attractive alternative occupation, a
student will be willing to pay for part or all of their
training. As one moves from the truly dedicated nurse
to those whose attachment to the profession is more
marginal, the amount they are willing to invest declines.*

—STUART H. ALTMAN

*A physician may want to hire a new health practitioner for a number of reasons. This could involve
either the provision of additional types of medical
services, such as preventive care or patient education, or more careful and systematic diagnosis for
those medical problems that require it. The ability to
give more thorough examinations may result in lower
hospitalization rates.*

—ALAN SORKIN

399

In this chapter we discuss the impact of federal policy on the market for nursing education. Whether the marginal price paid per additional nurse trained is a "good buy" as a federal program is discussed in the context of other current nurse labor market issues. The second half of the chapter surveys trends in nurse practitioner and physician assistants markets. Due in large part to a lack of physician acceptance, the physician extender market is faced with what many consider a paradox. The nation faces a shortage of primary care, low-cost providers in certain locations, yet many physician extender programs that emphasize such a social mission have had to close.

Since 1965 the federal government has been providing financial assistance for the training of registered nurses. Federal support began in 1964 with the passage of the Nurse Training Act (NTA); subsequent legislation has extended and expanded this initial commitment to nursing education. Government assistance for nurse training began as an attempt to increase the supply of RNs because health care institutions demanded more RNs on their staffs to meet the increased utilization of health services by the population. The provisions of the Nurse Training Act were specifically designed to increase the number of nurse graduates by subsidizing operating costs for nurse training programs and lowering tuition levels for nursing students. Support is awarded to training programs and students who meet certain criteria based on enrollment levels and financial need (DHEW, 1974). In addition, special project grants were available to (1) increase the quantity and quality of nurse training programs, (2) increase enrollment levels of disadvantaged students, (3) increase the supply of nurses in underserved areas, and (4) upgrade the skills of existing nurses.

Long-Standing Shortages: Fact or Fiction?

In the 1980s the willingness of federal and state government to support nurse education has declined for two basic reasons. First, governments do not have the financial resources to underwrite the promises of the past. Second, the prevailing belief in the need for government subsidies for the past two decades is dissipating as conventional wisdom concerning the nurse "shortage" erodes. Indeed, a 1983 Institute of Medicine study (IOM, 1983) concluded that the national nurse shortage is over. From 1962 to 1983, the number of nurses per capita grew 100 percent. The IOM report recommended continued, but increasingly targeted, funding of the Nurse Training Act. Direct funding for student aid was considered especially crucial, given that most students come from families with moderate incomes and that further federal support reductions could cause a future shortage of RNs.

Some analysts may argue that there has been no nursing shortage since 1969. For example, the principal stimulus for passing the NTA program was a 1963 Surgeon General's report that provided manpower targets. The report recommended (1) increasing the nursing supply to 675,000 (a figure actually achieved five years ahead of schedule in 1969) and (2) improving the quality of nursing education by expanding BSN (baccalaureate degree) programs. McNally (1981) estimated a "shortage of 1.3 RNs per hospital, hardly a situation which might be described as a crisis." However, for some health professionals, if the "correct number of nurses" does not exist on each and every shift to staff a unit at 85 percent target occupancy, even if actual patient occupancy is 20 to 30 percent less, a "crisis" shortage of nurses exists. Professional "guesstimates" of the need for nurses have ranged from 110,000 in 1945, 70,000 in 1955, 150,000 in 1969, and, most recently, 100,000 forecast for 1980. Estimates have not been developed by type of nursing program.

There are three basic educational training programs for the training of registered nurses. Each program is administered in a different educational setting and varies in length of time from start to completion. The two-year associate degree (AD) is earned at a community or junior college; the three-year diploma certificate is earned at a hospital-sponsored school of nursing; and the four-year baccalaureate degree (BSN) is earned at a college or university.

In 1983, BSN programs constituted 29 percent of all nursing programs and 36 percent of all graduates. The three-year diploma programs conducted in hospitals emphasize on-the-job training within the facility. In 1983, diploma programs constituted 21 percent of all nursing programs and 18 percent of all graduates. Total federal NTA subsidies per BSN student per year were twofold higher than support for AD and diploma students over the first 15 years. If the federal donors for nurse education had been interested only in maximizing the quantity of RNs, the government would have directed its expenditures to associate degree and diploma programs. The costs of educating a nurse in either AD or diploma schools is substantially less than the cost of a BSN degree in terms of money (as well as the opportunity costs of foregone labor). A measure of the cost of the quality objective was obtained by Edgren (1976) by comparing the cost of the subsidy program with what it would have cost to support diploma and AD programs exclusively. Edgren estimates that approximately 17,000 additional active RNs would have graduated from 1966 to 1972 if the decision to emphasize quality as well as quantity had not been made. Undoubtedly, there have been some positive shifts in educational and service quality, but some undetermined amount of these quality improvements may have occurred without NTA federal donations.

Changes in the Nursing Profession and the Schools

There have been three empirical estimates of the effectiveness of the NTA program in expanding the supply and type of nurses. In 1976, Edgren estimated that 7 percent of the total supply of RNs, or an additional 13,535 licensed RNs, can be attributed to the federal program from 1966 to 1972. Using an econometric simulation model initially developed by Deane (1971), Edgren produced a second estimate of the number of newly trained RNs produced by the federal program. In Deane's model, the number of entrants to nursing schools was a function of the wages of RNs, the wages of other professional women, and the number of female high school graduates. Using this equation, Edgren calculated the total change in graduations from schools of nursing between 1966 and 1972. Comparing the cumulative net change in graduates with predicted change, Edgren found approximately 6,813, or 3.5 percent, more graduates than expected because of the federal program. A third estimate, provided by Yett (1975), suggests that approximately 1,330 additional trained RNs graduated per year between 1968 and 1970 as a result of the NTA program. If these three estimates can be used as a range, anywhere between 1,300 and 3,000 extra RNs per year can be attributed to the NTA program during the initial seven years.

Edgren estimated that over the first decade, the costs of an NTA-subsidized education were roughly six times greater than his hypothetical alternative (a direct wage subsidy program). Thus, the cost of increasing the nurse labor force by one additional nurse was approximately $50,000 because of the federal policy. If a wage subsidy had been used, however, the cost of each additional RN would have been only $7,936 in 1969 dollars. This $7,936 estimate assumed that the wage elasticity of RNs with respect to nurse participation in the labor market was 1.0 (i.e., a 1 percent increase in wages produces a 1 percent increase in employment).

Various attempts to measure the accomplishments of the Nurse Training Act have concluded pessimistically that the increase in the supply of RNs resulting from the federal program does not appear to justify the cost. Health providers and nursing groups still contend, however, that federal support for nursing schools and students is necessary. Further research is required in view of the most recent substantial reductions in federal support. This chapter provides an empirical test of the enrollment behavior of nurse training programs. A viable policy for government support of nurse education must be based on reliable measurements of the sensitivity of nursing school enrollments to tuition, government subsidies, and educational costs. These measurements will permit estimates of the effects that future changes in subsidy levels will have on enrollment behavior and, ultimately, on the supply of registered nurses.

Donor Model for School Behavior

How have nursing schools responded to the NTA program and other subsidies? Nursing schools could have attempted to utilize subsidies to train more students, train the same number of students more intensively, engage in more community services, raise faculty salaries, or even purchase better office equipment. Without an economic model of the nursing school, we cannot test predictions of how schools respond to donations (including loans) from the government or the private sector. We shall adopt the donor model of medical school behavior developed by Hall and Lindsay (1980) to the nursing school context.

The single most important demanders of nursing education are the donors, including public agencies, which provide one-third to one-half of school revenues. The support for educational institutions is most frequently predicated on the distribution of "in kind" dividends to the gift givers (i.e., the donors) in the form of increased supply and quality of nursing manpower, and thus improved access to quality of health services delivery for the donors and society (Eastaugh, 1985).

In the Hall and Lindsay (1980) model, the public donors care about the quantity of school output, whereas the private donors are concerned with the quality of output. In the nursing education context, most of the donors are public sources, but they care about both the quantity and the quality of output as stated in the Nurse Training Act. One might hypothesize that nursing schools have more internal control because they have a less diverse stakeholder (donor) group.

Let us consider how nursing schools have reacted to the rise and fall of donor support. Because nursing schools have received few large private donations in the past, one might predict a reversal of this trend in the near future. In fact, there is evidence that this is already occurring. For example, the Kellogg Foundation committed $6.5 million to associate degree nursing education at two dozen schools from 1983 to 1986. Alumni are also becoming a more important donor group. However, the "giving power" of the typical middle-aged nurse is substantially less than the giving power of the "old boy" medical school alumnus.

Physician and nurse markets are very different, and the theories applicable to one may not be transferable to the other. It is the basic contention of the empirical portion of this chapter that the donor model is applicable to nursing education, even if donors' contributions to schools of nursing represent a smaller fraction of total school revenues (one-fourth to one-third; by comparison, one-half to two-thirds of medical school revenues come from government and private donors). In fact, a donor model of nursing school behavior might be as effective as the Hall and Lindsay medical school model for predicting behavior, for six basic reasons:

1. Nurses are less mobile and thus more likely to practice in the state in which they were trained and subsidized (a critical point for state government donors who want to donate for long-term increases in the state's supply of nurses).
2. Nurses exist in a more competitive job market with less control of their wages and demand functions.
3. Potential students face narrower variation in tuition across nursing schools; thus, the existence of a subsidy may determine whether a student goes into nursing. In contrast, potential medical students face a tenfold variation in tuition that allows a student to shop for a school with a lower price, ceterus paribus.
4. Once training is completed, nurses face fewer barriers to practice entry (e.g., licensure exams are easier and less frequently required than those for physicians).
5. Given the differences between medical and nursing students in socioeconomic backgrounds and given the perceived opportunity costs of foregoing short-term employment at $600 a month to go to school, a net $3,000 subsidy to a potential nurse may be more of a "lure" to that field than a much larger subsidy for a medical student with dreams of $80,000 annual income. In other words, the absolute levels of subsidy per student may be lower in nursing education, but the dollars may be more critical to an 18- to 22-year-old individual facing the decision of whether to enter or forego a career in nursing.

6. The number of nursing schools is much larger for hypothesis testing (Hall and Lindsay studied 16 of 128 medical schools; we shall consider data from 639 nursing schools in this analysis).

Nursing schools have good reasons to exercise discretion over matriculants (and their faculty). Analogously, just as baseball ticket buyers donate only one-fourth of the revenues to support the game, these "donors" largely determine the number and quality of the players. Donors may not be as important in the nursing education industry as they are in medical education, but their dollars do help determine the quantity and educational quality of our nursing labor force.

If nursing schools competitively produce trained licensed nurses for donors and their health programs, one can model the donors' demand for first-year students. Figure 15.1 graphically shows the three critical variables of the model: H is the demand curve of all hopeful applicants for first-year admission, D is the demand curve by that fraction of applicants judged qualified and allowed to matriculate, and M is the marginal cost of education per student

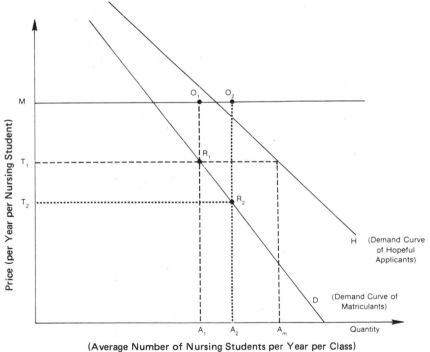

Figure 15.1   The Demand Schedule for Nursing Education as a Function of Tuition Supports (MT_1 MT_2) in Periods (T_1 T_2)

per year. A nursing school will select a class size of A_1 if it can collect T, R, A_1, and O dollars of tuition after budgeting for T, R, O, and M dollars of donations. If the dollars of donations expand to $T_2R_2O_2M$, as happened during the period 1965–1971, nursing schools can lower tuition (in real dollar terms) and expand enrollment (price T_2, class size A_2). Large numbers of potential nursing students are still rationed on a nonprice basis, but fewer qualified applicants are "available" than under equilibrium T_2.

One could hypothesize that during the period 1971–1974 we reached a new equilibrium (Figure 15.2) with donations at their maximum in real dollar terms ($T_3R_3O_3M$), tuition falling to T_3, and enrollment expanding to A_3. The demand for nursing services, and thus nursing education, shifted outward from D to D_3 thanks to increased medical technology and the demand-pull medical expenditure inflation fueled by expansion in Medicaid and Medicare coverage. Some would argue that during this "golden era," a large number of poorly qualified "marginal" nursing students were admitted, nearly one-third of whom did not graduate. Perhaps the correct equilibrium to trade off quality and quantity is point A_u.

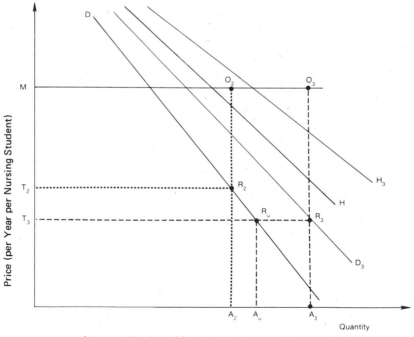

Figure 15.2 Demand Schedule for Nursing Education as the Tuition Supports Increase (to MT_3) and the Demand for Nurses and Consequent Demand for Nursing Education Increases

However, a steady retrenchment of donations occurred from 1974 to 1980 back to T_2, and a more drastic retrenchment during 1981 to 1984 back to T_1. Consequently, nursing school administrators have been pressured to raise tuition, which somewhat curtails class size (closer to A_u). Finally, nursing school faculty have become more highly trained and costly, driving up the marginal cost curve M. Increases in training costs created pressures to raise tuition and downsize enrollment. This simple model assumes it is equally costly to train each of the class levels (year 1, 2, 3, 4) within a given nursing program.

We shall next test the validity of the donor model for the nurse training equilibrium market where the supply and demand for medical training is determined by the level of donations (mostly government subsidies). In fact, the equilibrium price and quantity of training actually faced by prospective students and schools depends to a great degree on donor subsidies.

Data Analysis

Data were collected for 639 U.S. nursing schools for each of the academic years from 1974–75 through 1983–84. A fixed effects analysis of covariance was used to pool the time series, cross-sectional data. The dependent variables are tuition and first-year enrollments. The models involve simple linear approximations of the reduced form equations for nursing school tuition and enrollments. Annual subsidies, marginal training costs, and annual applications are the primary independent variables. The reduced form equations are estimated using two different model specifications, two functional forms (linear and semi-log), and two estimation procedures (ordinary least squares and instrumental variables).

We shall measure equilibrium enrollment (A) and tuition (T) as linear functions of donor subsidies (G), marginal training costs (C), and actual applications (H). In contrast to Hall and Lindsay (1980), we have the advantage of having data for application by school annually. Hall and Lindsay utilized aggregate applicants to all schools annually in combination with superior physician wage data to impute optimal physician stock. The nurse wage data from the Bureau of Labor Statistics are too spotty (they are irregular and do not include all of the school catchment regions), and the sample sizes are too small (50 to 100 respondents per area, rather than over 1,000 physicians per SMSA), to properly regress an optimal nursing labor stock. The number of applicants per school acts herein as the device to meter demand shifts directly.

In simplest forms, the initial regression specifications can be written as:

$$A = \beta_0 + \beta_1 H + \beta_2 C + \beta_3 G + e \qquad (15.1)$$

$$T = \alpha_0 + \alpha_1 H + \alpha_2 C + \alpha_3 G + u \qquad (15.2)$$

The model leads one to expect that regressions (15.1) and (15.2) will yield positive signs for β_1, β_3, α_1, and α_2 and negative signs for β_2 and α_3. The estimated coefficients from these equations allow one to test whether the derivatives of the true reduced-form equations for tuition and enrollment are nonzero and of the correct sign. One should point out that our reliance on actual observations of enrollment (A) and tuitions (T) to measure equilibrium levels assumes that changes in exogenous conditions are correctly antici-pated and that adjustments to such changes are made fully within each academic year. Nothing in the nursing literature suggests consideration of a more complex distributed-lag model (Eastaugh, 1986). The only variable in the analysis we shall lag is subsidies (G), which is assumed to affect school behavior the following year (year $n + 1$).

Next, we shall estimate the structural equations for the demand for nursing education (A) as a linear function of estimated tuition values $(\hat{T})$ from equation (15.2), as well as a function of applications (H). The regression specification for demand may be written as:

$$A = \delta_0 + \delta_1 \hat{T} + \delta_2 H + v \qquad (15.3)$$

Coefficients obtained from this equation will be used to calculate the elasticity of enrollment with respect to tuition and to achieve closer approximations to the partial derivatives of the true reduced form equation for enrollment.

Equation (15.1) can be estimated from data for each of the ten academic years, 1974–1983. The tuition data, however, are very poor prior to 1978; therefore, equations (15.2) and (15.3) are estimated over the six academic years 1978–1983. Two final caveats are in order. First, implicit in our definition of H is the assumption that the proportion of multiple applications to nursing schools remains relatively constant over the study period. Second, faculty salaries are used as a proxy for the marginal training cost (C) variable, for two reasons. First, as an Institute of Medicine study (1974) suggests, faculty salaries are 50 percent of total costs per student for a wide range of nursing schools, plus or minus 5 percent. Faculty salaries are clearly a consistent underestimate of marginal cost and average cost, but an error in variables estimation procedure is used to minimize this problem. Faculty are clearly the most elastic component of a nursing school's cost function.

Alternatively, one could also argue that salaries are a proxy for average cost, which is itself a proxy for marginal costs. Economists often use average cost as a proxy for marginal cost, under the assumption that returns to scale in the proportion of students are constant.

The total number of nursing programs has only increased 3 percent during the study period 1974–1983. The mix of program types, however, has changed significantly over this time period. The 50 percent decline in diploma programs has been offset by increases in both associate (up 55 percent) and baccalaureate degree programs (up 45 percent). Our sample represents 639 of the 650 largest nursing programs in 1974. These 639 schools matriculated 79 percent of the first-year RN enrollments in 1974 and 81 percent in 1983. Our sample includes 68 private BSN schools, 74 public BSN schools, 250 public AD schools, 28 private AD schools, 196 private diploma schools, and 23 public diploma schools. The sample represents the larger more stable nursing schools that were more likely to report financial data to the National League for Nursing (NLN). The NLN survey is annually administered to all state-approved schools of nursing each October. Because of its consistency across the period 1974–1983, it was used as the basis for developing the sample of nursing schools used in this chapter.

The data for the federal component of the variable *G* have been taken directly from the U.S. Department of Health, Education and Welfare, Bureau of Health Manpower's *Annual Directory of Grants, Awards and Loans to Schools of Health Professions*. These data reflect all award actions administered by the Bureau of Health Manpower in each fiscal year. Only those appropriations made specifically for the purpose of training nursing students, however, were included in the measurement of *G*. The data for the state, local, and private donation terms of *G* have been obtained from the National Center for Education Statistic's annual *Financial Statistics of Institutions of Higher Education Survey*. Due to the long lead time necessary for government funds actually to go into effect, the data for the public component of *G* have been lagged by one year.

Model Specification

The reduced form model that specifies individual school effects can be written as

$$y = X_{it}\beta + Z\alpha + u_{it} \tag{15.4}$$

where $y =$ a vector of observations on the dependent variable (i.e., annual tuition or first-year enrollment)

$X =$ observations on the regressors (i.e., applications H, marginal training costs C, and annual subsidies G)

$u =$ random error term

$Z =$ a design matrix for school effects.

Let $i = 1, 2, \ldots, 639$ cross-section units (schools), $t = 1, 2, \ldots,$ 10 years for enrollment and $t = 1, 2, \ldots, 6$ years for tuition. The total number of observations is 6,390 for enrollment and 384 for tuition. Assuming only cross-section effects are important and that X includes an intercept term, Z contains 628 dummy variables where each column is 1 for the respective ith school and 0 otherwise. Thus, Z is $6,390 \times 638$ for the enrollment equation and $3,834 \times 638$ for tuition, and α is 638×1 for both equations.

To estimate equation (15.4), one usually specifies dummy variables for each school in the sample. However, because N is large, an alternative approach was followed. The means of each variable were computed for each school from the unpooled observations. Performing ordinary least squares (OLS) on observations that have been modified in this way yields the same slope coefficients as those obtained by incorporating individual dummy variables into the model. Given results obtained from equation (15.4), the second reduced form model specification examined categories of effects, which permitted the variability of slope coefficients across financial control (public and private).

The expected signs of the coefficients of the three focus variables (G, C, H) vary across the tuition and enrollment equations. The subsidy variable (G) is expected to have a negative effect on tuition (charged less if subsidized more) and a positive effect on enrollment (more subsidy, more students). The expected sign of the marginal costs (C) coefficient is positive for tuition (more costly faculty, higher tuition) and negative for enrollment (expensive faculty, less student demand because of inability to pay their way). Finally, the applications (H) coefficient is expected to be positive for both equations (more applications, greater capability to raise tuition and enrollment). The structural equation for demand contains two focus variables. The expected sign of the estimated tuition variable (T) is negative, and the applications variable (H) is expected to be positive.

Empirical Results

The tuition equation results for public and private schools are presented in Tables 15.1 and 15.2, respectively. The signs of the coefficients are as expected for the three focus variables: G, C, H. The one exception is the negative but statistically insignificant sign for applications in the diploma school equation in Table 15.1.

With only 23 schools and 114 degrees of freedom, however, this result is hardly disturbing. The relatively small t ratios corresponding to the coefficients of H in the five equations indicate the lack of importance of applications in explaining tuition levels in public schools. One possible explanation for this is that public schools have much less internal control in pricing because of their more diverse stakeholder or donor group. Consequently, interaction between student demand for application and tuition prices is less pronounced relative to private schools.

One can place some confidence in the model, given the expected signs of the coefficients in Table 15.1. Although some variation is expected, no clear meaning can be given, for example, to the 3.5-fold variation in the slope coefficients of the subsidy variable across program type. These coefficients indicate that the effects of subsidies on tuition levels are approximately 250 percent higher for diploma programs than for associate programs. Interpreted in terms of the dependent variable, the coefficient of G in the aggregate equation indicates that annual tuition levels for public nursing programs would decrease by $1.10 to $1.23 if per school subsidy levels increased by $1,000 annually. The coefficient of C in this equation indicates that a $100 increase in marginal training cost will increase annual tuition levels by $12.31, ceteris paribus. However, this estimate may be low, and thus we shall reduce the effect of measurement error in C by reestimating the equation (line 3, Table 15.1) using the instrumental variables (IV) technique (Durbin's IV method; Eastaugh, 1985). These results, as reported in Table 15.1, show that the IV estimator increased the magnitudes of the coefficients of S and C and improved their corresponding t ratios compared to the OLS estimation of the same equation. The coefficients of C in this best equation for public schools indicate that a $100 increase in the marginal training cost will increase annual tuition levels by $19.82.

The tuition equations in Tables 15.1 and 15.2 are impressive in that they explain more than two-thirds of the variance. All coefficients are of the expected signs in Table 15.2. Private schools appear to be twice as responsive to subsidies and applications as public schools. The relatively small t ratios and coefficients of H in Table 15.2, however, indicate that subsidies (G) are more important in explaining tuition levels in private schools. The tuition levels for private nursing schools would be expected to decrease $2.69 for every $1,000 increase in subsidy per school per year. Each $100 of increase in marginal cost per student will, ceteris

Table 15.1 Regressions of Tuition Equations for Public Schools (*t* ratios in parentheses)

Equation	Number of Schools	(G) Subsidies[a]	(C) Marginal Training Cost	(H) Applications	BSN Dummy	Diploma[b] Dummy	Inter-cept	R^2	d.f.
Disaggregate									
associate	250	−.476 (−2.8)	9.25 (3.6)	.326 (1.7)			6.5	.798	(55, 1444)
baccalaureate	74	−1.274 (−4.1)	7.09 (3.9)	.156 (1.3)			28.7	.739	(49, 394)
diploma	23	−1.682 (−3.7)	20.36 (4.2)	−.064 (−.3)			34.8	.694	(23, 114)
Aggregate	347	−1.195 (−4.0)	12.31 (4.1)	.298 (1.2)	163.4 (9.3)	207.7 (10.4)	15.2	.715	(59, 2016)
Aggregate: IV estimation[c]	347	−1.231 (−4.5)	19.82 (4.8)	.340 (1.7)	159.7 (8.9)	198.7 (9.6)	9.9	—	(59, 2016)

[a] Coefficients of subsidy and marginal training cost have been multiplied by 1,000 and 100, respectively.
[b] All equations include state and time dummy variables not reported in this table.
[c] All coefficients are significant at the .05 level, except coefficient *H* (significant at .06).

Table 15.2 Regressions of Tuition Equations for Private Schools (*t* ratios in parentheses)

Equation	Number of Schools	(G) Subsidies[a]	(C) Marginal Training Cost	(H) Applications	BSN Dummy	Diploma[b] Dummy	Intercept	R^2	d.f.
Disaggregate									
associate	28	-2.261 (-2.0)	18.28 (1.8)	.285 (1.1)			456.5	.721	(26,141)
baccalaureate	68	-2.135 (-4.3)	38.79 (2.7)	.472 (1.9)			399.0	.596	(35,372)
diploma	196	-4.974 (-5.1)	25.91 (1.6)	.398 (2.0)			368.2	.640	(41,1134)
Aggregate	292	-2.508 (-4.9)	36.72 (4.5)	.550 (2.1)	302.7 (4.5)	302.7 (-6.2)	343.1	.686	(47,1710)
Aggregate: IV estimation[c]	292	-2.693 (-6.0)	47.40 (7.1)	.619 (2.4)	295.1 (4.2)	-438.3 (-6.3)	327.4	—	(47,1710)

[a] Coefficients of subsidy and marginal training cost have been multiplied by 1,000 and 100, respectively.
[b] All equations include state and time dummy variables not reported in this table.
[c] All five coefficients are significant at the .05 level.

paribus, increase annual tuition per student by $47.40. Private schools appear to be more responsive to market signals, such as declines in government subsidies or increases in educational costs. Before placing too much confidence in such a conclusion, however, one should consider potential sources of reporting bias between the two types of financial control. For example, private school tuition might more accurately reflect the actual costs of training a student.

The enrollment equation results for public and private schools are presented in Tables 15.3 and 15.4, respectively. The signs are in the expected directions, and the t ratios are more impressive than those of the tuition equations. The results of the instrumental variable estimation procedure again improve the magnitude of the coefficient and t ratios, especially for the intended target (C). The coefficient of C under IV estimation suggests that first-year public school enrollment would be expected to increase by one student if annual subsidies increased by approximately $19,600 per school. This benefit-to-cost ratio represents an improvement on the $50,000 estimate (1969 dollars) reported by Edgren (1976).

Applications appear to be more significant in determining the enrollment equation than impacting the tuition equation. The estimates in Table 15.3 suggest that first-year enrollment per school would increase by one student if applications at the margin increased by 4.2 per public school. However, BSN public nursing schools appear to be more selective—that is, less driven by applications. The coefficients for H indicate that, certeris paribus, the enrollment per public BSN program would increase by one student if applications increased by 7.1 per school per annum.

The results for the private school enrollment estimates are shown in Table 15.4. Private schools are even more sensitive to subsidies. The estimates suggest that first-year enrollment would be expected to increase by one student per $16,100 of subsidies added per school per year. The effectiveness ratio of subsidy programs is more dramatic if one factors inflation into the equation. Present valuing the Edgren estimates to the 1983 dollars, one nurse is added to the labor supply per $123,200 of NTA subsidies invested in the period 1966–1972. Expressed in 1983 dollars, one nurse is added to the first year of private nursing school programs for each $25,400 invested in NTA and other subsidies, and one graduated nurse is added to the nursing labor pool for each $35,800 of subsidies (1974–1983). In 1983 dollars, one nurse is added to the first year of public nursing school programs for each $30,485 invested into NTA and other subsidies (state, local, etc.), and one graduated nurse enters the labor supply for each $43,550 of subsidies (1974–1983). Although there are differences between the present study design and that of Edgren, nursing schools appear to have become three- to fourfold more efficient in producing nurses from donations during the more recent period 1974–1983 than during the years 1966–1972.

Two final points should be made regarding Table 15.4. The coefficient for C suggests that first-year enrollment should, all else being equal, decline by 3.19 students per school if marginal costs increased by $100. This suggests that private and public nursing schools are equally responsive to shifts in marginal costs. Second, the coefficient of H suggests that first-year enrollment would increase by 3.1 students per school. However, the coefficient of H for BSN schools is substantially lower (i.e., they are more selective). First-year BSN enrollment would increase by one student if applications at the margin increased by 7.94 students per school per year.

Enrollments for private schools appear to be 22 percent more sensitive to subsidy levels than public schools. One possible interpretation may be that a large portion of government subsidies are in the form of loans and scholarships that go directly to students. If this source of funding is cut back, rather than pick up the full (higher) tuition bill of a private nursing education, students would probably enroll in public nursing programs. Private schools could retain enrollment levels by cutting back on their marginal costs, but private schools appear to be no more successful at further improving educational productivity than public nursing schools. Annual private school expenditures on faculty salaries are, on average, $53 less per student per year in diploma programs, $151 less per student per year in associate programs, and $548 less per student per year in BSN programs than public school expenditures. Dramatic reductions in marginal costs may have to be made in the diploma programs, the dominant type of private schools, if they are to survive in the 1990s. Many will not survive because of downward pressure on hospital payment rates. The typical private diploma program in our sample has 10 students per faculty, in contrast to 15 for BSN programs and 18 for the few private associate programs. Thus, reducing faculty is the most obvious way in which a nursing school could cut its costs. As we observed in Chapter 14, medical schools will also have to cut faculty.

Finally, the results for the equation estimating the demand for education (first-year enrollment) as a function of price (tuition), applications, and type of program are presented in Table 15.5. Private school demand appears to be more sensitive to price. From the coefficients of T in Table 15.5, private school enrollments

Table 15.3 Regressions of Enrollment Equations, Dependent Variable A, for Public Schools[a] (*t* ratios in parentheses)

Equation	Number of Schools	(G) Subsidies[b]	(C) Marginal Training Cost	(H) Applications	BSN Dummy	Diploma[c] Dummy	Inter-cept	R²	d.f.
Disaggregate									
associate	250	.106 (36.7)	−2.88 (−9.9)	.276 (18.3)			39.3	.82	(59, 2440)
baccalaureate	74	.049 (19.2)	−1.79 (−7.4)	.141 (7.6)			62.4	.84	(53, 686)
diploma	23	.117 (31.3)	−1.52 (−4.9)	.310 (10.9)			21.9	.91	(27, 202)
Aggregate	347	.048 (22.5)	−2.52 (−7.5)	.207 (10.3)	19.2 (11.6)	5.2 (2.3)	45.9	.687	(63, 3394)
Aggregate: IV Estimation[d]	347	.051 (22.8)	−3.06 (−9.1)	.238 (10.3)	21.9 (10.8)	7.8 (3.0)	54.6	—	(63, 3394)

[a] Dependent variable first-year enrollment (A).
[b] Coefficients of subsidy and marginal training cost have been multiplied by 1,000 and 100, respectively.
[c] All equations include state and time dummy variables not reported in this table.
[d] All coefficients are significant at the .05 level.

Table 15.4   Regressions of Enrollment Equations, Dependent Variable A, for Private Schools[a] (*t* ratios in parentheses)

Equation	Number of Schools	(G) Subsidies[b]	(C) Marginal Training Cost	(H) Appli-cations	BSN Dummy	Diploma[c] Dummy	Inter-cept	R^2	d.f.
Disaggregate									
Associate	28	.184	−1.57	.329			1.7	.90	(30, 249)
		(17.0)	(−2.4)	(17.6)					
Baccalaureate	68	.058	−1.14	.126			48.4	.81	(39, 640)
		(6.6)	(−5.9)	(14.8)					
Diploma	196	.115	−2.39	.317			31.1	.762	(45, 1914)
		(13.5)	(−6.5)	(22.9)					
Aggregate	292	.060	−2.47	.294	−17.9	−15.7	53.2	.739	(51, 2880)
		(12.9)	(−6.5)	(23.5)	(−8.6)	(−8.2)			
Aggregate: IV Estimation[d]	292	.062	−3.19	.301	−17.1	−13.2	57.8	—	(51, 2880)
		(14.0)	(−9.2)	(23.4)	(−7.9)	(−6.3)			

[a]Dependent variable first-year enrollment (A).
[b]Coefficients of subsidy and marginal training cost have been multiplied by 1,000 and 100, respectively.
[c]All equations include state and time dummy variables not reported in this table.
[d]All five coefficients are significant at the .01 level.

Table 15.5   Regressions of Demand Equations (*t* ratios in parentheses)

Equation[a]	Dependent Variable	(T) Tuition[b]	(H) Applications	Dummy	Diploma Dummy	Intercept	d.f.
Private Schools	First-Year Enrollment	−.129 (−14.6)	.343 (31.2)	23.06 (8.0)	−27.95 (−10.3)	150.78	(46,1711)
Public Schools	First-Year Enrollment	−.094 (−7.0)	.229 (25.1)	49.52 (10.7)	38.66 (11.5)	37.20	(58,2017)

[a]All equations include state and time dummy variables not reported in this table.
[b]All variables are significant at the .01 level.

would increase by one student for each $7.75 decline in tuition, and public enrollments would increase by one student per $10.65 decline in tuition. Also, public school enrollment is less sensitive to applications (*H*) than private school enrollment. Public school applications would have to increase by 4.4 per school to yield an increase in enrollment of one student. However, the coefficient for private schools (correcting for type of program) suggests that applications need only increase by 2.9 to yield one more student per year. Because variable *H* may be a proxy for such effects as RN wage levels, marriage status, and so forth, this result could reflect a difference in the socioeconomic backgrounds of the students who attend private and public nursing schools. More research is needed to determine why students select nursing careers and how they select nursing schools (Hafer and Ambrose, 1983; Mechanic and Aiken, 1983).

A more complete examination of nursing school behavior should include factors that affect demand for education, such as expected future wages. How do prospective nurses acquire information on this issue? For example, one recent issue of *RN* magazine reported that (1) general duty nurses in Kansas City earn 21.1 percent less per hour than grocery cashiers and 28.4 percent less than head grocery clerks, (2) Boston nurses earn 28.6 percent less than head grocery clerks, and (3) Atlanta nurses earn 13.8 percent less than grocery cashiers and 29.8 percent less than head grocery clerks. The nursing profession seems insensitive to the two potential negative ramifications of such articles. First, young people pondering investment of time and money in nursing school might think twice after reading such information. Second, the nursing profession seems insistent that it operates independently of all other labor markets. While the health services sector is a "special" industry, one is nonetheless struck by the apparent difficulty of the nursing profession to respond proactively to the coming cuts in hospital-based nursing positions and wages. If the new Medicare

Prospective Payment System is going to withdraw $8 to 10 billion of reimbursement out of the hospital sector from 1987 to 1989, the principal losers will be nurses, not physicians or administrators. If the "nursing shortage" was the issue in the past, more bed closures and forced unemployment may become the nurse labor market issues for the 1990s.

In summary, the best statistical results for all four equations were obtained from the aggregate model, which allows the slope coefficients to vary across financial control and includes dummy variables for time, state, and program-type effects. A significant trend in our analysis of state effects is that California has the third highest tuition levels for private nursing schools but the second lowest tuition levels for public schools. The southern states, by contrast, appear to have relatively high public school tuitions. Concerning time effects, increases in private school tuitions exceeded those in public schools from 1978 to 1981. Furthermore, first-year enrollments have been declining since 1980 for both BSN and associate degree schools. The decline in enrollments for the 196 private diploma schools began in 1978. The moderate variability of the slope coefficients across program type for the disaggregated model suggests that the results reported in this section should be considered good approximations.

Nursing Schools and the Future

Two central measurement problems exist in this study. First, we did not have a good measure of marginal cost, but IV estimation procedures (Intriligator, 1978) minimized this problem. Second, we did not have wage data for the 300 nursing markets in which 639 schools operate. Applications served as a proxy for demand factors, especially wage levels. Given that nursing education is an input to the market for RNs, an examination of school behavior should include factors that affect demand for education, such as expected future wages. Prospective payment for hospital services may prove to have a downward impact on nurse wages and employment.

Despite the limitations of the regression, the equations strongly indicate that nursing schools respond to market signals from government and other donors, applicants, and faculty costs. These responses differed over the ten-year period for all three types of private and public schools. Schools appear to have improved their efficiency in producing nurses as a function of donations and loans since the Edgren study. Our estimates of an NTA effectiveness of

$35,800 to $43,550 per additional nurse graduated can be interpreted as the marginal price to the federal government of additional nurses produced. Whether this is too high a price to pay,
even if nursing schools have more than doubled their efficiency in
the 1970s, is a political decision. Most nursing educators hope that
the federal government will continue to be the final guarantor of
financial access to nursing school for students otherwise qualified.

Increasing subsidies in the 1960s and 1970s slightly increased
class size and lowered tuition (below what tuition would have
been), just as declining subsidies are now decreasing class size and
raising tuition. The Reagan administration questions the validity of
subsidizing nursing education in the absence of a nursing shortage
during an era when many inefficient hospital beds may have to
close. Nursing subsidies can be criticized for continuing the operation of inefficient and obsolete schools and promoting the training
of "marginal" nursing students. In contrast to medical education,
however, nursing schools do not have a large pool of excess
applicants; indeed, there are excess schools. Nursing educators
might refute the various arguments for discontinuing NTA subsidies by pointing to the fact that qualified students could not afford
the investment in a nursing education without government subsidy. Political support for the nursing loan program appears to be
dissipating in the face of vexing and persistent problems in collecting on the loans. Nursing loan defaults became a major issue when
the DHHS announced that if nurses merely paid the amounts they
are delinquent (not their total debt), another 24,000 nursing
students could receive loans. In dollar terms, in 1985, 27 percent
of the 181,000 nursing loans were delinquent a total of $19.1
million.

In attracting donors to substitute for declining federal support,
nursing school deans will have to address the issue of attrition and
educational standards to win the support of private donors. Deans
of medical schools have a somewhat easier task because the donors
are financially better off, plus donors may face less uncertainty in
the medical education business. A medical student admitted is a
practicing doctor down the educational pipeline, with very few
dropouts and voluntary inactivity from work. The nursing pipeline
can be much more leaky, with an average 30 percent dropout rate
in nursing school and up to one-third of licensed nurses not
working. There never has been an aggregate shortage of trained
nurses, just a presumed shortage of working nurses. Job satisfaction and wages are critically important in retaining practicing
nurses. Levels of dissatisfaction may increase, however, if education and training continue to far exceed practical needs and duties.

The progressive educator lobbies for providing nurses with more interesting and challenging duties and responsibilities.

Hospital Nursing: Vacancy Rates and Wages

The official DHHS policy under the past three administrations since 1975 has been that the aggregate supply of nurses is adequate. The American Nursing Association (ANA) acknowledged the American Hospital Association's (AHA) and state hospital associations' estimates of a nurse shortage of 100,000 in 1981. However, the ANA characterizes the market as geographically maldistributed, "crying out" for the specialized nurses with BSN training. Both the AHA and ANA have characterized the nurse shortage as "a crisis" as recently as 1983. The AHA reported that 88 percent of the nation's hospitals cannot fill their nursing vacancies. The long-standing "crisis" is most critical in certain states. In 1983, a number of state hospital associations reported especially high nurse vacancy rates: 13 percent in Illinois, 14 percent in Texas and Maryland, and 20 percent in California. However, one should suspect the validity of such "evidence." What are the social costs of not filling 20 percent of the maximum possible "full staffing" nursing slots given that 42 percent of the beds in California are empty on average? Statistics on budgeted vacancies are poor evidence of a shortage but could be indicative of a geographic or specialty-skill maldistribution in the market.

In pondering the "budgeted vacancy" issue, a number of points might be made regarding the major employer of trained nurses. Hospitals employ two-thirds of active nurses. Hospitals as a source of employment may enter an era of decline under prospective payment. Hospitals are monopsony buyers of nurse labor, and each hospital faces an upward-sloping labor supply curve (in contrast to a horizontal curve under perfect competition); thus hospitals are wary of raising nurse wages. For hospitals the short-run supply of nurses is inelastic. That is, increases in wages will yield only small increases in nurse labor available. Raising wages increases the entire nurse staff budget while yielding miniscule returns in terms of reentry by inactive nurses. Therefore, the rational hospital will purposefully control nurse wages at low levels (but not so low as to lose too many nurses to neighboring providers), and the hospital's state association can complain about a "crisis in budgeted vacancies."

State hospital associations might better spend their resources considering incentives to make more nurses careerists, such as increasing the differentials between beginning and top level salaries. Managers should trade off the costs of providing incentives to induce nurses to pursue a hospital-based career, versus the continuous high costs of retraining new nurses that turn over every three to four years. In the process of professional development, nurses have questioned the dated "doctor-knows-best" rules and replaced self-doubt with self-esteem. In the 1970s an assertive prospective nurse might have asked, "How can I fit into this hospital's goals?" Increasingly, nurses can ask "How will the hospital fit into my goals?" "How will it impact on my life style?" "Will the work be interesting?" and "Will I grow in my field of expertise?" Flexible employment opportunities, improved automated scheduling systems, and elimination of nonnursing tasks from the daily routine can be optimal for both nurses and employers. Nurses can stay in nursing and overcome home-career conflicts, and management can reduce nursing costs.

Over the last 15 years federal appropriations under the NTA have amounted to almost $3 billion in 1983 dollars. Table 15.6 lists the amounts of federal support appropriated to each provision of the Nurse Training Act over the last 15 years, representing 7 to 13 percent of the total expenditures for nursing education in any given year. According to the American Nursing Association inventory of registered nurses, the supply of nurses per 100,000 citizens has increased from 280 in 1960, to 356 in 1970, 506 in 1980, and an estimated 544 in 1986 (ANA, 1986). This 94 percent increase over 26 years in the fraction of the labor force working as nurses has brought with it a trend to specialize. Specialization in nursing has often focused more on high-technology inpatient care rather than on long-term care or primary care. However, the demand for hospital nurses has declined since 1983 and may continue to decline in the future. Nursing schools that adapt best to the emergence of growth markets, such as long-term care (discussed in Chapter 8), will be in the best position to place their students after graduation.

One final word of caution is in order concerning hospital managers setting nurse wages. Many hospital executives anxious to reduce labor costs incorrectly envision a long-run, large supply of unemployed nurses. This attitude may be true in the short run, but nurses are already shifting in large numbers to other care settings and may be less interested in a return to hospital nursing. The fraction of nurses working in hospitals may decline from 61 to 50 percent over the period 1986–1990, and hospital nurse wages may remain low over the period. However, a nursing wage "boom" to attract a sufficient supply of skilled hospital nurses may well emerge in the early 1990s.

Table 15.6 Nurse Training Act and Research Program Appropriations and Other Special Purpose Projects, 1969–1986, (in millions of dollars)

	Student Support (1–3)			4. Special Projects	5. Formula and Capitation	6. Advanced Nurse Training	7. Nurse Practitioner	8. Construction	Research (9–10)		11. Other	12. Total	Present Value of Total (12) in 1983 Dollars[b]
	1. Scholarships	2. Traineeships	3. Loans[a]						9. Fellowships	10. Grants			
1969	6.5	10.5	9.6	4.0	3.0			8.0	1.4	2.6		45.5	127.4
1970	7.2	10.5	16.4	8.4				8.0	1.4	2.6		54.4	139.6
1971	17.0	10.5	17.1	11.5				9.5	1.4	2.6		69.4	170.7
1972	19.5	11.5	21.0	19.0	31.5			19.7	1.4	2.5	12.0	138.0	329.1
1973	21.5	12.5	24.0	25.0	38.5			21.0	1.7	2.5	14.0	160.6	360.5
1974	19.5	13.0	24.4	19.0	34.3			20.0	1.4	2.5	5.4	139.5	282.3
1975	6.0	13.0	24.4	19.0	34.3			20.0		1.2	4.8	122.7	227.4
1976	6.0	13.0	23.5	15.0	44.0	2.0	3.0	1.0				107.5	188.4
1977	6.5	13.0	25.5	15.0	40.0	9.0	9.0					124.0	204.0
1978	9.0	13.0	24.0	15.0	30.0	12.0	13.0	3.5	1.0	5.0		125.5	195.2
1979	9.0	13.0	14.3	15.0	24.0	12.0	13.0		1.0	5.0		106.3	146.3
1980	9.0	13.0	14.3	15.0	24.0	12.0	13.0		1.0	5.0		106.3	128.8
1981		13.0	14.3	12.0	10.0	12.0	13.0		1.0	5.0		80.3	88.0
1982		9.6	7.66	6.18		11.5	11.5		.96	3.4		50.8	52.5
1983		9.6	1.61	6.33		13.2	11.8		.96	5.0		48.5	48.5
1984		9.6	1.56	6.40		13.8	12.0		.96	5.0		50.5	
1985		11.4	1.0	9.5		16.4	12.0		.65	5.0		56.0[c]	
1986		10.9		9.0		15.8	11.5		.53	4.8		52.7[c]	

SOURCE: Congressional Budget Office.
[a]Includes loan repayments.
[b]Brought to Present Value using the CPI, BLS.
[c]Figures do not include $6.2 million for the Center for Nursing Research and new projects; nor do they include in FY 1985 and 1986 the $800,000 per year for training nurse anesthetists.
NOTE: Some lines do not add due to rounding.

New Professionals: Physician Extenders

If the market for nurses and nursing education is in a turbulent
state in 1986, the market for physician extenders is in far worse
shape by comparison. Projections of 25,000 physician extenders in
practice by 1985 (Eastaugh, 1981) have not been realized. The
supply of physician extenders has become a captive of high-
technology medicine and not a substantial source of primary care
in underserved areas. Physician extender programs over the years
from 1981 to 1986 have closed or adapted to the "funding realities."
While limited funding support exists for primary care extenders,
most dollars are offered in high-technology areas—for example, the
FY 1986 federal budget contains $800,000 for nurse anesthetists
and $4 million for surgical assistants.

In theory, a set of new professionals was to emerge in order to
provide care in a fashion that is more conducive to serving consumer needs than traditional solo physician practice. Since 1971,
federal support of physician extender (PE) training programs has
been the primary federal response to the perceived shortage and
maldistribution of providers of primary care. The term *physician
extender* includes both nurse practitioners (NPs) and physician
assistants (PAs) with formal training that has equipped them for
functions beyond the scope of the traditional nurse. The rapid
growth in PE training programs in the 1970s was a by-product of
the unmet consumer demand for primary care and the perceived
neglect of the human side of medicine. PEs frequently take the
family approach to health education and contact the spouse or
relative of the patient in an attempt to improve patient compliance
with treatment and to convince the individual that a healthier life
style is attainable. With the growth in concern for the caring
function, prevention, health promotion, and care of the chronically
ill has come a fivefold increase in the supply of PEs from 1970 to
1980. In the current era of governmental retrenchment, concern
over the nation's medical bill should not *a priori* lead to a freeze at
the current annual level of the number of PEs trained. Physician
fears of competition should not change the fact that many underserved patients increasingly demand nonphysician personnel to act
as counselor, educator, and ombudsman.

The promise of PEs is best described in terms of improved
access to care, health education counseling, comprehensive planning in patient care management, and potential gains in productivity. PEs can meet a previously unmet need in two basic senses: If
not hospital-based, they are more likely than physicians to reside
in medically underserved areas, and they specialize in often ne-

glected areas of medical practice. Physician resistance to employing more PEs has called into question the service delivery rationale for federal funding of training programs. The intent of the following sections is to suggest that PEs can increasingly become a medically and economically popular solution to the problem of providing health care in underserved rural and inner-city areas. However, PE expansion into these markers has not occurred (1980–1986).

For nearly two decades the terms "doctor shortage" and "primary care shortage" have been bandied about. The "crisis" was defined in the 1970s as one of both geographic and specialty maldistribution. One of the most vexing questions asked by labor economists is whether, and to what extent, PEs act to improve productivity and decrease average costs by performing delegable tasks (Zeckhauser and Eliastam, 1974), or whether they free physician time to perform less necessary and more costly complex tertiary medical care. In the parlance of economics, to what extent do PEs act as substitutes and/or complements for physician time? Another, less tangible, unanswered question is to what extent have PE training programs had a positive spin-off effect on physician education—that is, making physicians more aware of primary care and the need for the caring function and preventive counseling. Any benefit-cost framework for assessing the projected expansion in the supply of PEs should not underestimate the tangible benefits to society of health promotion, self-care, and prevention activities.

Current Levels of Manpower Supply and Training Support

In January 1980 there were an estimated 11,000 physician assistants, including 1,000 certified PAs who did not graduate from a formal training program. The PA class size declined from 1,600 graduates in 1981 to only 700 graduates in 1986. An estimated 70 percent of certified PAs are presumed active. Most PA programs are university-based and require two years' training. Between 1972–1980 approximately 7,200 PA students received $66 million in direct and indirect federal support (Eastaugh, 1981). However, the level of federal support per annum has been frozen at approximately $8 to $11 million for the past eight years.

Certificate and master's NP training programs vary in emphasis over a range of disciplines: family medicine, pediatrics, maternity care, midwifery, and psychiatric care. In January 1986, an estimated 23,000 NPs had graduated from formal training programs. An estimated 80 percent are presumed to be active.* The American College of Nurse-Midwives estimates that 3,000 of the NPs are actively engaged in midwifery. Between 1972–1981, approximately 12,000 NP students and about half of the NP programs received $88 million from the Nurse Training Acts of 1971 and 1975. The level of federal support from the 1975 Nurse Training Act has been frozen at $49 to $51 million for the past five years. Only $1.1 million per annum has been awarded in direct traineeship support. Since 1978, the traineeships were awarded to individuals who were willing to perform postgraduate service in areas designated as underserved by DHEW.

One seldom mentioned benefit resulting from the emergence of PE training programs was the public questioning of the resistance of organized medicine to task delegation. Since 1847, the American Medical Association has committed itself to the trade union objective of promulgating restrictions on nurses or would-be doctors (Kessel, 1958). According to the report of the Macy Foundation (1976), the continued success of PEs will not only have a positive impact on the quality of health care, but will also encourage the development of other nonphysician competitors to physician subspecialist and solo practitioners. If consumers prefer high accessibility to care and cost containment, then training PEs seems a better bargain than training physicians at five times the cost.

Physician Supply and Reimbursement Issues

An Institute of Medicine (1978) study questioned the need to train additional PEs if the anticipated supply of physicians in 1990 is at least adequate and if the projected specialization trend is a return to family practice and primary care. While recognizing the need for a comprehensive strategy that coordinates the supply and distribution of PEs and physicians, it seems a shortsighted policy to presume that physicians in oversupplied areas will suddenly decide to serve the poor and less profitable locations. There is limited statistical evidence, however, that doctors have increasingly moved to rural underserved areas, thus alleviating some of the original impetus for many PE training programs. Physicians began to disperse to relatively underserved locations in response

---

* Data provided by the Bureau of Health Manpower, Division of Nursing, Public Health Service, DHEW.

to competitive pressures as early as 1979 (Newhouse et al., 1982). If Congress suddenly resolved to reimburse physicians on the basis of negotiated charges or DRGs rather than on the basis of prevailing charges, then the financial disincentives to work in a region of low physician density would be diminished. A mass exodus of physicians from the suburbs under this new reimbursement climate would seem highly unlikely. Despite the fact that personal life-style preferences dominate the physician's location decision, it seems poor public policy to pay more in areas where doctors are needed less and to pay less in areas where they are needed most.

Medicaid regulations typically permit reimbursement for PE services that are performed under "general" physician supervision. Some states are more liberal on this point—for example, the South Dakota legislature required health insurers to cover all PE services starting in 1980. Since 1976 the state of Nevada has directly reimbursed PAs at 100 percent of physician rates and NPs at 55 percent of physician rates. To liberalize the reimbursement climate among insurance payers in areas of physician shortage, Congress passed the 1977 Rural Health Services Act (P.L. 95-210), which provided Medicare and Medicaid reimbursement in certified clinics for PE services rendered without direct physician supervision.

Although one-fifth of PEs are employed in HMOs and clinics, the majority of PEs were employed by physicians in private practice until 1983. A number of outside surveys have suggested that physicians' reluctance to hire PEs might be accounted for by conflicting perceptions about the PE role (Prescott and Driscoll, 1979). Five rationales have been suggested to explain why physicians may hire PEs. First, they may wish to improve the quality of care by creating a less crowded and more comprehensive schedule. Second, they may want to increase the quantity (minutes) of care delivered per visit. Third, they may indulge in the purely economic desire to expand practice profits. Fourth, physicians may desire more leisure time and a shorter workweek. Last, employment of a PE may result in lower malpractice premiums in the long run, if improved patient rapport diminishes the incidence of nuisance suits.

Productivity and Cost Considerations

Many early comparative cost studies have tried to portray PEs either as a financial windfall or as a liability. Some of the earliest pro-PE studies came from HMOs in which nonphysician personnel provided care in a majority of the visits. Other studies were flawed because they loaded a large amount of overhead unnecessarily onto PE practices only (Nelson et al., 1975). The Systems Science (1978) study avoided such methodological pitfalls. The productivity component of their analysis focused on an economic efficiency measure, the number of ambulatory visits per $1,000 of cost. When the study considered group practices, it found no differential in economic efficiency between PE and non-PE comparison practices; both kinds of group practice produced 66 visits per $1,000 of cost. However, the Systems Science study found that solo physician practices produced 81 visits per $1,000 of reimbursable cost (cost to society) when a PE was part of the team, compared to 57 visits per $1,000 of cost in solo physician practices without a PE. Three other major conclusions of the study were that (1) the average charge per visit was lower in PE practices, (2) physician job satisfaction increased in PE practices as the perceived workload decreased, and (3) process measures of quality of care were better on average in the PE practices.

The demand for PEs is a function of the consumer demand for medical services, physician supply, physician reimbursement policy, PE reimbursement policy, and the willingness of physicians to hire PEs. For example, legal constraints, such as requirements for direct supervision of PEs by physicians, are cited by physicians as a rationale for not employing PEs. Another rationale for not employing PEs is the American physician's distaste for staff management. In estimating that physicians could profitably employ one to five PEs, Reinhardt (1972) suggests that physicians react with rather high psychic costs to employing a larger staff—that is, they hate to manage people. It is difficult to generalize these study results over time, but if we update the figures to 1980 dollars, Reinhardt estimates the marginal disutility of each additional PE employed to be between $200 and $260 per week. If the economic conditions of the 1980s erode a physician's ability to maintain a high living standard, the medical community may increasingly discount the marginal disutility of employing additional extenders and hire more PEs. However, the anticipated productivity gains may be overstated. For example, a study by Hershey and Kropp (1979) suggests that the productivity gain from employing a PA may be as small as 20 percent and the increase in net income may be negligible. The authors optimization-simulation model does not consider the possibility that shifts in the patient mix following addition of a PA might cause the measured productivity improvement to be understated. However, if income gain is negligible for the doctor in a period when office visits were increasing, the incentive to employ a PE is nonexistent in a market where visits per annum have declined (-6 percent per year, 1983–1986, Chapter 2), and the physicians often have empty appointment calendars.

Manpower Projections and the Appropriate Federal Role

The manpower projections in Table 15.7 (Eastaugh, 1981) are simple linear projections extrapolated from the points in time, 1973 and 1979. The projections are consistent with a study by Wallen (1980) suggesting that 8,000 more PEs or 4,000 to 5,000 physicians would be necessary to bring DHHS medically underserved areas up to the minimum supply ratios. Projected growth in nurse practitioners from 1980 to 1985 has been far short (less than half) of expectations. The medical profession, faced with an anticipated doctor glut, has been especially stringent in its advocacy of strict legal restrictions limiting the range of permitted activities and the possibility of free-standing reimbursement (Weston, 1984). Nurse practitioners have subspecialized to remain viable in the market. Pediatric nurse practitioners have proven valuable in rural areas and in urban medical centers. They can provide a wide range of functions vital to a multispecialty setting (Cruikshank et al., 1986). The normative ideals for pediatric NPs, as developed at three HMOs, were consistently higher than their actual job roles (Weiner et al., 1986). Nurse practitioners maintain their linkage to nursing by performing nursing functions—for example, patient advocacy, health education, and patient support (McNamara and Smith, 1984). Rather than acting as "junior housestaff" to supplement inpatient care, NPs and PAs might find greater growth potential in caring for the elderly (Chapter 8). The federal govern-

Table 15.7 Population Distribution and Supply Ratios per Population of Physicians, Physician Assistants, and Nurse Practitioners by Community Size, Projected for 1985

Community Size	Physicians per 10,000	PAs per 10,000	NPs per 10,000	Percent of U.S. Population
Under 10,000	10	.77	.54	18
10,000–49,999	22	.82	.54	16
50,000 plus	26	.42	1.14	66
National average	22	.56	.90	
Projected total supply in 1985	525,000	13,250	21,250	

SOURCE: Eastaugh (1981).

ment invested $220 million in NP and PA training programs to provide primary care, not produce a cheap source of labor for teaching hospitals. Geriatric medicine is one specialty area where the physician community may cede increasing independence for these physician extenders. Expansion of the physician extender workforce has been retarded by inadequate marketing, lack of community understanding, and lack of acceptance by community physicians (Kelly, 1985).

If the recent restrictive legislation limiting foreign medical graduates (representing at present one-fifth of the physician labor force) forces the physician supply to contract, and if specialists are increasingly successful in attracting PEs away from hospital practice, the total demand for PEs could increase.

The federal government might better serve the public interest by concentrating a higher proportion of PE funds into traineeships with a service obligation. As an added inducement to increase retention of PEs after completion of the service pay-back requirement, DHHS might subsidize the malpractice premiums and office equipment costs of individuals remaining in medically underserved regions. The DHHS could further target direct grants and contracts to programs that offer curricula that track students into primary care. Finally, the federal government should have an increased concern for research in the area of primary care manpower. For example, we need to ascertain the volume or critical mass of population necessary to allow an independent PE practice to attain financial self-sufficiency after three to five years of growth in an isolated rural area (Moscovice and Rosenblatt, 1979). Specifically, PAs have a proven ability to decrease per visit costs by up to 20 percent in large urban practices (Greenfield et al., 1978), but the introduction of PAs into smaller practices has not led to an equal reduction in unit cost or increase in patient volume (Frame et al., 1978).

Another potential area for further research is the difference in productivity between PAs and NPs. A study of 455 matched paired comparison practices suggested that PAs are 6 to 36 percent more productive than NPs, depending on practice arrangement (Mendenhall et al., 1980). The NPs in this study were employed in larger practices—practices with an average of 9.5 physicians compared to 4.7 in the average PA practice situation. However, the cause of the productivity differential was not explained by practice size.

The wisdom of increasing support for PE programs depends on judgments about future reimbursement incentives, PE responsiveness to required service location, PE retention in underserved areas following completion of the service requirement, and assumptions about competition in health care markets. In the short run if PEs merely add to the aggregate level of demand, they will, acting as an add-on, produce a net inflationary impact on medical costs. Although there are many reasons for the very slow emergence of PEs as a professsion, a dominant one is the concern for efficiency. Why must a $40 per hour physician spend 30 minutes with the anxious patient, when a $10 per hour PE can do an equally good or even better job in one hour at half the cost? Rather than spend a few rushed minutes with the physician, that patient can spend more time with a PE who can take the time to emphasize the caring function, yielding greater patient self-respect and improved rates of compliance. Managed care systems may well discover that PEs offer good value for their wage rate. Managed care systems, consumerism, and the emerging public desire for a low-cost health care adviser could promote a renaissance of interest in primary care PEs.

References

ALTMAN, S. (1970). "The Structure of Nursing Education and Its Impact on Supply." In H. Klarman (ed.), *Empirical Studies in Health Economics*. Baltimore: Johns Hopkins, 343.

American Nursing Association (1986). *Facts About Nursing*. Kansas City, Mo.: American Nurses Association.

BROWN, A. (1985). "The Uncertain Future of the Nurse Practitioner." *Health Matrix* 3:2 (Summer), 49–54.

BROWN, E. (1982). "Analyzing the Cost of Baccalaureate Nursing Education." *National League of Nursing Publication* 15–1880. New York: National League for Nursing, 13–25.

California State Division of Health Professions Development (1986). Annual Report to the Legislature, State of California Healing Arts Licensing Board, Sacramento: State of California.

CARLSON, R. (1975). *The End of Medicine*. New York: John Wiley.

CRUIKSHANK, B., CLOW, T., and SEALS, B. (1986). "Pediatric Nurse Practitioner Functions in the Outpatient Clinics of a Tertiary Care Center." *Medical Care* 24:4 (April), 340–349.

DEANE, R. (1971). "Simulating an Econometric Model of the Market for Nurses." Unpublished doctoral dissertation, Department of Economics, University of California, Los Angeles.

Department of Health, Education and Welfare (1974). *Report to the Congress: Nurse Training*, Publication (HRA) 75–41. Washington, D.C.: U.S. Government Printing Office.

EASTAUGH, S. (1985). "The Impact of the Nurse Training Act on the Supply of Nurses, 1974–1983." *Inquiry* 22:4 (Winter), 404–417.

EASTAUGH, S. (1981). "Physician Extenders: Potential for Improved Productivity." *Hospital Progress* 62:2 (February), 32–45.

EDGREN, J. (1976). "The Nursing Shortage and the NTA: Should the Federal Government Be Paying for the Education of Nurses?" Health Manpower Studies Group Working Paper A–12 (September). Ann Arbor, Mich.: School of Public Health, University of Michigan.

FELDSTEIN, P. (1979). *Health Care Economics*. New York: John Wiley, 375.

FRAME, P. S., WETTERAV, N. W., and PAREY, B. (1978). "A Model for the Use of Physician Assistants in Primary Care." *Journal of Family Practice* 7:12 (December), 1195–1204.

GREENFIELD, S., KAMAROFF, A., PASS, T., ANDERSON, H., and NESSIM, S. (1978). "Efficiency and the Cost of Primary Care by Nurses and Physician Assistants." *New England Journal of Medicine* 288:6 (February 9), 305–309.

HAFER, J., and AMBROSE, D. (1983). "Psychographic Analysis of Nursing Students: Implications for the Marketing and Development of the Nursing Profession." *Health Care Management Review* 8:3 (Summer), 69–76.

HALL, T., and LINDSAY, C. (1980). "Medical Schools: Producers of What? Sellers to Whom?" *Journal of Law and Economics* 23:2 (April), 55–80.

HERSHEY, J. C., and KROPP, D. H. (1979). "A Re-appraisal of the Productivity Potential and Economic Benefits of Physician's Assistants." *Medical Care* 17:6 (June), 592–606.

Institute of Medicine (1983). *Study of Nursing and Nursing Education*. Washington, D.C.: National Academy of Sciences.

Institute of Medicine (1978). *A Manpower Policy for Primary Health Care*. Washington, D.C.: National Academy of Sciences.

Institute of Medicine (1974). *Costs of Education in the Health Professions*. Washington, D.C.: National Academy of Sciences.

INTRILIGATOR, M. (1978). *Econometric Models, Techniques, and Applications*. Englewood Cliffs, N.J.: Prentice-Hall.

KELLY, K. (1985). "Nurse Practitioner Challenges to the Orthodox Structure of Health Care Delivery: Regulation and Restraint on Trade." *American Journal of Law and Medicine* 11:2 (December), 195–225.

KESSEL, R. A. (1958). "Price Discrimination in Medicine." *Journal of Law and Economics* 1:1 (October), 20–53.

LAMB, G., and NAPODANO, R. (1984). "Physician-Nurse Practitioner Interaction Patterns in Primary Care Practices." *American Journal of Public Health* 74:1 (January), 26–29.

Macy Foundation (1976). *Physicians for the Future: Report of the Josiah Macy Commission*. New York, 27.

MCNALLY, J. (1981). "Nursing Shortage: Fact or Fiction." *Hospital Financial Management* 11:5 (May), 16–25.

MCNAMARA, J., and SMITH, R. (1984). "Management Issues in an Ambulatory Care Consortium." *Journal of Ambulatory Management* 2:1 (January), 1–11.

MECHANIC, D., and AIKEN, L. (1983). "A Cooperative Agenda for Medicine and Nursing." *New England Journal of Medicine* 307:12 (September 16), 747–750.

MENDENHALL, R. C., REPICKY, P. A., and NEVILLE, R. E. (1980). "Assessing the Utilization and Productivity of Nurse Practitioners and Physician's Assistants: Methodology and Findings on Productivity." *Medical Care* 18:6 (June), 609–623.

MENNEMEYER, S., and GAUMER, G. (1983). "Nursing Wages and the Value of Education Credentials." *Journal of Human Resources* 18:4 (Winter), 32–48.

MOSCOVICE, I., and ROSENBLATT, R. (1979). "The Viability of Mid-Level Practitioners in Isolated Rural Communities." *American Journal of Public Health* 69:5 (May), 503–505.

National League for Nursing (1985). *NLN Nursing Data Book: 1984*. New York: National League of Nursing.

NELSON, E. C., JACOBS, A. R., CORDNER, B. A., and JOHNSON, K. G. (1975). "Financial Impact of Physician Assistants on Medical Practice." *New England Journal of Medicine* 293:11 (September 11), 527–530.

NEWHOUSE, J. et al. (1982). "Where Have All the Doctors Gone?" *Journal of the American Medical Association* 247:17 (May 7), 2392–2396.

PERRY, H. B. (1976). "Physician Assistants: An Empirical Analysis." Unpublished doctoral dissertation, Johns Hopkins University, Department of Social Relations.

PRESCOTT, P. A., and DRISCOLL, L. (1979). "Nurse Practitioner Effectiveness." *Evaluation and the Health Professions* 2:4 (December), 387–418.

RECORD, J., BLOMQUIST, R., BERGER, B., and O'BANNON, J. (1977). "Quality of PA Performance at a HMO." In A. Bliss and E. Cohen (eds.), *The New Health Professionals*, Chapter 12. Germantown, Md.: Aspen Systems.

REINHARDT, U. (1975). *Physician Productivity and the Demand for Health Manpower*. Cambridge, Mass.: Ballinger.

REINHARDT, U. (1972). "A Production Function for Physician Service." *Review of Economics and Statistics* 54:1 (February), 55–66.

SIMMS, L., DALSTON, J., and ROBERTS, P. (1984). "Collaborative Practice: Myth or Reality?" *Hospital and Health Services Administration* 29:6 (November/December), 36–48.

SORKIN, A. (1979). *Health Economics*. Lexington, Mass.: D. C. Heath.

Systems Sciences, Inc. (1978). *Survey and Evaluation of the Physician Extender Reimbursement Experiment*. Contract No. 55A-600-76-0167, Social Security Administration, Washington, D.C.

WALLEN, J. (1980). "Considerations in the Use of Nonphysician Health Care Providers in Physician-Shortage Areas." Unpublished report, Division of Intramural Research, National Center for Health Services Research, DHEW.

WEINER, J., STEINWACHS, D., and WILLIAMSON, J. (1986). "Nurse Practitioner and Physician Assistant Practices in Three HMOs: Implications for Future U.S. Health Manpower Needs." *American Journal of Public Health* 76:5 (May), 507–511.

WESTON, J. (1984). "Ambiguities Limit the Role of Nurse Practitioners and Physician Assistants." *American Journal of Public Health* 74:1 (January), 6–7.

YETT, A. (1975). *An Economic Analysis of the Nursing Shortage*. Lexington, Mass.: D. C. Heath.

ZECKHAUSER, R., and ELIASTAM, M. (1974). "The Productivity of the Physician Assistant." *Journal of Human Resources* 9:1 (Winter), 95–116.

Part Five

EFFICIENCY, EFFECTIVENESS, AND COST BENEFIT

Chapter 16

COST-EFFECTIVENESS AND COST-BENEFIT ANALYSIS

Nothing is pure and entire. All advantages are attended with disadvantages.

—DAVID HUME

It is better to put a fence at the top of the cliff than an ambulance at the bottom.

—JAMES MASON

Cost management means the delivery of all the care that is medically needed, for as long as it is needed, but not for a day or a dollar more.

—ROBERT SHELTON

Cost-effectiveness and cost-benefit analysis have been applied in many preventive, diagnostic, and treatment contexts. Over the past decade methods have improved for prospectively collecting better data sets and incorporating intangible quality-of-life valuations into the calculus for weighing benefits against costs. Further cooperation between clinicians, economists, and epidemiologists is a healthy trend. Political scientists are prone to argue over valuation in dollars, reflecting a basic misunderstanding of the trade-off concept and a need to combine and compare benefits and costs in comparable units. The purpose of this chapter is to review the state of the art of cost-effectiveness and cost-benefit analysis in evaluation of medical technologies. Economic evaluation of new or expensive technologies has become a central issue in the public debate about rising medical care costs. Historically, the growth in technology has stimulated a concomitant increase in the numbers and salaries of health care employees. Warner (1978) and Fuchs

437

(1986) characterize the new health technologies prior to 1955 as being cost-saving (physician time-saving and usually quality-enhancing), whereas the technologies introduced since 1955 have tended to be cost-increasing. Physicians and economists frequently express their hope that these expensive and/or physician-using technologies are partially justified by their quality-enhancing properties.

Basic Concepts

The objective of cost-benefit analysis is to maximize net benefits (benefits minus costs, appropriately discounted over time). The objective of cost-effectiveness analysis is to rank order the preferred alternatives for achieving a single goal or specified basket of benefits. Cost-effectiveness analysis is not any easier to perform than cost-benefit analysis if multiple varieties of benefit are specified (man-years, work-loss days, reduced angina), except that in doing cost-benefit one must value the intangible benefits in commensurate dollar terms. Operationally, ethical questions can be raised if the benefits and costs accrue to different social groups. For example, a clinic scheduling system that minimizes wasted time for the physician through multiple overlapping appointments may be a net benefit of a few hundred dollars per doctor at the expense of many more dollars of patient time.

In economic sectors where competitive markets fail to exist, such as the health care or water resource sectors, cost-benefit analysis aims to do what supply and demand forces accomplish in competitive markets. The price system will not equalize marginal benefits and marginal costs if market failure exists—that is, price disequilibrium occurs in highly insured consumer markets (Fuchs, 1986). Another criterion of choice is to maximize the ratio of benefits to costs, discounting the numerator and denominator to present value dollars. Alternative programs (or procedures or services) are then ranked by benefit-cost ratios, and the programs with the highest payoff ratios are selected until resources are exhausted or until the ratio equals one. This approach is equivalent to maximizing net present value within a budget constraint. A third, outmoded decision criterion is to support a project if the internal rate of return exceeds the predetermined discount rate. The internal rate of return criterion can lead to different resource decisions from the net present value criteria if programs are of different sizes or have varying time horizons.

If a technology is found to be the most cost-effective alternative, then the next question is whether it is cost-beneficial. For example, Acton (1973) first evaluates which of five program alternatives is most efficacious and which is most cost-effective in reducing deaths from heart attacks, which he follows by a valuation of life and intangible benefits to assess whether the benefits make the program worth the costs for society. One obvious advantage of cost-benefit analysis is that it leads to a positive (go) or negative (no go) net present value for the procedure being evaluated, and does not require a cost-effectiveness cutoff level to decide whether a project can be done within the resource constraints. However, many more complete cost-effectiveness analyses are performed than cost-benefit analyses, because intangible benefits pose difficulties with valuation and the choice of a discount rate is simpler in cost-effectiveness evaluations (Eastaugh, 1983).

If a technology is found to be cost-beneficial, the only question left is whether the risk is socially acceptable for public financing of the service. Society may have some preference for the social classes that are to face an unacceptable risk, even if it is known in advance that the total risk is insufficient to make the benefit-to-cost ratio less than one. Safety, as measured by risk analysis, is a relative concept. No test or therapy that provides any benefit has ever been completely safe. Physicians, like all professionals, have learned to live comfortably with the reasonable notion that we must forego some safety to achieve any net benefit.

The Merits of Prevention

One may consider the efficiency of medical care in a broader context by taking output as the overall health of the nation rather than simply as days of care. Victor Fuchs (1986) has stated that "when the state of medical science and other health-determining variables are held constant, the marginal contribution of medical care to health is very small in modern nations." In other words, one cannot simply add more doctors and hospitals and expect an equivalent improvement in health. Fuchs gives several reasons for this low marginal contribution. First, patients and physicians use more discretion when physicians are scarce—that is to say, patients seek medical care less often when it is difficult to obtain, and physicians tend to concentrate on those patients who need care most. Second, many highly effective treatments such as vaccinations do not require the huge amounts of resources required by many generally less effective treatments such as heart transplants. Third, as medical care proliferates, iatrogenic disease becomes a problem, exemplified by highly risky surgical interventions. And fourth, it is difficult to measure the output of medical care in terms of health, in that many factors other than medical care contribute to health—for example, nutrition and environment (Fuchs, 1986).

It is certainly not necessary to conduct economic analysis and randomized clinical trials on every new technology, and certainly not on most existing ones. However, the uncontrollable economic pressures for efficiency are apt to result in more careful economic analysis. Some of these studies will severely disrupt the conventional wisdom. For example, Russell (1985) studied a number of preventive programs, from immunization to exercise programs, and concluded that society's total health care costs increased (i.e., prevention was a cost add-on, not a cost-savings investment). Investments that are very low cost on a per person basis become very expensive when applied on a national basis. Russell cites the example of a blood pressure check, which is very inexpensive on an individual basis, but becomes very costly when applied to 20–30 million people. In a more recent study, Schelling (1986) suggests that smoking cessation programs may not be cost-beneficial for society.

Two basic truths seem apparent. First, society should not be oversold on prevention and health promotion as a strategy to slow (or reverse) the rise in national health expenditures. If health officials oversell their programs as a cost-savings vehicle, the inevitable disillusionment will cause excessive additional cuts in public health programs (i.e., a backlash against such programs). Second, prevention may not save money, but such programs can often be justified in terms of a worthwhile investment in improved quality of life. Keeping people happy is expensive, but quality of life is something worth paying for in the minds of most citizens. Analogously, while many medical technologies may be cost-increasing, they are strongly supported by the public. Schwartz and Aaron (1984) summarize this issue best with the following example: Hip replacements are much more expensive than providing an elderly person with aspirin and a walker, but wouldn't most people want the quality-of-life mobility of a new hip?

Phelps (1978) suggests that the reason prevention is not covered by insurance companies is that it may not be effective, or, if effective, it may not be cost-saving. Even in the event that preventive services are cost-saving, the gains may be so far in the future or the elasticity of supply in the industry may be so high that insurance companies are unable to reap any benefits. One of the problems with preventive screening examinations is that the cost of treating false-positive results, along with adverse psychological effects, may outweigh the benefits of detecting a disease in its early stages (Phelps, 1978). In the same vein, Fuchs has suggested that if expensive cancer treatment programs did not exist, people might be more likely to follow their own prevention programs (Fuchs, 1986). In this case, it might be more important to encourage a change in behavioral patterns rather than to support research into expensive cancer treatments. The critical need for better technology assessment studies was highlighted in the 1986 federal government decision to pay for heart transplants on a limited basis. If heart transplants were performed on all patients who could marginally benefit from them, the cost per year would be an estimated $8 billion; that estimate compares to an annual expense of $950 million for liver transplants.

The traditional basis of clinical medicine suggests that the physician should make every effort to provide all possible avenues of care to the patient. The idea of scarcity of resources has no role in this code of ethics, except during wartime. The medical ethic is increasingly being criticized relative to the public health ethic, which suggests that every clinician has an obligation to inquire about underserved potential patients and foregone man-years of life that go untreated because physicians serve a technological imperative and a profit imperative (that is, serve the patients who are technically interesting or profitable, then attend to the other cases). Decision-making is increasingly affected by computer monitoring, surveillance of the quality of care, and appropriateness review (Evans et al., 1986).

Methods of Analysis

There has been a high degree of public and political disenchantment with model builders who provide narrow definitions of direct benefits and ignore the limitations of their very crude data bases. The typical accounting costs of billed charges or incurred expenses are too narrow a definition of cost for the economic analyst. Confusion frequently exists when members of the medical profession attempt to do a cost analysis. For example, the cost to society of not having airbags must not exclude accident victims who are DOAs (dead on arrival). In the arena of cost-effectiveness analysis between medical treatment versus surgery, surgeons frequently omit DOTs (dead on table) from the analysis in order to make surgery look better relative to medical treatment. The tendency is to go far afield in counting benefits and to neglect some costs, such as the pain of surgery or the overhead costs of the operating room.

Cash expenditures are too limited a definition of cost. True cost to society can only be measured in opportunity cost terms. In the parlance of economics, the cost of any item or service is the foregone benefit that you sacrificed in order to obtain it.

Estimating the economic burden of a disease involves the measurement of prevalence, the assessment of impact on the individual's health status and other people's well-being, and the eventual quantification of direct and indirect costs associated with these impacts. For example, Berry and Bolond (1977) estimated the cost of alcohol abuse at $31.4 billion in 1971. Half of the alcohol abuse burden on the economy results from lost economic production ($14.9 billion), $8.3 billion is generated in direct health care service costs, and the residual $8.2 billion results from motor vehicle accidents, fires, crime, and other less tangible impacts. More recently, Hardy et al. (1986) estimated that the first 10,000 acquired immunodeficiency syndrome (AIDS) cases in the United States required 1.6 million hospital days, at a direct cost of $1.4 billion, and $4.8 billion in lost (foregone) wages from 8,387 lost years of work from disability and premature death. In most cases indirect costs can be the largest component of the analysis. Klarman (1965) estimated the present value of eradicating syphilis at $3.1 billion, with 42 percent of this total benefit accounted for by erasure of the "stigma" associated with the discovery of the disease. The study assumed that people were willing to forego 1.5 percent of their earnings to avoid the stigma associated with the disease.

Measurement of Indirect Benefits

Direct benefits of health services or public health programs are measured by the foregone medical care costs. Often the direct benefits of eliminating a disease are a fraction of the indirect benefits. For example, in 1979 HEW estimated the direct benefits of eliminating medical expenditures on smokers at $5 billion annually, and the indirect benefits were estimated at $12 billion in terms of foregone worker productivity. Mushkin (1962) separates indirect benefits of health programs into three categories: reducing premature death, avoiding lost working time (morbidity), and avoiding lost capacity to be productive after returning to work (debility). The first and second measures, mortality and morbidity, have been well researched. However, our ability to quantify debility remains a topic for future research. Expected earnings replaced income as the relevant measure of indirect benefits in the

1960s (Rice, 1966). Cooper and Rice (1976) produced annual tabulations of the present value of lost earnings due to mortality under alternative discount rates and annual estimates of the fore-gone earnings due to disability. In some cases potential morbidity reduction represents 90 percent of indirect benefits (skin diseases), and in other cases potential mortality reduction represents 90 percent of indirect benefits (neoplasms). Most recently, Rice et al. (1985) estimate the cost of illness at $455 billion: $211 billion for direct costs, $176 billion for mortality, and $68 billion for morbid-ity. Diseases of the circulatory system and injuries were the most costly conditions.

The value of housewives' services has also recently entered the benefit picture, although their services are still omitted from the gross national product. Klarman (1967) measured housewives' services by the wages they could earn (using alternative wages they could earn as an opportunity cost measure), while Weisbrod (1968) measured their replacement value by the cost of employing a housekeeper. The only strength of the Weisbrod approach is that it estimates housewives' worth as an increasing function of family size: A housewife is more expensive to replace in larger families. The opportunity cost concept is more persuasive, since housewife value is a function of education attainment and occupation. Fore-gone earnings as an estimate of indirect benefits is relatively easy to estimate, although some radical economists might question the assumption that earnings are a suitable measure of social benefit. The resultant biases implicit in measuring benefits in terms of earnings reflect imperfections in the labor market such as racism and sexism.

Most economists became disenchanted during the 1970s with the gross output approach of valuing a person's life as discounted expected future earnings. For example, concluding that visits to a rheumatology clinic were cost-beneficial only for males merely reflects an artifact of the sex bias in earnings data; women earn less (Glass, 1973). A variant of this approach, subtracting out consump-tion to yield net output, was considered ill advised, because killing elderly or handicapped individuals would be "valued" as an act that confers a net benefit to society. Fromm (1965) suggested a third approach, valuing life on the basis of the life insurance premiums one is willing to pay. However, the life insurance approach only measures a person's willingness to compensate others following death rather than the value set on one's own life.

The most prevalent assessment approach in the 1970s has been the "willingness to pay" approach suggested by Schelling (1968) and measured initially by Acton (1973). Both authors realized that quantity multiplied by price was at best equal to a minimum benefit of health services to the society, since it does not account for the many consumers who would be willing to pay more than the price.

Consumer Welfare

Consumer's surplus of benefit involves estimating a measurable proxy, the area under the entire demand curve. Figure 16.1 illustrates the concept of measuring benefit by the amount of money that each person is willing to pay rather than go without the service. For a hypothetical example of selling bone marrow transplants to people with aplastic anemia, Figure 16.1 shows some 48 individuals willing to pay $10,000 to receive the treatment.

All individuals are not willing to pay the same amount under hypothetical conditions of equal wealth across all individuals. Individuals face different risks; for example, the treatment is painful and often causes potentially fatal side-effects under which the new transplanted marrow cells attack the liver, skin, and other organs. The *ABC* shaded area above the price line *AB* is the sum of money equal to the consumer's surplus. The surplus represents a dollar measure of the excess of satisfaction over consumer dissatisfaction. Individuals 1–6 are willing to pay an extra $10,000 above the price ($10,000), individuals 7–11 are willing to pay an extra $8,000 each, individuals 12–15 are willing to pay an extra $6,000, individuals 16–25 are willing to pay an extra $4,000, and individuals 26–40 are willing to pay an additional $2,000 each. Consequently, the net benefits are $480,000 (price times quantity) plus $199,000 consumer's surplus.

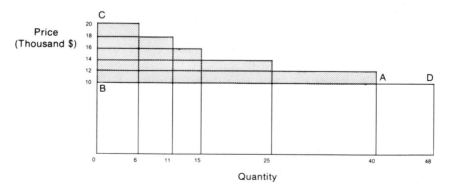

Figure 16.1 Hypothetical Demand Curve for Bone-Marrow Transplant Therapy (aplastic anemia patients). (The shaded regions represent the consumer's surplus.)

This analysis assumes that the consumer is well informed and that the social value of transplants for anemia patients is the sum of the individual values. One might argue for adding on a psychic benefit for expressing the value that all members of society place on the assurance that if they have this rare type of anemia, the bone marrow transplant will be available.

The next three chapters survey a number of normative economic models. The techniques, such as cost-benefit and cost-effectiveness analysis, are decision-making models designed to guide resource decisions, from building a facility to deciding what technique should be the standard operating procedure. The truth is, of course, that normative techniques are typically used to help provide better informed decisions at the margin, rather than dictate cook-book decision making. In our pluralistic society, the decision makers are wise to keep the experts on tap, rather than on top (Eastaugh, 1983). A number of willingness-to-pay techniques are presented in Chapter 18. The willingness-to-pay approach is an improvement relative to the economic theory of human capital developed by Becker (1964) and others. In contrast to the human capital approach for measuring foregone expected earnings, the willingness-to-pay approach provides a consumer measure of the sum total of indirect benefits and intangible benefits.

Economics and Patients

The critical point to convey to the reader is that cost-effectiveness and cost-benefit analysis are increasingly taking their appropriate position in the evaluation (pre-diffusion) stage prior to the marketing decision. The rationale of this emerging public policy is that the costs (in lives and in dollars) of foregoing economic and efficacy evaluation may often be much greater than the costs of a well-designed evaluation. One "consumerist" benefit of increasing reliance on economic evaluation is that it must force those in power to be explicit about (1) valuation of life biases (across social class) in cost-benefit calculations and (2) the resource cut-off level utilized in cost-effectiveness analysis.

As the public increasingly understands the degree to which medicine involves decision making under uncertainty, the doctor-god model must give way to a more realistic paradigm. Consumers might better think of their doctor as a "senior partner" (SP) in health care. This abrupt relabeling of the professional title, from MD to SP, highlights the rising popularity of health promotion and education, and the declining perception of infallibility in medicine. Moreover, outcome measures of quality and patient satisfaction and compliance are inseparable. Patient compliance is critical to improving health status (Eastaugh and Hatcher, 1982). SPs enhance patient compliance and provide a better level of informed consent; omniscient practitioners claim their "hands are touched by the god." Gods give out proclamations; SPs give probability estimates and explain them. For some patients, the explanation of odds and conditional probabilities may be so complex as to best be labeled "overinformed consent." The sensitive SP knows when to stop with the detail, whereas a god would never become schooled in such detail or provide it to a patient. The SP will wait for the junior partner (patient) either to say, "Enough detail, go for XYZ," or "What shall we do, doctor?"

Measurement of Intangible Benefits

Valuation is not a consideration in competitive markets, because marginal benefit is assumed to be equal to price. However, when prices fail to exist (water resources) or price is deemed a defective measure of value (health services), an attempt is made to impute value or "shadow price." Shadow price values can be imputed by asking individuals what they would be willing to pay for relief from pain, grief, discomfort, and disfigurement. For example, if a year of life is valued by a willingness-to-pay measure of $28,000, and a woman would sacrifice a year of life to avoid losing her breast(s) (Abt, 1977), this suggests a shadow price of $28,000 for a mastectomy. In this situation, Abt suggests that the additional costs for a few more drugs and drinks would bring the annual average shadow price of grief and worry to about $3,000. Often times the analyst can only identify the need to shadow price an intangible benefit. For example, one intangible that is difficult to shadow price is the benefit of restored fertility capacity that follows a successful kidney transplant.

The shadow price concept can also be applied to arrive at quality weights for adjusting the value of additional years of existence. Klarman (1965) utilized an analogous disease approach to measure the willingness-to-pay value of escape from early manifestations of syphilis by the proxy disease psoriasis, and the late manifestations of syphilis by the proxy of terminal cancer cases. Direct data acquisition for "unstigmatized" medical conditions like cancer and psoriasis was more easily accomplished than working directly with syphilis victims. Economists must work with physicians to develop proxies and weighting schemes for capturing the multiplicity of dimensions of health care outputs. Inappropriate priorities might be set if survival probabilities are not integrated with quality-of-life factors.

A growing number of physician surveys have focused on diagnostic decisions. Two suggested approaches present evidence as to just how advanced, and complex, medical risk assessment has become in the 1980s. Spiegelhalter and Knill-Jones (1984) favor computing diagnostic probabilities by forming a control group which is a combination of all the other diagnostic categories. This conceptual approach deals with the real world problem in which patients may possess several diagnoses simultaneously. Alternatively, Begg and McNeil (1985) suggest a decomposition in which each diagnostic group is separately treated with a baseline (normal) category as more appropriate in the absence of complex, equally critical, multiple condition, cases. Both approaches are equally valid, but the second approach may be more generalizable (and easier to explain to clinicians).

Individual physicians will not see a large number of specific instances of any specific rare condition in their practice, but individual subjective opinion is useful. As Kahneman et al. (1982) point out, most predictions contain an irreducible intuitive component. The intuitive threshold estimates of good clinicians contain useful information, even if biased in a predictable manner. Doctors often have more specific observations about the patient than can be evaluated by long-run statistical analysis. As Fryback (1985) has indicated, subjective probabilities are not just the "stuff we do before the statistician arrives."

Consumer surveys are prevalent in the area of consumer decisions (Eastaugh, 1983). The consumer utility literature has benefited from the recent development of more sophisticated scales for measuring preference functions and indifference curves. Stewart et al. (1975) and Grogono and Woodgate (1971) developed refined, but unvalidated, scales for measuring physical, social, psychiatric, and mobility limitations. The psychometric approach provided only marginal improvements over the 1948 Visick scales. Recently, multi-attribute utility theory has been applied to evaluate the benefits of treating sore throats (Giaque and Peebles, 1976) and cleft lips in children (Krischer, 1976). Indifference curve analysis has been suggested as another approach to quantifying benefits. Newhouse (1979) has described an indifference curve along which combined sickness, pain, and restricted activity day composite measures of suffering are weighted equally undesirable. The best practical application of these concepts is provided by Weinstein et al. (1977) in their assessment of quality-of-life considerations after coronary artery bypass surgery. Quality-of-life outcome measures include pain at rest, pain with minimal activity, pain with mild activity, pain with strenuous activity, and no pain. Quite predictably, a potential surgical patient places a higher utility value on no pain if he or she avoids exercise. A utility function to value outcomes was specified as a function of life-style and life expectancy. The data are highly subjective, but reliance on imperfect analysis provides more insights than analytical nihilism.

Cost-effectiveness analysis is more frequently completed because intangible benefits need only be estimated, not valued. Cost-effectiveness analysis requires only that all benefits be expressed in commensurate units so that the cost of achieving a specified level of benefits might be minimized. Cost-effectiveness is not any simpler than cost-benefit analysis if multiple varieties of benefit are specified (lives, years, pain), except that in doing cost-benefit analysis one must also value intangible benefits.

Net Present Value Analysis: Discounting

The uneven distribution of costs and benefits over time poses little conceptual difficulty for the analyst. One simply reduces the stream of future costs and benefits to net present value by discounting. The most common rationale for discounting social programs to present value reflects the uncertainty of the future: A benefit in hand is worth two in the future. In contrast, health economists have downplayed the business sector rationale for discounting, which is the time value of money. In the business sector uncertainty is always incorporated through the use of decision trees. A form of discounting, net present cost analysis, was used in Chapter 10 to evaluate buy/lease decisions for new equipment.

The discount rate is designed to reflect the opportunity cost of postponing benefits or expenditures for an uncertain future. Arrow and Lind (1970) posit that the yield on private investment can be properly regarded as the appropriate opportunity yield for public investment only if the subjective cost of risk-bearing is the same for the average taxpayer as it is for the private investor. Musgrave (1969) indicates that the benchmarks should be a function of the source of financing; private consumption has a higher discount rate than public investment. What is most frequently misunderstood by noneconomists is that inflation is only one part of the rationale for discounting. Even if all benefits were adjusted for the projected rate of inflation, discounting would still be necessary to account for the social rate of time preference. Discounting future years of life implies no utilitarian value judgment. It only presumes that benefits and costs must be juxtaposed and measured in commensurable dollar units at a single given discount rate. Choice of a discount rate is of no consequence for a short-lived program with benefits and costs concentrated within one to two years.

Selection of the rate of discount is a crucial parameter in most net present value calculations. For example, Jackson et al. (1978) reported that elective hysterectomy is only justified on tangible cost grounds if the discount rate is under 4 percent. Waaler and Piot (1970) reported in a cost-effectiveness analysis of tuberculosis control measures that discount rates greater than 6 percent favor case-finding and treatment, whereas a lower discount rate would favor a vaccination program. Discount rate selection is crucial for evaluating screening programs that yield benefits 20 to 60 years in the future. A prediction that technology will become more cost-increasing in the future argues for a lower discount rate selection in order to make lifesaving more valuable in future years. This viewpoint is supported by the suggestion that technology is reaching a state of diminishing returns where even an optimistic 50 percent reduction in the three leading causes of death (cardiovascular disease, cancer, and motor vehicle accidents) would add less than one year of life for people aged 15–65 (Tsai et al., 1978). There are three basic varieties of discount rates: (1) the corporated discount rate if the private sector borrowed the funds, (2) the government borrowing rate on bond issues in the marketplace, and (3) the social discount rate to enable programs and procedures with benefits far in the future to prove more acceptable.

The social discount rate is probably the most often used because of the strength of the intergenerational equity argument. For example, a $25 million one-shot project in 1990 with a payoff of $75 million in the year 2010 only has a positive net present value if the discount rate is 6 percent or less. The typical social discount rate is on the order of 4–6 percent. However, a bias against the value of future generations might still remain apparent to some futurists if they realized that at a 5 percent discount rate, 30 deaths in 2060 are exactly equivalent to 1 death in 1990. To those political scientists and welfare economists concerned with ethical issues, any discount rate will have some slight bias in favor of present generations (a counterargument might be Keynes's rejoinder that "in the long run we are all dead").

Opportunity cost principles argue for a high discount rate. The true cost of a health care investment is the return that could have been achieved if the resources had gone elsewhere in the private sector. For Mishan (1976) and Fisher (1973), the relevant comparison is not the expected rate of return but the expected rate of return net of the subjective costs of risk-bearing. The first option, the corporate discount rate, is obviously overinflated since it includes both a risk premium and a markup for corporate taxes. In order to achieve equivalent after-tax investor earnings, a corporation must offer stockholders a 10 percent return (that is, a 15 percent before-tax gross return) to compete with a riskless municipal bond returning 7.25 percent. Operationally, the second choice, government borrowing rates, serves as the upper bound in most analyses. Given the implicit assumption that the discount rate is not changing over time, the most prudent course of action is to perform a sensitivity analysis of the net present value under a range of discount rates. If a sensitivity analysis can demonstrate that selection of a discount rate does not affect the recommendations, then the tenuousness of the assumption will not be a source for concern.

The last discounting issue that must be considered is the selection of an appropriate downward adjustment to reflect the degree to which the medical price index exceeds the consumer price index (CPI). Klarman et al. (1968) were the first to incorporate a net discount rate adjusted downward by 1 to 2 percent to reflect the extent that growth in medical prices exceeded the growth in the CPI. Jackson et al. (1978) utilized a downward adjustment of 5 percent to reflect the excess of medical inflation relative to inflation in the general economy. This net discount rate factor reflects the value of direct health service foregone costs (benefits) that would also have increased by the excess of the medical price index over the CPI. If cost containment programs were to bring the medical inflation rate to parity with the CPI, then this adjustment would be unnecessary.

Applications of Cost-Benefit Analysis to Therapeutic Treatment

Both analysts and decision makers disagree over how to value the intangible benefits of health programs. Most decision makers find the valuation process in cost-benefit analysis difficult and do not trust analyses that depend on gross approximations, small samples, and a poor data base. These decision makers are willing to violate the efficiency criteria and invest more in hospitals and physicians than society receives as a return on the dollar. Society might profit from having a more healthy skepticism concerning therapeutic treatments. Many therapies will exhibit dramatic benefits on introduction and require no cost-benefit analyses. For example, the dramatic 90 percent decline in the fatality rate from heart block exhibited after introduction of cardiac pacemakers in 1968 is a classic example of a clearly cost-beneficial new treatment mode. However, as Lewis Thomas (1977) observed, modern medicine increasingly creates "half-way" technologies like bypass surgery or heart transplants and "complex" technologies like hemodialysis. Thomas reserves the label of a truly "sophisticated" technology for therapeutic treatments that eliminate the disease and restore the patient to prior health status. Consequently, a therapy like coronary artery bypass surgery is not sophisticated because it does nothing for the disease (arteriosclerosis). It has been assessed as having a low cost-effectiveness ratio because it does little to prolong life, but it almost always reduces chest pain for the 95–98 percent of patients surviving the operation (Weinstein et al., 1977).

Somewhere between 10 and 20 percent of new treatments might be prime candidates for cost-benefit studies to decide whether the benefits are worth the costs to society. A smaller percentage of established therapies might also deserve the same cost-benefit analysis. The policy issue is seldom one of cost-beneficial yes or no, but rather an issue of frequency. Obviously, if clinicians start treating more nonserious cases, the frequency of treatment skyrockets. For example, prophylactically treating slightly symptomatic conditions of appendicitis (Neutra, 1977), or completely asymptomatic conditions of disease without consequence (for example, cholecystitis; Ingelfinger, 1968) will dramatically decrease the benefit-to-cost ratio. It has been estimated that a program to treat asymptomatic silent gallstone carriers (15 million) would cost at least $45 billion (Fitzpatrick et al., 1977). One of the intangible benefits of doing an economic evaluation is that it may suggest to the medical community the benefits of decreasing overutilization by increasing the degree of discrimination through improved clinical interpretation skills. This policy is good medicine and good economics. For example, Neutra (1977) suggested that decreasing the removal rate of normal appendices will lead to slightly lower rates of perforation and other complications. One study in China reported a mere 0.2 percent mortality rate from nonsurgical treatment of appendicitis (China Medical Group, 1974).

Very few complete cost-beneficial studies have been published. Many times a limited cost-benefit analysis will lead to the most socially cost-effective clinical decision rules. For example, Schoenbaum et al. (1976) suggested that a single rubella vaccination at 12 years or at two ages would be better than the typical norm of a single vaccination for all children at an early age. Berwick et al.

(1975) suggested that hypercholesterolemia screening and treatment for children is more cost-beneficial than treatment and/or screening in adult years. This study also considered the issue of whether childhood screening is best done on the umbilical cord, all school-aged children, or high-risk school-aged children. The study suggested that selection of the discount rate determines whether the screen should be as liberal as 238 mgm for normal nonfamilial children or as conservative as 252 mgm for 10-year-old high-risk familial hypercholesterolemics. Sometimes the selection of a decision rule depends on how many intangible benefits are loaded onto the analysis. For example, prevention of Down's syndrome (mongolism) is a cost-beneficial screening venture for women over 40, but the screening for women age 35–39 is justified only if more disastrous psychological sequelae for the parents are postulated following the birth of an abnormal child.

Cost-benefit analysis can provide the justification for new or mandatory screening and treatment programs. Layde et al. (1979) reported a benefit-to-cost ratio of two ($4 billion/$2 billion) for a new multitiered alpha-fetoprotein screening program for detecting neural defects for a theoretical cohort of 100,000 American women. The mock analysis was necessary because the only existing data came from a small sample in Scotland. The study neglected many ethical issues and intangible benefit problems with a test that has only a 64 percent sensitivity—that is, the failure to identify an abnormality in a screened woman may result in more costly psychological sequelae than if the child had not been tested and declared healthy in utero.

Cost-benefit analysis can also be used to support expansion of an existing treatment program. Ward (1977) reported that an $8 billion hypertension control program would return a benefit to society of $10 billion. The suggestion that 6.1 million Americans with diastolic blood pressure above 105 mm undergo drug therapy was the by-product of a 1967–1969 controlled clinical trial on treatment effectiveness of males visiting Veterans Administration facilities. The two problems with hypertension control are the side effects of the drugs (dizziness, impotence, and malaise) and the problem of maintaining a high degree of patient compliance in nonexperimental situations. Finnerty et al. (1971) reported that patient compliance was 84 percent in the experimental situation but only 16 percent if the patient did not receive the "red carpet treatment." Before the nation spends $8 or $10 billion on hypertension, it seems reasonable to require that we make sure that the technology is effective (will not fail under normal conditions).

Frequently, the economic analyst is asked to perform a cost-benefit evaluation on a questionable treatment or mandatory screening program. For example, the Farber and Finkelstein (1979) cost-benefit study of mandatory premarital rubella-antibody screening dampened the initial enthusiasm for the program. In some cases, the evaluators need only look at the touted benefits in a more scientific fashion, with a randomized controlled trial, to conclude that the treatment has zero benefits. For example, the New York University 1973 study group, finding that hyperbaric oxygen provided no benefits for the elderly, eliminated enthusiasm for the treatment that had been stimulated by an unscientific study published in a nationally acclaimed journal in 1969 (Jacobs et al., 1969). The oxygen "treatment" cost $2,500 per week in 1970. The easy acceptance of a faulty, but profitable, treatment seems to be rather unprofessional if one views medicine as a science. For example, the time lag between general acceptance and proof of zero benefits was seven years in the case of gastric freezing as a cure for ulcers (1962–1969) and five years for internal mammary artery ligation surgery (1956–1961). The duration of the acceptance of faulty treatments was much longer in the early 1900s. For more than a quarter of a century, physicians tried to cure constipation with surgery (1906–1933) and treat menopausal symptoms with ptosis surgery (1890–1928) (Barnes, 1977).

Health education, which has been assailed by skeptics, is a popular current example of a new approach to improving the effectiveness of medical care. Table 16.1 represents the results of a limited benefit-cost comparison of four approaches to increasing patient compliance to antihypertensive medications. The study sample included 402 patients randomly assigned to experimental and control groups. The emphasis of the study concerned the efficacy of utilizing a triage process, whereby patients are subdi-

Table 16.1 Simple Benefit-to-Cost Comparisons of Triage Options Versus the Option Not to Triage in Achieving Improved Medication Compliance Among Hypertensives

Option	Triage	Type of Patients	IHC[a]	Health Education Intervention(s)	Benefit-Cost Ratio
1	Yes	High Level of Depression	65–26	Family Reinforcement (FR)	2.20[b]
2	Yes	Medium Level of Depression	58–33	FR + Message Clarification	1.15
3	Yes	No Depression	65–35	FR + Message Clarification	1.33
4	No	All Patients	60–32	FR + Message Clarification	1.24

SOURCE: Eastaugh and Hatcher (1982).
[a]IHC = Increase in number of high compliers with treatment versus control per hundred patients.
[b]Only option 1 has a significantly better ratio for triaging in comparison to not triaging.

vided into groups more predisposed to benefit from a given health education approach. The benefits of the triage method for achieving medication compliance clearly outweigh the cost only in the case of the highly depressed patients (24.3 percent of the sample), as defined by responses to five of the seven items used in the depression scale questionnaire. The benefit-to-cost ratio for the group (2.2) compares favorably with the average benefit-to-cost ratio of 1.24 for hypertension control for persons in the age range of 35–65 (option 4). In other words, triaging only the 24 percent highly depressed subpopulation and providing family member reinforcement is more cost beneficial than giving everyone the special health education intervention. Previous studies demonstrating a cost-benefit ratio in the 1.1 to 1.3 range may not stand the test of time in claiming a statistically significant ratio above the 1.0 level when applied to a larger population or applied to a nonexperimental population that will be less susceptible to the Hawthorne effect. Individuals are known to change their behavior more dramatically under experimental conditions due to the mere fact of being under concerned observation.

Applications of Cost-Effectiveness Analysis

The purpose of cost-effectiveness analysis in the therapeutic arena is to identify the preferred alternatives. Physician preoccupation with survival probabilities must not preclude measurement of quality-of-life factors in performing a cost-effectiveness analysis. Cost-effectiveness analysis still requires that intangible factors be measured; however, they do not have to be valued. Typically, the search for preferred alternatives involves comparisons of less invasive treatment versus radical surgery—for example, simple versus radical mastectomies; medical treatment versus bypass surgery; medical treatment versus doing a vagotomy for common duodenal ulcers; pyloroplasty versus antrectomy surgery for intractable duodenal ulcers; and internal urethrotomy versus uteral reimplantation for vesicoureteral reflux. In some cases the preferred alternative depends on treatment location—for example, home dialysis versus facility-based dialysis.

Cost-effectiveness analyses usually report either costs per unit of desired benefit achieved or units of tangible benefits per dollar expended. For example, Schweitzer and Keating (1978) report a cost-effectiveness ratio for bone-marrow transplants of $433,000 per leukemia patient saved ($22,000 per man-year saved) and $125,000 per aplastic anemia patient saved ($8,000 per man-year saved). Romm and McKeon (1979) report a cost-effectiveness measure of 81 visits per $1,000 for a solo doctor and physician extender compared to 57 visits per $1,000 for a physician operating in solo practice.

However, in some analyses, the need for computing any ratio is obviated by the lack of any differential in effectiveness between treatment modes. In such cases, the lower cost mode is preferable. One randomized study (Hill et al., 1978) of the cost-effectiveness of home versus hospital care in the coronary care unit (CCU) for heart attack victims (mild cases, originally seen at their homes) found no statistically significant difference in the six-week mortality between the two groups (13 percent). Another controlled trial (Hampton and Nicholas, 1978) that randomly allocated mobile coronary care unit (MCCU) and routine ambulances to answer emergency calls found no differential in prehospital coronary mortality rates (47 percent). Despite the comments on high costs of CCUs and MCCUs, and in view of the concern for lack of substantially improved outcomes following the public expenditure of more resources for such technologies, groups of cardiologists continue to support the more institutionalized modes of therapy. Coincidentally, the cardiologists derive higher fees from hospital utilization. The prudent decision maker might suggest that CCUs and MCCUs should continue to be utilized in carefully controlled pilot study settings until effectiveness can be clearly established. One does not want to impede innovation if a period of trial and improvement can produce a more cost-effective alternative.

Decision Analysis and Physician Involvement

Many physician-directed cost-effectiveness analyses ignore larger social issues in considering questions of whether a given procedure during an operation is worth the effort. For example, Skillings et al. (1979) rejected the concept of routine operative cholangiography since the technique detected only two unsuspected cases of "silent" gallstones at an average cost of $6,612. The authors rejected operative cholangiography if performed either routinely or for isolated silent small stones in the gallbladder. The Skillings study ignores the issues of false-positives (reported diseased when in fact healthy) yielding unnecessary surgery and mortality associated with increased time under anesthesia. However, including these negative benefits would only reinforce the case against operative cholangiography. Alon et al. (1979) performed a randomized trial and cost-effectiveness analysis of bypass patients treated under bubble oxygenators and membrane oxygenators. The more expensive membrane oxygenator brings no lasting benefits beyond the second postoperative day and is therefore only recommended for extended open heart procedures on high-risk patients. In some cases the analysis is touted as a cost-benefit analysis, when in fact it does not technically even qualify as a cost-effectiveness analysis. For example, a myringotomy with tube insertion is labeled cost-beneficial compared to the possibility of a foregone tympanoplasty simply because the relative fees are $75 and $925, respectively (Armstrong and Armstrong, 1979).

Decision analysis techniques incorporate the probabilities (assessed from data or expert opinion) of chance events and the values a patient or decision maker assigns to the benefits and risks to yield prescriptive thresholds (e.g., above or below this level, one would do X course of action). Decision analysis continues to be limited by the difficulties inherent in eliciting and quantifying willingness to pay dollar valuation for health status improvements (or deterioration). One increasingly popular alternative, threshold analysis, attempts to derive the thresholds that physicians actually use to guide their choices (Eisenberg et al., 1984). Unfortunately, there is no statistical method to compare the summary measure of thresholds that is derived from the distribution of doctors' thresholds (or patients' thresholds). Young et al. (1986) suggest two methods of developing a summary measure of the thresholds for groups of physicians. The first method, unweighted mean of the midpoints, indicates confidence limits of means and standard *t*-tests to compare different groups (e.g., cardiologists have higher thresholds than family practitioners). The second method, weighted standard error of the mean, involves the determination of confidence intervals and weighted regressions to compare weighted means of the midpoints of threshold ranges. Future research should compare derived thresholds (by either of the two methods), relative to the more familiar prescriptive thresholds obtained in decision analysis, to ascertain which technique holds more promise in health care.

One recent study in the fall of 1985 compared the expert opinion decision analysis approach versus the prescriptive threshold analysis approach, in the case of coronary bypass surgery. Decision analysis criteria were compared to the care strategy proposed by 61 randomly selected board-certified cardiologists (Manu and Runge, 1985). The 61 cardiologists surveyed demonstrated a fairly inaccurate factual knowledge regarding the probabilities involved in the diagnostic process. As a group, the 61 cardiologists performed suboptimally relative to decision analysis, underutilizing coronary angiography and overusing radionuclide exercise imaging for patients with unequivocally positive EKG stress tests. In addition, the intuitive thresholds for the use of angiography had little association with the judged probability of severe coronary artery disease. Unfortunately, valid and reliable decision analytical models only exist for a few dozen therapeutic and diagnostic situations. Decision analysis models, when updated with better quality expert opinion, can be utilized to educate, calibrate, and improve practitioner decision-making guidelines.

Policy Considerations

Cost-benefit analysis should increasingly assist government and third-party insurance carriers in inhibiting the financing of halfway technologies that provide palliative relief but not a definitive treatment. If it is politically difficult to underfinance therapies that are not cost-beneficial, then government can intervene on the development side to limit technological diffusion to a few well-evaluated pilot studies. If the evaluation suggests that the treatment mode is definitive and worth the price tag, then the new technology should diffuse through the medical sector.

An example of a complete and technically competent cost-effectiveness analysis is the comparison by Piachaud and Weddell (1972) of medical versus surgical removal of varicose veins. Fifty men and two hundred women were allocated at random to either surgery or injection-compression sclerotherapy. Direct costs were fourfold higher for the surgical group. The treatment in the medical group involved seven clinic visits, in comparison to the surgical treatment that required three to four days of hospitalization and two clinic visits. The time cost to the patient was 100 hours for surgery and 30 hours for medical treatment. The opportunity cost to the economy was 31 workless days for surgery and 7.5 days for medical therapy. After three years of follow-up, there existed no clinical basis for selecting either mode of therapy. There may be many treatments or procedures in medicine that, like varicose vein surgery, are effective, but less cost-effective than a recently developed alternative. The widespread disdain for randomized experimentation and the general acceptance of existing techniques among the physician community might retard the research and development of more efficient and equally effective alternatives.

Economic evaluation and decision analysis do not merit the unmitigated pessimism of Ransohoff and Feinstein (1976), who characterized it as a "computerized Ouija board." As Albert (1978) pointed out, the true role of evaluation in medicine lies between the pessimism of the Ouija board and the naive optimism of a "new Rosetta stone." The direct value of economic evaluation is that it can erode some of the areas of the unknown that surround the benefit-to-cost assumptions implicit in the behavior of physicians and administrators. Evaluation should be viewed as a consumerist cause if it forces those in power to be explicit about valuation assumptions in cost-benefit calculations and the resource cut-off level required in cost-effectiveness ranking decisions. The indirect benefit of economic evaluation is that it might teach health professionals to apply their craft only to the point where the marginal benefits equal the marginal costs. The credulity of economists and regulators has been taxed by the disorderly diffusion of every new unproven technology. A possible intangible benefit of the evaluation process lies in the hope that cost-effective clinical decision-making principles will seep into the subconscious cognitive process of American physicians and result in a less costly style of medical care.

It would take a high degree of naive optimism to suggest that economic analysis can produce a matrix of relative benefits, measured in quality-of-life points. Will quality improvements be cost-increasing, cost-decreasing, or self-financing, with the cost savings counterbalancing the cost increases? The conventional wisdom is that quality is cost-increasing. However, doing things right the first time should potentially diminish the cost of services per patient. Doing things incorrectly, unnecessarily, or repetitively is what costs money. Consider an example in the context of ordering diagnostic tests. If a large enough number of tests are ordered on a healthy person, just due to random variation one or more false-positive results will emerge. The experience will lead the patient on an anxiety-provoking, costly journey through unnecessary follow-up tests and procedures, only to be eventually discharged free of disease (provided the hospital did not provide an iatrogenic infection). This situation was labeled the "Ulysses syndrome" by Rang (1972) in memory of an individual who took a detour and was pulled into a series of unnecessary tests and dangerous adventures. By trimming the frequency of diagnostic and therapeutic misadventures, the resulting cost savings can more than outweigh the costs of investments in quality-control systems and continuing education.

More hospitalization costs per case do not always generate superior patient outcomes when studied over a time horizon of several months. Garber et al. (1984) compared the differences between faculty and private/community services within a university medical center for several DRGs. In a 12-month time frame, the faculty service had created higher levels of expense but had not improved patient survival relative to community physicians. Almost 30 percent more of the patients on the faculty service survived hospitalization, but at the end of 12 months the survival curves for the 48 pairs of matched patients were identical in both settings.

It is impossible to do a cost-benefit analysis of a hospital. Rather, hospitals should be viewed as flexible collections of medical technologies, where the benefit-cost possibilities of each technology need to be assessed separately. From the foregoing discussion it is clear that economists should be encouraged to address themselves to clinical applications of normative economic techniques (cost-benefit, cost-effectiveness, decision analysis). Aside from public health applications of cost-benefit analysis to polio and syphilis, few complete studies have been conducted to date. Many studies avoid the issue of valuation and perform limited cost-effectiveness analyses, and in the other cases the retreat is to provide only societal cost estimates of the impact of a disease or condition.

In view of the uncertainties implicit in any technological assessment effort, one might question whether medicine should lock itself into an expensive and unproven therapy, such as bone marrow transplants, as a type of standard treatment. A sliding fee schedule could be employed to make the utilization of expensive marginal technologies less profitable for the physicians. In order to create a positive incentive for physicians to evaluate and get experience with a new test or treatment, the fee could increase as the service is proven to be more valuable. This concept of a technology evaluation-sensitive fee schedule has already been suggested by Gaus and Cooper (1978). Another possible positive planning solution to stimulate less costly behavior may be the allowance of replacement cost reimbursement for depreciation at projected (higher) market prices if the hospital introduces cost-reducing technologies or tests, and/or phases out cost-increasing equipment and services of unproved efficacy. Negative planning solutions such as Certificate-of-Need program sanctions are another possible solution that are reviewed in Chapter 23. However, the coercion implicit in an effective negative planning approach inevitably adds to bureaucracy and creates barriers to innovation. Society should also fear any movement toward technology prohibition that creates disincentives for scientific inquiry merely because the economy cannot afford the implementation costs of every resulting procedure. The nation must strike some sort of balance between the relative risks of disorderly-promiscuous-diffusion versus orderly-slow-diffusion of new technologies, treatments, and tests.

References

ABT, C. (1977). "The Issue of Social Cost in Cost-Benefit Analysis of Surgery." In J. Bunker, B. Barnes, and F. Mosteller (eds.), *Costs, Risks, and Benefits of Surgery*. New York: Oxford University Press.

ACTON, J. (1973). "Evaluating Public Programs to Save Lives: The Case of Heart Attacks." Rand Corporation Report R-950-RC. Santa Monica: Rand Corporation.

ALBERT, D. (1978). "Decision Theory in Medicine: A Review and Critique." *Milbank Memorial Fund Quarterly* 56:3 (Summer), 362–400.

ALON, L., TURINA, M., and GATTIKER, R. (1979). "Membrane and Bubble Oxygenator: A Clinical Comparison in Patients Undergoing Bypass Procedures." *Herz* (German) 4, 56–62.

ARMSTRONG, B., and ARMSTRONG, R. (1979). "Tympanostomy Tubes: Their Use, Abuse, and Cost-Benefit Ratio." *Laryngoscope* 89:3 (March) 443–449.

ARROW, K., and LIND, R. (1970). "Uncertainty and the Evaluation of Public Investment Decisions." *American Economic Review* 60:3 (June), 364–378.

BAILEY, M. (1980). *Reducing Risks to Life: Measurement of the Benefits*. Washington, D.C.: American Enterprise Institute.

BARNES, B. (1977). "Discarded Operations: Surgical Innovation by Trial and Error." In J. Bunker, B. Barnes, and F. Mosteller (eds.), *Costs, Risks, and Benefits of Surgery*. New York: Oxford University Press.

BECKER, G. (1964). *Human Capital*. New York: National Bureau of Economic Research.

BEGG, C., and MCNEIL, B. (1985). "Response: To the Use of the Polychotomous Model." *Medical Decision Making* 5:1 (Spring), 123–126.

BERRY, R., and BOLAND, J. (1977). *The Economic Cost of Alcohol Abuse*. New York: The Free Press.

BERWICK, D., KEELER, E., and CRETIN, S. (1975). "Screening for Cholesterol: Costs and Benefits." Report from the Center for the Analysis of Health Practices, Harvard School of Public Health.

CASKEY, J. (1985). "Modeling the Formation of Expectations: A Bayesian Approach." *American Economic Review* 75:4 (September), 768–776.

China Medical Group (1974). Report of the Acute Abdominal Conditions Research Group, "Some Problems in Nonoperative Treatment of Acute Appendicitis." *China Medical Journal* 2, 21–40.

COCHRANE, A. (1972). *Effectiveness and Efficiency*. London: Nuffield Provincial Hospitals Trust.

COOPER, B., and RICE D. (1976). "The Economic Cost of Illness Revisited." *Social Security Bulletin* 39:1 (February), 21–36.

EASTAUGH, S. (1983). "Placing a Value on Life and Limb: Role of the Informed Consumer." *Health Matrix* 1:1 (Spring), 5–21.

EASTAUGH, S., and HATCHER, M. (1982). "Improving Compliance Among Hypertensives: A Triage Criterion with Cost-Benefit Implications." *Medical Care* 20:10 (October), 1001–1017.

EISENBERG, J., SCHUMACHER, H., DAVIDSON, P., and KAUFMAN, L. (1984). "Usefulness of Synovial Fluid Analysis in the Evaluation of Joint Effusions: Use of Threshold Analysis and Likelihood Ratios to Assess a Diagnostic Test." *Archives of Internal Medicine* 144:4 (April), 715–719.

EVANS, R., LARSEN, R., and BURKE, J. (1986). "Computer Surveillance of Hospital-Acquired Infections and Antibiotic Use." *Journal of the American Medical Association* 256:8 (August 29), 1007–1011.

FARBER, M., and FINKELSTEIN, S. (1979). "A Cost-Benefit Analysis of a Mandatory Premarital Rubella-Antibody Screening Program." *New England Journal of Medicine* 300:15 (April 12), 856–859.

FEINSTEIN, A. (1977). "Clinical Biostatistics: The Haze of Bayes, the Aerial Palaces of Decision Analysis, and the Computerized Ouija Board." *Clinical Pharmacology and Therapeutics* 21:4 (April), 482–496.

FELDSTEIN, M. (1970). "Choice of Technique in the Public Sector." *Economic Journal* 80:320 (December), 985–990.

FINNERTY, F., et al. (1971). "Reasons for Poor Clinic Attendance." *Clinical Research* 19:10 (October), 500–510.

FISHER, A. (1973). "Environmental Externalities and the Arrow-Lind Public Investment Theorem." *American Economic Review* 63:4 (September), 722–726.

FITZPATRICK, G., NEUTRA, R., and GILBERT, J. (1977). "Cost-Effectiveness of Cholecystectomy for Silent Gallstones." In J. Bunker, B. Barnes, and F. Mosteller (eds.), *Costs, Risks, and Benefits of Surgery*. New York: Oxford University Press, 246–261.

FROMM, G. (1965). "Civil Aviation Expenditures." In R. Dorfman (ed.), *Measuring the Benefits of Government Investment*. Washington, D.C.: The Brookings Institution, 172–230.

FUCHS, V. (1986). *The Health Economy*. Cambridge, Mass.: Harvard University Press.

GARBER, A., FUCHS, V., and SILVERMAN, J. (1984). "Casemix, Costs and Outcomes: Differences Between Faculty and Community Services in a University Hospital." *New England Journal of Medicine* 310:23 (May 17), 1231–1237.

GAUS, C., and COOPER, B. (1978). "Technology and Medicare: Alternatives for Change." In R. Egdahl and P. Grertman (eds.), *Technology and the Quality of Health Care*. Germantown, Md.: Aspen, 225–236.

GIAQUE, W., and PEEBLES, T. (1976). "Application of Multidimensional Utility Theory in Determining Optimal Test-Treatment Strategies for Streptococcal Sore Throat and Rheumatic Fever." *Operations Research* 24:5 (September-October), 933–950.

GIBSON, G. (1976). "Regionalization and Emergency Medical Services: The Dance of the Lemmings." In E. Ginzburg (ed.), *Regionalization and Health Care*. DHEW, Washington, D.C.: U.S. Government Printing Office.

GLASS, N. (1973). "Cost Benefit Analysis and Health Services." *Health Trends* 5:1 (January), 51–60.

GROGONO, A., and WOODGATE, D. (1971). "Index for Measuring Health." *Lancet* 2:7738 (November 1), 1024–1029.

HAMPTON, J., and NICHOLAS, C. (1978). "Randomized Trial of Mobile Coronary Care Unit for Emergency Calls." *British Medical Journal* 10:6120 (April 29), 1118–1122.

HARDY, A., RAUCH, K., ECHENBERG, D., MORGAN, W., and CURRAN, J. (1986). "Economic Impact of the First 10,000 Cases of AIDS in the United States." *Journal of the American Medical Association* 255:2 (January 10), 209–211.

HILL, J., HAMPTON, J., and MITCHELL, J. (1978). "A Randomized Trial of Home-versus-Hospital Management for Patients with Suspected Myocardial Infarction." *Lancet* 1:8069 (April 22), 837–844.

INGELFINGER, F. (1968). "Digestive Disease as a National Problem-Case V—Gallstones." *Gastroenterology* 55, 102–110.

JACKSON, M., LoGERFO, J., DIEHR, P., WATTS, C., and RICHARDSON, W. (1978). "Elective Hysterectomy: A Cost-Benefit Analysis." *Inquiry* 15:3 (September), 275–280.

JACOBS, E., WINTER, P., and ALVIS, H. (1969). "Hyperoxygenation Effects of Cognitive Functioning in the Aged." *New England Journal of Medicine* 281:13 (October 2), 753–757.

KAHNEMAN, D., SLOVIC, P., and TVERSKY, A. (1982). *Judgment Under Uncertainty, Heuristics and Biases*. New York: Cambridge University Press.

KLARMAN, H. (1974). "Application of Cost-Benefit Analysis to the Health Services and the Special Case of the Technologic Innovation." *International Journal of Health Services* 4:3 (Fall), 325–352.

KLARMAN, H. (1967). "Present Status of Cost-Benefit Analysis in the Health Field." *American Journal of Public Health* 57:11 (November), 1948–1953.

KLARMAN, H. (1965). "Syphilis Control Programs." In R. Dorfman (ed.), *Measuring Benefits of Government Investments*. Washington, D.C.: The Brookings Institution, 367–410.

KLARMAN, H., FRANCIS, J., and ROSENTHAL, G. (1968). "Cost Effectiveness Analysis Applied to the Treatment of Chronic Renal Disease." *Medical Care* 6:1 (January-February), 48–54.

KRISCHER, J. (1976). "The Mathematics of Cleft Lip and Palate Treatment Evaluation: Measuring the Desirability of Treatment Outcomes." *The Cleft Palate Journal* 13:4 (April), 165–180.

LAYDE, P., ALLMEN, S., and OAKLEY, G. (1979). "Maternal Serum Alpha-Fetoprotein Screening: A Cost-Benefit Analysis." *American Journal of Public Health* 69:6 (June), 566–573.

MANU, P., and RUNGE, L. (1985). "Testing Stable Angina: Expert Opinion Versus Decision Analysis." *Medical Care* 23:12 (December), 1381–1390.

MISHAN, E. (1976). *Cost-Benefit Analysis*. New York: Praeger.

MUSGRAVE, R. (1969). "Cost-Benefit Analysis and the Theory of Public Finance." *Journal of Economic Literature* 7:3 (September), 797–806.

MUSHKIN, S. (1962). "Health as an Investment." *Journal of Political Economy* 70:5 (October), 129–157.

NEUTRA, R. (1977). "Indications for the Surgical Treatment of Suspected Acute Appendicitis: A Cost-Effectiveness Approach." In J. Bunker, B. Barnes, and F. Mosteller (eds.), *Costs, Risks, and Benefits of Surgery*. New York: Oxford University Press, 277–307.

NEWHOUSE, J. (1979). *The Economics of Medical Care*. New York: Addison-Wesley.

PHELPS, C. O. (1978). "Illness Prevention and Medical Insurance." *The Journal of Human Resources* 13 (Supplement), NBER Conference on the Economics of Physician and Patient Behavior, 183–207.

PIACHAUD, D., and WEDDELL, J. (1972). "The Economics of Treating Varicose Veins." *International Journal of Epidemiology* 1:3 (Autumn), 287–299.

RANG, M. (1972). "The Ulysses Syndrome." *Canadian Medical Association Journal* 106:2 (January 22), 122–127.

RANSOHOFF, D., and FEINSTEIN, A. (1976). "Is Decision Analysis Useful in Clinical Medicine?" *Yale Journal of Biology and Medicine* 49:2 (May), 165–179.

RICE, D. (1966). "Estimating the Cost of Illness." Health Economics Series No. 6. Washington, D.C.: U.S. Government Printing Office.

RICE, D., HODGSON, T., and KOPSTEIN, A. (1985). "The Economic Costs of Illness: A Replication and Update." *Health Care Financing Review* 7:1 (Fall), 61–80.

ROMM, J., and McKEON, M. (1979). "Survey and Evaluation of the Physician Extender Reimbursement Study: Cost-Effectiveness." System Sciences Inc. Consultants Report to DHEW, Health Care Financing Administration.

RUSSELL, L. (1985). *Is Prevention Better Than Cure?* Washington, D.C.: Brookings.

SCHELLING, T. (1986). "Economics and Cigarettes." *Preventive Medicine* 15:5 (September), 549–560.

SCHELLING, T. (1968). "The Life You Save May Be Your Own." In S. Chase (ed.), *Problems in Public Expenditure Analysis*. Washington, D.C.: The Brookings Institution, 127–162.

SCHOENBAUM, S., HYDE, J., BARTOSHESKY, L., and CRAMPTON, K. (1976). "Benefit-Cost Analysis of Rubella Vaccination Policy." *New England Journal of Medicine* 294:6 (February 5), 306–310.

SCHWARTZ, W., and AARON, H. (1984). "Rationing Hospital Care: Lessons from Britain." *New England Journal of Medicine* 310:1 (January 4), 52–56.

SCHWEITZER, S., and KEATING, M. (1978). "The Cost-Effectiveness of Bone-Marrow Transplant Therapy." Paper given at the American Public Health Association Annual Meeting, Los Angeles, October 17.

SHELTON, R. (1986). "St. Louis Plans Cost Management Program." *Blue Cross and Blue Shield Consumer Exchange* (April), 3.

SKILLINGS, J., WILLIAMS, J., and HINSHAW, J. (1979). "Cost-Effectiveness of Operative Cholangiography." *American Journal of Surgery* 137:1 (January), 26–30.

SPIEGELHALTER, D., and KNILL-JONES, R. (1984). "Statistical and Knowledge-Based Approaches to Clinical Decision-Support Systems, with an Application in Gastroenterology." *Journal of R. Statistical Society* 147:1 (Series A), 35–77.

STEWART, A., WARE, J., and JOHNSTON, S. (1975). "Construction of Scales Measuring Health and Health-Related Concepts from the Dayton Medical History Questionnaire." In *The Conceptualization and Measurement of Health in the Health Insurance Study*. Santa Monica: Rand Corporation.

TSAI, S., LEE, E., and HARDY, R. (1978). "The Effect of a Reduction in Leading Causes of Death: Potential Gains in Life Expectancy." *American Journal of Public Health* 68:10 (October), 966–971.

VISICK, A. (1948). "A Study of the Failures After Gasterectomy." *Annals of the Royal College of Surgeons* 3, 266–281.

WAALER, H., and PIOT, M. (1970). "Use of an Epidemiological Model for Estimating the Effectiveness of Tuberculosis Control Measures." *Bulletin of the World Health Organization* 43, 1–16.

WARD, G. (1977). "National High Blood Pressure Program." Report from The National Institutes of Health to the Congressional Office of Technological Assessment.

WARNER, K. (1978). "Effects of Hospital Cost Containment on the Development and Use of Medical Technology." *Milbank Memorial Fund Quarterly* 56:2 (Spring), 187–211.

WEINSTEIN, M., PLISKIN, J., and STASON, W. (1977). "Coronary Artery Bypass Surgery: Decision and Policy Analysis." In J. Bunker, B. Barnes, and F. Mosteller (eds.), *Costs, Risks, and Benefits of Surgery*. New York: Oxford University Press, 342–371.

WEISBROD, B. (1968). "Income Redistribution Effects and Benefit-Cost Analysis." In S. Chase (ed.), *Problems in Public Expenditure Analysis*. Washington, D.C.: Brookings Institution, 177–209.

YOUNG, M., EISENBERG, J., WILLIAMS, S., and HERSHEY, J. (1986). "Comparing Aggregate Estimates of Derived Thresholds for Clinical Decisions." *Health Services Research* 20:6 (February 1), 763–780.

Chapter 17

THE ROLE OF MEDICAL TECHNOLOGY ASSESSMENT

> *Medline Research Service does not list the word "health" in its index. In a teaching hospital there is no such thing as a healthy patient. A healthy patient is one who has not been sufficiently worked up at high cost. Come to a teaching hospital as a Medicare patient with the complaint of "stiff hands in the morning" and we will send you to rheumatology for a workup to discover Lupus in one case per 1,000 screened.*
>
> —JOHN G. FREYMANN, M.D.

> *If humans are distinguished from other primates by their need to take drugs, then physicians must be distinguished by their need to order tests.*
>
> —WILLIAM OSLER, M.D.

Medical technology assessment is becoming an increasingly important topic for physicians and health policy makers (Institute of Medicine, 1985). Formal training in cost-effective clinical decision making for residents and medical students is a potential alternative to further coercive federal cost containment efforts. If further regulatory ventures are to be avoided, and the dual goals of cost containment and quality achieved, physicians should be taught in their formative clinical years to apply parsimony and efficiency principles in ordering tests and treatments. Many published physician reports misuse basic concepts (e.g., cost-effectiveness; Doubilet et al., 1986). This chapter examines the question of whether exposure to such instruction changes attitudes among medical students electing to take a course on decision analysis and health economics. Further research is needed as to the timing and

465

content of the most cost-effective means of promoting cost-effective clinical decisions. Ethical and social issues raised by cost-benefit and cost-effectiveness applications are also discussed. The chapter concludes with a survey of clinical protocols, physician profiles, and McNeil's (1985) innovative approach to preferred practice patterns (PPP).

Economics and Medicine

Future physicians must realize that cost-benefit analysis and cost-effectiveness analysis are tools that can produce better informed decisions. However, as we have seen in Chapter 16, these two analytical techniques have occasionally been oversold in the health sector because of the multiplicity of dimensions of health service output and the difficulty of comparing disparate types of health benefits. Economic techniques should not be sold as value-free mathematics. However, without such analysis, decision making will remain ad hoc, with the assumptions hidden and the value judgments implicit. Some decision makers may want their values and assumptions to be kept secret and free from refutation, rather than to be made public and explicit.

The Congressional Office of Technology Assessment (U.S. Congress, 1980) evaluation of cost-effectiveness and cost-benefit applications in the health field concluded that the conceptual and practical limitations of the techniques are such that they should not be considered definitive tools that produce "correct" decisions. For example, construction of a hospice may not be justified merely by the projected medical cost savings, but the humanitarian intangible benefits (bereavement support, etc.) might more than justify the investment. According to the Office of Technology Assessment report, the analyst's role is one of information-generation and decision-assistance, because limited resources typically preclude valuation of intangible benefits.

As we shall observe in Chapter 23, regulators and politicians have not been effective at rationing the availability of a new hospital technology through planning legislation. Traditionally, once the supply is in place we deal ineffectively with rationing decisions. For example, Rettig (1978) documented a classic case of the physician community's inability to cope with ethical issues in the rationing of renal dialysis care after Shana Alexander published the November 1962 *Life* magazine article, "They Decide Who Lives, Who Dies." The American tradition has been to make local selective choices through critical care committees rather than to implement an "all or none" rationing decision; that is, everyone is allowed access or no one is allowed access as with most European countries. A legal scholar in Boston wrote a hypothetical Supreme Court decision for the year 2000 that upholds the concept of a national lottery for distribution of artificial hearts (Annas, 1977). The author pointed out that American society cannot accept "all or none" rationing.

Frequently, economic evaluations consider questions of whether a procedure or treatment should be done more or less frequently. For example, Cole (1976) reported that performing one million prophylactic hysterectomies would save $1.4 billion (mostly in the form of 35,000 prevented cases of cancer), but cost $2.9 billion. The congressional study on unnecessary surgery estimated the cost of excess and inappropriate elective surgery at $4 billion in 1976 (U.S. Congress, 1976).

Since the reader may not have conceptualized excess utilization in graphic terms, Figure 17.1 illustrates three possible scenarios

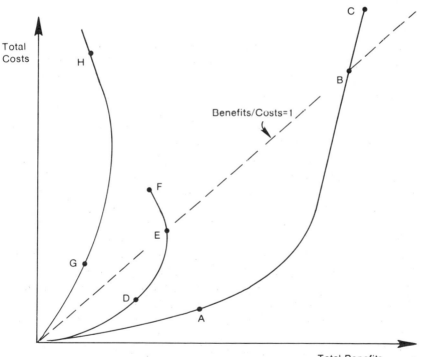

Figure 17.1   Three Hypothetical Production Functions of Total Treatment Benefits as a Function of Total Costs

for medical treatment production functions. Curve AB represents a cost-beneficial treatment mode such as heart pacemakers. If the technology were inappropriately utilized or prophylactically prescribed for an indiscriminately large fraction of the population, the assessed technology could move along the curve into the region BC where benefits do not justify costs. Hypothetical curve DE might represent the benefit-cost range when surgeons perform only 110,000 coronary artery bypass operations annually, but the treatment may appear unjustified (region EF) if the operative incidence increases to 180,000 annual bypass cases. More recently, Brott et al. (1986) suggested that many of the 60,000 annual carotid endarterectomies may be medically unnecessary. The number of endarterectomies increased 74 percent in the Cincinnati area from 1980 to 1984. In 1984, half of the procedures were performed in patients with asymptomatic carotid disease, at a combined stroke or death rate of 5.3 percent. This rate was higher than the 3.0 percent suggested rate for prophylactic carotid endarterectomies. Brott et al. (1986) called for a more conservative (less surgical) treatment of asymptomatic cases and future randomized clinical trials to assess the benefits of medical (antiplatelet agents and risk factor reduction) versus surgical treatment.

The third hypothetical curve GH is an example of a treatment mode that is never cost-beneficial (for example, gastric freezing for ulcers; Miao, 1977). Unfortunately, the public had to endure the fad from the introductory usage stage at point G (1962) to peak popularity at point H (1968), before the faulty treatment mode (gastric freezing) was finally discredited (1969).

Ethical and Social Issues

In the United States we allow any individual who can afford it to buy any technology, and we selectively finance transplants and less effective technologies from the public treasury. Questions of cost-benefit and resource limitations do disturb some American physicians and prompt the medical community to ask how we can afford dialysis and transplants during a resurgence of polio and other childhood diseases. In contrast to England, America has said that a citizen should not be barred from the opportunity to receive tertiary care services if he or she can afford them. Whereas England has made the slogan "health care as a right" operational by funding all primary and secondary care service activities, frequently individuals are not allowed to buy even proven technologies that are judged too expensive for the society. One of the demands during the British hospital strikes in the mid-1970s was that private pay patients not be allowed to have medically unnecessary services performed (Eastaugh, 1983). For the 91 percent of the British population utilizing the British National Health Service as their primary provider, publicly funded bypass surgery and heart and renal transplants are now available for those willing to wait two to four months. In America, obtaining most basic medical services is done through a process similar to the search for any other consumer good (that is, the family plans and budgets for the purchase), but obtaining very expensive new services is very often a matter of chance. It is possible that this situation reflects consumer preferences, in that the American consumer may value the assurance that comes with knowing that the nation can provide the utmost care for a given individual following the onset of a catastrophic disease.

Economic evaluation of common diseases will probably continue to receive more critical assessment than innovations for rare diseases that pose a less significant net financial burden in spite of the higher unit costs. An innovation like coronary bypass surgery has attracted the attention of the health services research community in the United States because expenditures have rocketed from zero to $5 billion per year within a single decade. Economic impact considerations should be a critical determinant in selecting the procedures for randomized clinical trials (RCT). Neuhauser (1979) has pointed out the dangerous limitations that short-sighted ethical considerations impose if they become the sole determinant of RCT experimentation. He argues that in some cases proposed sham operations (for example, telling the patient the operation was performed when in actuality it was not) should not be stopped by the local human subject committee of the hospital. For example, internal mammary artery ligation therapy was exposed by eight pairs of sham operations as an ineffective multimillion dollar mode of treatment. Neuhauser suggests an appropriate reward for the eight patients who saved our economy and the public chest: "Each should receive $1 million tax-free and be flown to the White House to shake hands with the President." The economy may be wasting tens of billions of dollars on unnecessary care because of the failure to perform RCTs.

The less tangible quality-of-life benefits comprise an increasing proportion of medical care benefits. For example, elective surgical expenditures are properly intended to achieve less tangible goals than mortality or morbidity rate reduction, such as relief of disability, pain, and disfigurement. Such quality-of-life factors are to be identified, then quantified in terms of their equivalent social

costs by shadow pricing, and finally balanced against commensurate shadow prices for quantity of life. Advocates of the "willingness-to-pay" approach suggest the maximization of lives saved as
the social objective function. Mishan (1971) has pointed out that
while our enlightened society can hardly avoid making these
analytical efforts, shadow pricing and value weighting present a
multitude of difficulties for research as we shall observe in Chapter
18. Because consumers are provided with imperfect information,
individuals' "willingness-to-pay" will sometimes be underestimated (e.g., vaccinations) and other times overestimated (e.g.,
laetrile).

Valuation problems still tend to plague most analyses. Subjective
questions concerning valuation and effectiveness are largely a
product of the values and occupation of the respondent. For
example, CAT (computerized axial tomography) scanner effectiveness to a radiologist is measured by whether the pictures are
clearer and the information is more detailed. The economist must
represent the public interest and ask whether there is a connection
between CAT scanning yielding better diagnosis, resulting in
better treatment, and ultimately improving patient outcome. The
radiologist's definition of effectiveness might argue for 7,000 CAT
scanners, with each hospital replacing its CAT machines every few
years because of marginal improvements (e.g., they "read spines
0.5 percent better").

A central dilemma that the economic analyst faces is the unsub-
stantiated thesis of ever-improving technology—that is, the assumption that any evaluation will be obsolete when completed
since medical science is improving so fast. Yet another problem
faced by the analyst attempting to do a prospective study is refusal
by the physicians to pursue randomized controlled trials if any hint
of inferiority among the alternatives can be raised as a "red
herring" to prevent the experiment. However, difficult decisions
will increasingly need to be made concerning the allocation of
scarce resources. Contrary to the conventional wisdom, the majority of Americans would like to place a dollar value on human life.
According to a 1981 national Harris Poll, 52 percent of the American public believe that government and the courts must attempt to
place an economic value on human life. Only 34 percent of the
national sample of the population disagreed with the need to put a
dollar value on life, and 14 percent responded "not sure" or "it
depends" (APHA, 1981).

Value judgments increasingly will have to be made by the
courts. For example, should patient X be provided with chloromy-
cetin if the drug is known to correlate weakly with fatal anemia.

Taking the drug increases the risk of dying from aplastic anemia from 1 in 500,000 to 1 in 40,000. How shall we decide when changing a probability distribution constitutes "causing" an event? This question has been raised in a wide range of circumstances, from auto safety to the case of swine flu vaccination side effects.

Consumer Cost Issues

The growth in third-party financing of medical care has frequently been criticized for funding excessive and/or inappropriate therapies. One postulated negative effect of health insurance is the increased financing of useless technologies like gastric freezing for ulcers. Another postulated negative by-product of the growth in health insurance is the utilization of treatments to an excess (see points C, F, H in Figure 17.2). The growth in health insurance coverage provided health care institutions with the wherewithal to expand service capability and produce service at the point where the cost exceeds the benefit. As health insurance becomes more comprehensive and the consumer's out-of-pocket cost falls to zero, health service institutions continue to provide care beyond the point where marginal cost is equal to marginal benefit (Q_2) up to point Q_3 (see Figure 17.2). The situation is somewhat analogous to

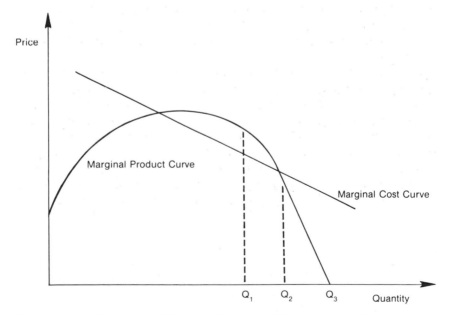

Figure 17.2   Hypothetical Marginal Benefit and Marginal Cost Curves

that of the consumer who visits an automobile showroom and asks
the dealer to select a car for him, price being no object. Because
the dealer's profit margin is higher if he provides a Mercedes
rather than a Mustang, the customer will never see the Mustang.

The present American economy cannot afford a Mercedes for
every consumer (point Q_3). In defense of production at point Q_3 is
the argument by the American medical establishment that it must
do the utmost for each patient irrespective of cost. Many economists argue that society can barely afford the Mustang unless we
decrease utilization rates by increasing the co-insurance paid by
patients. Future physicians should realize that relaxing the degree
of clinical discrimination and increasing the quantity of care provided per illness episode (intensity) will be curtailed by professional review organizations (PROs) and private utilization review
efforts. Moreover, doing the utmost for everybody will save a few
lives but at an ever diminishing rate. Production of Q_3 minus Q_1
additional units of medical service ignores the operative cost of
spending that money on housing or pollution control. Some analysts would hope that every dollar wasted in the medical economy
is a dollar not utilized on defense or nuclear power. However, it is
the broader health economy of prevention and public health that is
being squeezed by the growth in the medical economy.

Economic and Decision Theory Tools for Reducing "Little Ticket" Expenditures

A consideration to be dealt with in technology assessment is that
there is more to cost containment than simply preventing the
purchase of $500,000 machines. Many health planners assume that
the cost problem will disappear only if society can control the
purchase of "big ticket" items and so reduce the availability of
expensive therapeutic treatment approaches. A number of studies
in the 1970s (Maloney and Rogers, 1979) suggested that "little
ticket" items, such as laboratory tests and diagnostic procedures,
comprise the bulk of the cost crisis iceberg. Diagnostic charges
account for over 25 percent of total hospital expenditures, and
diagnostic testing costs have been increasing at almost double the
rate of total hospital costs (see Chapter 13). The efficiency and
increased costs of performing more diagnostic tests are central
issues in the public debate about rising medical costs. Twentyfold
variations in the number of diagnostic tests utilized by groups of
interns did not measurably affect the outcome following care for a
cohort of patients with ambulatory hypertensive disease (Daniels

and Schroeder, 1977). Providers continue to study little-ticket item volume. Consider the complete blood count (CBC), the laboratory test most often ordered in the emergency department. The $10 to $20 CBC test lacks the necessary specificity or sensitivity to benefit most emergency room patients (Young, 1986). Because absolute differential counts are more accurate than differential percentages, the clinician can rapidly enhance the data gained from any white blood count (WBC) and differential at no extra marginal cost. The absolute count of each leukocyte cell type is easily calculated from the total WBC count and the differential percentages reported by the lab. A little thinking can save a lot of little-ticket expenses for the patient and society.

The surgery study presented in Chapter 13 suggests that physician characteristics, such as degree of medical school affiliation and percentage of foreign medical graduates, are the best predictors of the number of elective tests ordered. John Knowles (1969) was one of the first physicians to link the cost and efficiency issues:

> *One should ask how many renal arteriograms in patients with hypertension have resulted in the surgical or medical cure of the patients' hypertension. . . . Increasingly we shall be asked to answer such questions, for our resources are not infinite nor is our share of the Gross National Product.*

Testing Specificity and Sensitivity

In considering the cost-effectiveness value of diagnostic tests, clinicians and medical students should be encouraged to consider three issues: (1) the reliability of test interpretation among physicians, (2) the specificity of the test, and (3) the marginal costs and benefits of additional testing. With respect to the reliability issue, there is wide disagreement among physicians over what constitutes a significant change in diagnostic test results for the same patient (Skendzel, 1978). The previously cited study by Daniels and Schroeder (1977) indicated a strong but not statistically significant correlation between poor clinical outcome and laboratory costs, suggesting that physicians who tend to be less competent use the laboratory more. A growing body of evidence indicates physician confusion in the interpretation and application of information contained in diagnostic tests (Eastaugh, 1981). This confusion tends to result in suboptimal patient care and high medical costs.

Obviously, diagnostic tests do not disclose the presence or absence of disease. They are merely tools to detect the presence or absence of particular signs or symptoms from which the presence or absence of a specific disease may be predicted. The following diagram illustrates the two-step sequence from testing to diagnosis.

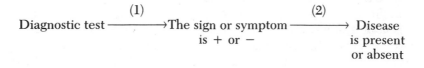

There are two points of potential slippage, each with its own implications, in the diagnostic testing procedure. Type one (1) breakdowns are often due to inadequate technology, which is translated into an inability to detect the target sign or symptom with adequate accuracy. It follows that these breakdowns often can be remedied by improving technology. Type two (2) breakdowns occur when the presence or absence of the target sign or symptom has a low predictive value for the presence or absence of disease. These breakdowns are inherent in the test and usually cannot be remedied.

Sensitivity and specificity analysis have traditionally been used to measure the efficacy of diagnostic tests. These values are determined by performing the test on two selected groups of subjects, those with disease and those without disease. They answer the questions: Given that the patient has the disease, how likely is he to have a positive test? Conversely, given that the patient doesn't have the disease, how likely is he to have a negative test? Sensitivity and specificity are rarely both 100 percent because diagnostic tests measure biologic variations that are then used to predict disease. These variations are usually distributed over a range of values roughly conforming to a normal curve. The curves representing the range of laboratory values of the diseased and the nondiseased population overlap. The more overlap, the greater the trade-off betweeen sensitivity and specificity.

Better specificity usually brings with it the trade-off of increases in the false-negative rate (erodes sensitivity). Determination of the patient sample size required to measure the false-negative rate to the researcher's specified degree of precision in two group comparison studies varies from 62 for a sensitivity of 0.80, to 298 for a sensitivity of 0.95, to a sample size of 1,552 for a sensitivity of 0.99 (Wears and Kamens, 1986). Such sampling concerns are important in projecting research costs and in estimating the smallest increase in false-negative rates that a study of a given size is likely to detect.

Diagnostic tests are used for at least three purposes: discovery, confirmation, and exclusion. Discovery tests must have high sensitivity and are used to detect disease in patients who seem healthy.

Confirmation tests must have high specificity and are used to verify disease in situations of strong suspicion.* Exclusion tests must have high sensitivity and are used to rule out disease in situations of suspicion, but are too expensive to use for discovery purposes. A test can be used for one, two, or all three purposes. Physicians and medical students should be encouraged to develop strategies utilizing combinations of tests that allow the achievement of both high sensitivity and high specificity.

Specificity and Fetal Monitoring

The importance of the specificity or false-positive issue has been raised recently in the context of fetal monitoring and renovascular disease screening among hypertensives. Banta and Thacker (1979) reported that the direct annual costs of electronic fetal monitoring in 1977 were $80 million, but that the indirect costs to both mother and child could exceed $300 million annually. The benefits of fetal monitoring are to be found in the degree to which early detection of fetal distress prevents mental retardation or death. The poor specificity of this diagnostic tool gives rise to many false-positive indications of fetal distress, contributing to 100,000 additional unnecessary Cacsarean sections in 1977 (costing $222 million). Future controlled clinical trials are necessary to determine whether there is a "best" mode of monitoring among the five (internal electronic monitoring, external electronic monitoring, diagnostic amniocentesis, scalp sampling, and ultrasonography). Banta and Thacker pointed to the need to acknowledge increased risk to the mother associated with pelvic infections or death from unnecessary operations, estimated at $58 million for 1977. In addition, there is another $50 million of estimated costs associated with the risk of infant hemorrhaging, respiratory distress, and infection at the site of the electrode.

The popularity of Caesarean deliveries has increased dramatically from 6 percent in 1972 to 25 percent of all births in 1986. According to many experts in the field, Caesarean deliveries (C-sections) and electronic fetal monitoring are being overutilized. Leveno et al. (1986) studied 35,000 deliveries in Dallas and found that continuous electronic monitoring of the fetal heart rate led to a significant increase in C-sections, but with no improvement in

---

* Sometimes it is better to avoid the confirmation test (e.g., a biopsy) and treat all highly suspect cases with the therapy [e.g., the anti-viral drug adenine arabinoside for herpes virus encephalitis (HVE)]. Braum (1980) demonstrated that it is better on the average to avoid the risk of brain biopsy and directly administer the drug on the basis of other tests.

health to the babies. C-sections obviously do harm to the health status of the mother, with more trauma and more resulting days off work. Regt et al. (1986) reported on a study of 65,600 deliveries at four Brooklyn hospitals that private physicians perform significantly more C-sections than doctors treating clinic patients, without improving the outcome for most babies. Demographic factors that have been related to higher rates of C-sections, such as percentage teenagers, medically complicated pregnancies, and low-birth weight, were all controlled for in these studies. Nonetheless, private patients had substantially higher C-section rates than clinic patients.

Payment incentives obviously feed the inflation in C-section rates and fetal monitoring utilization. Patient charges for C-sections are typically 90 to 120 percent higher than a normal vaginal delivery. One might suggest that if providers were paid the same rate irregardless of whether the delivery required a C-section or not, the C-section rate would decline substantially. However, the payment rate would have to be higher for hospitals treating more teenagers and poor patients, so as not to discriminate unfairly against hospitals with a high rate of necessary C-sections. Employers are already beginning to institute more stringent claims review and quality audits. Some employers and insurance plans in Maryland and California are beginning to deny payment for C-sections deemed unnecessary.

A potential explanation for why fetal monitoring became so popular in a matter of months might center on what Foltz and Kelsey (1978) call "the nation's ideology to support the maximum utilization of new technologies." Two clinical trials by Haverkamp et al. (1976, 1979) of the effectiveness of electronic fetal monitoring versus basic nurse monitoring found no significant differences. Our medical technology is all too quick to accept new diagnostic techniques that have been founded on faulty evaluations or have poor specificity in the average hospital. Two examples are the CEA (carcinoembryonic antigen) test for colonic cancer and the NBT (nitro-blue tetrazolium) test in the diagnosis of bacterial infection. Both tests were promoted to medical students in 1973, then found to be substantially less effective by 1975–1976 (Ransohoff and Feinstein, 1978).

A fourth case of the importance of considering the costs associated with poor test specificity has been provided by McNeil and Adelstein (1975). The effect of high sensitivity but poor specificity in the primary screening modality for detecting renovascular disease among hypertensives ($83 intravenous pyelogram plus $100 renography) can be improved by subsequent arteriography at a cost of $375 (1975 prices). This subsequent angiogram increases the specificity to a perfect 100 percent, but the new information is hardly worthwhile since case finding is not associated with improved survival figures, and surgical treatment following the angiogram was found to be no more efficacious than medical treatment prior to testing (McNeil, 1977). However, improved specificity and case finding through pulmonary angiography ($300) and perfusion lung scanning ($125) have been demonstrated to be worth the 40 percent increased costs for diagnosis of pulmonary embolism in young patients.

Marginal Costs and Benefits of Additional Testing

Having addressed the reliability and specificity issues in cost-effectiveness analysis, the third issue left for discussion is marginal costs. Neuhauser and Lewicki (1975) performed a marginal cost analysis on the value of doing a fifth or sixth sequential stool guaiac, in reaction to the recommendation by Gregor (1969) and the American Cancer Society (Leffall, 1974) that six guaiacs be done on all persons over 40 years of age to detect asymptomatic colon cancer. Even with a diagnostic test of high sensitivity (92.67 percent), the marginal cost of the sixth test ($47.1 million per cancer case detected) was 20,000 times the average cost per case discovered. Although six sequential stool guaiacs, followed by barium enemas for all positive guaiacs, will identify virtually all "silent" colon cancers, is it worth $47.1 million to detect that one rare case when the resources could be used elsewhere? Physicians are too oriented toward citing simple average costs ($4 for the first stool guaiac, and $1 for each subsequent guaiac) to recognize the devastating implications that the recommendation of up to six guaiacs could have on medical costs. For example, physicians would neglect the 41 percent of total diagnostic costs devoted to diagnosing incorrectly (false-positive) colon cancer and then ruling out presence of the disease with a $100 barium enema. Maximization of specificity (the minimization of false-positives) has the added benefit of reducing needless patient anxiety, in addition to the tangible benefits of reducing unnecessary care, iatrogenic morbidity, and mortality.

One final problem in assessing new tests or techniques concerns the issue of substitutability. New diagnostic procedures can seldom be judged 100 percent accurate, perfect substitutes for the old methods. For example, CAT scanning may be considered by physicians to be cost-effective simply because it replaces other costly, painful, and invasive diagnostic procedures. However, some radiologists have suggested that head scans cannot be considered merely a substitute for pneumoencephalography, arteriography, and other techniques. For example, many more CAT head scans are being performed than would be necessitated by replacement of all the prior techniques. The Office of Technological Assessment (U.S. Congress, 1978a) study suggests that hospitals with high percentages of negative scans are using the machine as a less than cost-beneficial blind screening tool.

More recently, magnetic resonance imaging (MRI) technology has been introduced to over 200 hospitals. MRI images are spectacular; they partially substitute (and complement) CAT technology and cost over $2 million (Evens, 1984). Both MRI and CAT scanning can have efficacy at the best quality hospitals but lack cost-effectiveness at the average or below-average hospital if utilized too frequently. In the short run, it is unlikely that hospitals will abandon outdated modalities in favor of MRI, as most modalities CAT scans were designed to replace still exist. Weinstein (1985) holds out the promise that in the long run hospitals employing MRI technology that are facing increased financial pressure will slowly phase out older, more invasive treatment modalities. Judging from a number of recent decisions, HCFA does not appear interested in fueling the diffusion of technology. For example, in the summer of 1986 HCFA ignored ProPAC's suggestion that Medicare should pay hospitals an additional amount for every case in which an MRI scan was used.

Rising Importance of "Big Ticket" Technologies

Scitovsky (1985) examined the effects of changing medical technologies on medical costs by comparing treatment patterns for a number of common illnesses at four points in time (1954, 1964, 1971, and 1981). While the results from 1954 to 1971 indicated that "little-ticket" items like lab tests and X-rays were driving up the cost of care, the new and expensive "big-ticket" technologies appeared to be the major inflationary factor. New modes of treatment and big-ticket technologies significantly increased the cost of myocardial infarction and breast cancer cases. For example, in 1981 dollars, treatment involving streptokinase infusion cost $19,206 per case, compared to $47,564 for bypass surgery and $10,094 for "conventional care." The increased reliance on an existing big-ticket technology, delivery by Caesarean section, significantly increased the average cost of maternity care. Hospital costs of a delivery by Caesarean section were 2.4-fold higher than a vaginal delivery, and nonhospital costs were 52 percent higher.

The Scitovsky findings are consistent with other recent findings. Showstack et al. (1985) studied ten diagnoses at one San Francisco teaching hospital for the years 1972, 1977, and 1982. They concluded that little-ticket laboratory tests did not contribute substantially to rising costs, and new imaging techniques were commonly substituted for traditional invasive procedures. The authors concluded that the primary driving force behind rising hospital costs were intensive treatments for the critically ill, provision of surgery to patients admitted with acute myocardial infarction, delivery, and newborn respiratory distress syndrome. Among the ten diagnoses studied, only for acute myocardial infarction patients did the use of imaging procedures increase substantially (2 percent cardiac catheterization in 1977, and 40 percent in 1982).

Little-ticket items still contribute to the rising cost of medical care. For example, the annual number of lab tests per case increased 7.1 percent for mastectomy cases, 4.4 percent for myocardial infarction (conventional care) cases, and over 3.0 percent per year for appendicitis and vaginal delivery. Tests usage per patient increased more than 3.0 percent per annum for a number of nonhospitalized patients: duodenal ulcer, pneumonia, and complete (adult) physical exam (Scitovsky, 1985). Attempts to trim little-ticket items also occur in radiology and the emergency room. For example, Clinton (1986) argues that application of more rigorous specific clinical indications will lead to continued major declines in the number of unnecessary chest radiographs performed.

Physician Involvement or Increased Federal Intervention?

The existence of growing federal regulation in the health field is a by-product of the observation that the imperfect private sector has been of little help in selecting the programs and services that are to be available as a reimbursable expense in the clinical armada. Consequently, as a matter of public policy, the Congressional Office of Technological Assessment (U.S. Congress, 1978b) has suggested a sequence for evaluating medical technology: Consider efficacy, cost-effectiveness, cost-benefit, and then safety. Efficacy is concerned with measuring the benefit of a technology under ideal conditions of use—for example, the Mayo Clinic and Johns Hopkins Hospital. Cost-effectiveness is a measure of the relative benefits and costs, to society, of various technologies applied to the same problem area under average conditions of use. Consequently, a technology can have efficacy in the best hospitals but be cost-ineffective for general use. Cost-effectiveness is measured by the ratio of costs to tangible benefits, expressed as cost per man-year saved or cost per quality adjusted man-year saved or cost per disability-year prevented.

The estimation of direct benefits is usually a simple process of measuring what costs are foregone as a result of the consumption of the service under evaluation. One frequently mentioned caveat to the problem of benefit estimation is double-counting or overestimating the benefit of eliminating one disease if there is a simultaneous presence of multiple diseases. Weisbrod (1961) was one of the first to recognize that patients who avoid one cause of death (cancer) may have a higher susceptibility to another competing cause of death (heart disease). The bias in the benefit estimation process is to overstate the benefits projected from reducing the prevalence or incidence of any single disease category—that is, the whole is smaller than the sum of the individual parts. The estimation of intangible benefits is also a major problem in most studies. One of the most overlooked intangible benefits is the patient reassurance factor. However, if the false-positive rate is too high, the intangible negative benefit of unnecessary patient distress could outweigh the net amount of patient assurance.

Physician involvement in the process of doing cost-benefit or cost-effectiveness research is crucial. Construction of a decision tree is the first step in most cost-effectiveness analyses designed to assist in the selection of alternative approaches to patient care. It allows the practitioner to incorporate the predictive values obtained from appropriate therapeutic procedures into a wider framework. This analysis is not purely mechanical and requires input from a group of experienced clinicians. The twin problems of "dirty" data and unreasonable assumptions could be eliminated if heavy-handed regulators allowed clinicians to have more input in the design phase, funded better epidemiological studies, and sponsored more randomized controlled clinical trials.

Physician Education Programs

Physician education programs have as their goal apprising doctors of the appropriate use of tests, procedures, and treatment options. Educational efforts come in a number of formats, offered in combination, including didactic lecture, order-form restructuring, cost feedback, concurrent or retrospective protocol review, and other retrospective medical record audits. The didactic course approach typically makes four basic points: (1) Do what must be done in a cost-effective way (e.g., home health, or ambulatory surgery), (2) perform a cost-benefit assessment of the case management alternatives, (3) avoid the unnecessary/outmoded/duplicative things, and (4) encourage preventive and health promotion activities. On this last point, Bartlett (1985) reported that health promotion can do more than reduce future illness; it can also reduce duration of stay, patient anxiety, and complications. Didactic examples work best if targeted to areas of interest for future practice (Philip et al., 1986). Historically, the problem with most didactic educational programs is that by themselves they tend to produce only short-run changes in behavior.

Restructuring the excessively convenient patient order forms was one of the first nondidactic approaches to be utilized successfully. For example, Wong et al. (1983) found didactic programs to be ineffective in reducing test usage unless the order form was redesigned to alter the test selection process. If the physician has to take an action beyond simply checking the entire row of boxes, less medically unnecessary tests are performed. Eisenberg and Williams (1983) decreased lab overuse by no longer allowing standing orders (i.e., a test would be done multiple times per day until discharge, whether the test was medically necessary or not). Under their program, all test orders are good only for the day they are written.

More recently, the medical staff of Boston City Hospital in 1985 reduced the volume of common labor-intensive lab tests 28 to 45 percent by requiring doctors to enter their reason for ordering each specific test on the test request form. This suggests that clinicians have the cognitive knowledge to select tests more efficiently but need a continuing reminder of the importance of cost-effective selection. Moreover, placing responsibility for parsimony on the physicians prevents resentment over perceived limits on physicians' exercise of clinical judgment. Detsky et al. (1986) confirm this second point, that there is no intrinsic reason why teaching hospitals need to order more tests per case—that is, there is no pure teaching effect.

A second nondidactic educational approach involves simply attaching a copy of the patient's cumulative bill to the last progress note (McPhee, 1984). Berwick and Coltin (1986) tested the effectiveness of cost feedback versus two other forms of feedback (didactic teacher feedback and yield feedback flags on abnormal test results). Studying internists' usage of 12 common blood tests and roentgenograms over four months, the authors concluded that test usage declined across the board 14.2 percent. Other studies have reported comparable success from pharmacy feedback, with the review process reducing ineffective, irrational, or excessively costly drug-prescribing habits.

There are few clinical trials documenting the long-run effectiveness of feedback techniques. Chassin and McCue (1986) reported results from one educational quality assurance program assigned randomly across 120 study and control group hospitals. Education concerning acceptable indications for X-ray pelvimetry reduced usage by 33 percent more in the study hospitals. Some of the more innovative chiefs of medical staff have initiated protocol development as a fourth alternative approach to cost-containment education. Within their institutions, protocol development has not always been a smooth developmental process. Protocols could be used for case management by hospital administrators, or even by, God help us, the federal government. The primary challenge for the chiefs of staff is to keep their fellow physicians happy or, if not happy, at least not too unhappy. Wachtel et al. (1986) designed protocols at Brown University's largest teaching hospital for four medical conditions (chest pain, stroke, pneumonia, and upper gastrointestinal hemorrhage). The protocols were implemented on 64 experimental patients who were compared to 64 control group (nonprotocol) patients. The protocols resulted in a 15 percent reduction in total charges per case (and reductions as high as 35 percent for EKGs and 20 percent for lab tests). The benefit of altering clinician behavior by using protocol standards developed by the medical staff could be substantial. However, other analysts have suggested that the medical staff should simply develop a brief manual with test characteristics or EKG information. For example, Marton et al. (1985) studied test usage among three intervention groups (detailed manual, manual plus feedback, and feedback) and found the most significant declines in utilization among the mixed strategy intervention (manual plus feedback).

One should not come away from this brief survey of protocols with the opinion that few conditions have been studied (Mohr et al., 1986). Decision analysts and clinicians have developed protocols for over 1,800 conditions; over 1,000 were developed in Pittsburgh alone. While protocol development clearly works best if developed by those who use them, there are conceptual problems with protocols. The failure of researchers to incorporate all aspects of a clinical problem into the protocol is analogous to the attempts of a blind man to ascertain the nature of an elephant by inspecting its trunk alone (Kassirer, 1986). Some protocols may cover 80 to 99 percent of their specific elephant, but the risks and benefits of all possible outcomes must be assessed. The challenge for those who promulgate protocols is to encompass the whole problem and avoid both the wild goose chase and the sometimes inappropriately "cheap" strategy of watch and wait.

Hospital Practice Privileges

Fewer than 1,000 physicians had their licenses suspended or revoked for inappropriate or unnecessary practice behavior in 1986. The federal peer review organizations (PROs) took sanction actions against less than 100 physicians during 1985–86. However, as hospitals win court cases related to staff privilege decisions, based on quality or efficiency concerns, hospital managers and medical staff are getting more selective about which physicians they allow admitting privileges. Self-serving members of the medical staff may want to close the doors on their hospital's medical staff in a crowded marketplace and force the institution to cease taking new applications from potential competitors. In negotiating compensation agreements with hospital-based physicians, the management clearly likes the leverage to negotiate from a large pool of potential replacement clinicians. All types of physicians have potential anticompetitive reasons for closing their segment of the medical staff (raising antitrust legal concerns); but hospital managers and trustees are more interested in the composition of their medical staff and their cost behavior relative to levels of payment.

Institutions may no longer allow physicians who erode the financial standing of the institution through imprudent wasteful use of hospital resources to admit patients. Hospitals that allow inefficient doctors to admit patients may go so heavily into debt that their survival is unlikely. In 1987–88, almost one-third of all hospital clinical departments will be closed to new medical staff appointments; most of these will be internally reviewing whether certain clinicians should not have their privileges renewed (legally it is easier to not renew privileges rather than actually revoke privileges). The percentage of physicians with admitting privileges at any hospital has been declining each year since 1982, according to AMA survey statistics. Any physicians losing their practice privileges at one hospital will have a tough time establishing a relationship with other local hospitals. Inefficient ordering and treatment habits are a liability for the individual doctor in a market that increasingly is paid prospectively (i.e., inefficiency is not a pass-through of costs for the hospital) and in which hospital privileges are in short supply. The practice profile cost per case experience of a doctor should be appropriately adjusted for DRG mix and case severity to make any data-based "credentialing" process fair (i.e., for medical staff membership). Physicians can be analyzed on whether they are inefficient on two basic dimensions: length of stay and ancillary cost per case (Figure 17.3).*

---

* The third dimension, appropriate admissions, was discussed in Chapter 2.

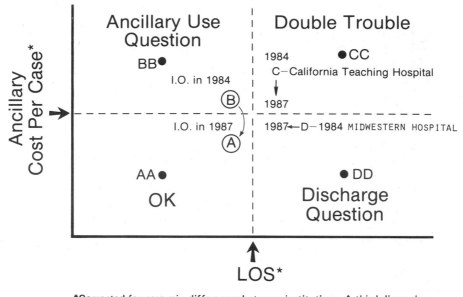

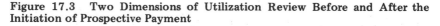

*Corrected for case-mix differences between institutions. A third dimension of utilization review would monitor physician billings.

Figure 17.3   Two Dimensions of Utilization Review Before and After the Initiation of Prospective Payment

If the individual physician is "double trouble" on both dimensions, the total cost per case (case mix adjusted) figure will be high. Many midwestern hospitals have been particularly effective at trimming lengths of stay relative to the national average since 1983 (Table 17.1). By point of contrast, West Coast hospitals historically tend to be very efficient on length of stay. However, West Coast investor-owned hospitals have been particularly high in generating ancillary costs per case. Such behavior was rewarded in an era of cost reimbursement or full charge payment, when the profit margins were highest in the area of ancillary tests. The hospital CFO's best physicians were the ones who ordered the most ancillary tests per case (earning the hospital more money). However, now the medical staffs have had to unlearn all the lessons of the 1969–1983 "maximization of reimbursement" period (outlined in Chapters 1 and 5), and become more efficient (move from point B to A in Figure 17.3). The medical staff is sometimes provided breakeven-point analysis by product line to provide a yardstick for target areas to trim cost behavior.

The concept of strategic product-line groupings was discussed in Chapter 9. The intent of Table 17.2 is to provide the medical staff with sensitivity estimates as to how much one has to trim in the

Table 17.1 Annual Percentage Change in Medicare Average Length of Stay and Admission Rates per 1,000 Enrollees, Short-Stay Hospitals, by Area FY 1981–1985

	A. Four Waiver States (N.Y., N.J., Md., Mass.)	B. 12 North-Central States[a]	C. 34 Other States and D.C.	D. USA Total
1. Medicare Length of Stay				
1982	−1.7%	−1.6%	−1.6%	−1.6%
1983	−3.2%	−3.2%	−3.1%	−3.1%
1984[b]	−3.9%	−13.5%	−9.4%	−8.9%
1985	−6.1%	−9.6%	−7.0%	−8.0%
2. Admission Rates per 1,000 Medicare Enrollees				
1982	2.8%	2.2%	2.0%	2.2%
1983	3.4%	2.5%	2.1%	2.3%
1984[c]	−0.9%	−5.3%	−2.9%	−3.5%
1985	−1.5%	−5.1%	−4.6%	−4.9%

SOURCE: Health Care Financing Administration, Bureau of Data Management and Strategy.

[a]North-central states include Iowa, Illinois, Indiana, Kansas, Michigan, Minnesota, Missouri, Nebraska, North Dakota, Ohio, South Dakota, and Wisconsin.

[b]The Behrens-Fisher statistic for comparing mean rates of increase in length of stay for waiver states exhibits no statistically significant differences prior to 1984—that is, there is no support for suggesting that waiver states were predisposed to have lower declines in length of stay.

[c]The Behrens-Fisher statistic for comparing mean rates of increase in admission rates for north-central states versus other nonwaiver states exhibits no prior statistically significant difference before 1984—that is, there is no support for suggesting that north-central states were predisposed to having the fastest declines in admission rates per 1,000.

Table 17.2   **Nine Additional Options for Achieving a Break-even Cost Behavior Profile for Strategic Product-line Grouping (SPG) 7: Beyond Simply Asking for a 15 Percent Reduction in Average LOS (SPG 7 consists of 16 DRGs produced by 13 attending physicians) (in percent)**

Option	LOS[a] Length of Stay	Inhalation[b] Therapy, IVs, and Misc. Therapy[c]	Lab[bc]	Radiology[c]
1	− 15.0	0	0	0
2	− 10.0	− 27.0	0	0
3	− 10.0	− 10.0	− 23.0	0
4	− 10.0[d]	− 10.0	− 10.0	− 18
5	− 5.0	− 20.0	− 24.0	0
6	− 5.0	− 20.0	− 10.0	− 19.0
7	− 5.0	− 16.8	− 16.8	− 16.8
8	0	− 27.0	− 22.0	− 39.7
9	0	− 29.8	− 29.8	− 29.8

[a]The semivariable and variable cost savings from reduction in LOS distributes .450 in foregone "hotel" costs, .271 in foregone nursing services, .133 in foregone therapy (inhalation therapy, IVs, medication, recovery room, OR, anesthesia, etc.), .085 in foregone lab tests, and .061 in foregone radiologic services.
[b]For this hospital, and this Strategic Product-line Grouping 7, the example is only atypical to the extent that overutilization of inhalation therapy was a major problem identified in peer review audits. Requiring a 27 percent aggregate reduction in inhalation therapy could be easily accomplished by a 75 percent reduction in usage by 4 (of the 13 doctors offering this SPG) clinicians, and no change in behavior was required of the other 9 attendings (who were already utilizing 24 to 32 percent less inhalation therapy than the 13 physician group average).
[c]utilization per diem
[d]The cost savings from a 5 percent drop in LOS equals a 27 percent drop in therapy per diem (for the reduced number of per diems remaining after the LOS reduction), which is equivalent to a 43 percent drop in lab tests per diem, and equates to a 59 percent drop in radiology usage per diem.

other three areas if, for example, the clinicians running SPG-7 decide they cannot improve length of stay (options 8 or 9), or adjust behavior in radiology (options 1–3, and 5). Such estimates are highly dependent on the blend of variable-to-fixed costs for the specific hospital under study. Therefore, the analysis must be done at each hospital every 1 to 3 to 12 months. In studying two of the hospitals sampled in Chapter 5, McNeil (1985, page 18) indicated that there is:

> *enormous variability in the fixed-variable cost ratios of tests done in chemistry labs, ranging from under 20 percent variable cost for some to over 90 percent for others. Information on the distribution of tests in the "highly fixed" cost category compared to those in the "highly variable" cost category should be useful in the design of educational programs for cost containment.*

The challenge for physicians and managers is not to break even on every product line. There will always be some cross-subsidization in the hospital sector. The real challenge is to have all parties work toward common goals: quality care, institutional financial health, and enough retained earnings to keep the hospital/doctor-workshop state of the art. One must balance this last goal against the broader social goal of not having too much wasteful excess capacity (Chapter 16) or excess patient admissions (Chapter 2).

Preferred Practice Patterns

Checklist protocols and decision rules are but one approach for the medical staff to define preferred styles of behavior. McNeil (1985) reported on the preferred practice pattern (PPP) study of Massachusetts General Hospital, Brigham Hospital, and New England Medical Center. The study team identified nine diseases or procedures, ranging from carotid endarterectomies to GI bleeding. The physicians were of the opinion that quality was equally good across all three hospitals, in which case the research question became measuring the efficiency of utilization (a concept originally pioneered by Neuhauser in the 1960s, Chapter 13) across the three hospitals. By looking across all cost items, the study group identified a lowest-cost, high-quality PPP based on the approach that it is best to have the "least resource usage for the same quality output." Detailed chart reviews were undertaken to assess the comparability of the patients, adjust for case severity, and ascertain the vagaries and errors in the discharge coding.

Many hospitals have eschewed equally careful concern for discharge abstract data, or patient severity, and developed crude profit-and-loss statements by DRG, groups of DRGs, and by physician. The idea of P&L (profit-and-loss statements) is only as good as the data (clinical and cost accounting). Good data can yield good PPP analysis. Needless to say, the phrase "preferred practice pattern" is more popular among clinicians than the more inflexible label, "standard protocol." However, without valid cost-accounting information and a severity measure, the analysis will be less than useful for many hospitals. Horn et al. (1986) reported that 37 percent of the physicians at one medical center would have errors, up (or down) of more than $10,000 in the apparent impact of the clinician on the hospital's profit and loss, depending on whether one incorporated the severity measure into the analysis. An amazing 14 percent of physicians would be labeled under- or overutilizers of hospital resources, relative to a $30,000 threshold of accuracy. For example, doctors with a terrible profit-and-loss profile could actually be efficient, but all the most severe cases within a given DRG may be channeled their way in the referral process. These results might pertain to a typical medical center, but the need to adjust individual performance for patient severity may not exist at most nonteaching hospitals.

Many clinical outliers will discuss details of their PPP and their individual performance relative to the PPP standard with the various utilization review committees. Judgments of individual practice habits will always involve some degree of uncertainty. For example, if doctor X appears to prophylactically order inhalation therapy, in varying amounts, the exact amount of unnecessary and controllable inhalation therapy may be difficult to determine from the medical record. Deliberate deviations from the PPP standard of care should be documented in the medical record such that the objective observer could follow the reasoning behind certain clinical decisions. The medical staff can make appropriate documentation of records a precondition for membership, and determine whether a given individual offers a pattern of deception to defend his or her inefficient performance relative to the PPP yardstick.

In 1986 a few hospitals began to make medical staff membership decisions on the basis of cost profiles plus forecast sales quotas as to how much volume the individual will "harvest." If the sales quota concept seems a bit aggressive, more radical approaches may come in the future. At the extreme, some hospitals may one day require that independent contractors (called physicians) pay the hospital a security deposit, or rent, in order to admit patients (e.g., the way some car mechanics pay their garage). If the physician is cost-effective from the hospital's viewpoint, the deposit or rent is returned to the physician. However, if the "body mechanic" wastes resources of the firm (garage or hospital) that he or she controls but does not own, then the professional (mechanic or doctor) must make good on any cost overrun. Unlike the imperfect garage analogy, one would want to take account for case severity and outliers (e.g., not penalizing the doctor for serving AIDS patients). However, if the physician harms the hospital's financial health on a regular basis, after repeated attempts at behavior modification, all or part of the rent or security deposit would be retained by the hospital.* The current payment system is clearly unfair for hospitals, in that business risk is borne by the hospital, yet it is the physician's behavior that dictates the amount of risk.

---

* This idea was originally suggested to the author by a garage mechanic and a Nobel prize winner in economics, which may or may not offer proof that great minds think alike when it comes to professional user fees.

Teaching Medical Students

The purpose of this section is to outline one approach to teaching cost-effective clinical decision making and to measure the degree of attitudinal change produced by a brief course in this area. The elective course was offered to third-year medical students at Cornell Medical College. As medicine has grown more technological, the decision process has also become more statistically complex. Unfortunately, the recent medical school graduate's statistical knowledge has not kept pace with the growth in medical science. In one early study at four Harvard teaching hospitals, only 20 percent of fourth-year medical students, 15 percent of internal medicine residents, and 20 percent of attending physicians correctly responded to a question that required the application of elementary statistical analysis to diagnostic test results (Cassells et al., 1978).

A potential benefit of injecting economic content into the medical school curriculum is that the new clinicians might informally utilize cost-effective clinical decision-making principles to provide equivalent quality of care at less cost. The Association of American Medical Colleges, the American Hospital Association, and the American Medical Association House of Delegates have all endorsed cost education for physicians during the undergraduate and postgraduate educational process.

Socioeconomic courses often take a back seat to the "hard sciences." One would hope that the progressive social and economic course content of residency and medical school programs will not fall to the budget ax. If we are to make intelligent decisions on how to improve the quality of care and contain the cost of services, it is our responsibility to discover the most effective means of training physicians to make economical decisions. The hope is that formal training in decision analysis and economics can yield more rational decisions, and perhaps better patient outcomes, or at least more informed choice if economy happens to conflict with the pursuit of the "highest possible" quality of care. The norm for the 1990s may have to be the provision of the best possible patient outcomes within the constraint of a given amount of available resources—for example, 12 percent of gross national product for health care. With the aging of the population, however, this 12 percent may be difficult to achieve.

If some of the principles of cost-effective clinical decision making would permeate into the subconscious cognitive processes of American physicians, a less costly style of medical care might result. Continuing education programs may affect practicing physicians' behavior, but it might be more cost-beneficial to bring formal discussion of these issues to medical students and help them reflect on their future role as clinicians. Most of the previous effort in this area has concentrated on house staff (AMA, 1978). The approaches include identifying those individuals with out-of-line utilization profiles, testing residents with a price list of hospital charges, and asking the young clinician if the marginal information gain of the test justified the cost (Lyle et al., 1979).

The next section reviews the results of the pre-course and post-course attitude survey of the students. The course had three major themes (Eastaugh, 1981). The first basic theme is that physicians must understand the role of cost-benefit analysis in "big ticket" resource priority decisions and other policy determinations. The second course theme is that physicians should increasingly utilize and participate in cost-effectiveness evaluations to constrain the proliferation of "little-ticket" expenses for tests and procedures. Third, clinicians should be interested in preserving professional autonomy by cooperating with the health policy decision makers rather than being co-opted by the growth in federal intervention. If further regulation is to be avoided and the dual goals of cost containment and improved patient care achieved, health practitioners must be taught to utilize diagnostic tests more appropriately and treatment modes more effectively.

Student Attitude Survey

There is inevitably an imperfect link between attitudes and behavior. Nevertheless, attitude shifts are taken as a proxy estimate of program effectiveness because researchers seldom have the option to wait five years and do a prospective field survey to measure shifts in postgraduate clinical behavior. The self-report attitudinal instrument utilized in this study did not rely on a single question to detect the depth or presence of an attitude. Instead, the four basic constructs (interest in reducing costs, concern with decision science techniques, concern with economics and biostatistics, and advocating maximum consumer information) were measured by a number of questions. Providing four-to-seven ordinal attitudinal (agree strongly, mildly, disagree mildly, strongly) items for each construct aids in minimizing the error that could result from student misinterpretation of single items.

The instrument was constructed so that the responses were anonymous, while allowing for the recognition of individuals before and after the course. The anonymity of the survey response was intended to minimize the potential bias that could occur if respondents were to hide their true attitudes and bend their answers to conform to the attitudes of the instructor. Of the 80 third-year Cornell Medical students based in New York City during the month in which the Cost-Effective Clinical Decision Making Course was offered, 56 filled out a pre-course questionnaire. Of these 56, 29 elected to take the course and completed a post-course questionnaire. The two basic research questions involved how the course affected the attitudes of the 29 course takers, and how the 27 respondents who elected not to take the course differed from the 29 course participants.

A number of nonparametric statistical tests demonstrated the significant impact of the course on attitudes and the selection bias between course takers and nontakers. The Kolmogorov-Smirnov Test* demonstrated that the sample of course takers was more predisposed to cost-effective clinical decision-making ideas compared to those electing not to take the course for six of the twenty items. Course takers were significantly predisposed to being pro-consumerists (two items significant at the 0.01 level), mindful of the need for medical cost containment (three items significant at the 0.05 level), and conscious of the necessity for decision analysis applications to medicine (one item significant at the 0.05 level).

In the case of the 29 students who completed questionnaires before and after the course, the Wilcoxon matched-pairs test provided a measure of the significance of attitudinal change. Those completing the course had not significantly shifted their ideas on consumerism and the need for cost containment. However, there was a significant shift with respect to applications of decision analysis to medicine (two items were significant at the 0.02 level, two additional items at the 0.05 level). Completion of the course also positively affected their respect for health economics (one item was significant at the 0.01 level, two additional items were significant at the 0.05 level).

The students most in need of a course in this subject area appeared to be the least likely to take the course. Multivariate discriminant analysis provided an accurate prediction of participation (yes, no) in the course. Of the 56 respondents, 78.6 percent were correctly classified, and the two groups were statistically different (Chi squared = 4.09, $p < 0.05$, d.f. = 1). In order to investigate further the question concerning the dichotomous variable of course selection, a probit model was tested for the 20 agree/disagree items. One of the early applications of this maximum likelihood technique in the health field was provided by Finney

---

* Siegel, S. (1956). *Nonparametric Statistics*. New York: McGraw-Hill.

(1972). In our situation, the model was statistically significant in explaining the course selection (Chi squared $= 51.78$, $p < 0.05$). The two items significant at the 0.01 level were: "Patients should have convenient access to their medical record," and "Physicians should answer the patient in a quantitative probabilistic fashion if the patient asks for such specific information." The only other statement responses significant at the 0.05 level were: "Appropriate applications of statistical tools in differential diagnosis can significantly lower medical costs," and "Understanding of statistical tools is necessary to properly interpret diagnostic test results." The results seem to argue for making the course a requirement since the students most in need of decision science materials are the least likely to select such a course voluntarily.

Conclusions

Health practitioners, especially physicians, must be taught more economics and biostatistics in order to use diagnostic information appropriately and effectively and arrive at the best treatment mode.* Formal training in decision analysis can be applied to improve patient care in a therapeutic setting as well as to assist medical practitioners in understanding the priority setting and policy determinations that society will make regarding the future medical practice.

Increasingly, house staffs (residents) and medical students are utilizing the computer for clinical education. New software systems developed in Texas, New Mexico, Massachusetts, and Pennsylvania assist the practicing physician to sort through possible differential diagnoses for 1,000 diseases, based on 1,600 signs and symptoms. Most systems are management tools that can track what is done and sequentially list what further studies are necessary to confirm a diagnosis. The computer interacts with the user by listing disease possibilities and distinguishing features and tests. These programs will also list a number of current approaches to treatment. The computer system is a time saver and aid to quality care—not a robotic competitor to the attending physician.

Attempts have been made to reform medical education over the past decade. Most of the informational content in medical text-

---

* Duncan Neuhauser has suggested that the Hippocratic oath be rewritten in the 1990s as follows: "I swear by Apollo, the physician, and Aesculapius, and health and all heal and all the Gods and Goddesses that, according to my ability and judgment, *and cost considerations,* I will keep this oath and stipulation."

books is still presented "upside down" in that the student is first informed of the diseases and then told of the probability of various signs and symptoms. Residents and students all too often minimize probabilistic concerns and search for that rare "zebra" condition, as with the search for lupus in the Freymann quote at the beginning of this chapter. The physician has to take this information and invert the order to go through a process that eventually leads to a diagnosis. A dozen American medical schools are now experimenting with a problem-oriented, computer-enhanced medical curriculum. Originally developed at MacMasters University in Ontario, the problem-oriented approach has spread from New Mexico to Harvard Medical School's "New Pathway" program for 24 students each year.

Criticism of statistical tools usually is based on the subjective estimates included in the formulas, alleging that what appears to be objective analysis is really no better than the examiner's best guess. This criticism will become less justified as decision makers begin to realize that (1) all decisions incorporate subjective estimations and (2) only through disciplined analysis can this subjectivity be evaluated. The recent proliferation of courses in the area of cost education or cost-effective clinical decision making is a healthy trend for those interested in evaluative research and medical cost containment. If we are to contain costs and maintain patient service quality, it is our responsibility to discover the most effective approaches to making economical clinical decisions.

References

AARON, H., and SCHWARTZ, W. (1984). *The Painful Prescription: Rationing Hospital Care*. Washington, D.C.: Brookings.

American Medical Association (1978). *Cost-Effective Medical Care*. Chicago: Resident Physicians Section, American Medical Association.

American Public Health Association (1981). "Poll Shows Americans Would Put Dollar Value on Life." *Nation's Health* 20:2 (February), 3.

ANNAS, G. (1977). "Allocation of Artificial Hearts in the Year 2002: Minerva v. National Health Agency." *American Journal of Law and Medicine* 3 (Spring), 59–76.

ARTHUR, W. (1981). "The Economics of Risks to Life." *American Economic Review* 71:1 (March), 54–64.

AVORN, J., and SOMERAI, S. (1983). "Improving Drug-Therapy Decisions Through Educational Outreach." *New England Journal of Medicine* 308:25 (June 25), 1457–1463.

BANTA, D., and THACKER, S. (1979). "The Premature Delivery of Medical Technology: A Case Report—Electronic Fetal Monitoring." DHEW, National

Center for Health Services Report, Rockville, Md.: U.S. Government Printing Office.

BARTLETT, E. (1985). "Accomplishing More with Less Under PPS Using Patient Education." *Healthcare Financial Management* 39:7 (July), 86–94.

BERKELHAMER, J. (1986). "Charges by Residents and Faculty Physicians in a University Hospital Pediatric Practice." *Journal of Medical Education* 61:4 (April), 303–307.

BERNER, E., COULSON, L., and SCHMITT, B. (1985). "A Method to Determine Attitudes of Faculty Members Towards Use of Laboratory Tests." *Journal of Medical Education* 60:5 (May), 374–378.

BERWICK, D., and COLTIN, K. (1986). "Feedback Reduces Test Use in a HMO." *Journal of the American Medical Association* 255:11 (March 21), 1450–1454.

BRAUN, P. (1980). "The Clinical Management of Suspected Herpes Virus Encephalitis." *American Journal of Medicine* 69, 895–899.

BROTT, T., LABUTTA, R., and KEMPCZINSKI, R. (1986). "Changing Patterns in Practice of Carotid Endarterectomy in Large Metropolitan Area." *Journal of the American Medical Association* 255:18 (May 11), 2609–2613.

CAHILL, N., and BELJAN, J. (1984). "Technology Assessment: Differing Perspectives." *Journal of the American Medical Association* 252:23 (December 21), 3294–3295.

CARELS, E., NEUHAUSER, D., and STASON, W. (eds.) (1980). *The Physician and Cost Control*. Cambridge, Mass.: Oelgeschlager, Gunn and Hain, Inc.

CASSELLS, W., SCHOENBERGER, A., and GRABOYS, T. (1978). "Interpretation by Physicians of Clinical Laboratory Results." *New England Journal of Medicine* 299:17 (October 26), 999–1001.

CHASSIN, M., and McCUE, S. (1986). "A Randomized Trial of Medical Quality Assurance." *Journal of the American Medical Association* 256:8 (August 29), 1012–1016.

CLINTON, J. (1986). "Chest Radiography in the Emergency Department." *Annals of Emergency Medicine* 15:3 (March), 254–256.

COLE, P. (1976). "Elective Hysterectomy: Pro and Con." *New England Journal of Medicine* 295:5 (July 29), 264–265.

DANIELS, M., and SCHROEDER, S. (1977). "Variations Among Physicians in Use of Laboratory Tests: Relation to Clinical Productivity and Outcomes of Care." *Medical Care* 15:6 (June), 482–487.

DETSKY, A., McLAUGHLIN, J., ABRAMS, H., LABBE, K., and MARKEL, F. (1986). "Do Interns and Residents Order More Tests Than Attending Staff?" *Medical Care* 24:6 (June), 526–534.

DOUBILET, P., WEINSTEIN, M., and McNEIL, B. (1986). "Use and Misuse of the Term 'Cost Effective' in Medicine." *New England Journal of Medicine* 314:4 (January 23), 253–255.

EASTAUGH, S. (1983). "Placing a Value on Life and Limb: The Role of the Informed Consumer." *Health Matrix* 1:1 (Spring), 5–21.

EASTAUGH, S. (1981). "Teaching the Principles of Cost-Effective Clinical Decision Making to Medical Students." *Inquiry* 18:1 (Spring), 28–36.

EISENBERG, J. (1986). *Doctors' Decisions and the Cost of Medical Care*. Ann Arbor, Mich.: Health Administration Press.

EISENBERG, J., and WILLIAMS, S. (1983). "Cost Containment and Changing Physicians Practice Behavior: Can the Fox Learn to Guard the Chicken Coop?" *Journal of the American Medical Association* 249:22 (May 11), 3074–3076.

EVENS, R. (1984). "Computerized Tomography: A Controversy Revisited." *New England Journal of Medicine* 310:18 (May 3), 1183–1185.

FINNEY, D. (1972). *Probit Analysis*, 3rd ed. Cambridge: Cambridge University Press.

FOLTZ, A., and KELSEY, J. (1978). "The Annual Pap Test: A Dubious Policy Success." *Milbank Memorial Fund Quarterly* 56:4 (Fall), 426–462.

GODDEERIS, J., and BRONKEN, T. (1985). "Benefit Cost Analysis of Screening." *Medical Care* 23:11 (November), 1242–1255.

GREGOR, D. (1969). "Detection of Silent Colon Cancer in Routine Examinations." *CA: Cancer Journal for Clinicians* 19:6 (November–December), 330–337.

HAVERKAMP, A., ORLEANS, M., LANGENDOERFER, S., MCFEE, J., MURPHY, J., and THOMPSON, H. (1979). "A Controlled Clinical Trial on the Differential Effects of Fetal Monitoring." *American Journal of Obstetrics and Gynecology* 134:4 (June 14), 399–408.

HAVERKAMP, A., THOMPSON, H., MCFEE, J., and CETRULO, C. (1976). "The Evaluation of Continuous Fetal Heart Rate Monitoring in High-Risk Pregnancy." *American Journal of Obstetrics and Gynecology* 125:3 (June 1), 310–318.

HORN, S., HORN, R., and MOSES, H. (1986). "Profiles of Physician Practice and Severity of Illness." *American Journal of Public Health* 76:5 (May), 532–535.

Institute of Medicine (1985). *Assessing Medical Technologies*. Washington, D.C.: National Academy of Sciences.

KASSIRER, J. (1986). "The Wild Goose Chase and the Elephant's Relevance." *Journal of the American Medical Association* 256:2 (July 11), 256–257.

KNOWLES, J. (1969). "Radiology: A Case Study in Technology and Manpower." *New England Journal of Medicine* 280:24 (June 12), 1323–1329.

LEFFALL, I. (1974). "Early Diagnosis of Colorectal Cancer." *CA: Cancer Journal for Clinicians* 24:3 (May–June), 152–159.

LEVENO, K., CUNNINGHAM, F., NELSON, S., ROARK, M., WILLIAMS, M., GUZICK, D., DOWLING, S., ROSENFELD, C., and BUCKLEY, A. (1986). "A Prospective Comparison of Selective and Universal Electronic Fetal Monitoring in 34,995 Pregnancies." *New England Journal of Medicine* 315:10 (September 4), 615–619.

MALONEY, I., and ROGERS, D. (1979). "Medical Technology—A Different View of the Contentious Debate over Costs." *New England Journal of Medicine* 301:26 (December 27), 1413–1419.

MARTON, K., TUL, V., and SOX, H. (1985). "Modifying Test Ordering Behavior in the Outpatient Medical Clinic: A Controlled Trial of Two Educational Interventions." *Archives of Internal Medicine* 145:4 (April), 816–821.

MCNEIL, B. (1985). "Hospital Response to DRG-Based Prospective Payment." *Medical Decision Making* 5:1 (January), 15–21.

MCNEIL, B. (1977). "The Value of Diagnostic Aids in Patients with Potential Surgical Problems." In J. Bunker, B. Barnes, and F. Mosteller (eds.), *Costs, Risks, and Benefits of Surgery*. New York: Oxford, 77–90.

MCNEIL, B., and ADELSTEIN, S. (1975). "Measures of Clinical Efficiency: The Value of Case Finding in Hypertensive Renovascular Disease." *New England Journal of Medicine* 293:5 (July 31), 221–226.

MCPHEE, S. (1984). "Lessons for Teaching Cost Containment." *Journal of Medical Education* 59:9 (September), 722–729.

MIAO, L. (1977). "Gastric Freezing: An Example of the Evaluation of Medical

Therapy by Randomized Clinical Trials." In J. Bunker, B. Barnes, and F. Mosteller (eds.), *Costs, Risks, and Benefits of Surgery.* New York: Oxford University Press, 198–211.

MISHAN, E. (1971). "Evaluation of Life and Limb: A Theoretical Approach." *Journal of Political Economy* 79:4 (July-August), 687–705.

MOHR, D., OFFORD, K., OWEN, R., and MELTON, J. (1986). "Asymptomatic Microhematuria and Urologic Disease." *Journal of the American Medical Association* 256:2 (July 11), 224–229.

MUSHKIN, S. (1979). *Biomedical Research: Costs and Benefits.* Cambridge, Mass.: Ballinger.

NEUHAUSER, D. (1979). "The Public Voice and the Nation's Health." *Milbank Memorial Fund Quarterly* 57:1 (Winter), 60–69.

NEUHAUSER, D., and LEWICKI, A. (1975). "What Do We Gain from the Sixth Stool Guaiac?" *New England Journal of Medicine* 293:5 (July 31), 226–228.

PERRY, S. (1986). "Technology Assessment: Continuing Uncertainty." *New England Journal of Medicine* 314:4 (January 23), 240–243.

PERRY, S. (1982). "The Brief Life of the National Center for Health Care Technology." *New England Journal of Medicine* 307:17 (November 1), 1095–1100.

PERRY, S., and KALBERER, J. (1980). "The NIH Consensus-Development Program and the Assessment of Health Care Technologies." *New England Journal of Medicine* 303:3 (July 17), 169–172.

PHILIP, J., WILFORD, R., and LOW, I. (1986). "Implications for Medical Education of Nonrational Prescribing by Residents." *Journal of Medical Education* 61:5 (May), 418–420.

RANSOHOFF, D., and FEINSTEIN, A. (1978). "Problems of Spectrum and Bias in Evaluating the Efficacy of Diagnostic Tests." *New England Journal of Medicine* 299:17 (October 26), 926–930.

REGT, R., MINKOFF, H., FELDMAN, J., and SCHWARZ, R. (1986). "Relation of Private or Clinic Care to the Cesarean Birth Rate." *New England Journal of Medicine* 315:10 (September 4), 619–624.

RETTIG, R. (1978). "Lessons Learned from the End-Stage Renal Disease Experience." In R. Egdahl and P. Gertman (eds.), *Technology and the Quality of Health Care.* Germantown, Md.: Aspen Systems, 153–173.

REUBEN, D. (1984). "Learning Diagnostic Restraint." *New England Journal of Medicine* 310:9 (March 1), 591–593.

SCITOVSKY, A. (1985). "Changes in the Costs of Treatment of Selected Illnesses, 1971–1981." *Medical Care* 23:12 (December), 1345–1357.

SHOWSTACK, J., STONE, M., and SCHROEDER, S. (1985). "The Role of Changing Clinical Practices in the Rising Costs of Hospital Care." *New England Journal of Medicine* 313:19 (November 7), 1201–1207.

SKARUPA, J., and MATHERLEE, T. (1985). *The Hospital Medical Staff, Closed Medical Staffs Are Not Inevitable.* Chicago, Ill.: American Hospital Publishing, Inc.

SKENDZEL, L. (1978). "How Physicians Use Laboratory Tests." *Journal of the American Medical Association* 239:11 (March 13), 1077–1080.

U.S. Congress (1976). 94th Congress, 2nd Session, Subcommittee on Oversight and Investigations of the Committee on Interstate and Foreign Commerce.

Report on the Cost and Quality of Health Care: Unnecessary Surgery. Washington, D.C.: U.S. Government Printing Office.

U.S. Congress, Office of Technology Assessment (1980). *Cost-Effectiveness and Cost-Benefit Analysis in Health Care: Methodology and Literature Review*, Vol. II. Washington, D.C.: U.S. Government Printing Office.

U.S. Congress, Office of Technology Assessment (1978*a*). "Policy Implications of the Computed Tomography Scanner." Report to the U.S. Congress, F. Robbins, Study Chairman. Washington, D.C.: U.S. Government Printing Office.

U.S. Congress, Office of Technology Assessment (1978*b*). *Assessing the Efficacy and Safety of Medical Technologies*. Washington, D.C.: U.S. Government Printing Office.

WACHTEL, T., MOULTON, A., PEZZULLO, J., and HAMOLSKY, M. (1986). "Inpatient Protocols to Reduce Health Care Costs." *Medical Decision Making* 6:2 (April), 101–109.

WEARS, R., and KAMENS, D. (1986). "A Simple Method for Evaluating the Safety of High-Yield Criteria." *Annals of Emergency Medicine* 15:4 (April), 439–444.

WEINSTEIN, M. (1985). "Methodologic Considerations in Planning Clinical Trials of Cost Effectiveness of MRI." *International Journal of Technology Assessment* 1:3 (Fall), 567–581.

WEISBROD, B. (1961). *Economics of Public Health*. Philadelphia: University of Pennsylvania Press.

WONG, E. et al. (1983). "Ordering of Laboratory Tests in a Teaching Hospital: Can It Be Improved?" *Journal of the American Medical Association* 249:22 (June 10), 3076–3080.

YOUNG, G. (1986). "CBC or Not CBC? That Is the Question." *Annals of Emergency Medicine* 13:3 (March), 367–371.

Chapter 18

BENEFIT EVALUATION: THE VALUE OF LIFE AND LIMB

An economist can tell you the prices of everything, but the value of nothing.

—WILL ROGERS

American doctors should begin to build up a social ethic and behavioral practices that help them decide when medicine is bad medicine: not simply because it has absolutely no payoff or because it hurts the patient, but also because the costs are not justified by the marginal benefits. To do this we are going to have to develop and disseminate better information. . . . Some small fraction of what we now spend on health care could be better spent to determine limits.

—LESTER THUROW

Harris Poll reveals that 52 percent of the public think that the government and the courts should place an economic dollar value on life—only 34 percent say No.

—*News Report*, February 1, 1981

Changing social and economic conditions over the past decade have spurred new concerns about medical cost containment. Consumers indirectly feel the impact of the medical cost-containment problem in the prices they pay for other goods. For example, production of the American automobile frequently contains more health dollars than steel dollars in the production process. Many consumers incurring catastrophic medical expenses have a more direct experience. As Senator Dennis DeConcini (D., Ariz.) re-

498

marked, "Nearly half of the personal bankruptcies filed each year in this country are the result of medical costs."

Physicians are increasingly realizing the opportunity cost implications of supporting more high-technology medicine for very rare diseases. The public also realized that the health economy and the American economy are not limitless. An opportunity for new transplant techniques will, by definition, prevent society from financing some other medical or social program. The objective of cost-benefit analysis is to maximize net benefits (benefits minus costs, appropriately discounted over time). The objective of cost-effectiveness analysis, as was observed in Chapter 16, is to rank order the preferred alternatives for achieving a single goal or a specified basket of benefits. Cost-effectiveness analysis is not any easier to perform than cost-benefit analysis if multiple varieties of benefit are specified (man-years, work-loss days, reduced angina), yet in cost-benefit analysis one must value the intangible benefits in commensurate dollar terms (Torrance, 1986).

Practitioners of cost-benefit analysis are accused in alternating years of either (1) stifling liberal attempts to build better service programs, (2) frustrating conservative attempts to reduce the regulatory burden on industry, or (3) browbeating liberals and conservatives who bring pork-barrel projects with low benefit-to-cost ratios to their home state. Whether the source of pork existed in the social service sector or industrial sector, practitioners of cost-benefit analysis are seen as an anathema by many interest groups. Economists have become increasingly skeptical of any political process that encourages waste and ignores careful analysis designed to incorporate all benefits, including intangible benefits, when making resource decisions. When fully identified prices fail to exist (water resources) or price is deemed an ineffective measure of value (health services), an attempt is made to impute value or to "shadow price." In economic sectors where competitive markets fail to exist, such as the health care or water resource sectors, cost-benefit analysis is an attempt to do what supply and demand forces accomplish in competitive markets (Eastaugh, 1983).

Analysts and decision makers disagree on how to value the intangible benefits of health programs. Most decision makers find the valuation process in cost-benefit analysis difficult and do not trust analyses that depend on gross approximations, small samples, and a poor data base. These decision makers are willing to violate the efficiency criteria and invest more in hospitals and physicians than society receives as a return on the dollar. Consequently, economic evaluation of new or expensive technologies has become a central issue in the public debate about rising medical care costs.

Risk Analysis: Experts Differ from Citizens

The average radiation exposure to residents 1 mile from the Three Mile Island accident (1 millirem) is as risky as 4 extra miles driven in a car or 4 city street crossings. This "bloodless" statistical comparison, while numerically correct, ignores the quality of those three relative risks. Experts worry about the quantity of risk, whereas typical Americans worry about the nature of the risk (whether involuntary, controllable, new, unknown, or known). Fear of nuclear radiation, for a citizen of any country, is increased by each of these quality or risk factors. In considering a list of two-dozen technologies and behaviors, nuclear power and swimming were ranked first and 24th in terms of risk by graduate students. However, the probability of morbidity and mortality is much higher for a voluntary behavior such as swimming than it is for a nuclear power accident.

McNeil and Pauker (1982) reported that patients are more willing to take a risk to avoid a sure loss. However, if the same risk is posed in terms of a potential gain, people are less willing to take the risk (e.g., radiation therapy). The effect of a physician's word choice may have a big impact on patient preference, even if all risk elements are statistically unchanged. For example, in lung cancer cases when the odds were presented in terms of dying, only 18 percent of people chose radiation treatment over surgery. However, if the odds were presented in terms of surviving, almost half of the subjects chose radiation treatment over surgery.

Seen in this context, terminally ill cancer patients seeking laetrile may be victimized, but they are not totally irrational. The terminally ill are risk-takers, as is any individual faced with the following situation: A tiger chases you to the bank of a 50-foot river filled with crocodiles; you leap into the water convinced that you can make it safely to the other side. You would never accept such odds if there were no tiger. Many cancer and AIDS victims are faced with this situation daily.

In order to preserve their sense of worth, many physicians also tend to underestimate the risks. The difference is that the physician only observes the risks and outcomes and doesn't have to live the risks first hand. Even in the case of elective surgery, with a mere 0.2 percent chance of dying, the typical surgeon understates risk. The surgeon may understate risk for the same reason a truck driver understates risk—it makes working and sleeping easier. A surgeon may look at the small per hour risk and forget that one "healthy" patient dies on the table statewide every 9 hours and even more die postoperatively. Each uncomplicated trip to the operating room may reinforce the idea that one is better than the average surgeon. Analogously, a truck driver may look at the tiny per trip risk and forget that 81 percent of truckers suffer a disabling injury during their career. Any professional, no matter how well educated, tends to look at risk in terms of low-risk short hops. Disabled truckers and surgeons forced into retirement might have something to teach their respective practitioners about tigers, crocodiles, continuing education, and when to quit.

The government does not make many macro-level resource decisions on the basis of cost-benefit analysis. By ignoring the necessity for making cost-benefit judgments for proposed OSHA standards, Congress and the courts have allowed this agency to make a number of extreme decisions. For example, the 1979 proposed OSHA benzene standard of one part per million would benefit society by one life every three years at a cost of $300 to $450 million per life saved. The public does not force Congress to legislate mandatory automobile restraint devices, even though such a program would have a benefit-to-cost ratio that is 3,000 to 6,000 times higher than the benzene standard.

The situations that are most ripe for cost-benefit study are those in which the benefit is incomplete and transient and the costs are high. For example, $12,000 per course of apheresis treatment for rheumatoid arthritis has been questioned (McCarty, 1981). McCarty raises the issue of whether the health economy can afford an additional $1.1 billion plus dollars to provide transient benefits by apheresis. The question is answered only clearly for the small subset of patients facing life-threatening side effects and obvious potential benefit (Jones et al., 1981).

For microdecisions made by the medical community, economic evaluation is frequently held in disrepute because physicians may have the elitist view that cost-benefit analysis is a less satisfactory alternative to ad hoc decisions of hospital committees (Turnbull et al., 1979). The American tradition has been to make local selective choices through critical care committees rather than to implement an "all or none" rationing decision. Under "all or none," as practiced in most European countries, everyone is allowed access or no one is allowed access (Annas, 1977). Physicians typically misunderstand the concepts and potential applications of cost-benefit analysis. Attitudes of these professionals are shaped and misshaped by the same sort of colorful but inaccurate portrayal of the topic by the media. For example, throughout the Robert Duvall film *THX-1138*, the king computer states the number of dollar units remaining in the Duvall retention account before the project shuts down and all activity to "save" the individual terminates. The movie thus conveys the viewpoint that approximately 14,000 resource units have been allocated by the economists and the king computer to save the individual, and once that ceiling is attained the project will be terminated. In real life, as in the film, the public is continually fed an inappropriate definition of both sunk costs and cost-benefit analysis.

Some humanitarians argue that if a small group of individuals report infinitely large intangible benefits, then society should place an infinite value on life. Indeed, in some situations society places the benefits of citizen health above benefit-cost concerns. For example, the June 1981 Supreme Court decision ruled that under the 1970 Occupational Safety and Health Act, OSHA does not have to consider the balance between benefits and costs when implementing regulations. The Reagan administration had argued that cost-benefit analysis should be implicit in any governmental activity. Justice W. J. Brennan interpreted the law as "placing the benefit of worker health above all other considerations save those practical concerns that might make attainment of this benefit unachievable." The OSHA regulations impose on firms a penalty that is in some degree proportional to the presence of unsafe working conditions.

Different groups provide vastly varied estimates of the benefit-cost impact of OSHA. The business community attacks OSHA as a $10 billion regulatory burden (over the years 1971–1981). In sharp contrast, the liberal Council on Economic Priorities research group supports OSHA because of a 23 percent reduction in chemical worker morbidity rates since 1972 at a "meager" cost of $140 per worker per year. Both groups agree that one should not underestimate the value of cost-benefit calculus. The process of analysis asks explicit questions of valuation that politicians might want to blur, such as why do we spend $40,000 to give one executive a bone marrow transplant or bypass operation while foregoing five years of life for 25 ghetto dwellers suffering from rheumatic fever or hypertension? When value judgments are quantified, although some groups dislike this process, unconsciously inaccurate or insidious assumptions are exposed. Public disclosure of the underlying assumptions in a given economic analysis may yield more informed and better quality ex ante "Who shall live?" decisions. Cost-benefit analysis should be an ex ante resource decision rather than an ex post bedside decision of whether to pull the plug.

Value-of-life issues play a major role in congressional budgeting issues. For example, conservatives who wish to abolish the Clean Air Act cite a 1978 study by the National Economic Research Associates, consulting economists, which reports negative $700 million net annual benefits if we assume life is valued at $560,000. However, supporters of the Clean Air Act report that under a $1,000,000 estimate of the value of life, the Clean Air Act becomes an attractive proposition with positive annual net benefits of $4.4 billion. (For a more detailed discussion of the Clean Air Act, refer to Perl and Dunbar, 1982.)

Four Techniques to Value Benefits

Some citizens may balk against any value-of-life measurement for religious reasons—that is, they may believe that the process debases the sanctity of life. These individuals would be shocked to learn that for the last two decades public and private agencies have been placing a value on life, ranging from $200,000 by Ford Motors to $250,000 by the Federal Aviation Administration to $287,000 by the National Highway Traffic Safety Administration (Hapgood, 1980). The approach taken by these groups involves measuring discounting future earnings (DFE). Foregone earnings as an estimate of indirect benefits is relatively easy to estimate, although some economists would question the assumption that earnings are a suitable measure of social benefit. The resultant biases implicit in measuring benefits in terms of earnings reflect imperfections in the labor market such as racism and sexism. For example, concluding that visits to a rheumatology clinic were cost-beneficial only for males merely reflects an artifact of the sex bias in earnings data: Women earn less (Glass, 1973). A variant of this approach—subtracting out consumption to yield net output—was considered ill-advised, because killing elderly or handicapped individuals would be "valued" as an act that confers a net benefit to society.

The most prevalent assessment approach for researchers in the 1970s has been the "willingness to pay" (WTP) approach suggested by Schelling (1968). Schelling emphasized the fact that quantity multiplied by price was at best equal to a minimum benefit of health services to the society, since it does not account for the many consumers who would be willing to pay more than the price. The initial WTP studies involved responses to hypothetical questions. However, the bulk of the recent studies concern imputed worker valuation of life based on their willingness to be paid to assume added occupational risk.

There are four basic methods to value life or limb:

1. paternalistic aggregate needs assessment
2. DFE observed

3. WTP hypothetical behavior in an opinion survey
4. WTP observed behavior in the labor market (LWTP)

Paternalistic Aggregate Needs Assessment

The first method of ad hoc valuations is often practiced by public
health professionals acting as "problem" definers—for example,
defining mental hygiene cases that "need" deinstitutionalization or
defining nutritional status as "inadequate." The definition of what
is needed or adequate varies tremendously across time and place.
This first method is paternalistic in the sense that it takes the
aggregate preferences of a single expert or small group of individuals and extrapolates their judgments to other groups of citizens.
These techniques are sometimes helpful in making cost-effectiveness decisions within a given discipline (Jones et al., 1979; Lestz,
1977). However, the aggregate assessment approach has little
utility in cost-benefit analysis since each discipline tends to overstate its case. If you bring together 50 experts from 50 separate
disciplines, all of them would have you believe that 10 to 20
percent of gross national product should be dedicated to their
field.

There are a number of strengths and weaknesses for the three
remaining valuation methods. Observed WTP measures may be
biased by an imperfectly informed wage earner who might bias the
responses downward. Hypothetical WTP measures leave room for
individual assessments of the intrinsic intangible benefits. However, the sample sizes are typically small and the analysis is
expensive—that is, the results cannot be derived from secondary
data like methods 2 and 4. The third method, hypothetical WTP
surveys, is limited by the usual problems with a survey: response
bias, problem with questionnaire phrasing, etc.

Discounting Future Earnings

The valuation method DFE has a long history, running back a few
hundred years (Fein, 1971; Mushkin, 1962; Shattuck, 1850). Expected earnings replaced income as the relevant measure of
indirect benefits in the 1960s (Rice, 1966). Cooper and Rice (1976)
produced annual tabulations of the present value of lost earnings
due to mortality under alternative discount rates and annual
estimates of the foregone earnings due to disability. In some cases
potential morbidity reduction represents 90 percent of indirect
benefits (skin diseases). In other cases potential mortality reduc-

tion represents 90 percent of indirect benefits (neoplasms). In many cases the direct benefits of eliminating a disease are a fraction of the indirect benefits (Eastaugh, 1983).

There are two basic accounting approaches to DFE studies: the incidence-based approach and the prevalence approach. The incidence-based approach is generally regarded as the superior method for evaluating how much human capital is foregone in the case of chronic or preventable diseases (Hartunian et al., 1981). A simple example will illustrate the differences between prevalence and incidence approaches. Consider an individual experiencing a stroke in 1988, who, over the following eight years, shares the expenses for his medical care with Medicaid, misses some work, and dies in 1996. The traditional prevalence approach assigns the medical expenses and foregone wages to the years in which they occurred and the lost future earnings due to premature death to the year 1996. The incidence-based approach present-values and assigns all the costs associated with the eight-year duration of the disease to the year of incidence (1988).

Both accounting approaches have comparable drawbacks, depending on the time frame of the relevant policy issue under study. For evaluation of preventive programs or programs aimed at arresting the progression of a chronic illness, federal officials utilize the incidence approach. The incidence approach provides the better estimate of the cost that may be avoided and, consequently, of the benefits that may be gained by efforts aimed at reducing disease incidence. The traditional prevalence-based viewpoint remains the best of the DFE approaches for decisions concerning the control of current service costs and absenteeism. While the accounting is nice and tidy, the basic flaw of DFE valuation is that it only accounts for society's loss in foregone national income and ignores the person's own value of life, including how much the individual, the direct family, and the overall community values the individual life (Schelling, 1968; Mishan, 1971).

Hypothetical Measures of Willingness to Pay

The WTP principle in normative economics states that the value of something is simply measured by what people are willing to pay for it. To paraphrase Mishan (1971) in his seminal article on the value of life and limb, economists are generally agreed as a canon of faith to accept the dictum that each person knows best his or her own interests. Cost-benefit analysis has to operate within the bounds of the individual's deficient information base, congenital optimism, or hypochondria and to accept the expressed consumer preferences as a more relevant measure of benefits than the expert opinions of an educated elite. Experts' presumption that the public is unable to properly assess its interests may be foiled on two counts. First, the observation that people respond in a biased emotional fashion may be irrelevant for policy-making purposes if the bias is unsystematic, since the extremes will cancel each other. Second, one could make the same argument that the public cannot understand the technical details necessary to purchase calculators, cameras, cars, and stereos. The public does not have to understand all the details, as long as a free flow of information creates some small cadre of amateur consultant-friends to help guide consumer choice behavior.

The most often cited early WTP study was done on a sample of 100 Boston residents by Acton (1973). Acton's most publicized question involving public attitude toward risk reduction and heart attacks read as follows:

> *Let's suppose that your doctor tells you that the odds are 99:1 against your having a heart attack. If you have the attack, the odds are 3:2 that you will live. The heart-attack program would mean that the odds are 4:1 that you live after a heart attack. How much are you willing to pay in taxes per year to have this heart-attack program which would cut your probability of dying from a heart attack in half (i.e., the chances are two per 1,000 you will have a heart attack and be saved by the program this year)?*

The median response of $56 suggests that 200 people would chip in $28,000 to save one of the group member's lives in the coming year. The scenario is reasonable because most health programs are risk-reduction efforts. One might also note that small changes in the question, reducing the risk to 0.001, increases the median imputed value of a life saved to $43,000. Both of the two aforementioned questions emphasize the individual's situation. When Acton posed the question in more probabilistic terms, focusing on the 10,000 people living around a hypothetical respondent, the median amounts were reduced by approximately 50 percent for equivalent risk-reduction levels.

The willingness-to-pay approach can be criticized on the grounds that life is probably valued much higher for identified individuals than for members of a hypothetical population. Consumers and physicians tend to value identified individual lives more than statistical anonymous foregone lives, yet physicians are often criticized for placing a substantially higher value on identified individuals than society, with its limited resources, can afford to place on the average citizen.

Labor Market Imputed Willingness to Pay

As a general proposition, WTP results may be substantially higher than DFE (Hirshleifer et al., 1974). The results in Table 18.1 are consistent with this assertion if one considers labor market WTP studies only (LWTP, studies 10–14). All of the LWTP studies are based on the presumption that workers perceive the full extent of the risks and have the potential mobility to shift occupations if they do not like a given dictated price for risk taking. Consequently, all of the estimates in Table 18.1 should be regarded as very rough approximations. Some perceptions of risk will be reviewed before surveying the specific LWTP studies.

The world is not a riskless environment. Every product and service used can be shown to be potentially hazardous in some way. For example, in an average month of January, four children die from hazards associated with Christmas toy chests. Should these toy chests be banned? What is the appropriate role for government in this situation? After much reflection, Kass (1975) concluded that the conventional wisdom of "a right to health flies in the face of good sense and serves to undermine personal responsibility." Kass might overestimate the degree to which we can improve the health of the population through personal responsibility and health education, but a riskless society maximizing our safety would surely be a joyless, totalitarian one. Workers have faced occupational risks for centuries, but only in the last century have they extracted a wage premium that is roughly proportional to the measured riskiness of the workplace. An extensive network of insurance reporting systems supplements the Bureau of Labor Statistics industrial accident reporting system for fatal and nonfatal incidents. The last five studies in Table 18.1 confirm the fact that occupations that are more likely to experience accidents tend to demand a larger risk premium at the bargaining table, presumably to compensate for the expected losses due to injury.

In theory, the LWTP approach provides a valid market measure of the sum total of indirect and intangible benefits. For example, the often cited Thaler and Rosen (1976) estimate for marginal valuations of safety for select hazardous occupations from the 1967 Survey of Economic Opportunity earnings data extrapolates the value of a life saved to $176,000. Utilizing actuarial data, the authors estimated that, on average, workers in certain high-risk occupations demanded an additional $176 a year to accept an extra death risk of 0.001 per year. Thaler and Rosen concluded that a society of workers would together be willing to pay $176,000 (in 1967 dollars) per life saved.

Table 18.1. *Value of a Life*—Three Basic Approaches: Human Capital Discounted Future Earnings (DFE), Hypothetical Willingness to Pay from Suggested Consumption Decisions (WTP), and Labor Market Willingness to Pay (LWTP)

Study	Approach	Data	Value of a Life[1]	Value of a Life in 1987 Dollars[2]
1. Dept. of Defense (1963)	DFE, discounted at 3 percent	U.S. Air Force captain's wages	$135,000 (1962 dollars)	$492,000
2. Dept. of HEW (1967)	DFE, nonmilitary personnel, discounted at 4 percent	a. black male, age 85 b. white male, age 25–29	$396 (1966) $136,121 (1966)	$1,440 $496,000
3. Ford Motor Company (1973)	DFE, study data for federal auto safety officials, discounted at 6 percent	1973 study of the average American DFE, released October 1979 at the Pinto trial	$200,000 (1971)	$584,000
4. Hartunian, Smart, and Thompson (1981)	DFE, discounted at 6 percent	a. male, 25–34 b. female, 25–34	$247,881 (1975) $153,131 (1975)	$527,000 $326,000
5. Schelling (1968) and Joksch	Hypothetical WTP poll	University-based polling to assess WTP to avoid large risks	$1–2 million (1967)	$3.4–6.8 million
6. Acton (1973)	Hypothetical WTP study for a heart attack ambulance program	a. value to avoid a 0.002 risk of death ($56 mean) b. value to avoid a 0.001 risk of death ($43 mean)	$28,000 (1971) $43,000 (1971)	$81,000 $125,000

7. Blomquist (1979)	WTP based on value drivers place on safety implicit in their demand for seat belts	Seat-belt questionnaire—usage reduces risk from 0.00025 to 0.00010	$257,000 (1975)	$548,000
8. Dardis (1980)	WTP based on consumer demand for smoke detectors, 1974–1979	Implicit valuation from sales and annualized costs for smoke detectors during the five-year period	$101,000 (1976–77)	$192,000
9. Portney (1981)	WTP assessment of life, home, and environmental quality	Tradeoffs implicit in pollutions impact on mortality and housing prices	$355,000 (1977)	$674,000
10. Thaler and Rosen (1976)	LWTP based on actuarial survey of very risky occupations, including all causes of death, not just accidents (no information on actual cause of death)	Observed wages $136 to $260 (mean $176) higher annually to accept an additional death risk of 0.001 per year	$176,000 (1967)	$603,000
11. Smith (1976)	Industrial LWTP risk data (BLS injury data) for hourly workers in manufacturing	a. Observed wages $120–$160 higher annually to accept an additional death risk of 0.00008 per year, 1973, manufacturing. The bias implicit in industrial injury data is that they limit slower causes of death captured in the actuarial data.	$1.5 million (1973)	$4.0 million

Table 18.1 (continued)

12. Viscusi (1978)	Industrial LWTP data controlled for a wide range of occupational characteristics	b. 1967, all Industries Industrial risk data, observed wages $60–$180 higher to accept an extra death risk of 0.0001 per year.	$2.5 million (1967) $600,000–$1.8 million (1970)	$8.85 million $1.8–5.4 million
13. Dillingham (1979)	LWTP based on occupational-and-industry-based risk data (wide sample of occupations)	Average observed wages $368 (on average) higher to accept the extra death of 0.001 per year	$368,000 (1969)	$1.18 million
14. Olson (1981)	Industrial LWTP merged with other occupational data for nonfatal accidents from 70 percent of the industries surveyed by the BLS	a. Average observed annual wages $350 higher to accept an additional risk of 0.000095 per year	$3.2 million (1973)	$8.5 million
		b. Nonunion workers observed annual wages $110 higher to accept an extra risk of 0.00008 per year	$1.4 million (1973)	$3.8 million
		c. Union workers observed annual wages $1140 higher to accept an extra risk of 0.00014 per year	$8.1 million (1973)	$21.6 million

SOURCE: Eastaugh (1983).

1"Most reasonable" estimate is reported in most cases; otherwise a range of low and high estimates is provided.

2The BLS Consumer Price Index is utilized to inflate all figures to 1987 dollars; 1987 inflation rate estimated at 3 percent.

The strength of the Thaler and Rosen study is that they used disaggregate individual actuarial death rate and wage rate data by occupation. However, their WTP assessment might be expected to understate the average citizen's WTP, since the data are for 37 very hazardous occupations. The WTP values of those in the very hazardous occupations might represent the viewpoint of the lowest decile of the general population (i.e., these "crazy" individuals have the lowest disutility toward risk in the population, and hence value their lives the least). The most basic potential problem with this type of analysis is the assumption that the worker has sufficient information to trade risk for earnings knowledgeably. Better informed boilermakers and lumbermen might have requested substantially higher wages. The workers might be under the delusion that they are benefiting from thousands of dollars in increased wages per 0.001 increment in risk. Workers might substantially raise the price of risk taking if they only had knowledge of the true degree of risk being faced (Eastaugh, 1983).

The Thaler and Rosen data provide no information on cause of death, nor verification for the assumption that the cause of death was work-related. In spite of the fact that Thaler and Rosen (1976) included all the relevant disclaimers and expressed little confidence in the precision of their estimate, Bailey (1980) embraced their estimates with total confidence. Given all the disclaimers, it is surprising that Bailey would simply adjust the Thaler and Rosen estimate to allow for inflation, indirect taxes, and special benefit programs (OSHA and worker compensation) and conclude that $303,000 (in 1978 dollars) was a more reasonable current estimate of the value of a life saved.

A subsequent study by Smith (1976) utilizing 1967 data offers the advantages of a more representative range of occupations and controls for the occupation of each worker. Unfortunately, Smith begged the question of allocating the wage compensation for risk between nonfatal and fatal injuries by assuming that more of the compensation is for simple injuries. Smith's definition of a high-risk industry is one with an annual death rate of 16 per 100,000 workers. A low-risk industry has an annual death rate of 8 per 100,000. Smith concluded that workers in high-risk manufacturing industries are willing to receive $1.5 million in pay to forego saving one industry member's life per annum. The basic problem with the Smith data is that one must assume that job risks in each industry are approximately uniform across occupations within that industry. This assumption may be invalid for many industries.

Subsequent work by Viscusi (1978) reestimated the equations of Smith (1976) using more detailed data for occupational characteristics within an industry. Viscusi's central estimate is roughly half the value of Smith's equation. A later dissertation by Dillingham (1979) replicated the Viscusi study with even more detailed data concerning occupations and risk. His estimates are one-third the central estimate of Viscusi, partially because of the more unfavorable arbitrary allocation of risk compensation between nonfatal injuries and death. Dillingham speculated that previous studies have overstated the variation in risk aversion across occupations.

A more recent study by Olson (1981) disagreed substantially with the aforementioned work of both Dillingham and Viscusi. The two main advantages of the Olson study relative to studies 10–13 in Table 18.1 are that the range of occupations is almost representative of the general economy (not just the most hazardous jobs) and a complex nonlinear risk-wage relationship is estimated. The most significant aspect of the Olson study is that he found a substantial interaction between risk premium and union status. The study year, 1973, represents a peak period for union power in the United States. In this context, the Olson study may overstate workers' WTP bodily to receive higher wages. The 1973 market situation with lower unemployment and industry operating at above 95 percent capacity might provide workers with the security to value a life above the 1982 level. In the less favorable 1982 economic climate the unemployment rate has risen to 10 percent and industrial capacity utilization has fallen below 76 percent (Eastaugh, 1983). Thus, workers might be much more willing to accept less wages for an equal incidence of accidents and fatalities. The wage settlements of British coal miners with the Thatcher administration reinforces this point. One might ask: Does the American medical sector ever make decisions with an $8.5 million benefit-to-cost ratio? Yes, in many cases. For example, Himmelstein and Woolhandler (1984) estimated the cost of cholestryamine per myocardial infarction death prevented as high as $9.3 million (1982 dollars).

The last WTP study we shall survey is the Blomquist study (1979) based on consumer preference for seat-belt usage (line 7, Table 18.1). This hybrid study has some of the attributes of a hypothetical WTP questionnaire in that the consumer responses concerning belt usage are self-reported, but the estimates also incorporate labor market valuation of the opportunity cost of time. Blomquist imputed a value of life based on belt usage and 13 household parameters. Avoiding injury is part of the rationale for usage, whereas discomfort and time consumption are part of the rationale for nonusage. Blomquist's estimates of the value of life vary from $142,000 to $488,000, with a central estimate of $257,000.

The disaggregate studies reporting a relatively low valuation of life (6–10 in Table 18.1) avoid one source of bias that hampers studies 11–14 in Table 18.1. These studies, in which analysis is based on aggregate risk assessment for groups rather than on individual risk data, will always significantly overestimate the value of a life. To demonstrate this point, consider hypothetical results from a 1982 update of the Olson study. The resulting sample consists of two groups of individuals: (1) 15 percent of the workforce in very high risk jobs, defined as an annual extra risk of mortality of 0.0009 and (2) the remaining 85 percent of the sample in zero-risk work situations. The problem with considering only an aggregate risk factor of 0.000135, equal to (0.15 × 0.0009) plus (0.85 × 0), is that a reported wage premium of $972 should not be assessed against the 0.000135 risk (yielding a falsely inflated value of life of $7.2 million). In this hypothetical example, the implicit value of life should in fact be calculated as $972 per 0.0009 of extra risk, or $1.08 million per life.

Some individuals may think the wide range of WTP valuations of life discredits the technique. For example, what would nonunion workers think of a valuation approach that values five nonunion lives as slightly less than one union life? Perhaps these figures reflect positively on the union's ability to act as an agent of the worker and extract the much higher risk premium. One should conclude from this brief survey that improvement in techniques is both possible and necessary. On balance, the public should come to recognize the necessity for making better decisions, and hence the necessity to experiment continually with WTP techniques. Three major attempts have been undertaken to reconcile the two styles of WTP studies with the traditional DFE approach (Conley, 1976; Bailey, 1978; Landefeld and Seskin, 1982). However, progress has been very slow in developing the theoretical basis for any hybrid technique that could simultaneously capture the positive aspects of both WTP and DFE approaches.

The success of the WTP approach may be somewhat limited, since the methodology is fraught with problems. However, to paraphrase Winston Churchill, the approach is terrible unless you stop and compare it to the alternatives (DFE, or do nothing). The WTP technique generates troublesome questions, but not nearly so troublesome as assuming a group is merely worth the amount its members can earn, or assuming political fiat is superior to economic measurement and evaluation. Those who favor political fiat over analysis may take pause to count the number of times pork-barrel projects acquired resources that could have gone to more broadly beneficial projects. Human service programs and productivity-enhancing projects are generally withering, while breeder reactors and bomber jets increasingly win out despite their unfavorable cost-benefit ratios.

Hypothetical WTP Survey Techniques

One central research issue that Arrow (1978), Thaler (1981), and others have identified is the timing of a willingness-to-pay evaluation. The issue is should respondents be surveyed ex ante under a veil of ignorance concerning the respondents' future disease prognosis, or should the survey be done ex post on consumers with limited information concerning the prognosis for themselves or members of their socioeconomic group? The problem to be considered is one of response bias, since the ex post WTP responses will surely be highly inflated—that is, the answers will be high because the opportunity costs of those remaining dollars, given the shortened amount of time, are low to the individual about to die. Obviously, people who have a fatal disease may answer with a higher WTP response than the average citizen. However, with some chronic conditions this assertion appears to be false—that is, the general population overstates the burden of all illness more than the actual victims do (Sackett and Torrance, 1978). In other words, ex post WTP responses by victims should be adjusted downward because their WTP is based, in part, on their increased chances of fatality. For example, the WTP for fire protection by store owners on the currently unaffected half of a burning city block would certainly be higher than the WTP of the average store owner in the city.* One could not plan a rational public service on the basis of the preferences of respondents undergoing a catastrophe.

In valuing lifesaving activities for statistical lives, the wording of the question is a very important issue. Consider an example outside the context of health care: If the government wants to help American companies with "incentives," 68 percent of the public favors the program; but if the government wants to provide "subsidies," then 60 percent are against it, even when the programs are exactly equivalent (Kinsley, 1981). Economists have discovered a number of elegant techniques to elicit consumer WTP preferences, but such questionnaires have yet to be utilized for making substantial resource allocation decisions. The most

---

* Utility preferences need not be linear or independent of wealth. Risk aversion and risk preference can be observed to change over time in the same individual, or concurrently in the same person under different hypothetical situations. However, very few models of lifetime utility functions have suggested a link between individuals' earnings and their WTP for risk reduction (Conley, 1976).

obvious practical problem with hypothetical WTP measures is that the questions could be considered too unreal to be treated seriously by some respondents. One way to avoid this problem is to present a plausible scenario that concerns a risky situation that has recently been reported on all news media. The survey instruments should also be short in length. Figure 18.1 is an example of such a WTP questionnaire (Eastaugh, 1983).

As with all surveys, the best WTP questionnaires would avoid the use of value-loaded wording. For example, one would not like to ask the question, "How much is your grandfather worth?" More reasonable answers will be given if 1,000 people facing a 0.002 chance of dying next year were asked, "How much would you pay to reduce your risk by 0.001?" In other words, the 1,000 individuals are willing to pay the total sum of their responses to save the one statistical life, not to be identified until next year. It is common knowledge that society places very high values on identifiable lives

---

Please think for a few minutes about the following five questions and then answer them as best you can. There are no right or wrong answers.

1. By attending class today you have been exposed to a rare, fatal form of Legionnaires disease. The disease has only been coming through the air vents for the past two hours. The probability that you have the disease is six in a thousand, .006. If you have the disease you will die a quick and painless death in one week. There is a cure for the disease that works 33.3% of the time but it has to be taken now. We do not know how much it will cost. You must say now the most you would pay for this cure. If the cure ends up costing more you won't get it. If it costs less, you will pay the stated price, not the maximum you stated.

   How much will you pay? _____

2. Same story as above *except* the risk of getting the disease is now .002 and the cure works 100 percent of the time.

   How much will you pay for the cure? _____

3. Same story as question one *except* the risk of getting the disease, thanks to the poor ventilation in this room, is now .250, and the newest cure works 100% of the time.

   How much will you pay for the cure now? _____

Assume for questions 4 and 5 that you have no prior exposure to the disease:

4. We are conducting experiments on the same disease for which we need subjects. A subject will just have to expose him or herself to the disease and risk a .002 chance of death. What is the minimum fee you would accept to become such a subject? _____

5. Same story as in question 4, except the risk of now getting the disease is .250. What is the minimum fee you would now accept to become such a subject? _____

Figure 18.1 Willingness-to-Pay Preference Questionnaire

facing a high probability of death or disfigurement. The media frequently reports a high level of psychic benefit accruing to the population following a heroic rescue attempt or attempt to aid an identified child. For example, individuals seem to experience more psychic benefits as a group in supporting the identifiable March of Dimes Poster Child than supporting Medicaid for multi-institutional charity hospitals. Schelling (1968) was the first to observe that individuals jump to help one 6-year-old identified life, but few shed a tear or write a check if a tax shortfall causes facilities to deteriorate, thereby causing a barely perceptible statistical increase in preventable deaths.

The most basic problem with WTP valuation is that the appropriate data base to make estimates with any adequate range of confidence does not exist. Three subsidiary problems concern (1) lack of physician input in identification of the subtle side effects that should go into the analysis, (2) lack of appropriate behavioral science survey instruments, and (3) lack of an appropriate populace to survey in many cases. As an example of this last problem, in doing a WTP analysis of benzene cleanup activities, how are people to be survey-selected—workers heavily exposed to benzene, all workers, all those who bear the burden of the cleanup? Should people with a given disease be sampled while hospitalized, or should potential candidates for the disease be surveyed, or should all citizens be queried? And how is the survey instrument to be written if researchers are unsure of whether benzene starts significantly to bring about increases in the incidence of leukemia by XYZ percent at prolonged exposure levels of 40 parts per million, 20 parts, or 1 part?

Another problem with WTP consumer preference surveys is that the results may not be very stable over time. The public may express a lower WTP for avoiding a relatively higher and familiar risk (like automobile fatality) than a lower but unfamiliar risk. Some individuals get alarmed over the prospect of a nuclear accident, yet tolerate much higher risks in their daily lives. Moreover, just because the public WTP to avoid uncertain risks is not in direct proportion to the nature and seriousness of some other risks does not mean that the public's preferences should be ignored.

Attempting to Improve Applications of WTP Theory

The WTP preferences of healthy adults were tested on three groups of health professionals using the questionnaire in Figure 18.1. The median results are presented (Table 18.2) so as not to

Table 18.2   Imputed Median Willingness to Pay (WTP) Value of a Life (Actual
Response Situation and Median Answers in Parentheses) for the
Three Groups of Health Professionals, 1980

Sample	Second-Year Masters Students in Health Administration	Hospital Administrators in Summer HA Program	Third-Year Medical Students
Age Range	22–34	30–55	24–31
Sample Size	25	23	29

A. Willingness to Pay to *Gain* Life Expectancy (Prolong Survival)

Q1, .333 cure rate	$250,000[a]	$375,000	$300,000
(.006 × .333)	($500)[b]	($750)	($600)
Q2, perfect 1.0 curve rate	$500,000	$1,000,000	$1,250,000
(.002 × 1.0)	($1,000)	($2,000)	($2,500)
Q3, perfect curve rate	$600,000	$1,000,000	$1,400,000
(.25 × 1.0)	($150,000)	($250,000)	($350,000)

B. WTP to *Lose* Expected Survival Time by Gambling as an
Experimental Subject

Q4, (exposure to	$25 million	$50 million	$35 million
a .002 risk?)	($50,000)	($100,000)	($70,000)
Q5, (exposure to	$4 million	$6 million	$4 million
a .25 risk?)	($1 million)	($1.5 million)	($1 million)

[a]Median imputed value of a life (in this case, the actual median response divided by the .006
× .333 risk).
[b]Median response to the preceding question in parentheses.

skew the results by overweighting the importance of the 4 to 8
percent of respondents who think their life is worth somewhere
between $1 billion to infinity. While there is nothing wrong with
some people perceiving their value as infinite, it makes the mean
response meaningless. The responses undoubtedly vary across
other professions. Within a given profession, the median value of
life probably varies with age, sex, and income. However, even
more interesting than median results across groups is the difference in response for a given individual. First, a pairwise comparison of questions 1 and 2 provides support for the certainty effect
(Thaler, 1981). Under the postulated certainty effect, WTP is less
for a reduction in probability from a small level (0.006) to an even
smaller level (0.004) than the WTP for an equivalent reduction in
probability (0.002) to zero. Of the three subjects groups in Table
18.2, 60 to 75 percent of the respondents in each group gave a
lower answer for question 1 relative to question 2, even though the
increase in survival probability was identical for each question.

Second, a pairwise comparison of questions 2 and 4, and questions 3 and 5, lends support for the so-called endowment effect. Of the 77 respondents, 51 percent of the sample reported fivefold higher responses for question 5 compared to question 3, and more dramatically, 92 percent of the sample reported fivefold higher responses for question 4 relative to question 2. This supports the assertion that people must be paid a substantially higher WTP bribe to risk their endowment of remaining life than to reacquire the same endowment they had already lost due to bad luck.

A third interesting result of pairwise response comparisons is the lack of clear evidence for the von Neumann-Morgenstern game theory axiom that a person should pay more per unit of risk reduction the higher the absolute level of risk (Luce and Raiffa, 1957). A respondent with no bequest motives who obeys the conventional axiom would be expected to pay more per 0.001 of risk reduction the higher the absolute risk (0.25 risk versus 0.002). This axiom is intuitive if one considers the case of how much one is willing to pay to remove one bullet in a 500-bullet gun. In the extreme case, a person pays the maximum to remove the 500th bullet and have some chance for life. Analogously, it seems plausible that a 0.002 risk reduction might mean more to a 70-year-old with a 0.3 chance of dying than to a 40-year-old with a 0.01 chance of dying in the next year. However, the scenario in Figure 18.1 may not be a fair test for this axiom, since the axiom might hold better in the high-risk section of the mortality probability curve (0.3–1.0) than in the flat of the curve (risks under 0.3). One could speculate that one of the reasons why middle-aged hospital administrators in column 2 (Table 18.2) have somewhat higher WTP responses than their administration student counterparts is that they are older (therefore, more subject to risk and more in touch with their mortality). An interesting ethical issue raised by these data is should the results be interpreted literally? Should those who value their lives the most be saved? Under such a WTP criteria, the life of a hospital manager in his forties would be saved before the life of a health administration student in his twenties, in contrast to the DFE higher relative valuation for the younger individual. Perhaps the WTP valuation is more indicative of the full value of individuals to their family, community, and society (Eastaugh, 1983).

In addition to valuing life, consumer preference surveys can assist in the selection of an optimum therapy. Most progressive physicians have at least recognized in theory that treatment decisions should attempt to incorporate patient values into the decision. However, most clinicians are untrained in the disciplines of economics and behavioral decision theory and cannot scientifically survey patient preferences. The sensitive clinician attempts a "quick-and-dirty" approach to get some handle on patient values by asking, "Would you rather have short-term certain survival for say five years, or gamble on an operation that has a low probability of death but offers an additional 20 years of life expectancy?" Physicians are increasingly coming to respect the value of asking such questions.

McNeil et al. (1978) assessed patient preferences for certain near-term versus potential far-term years of life with a hypothetical gambling scenario. For example, the individual would be given a choice of a 50/50 gamble: (1) a quick death or full life expectancy (25 years) or (2) a guaranteed period of survival (X years). A risk-neutral individual would be indifferent to whether he received 12.5 years of guaranteed survival or 25 years times 0.5 chances for survival. Individuals who select a value of X less than 12.5 are risk averse. A significant minority of patients (21 to 43 percent) are so highly risk averse that depending on their age, they would rather select radiation therapy with a far inferior five-year survival to the surgical alternative (McNeil et al., 1978). Physicians are revising their clinical decisions as they discover that many of their patients are risk averse and have made rational internal utility judgments—that is, they prefer definitely surviving over the near term to possibly surviving over the far term.

Surgeons show a high degree of willingness to let their clients trade short-term survival for long-term survival. Is it fair of the surgeon, in the interest of maximizing professional income, to corner patients into having surgery when the gamble runs counter to patient preferences? Perhaps most surgeons are willing to accept the principle that the best treatment for a given patient is the one with the higher net expected personal utility for the patient. Alternatively, the American surgeon could believe that patients' individual preferences have no place and that the best treatment is the one that adds the most man-years of human capital to the economy (i.e., surgery). This last aforementioned rule sounds more applicable to the ethos of a Soviet physician. American physicians and surgeons are much more interested in the individual quality of life for the patient after treatment.

Going Beyond Survival: Weighting the Quality of the Years

We have been reviewing techniques to value life, but there are also important valuation questions concerning the quality of survival. In this context, Stewart et al. (1975) and Grogono and

Woodgate (1971) developed scales for measuring physical, social, psychiatric, and mobility limitations. The psychometric approach provided only marginal improvements over the 1948 Visick scales. Recently, multiattribute utility theory has been applied to evaluate the benefits of treating sore throats (Giaque and Peebles, 1976) and cleft lips in children (Krischer, 1976). One of the best practical applications of these concepts is provided by Weinstein et al. (1977) in their assessment of quality-of-life considerations after coronary artery bypass surgery. Quality-of-life outcome measures include pain at rest, pain with minimal activity, pain with mild activity, pain with strenuous activity, and no pain. Quite predictably, a potential surgical patient places a higher utility value on no pain if he avoids exercise. A utility function to value outcomes was specified as a function of life-style and life expectancy. The data are highly subjective, but reliance on imperfect analysis provides more insights than analytical nihilism.

The less tangible quality-of-life benefits comprise an increasing proportion of medical care benefits. For example, elective surgical expenditures are properly intended to achieve less tangible quality-of-life goals such as relief of disability, pain, and disfigurement than mortality or morbidity rate reduction (Bunker et al., 1977). Such quality-of-life factors are to be identified, then quantified in terms of their equivalent social costs by shadow pricing, and finally balanced against commensurate shadow prices for quantity of life. Advocates of the willingness-to-pay approach suggest the maximization of lives saved (Zeckhauser, 1975) or, alternatively, quality-adjusted life years (QALY) saved as the social objective. The decision sciences improved the traditional health status indexes by multiplying life years by a weighting factor that reflects the quality of those years. The resulting QALY index was originally suggested by Fanshel and Bush (1970) and later developed by Torrance (1976) and Zeckhauser and Shepard (1976). QALY utility analysis presumes risk neutrality, utility independence, and a constant proportional trade-off between life years and health status.*

Zeckhauser and Shepard (1976) made arbitrary assignments of quality-adjusted life years saved (QALYs). They assigned a QALY value of 0.8 to the year in which a nonfatal heart attack occurs, and suggested a value of 0.95 for the second year because the patient's health has improved. If one dies, that year is given a QALY value of zero. One could speculate that even a coma patient experiencing

---

* A more general family of multiattribute utility functions that forego the risk neutrality assumption have been applied to coronary bypass surgery (Pliskin, Shepard, and Weinstein, 1980).

psycho-social death before the inevitable biological death would place some low value on man-years of life spent in a coma (perhaps 0.02 of a QALY, plus or minus 0.02). A typical terminal cancer patient treated with the typical American level of narcotics to dull the pain might value a man-year at 0.10. The counterpart English patient provided with much higher doses of narcotics may value life at double that level because he feels less pain and the high doses of narcotics, such as morphine, depress the respiratory function and shorten the painful dying process.

Research by McNeil et al. (1981) indicates that 20 percent of cancer patients in the sample group are interested in trading off some quantity of life to acquire more quality of life. In this study, one in five patients would forego surgery and the resultant improved average longevity to preserve their normal speech. The study group as a whole considers life without speech to be equal to 86 percent of life with it. The time trade-off technique for scaling consumer preferences for states of health has been tried in other contexts. Sackett and Torrance (1978) reported lower values of utility for a wide range of chronic conditions (tuberculosis, 0.68; mastectomy, 0.48; long-term depression, 0.44; and hospital dialysis, 0.32 of a lifetime without the disability; perfect health = 1, death = 0). A sample response might help clarify the technique.

If a 40-year-old woman with a life expectancy of 33 years were willing to equate 23 years in perfect health with 33 years of life with tuberculosis, the relative value of a life with tuberculosis would be 23/33 or 0.68 for the individual. Temporary conditions were valued as less of a burden. More recently, a variation of this technique was applied by Card (1980). Card asked the respondents to specify a maximum surgical mortality they would accept to avoid blindness. He reported that the average medical professional was willing to undergo a 20 percent risk to avoid complete blindness. The value of life with blindness was projected to be 0.80. McNeil and Pauker (1982) have reviewed the sources of bias in the two approaches. The time trade-off approach seems to understate the positive utility of a man-year with a given condition—that is, it overstates the disutility of having a disease. In our tuberculosis example, the woman may understate the value of losing 10 years of life (years 63–73), and consequently the 0.68 estimate for tuberculosis may be an underestimate. The surgical mortality to avoid the disease gamble posed by Card (1980) has the opposite bias— overestimating the utility of a man-year with a given disease. Many respondents may overreact in favor of living with any condition to avoid the distasteful alternative, instant surgical death, hence overstating the value of having a condition (i.e., 0.8 for complete blindness seems high).

The alternative shadow-price concept can also be applied to arrive at quality weights for adjusting the value of additional years of existence. Klarman (1965) utilized an analogous disease approach to measure the willingness-to-pay value of escape from early manifestations of syphilis by the proxy disease psoriasis, and the late manifestations of syphilis by the proxy of terminal cancer cases. Direct data acquisition for "unstigmatized" medical conditions like cancer and psoriasis was more easily accomplished than directly working with syphilis victims.*

Economists must work with physicians to develop proxies and weighting schemes for capturing the multiplicity of dimensions of health care outputs. Inappropriate priorities might be set if survival probabilities are not integrated with quality-of-life factors. Doctors agree that patient preference is important in some circumstances, but if clinicians do not know how to quantitate the trade-off, clinicians often overlook the issue of individual preference. A relatively unconventional but rational treatment, like wearing a truss for a hernia or trying radiation therapy for cancer of the larynx, is often ignored, downplayed, or misrepresented (relative to how "wonderful" surgery can be). Both society and the individual may not want to value all years of life equally. For example, a national artificial heart program in 1990 may cost $200,000 to $900,000 per man-year of life saved (Lubeck, 1982), and these man-years of life may only have a QALY value of 0.70 or 0.80. Alternatively, one might devote $1 billion to a nationwide cardiac disease prevention program like the Stanford Heart Disease Prevention Program's Three Community Study. The prevention alternative would be saving man-years of life with QALY values in excess of 0.95. The author (Lubeck, 1982) did not specifically take QALYs into account, but the issues of QALY weights may prove more critical in other cases (e.g., bone marrow transplants). The decision concerning a strategy to combat heart disease is a simpler case, since the benefit-cost ratio is somewhere between 20- to 200-fold higher in the preventive program relative to a heart implant program.

---

* One of the major shortcomings of the DFE approach is that to capture fully the intangible costs of losing a life or limb, these attributes must be shadow-priced. The results of economists' attempts to shadow-price such nonquantifiable attributes often sound ludicrous: "She will spend $3,000 more per year on alcohol, drugs, and other things to compensate for a lost breast," or "He will forego sexual experience valued at $40 per encounter, with a frequency of 50 times per year." Even if these costs are a small fraction of the total estimate, one can always discredit the technique by quibbling with the arbitrary price tags.

Fuzzy Reality and the Rationale for Listening to John Q. Public

Physicians and consumers typically deal with probabilities with a terminology that can best be defined as fuzzy semantics: very likely, unlikely, very rare, etc. The user of fuzzy probability statements often obscures the fact that the underlying uncertainty is possibilistic rather than probabilistic—that is, imprecise data lead to imprecise statements concerning possibilities.* Pathologists are unpopular with their fellow physicians for utilizing fuzzy language like "cannot be ruled out" or "consistent with." Recently, this fuzzy language has been defended on the basis of the accuracy with which it describes the conditional possibilities (Legg, 1981). This viewpoint is contrary to the statistical school of thought founded by Reverend Bayes. The Bayesian "true-believer" viewpoint is that all probability guesstimates are real numbers to be manipulated regardless of the imprecise nature of the limited data set.

Physicians do not like to be pinned down by patients on fuzzy issues such as, "What is the chance of improvement? Give me a number." Physicians who exhibit undue ex ante optimism concerning the prognosis for an individual patient are committing one of the most common human foibles. For example, economists have observed the phenomenon of overoptimism among poker players in overvaluing the chance of benefits (and prior winnings) and undervaluing the chance of losing (and understating prior losses). Adam Smith (1776) described this overoptimism in the context of health care:

> The overwhelming conceit which the greater part of men have of their own abilities is an ancient evil. . . . The chance of gain is by every man more or less over-valued . . . chance of loss is undervalued, and by scarce any man in tolerable health (seldom) values loss more than it is worth.

In considering WTP measures to value benefits, one should be cognizant of these potential respondent biases. However, that does not imply that we should ignore or downplay consumers' values as some have suggested. Future research should address the question of whether the excessive faith the public has in new medical technology makes WTP surveys highly sensitive to misleading

---

* The concept of probability is based firmly on recorded outcomes (as a proportion or likelihood), and possibility is a more abstract concept to describe "ease of compatibility." It is often said that a low possibility implies a low probability, but a high possibility need not imply a high probability (e.g., it is highly possible but not very probable that individual X has disease Y).

advertising campaigns or, alternatively, whether "blind" public faith in medicine is on the wane. The first position is supported by the Chicago Mount Sinai Medical Center 1977 market survey, which reports that area residents believe medicine has future miracle techniques and spare parts to fix them no matter how they live their lives. The second position—eroding faith in biomedical techniques and equipment—is supported by media reports concerning the frequency of malpractice. Public interest in medical problems and problems with the health services delivery system is evidenced by the fact that over half of the stories in *Reader's Digest* and *National Enquirer* concern health issues. The coverage in these magazines and others is getting increasingly pessimistic of new medical techniques.

Fighting Analytical Nihilism

One important motto that most politicians keep in mind is to "keep the experts on tap rather than on top." While it is good that we do not presently have a society run by technocrats, it seems reasonable to point out the shortcomings of our current political system. Politicians react to power rather than judiciously weighing all the facts and unquantifiable aspects of the issue. As a result, they have not been able to galvanize concern over the medical cost crisis to make simple benefit coverage limitation decisions. In this context, Blumenthal et al. (1982) outlined a number of difficulties the government may face in making health insurance benefit coverage decisions based on economic analysis. Given the rapidly expanding vista of new medical technology and the antiregulatory mood in Congress, it is hard to expect any one regulatory body to preempt the collective judgments of 6,000 hospitals and half a million clinicians.

The performance of the economics profession has not been without fault. There has been a high degree of public and political disenchantment with model builders who provide narrow definitions of direct benefits and ignore the limitations of their very crude data bases. Little theoretical work has been done to assess the degree to which workers weigh the price of risk taking and consider the probability of premature, work-related death as a variable that is subject to their control.

The multiplicity of quality-of-life dimensions for weighting health benefits will always require the use of consensus decision making and value judgments. How else can society weight the value of a 55-year-old's life saved against a 5-year-old's case of blindness prevented? Encapsulated in that classic quip that economists "know the price of everything and the value of nothing" comes the realization that there are theoretical limitations to either market prices or willingness-to-pay prices in valuing benefits (Torrance, 1986). Prices do not reflect the value of externalities and other assurances (of capacity if needed) enjoyed by nonusers of the service, and the imperfectly informed user of the service may fail to appreciate all the direct or indirect benefits accrued. If consumers valued health care as much as public health professionals, society could simply stop 60 million American smokers from puffing, and perhaps feed the tobacco plants to 5 million hungry livestock. The outcome of this scenario seems pareto optimal to some health officials—that is, 350,000 individuals are prevented from dying annually and the world is fed with a few extra million cattle annually. This rather simplistic analysis overlooks one very important item. Consumers of hazardous chemicals report many intangible personal benefits that far outweigh the personal health and social costs to them.

Mishan (1971) has pointed out that while our enlightened society can hardly avoid making WTP analytical efforts, shadow pricing and value weighting present a multitude of difficulties for research. If consumers are provided with imperfect information, individuals' willingness to pay will sometimes be underestimated (e.g., vaccinations) and other times overestimated (e.g., laetrile). Unfortunately, prima facie evidence does not exist to suggest that every patient should have his or her own family decision analyst to perform risk analysis.

How much consumers are willing to pay for a specific therapy is highly dependent on their current health status. For example, Thompson (1986) estimates that persons without difficulty in climbing steps would pay roughly 19 percent of their income (or $5,160 annually) for a cure to their arthritis. This same figure almost doubles (to 35 percent) for those unable to climb steps. Willingness to pay, not surprisingly, also correlated with pain (self-rated). Subjects without pain stated, on average, they were willing to pay 15 percent of their income to be cured of arthritis, in contrast to 32 percent for those with the highest-rated pain levels. The author reported reasonable, consistent, and rational patterns of response to the WTP survey for over 84 percent of the 247 patients with rheumatoid arthritis (Thompson, 1986). This pattern of plausibility reflects a good questionnaire design, in contrast to some earlier studies (Muller and Reutzel, 1984).

Conclusions

This review has summarized some of the reasons for the less than total enthusiasm for expanding the application of cost-benefit techniques. Cost-benefit analysis, despite all its shortcomings, can improve the quality of micro- and macro-resource decisions. No one wishes to appear to be, or intends to be, callous concerning the selection of a price level for valuing a human life. One could suggest that a more realistic projection of the future for cost-benefit analysis would surely involve cyclic periods of boom and bust. When the economy is in a boom period, cost-benefit will be in a bust period and vice versa. In economical boom periods, society will reject the arbitrary and capricious irrational decisions of our leaders that call for increased prudent use of cost-benefit techniques. In other words, society will be revulsed by the heartless cold decisions of those cost-benefiters in cyclic economical boom periods, but support increased reliance on a benefit-cost calculus in the bust periods. In time, a stable pattern of decision making will evolve and progress in treating disease will not depend solely on one political lobby against another (e.g., hemophiliac vs. renal research). There are no quick and easy answers to a number of technical problems raised in this chapter, and whether reasonably satisfactory solutions can be found remains unclear.

Members of humanitarian professions often provide outrageous reactions to what they describe as utilitarian econometric pyrotechnics for valuing life. The need for candor, consumerism, and a free flow of information to consumers has been implicit in the analysis. Contrary views predominate in many political science departments. For example, Rhoades (1978) has argued that "absence of total candor leaves the way open for the periodic appearance of ambitious reporters and politicians who expose the Dr. Strangelove-like analysts at the heart of the bureaucracy." However, an alternative plan of action invoking total candor, frequent consumer preference surveys, and open communication between the bureaucracy and the public might provide better prospects for the health economy in the 1980s. To label economists simply as Dr. Strangeloves and hope that Congress operates in the name of "doing good" is a highly suspect way of assuring that the health economy can compete with the defense economy.

In summary, the willingness-to-pay approach to cost-benefit analysis is one elixir that will not make decision making any easier, but at least the process could increase consumer input and illuminate the assumptions that currently prevail. The Institute of Medicine (1981*b*) review of the valuation question concluded that the "measurements" are better described as illustrations of methodology than as serious attempts to derive representative answers. The true role of cost-benefit valuation of life resides somewhere between the pessimism of the Institute of Medicine and the naive optimism of many in the economics profession.

References

ACTON, J. (1973). "Evaluating Public Programs to Save Lives: The Case of Heart Attacks." RAND Corporation Report R–950–RC, Santa Monica, Calif.

ALBERT, D. (1978). "Decision Theory in Medicine: A Review and Critique." *Milbank Memorial Fund Quarterly* 56:3 (Summer), 362–400.

ANNAS, G. (1977). "Allocation of Artificial Hearts in the Year 2002: Minerva v. National Health Agency." *American Journal of Law and Medicine* 3 (Spring), 59–76.

ARROW, K. (1978). "Risk Allocation and Information: Some Recent Theoretical Developments." *Geneva Papers on Risk and Insurance, Conference Proceedings* 8:1 (May), Geneva, Switzerland.

BAILEY, M. (1980). *Measuring the Benefits of Life-Saving*. Washington, D.C.: American Enterprise Institute.

BAILEY, M. (1978). "Safety Decisions and Insurance." *American Economics Review* 68:2 (May), 45–55.

BARZA, J., and PAUKER, S. (1980). "The Decision to Biopsy, Treat, or Wait in Suspected Herpes Encephalitis." *Annals of Internal Medicine* 92, 641–649.

BEERY, W., SCHOENBACH, V., and WAGNER, E. (1986). "Health Risk Appraisal: Methods and Programs." Department of Health and Human Services Publication PHS–86–3396. Washington, D.C.: U.S. Government Printing Office.

BLOMQUIST, G. (1979). "Value of Life Saving: Implications of Consumption Activity." *Journal of Political Economy* 87:3 (June), 540–558.

BLUMENTHAL, D., FELDMAN, P., and ZECKHAUSER, R. (1982). "Misuse of Technology: A Symptom, Not the Disease." In B. McNeil and E. Cravalho (eds.), *Critical Issues in Medical Technology*. Dover, Mass.: Auburn House, 163–174.

BROOKSHIRE, D., THAYER, M., SCHULZE, W., and ARGE, R. (1982). "Valuing Public Goods: A Comparison of Survey and Hedonic Approaches." *American Economic Review* 72:1 (March), 165–177.

BUNKER, J., BARNES, B., and MOSTELLER, F. (eds.) (1977). *Costs, Risks, and Benefits of Surgery*. New York: Oxford University Press.

CARD, W. (1980). "Rational Justification of Therapeutic Decisions." *Metamedicine* 1, 11–28.

CATLIN, R. (1981). "Does the Doctor Understand What I Am Asking?" *American Journal of Public Health* 71:2 (February), 123–124.

CONLEY, B. (1976). "The Value of Human Life in the Demand for Safety." *American Economic Review* 66:1 (March), 45–55.

COOPER, B., and RICE, D. (1976). "The Economic Cost of Illness Revisited." *Social Security Bulletin* 39:1 (February), 21–36.

DARDIS, R. (1980). "The Value of Life: New Evidence from the Marketplace." *American Economic Review* 70:5 (December), 1077–1082.

DECONCINI, D. (1978). "Medical Costs and Personal Bankruptcy: Capital Close Up." *Hospitals* 52:21 (November 1), 46–47.

DILLINGHAM, A. (1979). "The Injury Risk Structure of Occupations and Wages." Ph.D. dissertation, Department of Industrial and Labor Relations, Cornell University.

EASTAUGH, S. (1983). "Placing a Value on Life and Limb: The Role of the Informed Consumer." *Health Matrix* 1:1 (Spring), 5–21.

EASTAUGH, S., and HATCHER, M. (1982). "Improving Compliance Among Hypertensives: A Triage Criterion and Cost-Benefit Implications." *Medical Care* 20:8 (August), 1001–1017.

FADEN, R., BECKER, C., LEWIS, C., FREEMAN, J., and FADEN, A. (1981). "Disclosure of Information to Patients in Medical Care." *Medical Care* 19:7 (July), 718–733.

FANSHEL, S., and BUSH, J. (1970). "A Health-Status Index and Its Application to Health-Services Outcomes." *Operations Research* 18:6, 1021–1066.

FEIN, R. (1971). "On Measuring Economic Benefits of Health Programs." In *Medical History and Medical Care*. London: Nuffield Provincial Hospitals Trust, 181–217.

FEINBERG, H., and HIATT, H. (1979). "Evaluation of Medical Practices." *New England Journal of Medicine* 300:18, 1086–1090.

FEINSTEIN, A. (1977). "Clinical Biostatistics: The Haze of Bayes, the Aerial Palaces of Decision Analysis, and the Computerized Ouija Board." *Clinical Pharmacology and Therapeutics* 21:4 (April), 482–496.

FITZPATRICK, G., NEUTRA, R., and GILBERT, J. (1977). "Cost-Effectiveness of Cholecystectomy for Silent Gallstones." In J. Bunker, B. Barnes, and F. Mosteller (eds.), *Costs, Risks, and Benefits of Surgery*. New York: Oxford University Press, 246–261.

GIAQUE, W., and PEEBLES, T. (1976). "Application of Multidimensional Utility Theory in Determining Optimal Test-Treatment Strategies for Streptococcal Sore Throat and Rheumatic Fever." *Operations Research* 24:5 (September-October), 933–950.

GLASS, N. (1973). "Cost Benefit Analysis and Health Services." *Health Trends* 5:1 (January), 51–60.

Graduate Medical Education National Advisory Committee (1980). Report to DHHS Secretary, September, 123.

GREGORY, N. (1980). "Relative Wealth and Risk Taking: A Short Note on the Friedman-Savage Utility Function." *Journal of Political Economy* 88:6, 1226–1230.

GROGONO, A., and WOODGATE, D. (1971). "Index for Measuring Health." *Lancet* 2:7738 (November 1), 1024–1029.

HAPGOOD, F. (1980). "Risk-Benefit Analysis: Putting a Price on Life." In S. Rhoads (ed.), *Valuing Life: Public Policy Dilemmas*. Boulder, Col.: Westview.

HARRIS, P. (1980). Press Release, Office of the Secretary, Department of Health and Human Services, June 12, Washington, D.C.

HARTUNIAN, N., SMART, C., and THOMPSON, M. (1981). *The Incidence and Economic Costs of Major Health Impairment*. Lexington, Mass.: D. C. Heath.

HIMMELSTEIN, D., and WOOLHANDLER, S. (1984). "Free Care, Cholestyramine, and Health Policy." *New England Journal of Medicine* 311:23 (December 6), 1511–1514.

HIRSHLEIFER, J., BERGSTROM, T., and RAPPAPORT, E. (1974). *Applying Cost-Benefit Concepts to Projects Which Alter Human Mortality*. Los Angeles: University of California.

INGELFINGER, R. (1968). "Digestive Disease as a National Problem—Case V—Gallstones." *Gastroenterology* 55, 102–110.

Institute of Medicine (1981a). *Access to Medical Review Data: Disclosure Policy for PSROs*. Washington, D.C.: National Academy of Sciences.

Institute of Medicine (1981*b*). *Costs of Environment-Related Health Effects: A Plan for Continuing Study*. Washington, D.C.: National Academy of Sciences.

JONES, E., DENSEN, P., and McNITT, B. (1979). "An Approach to the Assessment of Long Term Care." In W. Holland, J. Ipsen, and J. Kostrzewski (eds.), *Measurement of Levels of Health*. Copenhagen: World Health Organization, Regional Office, Europe, 299–311.

JONES, J., CLOUGH, J., KLINENBERG, J., and DAVIS, P. (1981). "The Role of Therapeutic Plasmapheresis in the Rheumatic Diseases." *Journal of Laboratory Clinical Medicine* 97, 589–598.

KASS, L. (1975). "Regarding the End of Medicine and the Pursuit of Health." *Public Interest* 40 (Summer), 11–42.

KINSLEY, M. (1981). "Polls and People's Opinion of Hazards." *New Republic* (June 20), 15–19.

KLARMAN, H. (1965). "Syphilis Control Programs." In R. Dorfman (ed.), *Measuring Benefits of Government Investments*. Washington, D.C.: Brookings, 367–410.

KRISCHER, J. (1976). "The Mathematics of Cleft Lip and Palate Treatment Evaluation: Measuring the Desirability of Treatment Outcomes." *The Cleft Palate Journal* 13:4 (April), 165–180.

LANDEFELD, J., and SESKIN, E. (1982). "The Economic Value of Life: Linking Theory to Practice." *American Journal of Public Health* 72:6 (June), 555–566.

LEGG, M. (1981). "What Role for the Diagnostic Pathologist?" *New England Journal of Medicine* 305:16 (October 15), 950–951.

LESTZ, P. (1977). "A Committee to Decide the Quality of Life." *American Journal of Nursing* 77:5 (May), 862–864.

LUBECK, D. (1982). "A Cost-Effectiveness Analysis of Treatment and Prevention of Heart Disease." Working paper, Stanford University Medical Center and the Data Bank Network, Palo Alto, Calif.

LUCE, R., and RAIFFA, H. (1957). *Games and Decisions*. New York: John Wiley.

McCARTY, D. (1981). "Treating Intractable Rheumatoid Arthritis." *New England Journal of Medicine* 305:17 (October 22), 1009–1011.

McNEIL, B., and PAUKER, S. (1982). "Incorporation of Patient Values in Medical Decision Making." In B. McNeil and E. Cravalho (eds.), *Critical Issues in Medical Technology*. Dover, Mass.: Auburn House.

McNEIL, B., WEICHSELBAUM, R., and PAUKER, S. (1981). "Tradeoffs Between Quality and Quantity of Life in Laryngeal Cancer." *New England Journal of Medicine* 305:17 (October 22), 982–987.

McNEIL, B., WEISCHSELBAUM, R., and PAUKER, S. (1978). "Fallacy of the Five-Year Survival Rate in Lung Cancer." *New England Journal of Medicine* 299, 1397–1401.

MISHAN, E. (1971). "Evaluation of Life and Limb: A Theoretical Approach." *Journal of Political Economy* 79:4 (July-August), 687–705.

MULLER, A., and REUTZEL, T. (1984). "Willingness to Pay for Reduction in Fatality Risk: An Exploratory Study." *American Journal of Public Health* 74:8 (August), 808–812.

MUSHKIN, S. (1962). "Health as an Investment." *Journal of Political Economy* 70:5 (October), 129–157.

NEUTRA, R. (1977). "Indications for the Surgical Treatment of Suspected Acute Appendicitis: A Cost-Effectiveness Approach." In J. Bunker, B. Barnes, and F.

Mosteller (eds.), *Costs, Risks, and Benefits of Surgery*. New York: Oxford University Press.

OLSON, C. (1981). "An Analysis of Wage Differentials Received by Workers on Dangerous Jobs." *Journal of Human Resources* 16:2 (Spring), 167–186.

OSTER, G., COLDITZ, G., and KELLY, N. (1984). *The Economic Costs of Smoking and Benefits of Quitting*. Lexington, Mass.: Lexington Books, D. C. Heath.

PERL, L., and DUNBAR, F. (1982). "Cost Effectiveness and Cost-Benefit Analysis of Air Quality Regulations." *American Economic Review* 72:2 (May), 208–213.

PLISKIN, J., SHEPARD, D., and WEINSTEIN, M. (1980). "Utility Functions for Life Years and Health Status." *Operations Research* 28:1 (January-February), 206–224.

PORTNEY, P. (1981). "Housing Prices, Health Effects, and Value Reductions in Risk of Death." *Journal of Environment Economics and Management* 8:1 (March), 72–78.

RHOADS, S. (1978). "How Much Should We Spend to Save a Life?" *The Public Interest* 51 (Spring), 74–92.

RICE, D. (1966). "Estimating the Cost of Illness." *Health Economics*, Series No. 6. Washington, D.C.: U.S. Government Printing Office.

ROURK, M., HOCK, R., PURSELL, J., JONES, D., and SPOCK, A. (1981). "The News Media and the Doctor-Patient Relationship." *New England Journal of Medicine* 305:21 (November 19), 1278–1280.

SACKETT, D., and TORRANCE, G. (1978). "The Utility of Different Health States as Perceived by the General Public." *Journal of Chronic Disease* 31, 697–704.

SCHELLING, T. (1968). "The Life You Save May Be Your Own." In S. Chase (ed.), *Problems in Public Expenditure Analysis*. Washington, D.C.: Brookings, 127–162.

SHATTUCK, L. (1850). *Report of the Sanitary Commission of Massachusetts— 1850*. Cambridge, Mass.: Harvard University.

SMITH, A. (1776). *The Wealth of Nations*. London: London Press.

SMITH, P., KEYES, N., and FORMAN, E. (1982). "Socioeconomic Evaluation of a State-Funded Comprehensive Hemophilia Care Program." *New England Journal of Medicine* 306:10 (March 11), 575–579.

SMITH, R. (1976). *Occupational Safety and Health Act*. Washington, D.C.: American Enterprise Institute.

STARFIELD, B., WRAY, C., HESS, K., GROSS, R., and BIRK, P. (1981). "The Influence of Patient-Practitioner Agreement on Outcome of Care." *American Journal of Public Health* 71:2 (February), 127–131.

STEWART, A., WARE, J., and JOHNSTON, S. (1975). "Construction of Scales Measuring Health and Health-Related Concepts from the Dayton Medical History Questionnaire." In *The Conceptualization and Measurement of Health in the Health Insurance Study*. Santa Monica, Calif.: RAND Corporation.

THALER, R. (1981). "Precommitment and the Value of a Life." *Geneva Papers on the Value of Life and Safety, Conference Proceedings* 11:2 (April), Geneva, Switzerland.

THALER, R., and GOULD, W. (1982). "Public Policy Toward Life Saving: Should Consumer Preference Rule?" *Journal of Policy Analysis and Management* 1:2 (Winter), 223–242.

THALER, R., and ROSEN, S. (1976). "The Value of Saving a Life: Evidence from the Labor Market." *National Bureau of Economic Research* 40, 265–298.

THOMAS, L. (1977). "On the Science and Technology of Medicine." *Daedalus* 106:1 (Winter), 35–46.

THOMPSON, M. (1986). "Willingness to Pay and Accept Risks to Cure Chronic Disease." *American Journal of Public Health* 76:4 (April), 392–396.

THUROW, L. (1984). "Learning to Say No." *New England Journal of Medicine* 311:24 (December 13), 1569–1572.

TORRANCE, G. (1986). "Measurement of Health State Utilities for Economic Appraisal: A Review." *Journal of Health Economics* 5:1 (March), 1–30.

TORRANCE, G. (1976). "Health Status Index Models: A Unified Mathematical View." *Management Science* 22:9, 990–1001.

TURNBULL, A., GRAZIANO, C., BARON, R., SICHEL, W., YOUNG, C., and HOWLAND, W. (1979). "The Inverse Relationship Between Cost and Survival in the Critically Ill Cancer Patient." *Critical Care Medicine* 7:1 (January), 20–23.

URBAN, G., and HAUSER, J. (1980). *Design and Marketing of New Products*. Englewood Cliffs, N.J.: Prentice-Hall.

VISCUSI, W. (1978). "Wealth Effects and Earnings Premiums for Job Hazards." *Review of Economics and Statistics* 60:3 (August), 408–416.

WARNER, K. (1978). "Effects of Hospital Cost Containment on the Development and Use of Medical Technology." *Milbank Memorial Fund Quarterly* 56:2 (Spring), 187–211.

WEINSTEIN, M., PLISKIN, J., and STASON, W. (1977). "Coronary Artery Bypass Surgery: Decision and Policy Analysis." In J. Bunker, B. Barnes, and F. Mosteller (eds.), *Costs, Risks, and Benefits of Surgery*. New York: Oxford University Press.

WHITING, R. (1980). "Ventricular Premature Contractions: Which Should Be Treated?" *Archives of Internal Medicine* 140:10, 1423–1426.

ZECKHAUSER, R. (1975). "Procedures for Valuing Lives." *Public Policy* 23:4 (Fall), 419–464.

ZECKHAUSER, R., and SHEPARD, D. (1976). "Where Now for Saving Lives?" *Law and Contemporary Problems* 40:4 (Autumn), 5–45.

Part Six

DIVERSIFICATION, MULTIHOSPITAL SYSTEMS, AND ACCESS TO CAPITAL

Chapter 19

DIVERSIFICATION FOR THE SINGLE HOSPITAL

It is futile to attempt to eliminate risk, and questionable to try to minimize it. But it is essential that the diversification risks taken be the right risks.

—Peter F. Drucker

We are losing patients. This hospital cannot be just an acute care facility any more and stay in business.

—Teressa VanNorman

Just as the March of Dimes diversified out of the polio business, so should many hospitals diversify out of the hospital business.

—James L. Elrod

The most impressive organizational change in the health economy during the 1980s has been the emergence of health systems where the hospital represents the financial center of the system. Many hospitals view diversification into health and nonhealth (unrelated) ventures as being their only chance for survival into the 1990s. The hospital sector is a good example of the old French couplet, "That's a very bad animal, when it's attacked, it defends itself." The good news about all this talk of "diversification for a fighting chance at survival" is that it is not true in the majority of cases. Indeed, many hospitals diversify because they are cash rich (Eastaugh, 1984). The bad news is that for some hospitals this rhetoric is appropriate and accurate. The terrible news is that many hospitals have yet to discover that one cannot simply relabel a number of unsystematic, disjointed ventures as the hospital diversification plan. A health facility's strength cannot be built through coalescing weaknesses

535

and promoting a collection of uncoordinated joint ventures. Hospitals planning to diversify might consider the following three bits of advice:

1. Do not mess with structure before one has a comprehensive strategy.
2. Do not kill a new service line with insufficient initial capitalization and unreasonable expectations as to profitability.
3. When a mistake has been made, jettison the service line and "recommit the resources to the core business" (Eastaugh, 1985).

In this chapter we analyze the diversification trend in the hospital sector from an economic point of view. The emphasis is on diversification into related lines of business. Historically, many economists had assumed that hospitals maximized their cash flow (net revenue plus depreciation) in order to continually expand their facility. This tendency was often called "empire building" in the 1970s (see Chapter 23). However, in the 1980s the empire-building imperative has been directed away from building beds and toward generating cash flow outside the inpatient arena. Successful diversification can (1) allow accumulation of equity capital to offset anticipated lower capital and operating payment rates, (2) provide a storehouse of liquid assets for feeding the mothership hospital, and (3) generate wealth sheltered from the malpractice attorneys and rate regulators (which can also be channeled back to the mothership to cover unexpected contingencies). Diversification can also generate operational efficiencies for the hospital—for example, if the hospital controls the capacity of its home health agency or nursing home, it can facilitate better inpatient discharge planning.

Diversification: A Cautionary Note

A well-planned diversification program can allow a hospital to create a network of for-profit subsidiaries and holding companies (Gilbert, 1986; Sax, 1986). While diversification can save a hospital from a "plodder" or negative growth existence, poorly selected multiple diversification programs can result in loss of autonomy (takeover or closure). Hospitals have a vast range of technical abilities to analyze return on investment and operate as "active seekers" of emerging diversification options (Harris and Reutz, 1984; Eastaugh, 1984, 1985). The best options for diversification are those not yet documented in any journal article. In the parlance of an economist or organizational theorist (Porter, 1980), this is labeled the "advantage of being first" (or at least first in your market catchment area).

The statistical evidence concerning the advantage of being first is far from uniform. For example, Glazer (1985) reports that in large business firms first entrants are, on average, as likely to fail as second entrants. First entrants carry the risk of being at the early stage in the development of a service market, so that there is a greater danger that patient demand will not increase to the extent predicted. Business risk is not as easily quantifiable as pro forma income (Boles and Glenn, 1986), but the analyst should study the three basic factors: (1) effect on revenue stability (revenue risk), (2) effect on debt dependency and capital structure (financial risk), and (3) effect on the variability of the cost structure (expense risk).

If the new market does not reach the achieved critical mass and exceed the break-even point within a reasonable time, the first entrant will usually label the venture a failure. In the health context, the message might be: Do not try significant investment in a capital-intensive new technology (e.g., plasma apheresis) until one observes a first entrant succeed somewhere in the nation. If the initial investment is not substantial, hospitals need not be so risk averse. However, if the investment at risk is substantial, a second entrant in the market can often experience the safety of diversification into a proven market, soon to reach appreciable size (market demand). On the other hand, the first entrant may still reap some intangible benefits of better knowledge of the market and consumer tastes (preferences).

Any hospital should ex ante (up front) calculate the expected break-even point and a judgment of reasonable time to expect results (e.g., achieve break-even). Such calculations will be open to ex post judgment (e.g., as to whether a second injection of capital is needed to get the new service off the ground; Urban and Hauser, 1980). However, a good marketing survey of the external environment is probably the most critical determinant of successful diversification ventures. When a hospital seems to jump off a cliff, either through excessive diversification or total inaction, if the researcher inquires as to why, 99 percent of the time everything the individual managers did made perfect sense as a response to internal politics. In other words, the fatal mistake was to let internal pressures block out external reality concerning risk and payoff.

Diversification: The Upside

Diversification can produce a more adaptable, flexible health care system that offers the institution new avenues to equity markets (see Chapter 21) and patients greater continuity of care. Internal, strategic, and competitive benefits can be gained through new ventures. What is viewed at one hospital as a "burden that saps management talent" is viewed by a more adaptable institution as an invigorating challenge for management and staff. A diversification effort, when carried out appropriately, can be a powerful mode of altering the institution's competitive position, especially as management gains sufficient experience with assessing business risk. Optimally, diversification is not a risk strategy but, rather, a syndication of risk strategy. New venture strategies should be analyzed using the portfolio theory of business management, where multiple business concerns can dampen the extremes of variability in cash flow in any single business (e.g., inpatient care).

Diversification can be viewed as a strategic management issue in the development of a marketing plan. For example, the basic ways to build market share involve the development of (1) more markets for current service, (2) more services for current markets, (3) more use of current service by the current market, and (4) a mixed strategy of growth in the first three areas. Some argue that the hospital which fails to diversify will be relegated to a "plodder" or negative growth existence in the 1980s. Those hospitals most frequently employing the diversification and consolidation strategy (investor-owned or contract-managed hospitals) have doubled their market share of hospital beds over the past five years, while the rest of the industry talks of retrenchment.

In a classic business marketing text, Kotler (1976) argues that marketing posture decisions usually precede marketing mix decisions. Hospital marketing efforts seldom get by the initial posture decision stage. Hospitals make the choice about how broad or narrow a diversification effort should be made (posture decision) but almost never consider, at least prior to 1983, the strategic decision about whether to use a market penetration or market skim pricing strategy (Joskow, 1981; Eastaugh, 1984).

Hospital administrators frequently submit to tortuous, protracted debates concerning whether their posture decisions should be narrow (e.g., pediatric outpatient services) or broadly diversified (e.g., pediatric inpatient special unit, plus neonatal intensive care unit, plus an organized pediatric outpatient department).

Some types of diversification appear to be simple examples of imitative entry or "bandwagoning," such as the explosion of podiatric services or speech pathology services. Posture variables considered by administrators and trustees include whether the new proposed hospital-based service offers a favorable degree of product differentiation relative to the service offered by incumbents (physicians currently providing the service in private offices). For example, does the hospital offer better quality, better convenience to its intermediate consumers (doctors) to practice medicine more productively, better provision of consumer education to foster increased utilization of health services, or better access to the ultimate consumers (patients)? The hospital, as a centralized service distribution innovator, has the potential to reduce the time cost to physicians and the travel time cost to patients in the provision of many acute medical services.

The "new lines of business" we shall consider in this empirical study are all related ventures—that is, expanding existing medical product lines of service. From a research feasibility standpoint, we are fortunate for four reasons that the sample is limited to New York State and the time frame is prior to 1980. First, the New York reimbursement system only allowed diversification into the narrow medical range of new ventures. Second, New York had the advantage of a uniform reporting data base with stable accounting conventions (Prince, 1982). Third, if the time frame had extended beyond 1979, we would have to disentangle two changes in professional accounting practice (AICPA, 1979; ASD, 1981). And fourth, as a 1983 General Accounting Office (1983) study pointed out while surveying hospitals in California and Nevada:

> *The growth in related organization transactions starting in 1980 not only conceals unallowable costs and overpayments, but also increases the administrative burden on payers because of the need to identify and analyze such transactions. Because the transactions are often complex, Medicare and Medicaid paying agents miss some, and overpayments result.*

In summary, New York hospitals had not been allowed the opportunity to develop the broad array of holding corporations and for-profit subsidiaries that prove beneficial in the states lacking tough mandatory rate-setting programs.

A number of hospitals reportedly have benefited from diversification programs, even in tightly regulated states like New York. Galvagni (1981), for example, reports on two profitable diversification efforts that provided dental care for the handicapped and alcohol detoxification and counseling services to teenagers. Regulators should realize that the diversification trend is not simply motivated to collect profits, but any institution must collect enough retained earnings to render health services in the future and to rebuild and modernize facilities. Further, the product portfolio of the hospital can be diversified to include health promotion and health education activities such as programs designed to improve patient compliance (Eastaugh and Hatcher, 1982).

Analysis of Diversification Patterns

According to one early national study, a clear pattern of diversification develops. The five basic services,, always added prior to any others, are (1) clinical lab, (2) diagnostic x-ray, (3) operating room, (4) delivery room, and (5) emergency room. According to Berry (1973), after these basic services have been established, hospitals begin to add facilities that are characterized as "quality enhancing" (see Table 19.1). According to this descriptive model, derived from published AHA data from 4,295 hospitals, hospitals in stage 2 of their expansion add complexity-expanding services after the acquisition of the quality-enhancing services. These complex services, outlined in Table 19.1, are designed to expand the institution's capacity to treat a much wider variety of diseases, while still preserving an essentially inpatient-oriented institution. The final stage of expansion under the Berry model is to acquire community-oriented services. This stage 3 transformation from a single inpatient orientation to a broad community medical center focus can occur either sequentially or simultaneously with continued growth in the stage 2 acquisition of complex services. One might suggest a fourth stage of expansion for the 1980s—expansion into nonhealth-related, for-profit services to subsidize the core health institution. One major reason to diversify is to subsidize, at least in part, the less profitable inpatient mission of the hospital. However, opportunities to "make money on the side" to finance the under-reimbursed health care mission of the institution were severely limited in New York in the 1970s. Outside of the highly regulated northeastern states, this fourth stage of diversification, the so-called "low road" for diversification in Figure 19.1, is currently the most popular topic for financial feasibility studies.

We shall confine ourselves in this study to diversification ventures into patient-related services not already offered by the majority of New York hospitals in the base year 1974 (Table 19.1). For the purpose of this study, hospital diversification (*DIV*) is calculated as follows:

$$DIV = \frac{\text{number of services available in the hospital}}{\text{maximum number of services (32)}}$$

Table 19.1 Service-Specific Changes in Hospital Diversification between 1974 and 1979 (*n* = 62 New York hospitals, 31 pairs)

Type of Service	Deletions	Additions	Net 5-Year Change
Quality-Enhancing Services			
Diagnostic radioisotope facility	2	8	6
Blood bank	2	7	5
Histopathology lab	1	4	3
Premature nursery	4	5	1
Postoperative recovery room	0	1	1
Emergency department	0	1	1
Pharmacy with pharmacist	3	3	0
Complex Services			
Neonatal intensive care unit	3	23	20
Dental services	5	8	3
Electroencephalography	2	4	2
Pediatric inpatient unit	0	2	2
Cobalt therapy	0	2	2
Respiratory therapy department	1	2	1
Cardiac intensive care unit (CCU)	5	5	0
Psychiatric partial hospitalization program	3	3	0
Therapeutic radioisotope	3	2	(1)
Rehabilitation inpatient department	2	1	(1)
Psychiatric inpatient unit	2	1	(1)
Radium therapy	7	5	2
X-ray, therapeutic	7	4	(3)
Community Services			
Podiatric services	1	16	15
Speech pathology services	2	14	12
Occupational therapy department	3	10	7
Skilled nursing or long-term care unit	0	6	6
Organized outpatient department	2	8	6
Alcoholism/chemical dependency outpatient services	0	5	5
Rehabilitation outpatient department	1	5	4
Inpatient hemodialysis	0	4	4
Physical therapy department	0	3	3
Clinical psychology services	1	3	2
Psychiatric outpatient unit	2	2	0
Psychiatric consultation and education services	4	3	(1)

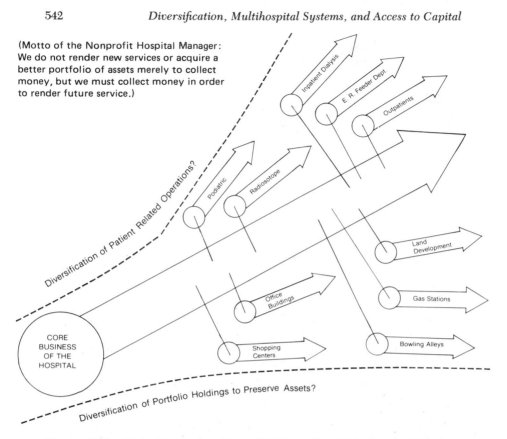

(Motto of the Nonprofit Hospital Manager:
We do not render new services or acquire a
better portfolio of assets merely to collect
money, but we must collect money in order
to render future service.)

Inpatient Dialysis

E. R. Feeder Dept.

Outpatients

Diversification of Patient Related Operations?

Podiatric

Radiosotope

Land Development

Office Buildings

Gas Stations

CORE BUSINESS OF THE HOSPITAL

Shopping Centers

Bowling Alleys

Diversification of Portfolio Holdings to Preserve Assets?

Figure 19.1   Two Roads for Diversification: The High Road? The Low Road? or Both Roads?

The maximum value of *DIV* prior to 1979 was 0.78, meaning that the hospital provided 25 of the 32 possible services. The utilization of a continuous variable *DIV* as a bounded natural index* ranging from 0 to 1.0, rather than an index for each individual type of service (quality-enhancing, complex service, community service), is supported by the work of Klastorin and Watts (1982). Klastorin and Watts expanded on Berry's (1973) study and found that hospitals still continue to add services in a well-defined order. However, in this most recent study, the process of adding services is done in a much smoother, continuous fashion, without distinct service clusters. The two authors conclude that hospitals have become increasingly differentiated over the past decade.

---

* Alternative weighted measures of DIV, weighted by dollars or occasions of service, made little difference in the subsequent regression analysis.

Developing a Model

The central problem in modeling hospital diversification and its impact on the operating ratio is that the relationship is interdependent. For example, diversification might improve the operating ratio in a causal fashion, but the baseline operating ratio might be inversely proportional to the hospital's self-perceived need to diversify. Conversely, a hospital might need a certain baseline operating ratio to afford to finance a diversification effort or to gamble. Diversification might also occur because of expectations as to change in the operating ratio.* In other words, the level of diversification and level of operating ratio are hypothesized to be jointly dependent or endogenous within the context of two simultaneous equations:

Operating Ratio, $M = f$ (Diversification, Exogenous Factors
           Influencing Market Share and
           Reimbursement, Disturbance Term)   (19.1)

Diversification, $DIV = f(M$, Exogenous Factors Impacting on
           Hospital Competition, Physician
           Demand, Financial Posture, Planners'
           Demands to Contain Capital Expansion,
           Disturbance Term)   (19.2)

It is important to note that if we are to study the interdependent endogenous variables DIV and M, and a number of other exogenous variables $(I_1, I_2, \ldots, I_7, I_8)$, it would be inaccurate and misleading to study a typical multiple regression equation:

$$DIV = f(M, I_1, I_2, \ldots, I_6, I_7) \qquad (19.3)$$

In this simultaneous equation situation we are dealing with the regression of a set, or in this case, a pair of dependent variables (DIV, M), regressed upon a set of independent variables:

Simultaneous Situation: $(DIV, M) = f(I_1, I_2, \ldots, I_6, I_7)$ (19.4)

The unit of analysis in this chapter is a matched pair of hospitals. The first stage in the nearest available matching process is to divide the 337 hospitals in New York State in the base period (1974) into nine clusters (three types of service control times three categories for teaching status) based on the following features:

1. Type of service control (short-term general medical and surgical) with the same AHA classification control code (vol-

---

* The subject of rational expectations as it affects hospital economics has been surveyed elsewhere (Battistella and Eastaugh, 1980).

untary paired with voluntary, church-operated paired with church-operated, investor-owned paired with investor-owned).

2. 1974 Teaching Status (pair high/COTH with a peer facility if both hospitals are members of the Council of Teaching Hospitals, pair "other" teaching hospitals with like "other" category, pair nonteaching with nonteaching).

The sampling frame only included hospitals that remained in operation throughout the time frame. Some 36 short-term nonfederal acute care hospitals closed or merged during the study period. Nearest available matching methods have been described elsewhere, both in the hospital context (Eastaugh, 1979, 1984) and within a more generalizable theoretical context (Rubin, 1970). In the second stage of the matching process, "best" pairs were developed on the basis of the 1974 values for the 10 variables in Table 19.2.

In pairing the hospitals, it is hoped that they may behave more nearly alike than do hospitals less closely related. The situation is analogous to designing an evaluation of a new drug, where patients whose prognosis appears to be about the same at the beginning of

Table 19.2   Ten Variables Utilized in the Nearest Available Matching of Hospitals into 31 Pairs ($n = 331$, 1974 Data)

Variable Category	Variable
Diversification	DIV
Output[1] severity	Percent families below poverty line
	Surgical intensity (operations per admission)
	Outpatient intensity (visits per patient treated)
Output complexity	Number of services in the following three (increasingly complex) categories in the Berry system of classification[2]
	Quality-enhancing services
	Community services
	Complex services
Financial health	M, Operating ratio
Other institutional factors fixed in the short-run	Hospital size
	Age of plant

[1]More direct case-mix measures, such as DRGs, are not available in the time period.
[2]The fourth category in the Berry (1973) scheme, labeled basic services, is irrelevant for purposes of our analysis since all New York hospitals had these services. In contrast, the data in Berry's national sample from the mid-1960s contained hospitals even lacking JCAH accreditation.

the study (1974) are paired. The patients are administered different dosage levels of the same drug and then evaluated at the end of the study period (1979). In the case of this hospital study, one asks how did the operating ratio change in response to changes in the dose of diversification? The analogy to the drug evaluation breaks down in one important respect: The hospitals are in control of their own dosage of diversification—that is, expansion is endogenous (within system control) within some exogenous (external, not predetermined by the hospital) regulatory and market constraints. Consequently, the evaluation design is similar to a pretest-posttest situation. However, the hospitals are not in experimental isolation, and a number of other intervening variables must be monitored during the five-year period, such as the introduction of more stringent local Certificate-of-Need programs within the eight different Health Service Areas. The hope is that if one monitors all the market characteristics that could have an intervening effect $(IV_1, IV_2, IV_3, \ldots, IV_m)$, and if the matching process adequately captures other intrinsic characteristics (V_1 through V_z), then the impact of diversification on operating ratio M can be measured as:

$$M = f(DIV, I_1, I_2, I_3, I_4, I_5) \qquad (19.5)$$

The advantage of this approach, rather than collecting data to estimate a more complicated regression equation, is that one need not worry about losing too many degrees of freedom in measuring attributes V_1 through V_z with I_{z+n} additional number of independent variables.

Two final caveats are in order before we proceed to develop a model. First, although the sample is not intended as a valid representative cross section of New York State hospitals, there are only two statistically significant differences between hospitals that could be well matched into pairs (62 hospitals) and the entire state (337 hospitals): (1) the sample consists of 32.2 percent teaching hospitals (statewide the percentage is 26 percent), and (2) the average bed size of the sample hospitals is 14 percent higher than the state average. Second, the accuracy of the matching technique should be cross-validated by comparing the 31 pairs of hospitals to the state reimbursement clusters for 1975. All hospitals in the 31-pair sample were in the same reimbursement cluster as their partner and almost equally positioned relative to being under or over the existing reimbursement ceilings for that cluster. Therefore, the pairing methodology does appear to neutralize any potential differential reimbursement effect. It is more critical to the analysis to note that the pairs of hospitals start with the same operating ratio, plus or minus 0.004, than to assume that their general reimbursement environment must be equivalent if both hospitals are in New York State.

Hypotheses Under Study

Eleven basic null hypotheses are under consideration in our analysis. Since a hospital may need a sufficient operating margin (M) to diversify, and a diversification effort should improve the reimbursement portfolio (assuming one selects above-average arenas in which to diversify) and consequently the operating margin, we hypothesize:

> *Hypothesis 1a:* A nonrecursive simultaneous model, where *DIV* is a function of operating ratio *M* and further, *M* is a function of *DIV*. In our model, *DIV* and *M* are endogenous since they are to a large extent dependent on other variables in the system and under the control of management. (One could alternatively have postulated a recursive model, where *M* does *not* directly or indirectly influence *DIV*, while *DIV* is an indirect or direct determiner of *M*. Instead, we are testing the strength of a nonrecursive model, where in terms of a path diagram, *M* and *DIV* are allowed to form a closed loop.)

Given that the hospital pairs start the time period with the same approximate bed size, diversification index (no pairs were more than 0.031 different in *DIV*), operating ratio (no pairs were more than 0.010 different in *M*), output complexity, output severity, plant age, and teaching affiliation status in base year 1974, we postulate that only three additional exogenous variables impact on operating ratio *M*:

> *Hypothesis 1b:* A positive influence of exogenous bed closings of neighboring hospitals on (increasing) the operating ratio of our paired sample hospitals. Over 6,000 hospital beds were closed with the assent and support of the state health planners during the study period. Bed closure by competitors has the postulated effect of improving the strong surviving hospital's market share, occupancy rate, and financial performance. For this reason, there is a strong theoretical argument for the "safe" hospitals to act as monopolists and support health planning (Havighurst, 1980).

None of the 62 paired hospitals in our analysis was closed. The hospitals that closed tended to be "isolates"—that is, radically different, single-hospital clusters that could not be reasonably paired with any other hospital. A 32nd potential pairing of two hospitals 100 miles apart geographically was not included in the analysis for two reasons: (1) the pairing was by far the most inferior, and (2) both hospitals were closed within three years (1977).

Hypothesis 1c: A positive influence of the exogenous variable *MCARE*, annual fraction of the county catchment area over 65, was postulated to have a positive influence on *M*. Ruchlin and Rosen (1980), in a study of reimbursement of New York hospitals, revealed that Medicare was a more profitable third-party payer, by 4 percentage points per annum, relative to Blue Cross or Medicaid. One should note that in other states Medicare is not always the most favorable payer. We need not consider subtle shifts in New York state regulations, since the effect is presumably constant across all pairs of hospitals.

One might postulate that New York regulations are biased in dealing with hospitals as a function of teaching status, and perhaps hospital size. However, since the hospitals were paired, this bias should presumably be equal across each member of the pair. Consequently, the net effect is irrelevant to our analysis since every variable in our analysis will be defined as the paired difference between the paired hospitals. Conceptually, 31 hospital pairings producing 155 observations over the five-year study period are equivalent to 155 first differences of logs. By matching hospital pairs, instead of having 62 observations with $10 + m$ independent variables (where m is a very large number of additional variables needed to measure the constructs captured in the matching process, including bias in the two years of New York rate reimbursement based on a cluster analysis breakdown by size and teaching status), one is left with 155 observations and 5 to 6 variables per equation.

Hypothesis 1d: A negative influence of the exogenous variable *NONWHITE*, annual fraction of the catchment area nonwhite, is postulated to have a negative influence on *M*. This variable is taken as a proxy measure for the likelihood of bad debt, given that there is a high positive correlation between nonwhites, illegal aliens, lack of insurance, and bad debt to the institution (Ruchlin and Rosen, 1981; Battistella and Eastaugh, 1980).

The logarithmic specification (ℓn) for the long-run operating ratio in year t, with a disturbance term u_t, equals:

$$\ell n\, M_t\, \ell nDIV_t + \beta_2\, \ell nE_t + \beta_0 + u_t \qquad (19.6)$$

where the set of exogenous explanatory variables (E) includes:

BEDCLOSE = reduction in number of beds per capita in the catchment area since 1973.

MCARE = fraction of population eligible for Medicare in the area.

NONWHITE = fraction of population that is nonwhite.

T = time trend variable (1974 = 1, 1975 = 2, etc.).

Five hypotheses are associated with the second equation in our simultaneous model. The academic literature on diversification in the hospital field is rather uneven and anecdotal (Goldsmith, 1980). The most universally mentioned variable in the recent literature is competition. The current concern for competition contrasts sharply with the liberal planning ethic of the last two decades. Planners hoped that if hospitals engaged in cooperative behavior patterns of sharing services and departments, then costs would be contained. Unfortunately, the steady growth in hospital assets per bed in real dollar terms has not slowed in the past 20 years (Eastaugh, 1982). Our purpose in this study is to test the link between more competition and increased diversification.

The search for an appropriate measure of competition has yielded little in the way of econometric performance. Russell (1979) has used the traditional four-firm concentration ratio (market share of the four largest hospitals) to proxy competition, with little success. An alternative index seems in order. Schmalensee (1977) reports that the four-firm concentration ratio is inferior to the Herfindahl index. The four-firm ratio can only be used with confidence when dealing with highly concentrated industries (e.g., automobiles). The Herfindahl index* summarizes the entire size distribution of firms in a market. The Herfindahl index can range from 1.0, by definition, for a natural monopoly situation (e.g., a very rural hospital) to a low of 0.09 in our sample. Since the Herfindahl measure is an index of noncompetition, we hypothesize:

> *Hypothesis 2a:* A higher Herfindahl index, as a proxy for less competition, will be associated with less diversification—that is, H should have a negative impact on *DIV*.

From a hospital manager's vantage point, the direction of change (increasing, decreasing) of this index for noncompetition may be more important than the absolute level of competition. One might postulate that the change in institutional pressures to diversify

----

*Herfindahl Index $(H) = \sum_{i=1}^{N} (P_i)^2$

[where P_i is the market share of the largest hospital in the catchment area (population size ranges 650,000 to 2,000,000), and P_2 is the share of the second largest hospital, and so on, in a market with N hospitals.] For more detailed information on the Herfindahl index refer to Dansby and Willig (1979). The nature of the noncooperative behavior between hospitals in more densely concentrated markets (with low H index) was originally outlined by Lee (1971).

over time might depend more on the recent direction of change in the level of competition. That is, if competition is on the upswing, a manager might be less risk averse and more likely to take a gamble on a diversification proposal. However, if the level of competition is stable or declining, the manager may be less likely to gamble. In other words, the impact of our anticompetitive index *H* on *DIV* might vary as a function of whether *H* had been decreasing in the recent past. We hypothesize:

> *Hypothesis 2b:* The coefficient for the *H* index is smaller and less significant when *H* has been declining (competition increasing) in the last two years, relative to the coefficient for *H* when the index has been stable or increasing. *H* is postulated to have a less negative influence on *DIV* when competition has been increasing (*H* declining), perhaps because the manager's aversion to risk taking would be diminished in the increasingly more competitive environment.

A number of analysts have suggested that the exogenous pressures to diversify are generated, in part, from medical specialists (Lee, 1971; Greer, 1982; Eastaugh, 1984). We hypothesize:

> *Hypothesis 2c:* The ratio of specialist physicians per 10,000 population in the area has a positive impact on diversification.

A third exogenous variable postulated to impact on diversification behavior is the ability of local health planning groups to retard the rate of hospital asset expansion. Moreover, even though all diversification efforts do not require equivalent amounts of major movable equipment and new plant assets acquisition, it does seem plausible to suggest that the areas with the tougher health planning programs could negatively affect the diversification index impact. Obviously, the markets with a higher rejection rate of Certificate-of-Need applications would be the more difficult areas in which to diversify for certain types of services. We hypothesize:

> *Hypothesis 2d:* Certificate-of-Need rejection rates in the local HSA area, as measured by a two-year moving average, will have a negative impact on DIV. The 1979 ex ante CON rejection rates based on 1977 and 1978 data are reported in Table 19.3.

The ninth hypothesis we wish to test is whether *M* has a differential impact on DIV, depending on whether the financial position of the hospital is improving or not. The argument is somewhat analogous to hypothesis 2b, in that, if financial position is on the upswing, the manager might be less likely to take a gamble on a diversification proposal. This null hypothesis could be labeled the "fat and happy" theory of "not rocking the boat" if the

Table 19.3   **Characteristics of the Eight Study HSAs in New York State, 1979 CON Rejection Rates, and 1979 Population**

HSA	1979 CON Rejection Rate (= PLAN)	1979 Projected Population	Percent of State Population
#1, Western New York	0.3113	1,751,000	9.7
#8, Nassau-Suffolk	0.2632	2,745,000	15.2
#2, Finger Lakes	0.2313	1,225,000	6.8
#4, N.Y.-Penn (for N.Y. only)	0.2195	324,000	1.8
#5, Northeastern N.Y.	0.1762	1,405,000	7.8
#6, Hudson Valley	0.1689	1,969,000	10.9
#3, Central N.Y.	0.1549	1,446,000	8.0
#7, New York City	0.1412	7,222,000	39.8

boat appears to be improving without further rebuilding or restructuring (Eastaugh, 1984). We hypothesize that:

> *Hypothesis 2e:* The coefficient for M is smaller and less significant when M has been increasing in the last two years, relative to the coefficient for M when the operating margin has been stable or on the decline.

This hypothesis was suggested by hospital administrators in the data collection process. The administrators managing consistently in the "bad year" column A of Table 19.4 complained that the few hospitals able to run in the black (column C) were the only hospitals that had the financial wherewithal to afford to diversify aggressively and consequently improve or preserve M over time

Table 19.4   **Operating Ratio *(M)* Trends for the Sample of Matched New York State Hospitals**

Year	Number of Matched Hospitals Operating Ratio (M)[1]			
	(A) Under .985 "Bad Year"	(B) .985 to .999 "Typical Year"	(C) Over 1.0 "Good Year"	Median Value M
1973	22	24	16	.986
1974	20	20	22	.992
1975	23	17	22	.988
1976	25	22	15	.989
1977	37	11	14	.978
1978	34	11	17	.981
1979	36	12	14	.977

[1]Operating ratio equals operating revenues divided by operating expenses, or 1.0 plus the operating margin. Bottom-line operating margins include nonoperating revenue in the calculation.

"against the onslaught of state rate regulators." The last point suggests two additional null hypotheses for inclusion in our analysis:

Hypothesis 3a: Time is postulated to have a negative impact on operating ratio M and a potential positive impact on the purely technology-driven component of diversification (*DIV*). The argument that uniform statewide rate regulation has deteriorated the average operating ratio over time has been well documented (HANYS, 1985; Cleverley, 1986).

Hypothesis 3b: Teaching status may interact with the management philosophy of the institution and consequently have an impact on the equation for *DIV* and M. Therefore, we shall run the analysis for the entire sample, and then rerun the analysis for the 10 pairs of hospitals that are teaching hospitals separate from the 21 pairs of hospitals that are nonteaching hospitals.

To summarize our equation for *DIV*, differential diversification between pairs of hospitals is taken as a function of one endogenous factor (operating ratio $= M$) and four exogenous variables. To test the hypothesis that diversification is more a function of $(DM)/(dt)$—the change in financial status over time—we test the efficacy of creating two variables:

$MUP = (-\sigma)(M) =$ Operating Ratio Increasing
$MSD = \sigma M =$ Operating Ratio Stable or Decreasing where $\sigma =$
  1.0 when $M_t < M_{t-1}$

The log-linear form will be utilized; thus all the estimated coefficients represent short-term elasticities. The diversification equation has the following specification, in time t with disturbance term v_t:

$$\ell n\ DIV_t = \gamma_1\ \ell n\ MUP_t + \gamma_2\ \ell n\ MSD_t + \gamma_3\ \ell n\ F_t + \gamma_0 + v_t \qquad (19.7)$$

where the set of variables F includes:

$HDOWN = \Theta\ H_t =$ Competition Increasing

$HSG = (1 - \Theta)\ (H_t) =$ Competition Stable or Declining
[where $H =$ Herfindahl index, and $\Theta = 1.0$ when $H_t < H_{t-1}$,
  otherwise $\Theta = 0$]

$SPECMD =$ specialists in the catchment area per 10,000 population

$PLAN =$ CONs rejected in the area/total CONs submitted in the
  area
[where CON $=$ CON proposals (involving expenditures) in years
$t - 1$ and $t - 2$].

$T =$ time trend variable (1974 $= 1$, 1975 $= 2$, etc.).

Analysis

The simultaneous system was estimated by means of two-stage least squares utilizing diversification and exogenous market data from 1974–1979. The model was also estimated by means of ordinary least squares (OLS). We estimated regressions of the simultaneous relationship between *DIV* and *M* using pools of the time-series observations for 31 pairs of hospitals. Statistical investigation did not reveal any heteroskedasticity problems of changing variance in the disturbance terms. The Durbin-Watson test revealed no apparent problems of serial correlation in the error terms (autocorrelation). Multicollinearity is not much of a problem in the analysis, since only one item in the correlation matrix has an absolute value in excess of 0.40 (*SPECMD* and *M* are negatively related, $r = -0.582$).

The results for the operating margin equation are reported in Table 19.5. Diversification has its predicted positive impact on operating ratio, and this is statistically significant in all six cases. Moderate support is presented for hypotheses 1b and 1c, in that the coefficients are positive for Bedclosure and Medicare variables, but the results are only significant at the 0.10 level. Strong support is provided for hypothesis 1d and hypothesis 3a. There seems to be a steady deterioration in the operating ratio under the influence of the state rate formula system, consistent with reports that New York hospitals are facing critical financial problems. However, for the average New York hospital in our sample, the -0.004 negative impact on *M* per year can be compensated for by $+0.0034$ per new service added. This suggests that diversification is one means to compensate for "cost-minus" reimbursement.

The results for the *DIV* equation, excluding the statistically insignificant *T* variable (rejecting hypothesis 3a), are reported in Table 19.6. Hypothesis 2a is supported, as a larger Herfindahl index is associated with less diversification. However, the negative impact of *H* on *DIV* was not statistically significant for the 29 percent of cases where competition was increasing (*HDOWN*), strongly supporting hypothesis 2b. All else equal in the equation, the 71 percent of hospitals not experiencing an increase in competition (*HSG*) were able to avoid adding two new services in the five-year time period relative to the other facilities (*HDOWN*, competition up). Neither the popular nor the economic concept of competition is adequately represented by the *H* index, but the results are suggestive. The impact of declining *H* or increasing *DIV* is approximately equivalent in teaching and nonteaching hospitals. One might speculate that as the hospital industry's noncompetitive

Table 19.5 Estimated Operating Margin Equations, for Teaching and Nonteaching Hospitals, Under Two Estimation Methods: Single Equation OLS and TSLS, Normalized Variable ℓn M

Type of Hospital[a]	Estimation Method	ℓnDIV	ℓnBEDCLOSE	ℓnMCARE	ℓnNONWHITE	T	Constant	R Squared
Teaching	TSLS	0.025[b] (.010)	0.021[b] (.012)	0.039[b] (.018)	−0.181[c] (.062)	−0.002 (.002)	0.021 (.076)	.821
	OLS	0.042[c] (.016)	0.019 (.013)	0.038[b] (.017)	−0.193[c] (.064)	−0.003[a] (.0017)	0.024 (.079)	.814
Nonteaching	TSLS	0.031[c] (.009)	0.010 (.018)	0.027[a] (.016)	−0.165[b] (.061)	−0.004[c] (.001)	−0.038 (.097)	.754
	OLS	0.62[c] (.013)	0.008 (.018)	0.025 (.017)	−0.169[b] (.059)	−0.004[c] (.001)	−0.040 (.098)	.741
All Pairs	TSLS	0.046[b] (.0019)	0.037[a] (.021)	0.029[a] (.016)	−0.196[c] (.053)	−0.003[b] (.0013)	0.014 (.100)	.847
	OLS	0.065[c] (.0025)	0.034[a] (.020)	0.028[a] (.016)	−0.198[c] (.053)	−0.004[c] (.0014)	0.006 (.106)	.845

NOTE: The estimated standard errors are in parentheses.

[a] The three clusters of hospitals have 44, 99, and 149 degrees of freedom, respectively.

[a] Statistically significant at the 10 percent level, utilizing appropriate t-test (Comanor and Wilson, 1974).

[b] Statistically significant at the 5 percent level.

[c] Statistically significant at the 1 percent level.

Table 19.6   Estimated Diversification Equation, for Teaching and Nonteaching Hospitals, Under Two Estimation Methods: Single Equation OLS and TSLS, Normalized Variable ℓn DIV

Type of Hospital[a]	Estimation Method	ℓnMUP	ℓnMSD	ℓnHDOWN[b]	ℓnHSG	SPECMD	ℓnPLAN	Constant	R Squared
Teaching	TSLS	0.843[c] (.449)	−0.034 (.027)	−0.011 (.046)	−0.760[d] (.303)	−0.109[c] (.065)	−0.142 (.178)	0.006 (.137)	.730
	OLS	0.852[c] (.454)	−0.019 (.020)	−0.019 (.048)	−0.765[d] (.304)	−0.113[c] (.064)	−0.136 (.181)	0.001 (.140)	.716
Nonteaching	TSLS	0.562[d] (.241)	3.067[e] (.859)	−0.096 (.068)	−0.583[d] (.264)	−0.172[c] (.097)	−0.396[d] (.153)	−0.012 (.090)	.698
	OLS	0.575[d] (.247)	3.412[e] (.961)	−0.089 (.063)	−0.596[d] (.271)	0.176[c] (.099)	−0.401[e] (.153)	−0.008 (.097)	.684
All Pairs	TSLS	0.674[d] (.312)	1.58[d] (.620)	−0.046 (.062)	−0.682[d] (.277)	0.024 (.016)	−0.270[c] (.154)	−0.009 (.123)	.732
	OLS	0.684[d] (.314)	1.93[e] (.723)	−0.051 (.065)	−0.689[d] (.275)	0.017 (.011)	−0.272[c] (.155)	−0.004 (.129)	.728

NOTE: The estimated standard errors are in parentheses.

[a]The three clusters of hospitals have 42, 97, and 147 degrees of freedom, respectively.

[b]H (Herfindahl index) declining means competition is increasing, whereas HSG stable or growing implies that competition is stable or declining.

[c]Statistically significant at the 10 percent level.

[d]Statistically significant at the 5 percent level.

[e]Statistically significant at the 1 percent level.

facade subsides in a neighborhood, contrary to hypothesis 3b, the managers of teaching and nonteaching hospitals are equally willing to take risks to maintain (or improve) financial position and market position.

There is little support for hypotheses 2c and 2d in most cases, except that the planners' rejection rate does appear to be significant at the 1 percent level in deterring diversification at the 21 nonteaching hospitals. However, planning appears to have no inhibiting impact on the teaching hospitals. One could speculate that teaching hospitals have more political power and a better ability to bargain with health planners (Lewis and Sheps, 1983). Moreover, equally consistent with hypothesis 3b is the finding that hypothesis 2e is only supported in the case of nonteaching hospitals. Surprisingly, the inverse of postulate 2e appears to be operating in the case of teaching hospitals. That is, teaching hospital managers only gamble on diversification if they are experiencing improved financial health (M increasing), but nonteaching hospital managers are more willing to gamble on diversification if their operating ratio is stable or declining. Nonteaching hospital managers are less concerned with gambling if they are "fat and happy" (high M) relative to the other 77 percent of the sample hospitals. Further research is needed to ascertain the differences between the three types of hospital management concerning (1) risk aversion, (2) ability to negotiate with planners, and (3) preferences for what services are best for diversification.

A growing army of lawyers and consultants are available in all 50 states to sell hospitals on a diversification plan. The plan is sometimes developed on a "turn key" basis—that is, all hospitals get approximately the same strategy advice with only marginal changes in where to diversify. Some naive hospital administrators buy the "unique" plan of the more unscrupulous (atypical) consultants: "Diversify, it's fail-safe, and you cannot help but make money." Such administrators would do well to study the failure rate of diversification programs in industry. Not enough hospitals do a complete analysis of future patient volume, cash flows, overhead, fixed startup costs, and the potential political and economic problem of undermining existing programs and clinics. Diversification is often sold with the simple argument that the more diverse the product lines, the greater the number of affiliated physicians, and, therefore, the more patients.

Future research into the increasingly costly world of hospital diversification might profit by considering the work of business economists. Biggadike (1979) suggests that a bold approach is necessary to make diversification into new product lines successful. Large-scale, aggressive ventures into broad scope product lines report the fewest negative short-run financial results and the best long-run returns on investment. A middle-road approach of medium breadth, and only moderate aggressiveness, yielded the worst of all possible worlds: the most negative financial results and a lack of managerial patience (e.g., kill new product lines if they are not profitable in two to three years). In private industry it is better to be either low or high in aggressiveness or scope of diversification than in the middle in the land of compromise. A number of analysts (Leontiades, 1980; Eastaugh, 1984) have speculated (1) that small-scale gambles with diversification require less than average managerial patience to see the project to conclusion since the maximum regret (loss) is low and (2) that large-scale gambles may require less than average patience because the initial commitment has been so large that management fears the long-run consequences of timidly "cutting our losses" and pulling back on diversification (retrench). Bowmann (1982) reports that troubled business firms continue to take more risks, thus contributing to the negative empirical association between risk and return.

Alternative Qualitative Models and Future Research

The quantitative results of this small study must be regarded as tentative. However, the results for nonteaching hospitals suggest a potential interesting interaction between planning, diversification, and competition. The qualitative model presented below explains the quantitative and qualitative (anecdotal) information collected in this study with a life-cycle hypothesis for hospital behavior. The qualitative model we shall employ is a cusp catastrophe model (Chidley, 1976), developed from the differential topology branch of pure mathematics. The word "catastrophe" implies sudden change and not necessarily a "bad" outcome. The strength of catastrophe models is that they explicitly recognize that hospital managers make interactive decisions, often with a jump (quick change, add two or three services), feedback, and imperfect incomplete information.* Two organizations in approximately the same position on

---

* This theory has been applied in developmental biology. Instead of changing gradually as one generation shades into the next, Harvard biology Professor Stephen Gould argues that evolution proceeds with a discrete lurch or jump. Supporters of Darwin have to defend the past existence of hypothetical "missing links," but under Gould's new theory there are not any gradual transitional forms and thus no need to postulate "missing links." Species can either have a positive "catastrophe" or "leap" for the better and improve, or a negative catastrophe and become extinct. Gould labels this theory the "punctuated-equilibrium theory of evolution."

paper may experience two entirely different short-run futures: pervasive rapid change or none at all. Given the infancy of such qualitative models, the best we can do is generate a reasonable descriptive model, invoke limited tests for plausibility, and, as always, suggest avenues for future research.

The financial ability and desire of a hospital to diversify changes suddenly, by fits and starts, in a fashion quite inconsistent with the typical linear regression analysis model. The qualitative pictorial catastrophe theory model for describing sudden change might better capture the interactions between competition, diversification, and external planning regulations. This model assumes that diversification behavior is controlled by two conflicting motivations, growth and retrenchment, as plotted in Figure 19.2 on the axes of the horizontal (control) surface. The behavior of the institution, which ranges from diversification to consolidation to contraction, is represented on the vertical axes. For any given point on the folded behavior surface [i.e., the surface (P,CM) equals the combination of pressures to retrench and pressures to grow and compete], there is usually one point of most probable behavior.

The point of most probable behavior is located directly above the point on the control surface (P,CM) and at an elevation directly proportional to the degree of diversification on the Y-axis. However, in the center of the figure, where pressures for competition and retrenchment are approximately in balance (E, Neutrality), there always exist two points of probable behavior (examples: A and AA, also B and BB). A small prior change in P or CM can produce a large change in behavior D (diversification). The higher of these two points on the behavior surface (A) represents an aggressive institutional philosophy ("Let the planners be damned") and the other point (AA) at a low value for diversification represents submissive inactivity ("Ignore the competition, please the regulators, and see what happens"). The intermediate point (A') represents the least likely of the three possible points, neutrality or status quo. This might be summarized in the homily, "It's hard to sit on a fence for long; things either have to fall right or left." In undertaking the diversification "catastrophe" to expand (jumping from B to BB), an institution faces the risk of having overdiversified and collapsing down through the contraction catastrophe (A to AA) in the future. Conversely, a facility that believes "things must get worse before they can get better" and resides at point AA for a time, may survive and have the opportunity to diversify into vacated markets at some future date.

If the hospital is pressured to compete but is not seriously hampered by the local Certificate of Need decision makers, then some aggressive action such as diversification could be expected. If

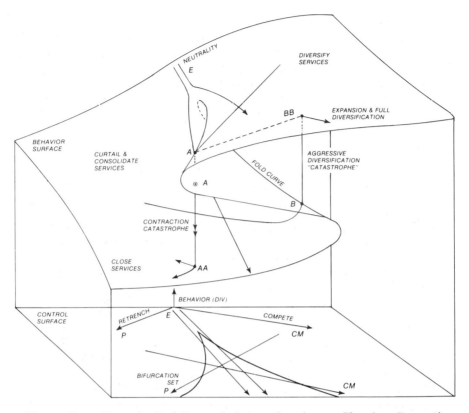

Figure 19.2   Hypothesized Dynamic Interaction Among Planning, Competition, and Diversification Behavior. The most diversified (aggressive) modes of behavior are assigned the highest values on the behavior axis (DIV) in this figure. For each point on the control surface (i.e., the surface (P, CM) equals the combination of pressures to retrench and pressures to compete) there is usually one point of most probable behavior. This point is located directly above the point on the control surface (P, CM) and at an elevation directly proportional to the degree of diversification. However, in the center of the figure where pressures for competition and retrenchment are approximately in balance (E, Neutrality), there always exists two points of probable behavior (examples: A and AA, also B and BB). A small prior change in P or CM can produce a large change in behavior DIV (diversification). The word "catastrophe" implies sudden change, and not necessarily a "bad" outcome.

the hospital is not pressured to compete or expand market share but is faced by the frequent negative decisions of the CON decision makers, then passive inaction toward advocates of diversification, both internal and external (i.e., consultants), could be expected. The interesting question is what if the institution were suddenly faced with a highly pressured environment to expand through diversification or contract under the planners' thumb in 1975? The two controlling factors, to compete or contract, are then in direct conflict. The regression models do not accommodate either discontinuity or the need to respond retroactively or proactively to these opposing pressures, thus predicting (inaccurately) that the two pressures tend to cancel each other (Eastaugh, 1984). In other words, the regression models tend to predict that the hospital will remain indifferent to countervailing forces and "stand pat" with the status quo. Such prediction of a neutral "canceling out" effect is indicative of the inaccuracy of regression models, since standing with the status quo is in fact the least likely behavior (i.e., 12 percent close, while two-thirds of those that remain move to diversify eventually, and one-fifth opt to reduce or contract services significantly).

The administrators of nonteaching hospitals in our subsequent telephone survey reported residing in one of three positions (Figure 19.3): (1) recovering from a period of unsuccessful diversification and planning slow strategic growth for the next few years (cloud *RRR* in Figure 19.3); (2) teetering on the brink of an aggressive move to diversify into two-to-four new services (cloud *BBB*); and (3) highly diversified and content with 19 to 23 of the services listed in Table 19.1 (cloud *FFF*). The order by which hospitals might cycle through a life history of expansion and contraction before reaching a final state of either closure or well financed fully diversified "nirvana" is outlined in the flow diagram in Figure 19.3.

In the recent past, increasing competition (*HDOWN*) appears to be statistically insignificant (not impacting *DIV* adversely). That is, many hospitals have made the leap from *BBB* to *FFF* (by way of point *B* and *BB* in Figure 19.3), whereas *HSG* appears to be statistically significant in suppressing *DIV* up to this point (1979) in time. Few New York hospitals have yet to arrive at point *A* to make the "leap" downward to *AA*, and eventually back to *RRR*. However, one might predict that some hospitals may consolidate back from *FFF* to *A* over the next five years if New York regulatory pressures remain strong, including the downward pressures on rates. Competition stable or declining (*HSG*) could become statistically significant as hospitals make the "leap" downward from *A* to *AA* (to consolidate). The natural life of hospitals may follow a cyclical period of boom and bust, moving from *BBB* to *B* to *BB* to *FFF* to *BB* to *A* to *AA* to *RRR* and back to *BBB*. The driving force behind this boom and bust would be the cycles of boom and bust for exogenous competitive, rate regulatory, and planning regulatory forces. The life-cycle concept is a popular topic in the burgeoning field of organizational theory and behavior (Shortell et al., 1985; Kimberly, 1980).

Our catastrophe life-cycle model demands further study in

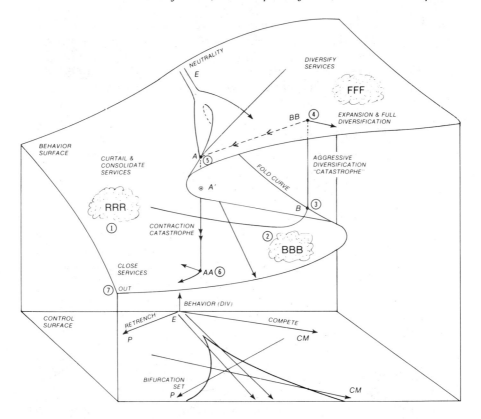

Note: The typical New York hospital started the cycle in positions RRR or BBB during the study period.

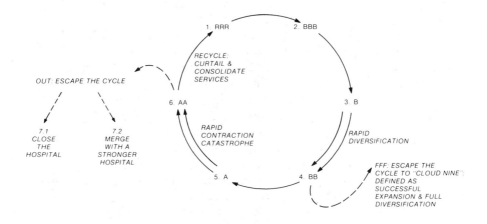

Figure 19.3   Hypothesized Life Cycle for Hospital Diversification Behavior

hopes that we may better understand the complex behavior of hospitals. One central strength of the cusp catastrophe model is the capacity to describe pictorially the complex dynamics of a multitude of interacting pressures. A second advantage is the ability of cusp models to describe a hospital behavior like diversification (dependent variable) that has two very different outcomes for *DIV* given the same exact underlying independent variables (competition, planning, etc.). Regression analysis distorts reality in this case by collapsing two distinct behavior points into one single function (linear or nonlinear). For example, regression modeling would be of little help in describing the discontinuous change in going from *A* to *AA* in Figure 19.2.

One critical element missing from our study is the manner in which physicians interact with management and trustees. A study by Meyer (1982) defines three different styles of management adaption to the short-term catastrophe of a doctor's strike. One hospital acted as a conservative status quo "defender." A second hospital in the area was characterized as the experimental playful "prospector" hospital willing to make small-scale gambles to improve its poor financial position. The third hospital was labeled as an "entrepreneurial-analyst" firm willing to make only a few large-scale commitments to new market niches and sheltering most of its substantial financial reserves. Future research might explore whether the hospital-based physician community splits into two basic divisions: (1) the diagnostic division containing equal numbers of prospectors and defenders and (2) the therapeutic division consisting of a multitude of defenders and a few entrepreneurial-analysts willing to "convince management to make that one large-scale bet." The hospital that grows in the 1980s under Medicare prospective payment may be the institution with the vision to follow the entrepreneurial-analysts into geriatric day care and home health care, as well as in service delivery keyed to particular human problems, such as alcoholism, hypertension, marital dysfunction, and wellness and health promotion. Hospitals may follow the example of U.S. Steel and drop inpatient care as their primary or core business. Due to a strong five-year diversification effort, in fiscal 1984 energy and chemicals replaced steel as the company's primary profitable product.

Policy Implications

The odds against diversification are high in many regulated markets. Indeed, some hospitals in moderately good financial health (relative to their neighbors) will find the odds for success in broadly diversifying very unattractive. For the financially well managed or financially destitute institution teetering on the edge of a catastrophe, the urge to gamble a little or a lot, respectively, may lead to diversification of services. In the first case, the management and trustees might be more interested in "having some fun" and "doing some good" by building a balanced corporate portfolio of service offerings. In the second case, the management might have to convince the trustees that "if we want to stay afloat in this regulated environment, we better find some money-making service areas to subsidize our money losers." The incentive compensation plans reviewed in Chapter 11 are one mechanism to assure that the hospital sector can attract education prudent risk-takers, whether they are administrators or clinical managers.

The hospital is an important civic enterprise in our society. Hospitals with broad and lateral interests in the health and well-being of their consumers are likely to grow through diversification into other medical arenas rather than expand into unrelated lines of business. The popularity of hospital restructuring plans has to be tempered by concern for direct and indirect administrative costs. The forward-looking diversified institution should be better able to adapt to unforeseen, and many times unforeseeable, changes in the regulatory climate. Unfortunately, the impact of competition and "financial health" on hospital diversification has usually been presented in a static and anecdotal fashion. Competition always seems to prompt diversification. The picture is most complex in the case of financial health, since a hospital with a good operating margin can, depending on whose anecdotes one believes, either (1) breed complacency because lack of necessity impedes innovation, or (2) breed rapid diversification because the operating margin provides the venture capital for the hospital to experiment. However, the numerous anecdotes from northeastern and sunbelt states ignore the more plausible existence of a dynamic interaction by the decision makers. In a dynamic situation, the first derivative of competition (increasing or decreasing) and financial health (improving or deteriorating) may be more crucial to the diversification issue than the absolute level of either competition or financial health.

The Current Context

Diversification is a delicate undertaking that involves many nonfinancial concerns. A rational portfolio framework must consider how to select new ventures, which internal and external partners are appropriate, and how much capital investment will be required. One should not oversimplify the situation and jump from a quick and dirty competitor analysis to decision. To paraphrase H. L. Mencken, for each complex alternative there is a simple explanation, and it is very often incorrect. The diversification plan can be accomplished through acquisitions, internal joint venture spin-offs, partial ownership joint ventures, contractual minority investments, or joint cooperative agreements. Every market situation is different, and generalizations about structure and process are often hazardous. A medical mall that may work as a profitable venture in some states may fail in the New York market.

The most substantial diversification activities that are likely to dampen the magnitude of revenue variability (e.g., from low DRG or HMO payments) are also the most fraught with risk. The trustees of each institution must counterbalance the risks against the rewards of improved financial autonomy. Initial and ongoing financial requirements of the diversification effort must be carefully assessed. In a highly regulated state like New York, most of the ventures are health related, but many might still carry a substantial risk. Just because a hospital is successful in heart surgery does not mean that it will be successful in mobile lithotripsey. Hospital managers should reflect on the fact that 60,000 businesses go bankrupt each year.

Since the initial study period (1974–1979), the same 31 pairs of hospitals were resurveyed during the summer of 1986. The second stage of diversification activities in these New York hospitals is summarized in Table 19.7. New York hospitals still cannot avail themselves of the benefits, and the risks, of substantial diversification into nonhealth-related services. Many of these new services are driven by community need (e.g., AIDS education), and obvious new developments in technology (e.g., MRI, Table 19.7).

Summary

Hospital diversification and its impact on the operating ratio were studied for 62 New York hospitals during the period 1974–1979. Diversification and operating ratio were modeled in a two-stage least squares (TSLS) framework as being jointly dependent. Institutional diversification was found to yield better financial position, and the better operating ratio allowed the institution the wherewithal to diversify. The impact of external government planning and hospital competition was also measured. An institution life-

Table 19.7   A Second Generation of Diversification, 1983–1986: 58 Surviving New York Hospitals (29 Pairs*)

Activity	1983	1986
Capital-Intensive Services		
CT scanner	9	21
Magnetic resonance imaging (MRI)	0	4
Lithotripter	1	7
Mobile lithotripter	0	1
Open-heart surgery	13	11
Cardiac catheterization	22	21
Ultrasound	41	50
Ambulatory surgery	1	29
Labor-Intensive Community Services		
Home care	12	30
Health promotion	33	42
Hospice	6	9
Chemical dependency	14	16
Psychiatry	16	17
Organized outpatient department	39	42
Rehabilitation	20	31
AIDS consultation and education services	0	7
Child-abuse assessment unit	3	9

*Of the original 31 pairs (62 hospitals), two pairs of hospitals (4 facilities) closed between 1979–1986.

cycle hypothesis was advanced to explain hospital behavior: boom and bust, diversification and divestiture, occasionally leading to closure or merger. However, one should be careful not to generalize these results beyond the New York State context. Restructuring of the organization, unrelated business ventures, and transactions with related organizations were not a problem in this sample. However, in 1983, many new corporations were set up so that their revenues do not become part of the hospital's revenues; their complex transactions conceal unallowable costs and maximize reimbursement. The chapter concluded with the presentation of a number of hypotheses concerning hospital administrators' attitudes toward risk.

We have not exhausted the range of ventures into which hospitals may diversify. Increasingly, efforts are more specialized and targeted to a specific patient segment (e.g., eating disorder units, diabetes fitness programs). Hospitals will find competition from a number of firms and institutions. For example, increasingly freestanding surgery centers are competing with hospitals. The number of independent surgicenters has grown from 41 in 1975, 130 in 1981, 410 in 1985, and an estimated 830 by 1990.

Ambulatory surgery has been one of the fastest growing diversification options. The fraction of hospitals operating ambulatory surgery facilities has increased from under 200 in 1983 to over 80 percent of American Hospital Association members in 1986. An estimated 30 percent of operations were done on an ambulatory basis in 1986. Some analysts project that 50 to 60 percent of inpatient surgery in 1991 could be conducted on an ambulatory basis. Payers favor ambulatory surgery for the obvious cost savings potential. Shannon (1985) estimates that 600 million inpatient days could be saved annually if 60 percent of operations were done on an ambulatory basis.

Another area for rapid diversification is primary care. The first emergicenter opened in 1973. According to the National Association for Ambulatory Care, the number of free-standing urgent care centers grew from 1,190 in 1983 to 3,000 in 1985, and an estimated 5,500 are projected by 1990. The gains can be substantial for those institutions that diversify into the "correct" service lines for their market. Careful analysis can increase the probability of success. A shotgun approach, with too many diversified ventures, will almost surely guarantee financial failure.

References

American Institute of Certified Public Accountants (1979). "Proposed Statement of Position, Clarification of Reporting Practices Concerning Hospital-Related Organizations" (August).

American Institute of Certified Public Accountants, Accounting Standards Division (1981). "Statement of Position 81-2, Reporting Practices Concerning Hospital-Related Organizations" (August). New York: AICPA.

BATTISTELLA, R., and EASTAUGH, S. (1980a). "Hospital Cost Containment." *Proceedings of the Academy of Political Science* 33:4 (Fall), 192–205.

BATTISTELLA, R., and EASTAUGH, S. (1980b). "Hospital Cost Containment: The Hidden Perils of Regulation." *Bulletin of the New York Academy of Medicine* 56:1 (January–February), 62–82.

BERRY, R. (1973). "On Grouping Hospitals for Economic Analysis." *Inquiry* 10:4 (December), 5–12.

BIGGADIKE, R. (1979). "The Risky Business of Diversification." *Harvard Business Review* 57:3 (May-June), 103–111.

BOLES, K., and GLENN, J. (1986). "What Accounting Leaves Out of Hospital Financial Management." *Hospital and Health Services Administration* 31:2 (March-April), 8–27.

BOWMANN, E. (1982). "Risk Seeking by Troubled Firms." *Sloan Management Review* 23:2 (April), 30–43.

BUZZELL, R., and WIERSEMA, F. (1981). "Successful Share-Building Strategies." *Harvard Business Review* 59:1 (January–February), 135–144.

CHIDLEY, J. (1976). "Catastrophe Theory in Consumer Attitudes Studies." *Journal of Marketing Resarch* 18:2 (April), 64–91.

CLEVERLEY, W. (1986). "Hospital Financial Condition Under State Rate Regulations." *Hospital and Health Services Administration* 31:2 (March-April), 135–147.

CODDINGTON, D., and POTTLE, J. (1984). "Hospital Diversification Strategies: Lessons from Other Industries." *Healthcare Financial Management* 38:12 (December), 19–24.

DANSBY, J., and WILLIG, J. (1979). "Industrial Performance Gradient Indexes." *American Economic Review* 69:2 (June), 249–260.

EASTAUGH, S. (1985). "Hospital Diversification and Business Risk." Keynote address to the Greater New York Hospital Association Annual Meeting (April 16).

EASTAUGH, S. (1984). "Hospital Diversification and Financial Management." *Medical Care* 22:8 (August), 704–723.

EASTAUGH, S. (1982). "The Effectiveness of Community-Based Hospital Planning: Some Recent Evidence." *Applied Economics* 14:3 (September), 475–490.

EASTAUGH, S. (1979). "Cost of Elective Surgery and Utilization of Ancillary Services." *Health Services Research* 14:4 (Winter), 290–308.

EASTAUGH, S., and HATCHER, M. (1982). "Improving Compliance Among Hypertensives: A Triage Criterion with Cost-Benefit Implications." *Medical Care* 18:10 (October), 1001–1017.

ELROD, J. (1986). "Can Municipal Bond Futures Contracts Minimize Financial Risk?" *Healthcare Financial Management* 40:4 (April), 40–45.

GALVAGNI, W. (1981). "Hospitals Diversify to Thrive in a Competitive Environment." *Hospitals* 55:7 (April), 131–136.

General Accounting Office (1983). "Hospital Links with Related Firms Can Conceal Unreasonable Costs." GAO/HRD 83-18 (January 19).

GILBERT, R. (1986). "Hospital Revenue Diversification: A Case Study in Joint Venturing." *Healthcare Financial Management* 40:4 (April), 46–53.

GLAZER, A. (1985). "The Advantages of Being First." *American Economic Review* 75:3 (June), 473–480.

GOLDSMITH, J. (1982). "Competition: How Will It Affect Hospitals?" *Health Care Financial Management* 12:11 (November), 64–74.

GOLDSMITH, J. (1980). "The Health Care Market: Can Hospitals Survive?" *Harvard Business Review* 58:5 (September-October), 100–112.

GREER, A. (1982). "Medical Technology and Professional Dominance Theory." Urban Research Reports, University of Wisconsin, Milwaukee.

HARRIS, J., and RUETZ, J. (1984). "Rate of Return: A Tool to Evaluate Diversification." *Healthcare Financial Management* 38:12 (December), 28–34.

HAVIGHURST, C. (1980). "Antitrust Enforcement in the Medical Services Industry: What Does It All Mean?" *Milbank Memorial Fund Quarterly* 58:1 (Winter), 89–124.

Hospital Association of New York State (1985). "13th Annual Fiscal Pressures Survey, 1981" (March), Albany, New York.

JOSKOW, P. (1981). "The Effects of Competition and Regulation on Hospital Bed Supply and the Reservation Quality of the Hospital." *Bell Journal of Economics* 11:2 (Autumn), 421–447.

KIMBERLY, J. (1980). *The Organizational Life Cycle: Issues in the Creation, Transformation, and Decline of Organizations*. San Francisco: Jossey-Bass.

KLASTORIN, T., and WATTS, C. (1982). "A Current Reappraisal of Berry's Hospital Typology." *Medical Care* 20:5 (May), 441–449.

KOTLER, P. (1976). *Marketing Management*, 3rd ed. Englewood Cliffs, N.J.: Prentice-Hall.

LEE, M. (1971). "A Conspicuous Production Theory of Hospital Behavior." *Southern Economic Journal* 38:7 (July), 48–59.

LEONTIADES, M. (1980). *Strategies for Diversification and Change*. Boston: Little, Brown.

LEWIS, I., and SHEPS, C. (1983). *The Sick Citadel: The American Academic Medical Center and the Public Interest*. Cambridge, Mass.: Oelgeschlager.

MEYER, A. (1982). "Adapting to Environmental Jolts." *Administrative Science Quarterly* 27:3 (December), 515–537.

PLACELLA, L. (1986). "Choosing a Growth Strategy: Diversification Versus Vertical Integration." *Trustee* 39:11 (November), 26–28.

PORTER, M. (1980). *Competitive Strategy: Techniques for Analyzing Industries and Competitors*. New York: Free Press.

PRINCE, T. (1982). "Changes in Accounting Practice." *Health Services Research* 17:4 (Winter), 391–398.

RUBIN, D. (1970). "The Use of Matched Sampling and Regression Adjustment in Observational Studies." Ph.D. dissertation, Harvard University.

RUCHLIN, H., and ROSEN, H. (1981). "The Process of Hospital Rate Regulation: The New York Experience." *Inquiry* 18:1 (Spring), 70–78.

RUCHLIN, H., and ROSEN, H. (1980). "Short-Run Hospital Responses to Reimbursement Rate Changes." *Inquiry* 17:1 (Spring), 42–53.

RUSSELL, L. (1979). *Technology in Hospitals*. Washington, D.C.: Brookings.

SAX, B. (1986). "Joint Ventures and Illegal Remuneration: The Pressure Is Growing." *Healthcare Financial Management* 40:3 (March), 38–43.

SCHMALENSEE, R. (1977). "Using the H-Index of Concentration with Published Data." *Review of Economics and Statistics* 59:2 (May), 186–193.

SHANNON, K. (1985). "Maximizing Outpatient Surgery Could Cut 600 Million Patient Days Yearly." *Hospitals* 59:10 (May 16), 61.

SHORTELL, S., MORRISON, E., and ROBBINS, S. (1985). "Strategy Making in Health Care Organizations." *Medical Care Review* 42:2 (Fall), 227–266.

THEIL, H. (1971). *Principles of Econometrics*. New York: John Wiley.

URBAN, G., and HAUSER, J. (1980). *Design and Marketing of New Products*. Englewood Cliffs, N.J.: Prentice-Hall.

Chapter 20

FOR-PROFIT MULTIHOSPITAL SYSTEMS

He profits most who serves the best.

—ADAM SMITH

Stirring visions of legendary entrepreneurial exploits enhance self-esteem while obscuring the implications of what is actually happening. The competitive strategy is akin to pouring new wine into old bottles.

—ROGER BATTISTELLA

The medical entrepreneurs are risking more than money. They may be risking the security and effectiveness of institutions people depend on to provide services. There is a moral as well as a business judgment involved in taking such risks. Corporations give us a strong national defense against the danger of a noncompetitive health system in which obsolete care is not replaced by modern medicine because public funds are unavailable and private capital is unappreciated.

—MICHAEL BROMBERG

We should not manage capital or labor any different in the nonprofit sector. Everybody used to think there was a great difference between business and universities because one is profit and one tax-exempt. As president of Carnegie-Mellon University I am as interested in the bottom line as any business.

--RICHARD CYERT

568

Many analysts have marked the trend away from individual independent hospital governance toward membership in investor-owned chains or tax-exempt multihospital systems. The fraction of community hospitals in multihospital systems increased from 20 percent in 1977, to 34 percent in 1984, and an estimated 50 percent by 1987 (Rosenstein, 1986; Brown and Klosterman, 1986). However, with the sale of 40 acute medical/surgical hospitals by investor-owned chains in 1986, many of these new health care conglomerates would be more accurately labeled multifacility health systems (providing care, and often offering an insurance product, HMOs, and PPOs). The hospital chains of five years ago are the health care corporations of today. The 1,100 for-profit nonpsychiatric hospitals comprise 19.2 percent of the beds and 13 percent of the hospitals (Table 20.1). The Institute of Medicine study (1986, p. 28) assessed the nature of 436 for-profit system acquisitions between 1976 and 1984. Of these 436 hospitals, 34 percent were formerly proprietary independent hospitals, and 46 percent were for-profit chain-owned. The remaining 20 percent were tax-exempt community or public hospitals, the majority of which were bought from 1981 to 1984.

Rapid growth of investor-owned chains became a hot topic for debate among tax-exempt hospital managers anxious for corporate capital or fearful of imminent loss of autonomy. However, for-profit managers have a growing number of problems: poor earnings, excessive reliance on debt, and high corporate overhead (Table 20.2). Certain chains had acquired a number of financially poor performing small tax-exempt hospitals (e.g., Hospital Corporation of America and American Medical International). However, as a general rule the large teaching hospitals were profitable the year prior to acquisition (sale or lease). In 1984–85, 10 tax-exempt teaching hospitals with 5,100 beds and 5 to 14 percent profit margins joined investor-owned hospital chains. Some analysts were fearful that investor-owned chains would take over the hospital industry.

Needless to say, the fears of a massive industry takeover were grossly overstated. The biggest continuing trend seems to be the growth of nonprofit hospital chains, ranging from tightly knit centralized secular chains to alliances such as Voluntary Hospitals of America (VHA) or American Healthcare Systems (AHS). By the end of 1986 such nonprofit systems may well have represented 21 percent of the hospitals and 27 percent of the hospital beds in the nation. Many tax-exempt chains are consolidating into larger firms. For example, Health Central and Health One Corporation are

Table 20.1 Investor-Owned Capacity, Number of Beds, Facilities, Occupancy Rate, and Market Share of Total, Nonfederal, Short-Term General Hospitals, 1946–1986

	Investor-Owned (For-Profit)			Total Nonfederal Short-Term General[a]			Investor-Owned Market Share	
Year	Number of Hospitals	Beds	Occupancy Rate	Number of Hospitals	Beds	Occupancy Rate	% Hospitals	% Beds
1946	1076	39,000	64.1	4444	473,000	72.1	24.2%	8.2%
1951	1190	41,000	61.6	5050	520,000	73.3	23.6	7.9
1956	990	37,000	60.0	5270	583,000	72.0	18.8	6.3
1961	856	38,000	65.5	5477	655,000	75.0	15.6	5.8
1966	852	48,000	69.0	5812	768,000	76.5	14.7	6.3
1971	750	54,000	71.0	5865	867,000	76.7	12.8	6.2
1976	752	76,000	64.8	5956	961,000	74.4	12.6	7.9
1981[b]	729[c]	88,000	66.4	5879	1,007,000	75.9	12.4	8.8
1986 est.	1100	123,000	48.0	5740	944,000	63.0	19.2	13.0

aDoes not include psychiatric facilities in either column (the investor-owned sector owns, leases, or contract manages 180 psychiatric facilities) (total number of hospitals 180 + 1,160).

bBetween 1961–1981, 75 percent of the investor-owned acquisitions were solo, free-standing investor-owned doctors' hospitals being bought by chains (no change in AHA control; investor-owned before and after). However, in the period 1981–1986, 65 percent of the acquisitions by investor-owned chains were tax-exempt (nonprofit) facilities, including 16 teaching hospitals.

cFigures include 149 independent proprietary hospitals (9,000 beds) that are not members of investor-owned chains.

Table 20.2 Scope, Capacity, and Financial Performance of Seven of the Eight Largest Investor-Owned Hospital Chains, 1986

	Owned (in U.S.) Hospital Beds	Managed (in U.S.) Hospital Beds	Owned or Managed (foreign) Hospital Beds	1986 Occupancy Rate (%)	Annual U.S. Pretax Profit per Acute Care Beds	Accounts Receivable Days 1986	Net Capital Expenditures 1985 ($ M)	Net Debt/Capital (%)	Interest Coverage Ratio 1985	1985 Corporate Management Costs as % of Net Revenue
1. Hospital Corp. of America[a]	36,400	24,389	3,320	50	$15,000	64	1,300	49	3.4x	2.5%
2. American Medical International Inc.	17,000	100	3,689	45	$13,900	84	700	48	3.9x	3.0%
3. Humana Inc.	16,389	0	707	49	$21,000	48	325	63	4.8x	2.0%
4. National Med. Enterprises[b]	11,762	3,746	822	53	$14,000	67	650	55	3.9x	3.2%
5. Charter Med. Corporation	5,862	321	362	44	$11,200	62	210	67	3.2x	2.8%
6. Republic Health Corporation[c]	5,181	2,017	0	39	$10,900	75	80	71	1.6x	3.3%
7. Am. Healthcare Management Inc.[d]	3,323	251	0	-	-	-	-	-	-	-
8. Universal Health Services Inc.	2,979	436	0	51	$14,400	56	115	71	2.0x	3.3%

[a]Statistics on uncompensated care vary by chain. HCA reports 4.4 percent of gross revenues go to bad debts. AMI reports 4.1 percent of gross revenues go to uncompensated care. Humana and NME both report revenue deductions of 3.2 percent of gross revenues.

[b]Includes Psychiatric Institutes of America, Brim & Associates.

[c]Republic has gone private; that is, as of September 1986 it is no longer a publicly held company. Private ownership, following the leveraged buyout, should allow the owners more degrees of freedom to cut costs and restructure the company.

[d]Firm 7 (AHI) is listed on the AMEX, but has not responded with further information. Firm 9 (Nu-Med Inc.) has 2,100 owned beds and 2,400 managed beds, and Paracelsus (firm 10) has 1,667 owned beds in the United States and 3,200 owned or managed in Germany (corporate headquarters) and other countries.

consolidating at the end of 1986 into one firm, with revenues of $295 million, combined assets of $406 million, and 34 hospitals. The rhetorical passion of the debate over corporate control reflects the fact that proponents of chains focus only on the desirable implications (e.g., better access to capital for modernization; Bromberg, 1984), while critics fanatically denounce handing the health care system over to an "army of promotors and financial speculators." Just as it is not informative to compare for-profit chains with a nonexistent ideal nonprofit hospital, it is equally silly to suggest that for-profit firms are perfect entrepreneurs. For example, the March 1986 National Council of Senior Citizens report lambasted for-profit medicine for "dumping patients on the street" and other unethical activities. Unfortunately, the report was inaccurate in one respect: Every example provided of for-profit medicine was in fact done by a tax-exempt nonprofit teaching hospital (e.g., Dallas-Fort Worth Medical Center, Rush-Presbyterian-St. Luke's).

Financial pressures have blurred the distinction between for-profit and tax-exempt facilities. Nevertheless, we shall survey the structural differences between the two sectors. Tax-exempt hospitals are generally responsible to a voluntary board of trustees (typically unpaid prior to 1984, often paid trustees in today's market). The managers who operate the tax-exempt facility have no claim on the assets; but since 1984 they are increasingly paid with incentive compensation plans that closely mirror the proprietary sector (see Chapter 11). Managers of for-profit firms often receive compensation in terms of preferred stock and a claim on certain assets. It is a moot point whether stock ownership provides for-profit managers significantly more incentive than tax-exempt facility managers (with incentive pay) to take action based on mainly economic grounds. Tax-exempt hospital boards are struggling to make their organizations as market-driven, businesslike, and incentive-based as possible. As the two quotes by Bromberg and Cyert at the beginning of this chapter suggest, the drive for a surplus of revenues over expenses has become an essential goal of both for-profit and nonprofit institutions.

As befits the academic controversy regarding for-profit health care and corporate organizations (chains, nonprofit, or proprietary), this chapter examines a wide array of facts, perceptions, and opinions. The demise of the nonprofit, nonbusinesslike hospital correlates, but has not been largely determined by, the rise of for-profit hospital chains in the early 1980s. One problem with the literature in this area is that the authors often falsely equate correlation with causality—that is, if for-profit medicine increased at a time when government retrenchment exacerbated the problem of uncompensated care, then some analysts lay the blame for "dumping" nonpaying patients on the corporate chains (irrespective of any direct evidence). Rising interest in institutional financial position, product-line planning, and the so-called "monetarization" of medicine (Ginzberg, 1984) seem to occur independently of whether the for-profit chains have a 0 to 50 percent market share (Institute of Medicine, 1986). One should obviously entertain alternative hypotheses. If a home radio fails to operate, you do not reject the hypothesis that radio waves still exist; you check the radio and the fuse.

If the academics who exhibit a distaste of for-profit institutions fail to separate correlation from causality, the advocates for investor-owned hospital systems also fail to test their assertions. Although standard economic theory was raised as an a priori fact to prove that for-profit concerns must have greater efficiency and lower patient costs, the opposite turns out to be the case (under cost reimbursement payment conditions 1975–1983; Institute of Medicine, 1986). Much of the overstated inflammatory rhetoric against investor-owned firms was the by-product of (1) false claims concerning cost efficiency and (2) claims that tax obligations serve as payment in full for all social and moral obligations (e.g., uncompensated care). On this second point, the Institute of Medicine study (1986, p. 203) cites the following Humana Certificate-of-Need application:

> *As a taxpayer, Humana contributes to the provision of indigent care through payment of property taxes, sales taxes, income taxes, franchise taxes, and other taxes. As a result of public policy and their status as taxpayers, Humana hospitals do not have the responsibility to provide hospital care for the indigent except in emergencies or in those situations where reimbursement for indigent patients is provided.*

Although the public finance argument that hospital chains pay taxes can be utilized to defend doing, say, 3.9 percent (of gross patient revenues) for charity care and bad debt, rather than 4.4 percent (as in the nonprofit sector, Chapter 6), chains would benefit from demonstrating how sensitive their admitting policies are toward local market conditions.* In the case of Hospital Corporation of America, Vraciu and Virgil (1986) report that uncompensated care amounts to 3.0 percent of revenues in areas of Kentucky where public hospitals exist, but is 4.8 percent of

---

* The Institute of Medicine study (1986) cites 1983 figures of 3.1 percent for investor-owned chains and 4.2 percent for tax-exempt facilities.

revenues in areas where HCA is the sole provider. For-profit chains may vary widely in their tendency to condone economically motivated transfers or admitting decisions.

Critics of "Commercial" Health Care

Relman (1980, 1983), Ginzberg (1984), and Fein (1986) decry entrepreneurialism in investor-owned hospitals, as they decry such commercialism by physicians and nonprofit hospitals. It is feared that something essential, compassionate, but not well defined will be lost if the service ethos is corrupted by a business ethic or conflict-of-interest situation (e.g., ownership of the facilities to which the provider refers patients). These concerns should be viewed in the context of a two-century old active debate about whether market self-interest can replace charity and compassion as the basis of a society, and whether important social values are eroded by industrialization and commercialization. Neoliberals and Marxists have argued that for-profit activity fundamentally undermines the moral foundation of society (obligation, trust, open access). The radical critics do not view front-line health workers as intrinsically any less ethical in corporate health systems, but they do postulate the existence of a corrupt business ethic in boardroom decisions as to what services should be offered in the community. According to these critics, the general interest of society and the local community become subservient to a distant corporate headquarters that views health care as merely a mechanism to generate profits and please stockholders. Ironically, such charges are seldom backed up with any supporting evidence. If the corporate chain does anything for the public good (e.g., American Medical International starting an 80-bed AIDS-only hospital in Texas), this action is dismissed by critics of for-profit medicine as being pure "public relations."

Advocates of for-profit medicine would counterargue that most of the big investors in health care are individuals with a career commitment to health care. Such investors, if they were merely interested in making money, would invest in something other than health care. Given that 80 percent of American industry groups earn higher profits and pay higher dividends than for-profit hospital chains in 1986, this explanation seems plausible. One could argue that 1986 was an atypically bad year for the investor-owned sector, with earnings declining 20 to 60 percent below 1985 levels. However, according to Value Line Investment Survey statistics, even in a good year for the investor-owned sector (1984), the profits of 62 percent of American businesses exceeded the performance of the hospital chains. While we can reject the myth of excess profitability in the for-profit hospital sector relative to the rest of our economy, one might postulate that investors may derive some nonmonetary "social dividend" in investing in health care. Any such social dividend must be small, declining, and insufficient for multihospital systems to rely on for future capital financing. The social dividend in the minds of owner/employees of the for-profit chains might well be described as "downward sticky" (slow to decline), given that they do not wish to sell their stock too quickly and drive down the price, or they hope that alternative strategies will improve future company returns (dividend yield, capital gains). We shall discuss a number of multihospital system strategies, such as divesting holdings in acute medical/surgical hospitals and diversifying into psychiatric care and long-term care.

Such a normative viewpoint of profitability relative to other for-profit concerns in the economy is not germane for critics of profits in health care (Buchanan, 1982). Critics of the for-profit sector question whether it is legitimate to make any profits from the misfortunes of the ill. Such a standpoint is particularly ironic when it comes from a physician, because doctors have always benefited from billing the ill. Moreover, nonsalaried physicians have always faced a conflict of interest situation earning more profits if they overtreat their patients. Critics are wise to be worried over whether for-profit firms will corrupt fee-for-service clinicians into both overadmitting patients and when prospectively paid (e.g., DRGs), undertreating the patient, so as to maximize hospital profits. However, from the survey of incentive plans in Chapter 11, only one investor-owned firm, based in West Germany, currently appears to be attempting such manipulations (Paracelsus). The rise of a market-driven competitive medical economy has certainly raised financial concerns to a primary goal for all types of hospitals. For some radical analysts, living in the shadows of the 10 best endowed teaching hospitals offers a "let them eat cake" condescension. It is much easier to be charitable and above mundane financial concerns when one has an endowment that exceeds $100 million (and covers the inflation-adjusted replacement value of the institution). Unfortunately, many recent studies have demonstrated that the vast majority of hospitals must be concerned with survival.

In a sellers' market, with rapidly inflating prices and few empty beds, hospital executives could act as if profit was a subordinate goal (Eastaugh, 1984). Reinhardt (1986) applies the same logic to physicians, arguing that with rapidly rising physician fees and fewer doctors, physicians could act as if income were a subordinate goal. Relman's (1986) response to Reinhardt argues that medical care has a crucial moral component that outweighs such crass commercial concerns. Private practitioners are not, as a group, ardent supporters of Relman's philosophy, largely because many individuals view medicine as an entrepreneurial activity (in addition to answering a professional "calling" to do good). Many physicians have invested in clinics, imaging centers, and hospital chains as a hedge to protect their financial futures against anticipated tightening in the payment system.

There are some interesting points of comparison between physician and hospital behavior. Physicians and hospitals are willing to provide some amount of uncompensated care as their social obligation. However, the two sectors have different reactions to a decline in consumer demand and growing oversupply. For-profit physicians seem willing to be saddled with more indigent patients in a market with unfilled appointment slots. In the jargon of economics, they will do more free care if the "opportunity cost" is lowered (Culler and Ohsfeldt, 1986)—they do not have a paying patient waiting to make room for indigent patients. However, a for-profit hospital may feel less sanguine about treating a charity patient and absorbing the unreimbursed variable costs, or treating a Medicaid patient under a program payment scheme that barely covers the marginal cost of such an effort. Only an ideologue could deny the danger of an insensitive for-profit ethos. However, the good news is that most health care providers in for-profit settings still appear to have a sense of ethics. The bad news for Relman's argument, according to Reinhardt (1986), is that excision of all for-profit enterprises from our health care system would not lead to restoration of the old social contract.

Defining Terms and the Search for Balance

Balanced presentation is an approach seldom offered by those engaged in a crusade for or against profit-seeking multihospital systems. The term "investor-owned" shall be used in this chapter to connote companies with a large number of stockholders. The word "proprietary" shall connote the solo, owner-operated institution with a relatively small number of shareholders (e.g., the traditional doctor's hospital, 410 of which have been absorbed by investor-owned chains since 1971). The term "for-profit" encompasses both investor-owned and proprietary facilities. The for-profit hospitals pay income taxes and property taxes. The property taxes are roughly 20 to 25 percent of income taxes.* The term "tax-exempt" is used to connote institutions that do not pay taxes but may retain earnings. The term "nonprofit" insufficiently describes institutions that "should" have no surplus of revenues over expenses. As we learned in Chapter 1, less than 18 percent of tax-exempt hospitals were nonprofit in 1985. In a bad financial year, the term "nonprofit" can describe either a tax-exempt or a for-profit institution.

The concept of profitless health care is moribund. A tax-exempt hospital must earn a profit to render future patient service and stay modern. The Catholic Hospital Association was the first to recognize the financial imperative in 1984 with the poignant slogan: No (profit) margin, no mission. An example of the old-style paternalistic view that deplores both finance and marketing was provided by Dr. Cecil Shepps at the November 1985 annual meeting of the American Public Health Association. Shepps stated that "nonprofit hospitals should be in the business of doing good, expanding a money losing department because it is the right thing to do; not breaking the rules, paying the fines, and making big profits." There are a number of potential areas for argument with those who are (1) quick to label all business concerns corrupt and unethical, (2) quick to treat patients as supplicants rather than valued customers, and (3) quick to reject the hypothesis that departments often lose money because consumers and local physicians steer clear of low-quality facilities (which in turn become unprofitable because they are empty—not because they are providing any better social good).

Shepps, Relman, and Ginzburg would be surprised to learn the degree of convergence among for-profit and tax-exempt hospitals in their board meetings and annual conventions (having attended eight of each since 1985, the author is hard pressed to recall a single point of difference between firms). Even tax-exempt institutions discuss tax issues, because their quasi-independent for-profit subsidiaries have to pay taxes. Managers in both sectors are equally anxious about generating capital to secure a better future for their institution, like university president Richard Cyert, quoted at the start of this chapter. Managers and clinicians view capital as the life blood for rebuilding, modernizing, and remaining state of the art as an institution. Indeed, it seems realistic to view private capital as a better bet than national health insurance or a second federal Hill-Burton program to revitalize the nation's hospitals.

There are still unique features in the investor-owned sector.

---

* Source: Sam Mitchell, Federation of American Healthcare Systems.

Such hospital chains have to pay dividends to their shareholders from profits. They have more of a growth imperative to satisfy stockholders' desire for a long-term capital gain. Students unfamiliar with finance are often surprised to learn that investor-owned capital is also more expensive relative to tax-exempt revenue bonds (about twofold more expensive on average). Consider two hospitals, each producing $1 million in retained earnings after one fiscal year. The tax-exempt hospital can translate this $1 million of current earnings into $2 to $3 million of additional financing (depending on its credit rating), making a total of $3 to $4 million available to improve the capital position of the facility. An overoptimistic spokesperson for the investor-owned chains cited in the Institute of Medicine study (1986, p. 61) claims that a chain could "easily" translate this $1 million in current annual earnings into $25 million of additional financing. In point of fact, the so-called multiplier effect may be half this amount. The future deals, not made with "ease," will be made at substantial cost (in terms of future expected earnings by the capital suppliers).

There are three basic problems with the logic of a 25:1 multiplier effect. First, a portion of the $1 million in current earnings must be paid to shareholders as a dividend (median value 20 percent in 1985 among the big-ten investor-owned chains). Therefore, only $800,000 of the current earnings will be available for leveraging additional capital financing. Second, in terms of additional equity financing through the sale of stock, recent price-to-earnings ratios in 1986 have declined to the 9 to 10 level (from the high flying 15 to 25 P/E ratios of a few years ago). Therefore, the chain will not have nearly the equity financing multiplier of the "heyday era" of hospital chains, circa 1982–1984. The minimally required return to investors is the chain's cost of equity capital (a "low" 16 percent in our hypothetical example in Table 20.3).

One should also consider the obvious fact that owning stock can be a risky venture. Under a debt financing contract the investor payback stream is prospectively fixed, enforceable, and relatively certain. In contrast, because of the risk inherent in being a shareholder, the cost of equity financing is typically double the cost of taxable debt financing (16 percent versus 7.25 percent in our example in Table 20.3). The 16 percent figure could be understated if investors rapidly become dissatisfied with their net yield (annual dividends plus capital gains). Investor-owned chains will differ widely in their messages to the marketplace. Some chains will soon claim they are paying declining dividends because they have implicitly shifted to greater reliance on long-run capital gains (typically promised for nonhospital operations). Other chains may

Table 20.3 **Superior Capital-Multiplier of Investor-Owned Hospitals Requires Compensation for Borrowers and Shareholders—Hypothetical Example, 33 percent corporate tax rate, 28% capital gains, 16% Rate of Return Acceptable to Investors (Dollar Figures 000s)**

	Day 1 1988	Day 2 1988	Day 3 1988	Day 4 1988	Years 1–14 (1989–2002)
Retained earnings from past 365 days	$1,000	800 (RE, retained earnings)	800		
Dividend paid by chain XYZ to shareholders (a "rental" for investing their $)		200			
XYZ sells stock on day 3 at a price/RE ratio of 9.0			7,200		
XYZ issues on day 4 long-term debt at 7.25% per year on $7.2 million in additional debt				7,200	
Capital available				15,200	

Future earnings required
to underwrite the $8 million
of additional equity financing (lines 1 + 3, day 3) assuming investors receive
16% rate of return

Returns 100% in the form of dividends	$1,870 per year
Returns 100% through capital gains in year 15	$2,530 per year

Future earnings required
to underwrite the $7.2 million

of additional debt financing (line 4)	541.3 per year
Additional pretax firm income required to pay shareholders and lenders (line 5, taxes)	$2,400–$3,000

Additional revenues required to generate this much

profit: assuming an 8% profit margin	$20–$25 million
assuming a 10% profit margin	$16–$20 million

be forced to pay a higher dividend yield because the investment community is not gullible enough to believe in unrealistic capital gains estimates.

In our case example in Table 20.3, the shareholders would at minimum (if they were willing to accept a very low 16 percent rate of return) require the chain to earn an additional $1.25 million per annum of after-tax earnings to keep them, as owners, financially secure. The firm would have issued at maximum $7.2 million in additional stock (given P/E ratios of 9 and current retained earnings of $800,000). Given an effective corporate tax rate of 33 percent, providing an annual $1.25 million return to shareholders, totally as a dividend yield, would require additional pretax profits of $1.87 million (line 5, Table 20.3). If the firm anticipated paying the investors through capital gains (taxed at 28 percent), then the future dividends would have to be 1.4-fold higher.

In addition to this $7.2 million of additional stock sold, the firm may be able to issue $7.2 million of additional long-term debt, given ample unused debt capacity. (Many chains do not have a debt-to-equity rate as low as 50 percent and are fighting to convert much of their long-term debt to equity shares.) The $7.2 million in new debt at 7.25 percent interest demands additional coupon interest of $541,300. This debt burden would have to be covered by additional after-tax earnings. On the date of maturity (2002 in Table 20.3), the principal would have to be repaid. The additional $15.2 million (7.2 + 7.2 + 0.8) of financing, hopefully utilized to transform/acquire $15.2 million-plus of income-yielding assets, will require additional annual pretax net income of 2.4 to 3.0 million per annum. In summary, the multiplier effect currently appears to be closer to 15 than 25. And more critically, given an 8 percent profit margin, the investor-owned hospital would have to find an additional $20 to $25 million in annual revenues to pay shareholders and lenders for the use of $7.2 million in each case.

Investor-owned firms have the mixed blessing of access to a unique and flexible, but more costly, source of capital (investor equity). The chain may, in the best case, utilize $1 million in current earnings to attract an extra $14.4 million in financing, but at an average cost of capital of 12 percent (16 + 7.25). If the investor-owned chain were to breach its past promises to shareholders, the cost of equity capital (16 percent) and cost of debt (7.25 percent) could rise significantly. Indeed, broken promises to institutional investors could do more to reverse the growth of for-profit hospitals than anything else on the policy front. In contrast, a tax-exempt hospital with a modest to good credit rating will be capable of parlaying $1 million in current earnings into $3 to $4 million in financing (by borrowing $2 to $3 million at 5.5 to 7.5 percent interest rates, and receiving tax-exempt philanthropy).

Uncertainty and Retrenchment

There are no currently available estimates as to what impact the 1986 federal tax reform act will have on investor-owned corporations. Nationally, corporations are projected to pay $120 billion more taxes over the period 1987–1992 as compared to prior years. However, the investor-owned hospitals might pay a disproportionately small share of this $120 billion (or actually pay less taxes). Investor-owned hospital chains paid atypically high effective tax rates (40 to 43 percent) relative to the statutory rate of 46 percent and the tax-paying firms' national average effective corporate tax rate of 22 percent. Consequently, reducing the statutory rate to 34 percent for all corporations and closing loopholes may yield an effective investor-owned tax rate of 30 to 33 percent by 1988. The effects of tax reform within the investor-owned firms will be far from homogeneous. In 1985, for example, Humana paid close to the statutory rate, whereas National Medical Enterprises (NME) was the most effective firm at tax avoidance and tax deferral. Federal taxes that were deferred, and therefore made available as working capital, represented 10 percent of NME's net working capital in that same year (1985).

In relative terms, tax reform may harm tax-exempt hospitals more than it assists tax-paying hospitals and corporate systems. Caps on bond volume per state, on a per capita basis, will hinder tax-exempt organizations' future access to the bond market. The estimated $1.3 billion of philanthropy paid to tax-exempt hospitals and hospital foundations in 1985 may also be reduced as the tax deduction value of a donor's contribution is worth less as individual tax rates are lowered (50 percent bracket to 28 percent). For the same reasons, the spread between taxable and tax-exempt borrowing rates will decline in the wake of tax reform. In the 50 percent tax bracket, a 7.0 percent tax-exempt return is equivalent to a 14 percent taxable investment. In the 28 percent tax bracket, a 5.25 percent tax-exempt return is the same as a 7.3 percent return on a taxable bond. On a structural level, the tax-exempt organizations that were typically borrowing from taxable institutions (investment companies, insurance firms, banks) may find fewer buyers, or buyers interested in a higher risk premium (higher interest rates) to compensate the firm for the increasing instability in hospital profit margins. To date it is somewhat ironic that taxable corporations often borrow from tax-exempt lenders, such as pension funds, whereas the tax-exempt sector has largely relied on taxable buyers of their tax-exempt debt. Pension funds may begin to question the appropriate risk premium and interest rates for lending to hospital chains with declining earnings rates and falling investor confidence in the stock market.

The biggest question among economic analysts is whether investor-owned hospitals can begin to produce patient care at lower costs than tax-exempt providers. It is no longer a smart strategy to cost more per diem or per admission, as it was when payment methods were dominated by cost-reimbursement principles. Members of the Institute of Medicine (1986) study team should not be surprised that investor-owned care costs 2 to 10 percent more per case based on pre-1984 data. For-profit hospitals achieved the standard of profit maximization simply through "maximization of reimbursement" by generating more costs. Most recently, Pauly (1986) views this 2 to 10 percent cost performance differential as "not of overwhelming practical significance, given the wide variations in costs and prices." For example, in the Watt et al. (1986) study, the initial statistically significant 17 percent difference in net patient service revenue per day fell to less than 10 percent difference (1982 data) once the taxes and contributions were netted out. If investor-owned hospitals prior to PPS had expenses that were 2 to 4 percent higher per admission, adjusting for DRG mix, the differential is inconsequential (as small as the "air turbulence caused by a butterfly in a hurricane"; Pauly, 1986). Table 20.4 surveys the major cost studies of investor-owned hospital expenses per case. Future researchers can test 1987 data to ascertain whether for-profit hospitals have started to cost less, relative to tax-exempt hospitals, by medical and surgical condition, after the rapid erosion of cost reimbursement. The DRG price payment system for Medicare has certainly severed the link between cost and revenues, thus providing incentives to cut costs.

One of the surprising findings of the Pattison and Katz (1983) study of California hospitals was that for-profit chain hospitals' costs per case were 5 percent higher than solo proprietary hospital costs, primarily due to higher corporate administrative and fiscal services expenses. On the face of it, this finding is inconsistent with the claims of multihospital system executives: that dollars and time will be saved (net) at the local hospital level by having the functions of highly specialized corporate experts delegated from headquarters. In theory, the costs of expensive high-quality experts could be spread among a large number cf hospitals and be more cost-effective than each hospital employing its own experts. One is left with two possible conclusions: Either central office is not such a cost-effective bargain or these cost comparisons are mere statistical artifacts of the "maximization of reimbursement" games (whereby the corporate overhead was distributed on paper to those hospitals with the highest cost-paying patient volumes— e.g., to "reap a high dollar yield from your Medicare cost report"). Again, we shall be able to ascertain which hypothesis is correct from future analysis of more unbiased cost reports.

Table 20.4   Investor-Owned Hospital Expenses, Relative to Tax-Exempt, Free-Standing Community Hospitals, Surveyed by the Institute of Medicine Study (1986)

Study	Higher Hospital Cost Per Admit in Independently Owned Facilities	Sample Frame
Lewin et al. (1981)	Chains 4% higher—Not statistically significant	1978 data, 53 matched pairs of hospitals (Calif., Fla, Texas)
Pattison and Katz (1983)	Chains 2% higher	1980 data, 280 California hospitals
Becker and Sloan (1985)*	Chains 8% higher—Per adjusted admit	1979 data, 2,231 AHA survey hospitals
Pattison (1986)	Chains 4–7% higher—Per adjusted admit	1977–1981 data, 230 small (under 250 beds) California hospitals
Watt et al. (1986a)	Chains 5% higher—Not statistically significant	1980 data, 53 Lewin pairs, plus 27 pairs from 5 other states
Watt (1986b)	Chains 4% higher—Not statistically significant	1980 data, 561 AHA survey hospitals
Coelen (1986)	Chains 4% higher—Nonchain proprietary hospitals were 2–3% lower per admission	1975–1981, Medicare cost reports and AHA survey

*Sloan and Vraciu (1983) report 4% lower costs per case in 44 chains hospitals in Florida (1979 data, under 400-bed nonteaching hospitals). Herzlinger (forthcoming) suggests that these studies fail to account for capital costs, not considering the age and real value of the younger for-profit hospitals' assets, and neglecting the public subsidies to tax-exempt hospitals. She factors in these considerations, and concludes that for-profits are less overstaffed, less costly per admission, and charge equivalent amounts per admission. However, her sample of 6 for-profit hospital chains and 8 nonprofit hospital systems excludes most urban inner-city hospitals and public hospitals and includes only the period 1977–1981.

Diversification Turns to Retrenchment

For the four largest investor-owned chains the 1983–1985 period was marked by rapid diversification into the HMO and insurance business. Earnings fell far short of expectations. Diversification to support falling hospital occupancy rates was replaced by hospital sales (e.g., in the spring and summer of 1986 HCA sold 19 hospitals, and NME sold 9). Three of the big four chains (with the exception of Humana) sold their interest in three to five HMOs that summer. For example, AMI reported $25.2 million in annual losses for its insurance division in August 1986. The next month AMI announced the total elimination of this unprofitable division. For the first time in 15 years Humana posted a decline in quarterly profits (8.9 percent for the fiscal period ending May 31, 1986). Humana "hung tough" in support of its HMOs and the insurance product "Care Plus," but a bottom clearly had not been reached in quarterly losses at the Care Plus* division (column 2, Table 20.5). Care Plus only makes sense for Humana in those markets where the firm also has empty hospital beds. Humana has stopped selling Care Plus in six markets where the firm does not own or lease hospitals, which is why the fourth-quarter enrollment figures in column 3 of Table 20.5 have declined.

The best productivity controls in the hospital market are behind the steadily increasing profits in column 1 of Table 20.5. At the least, the Care Plus division generates substantial investment income, in contrast to the Medfirst division with substantial capital costs. The 149 Medfirst free-standing emergent (or urgent) care

Table 20.5 **Eight Quarter Financial Performance of three Humana Divisions, FY 1985–1986**

| Time Period | 1. Hospitals' Pretax Profits | 2. Care Plus | | 3. Medfirst Losses |
		Losses	Enrollment	
1985, Q1	$94.8 million	$ − 1.7 m	56,300	$ − 2.2 m
Q2	98.8	− 2.3	125,900	− 3.3
Q3	108.4	− 1.9	212,000	− 4.6
Q4	111.4	− 3.7	294,500	− 4.6
1986, Q1	111.8	− 2.6	412,200	− 5.7
Q2	112.1	− 27.0	574,600	− 6.4
Q3	126.2	− 21.1	611,700	− 7.7
Q4	126.9	− 24.5	604,000	− 8.0
1985	413.4	− 9.3	294,500	− 14.7
1986	477.0	− 75.2	604,000	− 27.8

* Humana Care Plus is a family of insurance products tailored in each market to undercut traditional indemnity insurance costs by 12 to 20 percent and compete with local HMO and PPO rates. Care Plus promises employers that premiums will be kept in line with the general inflation rate. In the classic "make or buy" decision, HCA decided to "buy" and enter the prepaid market by purchasing firms that administer insurance claims for self-insured companies and converting subscribers to HCA's HealthPlan. NME's HealthPace and AMI's AMICARE also made the same decision to "buy" rather than "make" their insurance product.

centers reported substantial losses of $14.7 million in 1985 and
$27.8 million in 1986 (Table 20.5). However, as we observed in
Table 20.2, Humana is in the best capital position of any of the
investor-owned chains. Humana was purchasing in late 1986 a
Miami-based HMO with 131,000 Medicare enrollees among the
184,000 members. This network model HMO (International Medical Center) will allow managers to better channel patient flow to
Humana hospitals in contrast to IPA model HMOs. Humana
suffers from the same problems that all the chains encountered
when initiating a "Supermed" insurance product: (1) conflict of
goals (to fill beds or make money in insurance), (2) inexperience in
claims management and physician relations, and (3) the inability of
cost-sharing provisions (to have the patient pay more to go to a
non-Humana hospital) to dominate physician preference for nonchain hospitals in many markets (thus filling the beds of the
competition). This problem is particularly acute in markets where
physician relations are less than supportive (e.g., Humana's aggressive ad campaign for Medfirst in San Antonio led to a physician
boycott of three Humana hospitals).

Entrepreneurial vertical integration has to overcome corporate
bureaucracy, interdivision earnings pressure, and poorly integrated marketing efforts (e.g., would the Medfirst campaign adversely
affect Care Plus?). If Humana was the first chain to pursue the
Supermed (provider/insurer/national chain) strategy in 1983 (reviewed in Chapter 24), Humana may well be the last to drop this
strategy (or make it a brimming success story).* Unfortunately,
each of the large investor-owned chains appears to be, to varying
degrees, "rudderless" and "reactionless" (or what the Japanese
refer to as *shirake sedai*). Shall we erect a new savior and buy
psychiatric or rehabilitation hospitals while selling off acute medi-
cal/surgical facilities? Or shall we stick to the strategy of working
with physicians, bolstering insurance or primary care products,
and promoting stringent utilization review?

If scholars seriously debated in 1984 whether investor-owned
facilities would dominate the health care industry, they may soon
overreact in the opposite direction and ask: Will for-profit chains
survive in the 1990s? It is inevitable that investors will redistribute
their capital to nonhealth care industries if they believe the chains
are a poor investment relative to the expected low payment levels.
One might even speculate that the health of Americans in certain

---

* Humana was selected as an example because it had the lowest rate of declining
quarterly earnings (e.g., in Q2 of 1986 AMI reported a 59 percent decline in
earnings).

communities might decline due to the unplanned closure of certain for-profit facilities. For example, in 1986 Texas had 231 for-profit hospitals; California, 223; and Florida, 139. Society must continue to reinvest in the health care system to keep it going and to keep the population healthy. And although capital overinvestment is a problem in many states, for-profit facilities would also be sorely missed in 12 to 18 states. To ask whether profit or service is the primary objective of the firm is an interesting but not highly practical question in a capitalist economy.* People need services, and for-profit concerns can supply what is needed (if they remain decentralized and attuned to local consumer tastes and habits).

After a period of restructuring the balance sheet, taking write-offs on unproductive assets, and selling selected facilities, some of the investor-owned chains should bounce back in the near future. What will distinguish the winners from the losers are their abilities to promote productivity, encourage physician partnerships, integrate strategies, and recognize health care as a regionally consumed service (with widely varying market tastes).

Those who argue that the marketplace has made all hospitals, irrespective of ownership class, more profit-oriented must also consider the question of cause and effect. Those who argue that financial concerns should take a back seat to the professional dominance tradition of old may in fact be reactionary, but they have a clear villain in mind. For-profit chains are the clear villain, because in their rapid growth period (1980–1984) they presumably became the dominant leaders in the world of health care administrators (Longsdorf, 1985). To paraphrase Relman (1983), the rest of the market will be molded to the business ethos of that high-growth group, the for-profit manager. However, rather than cite the "business ethic" as some sort of endogenous source of pollution harming the health care system, it seems more likely that exogenous pressure was applied by the troika of industry, government, and the insurance industry on health care providers to contain costs. In other words, the payers were corrosive of such antibusiness pedestals of "cost is no object" and "resources are limitless." The tax-exempt managers discovered the for-profit efficiency ethos without any help from the for-profit chains. Scholars such as Relman (1983) and Starr (1982) might consider the problem of bias and whether they have an untested distrust of corporate culture.

---

* Many neoliberals still believe, as does Moammar Kadafi, that all forms of profit in health care are inherently exploitive. On the other hand, it is a nightmare for many to imagine that America's doctors would become "slavish" devotees of remote corporate officers whose prime responsibility is to their shareholders.

Tax-Exempt Hospitals Go for Profits

Chapter 19 highlighted the rapid diversification into for-profit ventures by tax-exempt firms. To the extent that the tax-exempt hospital is in reality a profit-seeking firm, there is no reason to expect behavior varying significantly from the proprietary norm. The for-profit corporations of a fully diversified tax-exempt hospital in 1986 are like tentacle feeders for the "nonprofit" (or lower profit) "mothership" hospital. The hospital may be a member of a tax-exempt multihospital system, alliance, consortia, or group purchasing arrangement. Members of this corporate culture, relatively new to the health care industry, are in an analogous position to Odysseus. This new breed of managers are caught between (1) the Charybdis of the consumerist's fears that they are as "greedy" and profit-oriented as the investor-owned chains and (2) the Scylla of the medical staff's noble hope that the hospital's original mission remains unaffected by structure. Most managers tend to side with their physicians and justify this massive restructuring of the hospital organization as a vehicle to maximize financial stability and insulate the myriad of facilities from future anticipated reimbursement reductions. Consumerists counterargue that charity care might be reduced to meet a financial bottom-line target. Odysseus could sail away to another land, but the health care manager will be perpetually attacked by physicians, consumers, and trustees for having insufficient capital, plant and equipment, and/or excessive profitability.

One intangible benefit of the proliferation of off-site nonhospital-based diversification is that many consumers reap the benefits of greater convenience. Reductions in patient travel time are often bolstered by the added benefit of a reduced price per unit of service. However, if not properly structured, these corporate spin-offs can threaten the tax-exempt status of the mothership hospital. One tax-exempt multihospital system (Intermountain Health Care, Inc. of Salt Lake) has had problems in this regard. In June 1985, the Utah Supreme Court (No. 17699) denied the tax-exempt status of a community hospital on the basis of its having evolved into a business that no longer satisfied the constitutional requirements for a charitable institution. Tax-exempt organizations are chartered under specific limited-purpose provisions (benevolent, educational, scientific, religious) for which their assets and income must be used. However, the vast majority of tax-exempt hospitals have restructured so as to minimize this threat to their tax-exempt status, and still act as more of a multiproduct, multiservice business concern. Nevertheless, if the courts begin to mirror the attitudes of most economists, there is increasing irrelevance in the distinction between for-profit and "nonprofit" hospitals.

A number of hospitals have sacrificed varying degrees of autonomy in pursuit of improved efficiency. Alexander and Rundall (1985) studied 80 hospitals under contract management and one to two years prior to contract management and observed a number of positive financial impacts. From an equity and access perspective, the hypothesis that contract-managed hospitals would cut back Medicaid and Medicare program participation received no empirical support. However, the data predate implementation of the PPS program and reduction in Medicaid benefits in many states. A wide variety of lease contracts have also been tried by some hospitals. For example, an arrangement can exist under a lease where a 20- to 40-year contract is made with a chain or company to provide full management, without ownership (or offering partial ownership* through joint venture capital projects). One should be careful to note that management does not imply the same economic incentives and behavior as management-plus-ownership.

The years 1984 and 1985 represented a window of opportunity for 10 teaching hospitals and the for-profit chains. The teaching hospitals needed better access to capital, and the chains were cash-rich (in stark contrast to their current financial position). These teaching hospitals were earning a substantial profit prior to acquisition—for example, Wesley Hospital in Kansas earned a $13 million operating profit prior to joining HCA, and Saint Joseph Hospital in Omaha earned a $17 million profit before joining AMI. Market focus continued to become more concentrated in geographic regions, and hospital chains desired high-status teaching hospital "flagships" to act as market "hubs" (leaders) for referrals from surrounding community hospitals. By acquiring currently profitable teaching hospitals, the chains hoped to minimize the risk of having the "hub" hospital evolve into a prestigious loss leader.

Nine of these teaching hospitals set up endowments or contract agreements to ensure that the facility would continue to do its historic share of indigent care. For example, the 1984 Saint Joseph's contract specified that (1) income earned by the net proceeds of the acquisition would be used to pay for $1 million of indigent care and (2) AMI would pay the balance (O'Brien and Haller, 1985). If an endowment is set up to cover indigent care, Coady (1985) cautions that the foundation's principal and invest-

---

* Joint ventures can also exist outside the context of a lease contract. For example, NME and Massachusetts General Hospital are developing a 340-apartment unit continuing care retirement community and 60-bed skilled nursing facility for $38 million.

ment income must be sufficient to pay for community service and charity care. Coady's estimates may understate the long-run risk to the hospital because the resources needed for such care continue to increase, whereas the foundation's return on investments has declined rapidly in the current market. Purchase contracts contained a buy-back clause to enable the original local authorities to regain control of the hospital if they are not satisfied with the investor-owned management (e.g., the chain would provide the authority 80 percent of the financing through low-interest loans in the buy-back). On the positive side, the teaching hospitals should be pleased with the high purchase prices they received in 1984–85, ranging from $185,000 to $388,000 per teaching bed. The typical community nonteaching hospital sold for $130,000 per bed in 1984; and chains have "dumped" 40 community hospitals in 1986 at an average sale price of $75,000 per bed. While teaching hospitals should certainly sell at a premium relative to the price of community hospital beds, few would argue that the prices of 1988–1990 will approximate the sale prices of 1984–1985. The chains that improve financial position sufficiently to be in an acquisition mode in the coming years may be a beneficiary of the "price wars" outlined in Chapter 9. If the chains continue to diversify away from inpatient medical/surgical beds, there may be no buyers of hospital beds in the short run.

Returns on Equity in the Hospital Business

The 1986 Consolidated Omnibus Budget Reconciliation Act (COBRA) will eliminate the Medicare return-on-equity payment to investor-owned hospitals 1987–1991. With cost reimbursement and a guaranteed return-on-equity profit factor any hospital chain could acquire hospitals, bill insurers for all costs, and collect a built-in profit. However, in the future it will be much more difficult to earn profits. Acquisitions will have to be based on standard financial analysis, like any other business (subject to tax concerns). With occupancy rates as low as those listed in Table 20.2, most chains are not in an acquisition mode in the short run. Stockholders react negatively to continued expansion of unused capacity (empty beds).

In 1986, Medicare will pay an estimated $211 million in return-on-equity payments. According to a May 1986 study released by HHS Inspector General Richard Kusserow (reviewed in Chapter 1), subtracting the return-on-equity payments from investor-owned hospitals would have reduced their profit margins (17.9

percent) to below the levels of tax-exempt hospitals (14.7 percent) in 1984. Kusserow utilized audited Medicare cost reports from 214 investor-owned facilities and 1,789 tax-exempt hospitals. Tax-exempt hospitals receive no return-on-equity payments. Subtracting off the $44 million in return-on-equity payments for the 214 investor-owned hospitals would have reduced their profit margins per Medicare case to 13.2 percent in 1984 (1.5 percent less favorable than the tax-exempt sector). Although one should not generalize too much from a limited sample, the investor-owned hospitals have their work cut out for them if they wish to compete against the tax-exempt hospitals on a level playing field [with neither group receiving any return-on-equity payments after the phase-out period (1991)].

A number of previous studies based on 1978–1981 data have suggested that for all patients (including Medicare) proprietary hospital profitability improves after joining a chain. Pattison (1986) studied nine California hospitals acquired during 1977–78 and reported a turnaround on profitability on average from an after-tax loss of $1.38 per diem to $23.70 after-tax profit per diem 27 to 33 months after acquisition. Consequently, proprietary hospitals joining an investor-owned chain improved profitability (prior to PPS). Profitability appears to improve due to better collections procedures (reduced bad debt from nonpoor patients), better productivity, and group purchasing.

However, a detailed descriptive study of 15 hospitals acquired in Florida (1979–1981) suggests that chains enhance profitability mainly be increasing prices (Brown and Klosterman, 1986). There is obviously more payer and consumer resistance to raising prices in the 1987–1989 marketplace. Competition through the proliferation of alternative delivery systems places a strong downward pressure on hospital prices. Future research should consider the question of profitability differences between chains, based on whether profitability is centralized in the hands of the system's corporate board or decentralized on the local level (Alexander and Fennell, 1986).

Although a number of chapters in this text have focused on profit margins, financial status is not easily captured by this unidimensional attribute. At minimum, financial health has two basic attributes: external slack and internal slack. Traditional measures of external slack include credit worthiness (ratings) and debt capacity (borrowing power). Internal slack measures include the capacity to pay incentive bonus compensation to management (and labor), dividends, and a full range of working capital measures. One can obviously trade off some external slack to purchase more internal slack as a firm. For example, a number of investor-owned companies have attempted in 1986 to convert long-term debt to shares of stock, thus improving external slack.

Investor Confidence and the Stock Market

Under cost reimbursement, the investor-owned firms seemed to live on the theory of perpetual earnings growth (PEG). The chains were growing on the back of cost reimbursement, a guaranteed return on equity, capital acquisitions, and aggressive harvesting of free-standing hospitals and smaller chains. The chains were not "birds of prey"; rather, the facilities acquired were willing sellers in most cases. In 1982, the six largest investor-owned hospital chains had price-to-earnings (PE) ratios that were 200 to 400 percent higher than the stock market average (PE = 9). This section documents the erosion of this aura of investor optimism over the period 1983–1986. By 1986, the stock market had an average PE of 16, which was 30 to 60 percent better than the PE range of the six largest health care chains. The chains were hurt by declining admissions and the failure of new insurance ventures and cost-cutting measures to produce earnings growth for investors. By October 1985, health care chains went from "modest riches" to relative poverty. In the second week of October, the stock value for the six big chains declined by $1.59 billion in value.

Analysis of investor confidence is an imperfect science, especially when the general market position has been so upbeat and the sector under study (health care) has experienced severe downbeat shocks (discussion of PPS, implementation of PPS, severe downturn in earnings trends, announced withdrawal of return-on-equity payments). In a downbeat period, the investors will favor firms that divest holdings in inpatient medical/surgical care and diversify into more profitable product lines. Many chains announced that while 50 to 65 percent of their revenues may be currently hospital-based, in three years this "dependence" will decline to 30 to 40 percent. The figures for the cost of equity contribution differ across the chains because of differences in perceived business risk. Clearly, the chains must offer investors higher financial returns than riskless financial assets such as treasury bills. One can employ a Sharpe-Lintner model whereby the dependent variable in the regression analysis is the risk premium in excess of the riskless rate observed for chain h in week t, and the independent variable is the risk premium in excess of the riskless rate observed for the pooled market index during week t. This section reports results from this standard capital assets pricing model (Lintner, 1965), based on stock market information, to measure the amount of erosion in investor confidence in the larger chains.

The upward movement in the general market is demonstrated by the substantial growth of the SP500, from $145 to $266 over the 44-month period January 1983 to August 29, 1986 (Table 20.6). In contrast to the SP500, by May 1983, the month following passage of PPS and the Medicare reforms, the stock prices for all the chains under study began to decline. Table 20.6 confirms standard economic theory concerning older established chains—that is, they exhibit less price volatility than the two newer chains (Universal and Republic). For the time series analysis a pooled market index (NYSE, AMEX, NASDAQ index) will be employed to broadly represent changes in American equity markets.

Beta is the standard measure for the risk of a security for which investors must be compensated with sufficient rate of return. Financial forecasters never project the rate of return with perfect accuracy (Harrington, 1983); therefore, one must consider the difference between actual and forecasted values, labeled the "abnormal rate of return." In the parlance of finance, the abnormal

Table 20.6   Monthly Stock Averages for the Six Chains Studied Under the Capital Asset Pricing Model

Month	SP500	*1* AMI	*2* HCA	*3* Universal	*4* Humana	*5* NME	*6* Republic
Jan. 1983	145	35.3	43.8	39.3	42.1	28.2	—
April 1983	166	32.8	49.8	45.6	22.6	33.8	—
July 1983	158	31.3	53.6	25.1	34.8	29.8	26.2
Oct. 1983	170	28.3	45.7	16.0	29.7	24.0	16.4
Jan. 1984	166	25.2	40.6	12.1	24.2	24.2	13.7
April 1984	158	24.3	39.3	11.7	24.9	20.1	12.1
July 1984	151	22.8	39.9	11.1	26.1	20.0	13.0
Oct. 1984	164	23.3	40.4	11.7	25.1	20.1	12.8
Jan. 1985	170	20.6	41.1	11.8	24.0	24.2	12.2
April 1985	180	23.8	38.3	13.4	24.8	27.0	14.4
July 1985	193	26.4	48.0	16.5	33.6	29.9	16.5
Oct. 1985	185	19.5	31.9	16.2	27.1	20.1	10.4
Jan. 1986	202	18.9	36.7	14.1	29.0	23.0	12.5
April 1986	240	19.8	41.3	14.5	30.3	24.3	16.8
July 1986	238	15.5	38.6	16.0	24.3	24.9	17.0
44-month (January 1983–August 1986)							
Mean		24.0	42.3	18.6	27.7	24.7	14.9
Standard Deviation		4.3	4.6	10.9	3.9	3.8	6.1

rate of return reflects the arrival of new information (e.g., bad news) during the investment period (one week), which causes a change in next week's price as investors revise expectations of future rates of return. If the period is marked by no new information, the abnormal rate of return will most likely take a "random walk," moving up and down, with no clear trend. All rates of return in the time series analysis were adjusted for stock splits and stock dividends and are converted to standard natural logarithm form.

The approach presented in Figure 20.1 assumes that the value of beta which is estimated for the first 52 weeks of data (1982) prior to congressional debate of PPS (early 1983) is immutable throughout the 243-week time period; then the market begins to wake up and react to new information on performance and future policy edicts. The expected risk premium on chain h for each successive week from early January 1983 to late August 1986 (191 weeks) is obtained by substituting the week's value for the market's risk premium, while using parameter estimates of beta and the average abnormal rate of return computed for the base period 1982. Since the trend was generally parallel, the Y-axis of Figure 20.1 reflects the cumulative abnormal rate of return for the six chains studied. [As suggested by Mandelker (1974), more sophisticated models were tried and confirmed the validity of a stability in beta values during 1982.]

Despite anecdotal reports suggesting that investors did not discount the ramifications of a passage of PPS in 1983, Figure 20.1 confirms that the information theory of the market (Fama, 1976) is operating as expected. The general market index increased 17 percent from passage of PPS (April 22, 1983, to December 1983), but the value of each of the six firms' stock fell below their January 14, 1983 values. The "disbelief theorem" of not trusting the regulators' expectations was confirmed, in that the stock values of all six chains increased from January to April 20, 1983 (PL 98–21). Most investors knew little of the content of the bill to save social security and reduce Medicare expenditures, but they did know the news was not positive.

Just as the investor response to the new Medicare system had played out in 1984, bad news concerning sharply declining earnings *below expectations* sent major shocks through the system in the five major downturns. The fourth downturn in Figure 20.1 correlated with the 1985 announcement of the future abolition of return-on-equity payments by Medicare. The reactivity of the market to bad news is impressive, especially when one considers that Medicare represents only 19 to 31 percent of the volume of patient days for these six chains.

In summary, one can reject the 1983–84 claims of the investor-

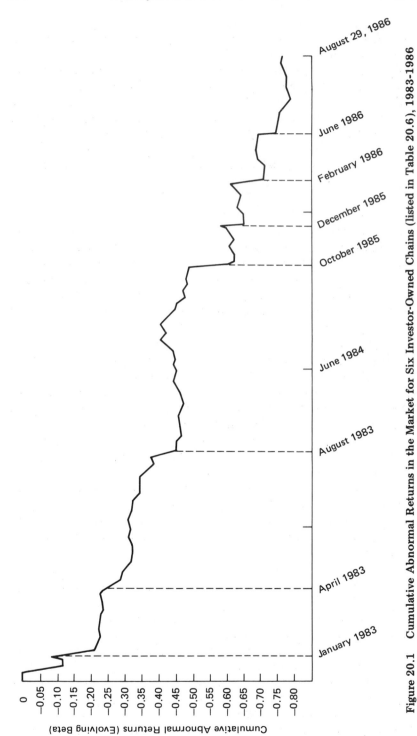

Figure 20.1   Cumulative Abnormal Returns in the Market for Six Investor-Owned Chains (listed in Table 20.6), 1983-1986

owned sector that their financial performance, and thus their stock performance, would not erode due to changes in the payment system. Depending on the chain and the model, investors in these six chains experienced an erosion of "expected" wealth of 20 to 44 percent in 1983, and 38 to 68 percent over the first three years of PPS. Chain-specific events, such as an inability to make a new insurance venture profitable, or varying degrees of success in implementing workload-driven staffing models, confound the effects of federal program changes. Moreover, changes in payment plans locally, such as Blue Cross and state Medicaid programs, confound the analyst's ability to separate internal and external events further in our time series analysis (Arzac, 1986).

Hybridization and Joint Ventures

The treacherous and complex payment climate demands creative joint venturing between chains, autonomous hospitals, insurance companies, HMOs, and consortia groups. We shall survey in Chapter 24 how some of this competitive activity may lead to very noncompetitive monopoly or oligopoly markets. Inpatient providers must soon realize they are not facing a minor recession but rather an old-fashioned dog-eat-dog shake-out. For-profit firms are considering a number of strategies for improving their attractiveness to investors. Interdependent strategies range from tighter operations (reduced overhead, better productivity), to converting long-term debt, to improving earnings per share by trading existing shares for a REIT (real estate investment trust) on company property. This last strategy will be attempted by two chains in 1987. Earnings per share will become more attractive because the number of shares outstanding will be cut in half, but the balance sheet erodes. Investors in the REIT will own the bricks and mortar on the hospitals, and the chain will continue to own the equipment. Annual interest expenses will decline by $8 million in one psychiatric chain because the amount of subordinated debt will decline from $163 million to $55 million, and long-term debt remains constant at $281 million. If the REIT is fully sold at the end of 1987, equity as a percentage of total debt at one chain will erode from 29 to 18.4 percent.

Ultimately, with the emphasis on cost control and debt reduction, investor-owned firms will shrink or expand according to their price competitiveness (especially as they enter more price-competitive markets like psychiatric care). Continued attempts to offer a capitation product, like Humana's CARE PLUS, offer a two-edged sword: the risk of financial failure but the possible benefit of revitalization of this mature industry. Hybridization is becoming a two-way street. Tax-exempt firms were the first to travel the road to multiple for-profit taxable subsidiaries, and investor-owned firms may donate failed ventures to the tax-exempt (if one cannot make a business profit or a tax profit from a failure, one might as well label it a "nonprofit" concern).

Hospital chains will continue to reduce exposure to the declining inpatient sector and reduce corporate overhead. But if they fail to raise earnings they will become ripe takeover candidates. In theory, the pooling of complementary strengths represents the hope behind the hybridization and joint venture trend. Many weaker chains, insurance firms, and hospitals may be swallowed up by the large surviving chains. Restraints on autonomy will be especially difficult for the acquired firm if the parent firm instinctively overmanages its new "teammate" (Starkweather, 1981).

While this chapter has been operations-oriented, it appears most appropriate to end with a few observations concerning business ethics. The pursuit of a nonmonetary ethos has been paradoxical: The more it is pursued, the more elusive it becomes. An obsession with the ownership issue produces a narrowness of vision and ignores basic issues such as survival and access to sufficient capital to promote quality care. Our search for capital, and joint ventures, may reap (given imperfect payment formulas) some unfortunate results if socially irresponsible firms do harm to community access to the poor. The solution is to not kill the "golden goose" and rail against nonphysician profit taking; rather, the solution is to enforce a social contract to force all concerned to bear their fair share burden of charity care. Firms that did their fair share in the 1980s will have a tougher time doing the equivalent volume of charity patients in the 1990s; however, they must.

References

ALEXANDER, J., and FENNELL, M. (1986). "Patterns of Decision Making in Multihospital Systems." *Journal of Health and Social Behavior* 27:1 (March), 14–27.

ALEXANDER, J., and RUNDALL, T. (1985). "Public Hospitals Under Contract Management: An Assessment of Operating Performance." *Medical Care* 23:3 (March), 209–219.

ANDERSON, G., SCHRAMM, C., RAPOZA, C., RENN, S., and PILLARI, G. (1985). "Investor-Owned Chains and Teaching Hospitals: Implications of Acquisitions." *New England Journal of Medicine* 313:3 (July 18), 201–204.

ARZAC, E. (1986). "Do Your Business Units Create Shareholder Value?" *Harvard Business Review* 64:1 (January–February), 121–126.

BATTISTELLA, R. (1985). "Hospital Receptivity to Market Competition." *Health Care Management Review* 10:3 (Summer), 19–26.

BECKER, E., and SLOAN, F. (1985). "Hospital Ownership and Performance." *Economic Inquiry* 23:1 (January), 21–36.

BROMBERG, M. (1984). "The Medical-Industrial Complex: Our National Defense." *New England Journal of Medicine* 309:21 (November 24), 1314–1315.

BROWN, K., and KLOSTERMAN, R. (1986). "Hospital Acquisitions and Their Effects: Florida, 1979–1982." In *Institute of Medicine, For-Profit Enterprise in Health Care*. Washington, D.C.: National Academy of Sciences.

BUCHANAN, R. (1982). "The Financial Status of the New Medical-Industrial Complex." *Inquiry* 19:4 (Winter), 308–316.

CITRIN, T. (1985). "Trustees at the Focal Point." *New England Journal of Medicine* 313:19 (November 7), 1223–1226.

COADY, S. (1985). "Not-For-Profits, Beware—Foundation Formed by Sale Could Be Short-lived." *Modern Healthcare* 15:7 (March 29), 138–140.

COELEN, C. (1986). "Hospital Ownership and Comparative Hospital Costs." In *Institute of Medicine, For-Profit Enterprise in Health Care*. Washington, D.C.: National Academy of Sciences, appendix.

COYNE, J. (1986). "A Financial Model for Assessing Hospital Performance: An Application to Multi-institutional Organizations." *Hospital and Health Services Administration* 31:2 (March-April), 28–40.

CULLER, S., and OHSFELDT, R. (1986). "The Determinates of the Provision of Charity Medical Care by Physicians." *Journal of Human Resources* 21:1 (Winter), 138–156.

DIMIERI, R., and WEINER, S. (1981). "The Public Interest and Governing Boards of Nonprofit Health Care Institutions." *Vanderbilt Law Review* 34:5 (May), 1029–1066.

EASTAUGH, S. (1985). "Organization, Scheduling Are Main Keys to Improving Productivity." *FAH Review* 18:6 (November–December), 61–63.

EASTAUGH, S. (1984). "Hospital Diversification and Financial Management." *Medical Care* 22:8 (August), 704–723.

ERMANN, D., and GABEL, J. (1985). "Changing Face of American Health Care: Multihospital Systems, Emergency Centers, and Surgery Centers." *Medical Care* 23:5 (May), 401–420.

FAMA, E. (1976). *Foundations of Finance*. New York: Basic Books.

Federation of American Health Systems (1987). *Directory of Investor Owned Hospitals and Health Care Management Companies*. Little Rock, Ark.: FAHS.

FEIN, R. (1986). *Medical Care, Medical Costs: The Search for a Health Insurance Policy*. Cambridge, Mass.: Harvard University Press.

GINZBERG, E. (1984). "The Monetarization of Medical Care." *New England Journal of Medicine* 310:18 (May 3), 1162–1165.

HARRINGTON, D. (1983). "Stock Prices, Beta, and Strategic Planning." *Harvard Business Review* 61:3 (May–June), 157–164.

HERZLINGER, R. (1987). "Performance of For-Profit and Nonprofit Hospitals." *Harvard Business Review* 65:1 (January–February), forthcoming.

Institute of Medicine (1986). *For-Profit Enterprise in Health Care*. Washington, D.C.: National Academy of Sciences.

LEWIN, L., DERZON, R., and MARGULIES, R. (1981). "Investor-Owneds and Nonprofits Differ in Economic Performance." *Hospitals* 55:13 (July 1), 52–58.

LINTNER, J. (1965). "The Valuation of Risk Assets and the Selection of Risky Investments in Stock Portfolios and Capital Budgets." *Review of Economics and Statistics* 47:1 (February), 13–37.

LONGSDORF, R. (1985). "The Medical-Industrial Complex: A Growing Problem for Health Care." *Private Practice* 11:2 (February), 39–41.

MANDELKER, G. (1974). "Risks and Returns: The Case of Merging Firms." *Journal of Financial Economics* 1:4 (December), 303–335.

McCUE, M., and FURST, R. (1986). "Financial Characteristics of Hospitals Purchased by Investor-Owned Chains." *Health Services Research* 21:4 (October), 515–528.

MINTZBERG, H. (1981). "Organizational Design: Fashion or Fit?" *Harvard Business Review* 59:1 (January–February), 103–107.

MORLOCK, L., ALEXANDER, J., and HUNTER, H. (1985). "Formal Relationships Among Governing Boards, CEOs, and Medical Staffs in Independent and System Hospitals." *Medical Care* 23:10 (October), 1193–1213.

O'BRIEN, R., and HALLER, M. (1985). "Investor-Owned or Nonprofit? Issues and Implications for Academic and Ethical Values in a Catholic Teaching Hospital." *New England Journal of Medicine* 313:3 (July 18), 198–201.

PATTISON, R. (1986). "Response to Financial Incentives Among Investor-Owned and Not-For-Profit Hospitals: An Analysis of the California Data, 1978–1982." In *Institute of Medicine, For-Profit Enterprise in Health Care*. Washington, D.C.: National Academy of Sciences, appendix.

PATTISON, R., and KATZ, H. (1983). "Investor-Owned and Not-For-Profit Hospitals." *New England Journal of Medicine* 309:6 (August 11), 347–353.

PAULY, M. (1986). "Advent and Implications of For-Profit Delivery." Paper presented at the EBRI Policy Forum, "The Changing Health Care Market" (June 3), Washington, D.C.

PEYSER, P. (1985). "Financial Dimensions of For-Profit Multihospital Systems: A Stock Market Analysis of Prospective Reimbursement Under Medicare." Paper presented at the International Health Economics Management Institute Conference (March 14), Rome, Italy.

REINHARDT, J. (1986). "The Nature of Equity Financing." In Institute of Medicine, *For-Profit Enterprise in Health Care*. Washington, D.C.: National Academy of Sciences, 67–73.

RELMAN, A. (1986). "Ethics and For-Profit Medicine." In Institute of Medicine, *For-Profit Enterprise in Health Care*. Washington, D.C.: National Academy of Sciences, appendix.

RELMAN, A. (1983). "Investor-Owned Hospitals and Health Care Costs." *New England Journal of Medicine* 309:6 (August 11), 370–372.

RELMAN, A. (1980). "The New Medical-Industrial Complex." *New England Journal of Medicine* 303:17 (October 23), 963–970.

RELMAN, A., and REINHARDT, U. (1986). "Debating For-Profit Health Care and the Ethics of Physicians." *Health Affairs* 5:2 (Summer), 5–29.

ROSENSTEIN, A. (1986). "Hospital Closure or Survival: Formula for Success." *Health Care Management Review* 11:3 (Summer), 29–36.

SHERLOCK, D. (1986). "A Wall Street Perspective on the Health Care Market." *Business and Health* 3:10 (October).

SHORTELL, S., FRIEDMAN, B., HUGHES, S., HUGHES, E., and MORRISON, E.

(1986). *The Strategy, Structure and Performance of Multi-Hospital Systems*. Unpublished paper, Center for Health Services and Policy Research (December), J. L. Kellogg Graduate School of Management, Northwestern University, Chicago.

SLOAN, F., and VRACIU, R. (1983). "Investor-Owned and Not-For-Profit Hospitals: Addressing Some Issues." *Health Affairs* 2:1 (Spring), 25–37.

STARKWEATHER, D. (1981). *Hospital Mergers in the Making*. Ann Arbor, Mich.: Health Administration Press.

STARR, P. (1982). *The Social Transformation of American Medicine*. New York: Basic Books, 146–153.

TEITELMAN, R. (1985). "Selective Surgery." *Forbes* (April 22), 75–76.

Utah County v. *Intermountain Health Care, Inc.*, Utah Supreme Court, (No. 17699), June 26, 1985.

VRACIU, R., and VIRGIL, P. (1986). "The Impact of Investor-Owned Hospitals on Access to Health Care." In R. Southby and W. Greenberg (eds.), *For-Profit Hospitals: Access, Quality, Teaching, Research*. Columbus, Ohio: Batelle Press.

WATT, J., and DERZON, R. (1986). "Effects of Ownership and Multihospital System Membership on Hospital Functional Strategies and Economic Performance." In Institute of Medicine, *For-Profit Enterprise in Health Care*. Washington, D.C.: National Academy of Sciences, appendix.

WATT, J., DERZON, R., RENN, S., SCHRAM, C., HAHN, J., and PILLARI, G. (1986). "The Comparative Economic Performance of Investor-Owned Chain and Not-For-Profit Hospitals." *New England Journal of Medicine* 314:2 (January 9), 89–96.

Chapter 21

ACCESS TO CAPITAL AND DEBT FINANCING

Starting in 1988 the typical hospital should be viewed as a more risky venture, and will pay higher interest rates unless they can demonstrate DRG profitability. Hospitals shall no longer have government as a "Sugar Daddy" paying the interest on their debt coupon by coupon. One thousand hospitals may close. We view such hospitals as "cross-eyed javelin throwers" in that they will not win any awards, but they will keep the attention of their fearful audience.

—*Investment Banker*

The penalty for a "wrong" decision a decade ago was usually no more than the effort of persuading some donor to make good a relatively small financial loss. The decisions were private affairs, usually made intuitively. Now they are public affairs involving large sums of borrowed money. Intuition has been replaced by discounted cash flows and debt capacity analysis.

—WALSH MCDERMOTT, M.D.

In many situations providers may have reached maximum debt capacity which implies that the next phase may be rapid aging and deterioration of present health facilities in this country. It seems inperative that a more equitable system of capital cost reimbursement be adopted.

—WILLIAM O. CLEVERLEY

A new era of total revenue controls and decreasing numbers of hospital beds does not preclude the need to allow hospital capital to keep pace with inflation and meet the demand for more tests and procedures per day of care. Debt financing has recently become the hospital's major source of funds for the purchase of new capital. Autonomy will be lost for those hospitals unable to maintain a reasonable income margin. To ensure against this, the payers should allow for a small but significant profit margin. Three equations are derived in this chapter to measure the impact that private-sector financing authorities could have on hospital growth as a function of various suggested financial ratio ceiling requirements. After a sensitivity analysis, it is concluded that a 3 percent operating margin would be barely sufficient to reduce the case study hospital's high dependence on debt. The definition of an adequate operating margin will vary among different size hospitals and ownership arrangements. Teaching hospitals may require a 4 to 6 percent margin. Payment formulas fixed in this manner would not only diminish the incentives for excessive reliance on debt financing but also allow new capital to be equally equity-financed (47 percent equity and 47 percent debt, instead of 81 percent debt and 13 percent equity). Philanthropy will continue to have a minor role to play (6 percent of new capital stock).

Shift from Equity to Debt Financing

In the 1970s we saw an explosion in the use of debt financing by hospitals to help support and expand their operations. Later in this chapter we will identify the reasons for an explosion in debt, the constraints on future increases in the debt ratio, and the implications of debt ratios for hospitals in a state of expansion or decline. In addition, the often neglected reimbursement issue concerning definition of an adequate rate of return on equity to assure sufficient private market financing of hospital capital needs will be discussed.

Two basic policy initiatives by the federal government fueled the 1972–1985 trend toward bonded indebtedness. First, Medicare and Medicaid substantially reduced the risk involved with debt financing by reimbursing 100 percent of interest and allowing full amortization of bonded indebtedness. Second, the Nixon administration, acting in the spirit of what it termed "off-budget financing," encouraged investment banking firms and local government to create tax-exempt financing authorities to issue tax-exempt hospital bonds in 42 states in the period 1970–1973. Tax-exempt bonds offered health facilities the advantages of longer payback periods, no down payment or equity requirements, and lower interest rates relative to taxable bonds.

Tax-exempt bonds as a percentage of hospital debt offerings increased from less than 10 percent in 1970 to 68 percent in 1974 to 87 percent in 1985 (Table 21.1).* The 1980 Congressional Budget Office Report entitled "Tax Subsidies for Medical Care" suggested either eliminating the tax-exempt. status of hospital bonds or containing the rate of issue of tax-exempt bonds by requiring that they be declared the general obligation issue of the state or local government unit issuing them. Placing hospital bonds under general obligation status would force hospitals to compete for capital with schools and public projects on an equal basis. Hospitals barely escaped this fate in the process of 1986 federal tax reform. Currently, state and local government units have no financial responsibilities for hospital bond issues; consequently, they have no direct interest in limiting them. However, the marketplace for general obligation bond issues would undoubtedly reduce the ability of hospitals to borrow. Some analysts have argued that the relative ease of borrowing in the hospital industry has exacerbated the shortfall of capital available to other public sector building projects.

Regardless of ownership type, responsibility for protection of assets, quality of care, and facility reputation rests with the governing board. Hospital trustees have a fiduciary responsibility for the preservation or enhancement of a facility's equity. When the equity capital of an institution is eroded due to insufficient reimbursement, inflation, and poor profitability, the ability of that facility to continue meeting community needs will be reduced or, even worse, eliminated. Some combination of insufficient payment rates and suboptimal financial management can create a shortfall in the retained earnings necessary to maintain sufficient replacement reserves. Cleverley (1986) reports that the average hospital only has enough equity funds to finance 15 percent of its present replacement needs. Therefore 80 to 85 percent debt financing is required to maintain the average facility adequately.

Philanthropy has declined from 21 percent (in 1968) of tax-exempt hospital capital project financing to 6 percent since 1984. Charitable contributions will not solve our future access to capital problems. Lenders do respect a successful fund-raising effort, as it may provide a proxy measure of community support and cash flow

---

* Hospitals financially strong enough to be undergoing a major building program, especially in the 1983–1986 era of declining inpatient demand, are somewhat less reliant on debt. For example, the $4.4 billion of construction in progress in the fall of 1984 was 60 percent debt financed, 24 percent coming from internal reserves, 8 percent equity, 4.4 percent philanthropy, and 3.6 percent from other sources.

Table 21.1 Summary of Debt Financing Trends for Hospitals, Selected Years 1974–1986 (thousands of dollars)

Year	A-1ᵃ Total Funding for Hospital Construction (thousands)	A-2 Total Debt from A-1 (thousands)	B-1 Total Debt Offerings in Hospitals (thousands)	B-2 Tax-Exempt Hospital Bond Offerings (thousands)	B-3 Tax-Exempt Offerings as a Percentage of B-1
1974	$3,231	$1,873	$2,215	$1,506	68%
1976	4,475	2,587	3,940	2,726	69
1977	3,729	2,331	6,312ᵇ	4,734	75
1978	3,318	2,031	4,226	3,123	74
1980	3,042	2,090	4,550	4,050	88
1982	3,864	2,453	10,741	9,021	84
1984	4,400	2,799	12,033	10,230	85
1985	4,250	2,804	34,360	29,900ᶜ	87
1986 est.ᵈ	1,500	900	7–8,000	4–5,000	50–70

SOURCES: Column A—American Hospital Association, Survey of Sources of Funding for Hospital Construction. Column B—Kidder-Peabody & Company, Inc. (1986).

ᵃDue to underreporting, this is probably an underestimate that should be inflated 50 percent. Even though the AHA figure includes construction costs plus some new equipment, plus refinancing, plus acquisition of land and architect fees, the Commerce Department figures for only hospital construction costs are $800 million higher in both 1977 and 1978. Commerce Department, *Construction Reporting: Value of New Construction Put in Place*, June 1979, Table F-1, U.S. Government Printing Office, Washington, D.C. The percentage of the funds in column A-1 from tax-exempt bonds increased from 28 percent in 1974 to 56 percent in 1979.

ᵇ1977 was a record setter because of a four-fold increase in the number of advance refundings in that year. Hospitals took advantage of the lower interest rates of 1977 because the rates were substantially lower than those of the recent past or projected future.

ᶜIn 1985 hospitals took advantage of declining interest rates and a last opportunity at arbitrage income before federal tax reform in 1986.

ᵈEstimates for 1986 are by the author.

for the institution; however, the sum total of charitable contributions and grants is less than 0.5 percent of the average tax-exempt hospital's revenues in 1985 (Institute of Medicine, 1986). Excessive reliance on debt is viewed by many hospital administrators as a critical problem. In the past few years, debt-to-equity ratios have increased dramatically. A facility's ability to issue debt is highly dependent on both the degree to which it is already leveraged and the capital market's estimation of the default risk of the firm. Under cost reimbursement, the tax-exempt hospital was not required to sell debt on the basis of profit yield; rather, hospital debt was issued on the basis of the risk-free nature of the investment.

With Medicare paying for its share of capital costs as a pass-through (whatever the facility spends it gets reimbursed, assuming interest expenses are reasonable), hospitals were viewed as relatively risk-free. However, as we observe from the *Investment Banker* quote at the start of this chapter, the risk-free days of the 1970s are over. Medicare will begin prospectively paying for capital as part of the DRG system of administered pricing sometime during FY 1988.* Once Medicare ceases to pay for capital at cost, this will end the perverse incentive under PPS to substitute capital for labor (labor costs are not passed through; rather, they are embodied in the DRG price). Not surprisingly, hospital capital spending increased at 15 to 20 percent per annum, whereas FTE employees declined at 60,000 to 70,000 per year (Chapter 1, AHA panel survey). The decline of cost reimbursement for hospital capital will harm both the financially distressed facilities (Ginzberg, 1986) as well as a broader range of hospitals with the unfortunate bad luck of being at the end of their investment life cycle (requiring a major modernization and replacement program soon after 1988).

Investment Life Cycles

Many published studies have suggested that hospitals make capital investments in identifiable life cycles (Eastaugh, 1984; Howell, 1984; Eastaugh, 1982). More basic research is needed concerning the length of these investment cycles, timing, and negative ramifications of deferred investment (Cohodes and Kinkead, 1984). A

---

* Table 21.2 indicates that hospital capital costs, as a percentage of total costs, averaged 7.14 percent in 1984. Capital spending might be closer to 9.0 to 9.2 percent of total costs by 1986. HCFA is currently assessing a less generous payment capital add-on that would on average pay 8.1 percent for urban hospitals and 6.3 percent for rural facilities.

number of professional estimates of the capital needs of the health care industry have been made. The estimates are highly dependent on the assumptions concerning the number of facilities that should survive, capacity utilization (occupancy), facility size, growth in technology, alteration of services, and expansion of different services (Cohodes, 1983; Anderson and Ginsburg, 1983; Kalison and Averill, 1985; Sykes, 1986). Even with health expenditure growth at 5 to 6 percent per annum, and technology growth at 1 to 2 percent per annum, capital needs from 1988 to 1993 could vary widely:

- $61 to $82 billion for hospital renovation and modernization
- $16 to 27 billion for hospital expansion
- $30 to 35 billion for skilled nursing facilities
- $15 to 20 billion for intermediate care and rehabilitation facilities

Will the health care sector receive the professionally defined estimate of capital needs? Will capital suppliers satisfy capital needs? As with every industry (except perhaps the defense industry from 1982 to 1985), effective capital demands will be some fraction of capital "needs." However, it may be important to the future health of the population that this fraction of demand-to-need be closer to 0.8 than 0.4 to 0.5. To paraphrase Iglehart (1986), the Reagan administration's proposal to reduce Medicare's total hospital capital payment by $11.53 billion from 1987 to 1991 is a far too harsh prescription. Capital financing availability will significantly shape the structure, access, quality, and cost of our health care system well into the 21st century.* Hospitals at the end of the investment cycle are most in need of capital for physical plant and modernization. At the level of individual programs, Brown (1986) suggests that certain "orphan investments" would be undercapitalized, such as preventive, social, and rehabilitative services. All

---

* In the fall of 1986, Congress began debating a cap (7–8 percent maximum for prospective capital payment, see Table 21.2) or fixed percentage reduction across the board of 3.5 percent per year (1987–1989) to reduce cost pass-through payments for hospital capital under the Medicare payment. This is designed to save federal dollars (and come closer to Gramm-Rudman deficit targets) and retard hospital capital spending. The General Accounting Office forthcoming report, GAO/HRD-86-93, suggests using minimum occupancy rates for hospitals to recover full capital costs. While any formula is arbitrary to some extent, this approach seems superior to the budget reconciliation bill of October 1986: to reduce Medicare payments for hospital capital expenses 3.5 percent in 1987, 7 percent in 1988, and 10 percent (below Medicare's fair share proportion of capital costs) in 1989.

Table 21.2   Hospital Capital Costs, as a Percentage of Total Costs, 1984

	Mean Percentage	Percentage of Hospitals with Capital Payments in Interval					
		Less Than 4	4–7.1	7.1–10	10–15	15–20	Greater Than 20
All hospitals	7.14	18.0	36.5	30.4	10.9	2.8	1.3
Ownership							
not for profit	7.6	13.6	31.4	35.1	15.0	3.5	1.4
for profit	8.3	7.8	27.7	51.3	8.3	2.6	2.2
state and local	5.5	31.6	50.8	10.4	5.0	1.7	0.6
Beds							
less than 50	5.9	23.1	58.9	10.7	4.4	1.4	1.4
50–100	7.3	17.3	35.6	32.6	9.4	3.2	2.0
100–200	7.9	13.2	29.0	39.4	12.8	3.9	1.6
200–400	7.8	13.4	25.1	39.6	17.8	3.5	0.6
more than 400	6.0	28.3	34.2	26.4	9.8	1.1	0.1
Expenses per day							
less than $250	5.8	28.7	43.6	23.0	2.9	0.7	0.9
$250–450	7.1	15.7	37.9	32.2	11.0	2.5	0.7
$450–525	8.1	11.8	30.0	34.0	17.7	5.0	1.5
more than $525	7.9	14.2	30.9	33.2	15.0	4.3	2.4
Occupancy rate							
less than 60%	7.2	15.9	40.4	30.0	8.9	2.9	1.9
60–70%	7.7	12.8	33.2	35.1	13.4	4.2	1.2
70–80%	7.2	14.9	36.9	31.3	14.0	2.1	0.7
more than 80%	6.0	33.6	29.9	25.1	8.9	2.1	0.5
Council of teaching hospitals							
member	6.7	15.5	46.2	24.6	11.2	2.1	0.3
not a member	7.1	18.1	36.0	30.8	10.9	2.9	1.3
Percent Medicare admissions							
less than 20	4.9	48.9	30.5	13.7	4.0	1.2	1.7
20–40	7.6	11.8	34.3	37.6	12.1	2.9	1.3
more than 40	7.1	15.6	43.9	24.2	11.9	3.5	1.0
Percent Medicaid admissions							
less than 5	7.1	21.5	28.7	31.6	12.8	3.8	1.6
5–15	7.2	14.3	39.4	32.2	10.4	2.6	1.0
more than 15	6.5	28.9	34.9	21.6	10.5	2.3	1.8
Census region							
Northeast	6.4	26.9	31.9	27.7	10.2	2.6	0.7
North Central	7.1	18.6	37.7	25.6	13.7	3.1	1.3
South	7.4	14.3	37.2	34.4	10.0	2.8	1.3
West	7.1	16.8	37.5	32.2	9.2	2.8	1.6

SOURCE: American Hospital Association, Annual Survey of Hospitals.

through the investment cycle, hospitals require capital for new program development, working capital, and debt service.

Cleverley (1986) reports that over the 1983–1985 period the average hospital reporting to FAS (Financial Analysis Service) has been increasing its working capital investment by about 17 percent per year. This healthy growth rate helped finance the diversification efforts outlined in Chapters 8 and 19. New product lines require sizable investments in working capital. If this growth rate is inevitably curtailed in the late 1980s due to lack of access to capital or market saturation (e.g., an oversupply of home health care suppliers), hospital managers may have to lengthen the investment life cycle.

The degree to which hospitals adjust their investment cycles may vary according to size, ownership, membership in a multihospital system, and the amount of retained earnings on hand. The capital investment cycle is crudely captured by the hospitalwide accounting age (under 9 years representing the "early stage," and over 24 the "late stage"). Accounting age is calculated as a ratio of accumulated depreciation to the original value of plant and equipment. There have been a number of simulation models of hospital investment cycles, including the Schneider-Mager (1986) study of 150 California hospitals, the ICF model of 4,000 American Hospital Association member hospitals, and the Krystynak (1985) study. For policy makers the most critical issue has been assigning an equitable capital add-on payment (CAPPAY), expressed as a percentage of operating revenues. A simple model would include the ratio of the first year's operating revenue to project cost R (e.g., 0.4 to .55), the life of the asset T (e.g., 28 to 35 years), the percentage of the capital investment debt financed B (e.g., 0.85), and the present value of capital reimbursement less principal and interest payments over the life of the asset expressed as a percentage of project cost CF (e.g., Cash Flow $CF = .22$). If $T = 28$ and $R = 0.47$, solving for CAPPAY:

$$CAPPAY = (B + CF) / (T \cdot R) = 0.081$$

There is substantial debate over what should be the appropriate level of capital payment for rural hospitals. The rural hospital generally has a longer effective asset life relative to an urban high-tech hospital. Generalization from a sample of 150 California hospitals (Schneider and Mager, 1986) may not lead to good public policy. The California hospitals are highly atypical relative to AHA panel survey trends (i.e., rural hospitals in the California sample are very profitable).

We shall consider a more representative sample of 112 north-

eastern and midwestern tax-exempt hospitals for purposes of simulating the impact of anticipated payment changes on hospitals over
the 10-year cycle 1984–1993. This sample of survey hospitals,
utilized in Chapters 5 and 19, offers the advantage of more typical
profit margins and bed size relative to the AHA data (Chapter 1),
when contrasted to the Schneider-Mager Office of Health Facilities sample. However, our sample does not include any for-profit
hospitals. Consequently, the foregoing analysis in Tables 21.3–21.5
will only be applicable to tax-exempt hospitals. Modeling the
capital investment cycle for eight future years of data based on
1984 and 1985 data requires estimation of the payment climate,
patient demand behavior, and disinvestment behavior (closing
product lines or beds; e.g., closing 20,000 beds per annum 1987–
1990 nationwide). The Medicare DRG prices were presumed to
have an inflation adjustment of 1.15 percent in 1987, and 2.5
percent per annum 1988–1993. Demand is projected using 24 to
30 months of data (1984 to June 1986), and the model simulates the
facility's income statement, including patient revenues, debt-service, and capital-related payments. The model simulates the organization's year-end balance sheet and capital-related sources and
uses. Final output of the model under various payment policies
includes new cumulative estimates of plant value, principal and
interest payments, and depreciation (as expense, not cash flow.)

The facilities with better financial position are clearly more
likely, ceterus paribus, to make major capital investments. Investment behavior also depends on accounting age, profit margin,
plant fund, retained earnings, fully funded depreciation accounts,
and occupancy rate. The variables are interrelated,* and it is
difficult to associate empirically the unique contribution of each
factor. For example, physicians and patients prefer newer facilities
(lower accounting age). This preference will in turn affect profitability and occupancy. Schneider and Mager (1986) assumed that for
every year's decrease in accounting age, a hospital's admission rate
will increase by 0.3 percent. In the microsimulation model presented in this text, we shall assume a more generous 0.5 elasticity
of facility age on admissions (Chapter 9) and present the model's
critical assumptions for investment probability in Table 21.3. Current and projected profit margins are increasingly critical factors in
whether a facility initiates a major capital project.

---

* It is more difficult to achieve higher occupancy rates in smaller hospitals. If one
assumes that half of the admissions are nonscheduled, both a 68 percent occupied
65-bed hospital and an 88 percent occupied 500-bed hospital are at 100 percent
occupancy three days a year.

Table 21.3 Capital Investment Probability as a Function of Hospital Accounting Age, Occupancy, Size, and Profitability

Accounting Age	Occupancy	Size (beds)	Operating Margin	Probability of Investment per Annum
25 +	GT* 50%	20–100	GT .015	0.010
	GT 60%	GT 100	GT .012	0.012
	any	any	GT .040	0.020
	other combinations		—	0.005
17–24	GT 50%	20–100	GT .025	0.011
	GT 60%	101–300	GT .020	0.014
	GT 70%	101–300	GT .050	0.090
	GT 70%	GT 300	GT .040	0.088
	GT 80%	GT 300	GT .060	0.170
	other combinations		GT .035	0.050
	other combinations		.0–.034	0.010
8–16	GT 50%	20–100	GT .025	0.007
	GT 60%	101–300	GT .020	0.009
	GT 70%	101–300	GT .050	0.040
	GT 70%	GT 300	GT .040	0.035
	GT 80%	GT 300	GT .060	0.070
	other combinations		GT .035	0.010
	other combinations		.0–.034	0.001
4–7	GT 80%	GT 300	GT .080	0.015
	other combinations			0.0

*GT denotes "greater than."

The smaller and less profitable hospitals in the 8 to 16 age category will not likely make a major capital investment in the coming decade (Table 21.3). Typically, hospitals with recent large capital investments have higher capital expenses and lower operating profit margins. However, hospitals that avoid replacement and modernization decisions also tend to have lower profit margins. This problem of underinvestment or delayed investment can be either involuntary (e.g., the facility is financially distressed) or voluntary (e.g., the trustees and managers are overly timid about the potential for new assets generating sufficient income). Organizations with moderate range capital expenses are usually the hospitals that have made recent major capital investments, but not in the immediate past.

In considering potential policies for Medicare prospective payment for capital, three scenarios shall be analyzed: (1) 8.1 percent capital add-on (best case scenario); (2) 6.3 percent capital add-on;

and (3) 6.3 percent capital add-on, or cost pass-through, whichever is lower (worst case scenario). Any cap on capital spending will naturally create incentives to spend up to that cap (at least on paper). Institutions may attempt accounting reclassifications to make operating costs into capital costs where possible (e.g., a capital lease, Chapter 22).

The administration could potentially justify the worst case scenario as a policy to expedite the closing of financially weak hospitals. For example, if a hospital spends 3 percent on capital in a given year, the payment formulas under scenario C would be based on Medicare's share of a 3.0 percent add-on (not paying hospitals for capital expenditures not made). Such a policy would be blatantly unfair to the hospital industry, as it discriminates against any and all facilities in the low-spending, late stage of their capital investment cycle.

The microsimulation assumes a six-year transition to national capital rates (1988–1993). This figure was selected as a compromise between the HCFA's suggested four-year transition, the Senate Finance Committee's seven-year transition, and the American Hospital Association's 15-year transition to fully phased-in prospective capital rates. Table 21.4 presents the simulated impact of each of the three scenarios on various types of hospitals. Teaching hospitals would receive the most generous dollar payments per bed for capital. (Historically they spend a lower percentage of total expense on capital, but the dollars per bed have always been highest in the teaching hospitals.) The facilities would have to rely increasingly on debt, even as capital spending is deferred somewhat, under the less generous scenarios B and C.

Given that urban hospitals have higher capital needs and a "tougher case mix" (higher unreimbursed patient severity), a hybrid policy would involve paying urban hospitals under scenario A and rural hospitals under scenario B. Table 21.5 presents results under such a two-tier capital payment policy (8.1 percent urban; 6.3 percent rural). Relative to scenario A, scenario B has only a marginal impact on rural hospitals' debt service coverage ratio and cash flow-to-debt ratio in Table 21.4. In 1993 rural hospitals would receive $453 per Medicare discharge for capital payments under scenario B. Urban hospitals would receive $722 per Medicare discharge for capital payments under scenario A (but only $491 under scenario B). Statistically, the most interesting finding in Table 21.5 is the significant correlation between accounting age and profitability. Perhaps the hospitals capable of completing a modernization and renovation project in the 1990s will be financially stronger (relative to builders in the 1980s) and less likely to

Table 21.4 Capital, Debt, and Liquidity Ratios in 1993, Under Three Capital Payment Scenarios, Phased in from 1988 to 1993

	Ownership				
	Public	Private Tax-Exempt	Urban and Teaching	Urban and Nonteaching	Rural and Nonteaching
Scenario A: 8.1% Capital Add-on					
Capital revenue per bed	$8,926	11,087	12,934	10,392	10,144
Debt service coverage[a]	3.79	4.32	3.56	4.40	4.84
Cash flow to total debt[b]	.476	.519	.498	.538	.479
Scenario B: 6.3% Capital Add-on					
Capital revenue per bed	$6,795	7,513	8,238	7,198	6,942
Debt service coverage[a]	3.61	3.80	3.26	3.83	4.48
Cash flow to total debt[b]	.458	.479	.472	.491	.462
Scenario C: 6.3% Capital Add-on or Cost Pass-Through (whichever is lower)					
Capital revenue per bed	$4,979	6,760	7,847	6,174	6,039
Debt service coverage[a]	3.23	3.67	2.98	3.63	4.29
Cash flow to total debt[b]	.431	.470	.454	.478	.445

[a]Sum of annualized cash flow plus annual interest expense divided by the sum of total principal plus interest payments.
[b]Annualized excess of revenues over expenses plus depreciation divided by the sum of current liabilities plus long-term debt.

**Table 21.5   Profit Margins as a Function of Accounting Age and Capital
Expense per Bed in the Late Years (1991–1993) and Early Years
(1988–1990) of a 8.1/6.3 Urban/Rural Capital Add-on Policy for
Medicare (FY 1988 +)**

	Operating Margin (1988–1990)	Operating Margin (1991–1993)
Accounting Age		
0–7	0.029	0.079
8–11	0.076	0.068
12–16	0.042	0.031
17–24	0.043	0.013
25 +	0.024	0.007
Annual Capital Expense per Bed (deflated to 1987 dollars)		
under $3,000	0.048	0.011
$3,000–$5,999	0.066	0.009
$6,000–$8,999	0.059	0.084
$9,000–$11,999	0.053	0.071
$12,000 +	0.019	0.034

SOURCE: Based on a simulation of 112 northeastern and midwestern hospitals (baseline FY 1984–1986).

see their profit margins erode. This may be a statistical artifact of decreased interest rates (two points lower than 1985), plus strong consumer sentiment for visiting the most modern available facilities. One-third of the surviving hospitals may face an era of capital starvation. Such facilities would be expected to lobby Congress for more generous capital payments and a second Hill-Burton capital spending program. Public policy analysts would need to assess the need for replacement beds in a maldistributed market, where in 1993 some areas may be underbedded, but some 190,000 to 210,000 empty acute care beds remain.

Historical Trends in Capital Spending

The ratio of capital expense to total operating expenses remained steady at between 6.6 to 6.9 percent during the decade 1971–1981. Since 1981, the ratio has increased substantially, from 6.6 percent to an estimated 9 percent in 1986. One small-scale survey of 121 hospitals by Ernst & Whinney in 1986 suggests that the capital-expense-to-total-expense ratios differ markedly by system affiliation. Free-standing tax-exempt hospitals had a ratio of 8.9, whereas chain hospitals had a ratio of 11.5 (Traska, 1986). Investor-owned chains may have a higher ratio due to newer facilities and past utilization of accelerated depreciation. The public data do not display the mix of capital costs reflected in acquisition prices versus expenditures to improve equipment and plant, nor do we know how much accounting age reflects timing of acquisitions versus facility age.* However, before one concludes that multihospital systems will be the hardest hit by prospective capital payment formulas, one should consider the flexibility of investment timing and cost allocation. Multihospital systems are better able to smooth out the "lumpiness" of investments by spacing them over time among chain members. Chains can allocate expensive new investments to member facilities that are currently operating under the capital cap (the payment add-on), and increasingly share such capital-intensive departments (e.g., MRI).

The upturn in capital spending was predictable in the context of what economists refer to as an "announcement effect." The federal government announced in 1983 that Medicare would end cost reimbursement by 1986 (the eventual date was extended to start for FY 1988). Hospital managers, as rational economic actors, made their capital investment decisions so as to maximize their Medicare payments before the "free lunch" of a cost pass-through ended. Indebtedness skyrocketed, especially in the tax-exempt bond market, where volume increased from $9 billion in 1982 to $9.9 billion in 1983, $10.2 billion in 1984, and $29.9 billion in 1985. According to the 1986 *Bond Buyer Statistical Supplement*, the average interest rate for new "A" rated hospital bonds declined from 12.82 percent to 7 percent in 1986.

Hospitals rushed to the bond markets to take advantage of the Medicare cost reimbursement formulas, to refinance old debt at lower rates of interest, and to hedge against any possibility that the tax reform in 1986 would eliminate or cap the volume of tax-exempt debt issued to health care facilities. Fortunately, tax-exempt hospitals were spared from most of the restrictions that were placed on tax-exempt bonds in the 1986 tax reform bill (the one major exception being the Dole provision concerning abusive arbitrage—that is, risk-free gain obtained by borrowing funds at a tax-exempt rate and investing these funds at taxable interest rates at a sure 2 to 3 percent profit). To cap the volume of hospital bonds at a fixed dollar amount per capita per state would have been a textbook example of "nude federalism"—that is, stripping state and local governments of the resources necessary to provide basic

---

* Technological or economic life is defined as the period of time the facility is expected to yield benefits to the owners or managers. This should not be confused with physical life, or the depreciable life set by the IRS or Medicare.

services (health care, schools, sewers, and other infrastructure programs).

Capital replenishment is a long-range issue that should not be subject strictly to short-run cost-cutting goals. Policy makers should consider the proverb of the old man who, in the interest of cost cutting, decided not to feed his ox. The ox did fine, so the man did not feed him for nine more days. The ox dropped dead on the tenth day. Do we as a society want the ox of medical technology that promotes quality patient care to drop dead? As with most analogies, this example is imperfect. The ox of quality care is more likely to erode slowly, almost imperceptibly, rather than drop dead suddenly. More critically, as we observe in Table 21.6, the hospital sector may be overcapitalized *on average*, but certain poor hospitals in poor neighborhoods are less well positioned to live under a 6 to 8 percent capital add-on program starting in 1988.

A formula cannot ensure that all hospital closings will be non-harmful (health planning program's ineffectiveness will be discussed in Chapter 23). Future developments in capital spending, the quality of service, and the health status of certain populations are difficult to foresee, and the need for monitoring changes is apparent. Kalison and Averill (1985) suggest allowing hospitals with high capital costs (defined as above 10 percent of total costs) to select a one-time capital-adjustment option patterned on accelerated depreciation. A reasonable phase-in-time for both fixed and movable capital assets would help minimize disruption of the investment cycle. In addition, HCFA needs to adjust the capital component of its Market Basket Input Price index, which is overly sensitive to declining interest rates, so that hospitals are allowed the appropriate adjustment for inflation in capital costs.

Reasons for the Increase in Debt Financing

Hospital administrators are not entirely to blame for the critical leverage problems facing their hospitals. Administrators had been blessed with large external sources of funds for many years. The abandonment of government programs such as Hill-Burton, the rise and fall of cost-reimbursement, and the dramatic drop in philanthropy have left hospitals groping for new capital sources.

Many factors underlie the shift from equity to debt financing. The most important factor is the shift from cost-plus to simple cost reimbursement. This has created a shortfall in both net income and working capital, forcing hospitals to seek funds externally. The Hill-Burton program, which provided federal funds for the con-

Table 21.6   Capital Costs as a Percentage of Revenues, Hospital Type and Occupancy Rates, Selected New York City Hospitals, 1986

Hospital Name	Hospital Type	Total Capital as Percentage of Total Revenue	Total Capital as Percentage of Operating Revenue	Occupancy Rate
Bayley Seton Hospital	Voluntary, church-operated	27.4	37.7	68.0
Doctors Hospital	Voluntary	18.0	21.9	77.8
Misericordia Hospital	Voluntary, church-operated	17.7	21.5	79.9
Methodist Hospital	Voluntary	17.7	21.5	77.9
Community Hospital (Brooklyn)	Voluntary	16.0	19.0	79.8
Catholic Medical Center	Voluntary, church-operated	15.7	18.6	81.0
Long Island College Hospital	Voluntary	15.6	18.5	80.5
Baptist Medical Center	Voluntary	3.5	3.6	90.8
N.Y. Eye & Ear Infirmary	Voluntary, Eye, Ear N & T	3.5	3.6	76.9
Doctors Hosp.-Staten Is.	Investor-owned, corporation	3.4	3.5	89.7
St. Clare's Hospital	Voluntary, church-operated	2.6	2.6	70.9
Flatbush General Hospital	Investor-owned, corporation	2.3	2.3	79.6
Joint Diseases North Gen.	Voluntary	2.0	2.1	85.4
Pelham Bay General Hosp.	Investor-owned, partnership	2.0	2.0	84.9
Physicians Hospital	Investor-owned, corporation	1.5	1.5	80.3
Rockefeller Univ. Hosp.	Voluntary, specialty hospital	1.6	1.6	66.0

struction of new beds, has been eliminated. Philanthropic contributions as a percentage of total contributions have declined. In 1968 philanthropy accounted for 21.1 percent of capital funds. By 1976 philanthropy accounted for just 7.5 percent of the funding for new projects (Lightle, 1981). One should also point out that states with hospital rate regulatory programs eroded the incentives to seek philanthropy by requiring hospitals to spend a fraction of such unrestricted funds on bad debts and charity care. On the supply side, 1986 tax reform diminishes the tax benefits of giving to tax-exempt organizations. Finally, new technologies and equipment obsolescence have put a strain on larger hospitals in particular to come up with the funds to maintain state-of-the-art technology. This drain on funds is frequently overlooked, yet the rapid turnover in new technologies has proven to be a major cause of increasing hospital costs.

The approach taken in the second half of this chapter will be to suggest why we might stimulate equity financing, rather than simply reduce the availability of debt options. Government and third-party insurance carriers have resisted the explicit recognition of an operating margin that would sufficiently cover capital replacement and the technological updating of equipment. Until 1988, interest on debt is an allowable cost passed through under the Medicare program. Hospitals that fund new equipment with debt find the actual cost of purchase to be much lower than the purchase price. To quickly see why, consider the following simplified example of a hypothetical hospital named ABC. Hospital ABC is anticipating the purchase of a new piece of capital equipment. It can fund the purchase through debt or internally generated funds. The financial officer considering these two alternatives faces the following cash flows. Hospital ABC could debt finance the equipment in 1977 through a 20-year bond issue paying interest of 10 percent per annum with repayment at maturity.

Three quarters of hospital ABC's revenues are paid by cost payers who reimburse for all interest expense. Therefore, 75 percent of interest payments will be reimbursed as allowable costs, and management would have assumed this percentage remains constant throughout the time period (1977–1996). The appropriate discount rate for computing the net present value of the cash flow is 10 percent—that is, the cost of borrowing. The effective cost of the debt-financed purchase to the hospital in 1977 is $36,148 (the $36,148 is composed of the net present value of the 25 percent unreimbursed interest payments equal to $21,284, plus the debt repayment of $100,000 in the year 2001, which has a net present value of $14,864). The effective cost of the internally funded purchase alternative in 1977 is $100,000. In summary, the time value of money and full reimbursement for interest expense create powerful incentives for hospitals to fund new capital acquisitions with debt. Decision makers had no way of projecting that by 1988 Hospital ABC's revenues paid by cost payers would decline to 40 to 50 percent, as Medicare refused to continue their pass-through of interest expense.

For some southern and western hospital markets, the incentive to debt finance is not as strong in the mid-1980s because only 50 percent of their patients pay costs—for example, half their patients are charge payers (self-pay) or represented by third parties that pay charges (commercial insurance companies, some Blue Cross and Medicare plans). If we assume that only 50 percent of the patient days are covered by cost payers, the effective cost of the debt-financed purchase in 1984 is $57,432. Consequently, it is still better to debt finance than equity finance the $100,000, but the differential has been reduced to $42,568. Although there are other cash flows involved in the capital purchase decision, such as reimbursement for depreciation, these cash flows would be the same for debt or internal fund financing alternatives, and thus are not relevant in the above comparisons.

Wanted: A Return on Equity

Analysts should draw a distinction between return *of* capital and the return *on* capital. Return of capital is embodied by the returns generated by the assets for the institution. It is a moot point whether an equitable return of capital would be based on the original cost or the state-of-the-art replacement cost of the capital asset. Price-level depreciation obviously keeps pace with advances in medicine but does not encourage better productivity among providers or manufacturers of hospital assets. Too generous a level of price-level depreciation would obviously be highly inflationary. However, historical cost depreciation erodes capital stock if inflation is greater than zero (Cleverley, 1982).

The return on capital is the effective cost of capital. In a for-profit firm, the cost of capital is the average rate per annum a company must pay for its equities. This figure changes over time with economic circumstances and shifts in perceived risk from investment in the facility (e.g., it may be 12 percent this year and 16 percent next year). As a firm believer in efficient capital markets, Conrad (1986) defines the cost of capital as the discount rate that equates the expected present value of all future cash flows to common stockholders with the market value of common stock at a given time. As we observed in Chapter 20, the stock market for investor-owned chains closely approximates a responsive, if not perfectly efficient, capital market. However, the problems with calculating a cost of capital for tax-exempt hospitals are more difficult.

The cost of capital for tax-exempt organizations is best shadow-priced by focusing on the motivation of donors (Pauly, 1986). Lenders clearly value parting with their capital at the interest rate negotiated in the deal. But donors, and certain generous third-party payers, may have other motivations. The key issue is whether the donors or quasi-donors want simply a tax deduction, or a tax deduction plus social dividends (e.g., the joy of seeing better health care delivered in their community). One could carry the argument to the extreme and suggest that if the donor is foregoing the dollar return from investing in the business world, then the donor does bear an opportunity cost equal to the competitive rate of return of for-profit equity capital.

Unfortunately for hospital managers, as a matter of public policy the government and other payers have not made reimbursement a "level playing field" by granting tax-exempt organizations a return on equity to match the for-profit chains. Instead, as was reported in Chapter 20, Medicare has decided to phase out paying any return on equity to the investor-owned sector by 1991. Silvers and Kauer (1986) effectively dismiss the regulators' traditional argument that paying hospitals a return on equity is a "forced" contribution to capital stock. Restoration of a return-on-equity (ROE) payment, one for for-profit hospitals and a lower ROE for tax-exempt firms, represents an ex post payment for a return on ex ante donated capital of contributors. To shadow-price contributions in a weighted average cost of capital as zero assumes the capital has no worth and will be equally easy to access each year in the future in perpetuity. Indeed, in this last respect, federal tax reform, by reducing the tax benefits of giving, may make it more difficult for hospitals to attract donations and grants.

Marketing the Debt

Financing authorities organized by state governments have greatly aided hospitals in issuing tax-free debt. The need for a debt service reserve fund has been eliminated in many cases. These securities typically offer high yields and have proven to be very attractive to fire and casualty companies, banks, and mutual funds. The federal government National Mortgage Association has similarly enabled hospitals to issue debt at reduced interest costs by reducing the riskiness of the security.

For the past decade a large number of private security brokers have been offering hospital securities. They have also helped hospitals to better tailor their debt to the needs of both the hospital and the lender. If the issue is large enough ($10 million or more), it will attract secondary market interest, which increases its liquidity and lowers its cost enough to make it competitive with other high-volume tax-exempt bonds (such as municipal bonds). The increased demand for debt financing has been matched by an enlarged infrastructure for the issuing of that debt.

Federal issuing agencies, institutional lenders, and bond rating agencies must evaluate the credit worthiness of the institution through quantitative measures (financial ratio analysis*) and qualitative (such as community support volunteers) criteria. The obvious objective of the credit analysis is to establish whether the borrower can generate sufficient cash flows to service its debt requirements and meet other financial obligations. As President Nixon contracted the Hill-Burton program and encouraged private borrowing, the hospital feasibility study developed as the document to assess credit worthiness. Such studies were first used in the mid-1970s by state and municipal authorities monitoring bond issues.

Government hospitals utilize general obligation (tax-exempt) bonds as their primary source of capital. For example, the state of Illinois, and the city of Chicago, may have to issue $350 to $380 million in general obligation bonds to rebuild a new 800-bed Cook County Hospital in the coming years. Tax-exempt hospitals do most of their borrowing with tax-exempt revenue bonds. Tax-exempt hospitals also used industrial development bonds (IDBs), a government-backed debt security, issued in amounts of $10 million or less, as an additional source of capital. Hospitals would frequently form proprietary subsidiaries and utilize the funds to build nursing homes, surgicenters, or ambulatory care centers. Starting in 1985, government restrictions and volume caps made IDBs a less attractive source of capital for the hospital industry.

---

* Ratio analysis should not be univariate. The superior alternative is to consider simultaneously the patterns in changes of a number of ratios over time. This approach has been labeled a multi-discriminant analysis methodology by Altman (1978). This method of multi-discriminant profile analysis reduces a number of problems of misclassification encountered in simple comparisons of single ratios.

Financial Constraints on Hospitals Issuing Debt

As a hospital becomes highly levered, it becomes increasingly susceptible to default. To protect themselves, lenders look at many financial indicators to determine the riskiness of a debt issue. Increasingly, hospitals find lenders placing restrictions on hospital finances to insure against the possibility of default. Constraints are often placed on financial ratios such as those mentioned above. Even if the constraints are not explicit in the loan agreement, hospitals find that if their leverage position deteriorates, the cost of new debt increases. Eventually, lenders will refuse to purchase any debt as the investment becomes too risky.

Hospitals must maintain their financial stability, as reflected in their leverage and coverage ratios, if they are to continue to finance growth through debt. If other sources of capital remain scarce, maintaining ceilings on financial ratios can severely limit hospitals in their ability to grow. Yet, such ceilings may be the only way to ensure the solvency of the hospitals.

Once a hospital has reached the limit of one of the constraints, it is possible to determine the maximum growth rate a hospital can maintain and still be within the constraint. This has been done before under some very limiting assumptions, but one can actually derive equations to solve for the maximum growth rate under more relaxed assumptions. We do assume that net income may be used to help meet capital requirements in the year it is earned. Additionally, we assume straight line relationships between revenue and the capital needed to generate that revenue and between net income and revenue. Under these two assumptions, it will be shown that in order to maintain a reasonable rate of capital expansion hospitals must rely on external sources of funds. The extent of this reliance on debt is determined largely by the hospital's ability to generate profits internally. The sensitivity of three key financial ratios to net income margin will be demonstrated in the next section.

How Financial Ratios May Restrict Hospital Growth

To demonstrate how a ceiling on the ratio of debt to total capital can restrict growth, consider the case of County General Hospital (CGH) currently operating with a debt-total capital ratio ceiling of 50 percent. CGH has a net income margin of 2 percent of revenues and requires $1.15 of capital investment (plant and equipment) and working capital to support each dollar of revenue. Under these conditions the hospital is constrained in the next year to a maximum growth rate in real dollar terms of 3.6 percent.

To see that this is so, let us say that CGH generates $1,000,000 in total revenues this year. Next year the hospital will generate total revenues of $1,036,000 (see Figure 21.1). Net income will be $20,720, which can be matched by $20,720 in new debt, maintaining the 50 percent debt/total capital ratio. The sum, $41,440, is exactly equal to (except for rounding off the growth rate) the additional working capital and capital investment required to generate the $36,000 of additional revenue. At higher growth rates the capital requirements exceed the total funds that can be obtained from debt and equity. The hospital would have to become more highly levered (issue more debt) to maintain a higher growth rate. At lower growth rates, the required new capital can be generated without reaching the debt financing limit.

A formal equation can be derived to calculate the maximum growth rate for any debt/total capital ratio. This equation can be used to see the effects each variable has on the growth rate.

$$G = \text{maximum growth rate}$$
$$CI = \text{\$ of capital investment required to support \$1 of revenues}$$
$$WC = \text{\$ of working capital required to support \$1 of revenues}$$
$$X = \frac{\text{debt/total capital}}{1 - \text{debt/total capital}}$$
$$= \text{maximum debt/equity ratio}$$
$$M = \text{net income margin}$$
$$\text{funds generated by growth} = \text{funds required to support growth}$$
$$(1 + X)(M + G)(M) = (CI + WC)G$$

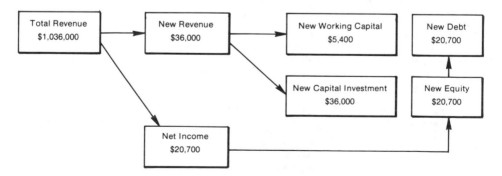

Figure 21.1   Capital Growth Under the Debt/Total Capital Restriction

$$G = \frac{(X + 1)(M)}{(CI + WC) - M - (X)(M)}$$

Table 21.7 presents the maximum allowable growth rates for various values of debt/total capital and $M \cdot CI + WC$ is assumed to equal 1.15 for the purposes of these calculations. Higher values of CI and WC would result in lower maximum growth rates.

Table 21.7 Maximum Growth Rates Under Debt/Total Capital Restriction

	Net Income Margin				
Debt/Total Capital	*0%*	*1%*	*2%*	*3%*	*4%*
0.50	0	2	4	6	8
0.67	0	3	6	9	12
0.70	0	3	7	10	13
0.75	0	4	8	12	16
0.80	0	5	10	15	21
0.90	0	9	21	35	53

Debt/Plant Ratio

This second constraint limits hospital growth in much the same way as the first constraint. If CGH was at its debt/plant limit of 0.67, it would be restricted to a maximum growth of 4.3 percent next year. This can be seen in Figure 21.2. Here, CGH generates $43,000 in new revenues and requires $43,000 in new plant and equipment and $6,450 in new working capital to support this growth—a total cash requirement of $49,450. Net income of $20,860 is generated during the year, leaving the debt requirement at $28,590. This maintains exactly the 0.67 debt/plant ratio.

If the growth rate exceeded 4.3 percent, the additional debt

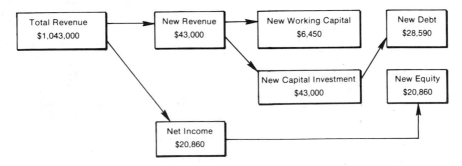

Figure 21.2   Hospital Growth Under the Debt/Plant Restriction

required to support operations would exceed 0.67 times the additional plant and equipment. A lower growth rate would reduce the debt requirement below the maximum allowable level. Again, we can derive an equation to determine the maximum growth rate for a hospital that has reached the limit of its debt/plant constraint.

$$G = \text{maximum growth rate}$$
$$CI = \$ \text{ of capital investment required to support } \$1 \text{ of revenue}$$
$$WC = \$ \text{ of working capital required to support } \$1 \text{ of revenue}$$
$$X = \text{maximum allowable debt/plant ratio}$$
$$M = \text{net income margin}$$
$$\text{funds generated by growth} = \text{funds required to support growth}$$
$$(CI)(X)(G) + M(1 + B) = (CI + WC)G$$
$$G = \frac{M}{(CI + WC) - (CI)(X) - M}$$

Table 21.8 presents the maximum growth rates for various values of X and M. $CI + WC$ is assumed to equal 1.15.

Debt Service Coverage

It is reasonable to expect a lender to want some guarantee that a hospital will generate enough income during the year to repay principal and interest. The ability to repay principal and interest is reflected in the debt service coverage ratio. This is the ratio of the cash flow available to repay debt to the required debt payments. Specifically, the debt service coverage ratio equals:

$$\frac{\text{Net Income} + \text{Depreciation} + \text{Interest}}{\text{Interest} + \text{Principal Payments}}$$

Depreciation is added because it is a noncash charge on the income statement.

Table 21.8   Maximum Growth Rates Under Debt/Plant Restriction

	Net Income Margin				
Level of Constraint: Debt/Total	*0%*	*1%*	*2%*	*3%*	*4%*
0.67	0	2	4	7	9
0.70	0	2	5	7	10
0.75	0	3	5	8	11
0.80	0	3	5	8	13
0.90	0	4	9	14	19

Typically, this ratio is required to be at least 1.0 to 1.5, with higher coverage ratios being more restrictive to the use of debt. Suppose CGH has a required margin of 1.50. Depreciable life on new capital investments at CGH averages 20 years, and any new debt would be paid back in equal principal payments over 20 years. If the current interest rate on debt is 10 percent, then it can be shown that the maximum allowable growth rate is just under 3.4 percent.

In this case, CGH would generate $34,000 in new revenues. This growth would require additional plant and equipment of $34,000, to be depreciated over 20 years at $1,700 per year. Additional working capital of $5,000 is needed as well. Net income for next year would be $20,680. Additional debt of $18,420 is required to support operations. The debt will be paid back in annual installments of $921. The first year's interest due is $1,842 and the total interest plus principal due in the first year is $2,763. We can now see that the coverage ratio will be maintained at 1.5.

Additional net income is $680. Depreciation is $1,700. Interest is $1,842. The sum is $4,222 which, except for rounding errors, is exactly 1.5 times the required interest and principal payments. Table 21.9 summarizes these figures. Again, faster growth would require additional debt, and CGH would be unable to maintain its coverage ratio.

Deriving an equation to determine the maximum growth rate under various situations is a simple task. The final equation is presented below.

G = maximum allowable growth rate
CI = $ of capital investment required to support $1 of revenue
WC = $ of working capital required to support $1 of revenue
C = required coverage ratio
I = rate of interest on debt
RP = repayment period of principal
M = net income margin
DL = depreciable life of new plant and equipment

Table 21.9   How County General Hospital Meets Its Debt Service Coverage Ratio

Cash Inflow	=	1.5 × Required Payments
Additional Net Income	$ 680	Principal $ 920
Additional Depreciation	1,700	Interest $1,842
		$2,762
Interest	1,842	
	$4,222 = 1.5 × $2,762	

$$G = [(C*M)/RP + (C*I*M) - (1*M)]/[((WC + CI)*C)/RP + ((WC + CI)*C*I) - M - (CI/DL) - ((WC + CI)*I)]$$

Table 21.10 presents the maximum growth rates for coverage ratios of 1.25 and 1.5. As the coverage ratio approaches 1 the maximum allowable growth rate approaches infinity.

For the purposes of calculations for Table 21.11, working capital and capital investment needs are assumed to be $1.15 for each dollar of revenue. The repayment period on new debt is 30 years, and the average depreciable life of new capital investment is 25 years. These are typical figures for most hospitals, although depreciable life in proprietary hospitals tends to be a bit shorter (21 years) and depreciable life in voluntary hospitals tends to be longer (27 years).*

As fewer patients are covered under a health plan that recognizes interest expense as an allowable expense for cost-based reimbursement, the coverage ratio as normally calculated in business increasingly reflects a hospital's ability to repay its debt. The figures used to calculate the coverage ratio should be the unreimbursable portion of the interest expense. Assume CGH has cash flows (which includes interest *expense*) of $20,000 and interest and principle payments of $15,000 or a coverage ratio of 1.33. If 50 percent of CGH's $5,000 in interest expense is reimbursed (because 50 percent of CGH's volume is reimbursed on a cost basis), then these figures should be adjusted to $17,500 [$20,000 − 0.5 (5,000)] in cash inflow and $12,500 [$15,000 − 0.5 (5,000)] in required debt service. The coverage ratio increases to 1.40. To calculate a maximum growth rate, use I' instead of I in the given equation, where $I' = I \times$ (percentage volume not cost-based).

Table 21.10 Maximum Growth Rates Under Debt Service Constraint

Prevailing Interest Rates	1.25 Coverage Net Income Margin				1.50 Coverage Net Income Margin			
	0%	*1%*	*2%*	*3%*	*0%*	*1%*	*2%*	*3%*
6%	0%/yr	3%/yr	10%/yr	93%/yr	0%/yr	2%/yr	4%/yr	8%/yr
8%	0	2	7	24	0	1	3	7
10%	0	2	6	15	0	1	3	6
12%	0	2	5	11	0	1	3	5
14%	0	2	4	9	0	1	3	5
16%	0	2	4	8	0	1	3	5

* Unpublished data provided by the Capital Finance Division of the American Hospital Association.

Table 21.11   Maximum Growth for Different Capital Investment Requirements

CI	Maximum Growth
0.8	12%/year
0.9	10
1.0	8
1.1	7
1.2	6

Under typical conditions, a hospital that has reached its debt ceiling and has a small net income margin will often be limited to an annual growth rate of 4 percent or less. For hospitals with a high percentage of revenues coming from uninsured indigent care patients, the net income margin is often 1 percent or less. In the future these hospitals will find it increasingly difficult to generate new funds from any source.

Hospitals that are not presently near their debt capacity may find their leverage positions weakening quickly as growth continues unabated. For example, if CGH currently has a debt-to-total-capital ratio of 0.5, annual revenue growth of 10 percent per year, and a net income margin of 2 percent, the debt-to-total-capital ratio would increase to 0.67 in just nine years. If the debt/plant ratio is currently 0.5, then under these conditions this ratio would increase to 0.67 in just six years.

Sensitivity Analysis

The growth rates presented in Tables 21.7, 21.8, and 21.10 are sensitive to changes in each of the variables used to derive the rates. Tables 21.11–21.14 indicate how small changes in these variables can affect the maximum growth rate under the debt service coverage constraint, which is the constraint most sensitive to small changes in a hospital's finances. Unless otherwise indicated, the variables will be assumed to have the following values:

$$CI = \text{capital investment} = 1.00$$
$$WC = \text{working capital} = 0.15$$
$$DL = \text{depreciable life} = 25 \text{ years}$$
$$RP = \text{repayment period} = 30 \text{ years}$$
$$I = \text{interest rate} = 0.10$$
$$M = \text{net income margin} = 0.02$$
$$C = \text{required coverage ratio} = 1.25$$

The results in Tables 21.11 and 21.12 indicate that small changes in the capital investment and working capital requirements can lead

Table 21.12   Maximum Growth for Different Working Capital Requirements

WC	Maximum Growth
0.10	10%/year
0.15	8
0.20	7
0.25	6

Table 21.13   Maximum Growth for Different Depreciable Lives of New Assets

DL	Maximum Growth
20 years	20%/year
23	10
25	8
27	6

Table 21.14   Maximum Growth for Different Repayment Periods of Debt

RP	Maximum Growth
20 years	4%/year
23	5
27	7
30	8

to pronounced changes in the constraint on growth. Increasing efficiency through better working capital management and general productivity increases can greatly reduce a hospital's dependence on debt.

Tables 21.13 and 21.14 demonstrate that long repayment periods for debt issues and a short depreciable life for new assets will place the least short-term financial strain on the institution. However, over the life of the debt these conditions may be more restrictive than typical conditions would be.

Philanthropic donations can improve a hospital's leverage position slightly. A hospital that receives enough donations to fund 11 percent of total capital expansion may increase its maximum annual growth rate by as much as a full percentage point or more, depending on the other variables.

Finally, these conditions assume level principal payments. If loans are paid back through level debt service (principal plus interest) instead, then the loan would prove less constrictive to growth in the first few years but would be more constrictive in the last few years of the debt. This is due to the different timing of the cash flows associated with each method of repayment.

A Federal Reserve Bank for Hospital Capital?

Many analysts claim that the hospital sector has reached the limits of its debt capacity, and will reach a point in the early 1980s when it is unable to generate enough capital to meet demand (Grimmelman, 1980). However, such analysis ignores the subtle difference between sufficient resources to meet capital maintenance and sufficient resources to meet the physicians' goal of unabated capital improvement. In other words, a national policy for cost containment might involve limiting the ability of hospitals to expand or improve their capital position and perhaps constrain their ability to maintain the high current levels of fixed capital assets. A number of studies in the United States (Fuchs, 1986) and England (Cullis et al., 1979) have argued that erosion of hospital capital will have negligible effects on quality, availability of nonelective care, and health status indices of the population. If hospitals do not cut back on their capital demands in the future, they may face financial disaster.

Brown and Saltman (1985) suggest a coordinated intervention into the hospital capital process. To allocate capital irrespective of the wealth of the patient mix, the authors suggest a local Federal Reserve style hospital capital bank, presumably to correct or substitute for marketplace imperfections of what some refer to as the current policy of "muddling through." Unfortunately, a hospital capital bank might be as inefficient an investment in the ideal of equity as community-based hospital planning. The "cure-all of regulation" does, however, appeal to small and poorly managed hospitals that are desperate for access to capital. Hospitals turned to debt financing because it was cheap and because other sources of funding (grants and gifts) had declined. As hospitals become more and more highly levered, new debt issues will be perceived as being more and more risky. Interest rates will increase, increasing the cost of hospital debt. Some of this increase will be passed along to consumers through reimbursement mechanisms, but hospitals will increasingly have to shoulder a lot of the burden themselves.

Hospitals that have small net income margins must become highly levered in order to maintain growth rates above 4 or 5 percent annually. Hospitals that have been unable to generate funds internally have brought themselves to the brink of default. The three important financial ratios considered herein do not define all conditions necessary to determine the correct operating margin for assuring the hospital sector of adequate private market financing. For example, the definition of an adequate operating margin will vary among hospitals as a function of size and owner-ship. It could be argued that the 3 percent operating margin suggested for the 200-bed case study hospital is niggardly for a 1,000-bed university medical center. Obviously, differences among hospitals do affect their capital needs and, consequently, the "correct" operating margins sufficient to freeze or reduce the amount of capital that is debt financed. The dependence on debt financing will increase if the third-party payers continue to prevent an adequate return on equity, fail to adjust depreciation schedules in line with inflation, and pay for only a miserly share of bad-debt cases.

References

ALTMAN, E. (1978). "Financial Ratios, Discriminant Analysis, and the Prediction of Corporate Bankruptcy." *Journal of Finance* 23:4 (September), 589–607.

ANDERSON, G., and GINSBURG, P. (1983). "Prospective Capital Payments to Hospitals." *Health Affairs* 2:3 (Fall), 52–63.

BROWN, J. (1986). "Hospital Capital Reimbursement in the Competitive Era." Department of Health Policy and Management (October), Harvard School of Public Health.

BROWN, J., and SALTMAN, R. (1985). "Health Capital Policy in the United States: A Strategic Perspective." *Inquiry* 22:2 (Summer), 122–131.

CLAIBORN, S. (1985). "Alternative Financing Approaches for Health Care Institutions." *Topics in Health Care Financing* 10:4 (Summer), 33–41.

CLEVERLEY, W. (1986). "The Ten Commandments of Financial Policy Development." *Healthcare Executive* 1:4 (May/June), 120.

CLEVERLEY, W. (1984). "A Proposal for Capital Cost Payment." *Health Care Management Review* 9:2 (Spring), 39–50.

CLEVERLEY, W. (1982). "Return on Equity in the Hospital Industry: Requirement or Windfall?" *Inquiry* 19:2 (Summer), 150–159.

COHODES, D. (1983). "Which Will Survive? The $150 Billion Capital Question." *Inquiry* 20:1 (Spring), 5–11.

COHODES, D., and KINKEAD, B. (1984). *Hospital Capital Formation in the 1980s.* Baltimore: Johns Hopkins University Press.

CONRAD, D. (1986). "Returns on Equity for Not-for-Profit Hospitals: A Commentary and Elaboration." *Health Services Research* 21:1 (April), 17–20.

CULLIS, J. G., FORSTER, D. P., and FROST, C. E. (1979). "Demand for Inpatient Treatment: Some Recent Evidence." *Applied Economics* 12:2 (December), 43–60.

DURENBERGER, D. (1986). "Capital Cost Pass-Through Phase-Out: A 6-Year Simplified Approach." Washington, D.C., United States Senate (January) (R., Minn.) (amended in S.2121, February 27, 1986, as a seven-year phase-in).

EASTAUGH, S. (1986). "Capital Financing and Refinancing." *Healthcare Financial Management* 41:1 (December/January), forthcoming.

EASTAUGH, S. (1984). "Hospital Diversification and Financial Management." *Medical Care* 22:8 (August), 704–723.

EASTAUGH, S. (1982). "Effectiveness of Community-Based Hospital Planning: Some Recent Statistical Evidence." *Applied Economics* 14:3 (September), 475–490.

ELROD, J., and WILKINSON, J. (1985). *Hospital Project Financing and Refinancing Under Prospective Payment*. Chicago: American Hospital Publishing.

FUCHS, V. (1986). *The Health Economy*. Cambridge, Mass.: Harvard University Press.

GINZBERG, E. (1986). "The Destabilization of Health Care." *New England Journal of Medicine* 315:12 (September 18), 757–761.

GRIMMELMAN, F. (1980). "Borrowing for Capital: Will It Empty Your Pockets?" *Hospital Financial Management* 6:12 (December), 19–25.

HOWELL, J. (1984). "Evaluating the Impact of CON Regulation Using Measures of Ultimate Outcome: Some Cautions from Experience in Massachusetts." *Health Services Research* 19:5 (December), 557–613.

IGLEHART, J. (1986). "Early Experiences with Prospective Payment of Hospitals." *New England Journal of Medicine* 314:22 (May 29), 1460–1464.

Institute of Medicine (1986). *For-Profit Enterprise in Health Care*. Washington, D.C.: National Academy of Sciences.

Institute of Medicine (1976). *Controlling the Supply of Hospital Beds*. Washington, D.C.: National Academy of Sciences.

KALISON, M., and AVERILL, R. (1985). "Building Capital into Prospective Payment." *Business and Health* 2:7 (JUNE), 34–37.

KIDDER-PEABODY & COMPANY (1986). *Tax-Exempt Hospital Revenue Bonds: A Database*. New York: Kidder-Peabody, Inc.

Kidder-Peabody & Company, The Health Finance Group (1985). Public report: *Review of Health-Care Finance*. New York: Kidder-Peabody, Inc.

KRYSTYNAK, L. (1985). "Prospective Payment for Capital: The Financial Nature of Capital Allowances." *Healthcare Financial Management Association Monograph*, Series 83, Oak Brook, Illinois.

LIGHTLE, M. (1981). "Changes in the Sources of Capital." *Hospital Financial Management* 11:2 (February), 42–47.

LONG, H. (1982). "Asset Choice and Program Selection in a Competitive Environment." *Health Care Financial Management* 12:8 (August), 34–50.

LYLES, A., and SCHNEIDER, D. (1984). "Development of the Office of Health Facilities Microsimulation Model for Hospital Financing Analysis: An Analysis of Investment Behavior in California." Research report, Center for Hospital Finance and Management (June), Johns Hopkins University.

PAULY, M. (1986). "Returns on Equity for Not-for-Profit Hospitals." *Health Services Research* 21:1 (April), 1–16.

SCHNEIDER, D., MAGER, R., and DUMMIT, L. (1986). "Hospital Investment Behavior: An Analysis Using the Office of Health Facilities (OHF) Model." Final report (October) under Health Resources and Services Administration HRSA–240–85–0060.

SILVERS, J. B. (1975). "How Do the Limits to Debt Financing Affect Your Hospital's Financial Status?" *Hospital Financial Management* 5:2 (February), 32–41.

SILVERS, J., and KAUER, R. (1986). "Returns on Equity for Not-for-Profit Hospitals: Some Comments." *Health Services Research* 21:1 (April), 21–28.

Standard & Poor's Corporation (1986). *Hospital Revenue Bonds and Debt Rating.* New York: S & P, Municipal Bond Department.

SYKES, C. (1986). "The Role of Equity Financing in Today's Health Care Financing Environment." *Topics in Health Care Financing* 11:3 (Spring), 1–3.

TRASKA, M. (1986). "Capital Proposal Hurts All Hospital Categories: E & W Study." *Hospitals* 60:13 (July 5), 60–62.

Chapter 22

EVALUATION OF FINANCING ALTERNATIVES

Under an easily identified set of circumstances, lease financing can be cost effective. Recent developments in finance make it possible to not only evaluate the financial attractiveness of a given lease, but also to accurately predict bounds within which the terms of the lease must fall. Hospital administrators armed with this information should be able to negotiate more favorable lease terms.

—Mark Bayless

Finance is somehow both the implicit culprit and the expected savior of an industry rapidly approaching bankruptcy. The health field, in large part, has been managed by professionals who often had a clear view of part of their external and internal environment without being able to relate these to financial realities.

—J. B. Silvers

Hospitals have an excessive reliance on debt relative to other sectors of the economy. Public utilities borrow on the average about 60 percent of total capitalization, and manufacturing firms about 40 to 50 percent. Hospital debt loads currently are in the 80 to 90 percent range. According to Kidder-Peabody and Company (1986), total debt offerings in the hospital industry increased from $2.2 billion in 1974 to $30 billion in 1985. As sources of philanthropy and free Hill-Burton funds dramatically declined, from 1972 to 1983, one out of two hospitals planning a capital expansion or modernization were forced into the private debt markets. In addition to the simple replacement concept of capital mainte-

632

nance, society may wish to consider adding on a technological maintenance factor to assure that the hospital has funds for updating capital to keep pace with peer institutions. Given that medical technology is likely to be cost-increasing in the future, preservation of capital position implies both capital replacement and a capital improvement concept that keeps pace with new technology.

In drawing comparisons between the degree of regulatory involvement in the hospital industry and public utilities, one encounters two important differences. First, the degree of regulatory involvement in hospitals is less rigid, more variable across state lines and Blue Cross catchment areas, and is handled in an illogical fashion that can best be described as muddling through. Consequently, the hospital sector has the benefit of being less regulated than most public utilities. Second, the ad hoc swings in the reimbursement rules have prevented many hospitals from preserving their capital purchasing power to anywhere near the degree that public utilities are allowed in order to assure future operations. In summary, hospitals have not received the same basic treatment that we accord to other highly regulated utility industries.

While capital costs are a relatively small percentage of total hospital costs (6 to 10 percent in most cases), the importance of equitable capital payment policies exceeds the per annum dollar volumes involved. Adequacy and stability are key in designing a fair payment system for financing both equipment (38 to 40 percent of capital costs annually) and plant. However, defining adequacy is not an easy task. After examining these issues, Chapter 22 concludes with an analysis of the impact of federal tax reform in 1986 on hospital capital financing decisions.

Accurate Self-Assessment of Risk and Return

After having taken full advantage of a 36-month slide in interest rates through 1986, hospital executives are beginning to realize that they cannot continue indefinitely increasing the leverage on a service that is leveling off or declining in both volume and earning power. However, borrowing power is needed so that expansion into areas other than inpatient care is not limited. The intrinsic advantage of moving hospitals onto a prospective capital payment scheme is in the capital budgeting process. Decisions will be made for rational economic reasons, and borrowing will not be done as a tool to write off some interest expense onto the Medicare program.

Decisions will be made on the basis of business risk, and the method of financing will not be largely driven by reimbursement concerns. Unfortunately, a genuine risk assessment of hospital executives on the late end of their hospital's investment cycle may, due to their facility's high accounting age, get dragged down with the poorly managed institutions. This would not happen because of poor judgment, but rather because HCFA refused to incorporate a rolling base of actual cost experience for hospitals with major capital projects.

Cleverley (1986) provides a simple linear regression analysis for assessing present and future capital expense levels under PPS. The most important determinant of his capital expense ratio (CER)— the ratio of capital to noncapital expense—is the accounting age of the hospital. Other variables in the analysis can include equity finance (current, projected), price-level adjusted fixed asset turnover, and replacement viability. In this context, Arnold (1986) would suggest that the organization cannot be too conservative in its assumptions. Oftentimes in other business sectors the worst case forecasts have proven far too optimistic. This is true in the case of the Stanford University debt capacity analysis (Hopkins et al., 1982). Because capital investment decisions are increasingly complex, a survey of the process is in order.

Designing a Capital Project

Major capital investments should be analyzed in five basic stages:

1. Capital requirements, benefits and opportunities
2. Project feasibility study stage
3. Assembly of a financing team and project plan
4. Credit assessment stage (e.g., bond ratings)
5. Completion of the financing (long run and short term)

Stage 1 involves identification of capital requirements to meet shifts in patient demand, clinician referral patterns, or the basic need to keep the facility state of the art (replacement, renovation, modernization, and expansion). The stimulus for assessing capital position may be reactive (e.g., market share is declining because the facility is outdated) or proactive. The opportunity to "be first" in a new service or in a new growing marketplace zone (location) is a proactive rationale for major new capital investment. As was pointed out in Chapter 9, this process is increasingly driven by consumer preference, supplanting the "empire-building complex" of trustees and medical staff to expand simply for expansion sake.

Stage 2, the feasibility study, involves a careful conservative assessment of projected cash inflows, cash outflows, the opportunity costs for the resources, and the economic life cycle of the project. The intent of this stage is to develop an accurate estimate of the financial viability and logistical complexity of the various capital project alternatives. What stage 2 requires is approximate answers to the precise problem—not precise answers to the approximate problem. When external consultants are brought in, they must be cognizant of the fact that there is little value in refining analysis that does not consider the most appropriate alternatives and assumptions for the hospital. The consultants can also point out unreasonable assumptions. If the hospital generates initial cash flow estimates that are too optimistic to convince their own paid consultants, the facility will have even less success trying to convince the bond rating agents at Moody's, Standard & Poor's, or Fitch Investor Services (very active in long-term care facility financing). Hospital managers and trustees must resist the human temptation among their peers to overstate excessively the growth potential of any new facility or service product line.

Stage 3 involves the formation of a financing team (bankers and lawyers, including hospital counsel, bond counsel, and issuer's counsel), plus other key actors in the project plan (e.g., from the architect to the construction manager). Coordination is important. For example, one would not want the architects to waste time and money designing a planned facility that is much too expensive for the debt capacity of the hospital. The individuals involved sometimes number in the hundreds. Consequently, the fixed transaction costs of issuing debt are substantial—that is, it would not be cost-effective to refinance old debt for financial reasons unless the interest rates declined 1.75 to 2.5 percent (depending on volume). Individuals have a number of roles to play and allegiances to parties other than the borrower (Elrod and Wilkinson, 1985).

The most critical broker of the deal is the commercial banker. Commercial bankers can perform three to four jobs in a single deal, including acting as the lender, investor, debt guarantor, underwriter, and bond or master trustee. Members of the financing team might suggest purchase of bond insurance to raise the credit rating for the hospital, thus decreasing the rate of interest, if the action is cost beneficial (without the bond insurance the required volume could not be sold in a reasonable time). Bond insurance clearly makes sense if the decline in interest expense discounted over the period is less than the cost of the insurance. Institutional investors do not shy away from buying the higher yield uninsured hospital bond issues, but individual investors often prefer the lower-risk, lower-yield hospital investment with bond insurance. The prevalence of bond insurance as a credit enhancement strategy increased from 9 percent of bond issues in 1983 to an estimated 55 percent in 1985. In summary, a hospital may have to pay $1.8 to $3.6 million on a bond insurance policy from the seven private sellers (not to mention the seldom used federal HUD 242 program), depending on its existing credit rating, but the cost is counterbalanced by lower interest expense or increased marketability of the bond or notes.*

Stage 4, the credit assessment stage, involves finalization of the financing documents, inviting in the bond rating agents for a review, on-site visit, and debt rating. If the issue is for more than $10 million, two independent ratings are required. Standard and Poor's (1986) describes a bond rating as a process to measure relative credit worthiness. Credit worthiness is measured from quantitative factors such as financial ratio analysis (normative time trend, past five years), competitive market position (market share), patient-payer mix, regulatory environment, and feasibility forecasts. To a lesser extent qualitative factors are also considered, such as the management focus of the governing board, characteristics of the medical staff (e.g., age, how faithful to the hospital), subjective institutional or demographic factors, and legal provisions of the indenture. Moody's summarizes the same concerns under four broad subject headings: debt factors, financial factors, bond security provisions, and hospital-specific factors.

The single most important component in the credit rating process, in addition to the obvious assessment of the nature of the project to be financed, is the financial ratio analysis of the institution. There are no hard and fast rules, but rating agents clearly prefer facilities with a high debt service coverage following completion of the project (above 3.0), and a healthy cash flow to total debt ratio (above 0.4). Other variables considered include the fund balance per adjusted patient day and operating profit margin. A hospital with a poor rating (e.g., BBB speculative) is likely to have a fund balance ratio of under $300 and a debt service coverage ratio below 1.7, whereas a AA-rated facility will most likely have a fund balance per diem above $700 and a debt service coverage ratio above 3.7.

Ratings are subject to appeal and may be changed even without

---

*In late 1985, Xerox, the parent corporation of the eighth private bond insurance company (Crum and Foster), stopped issuing such insurance. The reported reason was that the risks did not justify the returns. This points up a real policy issue for the post-1988 market: Who will bail out the bond insurers if any company has a few large bankruptcies?

a request from the hospital. Ratings may be improved or lowered, but in the current climate, most frequently the ratings are lowered. Rating agencies have a fiduciary responsibility to consider worst case scenarios in the "visible" future, after the demise of capital cost pass-through, rather than solely focus on a hospital's current financial position. One could neatly summarize the increasingly competitive field of capital finance as a transition from the world of Woody Allen ("90 percent of life is just showing up," often true in a rating or feasibility review during the easy era of cost pass-through) to a dog-eat-dog world of Oscar Wilde. Oscar Wilde often stated that "it is not enough to succeed, you have to hope your neighbors fail." German hospital administrators refer to it as *schadenfreude*, or joy in other people's failure. A capital project will no longer be viewed as financeable just because there exists local community support and a "community need"; the organization has to demonstrate that cash flow will be sufficient to make future debt service payments (Eastaugh, 1986).

In a market with many empty hospital beds, investors view financially weak hospitals as "cross-eyed javelin throwers," in that they will not win any awards but they will keep the attention of their fearful audience. David Winston (1986) of the 520-hospital Voluntary Hospitals of America (VHA) summarizes this issue as follows: "Trustees must resist the temptation of taking off their business hats and putting on their community service hats and making totally foolish decisions on behalf of their hospitals." Grand plans for capital needs often must be scaled back. As we noted in Chapter 20, there is strength in numbers when it comes to the capital markets. Multihospital systems utilize master trust indentures that cover all obligated issuers (members, or subsets* of the system), permitting a better credit rating and borrowing at lower rates of interest.

There is a clear distinction between "making the financial deal" in stages 3 and 4, and "doing the deal" in completion stage 5. In the closing period, bonds are printed, certificates written, bonds escrowed with the trustee, and the final boilerplate documents signed. The boilerplate is the basic language of all debt contracts— that is, obligation to pay, events of default, and indemnification. In the case of refinancing and refunding, the closing period also includes completion of legal documents to defease (pay, or set aside payment in an airtight escrow account) the prior bond issue

---

*The VHA cross-pledges assets from the 130 original partners. Members of the group are permitted to secure debt obligations on a parity with every other obligated issuer. VHA shareholders pay an initial fee of $200,000, and an annual fee of $50,000.

before issuing the new debt. Defeasance is the process of removing the liens of old bond documents by escrowing sufficient funds either from proceeds of a new bond issue or from the firm's cash into a special AAA-rated secure escrow trust. This defeasance escrow fund allows debt service payments to be made on the outstanding old bonds until they mature or can be called (redeemed prior to their stated maturity date).

Refundings are typically done with net cash defeasance (principal and related interest income in escrow is used to pay the principal and interest on the outstanding old bonds), although some hospitals have been forced by existing restrictive covenants to do either (1) full cash defeasance (principal in the escrow must pay principal plus interest on the old bonds) or (2) crossover refunding (principal amount in the escrow is used to pay outstanding bond principal, and interest income is used to reduce interest expense on the refunding bonds). Advance refundings have increased in popularity (107 hospitals in 1984, 306 in 1985) due to declines in interest rates, and also to relieve some hospitals from onerous debt covenants (restrictions, old bond documents that handcuffed the hospital in its efforts to diversify, transfer assets, and establish subsidiaries). In contrast to 1985, when the majority of refundings were variable rate put bonds, 1986 tax reform made fixed rate financing a must for advanced refunding.

In summary, the senior managers, trustees, and hospital counsel must address four major issues:

1. Will payment methods tighten in the future such that sufficient cash flow will not materialize?
2. Will the hospital be in "technical default" with a future modest downturn in patient demand?
3. How can additional debt be issued?
4. How flexible are the terms of the indenture?

Prior to 1986, movable equipment was typically financed with short-term variable-rate debt to minimize interest expense and maximize allowable arbitrage earnings. To expand available debt capacity, hospitals will have to continue to develop their joint-venture partnerships with their most wealthy client group: the physicians. However, the partnership must be sold on the basis of business risk versus return, and not on the basis of reducing an individual's tax liability. Tax reform also impacts on the hospital bond market. The transaction costs of borrowing will become increasingly expensive compared to 1985. Hospitals will have slightly narrowed access to more expensive borrowed money (even if interest rates remain low).

Living Within Limits

There are ways for hospitals to cope with the future limits on the availability of capital. Two frequently utilized strategies are sharing and leasing. The multihospital systems approach to health services management is potentially an effective structure if economies of scale can be captured by pooling financial resources and decreasing the duplication of services and facilities. In addition, multihospital systems make it feasible to hire more sophisticated management and offer an atmosphere conducive to long-range planning. These aspects of multi-institutional systems combine to raise credit ratings, decrease interest costs, and thus make capital financing less expensive and more feasible. The competitive financial advantages of multi-institutional systems in the future may contribute more to the regionalization of health care than health planning (surveyed in Chapter 23).

Leasing of equipment can reduce the immediate drain on funds associated with a major purchase. Often overall costs are even reduced as the hospital takes advantage of the economies realized by the leasing firm (Eastaugh, 1981). Until 1986 federal tax law encouraged leasing by third parties to nonprofit organizations in the following way. A vendor sold capital equipment to a proprietary intermediary. The intermediary got the benefit of the investment tax credit and accelerated depreciation and was able to lease to the nonprofit organization at a reduced price. The nonprofit organization benefited from this reduced price, whereas it would have reaped no benefit from buying the equipment itself, as the investment tax credit was worthless to an organization that does not pay taxes. In the case of hospitals, leasing provides additional advantages in the form of (1) a hedge against technological obsolescence, (2) an alternative source of funding when debt or equity funding is unavailable, (3) faster reimbursement, and (4) better service. On the downside, leasing companies will have to increase their prices to compensate for the negative impacts of federal tax reform in 1986.

The Advantages of Leasing

The rapid development of new medical products, in combination with consumer demands for more comprehensive insurance to cover the ever-expanding vista of medical technology, has pressured hospital administrators to replace their equipment more frequently and at a higher cost. Most corporate financial analysts are shocked to learn that hospitals lease less than 15 percent of their capital equipment. Given the nonprofit nature of more than 85 percent of the hospital industry, there are no tax incentives to discourage leasing and favor purchasing. The rule of thumb is that a nonprofit firm should lease most of its equipment. The resistance of hospital administrators to considering new financing options or performing net present value (NPV) analysis is especially appalling given the high rate of medical technological obsolescence. For example, only 8 percent of a 1973 sample of large complex hospitals calculated the NPV of a project (William and Rakich, 1973). Hopefully, this figure will surpass 80 percent in 1987.

The main advantage of lease financing is that it allows the health institution to be more flexible with regard to rapid technological changes in hospital equipment. The facility can lease equipment for the duration of the equipment's useful life, which is frequently less than the item's physical life. The possibility that the cost of future obsolescence will be built into the contract price is partly offset by the higher residual value the equipment may have for the leasing company, which has greater access to national resale markets.

Leasing is also attractive to the smart health facility administrator because of flexibility in financing. There is no requirement for a large initial payment. Moreover, even if the project is debt financed with low annual payments, the debt contract frequently involves restrictive clauses on future borrowing. Lease financing establishes a new line of credit that is useful as a supplemental financing source in times of high interest rates and limited borrowing opportunities. For example, leasing companies expanded following President Carter's May 1980 Executive Memorandum to all federal agencies asked for a moratorium on hospital bed construction and capital project financing in areas with more than 4.0 beds per thousand (the current national average is 4.3).

One indirect advantage of leasing is that the administrator may apply leverage on the leasing company through future lease payment options to force the lessee to provide better maintenance service. For example, hospital labs with leased equipment tend to have lower downtime and lower maintenance and repair costs.

Another advantage of leases is the treatment of lease costs by third-party payers.* By leasing, the hospital can utilize the services of the asset and be reimbursed for the periodic lease pay-

---

*Some state rate regulators in Massachusetts and New Jersey have argued that leasing should be discouraged, so as to force hospitals that have purchased equipment that became prematurely obsolete to suffer the full costs of their actions.

ments. When equipment is bought outright, straight-line depreciation is normally required. Thus, the early large cash inflows associated with reimbursement for accelerated depreciation are not realized. This is important in view of the increasingly high time value of money. Moreover, no third-party payers' reimbursement policies include full price adjustments for inflation over the economic life of the equipment. These negative effects of third-party reimbursement can be avoided when a true lease is used for financing.

There is one other potential reason why leasing may be financially superior to buying. It is currently a moot point to argue whether tax concerns have favored lease or buy decisions. Some analysts argue that the for-profit lessor benefits from the ability to utilize accelerated depreciation and tax credits (not available as of 1986) and consequently passes on partial benefits (in the form of slightly lower lease payments) of this asymmetry in the tax treatment to the lessees. On the other hand, some analysts have argued that the lessor simply charges an amount equal in present value terms to the cost of buying the equipment plus whatever taxes must be paid. This last scenario suggests that it would be financially advantageous for a tax-exempt lessee to buy rather than lease (and pay the lessor's taxes). There is clearly a need for future research to determine which of the two viewpoints is correct (Bayless and Diltz, 1985). One might suggest that the former scenario may occur more frequently, especially in urban markets that have many competing medical leasing companies.

Capital Leases and Operating Leases

There are two types of leases from the standpoint of the lessee: operating leases and capital leases. A *capital lease* is viewed as a purchase agreement whereby the risks and benefits of ownership of the asset are transferred to the lessee. This type of lease is not cancellable and is fully amortized so the asset, and related debt, must be recorded on the balance sheet.

Under an *operating lease*, the risks and benefits of ownership are not transferred to the lessee, and the payments under the lease contract are not sufficient to purchase the leased equipment. Thus an operating lease is not fully amortized and does not affect the balance sheet. Operating leases usually contain a cancellation clause and may call for the lessor to maintain and service the equipment.

Two organizations have attempted to classify leases according to whether the contract entered into is viewed as more of a purchase agreement or an actual lease/rental type of agreement. The FASB (Financial Accounting Standards Board) rule 13 distinguishes between a *capital lease*, which is a purchase agreement, and an *operating lease*, which is a rental agreement. On the other hand, the IRS uses the term *financial lease* to signify a purchase, and *true* lease to signify a lease agreement. However, because the FASB is more stringent in their criteria, it is possible for a *capital lease* by FASB standards to be classified as a *true lease* by the IRS (Table 22.1). This inconsistency on the part of the two agencies has led to some confusion in reimbursement by cost-based third-party payers.

The FASB standards must be used for financial statement re-

Table 22.1 FASB Criteria for a Capital Lease and IRS Criteria for a Financial Lease

FASB Criteria for a Capital Lease (Financial Accounting Standard 13)

  i. Ownership is transferred to the lessee by the end of the lease term.
 ii. The lease contains a bargain purchase option.
iii. The lease term is equal to 75% or more of the estimated economic life of the leased property.
 iv. The present value at the beginning of the lease term of the minimum lease payments equals or exceeds 90% of the excess of the fair value of the leased property over any related investment tax credit retained by the lessor.

IRS Criteria for a Financial Lease (Rule 55-540)

  i. The lessee will acquire title upon payment of a stated amount of "rentals" under the contract, i.e., portions of periodic payments are used to establish an equity position to be acquired by the lessee.
 ii. The "rental" payments materially exceed the current fair rental value, which indicates that the payments include an element other than compensation for the use of property.
iii. The total amount which the lessee is required to pay for a relatively short period of use constitutes an inordinately large proportion of the total sum required to be paid to secure transfer of title.
 iv. Some portion of the periodic payment is specifically designated as interest or is otherwise readily recognizable as the equivalent of interest.
  v. The property may be acquired under a purchase option at a price which is nominal in relation to the value of the property at the time when the option may be exercised, as determined at the time of entering into the original agreement, or which is a relatively small amount when compared with the total payments which are required to be made.

porting purposes. However, for third-party reimbursement purposes (Blue Cross and Medicare) the IRS standards are usually applied. If a contract qualifies as a true lease, the rental payments may be expensed on a periodic basis. If the contract is considered to be a purchase agreement (or conditional sale), the allowable expenses are interest and depreciation, as period costs.

Reimbursement

Current reimbursement policy among third-party payers favors true leases over capital leases if revenue maximization is the objective. The capital lease is treated in a fashion similar to debt, with allowable costs being determined for depreciation and interest in a fashion that may not reflect the full costs of the contract.

Medicare and most third-party reimbursement schemes create a disincentive for capital leasing by not allowing the depreciation of an asset below its estimated salvage value, and limiting historical cost to the lower of fair market value or purchase at the current cost of replacement (adjusted only by straight-line depreciation and prorated over the useful life of the asset). On the other hand, a contract defined as a true lease allows full reimbursement of both operating costs and the entire lease payment (Reed, 1985). Consequently, true leases give full reimbursement for the current costs of ownership. As a rule, most third-party payers follow the lead of Medicare in creating incentives that favor leasing over purchase. If the machine is purchased with either debt or equity capital, third-party payers reimburse a hospital for depreciation and operating costs. When the machine is financed by debt, hospitals are additionally reimbursed for interest. Depreciation is usually done by the straight-line method. For most movable scientific equipment, the life of the asset as established by the American Hospital Association is assessed as eight to ten years. Medicare has "an unnecessary borrowing" provision which, if applied to include capital leases in the 1980s, could require that the hospital use all unrestricted liquid assets, including future capital expansion funds, to reduce the amount of the debt lease.

Fortunately for the hospital industry, most third-party payers and Medicaid plans have been slow to adopt the four FASB criteria. Consequently, if the lease is defined as a true lease in the reimbursement contracts, the total rental payment is fully expensed on a period basis, even if the lease is classified as a capital lease for FASB reporting purposes. However, the FASB criteria are being adopted, and interpreted in a less flexible fashion, by third-party payers concerned with cost containment. What previously passed as a true lease contract allowing for transfer of ownership title at a nominal fee, in violation of FASB criteria two, is increasingly being appropriately labeled as a variant of the capital lease known as a conditional sales contract or financial lease. An institution that selects a capital lease should require the lessor to document explicitly the interest charges implicit in the lease. The hospital would then have a point of defense against the third-party payer that attempts to impute unfairly low interest costs.

Potential Changes in Reimbursement Incentives

Cleverley (1979) suggested two interesting alternatives to the currently popular method of treating depreciation. The first alternative Cleverley suggested is a form of replacement cost depreciation (RCD) with debt financing adjustment. In the case of RCD, debt financing adjustment, it is assumed that third-party payers will reimburse totally for the debt service costs, both principal and interest. In addition, replacement cost depreciation will be reimbursed, but not totally. The amount of allowed reimbursement will equal replacement cost depreciation times the desired proportion of equity financing—for example, a target proportion of 0.20 in each of the 10 years. This would stimulate containment of total capital financing costs, since debt would be used to supplement somewhat lower levels of reimbursement. The use of a given proportion of debt is desirable because the nonprofit hospitals can take advantage of the availability of lower tax-exempt interest rates. Moreover, the hospital can adjust the desired equity financing ratio to suit its financial needs. In the example provided by Cleverley, the target proportion of 0.20 over 10 years resulted in an effective 0.016 decline in the proportion at the end of the period. This decline occurred because the inflation rate was 2 percent higher than the presumed investment income rate. Thus, one disadvantage of this RCD alternative is that if surplus reimbursement funds cannot be invested at a rate of return greater than or equal to the inflation rate, the targeted equity ratio would have to be continually increased to achieve the desired target ratio.

The second practical alternative suggested by Cleverley is an annuity deposit. Under this method, the amount of equity financing necessary to purchase replacement equipment can be accumulated over the life of the present asset. This would allow for replacement of equipment while minimizing financial incentives for overcapitalization. A third alternative is to allow a capital maintenance factor in the reimbursement formulas—that is, a fixed percentage levied against all patients to finance the maintenance of equivalent state-of-the-art equipment and plant assets. This percentage surcharge might range from 3 to 5 percent.

One infrequently mentioned advantage of total replacement cost depreciation, or price-level depreciation, is that it reduces the long-term cost of services to the public. Replacement cost depreciation has been reported in a large number of corporate financial statements since FASB Statement Number 33 in 1979 (Cleverley, 1984). In basic economic terms, future capital funds are best held in the hands of the institution that can earn a higher rate of return on the investment over time. The average hospital, because it is a large, nonprofit firm, can earn a rate of return on its investments that is typically more than 4 percentage points higher than the average individual, whom we shall call John Q. Public. To make this point clear, let us consider the hypothetical example of a hospital that must replace a piece of equipment in the diagnostic radiology department in five years. The original equipment costs $500,000 in year zero (1987). The equivalent state-of-the-art replacement appreciates in value at the rate of 15 percent per year, and will cost $1,006 thousand ($1.006 million) in 1992. At the end of the time period the hospital can finance the new equipment in one of two ways: (1) historical cost depreciation of $100,000 per year for five years with a bonus to make up the difference from the rate setters in year 5 (this bonus is called the Planned Capital Service Component in some states), or (2) allow price-level depreciation (with cash inflows of $115,000, $132,000, $152,000, $175,000, and $201,000 for the five years, to net, after adding in the accumulated interest at 12 percent per year from the depreciation fund, a total of $1,006 thousand).

In the first case the control over the equity of the institution is effectively out of the hands of the trustees and vested under the control of the rate commission. If the hospital receives $100,000 each year for five years and earns 12 percent annual interest on those funds, it will accrue $635,285 at the end of the period (1992). The differential between replacement costs and accumulated depreciation funds ($370,715) will have to be paid by the consumers in the form of increased rates. If the public had to budget for that difference over the same five-year period, earning 8 percent per annum on the funds, John Q. Public would collectively have to save $63,191 per year for five years to finance the $370,715. However, if hospitals were reimbursed on the basis of price-level depreciation, they could invest the funds at 12 percent interest, and need save only $58,354 per year for the five years to achieve the \$370,715 at the end of 1992. Consequently, it is \$31,002 less expensive (future value of savings in 1993, discounted at 12 percent) in the long run for consumers to keep the funds in the hands of the hospital, rather than underreimburse the hospital and pay out the bonus differential (\$370,715) in year 5.

Some cynics argue that politicians support rate-setting commissions because they do apparently save money in the short term, irrespective of whether they are perhaps inflationary in the long run. Supporters of rate regulation and planning argue that society could save money in the long run if it could only force some hospitals not to purchase replacement equipment. The econometric results reported in Chapter 23 indicate that planners have not been successful in curtailing the hospital sector's annual growth in assets. Consequently, one might advocate cost containment and still question the wisdom of a regulatory system that treats hospital management like a beggar with a tin cup, where the government rate commission has the right to determine how full the cup should be. Allowing the hospital a return on equity capital is more efficient than letting the government arbitrarily decide how much each hospital deserves and when it should receive the funds.

Blue Cross plans in eight states and one state rate commission currently recognize some form of price-level depreciation. There is an irony that the one state government (New Jersey) that is progressive concerning the need for inflation-adjusted depreciation has become equally regressive in disallowing reimbursement for future lease contracts. Each New Jersey hospital is allowed a sinking fund for accumulating annually 10 percent of the price level depreciable value of the equipment. The New Jersey rate experiment explicitly discourages both leasing and borrowing in future capital decisions. Future lease contracts in New Jersey were not reimbursed by cost payers as of 1982. Fortunately, the climate for reimbursement of leases is much better for hospitals outside of New Jersey and Massachusetts.

The Financial Cost of Leasing

Leases are not always a cost-beneficial mode of capital financing. One common misconception about leasing is that it conserves capital. For example, the lease payments are frequently larger than the combined principal and interest payments on debt necessary to buy equipment, especially in southern states where leasing companies have a natural monopoly. Henry and Roenfeldt (1978) report that the majority of hospital financial managers did not know how to correctly determine the charges associated with leasing.

Lack of financial expertise did not inhibit the estimated doubling in assets leased by the hospital sector from 1975 to 1978 (Standard and Poor's, 1978). Growth in hospital equipment leases continued at an annual 16 percent rate from 1979 to 1986. According to the American Rental Association, in 1986 gross revenue for hospital equipment leases exceeded $3 billion. Hospital financial managers should force leasing company representatives to break out the costs that can be expensed rather than capitalized. Such costs include service arrangements, shipping and installation charges, training, and supply fees. Reed (1985) reports that hospital management must still frequently rely on the skills of their bankers and financial consultants.

Another common misconception among hospital managers is that leasing has an intrinsic cash-flow timing advantage. However, some lease contracts require the institution to borrow a sum (for security purposes) in advance, which is comparable to a loan repayable in arrears in annual installments. Consequently there is no cash-flow advantage to a leasing agreement if correctly compared to a loan of equivalent interest cost and a comparable schedule for repayment. The one advantage that leasing has over purchasing is that the interest costs are typically one or two percentage points lower. Probably, the most widely held misconception concerning leasing is that it represents an undetected mode of debt financing, hidden from regulatory oversight. The hidden debt argument is at best cosmetic, and at worst a zero-sum manipulation in that neither the asset, nor the future liability for the lease payments, appears on the balance sheet.

Another unanticipated side effect of defining true leases as capital leases is that a number of the financial ratios used to assess the credit worthiness of the facility deteriorate. If the debt ratio or interest coverage ratio diminishes, then the hospital's bond rating deteriorates, causing the public to pay for incrementally higher interest rates on future capital purchases. We have reviewed the subject of credit ratings and the limits of debt financing in Chapter 21.

Claims by lessors that leasing rates are lower than borrowing rates are not always valid. For example, miscellaneous leasing charges can significantly increase the effective interest rate over the quoted rate for the term of the lease. Leases often include hidden charges such as late payment penalties. The calculated salvage value of the asset also affects the effective interest rate. This means that careful analysis of the net present cost (NPC) of a lease must be carried out to find the effective rate of interest, in order to compare this mode of financing with other alternatives.

Net Present Cost Analysis of Leasing, Debt Financing, and Equity Financing Alternatives

There are no simple rules to suggest one form of financing is uniformly superior to another. For example, leases are purported to transfer the risk of medical equipment obsolescence to the leasing firm. However, the hospital could carry 110 percent (or 90 percent) of the risk in the form of higher (or lower) than "fair" lease payment terms. One cannot adopt a simple decision rule, such as "purchasing is best because it adds to the hospital's asset base on the balance sheet." Capital leases also add to the asset base, and the asset base is not critical by itself (that is, increases in assets are offset by increases in long-term debt on the same balance sheet).

In the following example, we consider four modes of financing a $100,000 blood analyzer. We assume that the hospital's objective function is to minimize the net present cost to the institution. One way to do this, although not the only way, is by selecting the method of financing that maximizes reimbursement from third-party payers. One could also minimize net present cost (NPC) by selecting the alternative that has a lower present cost because it had a lower initial cost, whether or not it had higher reimbursement. The net present cost estimates that we derive are sensitive to discount rates, interest rates, the time span of the lease or loan, the size of the down payment, the percentage of cost-based reimbursement, and the estimated salvage value.

In considering the cash flows for the four financing options in Tables 22.2 and 22.3, we have assumed that the hospital uses straight-line depreciation. The blood analyzer is assumed to have a useful life of five years and a book life of ten years. The debt financing option calls for a $20,000 down payment, payments on principal of $8,000 per year for ten years, and an interest rate of 15 percent.

In the case of both the capital and true (operating) leases, the lease contract is for a period of five years. The payment is at the beginning of the year for both leases. An interest rate of 13 percent is implicit in the capital lease and the bargain purchase option (nominal $1) is exercised. The reimbursement rate for the following example is taken as 50 percent; 50 percent of patients are cost-payers covering three-quarters of allowable costs. This reimbursement rate is assumed to be constant over the ten-year period.

Given these assumptions, the true lease* is the best alternative

---

*Discounted at the incremental borrowing rate of 15 percent, the true lease meets the requirements of having a net present value of less than 90 percent of the fair value of the equipment if $2,666 per year is allocated for maintenance, insurance, and service (as required under FAS 13).

given a discount rate of either 8 percent or 12 percent without salvage value. However, it is important to remember that the choice of alternative is sensitive to the assumptions that were made at the beginning. For example, debt financing can be brought into parity with the true lease option if the interest charge were to

Table 22.2   Net Present Cost Calculations with an 8 Percent Discount Rate

	A *True Lease*[a]	B *Capital Lease*[b]	C *Debt Financing*[c]	D *Equity Financing*
1. Principal Payments	—	—	73,680	—
2. Interest Payments	—	—	49,348	—
3. Maintenance (at $2000/yr.)	—	7,985	7,985	7,985
4. True Lease Payments	112,116	—	—	—
5. Capital Lease Payments	—	108,496	—	—
6. Cash Purchase	—	—	—	100,000
Net Outlay	112,116	116,481	131,013	107,985

7. Reimbursement for
     Depreciation (years
     1–5)[d]
	—	14,973	14,973	14,973

8. Capital Asset[e] Write-off ($50,000)[f]	—	12,761	12,761	12,761
9. Reimbursement for Maintenance (at 50%)	—	3,993	3,993	3,993
10. Reimbursement for Interest (at 50%)	—	11,045	24,674	—
11. Reimbursement of True Lease (at 50%)	56,058	—	—	—
Net Reimbursement	56,058	42,772	56,401	31,727
12. NPC without Salvage Value	56,058	73,709	74,612	76,258
Ranking	1	2	3	4
13. Salvage Value ($25,000)	—	17,015	17,015	17,015
14. NPC with Salvage Value	56,058	56,694	57,597	59,243
Ranking	1	2	3	4

[a]$26,000 per year for five years (includes maintenance, service, and insurance). The FASB term is operating lease.
[b]13 percent interest, five equal payments of $25,160.58 per year. The IRS term is *financial lease*.
[c]15 percent interest and 20 percent down payment.
[d]($75,000 ÷ 5) × 0.5 = 3,750 per year for five years.
[e]The asset is not fully depreciated at the time at which the useful life of the asset expires, so the remaining value of the asset must be written off.
[f]$7,500 × 5 × 0.5 = $18,750.

Table 22.3   Net Present Cost Calculations with a 12 Percent Discount Rate

	A *True Lease*[a]	C *Debt Financing*[b]	B *Capital Lease*[c]	D *Equity Financing*
1. Principal Payments	—	65,202	—	—
2. Interest Payments	—	43,496	—	—
3. Maintenance (at $2000/yr.)	—	7,209	7,209	7,209
4. True Lease Payments	104,972	—	—	—
5. Capital Lease Payments	—	—	101,582	—
6. Cash Purchase	—	—	—	100,000
Net Outlay	104,972	115,907	108,791	107,209
7. Reimbursement for Depreciation (years 1–5)[d]	—	13,519	13,519	13,519
8. Capital Asset Write-off ($50,000)[e]	—	10,640	10,640	10,640
9. Reimbursement for Maintenance (at 50%)	—	3,605	3,605	3,605
10. Reimbursement for Interest (at 50%)	—	21,749	10,284	—
11. Reimbursement of True Lease (at 50%)	52,486	—	—	—
Net Reimbursement	52,486	49,513	38,048	27,764
12. NPC without Salvage Value	52,486	66,394	70,743	79,445
Ranking	1	2	3	4
13. Salvage Value ($25,000)	—	14,186	14,186	14,186
14. NPC with Salvage Value	52,486	52,208	56,557	65,259
Ranking	2	1	3	4

a$26,000 per year for five years (includes maintenance, service, and insurance).
b15 percent interest and 20 percent down payment.
c13 percent interest, five equal payments of $25,160.58 per year.
d($75,000 ÷ 5) × 0.5 = 3,750 per year for five years.
e$7,500 × 5 × 0.5 = $18,750.

decrease relative to the discount rate by more than two to three percentage points. Likewise, debt would be the preferred option if the salvage value were to increase to more than $28,000 or 28 percent, or if the down payment were 10 percent or less given a 25 percent salvage value.

    In this example capital leases were assumed to have a 13 percent interest rate; however, such leases are not competitive with true leases, even if the interest rate is dropped substantially. Capital leases are basically debt financing with a higher down payment (in this example). Thus capital leases are intermediate between equity and debt financing, because as the down payment increases, reimbursement for interest decreases. Why then do so many hospitals currently hold capital leases? Their popularity is largely due to clever marketing efforts on the part of leasing companies that are able to obscure the actual cost of the lease by quoting low interest rates and then adding on miscellaneous charges. It may also be that hospitals that cannot obtain debt financing go instead with a capital lease. Prior to the adoption of FAS 13 in 1977, hospitals had the cosmetic advantage that the debt incurred through a capital lease did not affect their financial ratios; however, this is no longer the case.

A number of factors have been ignored in this simple analysis. The really crucial decision might not be how to finance the $100,000 blood analyzer, but rather: "Shall we purchase the new blood analyzer under any conditions?" The answer to this question is normally "yes" if the net present value is greater than zero, or if the net present cost is less than zero. In the example above, any income streams associated with the purchase of the blood analyzer have not been considered, other than the cash inflows associated with 50 percent cost-based reimbursement. If such income is considered, a net present cost of less than zero is required if a decision to purchase the machine is to be made on purely financial grounds.

The choice of discount rate is critical in determining the net present cost or net present value of a proposal (Bower and Oldfield, 1981). There are two factors to consider when determining the appropriate discount rate: the cost of funds and the yield from alternative uses of the funds. The correct figure to use depends on where the money is coming from. If equity is being spent (anything that is not debt), then the appropriate discount rate is the return from the best alternative use of the funds (including depositing the money in a bank). If the money is obtained via a debt issue, then the appropriate discount rate for evaluating a specific project is the borrowing rate or the rate of return for the best alternative use of funds, whichever is higher. If the rate of return for the best alternative project and the rate of return on the proposed project both exceed the borrowing rate, then both projects should be completed if enough money can be borrowed (otherwise do the one with the higher NPV).

Reed (1985) argues that a complete financial analysis should include a multivariate sensitivity analysis for a range of interest rates, purchase functions, lease cost functions, salvage values, and discount rates. Burns and Bindon (1980) pointed out the potential for linear programming applications in buy-lease decisions. However, these models are severely limited by our ability to estimate discount rates and the age at which obsolescence will occur.

The trend toward heavier debt financing may be replaced by a trend toward leasing options in the 1990s. The decision to lease rather than buy-borrow should be analyzed in each individual case. We have reviewed the important net present cost analysis assumptions that must be made explicitly.

Impact of 1986 Federal Tax Reform

The most intellectually honest thing to say about tax reform is that it could have been much worse for hospitals. The 1986 tax reform act exempts hospitals from a per capita quota for each state as to how many dollars of tax-exempt bonds may be issued. However, many state officials and members of Congress would like to bring this issue up in 1987–88 and target a $50 per capita statewide bond volume cap for tax-exempt organizations, including hospitals. In one scenario, hospitals and universities would be competing for a pot of money far smaller than their capital needs. In a more restrictive worst case scenario, some officials have suggested having private-purpose airports and nuclear power plants compete with public-purpose schools and health care facilities for a very restrictive pot of tax-exempt bonds.

Provisions of the 1986 tax reform act restricted or increased the cost of doing business in the tax-exempt bond markets in several important respects. An overall lifetime cap of $150 million, including bonds already issued, is placed on bonds used for nonhospital tax-exempt organizations (nursing homes, surgicenters, ambulatory care centers, day care centers, HMOs, medical school facilities). This cap is very restrictive for large tax-exempt multifacility systems. Many multistate organizations may have to incorporate into smaller regional systems to come in under this $150 million capital cap. All health care organizations are harmed by the restrictions on arbitrage income (and the harm this does to the working capital position of the organization). Arbitrage profits must be rebated to the federal treasury, but credit enhancement fees are treated as an interest expense to the extent they represent a charge for the transfer of credit risk.

Prior to 1986, a hospital could earn income on its construction fund and the debt service reserve fund (equal to the maximum one year of interest plus principal required under the bond issue). Under an arbitrage situation, bonds are issued at tax-exempt rates, and the proceeds are reinvested at higher taxable borrowing rates to earn money for the hospital. Without this arbitrage income, hospitals will have to borrow larger amounts. Some hospitals may defer borrowing. Wetzler (1986) estimates that 40 percent of the $29.9 billion tax-exempt financings in 1985 were done for arbitrage reasons. Under the 1986 Tax Reform Act all borrowers must disgorge (pay to the federal treasury) all the arbitrage profits earned. All arbitrage earnings are lost, except funds used for credit enhancement purposes (bond insurance or a letter of credit*). Firms that sell bond insurance or deal in letters of credit are happy with this stated exception. In summary, arbitrage profits for generating working capital, thus keeping down the costs of the total project, are destroyed by the 1986 tax act. Government economists would retort that this will eliminate borrowing done primarily for arbitrage purposes, which is essentially true by definition. However, the new rules also hurt those hospitals that are borrowing for reasons of improvement in plant and equipment, and it makes the cost of their project more expensive (they may in most cases still do the project, but capital costs will be higher; and there is no evidence that capital reimbursement will become more generous).

The cost of doing advanced refundings went up with the passage of tax reform—for example, legal counsel and consulting fees were essentially "free" as a cost pass-though, but now they will diminish the yield (become a cost of doing business). Prior to 1986, hospitals spread out their 25- to 35-year debt amortization by issuing long-term bonds to finance new equipment. Under the 1986 rules, restrictions are set on the average maturity of the bonds in proportion to the expected life of the financed property. Consequently, 25- to 35-year bonds cannot be used in most circumstances to finance 7- to 10-year equipment investments.

The volume of tax-exempt hospital bonds in the first nine months of 1986 was essentially nil. Because of the possibility of retroactivity back to January 1, 1986, no legal counsel was willing

---

*Banks with AAA or AA ratings often provide letters of credit to hospitals needing access to the bond market. Without paying for this letter of credit, many hospitals would not be able to assure liquidity and credit worthiness necessary to reimburse bondholders on demand. Hospitals with a lower credit rating receive the backing from a higher-rated bank, resulting in interest savings that more than offset the cost of the line of credit. Hospitals with the worst financial position, very speculative or nonrated, have to resort to private placement: private deals with higher rates of interest and "junk" bond funds.

to render opinions that tax-exempt bond issues would in fact be exempt from taxes. In all probability the volume of tax-exempt debt for the two-year period 1986 and 1987 will be less than half of the 1985 volume ($29.9 billion). Those facilities that needed to borrow in the late 1980s, or wanted arbitrage profits, probably borrowed in 1985. One would expect a steady growth in bond volume from 1986 to 1989. The next section surveys alternative debt arrangements for financing equipment, given that 25- to 35-year bonds can no longer be a primary source of capital finance.

Loan Pools to Finance Equipment

The concept of loan pools to finance equipment began in 1981, typically with fixed interest rates and a 5- to 7-year average maturity. Multisponsor "blind capital pools" to accumulate funds and higher investment yields without designating how the resources will be spent tended toward variable rate financing as interest rates declined in 1983. The loan pools required liquidity and credit support and had longer 7- to 10-year maturities (Graham, 1985). Because arbitrage rules were utilized to generate substantial earnings from 1981 to 1985, many loan pools became very large ($50 to $90 million). The main restriction to growth in loan pools was that hospitals must refund existing debt before they participate in loan pools. Loan pools also suffer, as with service-sharing agreements, from difficulties in public relations presentation (explaining the arrangement to physicians, community leaders, and hospital trustees). According to Sandrick (1986), the typical loan pool receives applications from 13 hospitals, actually makes loans to 10 hospitals (and some HMOs), and is required by the IRS to distribute the funds within three years.

 With the elimination of arbitrage profits, one would expect the cost of doing business in loan pools to increase. Prior to 1986, the administrative costs of loan pools were paid through arbitrage earnings. The next generation of loan pools in the future may involve long-term "revolving pools," with 15- to 20-year maturities that continue to make loans to a wider array of health providers throughout the life of the bonds.

References

ARNOLD, J. (1986). "Assessing Capital Risk: You Cannot Be Too Conservative."
    Harvard Business Review 64:5 (September-October), 113–121.
BAYLESS, M., and DILTZ, J. (1985). "Leasing Strategies Reduce the Cost of

Financing Healthcare Equipment." *Healthcare Financial Management* 15:10 (October), 38–48.

BERMAN, H., and WEEKS, L. (1982). *The Financial Management Hospitals*, 5th ed. Ann Arbor, Mich.: Health Administration Press.

BOWER, R. and OLDFIELD, G. (1981). "Of Lessees, Lessors, and Discount Rates and Whether Pigs Have Wings." *Journal of Business Research* 9:1 (March), 29–38.

BURNS, J., and BINDON, K. (1980). "Evaluating Leases with Linear Programming." *Management Accounting* 61:8 (February), 48–53.

CLAIBORN, S. (1985). "Alternative Financing Approaches for Health Care Institutions." *Topics in Health Care Financing* 10:4 (Summer), 33–41.

CLEVERLEY, W. (1986). "Assessing Present and Future Capital Expense Levels Under PPS." *Healthcare Financial Management* 40:9 (September), 62–72.

CLEVERLEY, W. (1984). "A Proposal for Capital Cost Payment." *Health Care Management Review* 9:2 (Spring), 39–50.

CLEVERLEY, W. (1979). "Reimbursement for Capital Costs." *Topics in Health Care Financing* 6:1 (Fall), 127–139.

COHODES, D. (1983). "Which Will Survive? The $150 Billion Capital Question." *Inquiry* 20:1 (Spring), 5–11.

CONLEY, C., and PEPPE, R. (1984). "Municipal Bond Insurance May Create Two Tiers of Healthcare Borrowers." *Modern Healthcare* 14:9 (September), 182–192.

Council of Economic Advisers (1986). *Economic Report of the President, 1986*, including data from the American Hospital Association Annual Survey. Washington, D.C.: U.S. Government Printing Office.

DANDION, J., and WEIL, R. (1975). "Inflation Accounting: What Will General Price Level Adjusted Income Statements Show?" *Financial Analysts Journal* 15:1 (January–February), 30–38.

EASTAUGH, S. (1986). "Capital Financing and Refinancing." *Healthcare Financial Management* 40:11 (November).

EASTAUGH, S. (1984). "Hospital Diversification and Financial Management." *Medical Care* 22:8 (August), 704–723.

EASTAUGH, S. (1981). *Medical Economics and Health Finance*. Dover, Mass.: Auburn House.

ELROD, J., and WILKINSON, J. (1985). *Hospital Project Financing and Refinancing Under Prospective Payment*. Chicago: American Hospital Publishing.

Financial Accountings Standards Board (1979). *Professional Standards: Accounting*, Vol. 3. Chicago: Commerce Clearing House.

GRAHAM, J. (1985). "More States Selling Bond Issues to Funded Pooled Equipment Programs." *Modern Healthcare* 15:15 (July 19), 76.

GRIMMELMAN, F. (1980). "Borrowing for Capital: Will It Empty Your Pockets?" *Hospital Financial Management* 6:12 (December), 19–25.

GROSSMAN, R. (1983). "Leasing Versus Buying Equipment." *Applied Radiology* 12:6 (November–December), 69–72.

GUY, A. (1976). "Six Leasing Considerations." *Hospital Financial Management* 6:6 (June), 40–46.

HENRY, J., and ROENFELDT, R. (1978). "Cost Analysis of Leasing Hospital Equipment." *Inquiry* 15:1 (March), 33–42.

HOPKINS, D., HEATH, D., and LEVIN, P. (1982). "A Financial Planning Model for

Estimating Hospital Debt Capacity." *Public Health Reports* 97:4 (July–August), 363–372.

HORVITZ, R. (1979). "Accounting Management Impact of FAS 13." *Hospital Financial Management* 9:8 (August), 16–21.

JOSKOW, P. (1980). "The Effect of Competition and Regulation on Hospital Bed Supply and the Reservation Quality of the Hospital." *Bell Journal of Economics* 11:2 (Autumn), 421–447. Kidder-Peabody & Company, The Health Finance Group (1986). Public report: *Review of Health Care Finance*. New York.

MARR, J., and PATRICOLA, S. (1984). "FHA Mortgage Insurance for Health Care Providers." *Health Care Financial Management* 14:10 (October), 52–58.

MIDYETTE, S., and PRYOR, W. (1978). "Equipment Ownership Financing Has Advantages for Hospitals." *Hospital Financial Management* 8:3 (March), 64–69.

MILLER, J. (1979). "Hospital Equipment Leasing: The Breakdown Discount Rate." *Management Accounting* 25:3 (July), 21–25.

MODIGLIANI, F., and MILLER, M. (1958). "The Cost of Capital, Corporation Finance and the Theory of Investment." *American Economic Review* 48:2 (May), 261–297.

REED, J. (1985). "How Bankers Can Help Their Customers Decide Whether to Lease or Buy." *Journal of Commercial Bank Lending* 22:3 (March), 28–40.

SANDRICK, K. (1986). "What If Equipment Loan Pools Dry Up?" *Hospitals* 60:2 (January 20), 60.

SIMPSON, J. (1978). "The Health Care Dilemma and Corporate Debt Capacity." *Hospital and Health Services Administration* 23:3 (Summer), 54–67.

Standard and Poor's (1986). *Hospital Revenue Bonds and Debt Rating*. New York: S & P, Municipal Bond Department.

Standard and Poor's (1978). "Evaluation of Future Hospital Capitalization." *Standard and Poor's Report*, New York.

SURER, J., and NEUMANN, B. (1978). "Cost of Capital." *Hospital Financial Management* 8:2 (February), 20–26.

TOOMEY, R. E., and TOOMEY, R. C. (1976). "Political Relations of Capital Formation and Capital Allocations." *Hospital and Health Services Administration* 21:2 (Spring), 11–27.

WETZLER, D. (1986). "Tax-Exempt Financing for Hospitals." Address at the 29th Congress of Administration, Annual Meeting, American College of Healthcare Executives (February 12), Chicago.

WILLIAM, J., and RAKICH, J. (1973). "Investment Evaluation in Hospitals." *Financial Management* 23:2 (Summer), 30–35.

WINSTON, D. (1986). "Access to Capital: The Health Care Market in Flux." Keynote address at the Washington Health Letter Conference on Capital (February 6), New York.

WOOD, S. (1986). "Survey Shows Changing Sources of Capital." *Hospital Capital Finance* 3:3 (Fall), 4–6.

Chapter 23

HEALTH PLANNING AND COST NONCONTROL

> *We have no system for closing out excess capital. We don't let hospitals fail, which keeps the pathology in the system, and that drives the costs up.*
>
> —Eli Ginzberg

> *Regulation inevitably operates at the periphery of the decision-making process.*
>
> —Alfred E. Kahn

The excessive growth in hospital expenditures has increased the burden of health care costs on employees, employers, and both federal and state governments. Between 1971 and 1979 three administrations have sought to impose mandatory cost controls on hospitals while simultaneously trying to deregulate the general economy. In the case of the last two legislative attempts in 1979, the Carter bill to contain hospital revenue increases per annum to 9.7 percent, or the Kennedy proposal for a 10.9 percent cap, both approaches implicitly assumed that economies would be obtained through fiscal starvation (that is, administrators would not run deficits for long periods), thereby forcing economic discipline upon a highly undisciplined market that exploits the current anarchy of multiple payers. Hopes that federal rate regulation could cool the rate of inflation in the hospital industry (15 percent in the period 1977–1979) were fueled by the supposed success of state rate-setting programs.

Many studies have demonstrated that state rate regulatory programs had a negative impact on their hospitals' financial position (Cleverley, 1986). However, the natural regression to the mean phenomenon may significantly bias regression studies like

657

that of Morrisey et al. (1983) which attempt to estimate the differential effectiveness of various state rate programs. The high-cost states tend to be more regulated and report more "savings" from hospital rate-setting activities. The Dranove and Cone (1985) study of 48 states over 12 years indicates that states did tend to regress significantly toward the mean. Point estimates based on the residuals from the regressions suggested that the laws in Massachusetts owe a substantial part of their apparent effectiveness to regression to the mean (each of these states did not meet the HCFA criteria for a waiver by 1985 and joined the PPS program in 1986). According to Dranove and Cone (1985), the New Jersey program appears to be more effective than the New York rate system, reversing the conclusion of Morrisey et al. (1983). These more recent results are also supported by the findings of Rosko and Broyles (1986) in New Jersey.

If state rate programs were at best a limited success in a few states, capacity regulations and community-based health planning are even more of an unproven cost-control strategy. Before we review the efficiency and effectiveness of existing cost-control regulations, some economic theories for analyzing regulation in other sectors of the economy will be introduced. The chapter ends with an econometric model for assessing the impact of two planning programs, Certificate-of-Need (CON) and Federal-State review Section 1122 of the Social Security Act (SS1122) signed under P. L. 93-641, on hospital costs in the period 1974–1978.

Regulation of Medical Resource Allocation

The scope of regulation in the health field is broad and complex. The Carter administration's hospital cost-containment proposal employed neomarket principles to control costs by containing revenues. This orientation, derived from economic theory and techniques, is perceived by many to be at odds with the type of consensus planning favored by political scientists. Consensus planning in health care was begun in this country in 1966 with the passage of the Comprehensive Health Planning (CHP) Act, and strengthened in 1974 by passage of the National Health Planning and Development Act that created 203 regional Health Systems Agencies (HSAs). The Carter administration's assumption that revenue starvation would curtail hospital cost inflation and force management to get tough with doctors was not supported by the behavioral response of hospitals to price controls (1971–1974). The physician community is in a stronger position as captain of the ship than the typical hospital administrator. Fiscal starvation through revenue controls to date has only produced an explosion in deficit spending and debt financing. For example, the percentage of new capital dollars financed through debt instruments grew from 25 percent in 1965 to 75 percent by 1978 (see Chapter 21).

The presence of market failures in the health economy is the most common justification given by economists for placing controls on physicians and hospitals. The most frequently cited example of market failure is the way consumers become myopic about price-consumption decisions in this highly insured sector of the economy. The physician is in the unique position of affecting both supply and demand. Acting as an input broker for their patients, doctors demand service from the hospital; at the same time they are the supplier of personal service to their patients.

The next two sections survey two economic arguments concerning the efficacy of regulation and conclude with an econometric study of the impact of two hospital capital containment strategies.

The Theory of Rational Expectations

The theory of rational expectations has been widely heralded in the popular press as one of the most exciting advances in economic theory. However, older economists have always considered anticipatory behavior and announcement effects as being key hypotheses within the classical theory of the firm. Social scientists will find this "new" theory of the firm entitled "rational expectations" to be similar to a more familiar concept of the self-fulfilling prophecy. Simply stated, the theory of rational expectations postulates that people and institutions will take action based on how they expect outsiders, including government, to behave. In the process of attempting to predict or foresee the timing and details of new regulations, hospital administrators, commensurate with the theory, are believed to behave with anticipatory actions. Administrators who rush into new purchases of hospital equipment are eschewed as "irrational" by regulators, but if their behavior stems from anticipatory actions designed to increase the reimbursement base, such behavior may be considered a rational measure of self-protection. The smart administrator learns to anticipate future edicts from the rule makers and merely devises a new set of games for co-optation of future rules. For example, Hellinger (1976) suggested that hospital administrators invested in a large amount of new capital the year before enactment of state Certificate-of-Need legislation that would regulate purchases above $100,000.

Another rational game to engage in is to raise per diem hospital room rates excessively prior to federal price controls and the enactment of local price controls.

Hospital administrators are not the only health professionals to engage in anticipatory defensive behavior. Many physicians raised their prices excessively in 1971 to anticipate a federal price control program designed to cap increases at below 3 to 3.5 percent per annum. Physicians and administrators behave idiosyncratically in the eyes of the regulators, when in fact their behavior should be viewed as rational because it is governed by a best estimate of how the government and the insurance industry intend to change the reimbursement rules. The nationwide trend in the early 1970s from cost-plus to simple cost reimbursement rendered it difficult for any hospital to survive intact if it did not play games (Chapter 5). The lag and indecision in achieving a concerted public policy over how to contain health spending contribute to misunderstanding of the cost crisis and increased distrust of government in a time of weakening confidence in social institutions in general. It is surprising that the regulators complain of anticipatory co-optive behavior. After all, the value system of the regulatory strategist exhorts hospital administrators to behave more like businessmen, which is what in fact they are doing.

Capture of the Regulators by the Regulated

The capture theory of regulatory behavior is the most prevalent regulatory model among American economic theorists (Eastaugh, 1982). According to the capture notion, the regulated group gradually comes to dominate the decisions of the regulators until the watch dog agency is converted to an ally, or even subsidiary, of the private sector group. Truman (1951) was one of the first to point out that capture is a natural process in the life of any federal agency. Truman argued that the regulated have more cohesion than the bureaucrats, that they keep closest track of the agency, that they are sure to reveal any malfeasance by the agency at the annual budget hearings, and consequently little will be done by the agency beyond what is desired by the regulated group.

Bernstein (1955) carried the Truman argument further and suggested that all agencies pass through a life cycle from early zeal to a period of debility and decline in which the regulators become the captive of the regulated. Capture is not necessarily bad if efficient decision making requires cooperation between industry and government. Effective cooperation must be a two-way street, rather than a one-way dominance of the industry by regulators. Social reformers who often get carried away by the one-way street view of regulation should pause to reconsider the value of regulators as adversaries (Battistella and Eastaugh, 1980). The social and economic cost of an antagonistic relationship between regulators and the industry may be much higher than society is willing to bear. If you destroy the motive of the regulated to cooperate, what is the result? More regulation and lower productivity?

Three new variants of the capture theory have appeared recently in the literature. One moderate variant of the capture concept advanced by Peltzman (1976) postulates "bureaucratic survival through politics" in observing that agencies respond primarily to the politicians in control of their budget. Maintaining the proper balance in the relationship is not always easy. There is a danger that the regulated can become the determining voice at the budgetary hearing, especially in the current era of antiregulatory spirit. In this regard, Cohen (1975) suggested a second variant to the capture theory. He postulated that after initial popular support for regulation has waned, the regulated become the only substantive and ongoing interest group concerned with the agency. Thus, over time, some degree of capture is inevitable if the industry exercises its monopoly power. A third theory of regulatory behavior as advanced by Hilton (1972) is "minimal squawk," or, in other words, the "squeaky wheel gets the grease." The key idea is that the regulator acts to minimize complaints. Bureaucrats are viewed as rational economic individuals operating in a complex political environment and attempting to minimize the sum total of government-consumer-industry dissatisfaction with regulatory policies. According to this view, the regulatory agencies and staff that experience the longest tenure pursue the most purely reactive policy possible. Agencies that follow the path of least resistance are destined to become less combative and avoid the ire of politicians on whom their survival depends.

Evidence as to whether the capture theory holds for regulation in the health field is mixed. Evaluation of programs that attempt to limit capital growth are criticized for two reasons. First, the regulators are often thought to be under the thumb of the hospital industry. Second, the Salkever and Bice (1976) study found no regulatory effect on total investment dollars, as dollars not used on new beds were shifted to the purchase of new equipment. This discouraging evaluation of regulatory effectiveness has provided impetus for price-revenue caps and other neomarket controls. However, one must balance the short-term direct cost savings against the cost of regulation, increased debt financing, cannibalization of endowment, and the intangible cost of reduced employee morale. For example, state government will be ill-served if tough health regulation bankrupts hospitals heavily in debt to the state treasury. Few regulators have considered studying the costs associated with forced postponement of maintenance and capital investment during a period of fiscal starvation. The neglect of equipment and facility maintenance will probably require larger future expenditures of resources simply to revitalize the surviving hospitals in the 1990s.

Another contributing factor to the possible conservatism of regulatory agencies with experience and tenure is the fear of court reversals. In the late 1970s the hospital industry utilized its due process safeguards, along with the overcrowded court calendar situation, to engage in lengthy legal delaying tactics to wear the regulators down (Eastaugh, 1982). The word is out in the hospital industry that it is better to get even than to get mad. For example, a hospital can tie up state revocation of its license for more than a decade in court (Eastaugh, 1982). Rather than experience the high opportunity costs of lengthy legal proceedings, perpetually understaffed regulatory boards prefer to negotiate a quick settlement, almost always to the advantage of the hospital industry. In addition to the dollar costs of court appeals, regulators fear the loss of credibility and erosion of public trust resulting from court reversals. Thus the major effect of due process safeguards is to foster conservatism among the regulators. Ironically, the more technological and less consumer-responsive hospitals are better situated to withstand the legal costs and win the court battles with the regulators. The financially weak hospitals providing a disproportionately higher share of primary patient care in the region are the least likely court participants, and consequently hold less clout in the eyes of the regulatory forces.

Rationale for Evaluation of CON

Despite widespread support for CON program effectiveness among health care officials, the evidence was always highly anecdotal, theoretical—"CON reduces duplication so it must save millions"—and inevitably led to the conclusion that CON saves money. A highly publicized example of the latter phenomenon was provided by the American Health Planning Association (AHPA) February 1979 report that CON activities saved $3.4 billion. The General Accounting Office (1980) was quick to point out that $1.2 billion of that total was attributed to one consultant's estimate of the capital expenditures avoided in the Los Angeles HSA region during the study period 1976–1978. It should be pointed out that during this period there was little CON program activity and no stable HSA active in the region.

The AHPA questionnaire contained biased statements asking for urgently needed cost-savings estimates to help get a larger budget for HSAs from Congress. The HSAs responded by including many questionable items as savings. The GAO report estimated that 45 to 65 percent of the $3.5 billion savings was not supportable. The GAO identified four basic types of errors in the AHPA tabulation of "savings":

1. Projects initially disapproved, then later approved.
2. Projects built despite the disapproval.
3. Projects withdrawn because of an inability to acquire debt financing.
4. Multiple counting of projects disapproved each time they were disapproved.

As an example of the first and second type of errors, the GAO reported that of the 16,000 hospital beds saved (not built), more than half were actually built in the period 1976–1978. The AHPA report also included 114,000 nursing home beds as saved by planning, when in fact 60 percent were built.*

Some planners are under the delusion that "analysis" consists of wild overestimates of what projects would have been undertaken in the absence of CON. Likewise, economists should not underestimate CON program benefits by acknowledging only the dollar-and-cents effect it has on total plant assets and beds. However, as a first approximation we shall consider whether this form of regulation has proven effective as a cost-control device. This approach neglects the fact that CON programs have had indirect benefits. For example, the high status teaching hospitals in Boston may have gotten 95 percent of what they requested in the CON application, but the CON agency slowed the process for 18 to 24 months until the hospital agreed to a "low status" primary care satellite project for the poor. It would be difficult to assess in dollar terms the intangible benefit of doing "something extra for the poor" as a quid pro quo requirement for the hospital getting the CON approval. Richard Nathan at the Brookings Institution is one of the few economists to take a case-by-case approach to this type of question,

---

*The GAO report was not above reproach. The irrational stratified sampling design that was employed violated all established statistical principles.

in another context (community development block grants; Nathan and Dommel, 1978). This approach deserves further research, and has been encouraged by Rashi Fein* and others (Institute of Medicine, 1980). The case study approach should examine small areas within HSAs across the nation to evaluate the degree to which hospitals collude or compete for regulatory favor in the CON process.

In the evaluation of capital expenditure controls, we first should set aside the presumption that planners are "special" and need to be evaluated only on the basis of activities, irrespective of outcomes. Bureaucrats have a tenacious notion that what counts is the act of pushing paper or producing great plans, rather than providing results. One must study the existence of any benefits (such as reduced assets or beds) across states with mature CON programs, new CON programs, new SS1122 programs, or no programs. A total of 43 states had some degree of experience with regulatory attempts to constrain hospital capital expansion (CON and/or SS1122) prior to December 1978. The wave of enthusiasm for capital supply-side constraints has not been based on the available evidence. Salkever and Bice (1976) reported on the 1968–1972 experience with CON programs and concluded that the net effect of the program over the four-year period was to reduce the growth in beds by a meager 5 to 9 percent, while assets per bed increased by 15 to 20 percent. The authors were quick to point out that the study evaluated CON program effects at a very early stage of implementation: Only five states (New York, Maryland, Rhode Island, Connecticut, and California) had mature operating programs.

The national trend data on hospital assets in Table 23.1 (American Hospital Association, 1986) reflect changes in hospital accounting designed to provide a more complete accounting of asset values after 1969. Despite the lack of uniformity, two trends are discernible. First, the expansion of health insurance with the passage of Medicaid and Medicare allowed hospitals to continue expanding assets at the rate of 2 to 3 percent per year in real dollar terms. The tougher state and federal reimbursement policies and the growth of CON programs in the 1970s did not precipitate a decline in hospital assets. Further study of the cost-containment impact of CON programs is needed. If CON programs were effective, the states with long-standing active CON programs would have retarded asset expansion in comparison to states without CON. The question posed is whether CON and Section 1122 programs con-

---

*Rashi Fein suggested the Nathan case study approach to the author.

Table 23.1　Plant Assets, Total Assets, Assets per Bed and the Five-year Percentage Increase, at Non-Federal Short-term General Hospitals, for Selected Years 1950–1979

Year	Hospitals	Plant Assets (in millions)	Total Assets (in millions)	Total Assets per Bed	5-Year Percentage Increase	
					Assets per Bed	APB in Real Dollars[a]
1950	5,031	$ 2,782	$ 4,349	$ 8,612	n.a.	n.a.
1955	5,237	5,188	6,985	12,298	42.8	28.4
1960	5,407	8,292	10,858	16,992	38.2	24.9
1965	5,736	12,316	16,364	22,084	30.0	22.0
1966	5,812	12,989	17,783	23,155	26.5	16.6
1970	5,859	18,132	26,674	30,766	39.3	13.2
1974	5,977	28,059	41,840	44,941	53.7	14.3
1975	5,979	31,655	47,256	49,901	62.2	17.0
1977	5,973	39,946	61,133	62,765	65.0	13.9
1978	5,935	42,141	68,248	70,004	74.2	18.7
1979	5,923[b]	45,937	76,151	77,076	71.5	16.5
1980	5,905					
1981	5,879					
1982	5,863					
1983	5,843					
1984	5,810					
1985	5,761					
1986 est.	5,711					

SOURCE: *Hospital Statistics, 1978* (1979). The AHA stopped publishing data on assets in 1978. The 1978 and 1979 unpublished figures were provided by the AHA.

[a]Deflated by the Consumer Price Index, U.S. Department of Labor, Bureau of Labor Statistics.

[b]The AHA questionnaire was changed in 1978 and 1979. Consequently these figures are underestimates, since 1,150 hospitals chose not to report data concerning restricted funds.

strained costs and achieved a more desirable allocation of hospital capital.

Historical Context

Planning has historically been regionalized in the United States. The Hill-Burton program (1948–1976) for hospital bed construction was implemented through 48 state hospital planning councils. The Regional Medical Programs (1966–1974), designed to diffuse new medical technological discoveries to the community physicians, were implemented by 56 Regional Advisory Groups. Concurrently, Comprehensive Health Planning (CHP) was attempted in the spirit of consensus planning through 50 state "a" agencies and 200 areawide CHP "b" agencies. Since passage of the 1974 National Health Planning and Resources Development Act (P.L. 93-641), the role of areawide planning fell to the 203 federally designated Health Systems Agencies (HSAs).

The HSAs were nonprofit corporations with boards comprised of representatives from the public, providers, third-party payers, and politicians. Marmor and Morone (1980) questioned the assumption that HSAs, which are at least 51 percent consumers, can represent the wider public interest. There is little incentive for the local HSA to reduce health service production costs if the social costs are borne by that area alone, whereas the benefits are distributed nationwide and are not perceivable by the local citizens. Given the present mode of financing hospitals, local HSAs have many more disincentives to close facilities and increase unemployment if the benefits of these actions accrue largely to over 100 million Americans paying taxes and insurance premiums. In the language of economics, there was little incentive for HSAs to get tough if all the costs were internalized locally and most of the benefits were externalized nationwide.

The relationship between the HSAs and the 50 State Health Planning and Development Agencies (SHPDA) is analogous to the relationship between the CHP "b" and "a" agencies prior to 1974. The important difference in the current planning infrastructure is that P.L. 93-641 inserted two layers of new bureaucracy into the picture. The State Health Coordinating Council (SHCC) was inserted between the HSAs and the SHPDA to act as an advisory body to the SHPDA and the governor. The other layer of bureaucracy, inserted at the top of the bureaucracy, was the federal National Health Planning Council acting in an advisory capacity to the Secretary of the Department of Health and Human Services.

The 1979 three-year extension (P.L. 96-79) of the 1974 Health Planning and Resources Development Act pushed health planning into a new phase. Planners had to face foreign new concepts such as "promoting competition" and "health marketing." Moreover, the HSAs had trouble convincing Congress of their effectiveness. Most HSA board members were not vocal about the contradictory objectives contained in their lists of goals and objectives. For example, the process of plan writing and implementation created new provider goals and consumer wants for a more inflationary style of medical care, yet all 198 fully designated HSAs in 1980 had cost containment as a major goal. In this regard, David Kinzer (1977), President of the Massachusetts Hospital Association, cited the HSAs for spreading wants and adding to the hospital cost problem. A second paradox in the HSA mission is the goal of keeping new construction below a maximum level X without realization of the long-run inflationary possibilities implicit in that strategy: (1) freezing out new low-cost competitors such as HMOs and surgicenters and (2) allowing a nearly 95 percent rate of approval of expansion projects in existing facilities (Lewin and Associates, 1975). Concerning this second point, the Abt (1976) study corroborates Lewin's suggestion that local agencies have difficulty turning down high-technology equipment requests from existing providers. One class of new entrants trying to break into the marketplace was exempted from the planning process by the 1979 Amendments (P.L. 96-79). Federally designated HMOs with more than 50,000 enrollees or new HMOs were made exempt from the Certificate-of-Need process. Small existing HMOs are still subject to the CON process, but at least one factor inhibiting new HMO development has been eliminated. Growth of existing small HMOs will still be inhibited to some degree by the planning process.

The major policy question in the late 1970s was not the overall effectiveness of CON or 1122 regulatory efforts. The big issue was whether such modes of providing regulatory teeth to the health planning movement were counterproductive in terms of restraining competition. CON regulation in particular was criticized for blocking entry of lower cost alternatives such as HMOs and ambulatory surgicenters (Havighurst, 1980). The anecdotal reporting of planners favoring the existing providers at the expense of new entrants is consistent with all variants of the capture hypothesis.

Defenders of capital expenditure controls would argue that the CON programs need more time, have only been half-heartedly supported, and are seriously understaffed. While the CHP boards and the early HSAs could argue that they were underbudgeted, the resource flow to HSAs more than doubled in the 1976–1978 period. Given that HSAs have attempted to meet an expanded list of functions during a recalcitrant antiregulatory period between 1979 and 1981, it may be better to evaluate their performance between 1974 and 1978.

Impact of CON and Section 1122 Regulatory Controls

Tests of the investment impact of capital expenditure analysis (CON and SS1122) were derived from a cross-sectional multiple regression analysis. The data employed in the analysis pertained to 50 states. Three dependent variables were defined over the 1974–1978 period. The first dependent variable, plant assets,* was viewed as a total dollar value of investment. The second variable, beds, was considered a measure of the capacity of 5,973 short-term general hospitals. The third variable, plant assets per bed, was viewed as an index of capital intensiveness or technological sophistication. The advantages of the four-year time period 1974–1978 were twofold: (1) it included enough long-term exposure to CON and widespread exposure to SS1122 to retire the argument that "planners everywhere need more time to become effective" and (2) it excluded the confounding influence of the federal Economic Stabilization Program controls.

The regression approach taken was to estimate an investment function (K) for each of the three dependent variables as a function of six measures of the availability of funds (F), 14 measures of factors determining hospital demand (D), two regulatory factors $(CON, SS1122)$, two structural factors $(MULTI, AFFO,$ and a cost-of-construction variable (CW) (Table 23.2). The equation estimated was of the general form:

$$K = \beta_0 + \beta_{1\text{-}6}F + \beta_{7\text{-}20}D + \beta_{21}CON + \beta_{22}SS1122 + \beta_{23}MULTI + \beta_{24}AFF + \beta_{25}CW + E$$

The intercept term is β_0 and the error term is E.

Two specific forms of this equation were estimated: (1) linear percentage change and (2) linear logarithmic change. The major advantages of these two specifications were that they have been

---

*External accounting reports deduct depreciation to arrive at net plant assets. If there existed a centralized data source on annual depreciation charges, we could add depreciation back into net plant assets to get more accurate figures for capital investment trends.

tried and tested in previous studies by Salkever and Bice (1976) and Muller et al. (1975), and they restrict the absolute impact on scale-free independent variables that are correlated with state size. Two of the scale-free variables that have not been previously analyzed are *SS1122* and *MULTI* (Table 23.2). The scale-free variable with the highest positive correlation with state size was per capita income. As the independent variables employed here were similar to those utilized in the two cited studies, they require little comment. The *SS1122* and *MULTI* variables were expected to have a negative impact on duplication of services and all three dependent variables. An attempt was made to improve the measurement precision of the two crucial regulatory independent variables *CON* and *SS1122*. For example, in the previously cited Salkever and Bice (1976) study, the crucial date of regulatory impact was the date of enactment of the legislation. However, a state like Kansas that passed a CON program in 1972 should not be counted as having CON in effect for year 1972 if the program was not made operational until 1974.

A telephone survey of the 34 states enacting a CON law prior to 1978 was attempted. The original intent of the telephone survey was to collect proxy measures for regulatory effort—for example, applications reviewed or full-time CON staff per hospital. The variability in program implementation was high, and the inability of CON staff to provide data concerning their productivity was less than reassuring. We learned that some states with CON programs (Georgia is one) were designed to review only nursing homes and consequently could not be expected to have any impact on hospital investment. In the final analysis, the *CON* variable was taken as percentage of time the state actually had a CON program in operation during the 1974–1978 period (28 states). The telephone survey revealed that 13 states started Section 1122 reviews prior to 1974, and 17 states initiated Section 1122 reviews during the 1974–1978 period. The *SS1122* variable was taken as the percentage of time the state actually participated in 1122 review processes during the 1974–1978 period (30 states, 15 of which did not have operating CON programs).

The regression results presented in Tables 23.3 and 23.4 are summarized as follows:

1. Capital expenditure regulation (CER) appeared ineffective in constraining plant assets, beds, and assets per bed. The CON program effect appears to add significantly to plant assets and assets per bed in two of the specifications. The sign of the *SS1122* coefficient was more uniformly negative, but still insignificant

Table 23.2   Variables Included in the Regression Analysis of the Impact of Planning Regulations on Hospital Investment

	Percentage Change Equations		Logarithmic Change Equations	
	Form of Variable	*Name*	*Form of Variable*	*Name*
Dependent Variables				
Change in Plant Assets, 1974–1978	a	D6PA	c	D6LPA
Change in Beds, 1974–1978	a	D6BD	c	D6LBD
Change in Plant Assets per Bed, 1974–1978	a	D6PAB	c	D6PAB
Availability of Funds Variables				
Ratio of Total Hill-Burton Allocations to 1974 Plant Assets				
1975–1978	b	R8HB	d	LR8HB
1971–1974	b	R1HB	d	LR1HB
1971–1978	b	RTHB	d	LRTHB
Ratio of Total Hospital Net Revenues to 1974 Plant Assets				
1974–1978	b	R6NR	d	LR6NR
1970–1974	b	R2NR	d	LR2NR
1970–1978	b	RTNR	d	LRTNR
Demand Variables				
Change in Population				
1974–1978	a	D6POP	c	D6LPOP
1970–1974	a	D2POP	c	D2LPOP
Change in Mean per Capita Income				
1974–1978	a	D6INC	c	D6LINC
1970–1974	a	D2INC	c	D2LINC
Occupancy Rate in 1974	b	OCC	d	LOCC
Change in Occupancy Rate, 1970–1974	a	D2OCC	c	D2LOCC
Change in Proportion of Population with Blue Cross or Medicare Hospital Coverage				
1974–1978	a	D6BCM	c	D6LBCM
1970–1974	a	D2BCM	c	D2LCBM
Change in Proportion of Population with Hospital Insurance				
1974–1978	a	D6PH	c	D6LPH
1970–1974	a	D2PH	c	D2LPH

Table 23.2   (continued)

	Percentage Change Equations		Logarithmic Change Equations	
	Form of Variable	*Name*	*Form of Variable*	*Name*
Change in Number of Physicians				
1974–1978	a	D6MD	c	D6LMD
1970–1974	a	D2MD	c	D2LMD
Change in Number of Specialists				
1974–1978	a	D6SP	c	D6LSP
1970–1974	a	D2SP	c	D2LSP
Other Independent Variables				
Percentage of the 1974–1978 Period with CON Program in Effect	b	CON	d	CON
Percentage of the 1974–1978 Period with Section 1122 Agreement in Effect	b	SS1122	d	SS1122
Percentage of Beds in a Multi-hospital System in 1977–1978	b	MULTI	d	MULTI
Annual Construction Wages in 1976 (in thousands of dollars)	b	CW	d	LCW
Residents and Interns per Hospital Bed, 1976	b	AFF	d	LAFF

a   Percentage of change
b   Level
c   Change in logarithms
d   Logarithm

statistically. There is no evidence suggesting that CON or SS1122 activity is effective or efficient. On the other hand, it is equally true that there is no indication that SS1122 regulation is inefficient.

2. Occupancy rate has a negative impact on total investment per bed—that is, the higher the occupancy, the smaller the investment per bed. This occupancy effect appears to be the result of significant increases in bed capacity combined with insignificant reductions in other types of investment in plant assets.

3. The supply of physicians per capita had a negative impact on all three measures of hospital investment. This agrees with the Salkever and Bice (1976) findings and adds support for the theory advanced by Greer (1980) that specialists have more interest in hospital capital than the typical physician. If generalists appear to

Table 23.3 Regression Coefficients for Percentage Change, Hospital Investment Equations 1974–1978 (t-statistics in parentheses)

Equation No.	3.1	3.2[1]	3.3	3.4	3.5[1]	3.6	3.7	3.8[1]	3.9
Dep Var.	D6PA	D6PA	P6PA	D6BD	D6BD	D6BD	D6PAB	D6PAB	D6PAB
Constant	-0.071	0.237	-0.259	-0.267	0.104	-0.310	0.396	0.361	0.519
CON[2]	0.112	0.150[4]	0.048	-0.006	0.019	-0.027	0.122[4]	0.154[4]	0.090
	(0.84)	(1.49)	(0.45)	(0.18)	(0.66)	(0.91)	(1.31)	(1.62)	(0.89)
SS1122[2]	-0.018	-0.046	-0.085	0.011	-0.013	-0.009	-0.030	-0.039	-0.088
	(0.02)	(0.39)	(0.72)	(0.36)	(0.43)	(0.30)	(0.24)	(0.32)	(0.86)
MULTI	-0.014			-0.010			-0.005		
	(0.28)			(0.35)			(0.09)		
D6POP	0.762	0.821	1.084	0.195	0.046	0.086	0.599	0.815	0.970
	(0.95)	(0.79)	(1.00)	(0.53)	(0.09)	(0.39)	(0.71)	(0.68)	(0.82)
D2POP	0.847	0.216	1.292[4]	0.552[4]	0.626[5]	0.145	0.316	-0.423	1.265[4]
	(0.79)	(0.13)	(1.46)	(1.47)	(1.76)	(0.60)	(0.58)	(0.39)	(1.31)
D6INC	-0.273	-0.428	-0.241	-0.018	-0.013	-0.016	-0.233	-0.470	-0.282
	(0.64)	(1.24)	(0.61)	(0.07)	(0.09)	(0.09)	(0.96)	(1.14)	(0.86)
D2INC	-0.507	-0.258	-0.356	-0.154	-0.085	-0.004	-0.371	-0.223	-0.329
	(1.08)	(0.34)	(0.94)	(1.26)	(0.43)	(0.03)	(0.57)	(0.46)	(0.74)
OCC[3]	-0.031		-0.008	0.017[4]		0.047[5]	-0.049		-0.063[4]
	(0.41)		(0.15)	(1.39)		(2.39)	(0.61)		(1.35)
D2OCC		-0.222			0.217			-0.436	
		(1.17)			(0.74)			(0.91)	
D6PH	0.320		0.478[5]	-0.052		-0.040	0.415[4]		0.466[5]
	(1.16)		(1.79)	(0.36)		(0.38)	(1.56)		(1.70)
D2PH	0.119		0.273	0.459		0.216	-0.348		0.094
	(0.45)		(0.88)	(0.50)		(1.11)	(1.23)		(0.25)

Table 23.3 (continued)

Equation No.	3.1	3.2[1]	3.3	3.4	3.5[1]	3.6	3.7	3.8[1]	3.9
D6BCM		-0.735[4] (1.36)			-0.495[6] (2.81)			-0.159[5] (1.73)	
D2BCM		0.178[4] (1.40)			0.079[4] (1.66)			-0.090 (1.06)	
D6MD	-0.561 (0.38)			-0.227 (1.18)			-0.367 (0.26)		
D2MD	-1.378[5] (1.70)		-1.659[5] (1.81)	-0.363[4] (1.58)		-0.183 (1.02)	-0.881[5] (1.94)		-1.469[5] (2.02)
D6SP		-0.324 (0.75)			-0.385 (1.21)			0.117 (0.36)	
D2SP		0.524[4] (1.61)			0.275 (0.86)			0.247 (0.71)	
R8HB	-2.014[5] (2.37)			-3.017[6] (6.54)			0.890 (0.97)		
R1HB	4.874[5] (1.82)			4.162[6] (5.83)			0.689 (1.16)		
RTHB		1.217[5] (1.90)	3.632[6] (5.19)		-0.074 (0.57)	0.653[6] (2.88)		1.304[5] (1.76)	2.816[6] (3.32)
R6NR	0.157 (0.63)			0.064 (0.78)			0.103 (0.29)		
R2NR	-0.011 (0.03)		0.241 (0.57)	-0.034 (0.29)		0.041 (0.43)	0.014 (0.07)		0.180 (0.72)

Table 23.3 (continued)

Equation No.	3.1	3.2[1]	3.3	3.4	3.5[1]	3.6	3.7	3.8[1]	3.9
RTNR		0.199			0.058			0.136	
		(0.75)			(0.47)			(0.68)	
CW	0.009	0.014	0.022[4]	-0.017[5]	-0.019[5]	-0.019[5]	0.031	0.039	0.043[4]
	(0.75)	(0.92)	(1.46)	(1.94)	(2.06)	(2.17)	(1.10)	(1.26)	(1.31)
AFF		0.836[5]			0.061			0.728[4]	
		(1.69)			(0.53)			(1.45)	
R-Squared	0.464	0.451	0.487	0.642	0.719	0.748	0.423	0.406	0.450

[1] Nevada and Wyoming are excluded because of undefined values for independent variables.
[2] Coefficients shown are actual coefficients multiplied by 100.
[3] Coefficients shown are actual coefficients multiplied by 10.
[4] Significant at the 0.1 level (one-tailed test).
[5] Significant at the 0.05 level (one-tailed test).
[6] Significant at the 0.005 level (one-tailed test).

Table 23.4 Regression Coefficients for Logarithmic Change, Hospital Investment Equations 1974–1978 (*t*-statistics in parentheses)

Equation No.	4.1	4.2[1]	4.3	4.4	4.5[1]	4.6	4.7	4.8[1]	4.9
Dep Var.	D6LPA	D6LPA	D6LPA	D6LBD	D6LBD	D6LBD	D6LBD	D6LPAB	D6LPAB
Constant	-0.302	0.518	-0.490	-0.406	0.071	-0.561	0.575	0.597	0.723
CON[2]	0.054	0.071[5]	0.025	-0.003	0.010	-0.013	0.046[4]	0.062[4]	0.035
	(0.91)	(1.69)	(0.73)	(0.16)	(0.52)	(0.78)	(1.43)	(1.58)	(1.16)
SS1122[2]	-0.011	-0.024	-0.038	0.008	-0.005	-0.004	-0.016	-0.017	-0.036
	(0.09)	(0.45)	(0.81)	(0.24)	(0.26)	(0.20)	(0.18)	(0.21)	(0.57)

Table 23.4 (continued)

Equation No.	4.1	4.2[1]	4.3	4.4	4.5[1]	4.6	4.7	4.8[1]	4.9
MULTI	-0.031 (0.45)			-0.020 (0.29)			-0.009 (0.15)		
D6LPOP	0.547 (0.48)	0.409 (0.38)	0.562 (0.72)	0.106 (0.78)	0.094 (0.30)	0.077 (0.65)	0.473 (0.59)	0.345 (0.29)	0.359 (0.40)
D2LPOP	0.620 (0.82)	0.082 (0.15)	1.284 (1.28)	0.535[4] (1.34)	0.758[4] (1.60)	0.196 (0.54)	0.084 (0.42)	-0.651 (0.87)	1.098 (1.23)
D6LINC	-0.255 (0.67)	-0.602[4] (1.45)	-0.267 (0.79)	-0.173[4] (1.40)	-0.104 (0.55)	0.012 (0.06)	0.091 (0.50)	-0.499[4] (1.33)	-0.256 (0.79)
D2LINC	-0.386 (0.89)	-0.079 (0.21)	-0.228 (0.80)	-0.163 (1.19)	-0.106 (0.61)	0.019 (0.05)	-0.227 (0.54)	0.024 (0.06)	-0.210 (0.63)
LOCC	-0.105 (0.47)		-0.054 (0.31)	0.085[5] (1.92)		0.060[5] (2.17)	-0.208 (0.85)		-0.074[4] (1.52)
D2LOCC		-0.152 (0.64)			-0.014 (0.10)			-0.139 (0.43)	
D6LPH	0.284[4] (1.37)		0.296[4] (1.53)	-0.051 (0.46)		0.008 (0.01)	0.277[4] (1.45)		0.296[4] (1.58)
D2LPH	0.107 (0.49)		0.315 (0.91)	0.482 (0.43)		0.197 (1.06)	-0.375[4] (1.32)		0.120 (0.43)
D6LBCM		-0.568 (1.27)			-0.385[6] (3.13)			-0.192[5] (1.85)	
D2LBCM		0.236[4] (1.50)			0.107[5] (1.84)			0.128[4] (1.45)	
D6LMD	-0.492[6] (0.36)			-0.231 (1.26)			-0.262 (0.57)		

Table 23.4 (continued)

Equation No.	*4.1*	*4.2*[1]	*4.3*	*4.4*	*4.5*[1]	*4.6*	*4.7*	*4.8*[1]	*4.9*
D2LMD	−0.898[4]		−1.281[4]	−0.329[4]		0.195	−0.609[5]		−1.487[5]
	(1.57)		(1.65)	(1.47)		(1.17)	(1.76)		(1.83)
D6LSP		−0.079			−0.148			0.068	
		(0.37)			(1.06)			(0.16)	
D2LSP		0.408[4]			0.239			−0.176	
		(1.59)			(0.68)			(0.94)	
LR8HB	−0.475[5]			−0.693[6]			0.245[4]		
	(2.11)			(4.97)			(1.42)		
LR1HB	0.516[4]			0.444[5]			0.087		
	(1.62)			(2.59)			(0.85)		
LRTHB		0.159[6]	0.452[6]		0.035	0.074[5]		0.125[4]	0.377[6]
		(2.94)	(4.76)		(0.69)	(2.60)		(1.67)	(2.94)
LR6NR[3]	0.153			0.090			0.062		
	(0.59)			(1.01)			(0.24)		
LR2NR[3]	−0.046		0.157	0.087		0.093	−0.135		0.061
	(0.10)		(0.46)	(0.42)		(0.61)	(0.72)		(0.04)
LRTNR[3]		0.127			0.031			0.096	
		(0.70)			(0.42)			(0.63)	
LCW	0.046	0.071	0.112[4]	−0.067[4]	−0.074[5]	−0.076[5]	0.115	0.148[4]	0.210[4]
	(0.92)	(1.03)	(1.57)	(1.66)	(1.89)	(2.01)	(1.16)	(1.37)	(1.34)
AFF		0.614[5]			0.106			0.513[4]	
		(1.78)			(0.64)			(1.41)	
R-Squared	0.515	0.472	0.429	0.704	0.696	0.601	0.558	0.480	0.472

[1] Nevada and Wyoming excluded because of undefined values for independent variables.
[2] Coefficients shown are actual coefficients multiplied by 100.
[3] Coefficients shown are actual coefficients multiplied by 10.
[4] Significant at the 0.1 level (one-tailed test).
[5] Significant at the 0.05 level (one-tailed test).
[6] Significant at the 0.005 level (one-tailed test).

consider hospital investment as a substitute for professional service, specialists treat hospital capital as a complementary resource. The supply ratio of specialists has a significantly positive impact on plant assets in one equation and a uniform (but statistically insignificant) impact on assets per bed.

4. The coefficient to measure strength of affiliation and teaching activities *(AFF)* conforms to the expectation that teaching hospitals are more strongly concerned with assets per bed than number of beds. This is consistent with the previous work of the author (1980) and Salkever and Bice (1976).

5. The coefficient for percentage of beds in multihospital systems has the expected negative impact on beds, assets, and assets per bed. Unfortunately the coefficients are insignificant and disappointing. One would have hoped that multihospital systems would have stimulated enough sharing of services, and elimination of capital duplication, to alter significantly the hospital investment profile.

Returning to the question posed in the middle of the chapter, the results suggest that states with active CON programs have stimulated investment in sophisticated technology and modernization projects, without affecting the number of existing beds. The assessment of the SS1122 program is only a bit less pessimistic, in that the program has not had a significant effect on beds, assets, or assets per bed. Consequently, one can only conclude that these two regulatory efforts have been a failure in retarding hospital investment. The potential reasons why the Section 1122 program may have been less of a failure, in the sense that it stimulated no excess investment, are threefold: (1) the uniform 1122 Social Security program was never successfully challenged in the courts, in contrast to a dozen CON programs that had sanctions invalidated in court; (2) Medicare auditors provided an established uniform national system of checkers to detect all facilities trying to avoid SS1122 review; and (3) SS1122 is as broad or broader in scope of expenditures reviewed than state CON programs. When the final revised SS1122 regulations were published in 1981, the overlapping inconsistencies between CON local activities and 1122 programs were almost eliminated, thus reducing the costs involved in operating two duplicate review programs. However, Congress and the public should question the value of operating any inflationary regulatory activity, much less one that operates with duplicate inefficiencies. Further study seems warranted concerning the efficacy and effectiveness of two other objective functions of SS1122 programs: health plan implementation and regionalization.

Failure and Co-optation

Community-based health planning is not exactly a growth industry. As of the fall of 1986, only 16 states had SS1122 review programs (even though the President's decision to continue cost payment for capital through 1987 mandates that all states reinitiate their SS1122 planning programs). From 1984 to 1986, seven states have let their Certificate-of-Need (CON) laws lapse: Arizona, California, Idaho, Kansas, Minnesota, Texas, and Utah. Planners in each of these states try to defend their profession. For example, planners in Utah point to an "alleged" surge in capital spending applications as proof that health planning saved money (based on evidence that developers have proposed building 60 new health facilities). However, proposing is a lot different from building, and access to sufficient capital holds back building plans more effectively than an army of health planners. Planners are privy to the struggle over capital accumulation in the health arena, but they have never been proven to affect the cost of care or the bed composition of the acute care health industry (Eastaugh, 1982). Planners might have had some limited effect of increasing the cost of a capital project by delaying the date of project initiation with paper roadblocks. However, the investor community largely determines the size of a firm's debt capacity (and net available capital stock), and the firms simply bombard the planners with spending proposals until the funds are exhausted. Health planning may still prove cost-effective in a cost-reimbursed market (e.g., nursing homes), but in a price payment hospital market the business risk associated with a proposal will determine whether the capital venture is good or bad for the institution. Corporate planning imperatives have essentially replaced community-based planning. Moreover, as many hospital chain managers can attest, only an idiot builds financially unnecessary bed capacity and equipment.

The previous sections reported minimal discussion of the adaptive responses that hospitals might pursue in highly regulated situations. Hospital administrators have three methods of co-opting the regulatory process. First, they can purchase equipment that is below the CON program review ceiling (section D, Figure 23.1). For example, depending on the state, these are items costing less than $100,000 to $200,000. Second, if the administrators cannot spend money on new bed construction or modernization, they can bombard the CON agency with a number of capital equipment requests (Section F, Figure 23.1). Failing at either of these strategies, the administrator can hire an excessive number of LPNs or grant above-average wage increases (Section G, Figure

23.1). This third phenomenon is consistent with all nonprofit models of hospital behavior and has been observed in a sample of 1,228 hospitals, 1970–1975, by Sloan and Steinwald (1980). In summary, the compensatory response to regulation can occur on both the capital and wage side of the patient care production process. The regression results presented in this chapter only assessed the nonlabor response and essentially support the earlier findings of Salkever and Bice (1976).

Regulation, Competition, and Sharing

There is a lively debate beginning to develop concerning the question of whether competition will bring higher or lower capital costs in the hospital industry. Most analysts agree that the effect will be inflationary in the short run. The advocates of competition are less concerned with the liberal disdain for profits in a largely nonprofit industry and counterargue that competitors will force inefficient providers to close up shop and sell their capital at low salvage prices, thus reducing the capital costs in the hospital industry. One might even go so far as to suggest a planned-competitive solution, whereby the new competitor would get an apportionment of capital at least equal to the new competitor's market share after five years of operation, and the federal hospital capital bank (like the Federal Reserve; Brown, 1986) would reduce the capital apportioned to the existing nonprofit providers. Society must face the two political questions as to how much short-term "excess" capital we will allow new competitors to purchase and how many inefficient providers we will allow to go bankrupt. The competitive solution may require "unacceptable" lead and lag times and hospital labor union unrest (Eastaugh, 1982).

Most health policy makers doubt that the competitive market allocation of hospital capital is as effective as a fully planned allocation system based on the CON process. Unfortunately, regional planning in the United States has not achieved its goal. Planners have inadvertently kept many cost-containing competitors out of the market in the name of planning. Given the recent experience with CON, one still has reason to doubt the ability of planners to reduce costs while not adversely affecting the nonprofit hospitals, and while not inhibiting surgicenters, HMOs, and new proprietary hospitals.

Devotees of the health planning process still scoff at the notion that CON activities have been ineffective or cost-increasing (Rodwin, 1984). Planners have always argued that they are under-

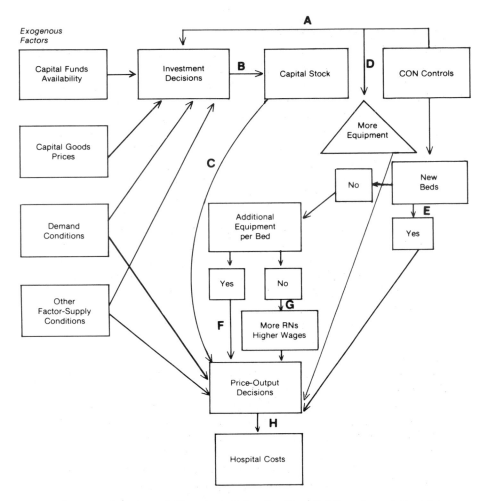

Figure 23.1   Conceptual Framework for the Hospital Investment Decision-Making Process

staffed and constantly receive an expanded list of review responsibilities from Congress every few years. However, the HSAs and CON agencies had significant staff budget expansions in the mid-1970s, and they cannot blame the budget cuts of 1981–1983 for the failures of 1974–1978. Planners are quick to argue that even if HSAs operate as an organizational "mess," with interrelationships among functions usually poorly defined and inadequately coordinated, they have identified some significant shortfalls or gaps in health resource supply.

Rodwin (1984) predicted the rebirth of health planning in hopes that the development of a rational system of health services could "guarantee that planners would make care accessible to all those in need of service." Rodwin also predicted a trend toward regionalization. However, in the current American context, one views little evidence of this regionalization trend coming from the plans of health planners. In point of fact, the trend toward regionalization emerging in 1986 has come from the price system and not health planners (Chapters 1 and 9). Institutional managers and multihospital system managers are learning about product-line regionalized marketing from the business community. As we observed at George Washington University Hospital from 1983 to 1986, the four largest hospital chains knew very little about regionalization, hub and spoke referral networks, and complementary marketing. Health managers are learning more about these topics from the airlines (Chapter 9). Rodwin's (1984) characterization of hospital managers as feudal "barons of the health sector" may be highly inaccurate. In the context of the Alfred Kahn quote at the start of this chapter, it was the health planners who acted as feudal barons on the periphery of the decision-making process of institutions, who have outlived their usefulness in a market-driven health economy. The price system can empty, and close, more beds than the health planners ever dreamed possible in the 1970s. The government's role should still assure that the price system does not close the "wrong beds" in potentially medically underserved neighborhoods.

One of the potential negative impacts of declining support for health planning CONs 1979–1982 may have been reduced pressure among hospitals to share services. Where the CON process had been strong, hospitals often decided that if only one license to operate a given high-tech service would be granted, they would work together and share the service. If these anecdotal reports are correct, one would project a decline in shared services for the period 1978–1982. The American Hospital Association did a survey of shared service capacity in 1978 and 1982, and the number of voluntary nonprofit hospitals sharing services declined from 2,598 in 1978 to 2,189 in 1982 (Smith and Cobb, 1983). If the financial pressures on hospitals are sufficient, perhaps we shall experience a rebirth in shared services for the period 1987–88. If many institutions bind together as a cooperative group, duplication of marketing research efforts is avoided. To achieve the best allocation of resources, the group can divide the service area among themselves and develop a vertically integrated sharing agreement where each institution provides the service at which it is the most proficient. However, even if the financial pressure to share services is strong, in a highly competitive market, with low occupancy rates and rampant fears of patients being "stolen," the prevalence of shared service arrangements may actually decline over time.

References   •

Abt Associates, Inc. (1976). "Incentives and Decisions Underlying Hospitals' Adoption and Utilization of Major Capital Equipment." NTIS No. PB–251–631. Washington, D.C.: DHEW, Health Resources Administration.

American Hospital Association (1986). *Hospital Statistics 1986*. Chicago, Ill.: AHA.

BATTISTELLA, R., and EASTAUGH, S. (1980). "Hospital Cost Containment." *Proceedings of the Academy of Political Science* 33:4 (Winter), 192–205.

BAUER, K. G. (1977). "Hospital Rate Setting—This Way to Salvation?" *Milbank Memorial Fund Quarterly* 55:1 (Winter), 117–158.

BERNSTEIN, M. (1955). *Regulating Business by Independent Commissions*. Princeton: Princeton University Press.

BROWN, J. (1986). "Hospital Capital Reimbursement in the Competitive Era." Unpublished working paper, Harvard School of Public Health.

COHEN, H. S. (1975). "Regulatory Politics and American Medicine." *American Behavioral Scientist* 19:1 (September/October), 122–136.

Congressional Budget Office (1979). "The Hospital Cost Containment Act of 1978." Staff Report (May). Washington, D.C.: U.S. Government Printing Office.

CLEVERLEY, W. (1986). "Hospital Financial Condition Under State Rate Regulatory Programs." *Hospital and Health Services Administration* 31:2 (March–April), 135–147.

DRANOVE, D., and CONE, K. (1985). "Do State Rate Setting Regulations Really Lower Hospital Expenses." *Journal of Health Economics* 4:2 (June), 159–165.

EASTAUGH, S. (1982). "Effectiveness of Community-Based Hospital Planning: Some Recent Evidence." *Applied Economics* 14:3 (September), 475–490.

EASTAUGH, S. R. (1980). "Organizational Determinants of Surgical Lengths of Stay." *Inquiry* 17:2 (Spring), 85–96.

EASTAUGH, S. R. (1979). "President's Hospital Cost Containment Proposal." Subcommittee on Health Hearings, Committee on Ways and Means, 96th U.S. Congress, First Session, April 2, 1979, Part 2, Serial 96–19. Washington, D.C.: U.S. Government Printing Office, 396–418.

General Accounting Office (1980). "Unreliability of the American Health Planning Association's Savings Estimate for the Health Planning Program." GAO Report HRD-80-49. Washington, D.C.: U.S. Government Printing Office.

GREER, A. (1980). "Medical Technology and Professional Dominance Theory." University of Wisconsin–Milwaukee: Urban Research Center Reports.

HAVIGHURST, C. (1980). "Antitrust Enforcement in the Medical Services Industry: What Does It All Mean?" *Milbank Memorial Fund Quarterly* 58:1 (Winter), 89–124.

HELLINGER, F. J. (1976). "The Effect of Certificate-of-Need Legislation on Hospital Investment." *Inquiry* 13:6 (June), 187–193.

HILTON, G. W. (1972). "The Basic Behavior of Regulatory Commissions." *American Economic Review* 62:2 (May), 47–54.

Hospital Association of New York State (1986). "Fourteenth Annual Fiscal Pressures Survey, 1985." Albany, New York.

Institute of Medicine (1980). *Health Planning in the United States: Issues for Guideline Development*. Washington, D.C.: National Academy of Sciences.

Institute of Medicine (1981). *Health Policy in the United States: Selected Policy Issues*, vol. 1. Washington, D.C.: National Academy of Sciences.

KAHN, A. (1971). *The Economics of Regulation: Principles and Institutions*, volume II, "Institutional Issues." New York: John Wiley.

KASSIRER, J., and PAUKER, S. (1978). "Should Diagnostic Testing be Regulated?" *New England Journal of Medicine* 299:17 (October), 947–949.

KINZER, D. (1977). *Health Controls Out of Control: Warning to the Nation from Massachusetts*. Chicago, Ill.: Teach'em.

LEE, L. (1980). "A Theory of Just Regulation." *American Economic Review* 70:5 (December), 848–862.

Lewin and Associates, Inc. (1975). *Evaluation of the Efficiency and Effectiveness of the Section 1122 Review Process*. Washington, D.C.: Lewin and Associates.

MARMOR, T. R., and MORONE, J. A. (1980). "Representing Consumer Interests: Imbalanced Markets, Health Planning and the HSAs." *Milbank Memorial Fund Quarterly* 58:1 (Winter), 125–165.

MORRISEY, M., SLOAN, F., and MITCHELL, S. (1983). "State Rate Setting: An Analysis of Some Issues." *Health Affairs* 2:2 (Summer), 36–47.

MULLER, C., WORTHINGTON, P., and ALLEN, G. (1975). "Capital Expenditures and the Availability of Funds." *International Journal of Health Services* 5:1 (Winter), 143–157.

NATHAN, R. P., and DOMMEL, P. R. (1978). "Federal-Local Relations Under Block Grants." *Political Science Quarterly* 93:3 (Fall), 421–442.

PELTZMAN, S. (1976). "Toward a More General Theory of Regulation." *Journal of Law and Economics* 19:3 (August), 211–248.

POSNER, R. A. (1975). "The Social Costs of Monopoly and Regulation." *Journal of Political Economy* 83:4 (August), 807–827.

RODWIN, V. (1984). *The Health Planning Predicament: France, Quebec, England and the United States*. Berkeley: University of California Press.

ROSKO, M., and BROYLES, R. (1986). "The Impact of the New Jersey All-Payer DRG System." *Inquiry* 23:1 (Spring), 67–75.

SALKEVER, D. S., and BICE, T. W. (1976). "The Impact of Certificate-of-Need Controls on Hospital Investment." *Milbank Memorial Fund Quarterly*, 54:2 (Spring), 195–214.

SLOAN, F. A., and STEINWALD, B. (1980). "Effects of Regulation on Hospital Costs and Input Use." *Journal of Law and Economics* 23:1 (April), 81–109.

SMITH, K., and COBB, D. (1983). "Are Hospitals Still Sharing?" *Hospitals* 57:17 (September 1), 67–70.

STIGLER, G. J. (1971). "The Theory of Economic Regulation." *Bell Journal of Economics and Management Science* 2:1 (Spring), 3–21.

TRUMAN, D. R. (1951). *The Government Process: Political Interests and Public Opinion*. New York: Alfred Knopf.

Part Seven

FUTURE POLICY TRENDS

Chapter 24

CAPITATION, CONSOLIDATION, AND UNIVERSAL ENTITLEMENT

> *Demands are infinite, whereas the resources are finite, regardless of whether the care is funded through health insurance or from public funds. The marketplace system encourages demand and diversity, whereas the controlled system leads to uniformity, rationing, and possibly mediocrity.*
>
> —JOHN LISTER, M.D.

> *Our current problems are past solutions.*
>
> —JOHN D. THOMPSON

Compared with other countries, America has a schizophrenic attitude concerning the production and financing of medical services. Some liberals would go so far as to argue that medical services are a merit good, so crucial to preserving the general welfare of society that the services should be financed by government even if they are not cost-beneficial.* Such an attitude is maintained in the Netherlands and Sweden, where medical care is produced and financed as if it were a public good—a social service

---

*A classic example of this thinking would be the Netherlands. The Netherlands has the highest medical cost inflation rate of any OECD member (OECD, 1986). By contrast, England takes the viewpoint that certain medical services are not cost-beneficial and should not be included in the National Health Service. The American tradition is to seldom support the classic externalities argument for supporting medical services as a public good. There are few services where one can demonstrate that the society as a whole earns more if the co-workers are kept healthy through preventive medicine (Eastaugh, 1981). However, most medical dollars go to curing and caring, not prevention.

687

too important to be rationed on market principles. Other countries, like Japan, France, and Switzerland, produce and finance medical services as if they were normal consumer goods. Insurance is available for expensive medical services, but the coinsurance rates range as high as 30 to 50 percent.

However, the United States has one of the most inconsistent policies toward medical service: We produce it as a consumer good, finance it as a public good, and complain when providers react in a rational way, promoting excess demand and behaving in an inflationary "quality is all important" style of care for the subsidized service. A decade ago American health care providers were best described as a fragmented group of fiercely independent organizations. Over 90 percent of the physicians were independent operators in private practice, and hospitals engaged in cost-increasing fierce competition for prestige and the newest capital equipment. Now physicians and hospitals are being subjected to a cost-decreasing mode of competition that is both consumer-driven and payer-driven. The nature of health services delivery is changing. We can no longer deny that health care is a blend of art, business, life-style, and science. Providers' traditional objectives have been expanded to include consumer-sensitive service, in a more economical style, promoting patient compliance and health promotion, while offering the best technical quality of care. Overemphasis on any one aspect may spell disaster for the provider. Providers who pursue only business interests will be no more protected, or respected, than a used car dealership. Likewise, those who disrespect business skills, marketing, and consumers' shifting tastes may face an early retirement in the 1990s.

Few hospital managers in the summer of 1983 expected that by 1986 their inpatient census would decline 15 percent and their operating profit margins would improve 1.5-fold. Both things could not possibly happen, but they did for the average hospital. Despite three years of Medicare payment freezes, many hospitals are reaping a higher return, with more controlled revenues, by managing their cost behavior. Changes in payment systems occur so rapidly that providers and medical suppliers are hard put to keep pace and react, much less plan proactively. There is still room for improved efficiency in a health sector that spends $1 billion every 19 hours. Some of the resources do little good, but the majority of the care averts death, pain, and erosion of functional health status. However, we must be careful not to discount quality or access in the name of economic efficiency. There is a delicate balance to maintain between health care as a social good and health care as a consumer good.

Innovation or Stagnation Plus Unbalanced Growth

The health economy should not be viewed as completely independent from the general economy. The health sector is in some sense
a microcosm of Baumol's model of unbalanced growth for the
economy (Baumol et al., 1985). An oversimplified health economy
might divide into three productivity growth sectors, one "stagnant" (inpatient), and two "progressive" sectors (ambulatory care
and long-term care). The share of the total economy gross national
product devoted to inpatient care may rise to above 5 percent. We
will spend more on the "miracles of modern medical technology,"
but the hospital census may remain in a permanent recession
relative to 1980–1983 levels. The share of health expenditures
invested on the stagnant inpatient sector may increase in the long
run as our appetite for transplant and high-tech medicine expands.
However, the progressive sectors' share of the labor force might
increase with the aging of the population and the decline in
hospital workers (from 3.17 million in 1983 to 2.5 million in 1993).
Productivity improvements may have to underwrite the volume
expansion in numbers of services within the two progressive
sectors. The progressive ambulatory care clinics are already inno-
vating themselves out of their cost-dominating market position
(Kotler, 1986). If shoddy quality operators tarnish the service
reputation of certain market segments, interest in universal entitlement and regulatory solutions may experience a rebirth.

Will Supermeds Rule the World?

When Tom Peters, co-author of *In Search of Excellence*, spoke to
the American College of Hospital Administrators' annual meeting
in 1983, his central message was "stick to the knitting." Hospitals
were advised to abide by this principle, one of eight principles
highlighted in the book, and not wander into the insurance business or ambulatory care. Humana realized in 1983 (closely followed by two other national hospital chains in the fall of 1984) that
the better strategy would involve going "beyond the knitting"
(inpatient care). The hospital groups that ignored the conventional
wisdom of 1983 should perform the best in 1986–1990, through
vertical integration into ambulatory care and insurance products.

Paul Elwood's "Supermed" theory predicts that rapid consolidation should soon produce eight major health corporations providing and insuring 80 to 90 percent of the health services in the
nation by 1995 (Elwood, 1986). Elwood suggests that only one of

these eight firms will be nonprofit. A nonbeliever in both the Supermed theory and the conventional wisdom should consider past examples of markets where the experts predicted rapid consolidation. In 1960 the experts predicted that we would have only two auto companies worldwide by 1968; yet we now have six dozen. In 1968 the experts predicted we would have 90 percent fewer microchip firms by 1975; yet we now have 950 percent more in 1986. Experts like to predict consolidation in the name of a well-ordered world, but the world continues to be a messy and complex place.

In the context of hospital care, local hospitals need not always join a for-profit chain or the nonprofit group with 600 member hospitals if they can find a local market niche. This point is doubly true in a local service delivery industry like health care, in contrast to microchips and automobiles where there is less concern for distance between the firm and the customer. By 1995 some 20 megasystems may control 50 percent of the market, but 200 to 400 local minisystems may control 60 to 80 percent of their local market shares with a locally developed and controlled insurance product. Consolidation begins to offer few advantages when the service cannot be stockpiled as inventory, and the central office becomes too removed from the local community. Minisystems should be capable of outcompeting against the megasystems if they remain flexible, adaptive, and nonbureaucratic in response to their market (Peters and Austin, 1985).

Individual hospitals or nursing homes may have less to fear from "takeover fever" than the corporate giants. American Medical International, HCA, CIGNA, and even Blue Cross may experience takeover attempts by the Marriott Corporation, Quality Inns, Sears, General Motors, Deere and Company, McDonnell Douglas, or South Korean Shipping. Nonhealth concerns with the venture capital to buy those familiar names may believe profits are to be made (or preserved) through the provision of cost-effective care to their employees and millions of other Americans. There may be a severe downside to having corporate shareholders assume too much power in health services delivery. The largest block of buyers, the institutional fund managers, tend to overemphasize short-term profits and ignore quality. One 1986 survey of institutional fund managers indicated that when selecting stocks, only 3 percent considered the quality of the firm's services and products. Firm managers tend to place "creating shareholder value" and short-run profits far above long-run competitiveness and quality in ranking their corporate objectives.

If the current owners of for-profit health systems do not succumb to the "short-term syndrome" of other corporate managers and owners, the new buyers of such firms may bring this disease into the health sector. Large corporations that get into health care as an unrelated business venture in the 1990s could care less about the future. Short-run profit taking will likely divert resources from quality-enhancing investment. Our two best hopes against such a hostile future environment involve (1) sufficient payment rates of return on equity to for-profit and tax-exempt providers (so that they will not be so "capital poor" as to require a sale to distant unrelated corporate buyers in the 1990s) or (2) hope the unrelated business acquisitions experience financial failure. Given that payers seem averse to reimbursement of a fair return-on-equity payment to providers, we may experience severe market disruption under the second scenario. The failure/divorce second scenario will permanently realign the core mission and business focus of the surviving providers. To paraphrase one federal economist, disputing Attorney General Edwin Meese's push for corporate mergers, "You don't put two turkeys together and get an eagle." Marriages of unrelated business concerns have in the past often led to divorce, so scenario 2 seems probable if the patients and physicians effectively protest corporate/bureaucratic health service delivery.

Universal Entitlement Someday?

Long-time advocates of national health insurance will seize on any prediction of major disruptions in the industry as a rationale for passing just such a universal program. In the near future their hopes and dreams may come to fruition if the clamor for quality care and indigent care peak. The issue attention cycle has gone up and down in support of universal health insurance coverage. National health insurance has appeared forever imminent on a number of occasions between 1933 and 1975 (Fein, 1986). If the current push for competition results in too many scandals of poor quality or poor access, the politicians might pass a national program. However, a national entitlement program could be structured in a number of different ways.

Some analysts advocate a public utility incremental approach to reregulating the health sector through expansion of PPS price controls from Medicare to all payers. The disadvantages of utility regulation are many, including the administrative costs, cumbersome technological updates for rates, and the basic risk that quality may be reduced to the lowest common denominator. At the most extreme, advocates of utility regulation for health providers argue for a totally federalized Medicaid system and a national quality standards review board (restructured PROs). However, price controls and quality assurance bureaucracy may not represent our best bet for achieving efficiency and equity in health care delivery. After reviewing a number of unequitable aspects of PPS price controls, a variant on the standard competitive theory (Enthoven, 1980) of capitated health systems will be presented. Capitated health plans that bid on both price and quality, with retrospective payments for measurable quality improvements in patient care, may represent a superior compromise between unfettered competition and utility price-control regulations. Advocates of more government may decry private operators cutting corners and reducing service quality, but the medicine of sanctions and review boards has less than an admirable track record in military and federal hospitals. The answer may not reside with more regulation, but rather better structured bidding procedures to enhance quality plus contain costs.

Uneven Prospective Poverty and Profit

One should consider ways to design a PPS scheme that better protects the four basic dimensions of equity:

1. Vertical equity, ensuring that different types of hospitals, such as specialty hospitals or teaching facilities, are treated equally.
2. Horizontal equity, ensuring that within a peer category, the facilities with equivalent case mixes are paid equally.
3. Financial equity, ensuring that pay is for performance, considering service quality and volume, and not just in proportion to the number of cases.
4. Geographic equity, ensuring that national DRG rates do not let "windfall profits" accrue beyond what is judged fair, given operating efficiency and effectiveness.

This fourth aspect of equity is what Stuart Altman refers to as the coming "re-creation of the Civil War." In such increasingly difficult times, the solidarity of the hospital industry may become volatile. The losers under PPS could claim that Medicare is paying windfall profits that could be better spent on the financially distressed. These problems could be partially helped by inclusion of a severity index with DRGs and more special funding for charity care. However, the political system has to allow 30 percent of the hospitals in some states to go bankrupt under the prospective poverty system (PPS–1), while 75 percent of the hospitals in other states make in excess of 10 percent profit per Medicare case under the prospective profit system (PPS–2). Rather than drown quietly in an ocean of red ink, the financially distressed hospitals will call for redistribution of the Medicare dollar. While complaints of "windfalls" are not popular in the Reagan administration, conservatives do have to play the prudent and fair buyer. Consequently, enacting a sealed bid contracting mechanism to squeeze out overpayments under PPS-2 solves part of the geographic equity problem. Subsidizing charity care through surcharges or block grants will reduce the PPS-1 problem. Including a severity measure in DRGs would help ensure that profit or loss occurs for reasons of efficiency and effectiveness. Moreover, as Stern and Epstein (1985) have pointed out, without a severity correction the distinction between specialization and "skimming" may be difficult to make.

For the true believers in the market, talk of unfair profits is absurd: All profits are fair, and windfalls are deserved. This viewpoint misses the critical point that PPS is a system of administered price controls and does not reflect the market. Prices are set by the HCFA computer, not by shifts in consumer behavior. One way to make PPS more like a market is to complement the HCFA computer with the monopsony power of a HCFA price czar taking sealed DRG price bids from hospitals in a PPS-2 area. With this mechanism one could squeeze some of the windfall profits from certain areas and redistribute the funds to hospitals that are unfairly underpaid. HCFA would have to make sure these windfall profits were redistributed, and not simply soaked up and dedicated to deficit reduction.

Competitive Bidding to Redistribute Windfall Profits

In the rush to become a prudent buyer, the Reagan administration is not about to delay the movement to national DRG rates for Medicare. Medicare has experience with three types of pricing: payback at allowable cost, administered prices (DRGs), and competitive bidding. A hybrid fourth pricing mechanism is a more fair and efficient alternative: Use administered prices as the maximum or ceiling price and use competitive bids to buy a sufficient supply of inpatient beds at or below the price line. However, implementing such an idea on a national scale has one major flaw. Such a bidding procedure might cause quality to stagnate or decline if hospitals "underbid." In a market with many half-empty hospitals, some might underbid the price necessary for quality service delivery and overpromise gains in efficiency and effectiveness in a game of "liar's dice." This could have a malignant effect on outcomes and cost as has been observed in eroding defense systems' quality control. Lower-quality firms have less leeway in discounting quality to pursue a contract.

Hospitals will break up into five essential groups:

1. Winners, or those that received a contract and on average made a profit per case.
2. Questionable winners, or those that obtained a contract but made it profitable only through discounting quality.
3. Losing winners, or those that obtained a contract but, because of resulting cost behavior that yielded a price that was only sufficient to cover marginal costs, did not earn a profit.
4. Losers, or those that submitted bids that were rejected.
5. Nonplayers, or those that did not submit bids.

Increased reliance on a system of competitive bids would relieve Medicare officials of the burden of defending the fairness of the DRG price list. Administered price control systems fail because the regulatory experts are incapable of monitoring and leading the industry. Failure has always occurred, even in much simpler industrial sectors, when the experts have trouble tracking, for example, innovation in plumbing codes, fire codes, or concrete manufacturing mixing codes. It would be absurd to suggest that bureaucrats could design a surgical code, medical code, or neurological code and price list. HCFA officials could collect sealed bids and decide the point at which they have purchased sufficient capacity and the right mix to serve the elderly, but judgment of whether the bid was good enough to receive a contract should include broader social concerns, such as the long-run viability of the medical education system or the facility's monopoly in the catchment area for some service.

Quality-Enhancing Bidding

Ideally, one would want a payment system that fosters improvement in quality of care, pays less than average price for less than average quality, and stimulates closure of unnecessary low-quality hospitals. A reform in the current PPS should offer incentives for low-quality performers to improve and should provide punishment for those who do not improve their quality and efficiency. A quality-enhancing bidding (QEB) system could achieve these stated goals, minimize extra administrative costs, and address the issues of geographic inequity and windfall profits. Under a QEB system, Medicare could receive annual sealed competitive bids along the lines of the California MediCal system (Johns et al., 1985; Christianson, 1985). QEB would differ from MediCal contracting in three crucial ways:

1. The sealed bids would not involve catch-all per diems, but rather average payment per DRG with a cost weight equal to one (e.g., if the bid were $4,000 and the DRG weight for that condition equaled 1.25, the payment would be $5,000).
2. Hospitals would be required to bid if they were judged to have below-average quality by their local PRO, and in the pilot test phase of QEB if they existed in a windfall profit state.
3. Retrospective incentive compensation for quality improvements would be offered one to two years later (e.g., if a hospital bid $4,100 in a market where the national price would have been $4,900 and it improved its quality rating by 10 percent relative to the PRO moving average, the hospital would receive a retrospective 10 percent kicker bonus for quality improvement). The sum total payment would not exceed national DRG prices, so this proviso is budget neutral.

Some representatives of the hospital industry are likely to object to QEBs by claiming that "capping the most costly institutions always erodes quality," based on the false premise that the "most costly hospitals are the best and serve the most severely ill." However, equitable compensation for severity can be incorporated into the bidding system either (1) directly, by continuous measurement of severity as a new sixth digit code or (2) indirectly, on a sampling basis by factoring a reasonable incidence of retrospectively measured case severity into each class of hospital (university medical center, major teaching, moderate teaching, minor teaching, and nonteaching). Quality does not increase cost as a general rule, but rather decreases cost: The skilled and adroit are more cost-efficient than the slow and clumsy users of excess procedures or inappropriate therapeutic adjuvants. It is necessary to invest in quality by designing a bidding system that constrains costs and encourages better service and convenience. The quality-oriented PPOs and HMOs already aggressively seek competitive bids for referral hospital care based on the cost/quality/convenience mix their enrollees desire. The elderly and poor should be equally protected, with PROs defining a floor on quality and HCFA managing the bidding process.

Quality-enhancement payments would give physicians more leverage to go to trustees and management and say, "Do not forego this quality improvement investment." If it helps patient care, the facility will get paid for it. To avoid the liar's dice dilemma, QEB would encourage the development of quality and efficiency in tandem. Restricting QEB to low-quality hospitals is important because these hospitals have the greatest potential for improvement, much as the worst-run companies are often the easiest to turn around. At least until QEB is judged cost-beneficial (Eastaugh and Eastaugh, 1986), incentive pay to improve quality should be restricted to those hospitals where the investment is most likely to change behavior. Wringing the windfall profits out of suboptimal hospitals—and redistributing the resources to more efficient, quality-enhancing providers—represents financial equity at its best. A QEB program would help inject the Smith-Barney slogan into medicine: "We earn patients the old fashioned way: We treat them better."

Is the Health Care Revolution Over Yet?

As in all revolutions, it is a time of confusion for the players, large and small. The overriding question is, "Do we want our health care sector to be controlled mainly by government or by market competition?" Familiarity with rate regulation and health planning has bred contempt. Will the next 10 years of familiarity with managed care systems breed equivalent contempt and government reregulation of the market? Under competitive conditions there is an "invisible hand" with which to shop for value, but no decision makers to whom the public can turn to "do the right thing." As Fein (1986) points out, a central problem with the "invisible hand" of competition is that it is also connected to an "invisible body," thus offering citizens no avenue of appeal to redress grievances. However, under government control there is an ample supply of decision makers to whom the consumer can appeal and from whom consumers can experience inaction, insensitivity, and occasionally relief. This last school of thought is best captured in the 1974 bumper sticker: "If you love the post office, you will love national health insurance." To hope that government can be reformed by idealists replacing insensitive bureaucrats is to root for the Christians to have a big fourth quarter against the lions. Nice idea, but the lions are as effective as the bureaucrats at capturing or killing idealists.

Pessimism is rife, fear of the future reigns, but a number of alternatives remain to be tried. Some of the new vertical integration arrangements will be poorly conceived and short lived, but many will thrive. Backward integration—for example, a hospital chain (HCA) attempting to buy a hospital supply company (American Hospital Supply)—will be judged harshly in the marketplace. Joint venturing through forward integration represents the only way hospitals and hospital chains can avoid getting stuck with only a few product lines to be wholesaled to managed care systems at a discount. Hospital chains are no longer hospital management companies; they are full-service health care corporations that have partially diversified into health insurance provision and sales. Analogously, nursing home chains are not simply staying in the nursing home business at wholesale public and private rates. Nursing home systems are selling retail and wholesale a portfolio of products from life care to home care. Many locally controlled hospital minisystems will joint venture with these nursing home chains.

Small Hospitals Band Together with Medical Centers

Single free-standing hospitals are much like the "Ma and Pa" grocery stores of old; many survived by banding together. The strategy typically goes beyond simple horizontal integration of like institutions. The strategy usually involves vertical integration, through common ownership or control of multiple (nonequivalent) enterprises, one of which can use as its input the output of another. Some analysts have argued that informal networking and formal systems development can provide small and costly rural and urban hospitals with the only opportunity to retain local community control (Grim, 1986). High-cost medical centers increasingly seize the opportunity to sell their expertise in alternative care services to lower-cost local hospitals and facilitate formal referral patterns for easy cases out of the medical center (so their managed care contracts can remain cost competitive). This builds a minisystem strong enough to withstand pressures to sell or close. Autonomous hospitals can band together locally, go it alone, or become a franchise in a national firm. In either of the last two cases hospitals should avoid going so heavily into debt that their survival is unlikely. Johns Hopkins Hospital, Northwestern, Rush-Presbyterian-St. Luke's Medical Center, and the Mayo Clinic expanded into small hospital groups in their respective cities during 1986. But few hospitals have such access to capital. Avenues for capital include insurance companies interested in regional or local health systems, ex-partners of failed Supermed ventures, nursing home chains, local dominant employers in the city, and ultimately the individual hospital's medical staff. As to this last point, the marketing points to the physician community could include: "You don't want to become an AMI or Humana physician? Then make a financial investment in your local hospitals."

Experts are nearly united in predicting substantial increases in multihospital systems' market share. In this era of rapid change, there is so much written about what "will be" that it is easy to forget current market conditions. Sixty percent of hospitals are still not members of multihospital systems in 1986. In times of stress, we often "circle the wagons" and join together in groups, but the circle need not be too large. One should question whether economics suggests that consolidations favor large over small groups of hospitals. Consider an analogy to another market, the toaster industry. Contrast this sector to health care, where quality is more heterogeneous and costs are more labor-intensive. Unlike the kitchen toaster market, the product/service varies widely in quality across geographic regions of the country in health care—that is, the Humana brand of quality service varies more widely than the GE brand of toaster. Unlike a stockpiled manufactured good, health services are produced and consumed locally. The postulated economies of scale in running a big chain are likely due to the fact that the principal cost input is locally sourced labor. Consequently, if a small hospital reaps purchase discounts through membership in a group buying agreement, the facility need not experience inferior scale economies relative to a 50,000 bed hospital chain. The one comparative advantage that consolidation offers is better access to capital at lower capital costs. However, the disadvantage of membership in a chain is that the corporate staff might add $15 to $25 per diem to the costs of care (Watt et al., 1986) in the form of increased overhead, salaries, and "gold-plating" (e.g., Humana headquarters' architectural opulence).

The principal disadvantage of small hospital minisystems is the aforementioned reduced access to low-cost capital. However, this is counterbalanced in that local control and small size offer the ability to be quick and flexible in adapting to changing community needs (Peters and Austin, 1985). Flexibility often beats size, and size often breeds rigidity and bureaucracy. The investor-owned megasystems are beginning to respond to this last point and are attempting to trim corporate staff and lone (single) hospitals with poor profitability. Local hospitals must sacrifice a little autonomy, initiate master limited partnerships, and band together as minisystems.

Offering stock in a firm or franchise was an unusual financing arrangement until passage of tax reform in October 1986. Even well-known firms, such as the Boston Celtics professional basketball team, were selling up to a 40 to 49 percent stake in the franchise under a master limited partnership in the fall of 1986. Most hospitals do not have the national marketability of the Boston Celtics or the Mayo Clinic, but they have a local captive group of potential investors—their physicians. The master limited partnership could be presented to the medical staff in general terms—that is, if you do not invest in this facility, the workshop where you perform patient care will erode (i.e., plant and equipment will become obsolete). In addition, one could appeal to clinicians' specific (individual) self-interest with various "perks." For example, physicians who invest in the partnership would be provided the best operative time slots, work schedules, and relief from bureaucratic burdens. Financially distressed facilities may have to charge those who do not invest in the master limited partnership a monthly "rent" for the right to admit their private pay patients to the hospital. At the extreme, those doctors not wishing to invest cash in their workshop/hospital would have to pay with their time for the right to be on medical staff and have admitting privileges. The shift from a field dominated by doctors as nonpaying "partners" (keeping the hospital at financial risk) to one where they must invest their funds to keep the facility state-of-the-art destroys the obsolete philosophy of professional dominance.* Moreover, the organizations that employ or rent admitting rights to physicians will demand that managers share in decisions regarding professional roles, and managers dominate decisions involving capital acquisitions. In a world where the climate for dialogue between payers and providers has never been worse, the opportunity for joint deals between hospitals and physicians has never been better.

Oligopoly of Minisystems or Duopoly?

Some hospital executives may ask, apart from the local control question, what difference does it make as to whether the market is

---

*One would hope that most hospitals could still base medical staff membership decisions on the professional input and not the financial input of the individual doctor. However, in a basic economic sense, if the hospital and the doctor are involved in joint production, and the hospital is under severe financial pressure, the institution may have to demand financial resources from the producer group experiencing higher rates of return—the physician community. Lower physician investment will lead to more hospital closings, longer travel time to reach the workshop/hospital, or perhaps many physicians will lack admitting privileges at any hospital.

dominated by minisystems or megasystems? A few hundred mini-systems may create rural/duopoly (monopoly of two, such as a minisystem and a single hospital) and urban/oligopoly. However, eight supermeds may well produce rural monopolies (and raise antitrust concerns) and urban duopolies (of two big supermeds in most cities).* The 10 biggest cities may experience, under the supermed theory, an oligopoly of three to six competing megasys-tems. All eight supermeds would not compete in every market, but five to six might enter the larger markets (New York, Los Angeles, and Chicago). It does make a difference, in terms of economic performance and quality of care, if we seek the ideal of competition and fall far short because of a failure to provide sufficient consumer information.

Under perfect competition, a large number of buyers and sellers will drive the producers to outprice, outvalue, and outmaneuver each other to the benefit of all consumers (with the ability to pay). Under an oligopoly the market is composed of a handful of producers whose pricing decisions are interdependent, and thus higher than purely competitive market prices (Eastaugh, 1981). If a chain has a monopoly on the area market, due to a natural monopoly (e.g., a one-hospital town) or because antitrust enforce-ment is weakened, it has no competitors to dissuade it from charging higher prices and reaping classic monopoly profits. In the case of a duopoly, the two firms can better collude to reap more profits than in an oligopoly situation. Consolidation of the health sector into a few supermeds may have some advantages for large corporations (reaping super discounts), but competition is not among them. Minisystems and the preservation of the free-stand-ing autonomous hospital will best assure a competitive market, if and only if such facilities fight hard to trim excess costs and invest in quality-enhancing activities. The aforementioned quality-en-hancing bidding scheme (QEBs) may support this more competi-tive marketplace.

Capitation: The Medicine to Cure Unbundling

Many employers and government regulators fear that unbundling of services has co-opted attempts at stringent price controls, discount purchasing, and rate regulation. Capitation payment is

*In 1986, 23 percent of hospitals were in a natural monopoly situation with no neighboring hospitals within 1,000 square miles (17.7 mile radius). In contrast, 21 percent of hospitals were in a relatively competitive market, with more than five neighboring hospitals within 17.7 miles.

the ultimate defense against unbundling. Without capitation, when payers squeeze down on one end of the cost-inflation problem, the balloon pops up on the other end in the form of increased quantity of different transitional care services. The problem may not be solved through invention of a better regulatory control system. For example, tinkering with the DRGs by adding a severity measure may only open a trapdoor to bottomless grief. The price system may be made more equitable, but does this substantially reduce the incentive to game the system? Capitation cures the potential for gaming the system through inflated transitional care and leaves the health system partners the discretion for dividing fair payment rates between institutions and individuals.

Capitation systems will pay providers a fixed fee per person or per family to take care of a group of potential patients regardless of their health status. Corporations, not the federal government, appear to be taking the lead in this area. Federal researchers have attempted to incorporate the desirable incentives of capitation selectively into the Medicare system, but the development of per capita prices is no easy task. Thomas and Lichtenstein (1986) report that new models which include measures of prior years' cost and utilization experience predict Medicare payments significantly better than the current demographic formula of adjusted average per capita cost (AAPCC). In examining 2,000 randomly selected Medicare beneficiaries, the authors indicate that inclusion of instrumental activities for daily living (IADL) as a measure of beneficiaries' functional health status can further improve the fraction of explained variation in cost per capita. However, it may not be worth the data collection costs of adding extra measures to improve the explained variance by a few percentage points when more than 77 percent of the variance remains unexplained (even with 20 factors in the equation).

Capitation Fever from Norway to North Dakota

Employers may have an easier time of deriving per capita rates for employed populations, with lower coefficients of variation in health status per person compared to the elderly population. A crude morbidity adjustment, in the aggregate, for nonelderly groups may be sufficient to set capitation rates in an AAPCC formula. The current American climate of enthusiasm for substantial payment reform may follow the path in 1990 that Norway followed in 1980. After eight years of a prospective payment price system, Norway initiated a population-based morbidity-adjusted capitation formula in 1980 (Crane, 1985). This capitation approach achieved a more equitable distribution of resources among the 89 hospitals and redistributed more resources to chronic long-term care services.

The apparent ineffectiveness of the old Norwegian PPS system to contain rising admission rates in the late 1970s should lead the American audience to expect significant rates of increase in PPS admissions in the late 1980s. Rising PPS admissions would hasten the day in which the federal government turns to a full capitation approach. A winter 1986 Office of Technology Assessment report on physician payment systems singled out capitation as the best long-term solution to paying for care. However, in the fall of 1986 less than 3 percent of Medicare enrollees will be paid on a per capita basis. Three western states and Maryland have entered into discussions with HCFA concerning the possibility of statewide geographic capitation experiments in 1988. In the American spirit of piecemeal movement toward a major policy shift, we may move state by state, and employer by employer, to a fully capitated health care system sometime in the 1990s. Gradualist policies will not bring the majority of public patients under capitation in the near future, but future success with private managed care systems might prompt all payers to push for capitation.

Some regions already have experience with capitation payments. Two rural hospitals in Maryland are paid on a per capita basis by the state rate-setting commission. Blue Cross and the Hartford Foundation have financed a number of additional capitation experiments (Eastaugh, 1981). A capitation experiment for rural inpatient care was initiated in North Dakota (five hospitals and a sixth hospital over the state line in Minnesota) and in Massachusetts (four hospitals) in 1981. Mangion (1986) reports on the results from one hospital. Significant savings were produced in the first three years, with the hospital retaining 75 percent of the savings and Blue Cross retaining the balance. Employer-based managed-care systems will undoubtedly be less generous than Blue Cross in setting the rates and dividing any cost savings, but the hospital would be fully at risk to retain 100 percent of the savings (or losses). The per capita fixed payment programs provide hospitals with obvious incentives to economize.

Returns from Better Information

Some health policy makers have tended to reduce health economics to the level of a forensic science, full of rhetoric and devoid of research results. A main objective of this book has been to engage the interests of policy makers and managers in the research results of academicians. Policy makers, like institutional managers, are too occupied with putting out daily brush fires and reacting to symptomatology to adequately keep abreast of the health services research literature.

The health industry and the regulators have taken a largely defensive stand. Each party has become preoccupied with the actions and expectations of the other. However, an internal cost containment ethos and fair reimbursement of total institutional financial requirements are necessary if we are to develop a more rational national health policy; rhetoric concerning "fat" providers and mindless "bureaucrats" is counterproductive. Will the 1980s be a period of uncontrolled growth and expansion of the health economy? Can the recent record of poor performance and sluggish productivity be reversed? The public has come to recognize that the key problems for health policy are cost containment and access to care. The solution to containing costs may be found in better implementation of management strategies and better research in the areas of finance and health economics. In our pluralistic society, better information is a necessary, but not sufficient, condition for achieving a more healthy health economy.

Physician Reaction to "Too Much Change"

Many conservative clinicians feel that 1984 ushered in the spirit of Orwell's novel, *1984*, into medicine. Such doctors fear that they will be stripped of admitting privileges if their practice profile exhibits an inability to adjust to the "new medicine" of decision analysis, PPS, PPOs, and HMOs. These clinicians argue that "personal care" gets lost in the shuffle as DRG trees, software, outliers, economic grand rounds, and "think-adjustment" sessions force professionals toward "cookbook medicine." Carrying their case to the extreme, four points are often made by conservative physicians:

1. If the practice profile is too expensive relative to excessively low government or third-party payment rates, the doctor is labeled "a dyscodic outlier heterogenicist" (Burnum, 1984) and faces loss of admitting privileges.
2. "True" doctors cannot join a PPO or a system because they are "neither providers, nor are they preferred" (medicine is a "calling," not a commercial enterprise, and should be preferred for quality caring, not price discounts).
3. Doctors are forced to provide only the admissions that are profitable to the hospital and jettison the nonprofitable services.

4. Doctors are forced to abide by market analysis and selling
strategies.

Hospital managers and medical staff leaders should develop a
cogent response to each of these four points of misunderstanding.

First, data-based "credentialing" for membership on the medical
staff is a negotiated process. If the chief of medical staff can build a
reasonable case for retaining an individual whose practice habits
are more expensive for uncontrollable reasons (for receiving more
severely ill cases than evidenced simply by the DRG or for
specializing in treatment of intrinsically unprofitable DRGs the
trustees want admitted), then the doctor should be retained on the
medical staff and not declared a "shameless statistical deviate." As
to the second point, patients do value economic attributes, such as
lower out-of-pocket payments for health care, lower premiums,
and higher wages because costs are more under control (i.e., so the
employer doesn't have to pay much of the wage increase to health
care providers).

In response to the third point, hospital executives should point
out that cost accounting is required to financially plan the institution's future. Moreover, clinicians should rid themselves of the
myth that hospital charges are highly correlated with actual resource costs. All parties concerned need accurate standard cost
accounting, as was pointed out in Chapter 5. It is never required to
have the hospital make a profit on each service product line.
However, trustees need to know how much they lose on certain
product lines, so they can expand or initiate money makers, such
that the final bottom line is sufficient to maintain a quality hospital.
If clinicians do not trust the dollar figures derived from accounting
or the CFO, the data can be presented in opportunity cost terms.
A nonphysician manager should never say the "unthinkable" and
claim that a given product line is a $500,000 example of "economic
malpractice." Instead, the clinicians working in this inefficient
service area can be told that the "opportunity costs of this service
require that we fire 20 people hospitalwide plus your postgraduate
fellow to underwrite the cost of this money-losing product line."

As to the fourth point, physician disdain for marketing is both
archaic and antipatient. Health marketing places the consumers as
kings and asks how best to meet their medical needs with quality
service at an affordable cost. Marketing is simply doing right by the
patients, channeling them to the service mode of delivery that is
most appropriate. Effective marketing is not "hucksterism" or
selling. Good marketing involves open communication, development of trust, and instilling in the public the differential advan-

tages and abilities offered by a given provider. Social marketing programs determine what consumers need, tailor services to meet those needs, and suggest that patients utilize services in a timely preventive manner—that is, before something more serious develops.

The Road Ahead

Some members of organized medicine express fear that prepaid Medicare is an invitation to create medical ghettos for the elderly. One noted economist argues that we may soon turn to a false form of national health insurance—one offering a voucher for minimum coverage but leaving the individual to fend for a large share of medical costs (Ginzberg, 1986). Politicians frequently seek headlines by claiming that the bulk of the medical cost problem is caused by the fraud and abuse of a few providers. This contributes to piecemeal attention being given to such infrequent problems as Medicaid kickbacks and HMO scandals, rather than the more insidious problem of inflationary or quality-eroding incentive structures. A quality-enhancing bidding system would go a long way toward promoting good medicine and good economics.

In visiting Chinese hospitals and medical schools in 1980, it was interesting to discover that the ancient proverb, "May you live in interesting times," was often misinterpreted by Caucasian visitors as a curse. The opportunity for substantial reform is best in just such times of stress and strain. In point of fact, the Chinese term "Wei Ji" has a simultaneous dual interpretation: opportunity and danger. Our health system faces over the next five years immense opportunity and danger in a reformation on four fronts: access, efficiency, effectiveness, and quality of life. The challenge for providers and managers during this period of unparalleled opportunity is to win a clear victory on all four fronts, and not erode either access or quality in the name of efficiency. This is a clear challenge for both managers and policy makers. The job is doubly tough for our physicians. The challenge to physicians will be to carry on one shoulder life-saving technology and the concomitant financial burden and, on the other shoulder, the will and imagination to apply modern management techniques.

How well the physicians and managers work together will determine whether we experience the bad or good side of the "invisible hand." Bad competition will result in overemphasis on a narrow business focus and attempt to avoid provider's social obligations. This dark side of competition attacks the special moral importance of health care in society. Daniels (1986) argues that health care derives its moral importance from its impact on the normal range of opportunities in society; and opportunity is reduced when illness impairs functioning. However, any balanced view of health care should be viewed as both a social good and a consumer good. Good competition shall invoke a broader business focus and health delivery orientation. Good competition can stimulate neighboring providers to offer better services at more reasonable expense, through specialization, economies of scale, and quality assurance. This process can improve, and not erode, patient access to quality services throughout all market segments.

References

AVERILL, R., and KALISON, M. (1986). "The Next Step: Introducing Competitive Pricing into PPS." *Healthcare Financial Management* 40:8 (August), 58–63.

BAUMOL. W., BLACKMAN, S., and WOLFE, E. (1985). "Unbalanced Growth Revisited: Asymptotic Stagnancy and New Evidence." *American Economic Review* 75:4 (September), 806–817.

BURNUM, J. (1984). "The Unfortunate Case of Dr. Z: How to Succeed in Medical Practice in 1984." *New England Journal of Medicine* 310:11 (March 15), 729–730.

CHRISTIANSON, J. (1985). "Competitive Bidding: The Challenge for Health Care Managers." *Health Care Management Review* 10:2 (Spring), 39–53.

CRANE, T. (1985). "Hospital Cost Control in Norway: A Decade's Experience with Prospective Payment." *Public Health Reports* 100:4 (July/August), 406–417.

DANIELS, N. (1986). "Why Saying No to Patients in the United States Is So Hard: Cost Containment, Justice, and Provider Autonomy." *New England Journal of Medicine* 314:21 (May 22), 1380–1383.

EASTAUGH, S. (1981). *Medical Economics and Health Finance.* Dover, Mass.: Auburn House, 318–322.

EASTAUGH, S., and EASTAUGH, J. (1986). "Prospective Payment Systems: Further Steps to Enhance Quality, Efficiency, and Regionalization." *Health Care Management Review* 11:4 (Fall), 37–52.

ELWOOD, P. (1986). "Supermed Concept Gaining Ground." *Federation of American Executives Review* 19:2 (March/April), 69–71.

ELWOOD, P., and PAUL, B. (1984). *Here Come the SuperMeds.* Excelsior, Minn.: Interstudy.

ENTHOVEN, A. (1980). *Health Plan.* Reading, Mass.: Addison-Wesley.

FEIN, R. (1986). *Medical Care, Medical Costs: The Search for a Health Insurance Policy.* Cambridge, Mass.: Harvard University Press.

GINZBERG, E. (1986). "Is Cost Containment for Real?" *Journal of the American Medical Association* 256:2 (July 11), 254–255.

GRIM, S. (1986). "Win/Win: Urban and Rural Hospitals Network for Survival." *Hospital and Health Services Administration* 31:1 (January–February), 34–42.

JOHNS, L., ANDERSON, M., and DERZON, R. (1985). "Selective Contracting in California: Experience in the Second Years." *Inquiry* 22:4 (Winter), 335–347.

KOTLER, P. (1986). "Megamarketing." *Harvard Business Review* 64:2 (March-April), 117–124.

LISTER, J. (1986). "The Politics of Medicine in Britain and the United States." *New England Journal of Medicine* 315:3 (July 17), 168–173.

MANGION, R. (1986). "Capitation Reimbursement: A Progress Report." *Hospital and Health Services Administration* 31:1 (January–February), 99–110.

Organization for Economic Cooperation and Development (1986). *National Accounts of OECD Countries 1950–1985*. Paris: OECD.

PETERS, T., and AUSTIN, N. (1985). *Passion for Excellence*. New York: Random House.

PETERS, T., and WATERMAN, R. (1982). *In Search of Excellence: Lessons from America's Best Run Companies*. New York: Harper & Row.

STERN, R., and EPSTEIN, A. (1985). "Institutional Responses to Prospective Payment Based on DRGs." *New England Journal of Medicine* 312:10 (March 7), 621–627.

THOMAS, J., and LICHTENSTEIN, R. (1986). "Functional Health Measure for Adjusting HMO Capitation Rates." *Health Care Financing Review* 7:3 (Spring), 85–95.

WATT, J., DERZON, R., RENN, S., SCHRAMM, C., HAHN, J., and PILLARI, G. (1986). "The Comparative Economic Performance of Investor-Owned Chain and Not-for-Profit Hospitals." *New England Journal of Medicine* 314:2 (January 9), 89–96.

SUBJECT INDEX

AUTHOR INDEX